SHOW JUMPING

RECORDS, FACTS AND CHAMPIONS

Judith Draper

GUINNESS BOOKS

Editor: Beatrice Frei
Design and Layout: Ian Wileman

Published in Great Britain by Guinness Superlatives Ltd,
33 London Road, Enfield, Middlesex

Typeset in Times and Helvetica
by Wyvern Typesetting Ltd
Printed and bound in Great Britain by Bath Press, Bath

British Library Cataloguing in Publication Data

Draper, Judith
    Guinness show jumping: records, facts and champions
    1. Show jumping—Records
    I. Title
    798.2'5'09   SF295.5

    ISBN 0-85112-473-9

Contents

Foreword   4
Introduction   5
Acknowledgements   6
Key to abbreviations   7
Milestones   9
Olympic Games   13
World Championships   48
World Cup   60
Nations Cups   74
The President's Cup   130
Highest and Widest   132
　　World High Jump Record   132
　　World Long Jump Record   133
　　Puissance Records   134
European Championships   136
Pan American Games   149
Balkan Championships   154
Mediterranean Games   166
Asian Games   168
Masters Games   169
Young Riders Championships   170
　　European   170 ·
　　American   173
Junior European Championships   178
Junior American Championships   194
Pony European Championships   198
Grand Prix   203
Derbies   215

FEI International Competition   218
National Championships   229
Index   237

GREAT NAMES
Riders
　　Federico Caprilli   58
　　Hans-Heinrich Brinckmann   72
　　Humberto Mariles Cortés   86
　　Pat Koechlin-Smythe   108
　　Pierre Jonquères d'Oriola   158
　　Piero and Raimondo d'Inzeo   175
　　Hans Günter Winkler   200
　　William Steinkraus   224
　　Jan Kowalczyk   234

Horses
　　Foxhunter   22
　　Meteor   47
　　Broncho   79
　　Halla   98
　　The Rock   100
　　Stroller   129
　　Merely-a-Monarch   135
　　Boomerang   153
　　Chilena   167
　　Mare's Nest   168

BUCKINGHAM PALACE.

The association between man and horse must go back thousands of years but it is somewhat ironic that so many of the horse sports only really began to flourish long after the horse had lost its practical utility. People have been jumping horses for generations, but it was only relatively recently that the Italians developed a technique which revolutionised the sport of showjumping.

Increasing affluence has allowed more people to participate in the horse sports, modern transport facilities have allowed more competitors to travel abroad and television has allowed many more people to become spectators at major events. Together, these factors have generated a demand for more international competitions and championships and they have also ensured a steady improvement in standards.

The history and the facts and statistics about showjumping are all in this book. I am sure it will be very useful for reference purposes, but I hope it will also be much enjoyed by enthusiasts.

1987

Foreword by HRH The Duke of Edinburgh K.G., K.T., O.M., C.B.E., Q.S.O.

Introduction

With the one notable exception of racing, equestrian sports have been extremely poorly served over the years from the point of view of official record keeping. Show jumping had been growing in popularity for the best part of two decades, and had been included in the Olympic Games, before the formation of an international governing body. Even the latter, the Fédération Equestre Internationale (founded in 1921), has no results for the sport prior to the 1930s, and thereafter its archives are far from complete, revealing total blanks for many years.

Wherever possible the material for this book has been obtained from official sources: from the FEI, from the national federations of the various countries concerned and from the archives of organizing bodies of events such as the Olympic Games and regional championships. However, in many cases formal records do not exist. Some have simply been thrown away; others have been damaged or totally destroyed by war, fire, flood—even, in one instance, by mice! Of the then 85 FEI affiliated national federations in the world, each one of whom was invited to supply information on the sport in their country, only 20 responded. Therefore, much material has necessarily been gleaned from contemporary reports in newspapers and periodicals. A major problem has been the ironing out of inconsistencies, which are to be found everywhere, even in official records. In some instances—notably one or two regional championships, such as the Bolivarian and Central American and Caribbean Games—the available results are so fragmented that I have decided, regretfully, to omit them altogether.

Piecing together the facts has been a fascinating, if frustrating, exercise, and the material in this book is as complete and accurate as I have been able to make it in the time available. I hope that it will be of interest to show jumping enthusiasts everywhere. Equally, I hope that if any readers have further information to offer on the competitions recorded here, they will contact me—I should be delighted to hear from them.

Judith Draper

Acknowledgements

I would like to express my gratitude to the staff of the British Newspaper Library, Colindale, for their wonderfully efficient and courteous service; likewise the library staff at the British Olympic Association, Wandsworth; to Max E. Ammann, for his invaluable help and advice; to the Secretary General, Fritz O. Widmer, and staff of the Fédération Equestre Internationale in Bern, for access to their archives; to Michael Clayton, Editor of *Horse and Hound*, for constant access to the back numbers of that publication; to Julian Humphrys, Librarian of the National Army Museum, London; to Raymond Brooks-Ward, for access to the schedules of the International Horse Show, Olympia; to the National Federations of Australia, Canada, Denmark, Finland, The Federal Republic of Germany, Greece, Ireland, Lebanon, Liechtenstein, New Zealand, Poland, Portugal, Rumänia, South Africa, Spain, Sudan, Sweden, Turkey, the USA and Zaïre, and especially to Colonel António Crespo, Secretary General of the Portuguese Equestrian Federation; to Ata Atabek, President of the Turkish Equestrian Federation and Dr Kr. Rashkov, Secretary General of the Bulgarian Equestrian Federation, for the tremendous efforts they made to rediscover the lost Balkan Championships results; to Nikos Filaretos, Secretary General of the Comité International des Jeux Méditerranéens; to the many friends, colleagues and riders who gave their assistance, particularly Maymes Ansell, Vivienne Burdon, Colonel Dan Corry, Findlay Davidson, Raimondo d'Inzeo, Witold S. Domański, Pierre Jonquères d'Oriola, Ted Dwyer, Vivienne Keall, Pat Koechlin-Smythe, Bill Landsman, Alan Smith, William Steinkraus, Hans van der Kolk and Hans Günter Winkler; and to the people who loaned their often valuable reference books, notably Bill Day, Findlay Davidson, John Kerr, Leslie Lane, Sir Harry Llewellyn and Pat Lucas.

Special thanks go to Norman Bailey, CBE, and his son, Richard, without whom the mysteries of the computer would not have been revealed. And last, but most important of all, I owe a huge debt of gratitude to my husband, Larry, who for two years was a 'Guinness widower', a fate he endured with (almost) unfailing good humour. Without his help and support this book could not have been written.

Four publications were of particular value for purposes of cross-reference: Max E. Ammann's magnificent *Geschichte des Pferde-Sports; L'Année Hippique* 1946–72, 1978–79, 1984–86; and Erich Kamper's *Enzyklopädie der Olympischen Spiele* and *Lexicon der 14,000 Olympioniken.*

Abbreviations

General

CHIO = Concours Hippique International Officiel (official international show staging more than one discipline, e.g. show jumping and dressage)

CSA = Concours de Saut d'Obstacles d'Amitié (friendly jumping show, open to riders from the host country and from up to four foreign countries)

CSI = Concours de Saut d'Obstacles International (international jumping show, open to riders from the host country and any number of foreign countries)

CSIO = Concours de Saut d'Obstacles International Officiel (official international jumping show, that is one at which a Nations Cup may be staged)

D = Disqualified

E = Eliminated

FEI = Fédération Equestre Internationale

h.h. = Hands high (1 hand = 4 in)

NP = Did not take part

R = Retired

Table A = A competition in which a horse's score is calculated by adding together the faults incurred at the obstacles and any time penalties. Time may be taken into consideration to separate equality for first place and/or lower places according to the conditions laid down for the competition.

Table C = A competition in which faults are penalized in seconds which are added to the time taken by the competitor to complete his round. The penalty for each jumping fault is fixed in seconds in relation to the length of the course and to the number of jumps to be made by the horse during the round.

W = Withdrew

Scores

Wherever possible the scores of the riders or teams listed in the results sections are included. In the majority of cases the scores are in *faults*. However, in some championships, and in a number of early competitions, *plus points* were awarded instead of faults, hence in some instances the winner is the rider or team with the highest, not the lowest, score.

Where times are given, they are normally in *seconds*, e.g. 36.54 = 36.54 seconds. However, some official records give times in *minutes and seconds*, and where this applies the same style has been followed in this book, e.g. 1:62,30 = 1 minute 62.30 seconds.

Where the scores for several rounds are given, as for instance in individual championships, the faults for the various rounds and jump-offs are given in sequence. If the deciding factor in the final round is *time*, this is given after the last score. For example: 0.00–0.00–4.00/36.47 = two clear rounds, followed by a final round for 4 faults in 36.47 seconds.

In show jumping, times are normally taken to one-hundreth of a second. On the rare occasions when they have been taken to one-tenth or one-thousandth of a second, these have of course been retained in this book.

Scores in brackets = discard scores.

Countries

Alg = Algeria
Arg = Argentina
Aus = Australia
Aut = Austria
Bel = Belgium
Ber = Bermuda
Bol = Bolivia
Bra = Brazil
Bul = Bulgaria
Cam = Cambodia
Can = Canada
Chi = Chile
Chn = China
Col = Colombia
CRC = Costa Rica
Cyp = Cyprus
Czech = Czechoslovakia
Den = Denmark
Ecu = Ecuador
Egy = Egypt
Esa = El Salvador
Fin = Finland
Fra = France

FRG = Federal Republic of Germany (West Germany)
GB = Great Britain
GDR = German Democratic Republic (East Germany)
Ger = Germany (pre-1949)
Gre = Greece
Gua = Guatemala
Hun = Hungary
Ina = Indonesia
Ind = India
Ire = Ireland
Ita = Italy
Jap = Japan
Kor = Korea
Kuw = Kuwait
Lux = Luxemburg
Mal = Malaysia
Mex = Mexico
NL = The Netherlands
Nor = Norway
NZ = New Zealand
Per = Peru
Phi = The Philippines
Pol = Poland
Por = Portugal
Pur = Puerto Rico
Rum = Rumania
Rus = Russia (until 1918)
SA = South Africa
Sin = Singapore

Swe = Sweden
Switz = Switzerland
Syr = Syria
Tpe = Chinese Taipei
Tun = Tunisia
Tur = Turkey
UAR = United Arab Republic
Uru = Uruguay
USA = United States of America
USSR = Union of Soviet Socialist Republics (since 1918)
Ven = Venezuela
Yug = Yugoslavia
Zai = Zaïre
Zim = Zimbabwe

Names

In the case of a woman who has married, and then resumed competing under her married name, her maiden name is given in brackets.

Inconsistencies in the spelling of names occur frequently in show jumping records (even official ones) and particularly where names have been transliterated from one alphabet into another. In this book, wherever possible these inconsistencies have been ironed out. Where it has not been possible to verify spellings, the author has retained those which appear in the official records of the events concerned, hence occasional variations.

Milestones

1864 The first of two trial horse shows is held on Leinster Lawn, Dublin. The shows include the High Jump and the Wide Leap, intended primarily to test the qualifications of the hunters.

1866 France stages her first 'concours hippique'.

1868 Birth of Federico Caprilli, 'the father of modern riding'.

Following the success of the trial shows in 1864 and 1866, The Royal Dublin Society stages its first annual horse show.

1881 The Dublin Horse Show moves to Ballsbridge. Belgium holds her first 'concours hippique'.

1883 Inauguration of the National Horse Show, New York.

1886 The Netherlands stages a 'concours hippique' for the first time.

1900 Jumping events—'prize jumping', high and long jump—are included in the Olympic Games for the first time.

1902 Inauguration of the first Turin 'concorso ippico internazionale', a major military equestrian meeting which did much to popularize the Caprilli system of riding over fences.

Heatherbloom jumps 2.515 metres (8 ft 3 in) in Richmond, Virginia.

Jumping at the Dublin Horse Show in 1881. At the stone wall, a feature of the show for many years, horses were penalised according to the number of loose stones which they dislodged. (The Illustrated London News)

1906 Count Clarence von Rosen (Sweden) proposes to the Congress of the International Olympic Committee that equestrian events should be officially included in the Olympic Games. Encouraged by Baron Pierre de Coubertin, progenitor of the Modern Olympics, von Rosen sets about devising suitable competitions.

1907 London's first International Horse Show takes place in the Grand Hall, Olympia.

Thanks to the persistence of Count Clarence von Rosen, equestrian events are included in the plans for the 1908 Olympic Games, to be hosted by Great Britain. In the event, the organizing committee decides it cannot cope, and the horse sports are dropped from the Games.

1909 The International Horse Show at Olympia stages the world's first Nations Cup: a gold international challenge cup (value £500) is presented by King Edward VII for jumping the course by a team of three officers of the same nationality and riding in uniform.

The world's second Nations Cup is held at San Sebastián in Spain.

An official team from Argentina competes in Europe for the first time.

International shows are held in Lucerne, Switzerland, and Lisbon.

New York's National Show is open to international riders for the first time.

1910 Belgium's first Nations Cup is competed for at Brussels.

1911 For the first time a team from the United States competes at Olympia.

Inaugural running of the New York Nations Cup.

Nations Cups are staged in Italy at Turin and Rome.

1912 The first Olympic Nations Cup is staged at the Stockholm Games.

Confidence, ridden by Jack Hamilton, jumps 2.45 metres (8 ft ½ in) at the Central Canadian Exhibition in Ottawa.

A Nations Cup is competed for at The Hague in The Netherlands.

1920 The first Nations Cup show following the Great War is held at Olympia.

The first Hamburg Derby takes place, a new type of competition devised by the well-known German rider Eduard F. Pulvermann.

1921 The Fédération Equestre Internationale is founded, following a preliminary meeting held in

A military jumping competition at Jerez de la Frontera, Spain, in 1913. (The Illustrated London News)

Lausanne, Switzerland, chaired by Baron de Coubertin and attended by representatives of 10 countries. On 24 November the first Congress of the new Federation is held in Paris, with the first eight member nations present: Belgium, Denmark, France, Italy, Japan, Norway, Sweden and the United States. The Frenchman Baron du Teil is elected as the FEI's first President, with Cdt Georges Hector as Secretary General.
Inauguration of the Nice International Show in France.

1923 Great Heart jumps 2.46 metres (8 ft ⅞ in) in Chicago.
Finland and Switzerland become affiliated to the FEI.

1924 For the first time the equestrian events at the Olympic Games are held under the jurisdiction of the FEI.
A national horse show is staged for the first time at Aachen, W. Germany.
Spain, Poland and The Netherlands become affiliated to the FEI.

1925 Canada's first Nations Cup is held at Toronto.
A two-day international show is held at Aachen, W. Germany.
Great Britain becomes affiliated to the FEI.

1926 The Aga Khan Trophy (Ireland's Nations Cup) is competed for for the first time at the Dublin Horse Show.

1927 Germany, Hungary and Czechoslovakia become affiliated to the FEI, and the Dutchman Oberst Maris is elected to the Federation's presidency.
Spain, Poland and Switzerland run Nations Cups in Madrid, Warsaw and Lucerne/Geneva, respectively.
Inaugural running of the Aachen Grand Prix.

1928 Argentina, Austria, Bulgaria and Portugal become affiliated to the FEI.

1929 Major J. K. Quarles van Ufford (The Netherlands) is elected to succeed Oberst Maris as President of the FEI.
Portugal's first Nations Cup is contested at the Lisbon Show, Hungary's at Budapest. Germany holds two Nations Cup shows, at Aachen and Cologne.

1930 Rumania and Yugoslavia become affiliated to the FEI.

1931 Ireland becomes affiliated to the FEI.
The FEI publishes its first comprehensive rule book, including rules for Nations Cups and for record breaking attempts in the high and long jump competitions, and also its first Bulletin. Guy V. Henry (USA) is elected to take over as President. In its 10th year, the membership of the Federation stands at 24.
Austria and Latvia stage their first Nations Cups, in Vienna and Riga, respectively.

1932 Turkey becomes affiliated to the FEI.

Miss Susanne de Strasser, riding side-saddle, competing in Budapest in 1925. Hungary, a country with a strong equestrian tradition, became affiliated to the FEI two years later. (The Illustrated London News)

1935 General Max von Holzing-Berstett (Germany) is elected FEI President.
Brazil and Chile become affiliated to the FEI.

1937 Cuba becomes affiliated to the FEI.

1938 Greece and Mexico become affiliated to the FEI.

1940 Official international events are held only in Rome and New York.

1941 New York stages the last official international show to be held during the Second World War. At the Cairns Show, in Queensland, Rukin Lass and Peninsula both clear 2.565 metres (8 ft 5 in) to set a new Australian high jump record.

1946 International shows resume in Europe and North America, with Nations Cups being contested at Dublin, New York and Toronto.
The FEI Congress is held for the first time since 1939. General Baron Gaston de Trannoy of Belgium, who had competed in the Olympic Games of 1912 and 1920 is elected President.
Egypt becomes affiliated to the FEI.

1947 Colombia, South Africa and Venezuela become affiliated to the FEI.

1948 At the FEI Conference in Paris it is decided to establish only two categories of rider, amateur and professional, and to abolish the third category, that for 'officers and gentlemen'.

1949 Huaso clears 2.47 metres (8 ft 1¼ in) in Santiago, Chile, to set a new official (i.e. ratified by the FEI) world high jump record.

Guatemala becomes affiliated to the FEI.

1950 Australia and Canada become affiliated to the FEI.

1951 New Zealand becomes affiliated to the FEI.

1952 The death of Cdt Georges Hector, Secretary General of the FEI from 1921–51.

In Ostend the first Junior European Championship is held.

Korea, Peru and the USSR become affiliated to the FEI.

1953 The first World Championship (for men, with a change-horse final) is staged in Paris.

1954 Prince Bernhard of the Netherlands is elected President of the FEI.

1956 Because quarantine restrictions make it impossible for horses to travel to Australia, for the first time the equestrian events of the Olympic Games are held separately from the main Games—in Stockholm, at the same stadium used for the 1912 Olympics.

Women are permitted to ride in the Olympic Games Nations Cup for the first time. Britain's Pat Smythe becomes the first woman to win a medal—a team bronze.

Luxemburg and Rhodesia become affiliated to the FEI.

1957 European Championships for senior riders are held for the first time, one event for men, another for women.

Ecuador and Lebanon become affiliated to the FEI.

1958 Morocco becomes affiliated to the FEI.

1959 Bolivia and Iran become affiliated to the FEI.

1960 Uruguay becomes affiliated to the FEI.

1961 Senegal and Tunisia become affiliated to the FEI.

1963 Algeria becomes affiliated to the FEI.

1964 HRH Prince Philip is elected President of the FEI.

Pierre Jonquères d'Oriola becomes the first and only rider to win two individual Olympic gold medals for show jumping.

Puerto Rico becomes affiliated to the FEI.

1965 The FEI introduces the President's Cup, honouring the most successful Nations Cup team of the year. The Federation also decides on the still valid rotation of Championships: in the even non-Olympic years World Championships are held, while in the odd years Continental Championships may be organized.

The first Ladies' World Championship is held.

The German Democratic Republic becomes affiliated to the FEI.

1967 Pat Koechlin-Smythe becomes the first woman chef d'équipe (to the British team at Aachen).

1968 The first Balkan Championships are held in Istanbul.

1970 Libya becomes affiliated to the FEI.

1971 India and Syria become affiliated to the FEI.

1972 Hans Günter Winkler wins an unprecedented fifth gold medal at the Olympic Games.

El Salvador becomes affiliated to the FEI.

1973 The Washington International Show stages a Nations Cup for the first time.

Costa Rica becomes affiliated to the FEI.

1975 Mrs I. G. van der Merwe's Something sets a new official world long jump record of 8.40 metres (27 ft 6¾ in) in Johannesburg.

Introduction of the first European Championship open to men and women (to replace the previous separate events) and the first Championship for teams.

Chinese Taipei, Indonesia, the Philippines and Singapore become affiliated to the FEI.

1976 Bermuda becomes affiliated to the FEI.

1977 Iraq and the Virgin Islands become affiliated to the FEI.

1978 Introduction of the World Cup.

Introduction of the first World Championship open to men and women (to replace the previous two separate events) and the first Championship for teams.

The Bahamas and Hong Kong become affiliated to the FEI.

1979 Introduction of the FEI International Jumping Competition designed to enable riders in all countries to compete against each other over identical courses without having to travel abroad.

The first World Cup final takes place in Gothenburg, Sweden.

Dominican Republic and Sudan become affiliated to the FEI.

1980 Kuwait, Paraguay and Zaïre become affiliated to the FEI.

1981 The FEI creates a new category of Young Riders (aged 16–21) as a bridge between the Juniors (14–18) and Seniors (over 18).

Malaysia and Zambia become affiliated to the FEI.

1982 Cyprus, Pakistan and Qatar become affiliated to the FEI.

1983 Jamaica, the People's Republic of China and Thailand become affiliated to the FEI.

1984 Liechtenstein becomes affiliated to the FEI.

1985 Bahrain, Honduras and the United Arab Emirates become affiliated to the FEI.

1986 Canada's Gail Greenough becomes the first woman to win the World Championship open to men and women.

At the FEI General Assembly, held in London in December, HRH Princess Anne is unanimously elected to succeed her father as President of the Federation.

Netherlands Antilles and Oman become affiliated to the FEI, bringing the total of affiliated nations to 86.

Olympic Games

Equestrian sports became part of the modern Olympics for the first time in Paris, in 1900. They included a 'prize jumping' competition, a high jump, a long jump, and polo. The jumping events attracted 24 riders from Belgium, France, Italy and the United States. However, the sport was still very much in the embryo stage. There was no overall governing body and international rules had yet to be formulated.

Polo featured in the 1908 Games in London, but it was not until 1912 that jumping appeared again. These Stockholm Games saw the introduction of the three Olympic 'disciplines' which we know today—show jumping, three-day eventing and dressage. In that first year there were separate jumping competitions for individuals and teams (the Prix des Nations or Nations Cup). Nowadays, the jumping is again run in two separate events, but for many of the intervening years there was only one competition to decide both individual and team medals.

Until 1980 the Nations Cup was, by tradition, the last competition of the Games. Following the completion of the track and field events the main stadium would be transformed into a show jumping arena and upwards of 100 000 people would become engrossed in what was for many a totally new sport.

This undoubtedly did much to popularize show jumping around the world. In 1980 the Russians broke with tradition by staging the Nations Cup in their specially built equestrian stadium and putting the individual competition into the main Olympic stadium. In 1984, for the first time, no equestrian event was run in the main stadium, the Americans having obtained permission to stage both the jumping events at Santa Anita racecourse, where a special complex had been built for the equestrian Games.

Because of their very specialized needs, there is a case for running equestrian sports away from the rest of the Games. In 1956, when the Olympics were held in Melbourne, the stringent Australian quarantine restrictions made it necessary to stage the equestrian Games elsewhere. They were run as a totally separate entity in Stockholm. Many people still remember them as the most enjoyable and successful equestrian Games of all.

Wilf White (right), Pat Smythe and Peter Robeson, followed by the British three-day event and dressage riders, at the opening ceremony of the 1956 Stockholm Games. Present at the ceremony were King Gustaf and Queen Louise of Sweden, and Queen Elizabeth II and the Duke of Edinburgh. (The Photo Source)

Olympic Games: explanatory note

Figures in brackets in the far right-hand column indicate the rider's position in the Nations Cup. At Games where only one competition was held these, of course, also indicate the individual placings. In years when a separate individual contest was staged, they are merely of academic interest.

At the 1912 Olympics Belgium's Captain de Blommaert riding Clonmore took part in all three equestrian events: the Prize Jumping (show jumping team and individual competitions), the Military (three-day event) and the Prize Riding (dressage with jumping).

1900 Paris

Prize Jumping

	Faults	Time
1 Aimé Haegeman (Bel)—Benton II	0.00	2:16,0
2 Georges van de Poële (Bel)—Windsor Squire	0.00	2:17,6
3 Louis de Champsavin (Fra)—Terpsichore	0.00	2:26,0

Number of starters: 17

High Jump

	Metres
1 Dominique Maximien Gardères (Fra)—Canela	1.85
2 Gian Giorgio Trissino (Ita)—Oreste	1.85
3 Georges van de Poële (Bel)—Ludlow	1.70

Number of starters: 18

Long Jump

	Metres
1 Constant van Langendonck (Bel)—Extra Dry	6.10
2 Gian Giorgio Trissino (Ita)—Oreste	5.70
3 Lt de Bellegarde (Fra)—Tolla	5.30

Number of starters: 13

1912 Stockholm

Nations Cup

(1 round, teams of 4, best 3 scores to count)

	Points (max. 190)	
1 **Sweden** 545		
Carl Gustaf Lewenhaupt—Medusa	188	(=1)
Gustaf Kilman—Gåtan	180	(=6)
Hans von Rosen—Lord Iron	177	(=8)
Fredrik Rosencrantz—Drabant	(171)	(=16)
2 **France** 538		
Michel Dufort d'Astafort—Amazone	185	(3)
Jean Cariou—Mignon	182	(4)
Bernard Meyer—Allons-y	171	(=16)
G. Seigner—Cocotte	(170)	(18)
3 **Germany** 530		
Sigismund Freyer—Ultimus	181	(5)
Wilhelm von Hohenau—Pretty Girl	177	(=8)
Ernst Deloch—Hubertus	172	(=13)
Friedrich Karl von Preussen—Gibson Boy	(166)	(20)
4 **USA** 527		
John C. Montgomery—Deceive	180	(=6)
Guy V. Henry—Connie	174	(11)
Benjamin Lear, jnr—Poppy	173	(12)
(no fourth rider)		
5 **Russia** 520		
Alexander Rodzianko—Eros	176	(10)
Michel Plechkov—Eveta	172	(=13)
Alexis Selikhov—Tugela	172	(=13)
Dimitri Pavlovitch—Unité	(169)	(19)
6 **Belgium** 510		
Emmanuel de Blommaert de Soye—Clonmore	188	(=1)
Gaston de Trannoy—Capricieux	162	(21)
Paul Convert—La Sioute	160	(22)
(no fourth rider)		

Number of teams: 6

Individual

(Separate competition, 1 round)

	Points (max. 190)	Jump-off (faults)
1 Jean Cariou (Fra)—Mignon	186	5
2 Rabod Wilhelm von Kröcher (Ger)—Dohna	186	7
3 Emmanuel de Blommaert de Soye (Bel)—Clonmore	185	
4 Herbert Scott (GB)—Shamrock	184	
5 Sigismund Freyer (Ger)—Ultimus	183	

Captain Jean Cariou of France and Mignon, winners of the individual gold medal at the 1912 Games. (Max E. Ammann)

= 6	Wilhelm von Hohenau (Ger)	
	—Pretty Girl	181
	Nils Adlercreutz (Swe)—Ilex	181
	Ernst Casparsson (Swe)—Kiriki	181
= 9	Dimitri Pavlovitch (Rus)—Unité	180
	Charles Lewenhaupt (Swe)—Arno	180
	Ernst Deloch (Ger)—Hubertus	180
	Carl Gustav Lewenhaupt (Swe)	
	—Medusa	180
= 13	Michel Dufort d'Astafort (Fra)	
	—Amazone	179
	Carl Axel Toren (Swe)—Falken	179
15	Charles von Rommel (Rus)	
	—Siablik	178
= 16	Alexander Rodzianko (Rus)—Eros	176
	Enrique Deichler (Chi)—Chile	176
= 18	Ernst Grote (Ger)—Polyphem	174
	Serge Zagorsky (Rus)—Bandoura	174

	Friedrich Karl von Preussen (Ger)	
	—Gibson Boy	174
21	Michel Plechkov (Rus)—Eveta	173
= 22	Åke Hök (Swe)—Mona	170
	Alexis Selikhov (Rus)—Tugela	170
24	Karl Kildal (Nor)—Garcia	168
25	Elias Yanes (Chi)—Patria	166
26	Jörgen Jensen (Nor)—Jossy	165
27	Paul Kenna (GB)—Harmony	162
28	Jens Chr. Falkenberg (Nor)	
	—Florida	161
29	Edward Radcliffe Nash (GB)	
	—The Flea	153
30	Guy Reyntiens (Bel)—Beau Soleil	147

Eliminated: Bernard Meyer (Fra)—Ursule

Number of riders: 31
Number of nations represented: 8

1920 Antwerp

Nations Cup

(1 round, teams of 4, best 3 scores to count)

		Faults	
1	**Sweden** 14.00		
	Claes König—Trésor	2.00	(2)
	Hans von Rosen—Poor Boy	6.00	(= 5)
	Daniel Norling—Eros II	6.00	(= 5)
	Frank Martin—Kohort	(10.00)	(11)
2	**Belgium** 16.25		
	Henri Laame—Biscuit	2.75	(3)
	André Coumans—Lisette	5.25	(4)
	Herman de Gaiffier d'Hestroy—Miss	8.25	(9)
	Herman d'Oultremont—Lord Kitchener	(30.00)	(18)
3	**Italy** 18.75		
	Ettore Caffaratti—Tradittore	1.50	(1)
	Alessandro Alvisi—Raggio di Sole	6.25	(7)
	Giulio Cacciandra—Fortunello	11.00	(12)
	C. Asinari di San Marzano—Varone	(33.00)	(19)
4	**France** 34.75		
	Auguste de Laissardière—Othello	7.50	(8)
	Henri Horment—Dignité	13.25	(14)
	Théophile Carbon—Incas	14.00	(= 15)
	Pierre Le Moyne—Flirt	(14.00)	(= 15)
5	**USA** 42.00		
	Harry D. Chamberlin—Nigra	9.00	(10)
	Karl C. Greenwald—Moses	12.00	(13)
	Vincent P. Erwin—Joffre	21.00	(17)
	Sloan Doak—Rabbit Red	E	

Number of teams: 5

The victors in 1920, Tommaso Lequio di Assaba, of Italy, and Trebecco. (Max E. Ammann)

Individual

(Separate competition, 1 round)

		Faults
1	Tommaso Lequio di Assaba (Ita)—Trebecco	2.00
2	Alessandro Valerio (Ita)—Cento	3.00
3	Carl Gustaf Lewenhaupt (Swe)—Mon Coeur	4.00

4	Paul Michelet (Nor)—Raon	5.00
= 5	Ferdinand de la Serna (Bel)—Arsinoe	6.00
	Lars von Stockenström (Swe)—Reward	6.00
= 7	Henry T. Allen, jnr (USA)—Don	7.00
	Santorre de Rossi di Santa Rosa (Ita)—Neruccio	7.00
	Roger Moeremans d'Emaus (Bel)—Sweet Girl	7.00
= 10	Garibaldi Spighi (Ita)—Virginia	8.00
	Edmond L'Hotte (Fra)—Kabyle	8.00
12	John W. Downer (USA)—Dick	8.50
13	Eugen Johansen (Nor)—Nökken	9.00
14	Åge Lundström (Swe)—Eros I	9.75
= 15	Gustaf Kilman (Swe)—Irving	10.00
	Jules Bonvalet (Bel)—Weppelghem	10.00
17	Ruggero Ubertalli (Ita)—Proton	10.25
18	William W. West, jnr (USA)—Prince	12.00
19	Emilio Benini (Ita)—Passero	13.00
20	Jacques Alquir-Bouffard (Fra)—Dahlia	13.25
21	Thierry de Briey (Bel)—Perfect Gentleman	13.50
22	Frank Tisnes (Fra)—Ugolin	17.00
23	Nils Akerblom (Swe)—Heikki	19.50
24	Allan Ekman (Swe)—Tagore	21.50
25	Jacques Misonne (Bel)—Gaucho	23.25

Number of riders: 25

Number of nations represented: 6

1924 Paris

Nations Cup

(1 round, teams of 4, best 3 scores to count)

Faults

1 Sweden 42.25

Åke Thelning—Loke	12.00	(6)
Axel Ståhle—Cecil	12.25	(7)
Åge Lundström—Anvers	18.00	(11)
Georg von Braun—Diana	(23.50)	(19)

2 Switzerland 50.00

Alphonse Gemuseus—Lucette	6.00	(1)
Werner Stuber—Girandole	20.00	(14)
Hans E. Bühler—Sailor Boy	24.00	(20)
Henri Von der Weid—Admiral	(24.00)	(21)

3 Portugal 53.00

Anibal Borges de Almeida—Reginald	12.00	(5)
Helder de Sousa Martins—Avro	19.00	(12)
José Mousinho de Albuquerque—Hetrugo	22.00	(17)
Luiz de Menezes Margaride—Profond	(36.00)	(31)

4 Belgium 57.00

Nicolas Leroy—Vif Argent	14.75	(8)
Jacques Misonne—Torino	19.50	(13)
Gaston Mesmaekers—As de Pique	22.75	(18)
Jeans Breuls—Acrobate	(24.00)	(22)

5 Italy 57.50

Tommaso Lequio di Assaba—Trebecco	8.75	(2)
Leone Valle—Sbruffo	20.00	(15)
Alessandro Alvisi—Grey Fox	28.75	(26)
E. Beraudo di Pralermo—Sido	E	(—)

6 Poland 58.50

Adam Krolikiewicz—Picador	10.00	(3)
Karol von Rommel—Faworyt	18.00	(10)
Zdzislaw Dziadulski—Zefer	30.50	(28)
Kazimierz Szosland—Jacek	(39.25)	(32)

7 Great Britain 65.75

Philip Bowden-Smith—Billy Boy	10.50	(4)
Capel Brunker—Peter	25.50	(24)
Geoffrey Brooke—Daddy Long Legs	29.75	(27)
Keith Wilson Hervey—Wanton	E	(—)

8 Spain 73.75

José Alvarez de Bohorques—Acabado	18.00	(9)
Nemesio Martinez Hombre—Zapatillero	22.00	(16)
José Navarro Morenés—Grande Couronne	33.75	(30)
Emilio Lopez de Letona—Modiran	E	(—)

Eliminated: USA, Czechoslovakia, France.

Number of teams: 11

Individual

(No separate competition)

	Faults	Time
1 Alphonse Gemuseus (Switz)—Lucette	6.00	2:24,4
2 Tommaso Lequio di Assaba (Ita) —Trebecco	8.75	2:42,0
3 Adam Krolikiewicz (Pol)—Picador	10.00	2:38,4

Switzerland's only winner of the Olympic title, Alphonse Gemuseus on Lucette, winners in Paris in 1924. (Max E. Ammann)

		Faults	Time
4	Philip Bowden-Smith (GB)—Billy Boy	10.50	2:41,4
5	Anibal Borges de Almeida (Por)—Reginald	12.00	2:28,8
6	Åke Thelning (Swe)—Loke	12.00	2:30,4
7	Axel Ståhle (Swe)—Cecil	12.25	2:40,0
8	Nicolas Leroy (Bel)—Vif Argent	14.75	2:42,2
9	José Alvarez de Bohorques (Spa) —Acabado	18.00	2:31,0
10	Karol von Rommel (Pol)—Faworyt	18.00	2:38,2
11	Åge Lundström (Swe)—Anvers	18.00	2:38,4
12	Helder de Sousa Martins (Por)—Avro	19.00	2:31,4
13	Jacques Misonne (Bel)—Torino	19.50	3:05,4
14	Werner Stuber (Switz)—Girandole	20.00	2:32,4
15	Leone Valle (Ita)—Sbruffo	20.00	2:36,6
16	Nemesio Martinez Hombre (Spa) —Zapatillero	22.00	2:17,2
17	José Mousinho de Albuquerque (Por) —Hetrugo	22.00	2:21,0
18	Gaston Mesmaekers (Bel)—As de Pique	22.75	2:50,0
19	Georg von Braun (Swe)—Diana	23.50	2:45,6
20	Hans E. Bühler (Switz)—Sailor Boy	24.00	2:20,0
21	Henri Von der Weid (Switz)—Admiral	24.00	2:39,8
22	Jean Breuls (Bel)—Acrobate	24.00	2:44,4
23	Rudolf Popler (Czech)—Eldorado	24.50	2:45,8
24	Capel Brunker (GB)—Peter	25.50	2:45,0
25	John A. Barry (USA)—Nigra	27.25	2:40,0
26	Alessandro Alvisi (Ita)—Grey Fox	28.75	2:42,4
27	Geoffrey Brooke (GB)—Daddy Long Legs	29.75	3:02,6
28	Zdzislaw Dziadulski (Pol)—Zefer	30.50	2:49,4
29	Sloan Doak (USA)—Joffre	32.00	2:23,0
30	José Navarro Morenés (Spa) —Grande Couronne	33.75	3:02,4
31	Luiz de Menezes Margaride (Por) —Profond	36.00	2:17,2
32	Kazimierz Szosland (Pol)—Jacek	39.25	3:20,0
33	Pierre Clavé (Fra)—Le Trouvère	41.00	3:23,0
34	Oldrich Buchar (Czech)—Esperanto	45.00	2:37,6

Eliminated: Keith Wilson Hervey (GB)—Wanton; Michel Bignon (Fra)—The Doctor; Théophile Carbon (Fra)—Incas; Henry de Royer (Fra)—Rosette XIV; E. Beraudio di Pralermo (Ita)—Sido; Emilio Lopez de Letona (Spa)—Modiran; Josef Rabas (Czech)—Arab; Frederic H. Bontecou (USA)—Ballymacshane; Vernon Padgett (USA)—Little Canada.

Number of riders: 43

Number of nations represented: 11

The winning Swedish team in 1924 (from left), Axel Ståhle, Georg van Braun, Åge Lundström and Åke Thelning. (Max E. Ammann)

Jumping in progress in the Olympic Stadium, Amsterdam 1928. (Max E. Ammann)

1928 Amsterdam

Nations Cup

(1 round, teams of 3, all 3 scores to count)

		Faults	
1 Spain 4.00			
José Navarro Morenés—Zapataso		0.00	(5)
José Alvarez de los Trujillos—Zalamero		2.00	(=10)
Julio Garcia Fernández—Revistade		2.00	(12)
2 Poland 8.00			
Kazimierz Gzowski—Mylord		0.00	(4)
Kazimierz Szosland—Alli		2.00	(13)
Michael Antoniewicz—Readglet		6.00	(20)
3 Sweden 10.00			
Karl Hansen—Gerold		0.00	(6)
Carl Björnstjerna—Kornett		2.00	(9)
Ernst Hallberg—Loke		8.00	(25)

	Faults	
=4 Italy 12.00		
Francesco Forquet—Capinera	0.00	(7)
Alessandro, Conte Bettoni-Cazzago—Aladino	6.00	(=21)
Tommaso Lequio di Assaba—Trebecco	6.00	(24)
=4 France 12.00		
Pierre Bertran de Balanda—Papillon XIV	0.00	(2)
Jacques Couderc de Fonlongue—Valangerville	4.00	(=17)
Pierre Clavé—Le Trouvère	8.00	(26)
=4 Portugal 12.00		
Luiz Ivens Ferraz—Marco Visconti	4.00	(15)
Helder de Sousa Martins—Avro	4.00	(16)
José Mousinho de Albuquerque—Hebraico	4.00	(19)

7 Germany   14.00

Eduard Krueger—Donauwelle	2.00	(=10)
Richard Sahla—Correggio	4.00	(14)
Carl Friedrich von Langen—Falkner	8.00	(28)

8 Switzerland   18.00

Charles Kuhn—Pepita	0.00	(3)
Alphonse Gemuseus—Lucette	2.00	(8)
Pierre de Muralt—Notas	16.00	(37)

9 USA   22.00

Harry D. Chamberlin—Nigra	4.00	(=17)
Frank L. Carr—Miss America	6.00	(=21)
Adolphus W. Roffe—Fairfax	12.00	(33)

10 Netherlands   26.00

Gerard de Kruijff—Preten	8.00	(27)
Anton Colenbrander—Gaga	8.00	(29)
Charles Labouchère—Copain	10.00	(30)

11 Norway   34.00

Knut Gysler—Sans Peur	6.00	(=21)
Anton Klaveness—Barrabas	12.00	(32)
Bjart Ording—Fram I	16.00	(36)

12 Argentina   58.25

Amabrio del Villar—Talán-Talán	12.25	(34)
Raul Antoli—Turbion	20.00	(40)
Victor Fernández-Bazán—Silencio	26.00	(42)

13 Hungary   62.00

Lajos de Malanotti—Ibolya III	12.00	(31)
Antal de Kánya—Gólya	20.00	(39)
Coloman von Cseh de Szent-Katolna —Beni	30.00	(43)

14 Belgium   64.25

Gaston Mesmaekers—As de Pique	14.00	(35)
Jacques Misonne—Keepsake	16.00	(38)
Baudoin de Brabandère—Miss América	34.25	(44)

Eliminated: Czechoslovakia

Number of teams: 15

František Ventura of Czechoslovakia riding Eliot. This pair jumped three clear rounds to win the 1928 Olympic title. (Max E. Ammann)

Individual

(No separate competition)

	Faults	Time	Jump-off One	Two
1 František Ventura (Czech)—Eliot	0	1:34	0	0
2 Pierre Bertran de Balanda (Fra) —Papillon XIV	0	1:21	0	2
3 Charles Kuhn (Switz)—Pepita	0	1:38	0	4
4 Kazimierz Gzowski (Pol)—Mylord	0	1:33	2	
5 José Navarro Morenés (Spa) —Zapataso	0	1:36	2	
6 Karl Hansen (Swe)—Gerold	0	1:39	2	
7 Francesco Forquet (Ita) —Capinera	0	1:33	D	
8 Alphonse Gemuseus (Switz) —Lucette	2.00	1:27		
9 Carl Björnstjerna (Swe)—Kornett	2.00	1:30		
=10 José Alvarez de los Trujillos (Spa) —Zalamero	2.00	1:33		
Eduard Krueger (Ger) —Donauwelle	2.00	1:33		

12 Julio Garcia Fernández (Spa) —Revistade	2.00	1:37
13 Kazimierz Szosland (Pol)—Alli	2.00	1:40
14 Richard Sahla (Ger)—Correggio	4.00	1:15
15 Luiz Ivens Ferraz (Por) —Marco Visconti	4.00	1:26
16 Helder de Sousa Martins (Por) —Avro	4.00	1:31
=17 Harry D. Chamberlin (USA) —Nigra	4.00	1:34
Jacques Couderc de Fonlongue (Fra)—Valangerville	4.00	1:34
19 José Mousinho de Albuquerque (Por)—Hebraico	4.00	1:42
20 Michael Antoniewicz (Pol) —Readglet	6.00	1:31
=21 Knut Gysler (Nor)—Sans Peur	6.00	1:38
Alessandro, Conte Bettoni-Cazzago (Ita)—Aladino	6.00	1:38
Frank L. Carr (USA) —Miss America	6.00	1:38
24 Tommaso Lequio di Assaba (Ita) —Trebecco	6.00	1:48
25 Ernst Hallberg (Swe)—Loke	8.00	1:31
26 Pierre Clavé (Fra)—Le Trouvère	8.00	1:33
27 Gerard de Kruijff (NL)—Preten	8.00	1:41
28 Carl Friedrich von Langen (Ger) —Falkner	8.00	1:42
29 Anton Colenbrander (NL)—Gaga	8.00	1:46
30 Charles Labouchère (NL) —Copain	10.00	1:44
31 Lajos de Malanotti (Hun) —Ibolya III	12.00	1:28
32 Anton Klaveness (Nor) —Barrabas	12.00	1:35
33 Adolphus W. Roffe (USA) —Fairfax	12.00	2:04
34 Amabrio del Villar (Arg) —Talán-Talán	12.25	1:49

35 Gaston Mesmaekers (Bel)		
—As de Pique	14.00	1:37
36 Bjart Ording (Nor)—Fram I	16.00	1:30
37 Pierre de Muralt (Switz)—Notas	16.00	1:48
38 Jacques Misonne (Bel)		
—Keepsake	16.00	2:04
39 Antal de Kánya (Hun)—Gólya	20.00	1:33
40 Raul Antoli (Arg)—Turbion	20.00	1:45
41 Josef Rabas (Czech)		
—Daghestan	22.50	2:14
42 Victor Fernández-Bazán		
(Arg)—Silencio	26.00	1:27

43 Coloman von Cseh de Szent-		
Katolna (Hun)—Beni	30.00	1:56
44 Baudoin de Brabandère (Bel)		
—Miss América	34.25	2:29

Eliminated: Rudolf Popler (Czech)—Denk; Shigetoma Yoshida (Jap)—Kyuzan.

Number of riders: 46

Number of nations represented: 16

1932 Los Angeles

Nations Cup

(1 round, teams of 3, all 3 scores to count)
No awards (no team completed the course with three riders).
Number of teams: 3 (Mexico, Sweden, USA)

Individual

(No separate competition)

	Faults	Time
1 Baron Takeichi Nishi (Jap)—Uranus	8.00	2:42,2
2 Harry D. Chamberlin (USA)—Show Girl	12.00	2:38,2
3 Clarence von Rosen, jnr (Swe)—Empire	16.00	2:19,2
4 William B. Bradford (USA)—Joe Aleshire	24.00	2:26,4
5 Ernst Hallberg (Swe)—Kornett	50.50	3:31,6

Eliminated: John W. Wofford (USA)—Babe Wartham; Arne Francke (Swe)—Urfé; Yasushi Imamura (Jap)—Sonny Boy; Procopio Ortiz Reyes (Mex)—Pinello; Andres Bocanegra (Mex) —El As; Carlos Mejia (Mex)—Kanguro.

Number of riders: 11

Number of nations represented: 4

Japan's Baron Takeichi Nishi and Uranus, winners of the only jumping gold medal awarded at the 1932 Games. (Max E. Amman)

1936 Berlin

Nations Cup

(1 round, teams of 3, all 3 scores to count)

	Faults	
1 **Germany** 44.00		
Kurt Hasse—Tora	4.00	(1)
Marten von Barnekow—Nordland	20.00	(=16)
Heinz Brandt—Alchimist	20.00	(=16)
2 **The Netherlands** 51.50		
Johan Jacob Greter—Ernica	12.00	(=6)
Jan Adrianus de Bruine—Trixie	15.00	(=11)
Henri Louis van Schaik—Santa Bell	24.50	(23)
3 **Portugal** 56.00		
José Beltrão—Biscuit	12.00	(=6)
Luis Marquez do Funchal—Merle Blanc	20.00	(=16)
Luis Mena e Silva—Faussette	24.00	(=21)
4 **USA** 72.50		
Carl Raguse—Dakota	8.00	(5)
William Bradford—Don	27.00	(=25)
Cornelius C. Jadwin—Ugly	37.50	(34)
5 **Switzerland** 74.50		
Arnold Mettler—Durmitor	15.00	(=11)
Jörg Fehr—Corona	29.00	(30)
Hans Iklé—Exilé	30.50	(31)

6 **Japan** 75.00

Manabu Iwahashi—Falaise	15.25	(14)
Takeichi Nishi—Uranus	20.75	(20)
Hirotsugu Inanami—Asafuji	39.00	(35)

7 **France** 75.25

Xavier Bizard—Bagatelle	12.00	(=6)
Maurice Gudin de Vallerin—Ecuyère	12.00	(=6)
Jean de Tillière—Adriano	51.25	(38)

Eliminated: Belgium, Italy, Austria, Rumania, Czechoslovakia, Great Britain, Norway, Poland, Sweden, Turkey, Hungary.

Number of teams: 18

Individual

(No separate competition)

		Jump-off
	Faults	F/Time
1 Kurt Hasse (Ger)—Tora	4.00	4/59.2
2 Henri Rang (Rum)—Delfis	4.00	4/72.8
3 Jozsef von Platthy (Hun)—Sellö	8.00	0/62.6
4 Georges Ganshof van der Meersch (Bel)		
—Ibrahim	8.00	0/69.0
5 Carl Raguse (USA)—Dakota	8.00	4/62.4
=6 Xavier Bizard (Fra)—Bagatelle	12.00	
Maurice Gudin de Vallerin (Fra)		
—Ecuyère	12.00	
Cevat Koula (Tur)—Sapkin	12.00	
Johan Jacob Greter (NL)—Ernica	12.00	
José Beltrão (Por)—Biscuit	12.00	
=11 Henry de Menten de Horne (Bel)		
—Musaphiki	15.00	
Jan Adrianus de Bruine (NL)—Trixie	15.00	
Arnold Mettler (Switz)—Durmitor	15.00	
14 Manabu Iwahashi (Jap)—Falaise	15.25	
15 Renzo Bonivento (Ita)—Osoppo	18.75	
=16 Gerardo Conforti (Ita)—Saba	20.00	
Marten von Barnekow (Ger)—Nordland	20.00	

Lt. Kurt Hasse and the mare Tora, individual and team gold medallists in 1936. Although bred in Schleswig-Holstein, Tora was by an English Hackney stallion, Capenor Mormal Forester. (BBC Hulton Picture Library)

=16 Heinz Brandt (Ger)—Alchimist		20.00
Luis Marquez do Funchal (Por)		
—Merle Blanc		20.00
20 Takeichi Nishi (Jap)—Uranus		20.75
=21 Luis Mena e Silva (Por)—Fausette		24.00
Heinrich Sauer (Aut)—Gloriette		24.00
23 Henri Louis van Schaik (NL)—Santa Bell		24.50
24 Arthur Qvist (Nor)—Notatus		25.00
=25 Arne Francke (Swe)—Urfé		27.00
William Bradford (USA)—Don		27.00
=27 Miloslav Buzek (Czech)—Chroust		28.00
Saim Polatkan (Tur)—Schakal		28.00
29 Constantin Apostol (Rum)—Dracustie		28.75
30 Jorg Fehr (Switz)—Corona		29.00
31 Hans Iklé (Switz)—Exilé		30.50
32 Rolf Örn (Swe)—Kornett		31.75
33 Ottmar Szepessy-Schaurek (Hun)		
—Pókai		35.00
34 Cornelius C. Jadwin (USA)—Ugly		37.50
35 Hirotsugu Inanami (Jap)—Asafuji		39.00
36 Janusz Komorowski (Pol)—Dunkan		47.25
37 Gerhard Egger (Aut)—Mimir		47.50
38 Jean de Tillière (Fra)—Adriano		51.25

Eliminated: Yves van Strydonck (Bel)—Ramona; Capel Brunker (GB)—Magpie; William Carr (GB)—Bovril; Jack Talbot-Ponsonby (GB)— Kineton; Fernando Filipponi (Ita)—Nasello; Halfdan Petterøe (Nor)—Schamyl; Henrik Skougaard (Nor)—Felicia; Rudolf Trenkwitz (Aut)—Danubia; Michael Gutowski (Pol)—Warszawianka; Tadeusz Sokolowski (Pol)—Zbieg II; Tomo Tudoran (Rum)—Hunter; Prinz Gustaf Adolf (Swe)—Aida; Julius Čoček (Czech)—Chostra; Josef Seyfried (Czech)—Radmila; Cevat Gürkan (Tur)—Güdük; Elemer von Barcza (Hun)—Kopé.

Number of riders: 54

Number of nations represented: 18

1948 London

Nations Cup

(1 round, teams of 3, all 3 scores to count)

Faults

1 Mexico 34.25

Humberto Mariles Cortés—Arete	6.25	(1)
Rubén Uriza Castro—Hatuey	8.00	(2)
Alberto Valdés Ramos—Chihuahua	20.00	(=10)

2 Spain 56.50

Jaime Garcia Cruz—Bizarro	12.00	(=5)
José Navarro Morenés—Quorum	20.00	(=10)
Marcelino Gavilán y Ponce de Léon —Forajido	24.50	(16)

3 Great Britain 67.00

Harry Llewellyn—Foxhunter	16.00	(=7)
Henry Nicoll—Kilgeddin	16.00	(=7)
Arthur Carr—Monty	35.00	(19)

Eliminated: Ireland, Sweden, France, The Netherlands, Italy, USA, Argentina, Portugal, Brazil, Denmark, Turkey.

Number of teams: 14

Individual

(No separate competition)

		Faults	Jump-off F/Time
1	Humberto Mariles Cortés (Mex)—Arete	6.25	
2	Rubén Uriza Castro (Mex)—Hatuey	8.00	0/49.1
3	Jean d'Orgeix (Fra)—Sucre de Pomme	8.00	4/38.9
4	Franklin F. Wing (USA)—Democrat	8.00	4/40.1
=5	Jaime Garcia Cruz (Spa)—Bizarro	12.00	
	Eric Sörensen (Swe)—Blatunga	12.00	
=7	Henry Nicoll (GB)—Kilgeddin	16.00	
	Harry Llewellyn (GB)—Foxhunter	16.00	
	Max Fresson (Fra)—Décamètre	16.00	

=10	José Navarro Morenés (Spa)—Quorum	20.00
	Alberto Valdés Ramos (Mex) —Chihuahua	20.00
	Franco Pontes (Bra)—Itaguai	20.00
13	Johan Greger Lewenhaupt (Swe) —Orkan	20.75
14	Dan Corry (Ire)—Tramore Bay	21.25
15	Rafael Campos (Arg)—Santa Fe	24.00
16	Marcelino Gavilán y Ponce de Léon (Spa)—Forajido	24.50
17	Fred Ahern (Ire)—Aherlow	25.50
18	Henrique Callado (Por)—Xerez	26.00
19	Arthur Carr (GB)—Monty	35.00
20	Joachim Joseph Gruppelaar (NL) —Random Harvest	36.00
21	John W. Russell (USA)—Air Mail	38.25
22	João Correia Barrento (Por)—Alcoa	42.50
23	Tauno Rissanen (Fin)—Viser	56.00

Eliminated: Nestor Alvarado (Arg)—Mineral; Pascual Pistarini (Arg)—Canguro; Eloy Massey Oliveira de Menezes (Bra)—Sabu; R. Continentino Dias Ribeiro (Bra)—Bon Soir; Otto Acthon (Den)—Please; J. J. Ladegaard Mikkelsen (Den)—Atom; Torben Tryde (Den)—Attila; Veiko Vartiainen (Fin)—Pontus; Pierre de Maupeou d'Ableiges (Fra)—Nankin; Jan de Bruine (NL)—Romanichel; Jakob Rijks (NL)—Master; John Lewis (Ire)—Lough Neagh; Alessandro, Conte Bettoni-Cazzago (Ita)—Uranio II; Gerardo Conforti (Ita)—Furore; Piero d'Inzeo (Ita)—Briacone; Helder de Souza Martins (Por)—Optus; Karl Ake Hultberg (Swe)—Ismed; Selim Cakir (Tur)—Gitchluv; Kudret Kasar (Tur)—Siyok; Eyrup Oncü (Tur)—Yildiz; Andrew A. Frierson (USA)—Rascal.

Number of riders: 44

Number of nations represented: 15

After their arrival in England (together with 55 tons of feed), the Argentinian horses make their way across Barnes Common to Roehampton to their 1948 Olympic Games quarters. (Popperfoto)

Foxhunter

In the late forties and early fifties there could have been few people with any interest in equestrian sports who had not heard of Foxhunter, the horse who saved the day for Britain at the Helsinki Olympics; who was three times winner of the King George V Gold Cup, and who was full-back of the British team in many a Nations Cup.

Born in 1940, on 23 April—an auspicious day if ever there was one, being St George's Day and Shakespeare's birthday—he was a native of Norfolk, though he was living in Leicestershire when Harry Llewellyn, now Sir Harry, acquired him as a six-year-old. A big, quality bay gelding, Foxhunter made such rapid progress as a show jumper that he was selected to represent Britain at the 1948 Olympic Games in London. He finished in equal seventh place, winning a team bronze medal in the process. A few days later he won the coveted King George V Gold Cup at London's International Horse Show for the first time.

In the years that followed he won Grand Prix and puissances at many of the world's most important shows; he was in 12 winning Nations Cup teams, and he won the King George V Gold Cup on two more occasions, in 1950 and 1953. He remains the only horse to have achieved a hat-trick in that event.

Harry Llewellyn schooling Foxhunter at home in Monmouthshire. (Popperfoto)

The highlight of his career, however, came in 1952 at the Helsinki Olympics. Up to the time of the Nations Cup, the last event of the Games, Britain had failed to win a gold medal. At the end of the first round the USA was leading on 23.00 faults, followed by Portugal (24.00), Argentina (28.00), Brazil (28.50) and Britain (32.75). Foxhunter, who was over-fresh, had gone least well of the three British horses, had very nearly unseated his rider at one point, and was lying in 36th place on 16.75 faults. But in the second round the situation changed radically. Wilf White and Nizefela repeated their brilliant first-round performance for only 4.00 faults and a total of 8.00. Duggie Stewart and Aherlow also made only one mistake for a two-round total of 16.00. Britain had pegged back the lead of the other countries to such effect that the gold medal itself was within reach.

When he started his second round, Harry Llewellyn knew that he could afford to have one fence down and the team would still win the gold. Two down, and victory would go to Chile. As if to make up for his first-round debacle, Foxhunter jumped one of the most immaculate rounds of the entire contest to record one of only four clears that day. The gold medal was Britain's. Nizefela had proved himself the best of the British trio and was unlucky not to win the individual gold, too—a controversial water-jump fault forced him to jump off against four others and he finally finished fifth. Foxhunter had redeemed himself, and in spectacular fashion. Britain has not won an Olympic gold medal for show jumping from that day to this.

Since the great horse's retirement, and his subsequent death in 1959, the name of Foxhunter has lived on thanks to the competition devised by Harry Llewellyn, initially as a means of giving away some of the numerous silver trophies the horse had won and which Harry's wife said she was not going to clean! The Foxhunter Jumping Championship is designed to introduce promising young horses and riders in Great Britain to top level competition. In 1987 some 46 000 horses competed in nearly 1600 preliminary Foxhunter competitions, followed by 15 Foxhunter regional finals, and leading to the Foxhunter Championship at the Horse of the Year Show, Wembley. Horses who have made their way to the top via the Foxhunter Championship include Beethoven, World Champion in 1970. There could be no more fitting memorial to a great and much-loved horse.

1952 Helsinki

Nations Cup

(2 rounds, teams of 3, all 3 scores to count)

	Round One	Two	Total	
		Faults		

1 Great Britain 40.75

	One	Two	Total	
Wilf White—Nizefela	4.00	4.00	8.00	(5)
Duggie Stewart—Aherlow	12.00	4.00	16.00	(=12)
Harry Llewellyn —Foxhunter	16.75	0.00	16.75	(15)

2 Chile 45.75

Oscar Cristi—Bambi	4.00	4.00	8.00	(2)
Cesar Mendoza—Pillan	12.00	0.00	12.00	(=7)
Ricardo Echeverria —Lindo Peal	17.75	8.00	25.75	(28)

3 USA 52.25

William Steinkraus —Hollandia	4.00	9.25	13.25	(11)
Arthur McCashin —Miss Budweiser	12.00	4.00	16.00	(=12)
John W. Russell —Democrat	7.00	16.00	23.00	(24)

4 Brazil 56.50

Eloy Massey Oliveira de Menezes—Biguá	4.00	4.00	8.00	(4)
Renyldo Guimarães Ferreira—Bibelot	12.50	8.00	20.50	(23)
Alvaro Dias de Toledo —Eldorado	12.00	16.00	28.00	(=31)

5 France 59.00

Pierre Jonquères d'Oriola —Ali-Baba	8.00	0.00	8.00	(1)
Bertrand Pernot du Breuil —Tourbillon	12.00	8.00	20.00	(=16)
Jean d'Orgeix—Arlequin D	16.00	15.00	31.00	(34)

The individual medallists in Helsinki, Pierre Jonquères d'Oriola (centre), Oscar Christi (left) and Fritz Thiedemann.

6 Germany 60.00

Fritz Thiedemann—Meteor	0.00	8.00	8.00	(3)
Georg Höltig—Fink	8.00	12.00	20.00	(=16)
Hans Hermann Evers —Baden	24.00	8.00	32.00	(=35)

7 Argentina 60.75

Sergio Dellacha—Santa Fe	8.00	4.00	12.00	(=7)
Argentino Molinuevo —Discutido	4.00	8.00	12.00	(=7)
Julio Cesar Sagasta —Don Juan	16.00	20.75	36.75	(38)

8 Portugal 64.00

Henrique Callado —Caramulo	8.00	12.00	20.00	(=16)
João Craveiro Lopes —Raso	12.00	8.00	20.00	(=16)
José Carvalhosa —Mondina	4.00	20.00	24.00	(=25)

9 Mexico 64.75

Humberto Mariles Cortés —Petrolero	4.00	4.75	8.75	(6)
Victor Saucedo Carillo —Resorte II	12.00	12.00	24.00	(=25)
Roberto Viñals Contreras —Alteño	20.00	12.00	32.00	(=35)

10 Spain 67.25

Jaime Garcia Cruz —Quorum	12.00	8.00	20.00	(=16)
Manuel Ordovas— —Bohemio	8.00	12.00	20.00	(=16)
Marcelino Gavilán y Ponce de Léon—Quoniam	20.25	7.00	27.25	(30)

11 Sweden 80.00

Gunnar Palm—Lurifax	12.00	8.00	20.00	(=16)
H. Börje Jeppsson —Spitfire	12.00	16.00	28.00	(=31)
Carl Jan Hamilton—Halali	12.00	20.00	32.00	(=35)

12 Egypt 80.25

Mohamed Khairy —Insh Allah	8.00	8.00	16.00	(=12)
Gamal El Din Haress —Sakr	8.00	16.00	24.00	(=25)
Mohamed Selim Zaki —Sali al Nabi	28.25	12.00	40.25	(41)

13 Rumania 180.25

Georghe Antohi—Haimana	16.00	22.25	38.25	(39)
Ion Jipa—Troika	8.00	31.00	39.00	(40)
Ion Constantin—Vagabond	70.00	33.00	103.00	(48)

14 USSR 201.75

Michail Vlasov—Rota	40.00	16.00	56.00	(43)
Nikolai Shelenkov—Atiger	41.75	20.75	62.50	(46)
Grigori Budenny—Yeger	23.00	60.25	83.25	(47)

Eliminated: Italy, Finland.

Number of teams: 16

Individual

(No separate competition)

		Round One Faults	Round Two Faults	Total	Jump-off F/Time
1	Pierre Jonquères d'Oriola (Fra)—Ali-Baba	8.00	0.00	8.00	0/40.00
2	Oscar Cristi (Chile)—Bambi	4.00	4.00	8.00	4/44.00
3	Fritz Thiedemann (Ger)—Meteor	0.00	8.00	8.00	8/38.50
4	Eloy Massey Oliveira de Menezes (Bra)—Biguá	4.00	4.00	8.00	8/45.00
5	Wilf White (GB)—Nizefela	4.00	4.00	8.00	12/43.00
6	Humberto Mariles Cortés (Mex)—Petrolero	4.00	4.75	8.75	
=7	Cesar Mendoza (Chi)—Pillan	12.00	0.00	12.00	
	Argentino Molinuevo (Arg)—Discutido	4.00	8.00	12.00	
	Raimondo d'Inzeo (Ita)—Litargirio	4.00	8.00	12.00	
	Sergio Dellacha (Arg)—Santa Fe	8.00	4.00	12.00	
11	William Steinkraus (USA)—Hollandia	4.00	9.25	13.25	
=12	Mohamed Khairy (Egy)—Insh Allah	8.00	8.00	16.00	
	Arthur McCashin (USA)—Miss Budweiser	12.00	4.00	16.00	
	Duggie Stewart (GB)—Aherlow	12.00	4.00	16.00	
15	Harry Llewellyn (GB)—Foxhunter	16.75	0.00	16.75	
=16	Henrique Callado (Por)—Caramulo	8.00	12.00	20.00	
	Jaime Garcia Cruz (Spa)—Quorum	12.00	8.00	20.00	
	Bertrand Pernot du Breuil (Fra)—Tourbillon	12.00	8.00	20.00	
	João Craveiro Lopes (Por)—Raso	12.00	8.00	20.00	
	Georg Höltig (Ger)—Fink	8.00	12.00	20.00	
	Manuel Ordovas (Spa)—Bohemio	8.00	12.00	20.00	
	Gunnar Palm (Swe)—Lurifax	12.00	8.00	20.00	
23	Renyldo Guimarães Ferreira (Bra)—Bibelot	12.50	8.00	20.50	
24	John W. Russell (USA)—Democrat	7.00	16.00	23.00	
=25	Gamal El Din Haress (Egy)—Sakr	8.00	16.00	24.00	
	José Carvalhosa (Por)—Mondina	4.00	20.00	24.00	
	Victor Saucedo Carillo (Mex)—Resorte II	12.00	12.00	24.00	
28	Ricardo Echeverria (Chi)—Lindo Peal	17.75	8.00	25.75	
29	Bjart Ording (Nor)—Fram II	4.00	23.00	27.00	
30	Marcelino Gavilán y Ponce de Léon (Spa)—Quoniam	20.25	7.00	27.25	
=31	H. Börje Jeppsson (Swe)—Spitfire	12.00	16.00	28.00	
	Alvaro Dias de Toledo (Bra)—Eldorado	12.00	16.00	28.00	
	Salvatore Oppes (Ita)—Macezio	8.00	20.00	28.00	
34	Jean d'Orgeix (Fra)—Arlequin D	16.00	15.00	31.00	
=35	Carl Jan Hamilton (Swe)—Halali	12.00	20.00	32.00	
	Roberto Viñals Contreras (Mex)—Alteño	20.00	12.00	32.00	
	Hans Hermann Evers (Ger)—Baden	24.00	8.00	32.00	
38	Julio Cesar Sagasta (Arg)—Don Juan	16.00	20.75	36.75	
39	Georghe Antohi (Rum)—Haimani	16.00	22.25	38.25	
40	Ion Jipa (Rum)—Troika	8.00	31.00	39.00	
41	Mohamed Selim Zaki (Egy)—Sali al Nabi	28.25	12.00	40.25	
42	Alexander Stoffel (Switz)—Vol-au-Vent	40.25	4.00	44.25	
43	Michail Vlasov (USSR)—Rota	40.00	16.00	56.00	
44	Pyung-sun Minn (Kor)—Parcifal	35.75	24.00	59.75	
45	Toshiaki Kitai (Jap)—Ulysse	50.00	12.00	62.00	
46	Nikolai Shelenkov (USSR)—Atiger	41.75	20.75	62.50	
47	Grigori Budenny (USSR)—Yeger	23.00	60.25	83.25	
48	Ion Constantin (Rum)—Vagabond	70.00	33.00	103.00	

Eliminated: Mauno Roiha (Fin)—Roa; Viktor Jansson (Fin)—Jessa; Henrik Lavonius (Fin)—Lassi; Piero d'Inzeo (Ita)—Uruguay (d'Inzeo missed his start).

Number of riders: 52

Number of nations represented: 20

In the individual competition at the 1912 Olympics, 15 of the 31 horses were British bred; five were bred in Sweden, four each in France and Russia, and three in Germany.

The first woman to win an Olympic silver medal for show jumping was Janou Lefèbvre. Riding Kenavo D, she was a member of the French team which finished runners-up in the Nations Cup at Tokyo in 1964.

Arete, the horse on whom Humberto Mariles Cortés of Mexico won individual and team gold medals at the 1948 Olympic Games in London was blind in one eye.

1956 Stockholm

Nations Cup

(2 rounds, teams of 3, all 3 scores to count)

	Faults Round One	Two	Total	
1 Germany 40.00				
Hans Günter Winkler				
—Halla	4.00	0.00	4.00	(1)
Fritz Thiedemann				
—Meteor	8.00	4.00	12.00	(=4)
Alfons Lütke-Westhues				
—Ala	16.00	8.00	24.00	(=11)
2 Italy 66.00				
Raimondo d'Inzeo				
—Merano	8.00	0.00	8.00	(2)
Piero d'Inzeo—Uruguay	8.00	3.00	11.00	(3)
Salvatore Oppes				
—Pagoro	23.00	24.00	47.00	(24)
3 Great Britain 69.00				
Wilf White—Nizefela	8.00	4.00	12.00	(=4)
Pat Smythe—Flanagan	8.00	13.00	21.00	(10)
Peter Robeson—Scorchin	16.00	20.00	36.00	(=19)
4 Argentina 99.50				
Carlos Delia—Discutido	15.00	4.00	19.00	(8)
Pedro Mayorga				
—Coriolano	16.00	16.00	32.00	(17)
Naldo Dasso—Ramito	16.00	32.50	48.50	(25)
5 USA 104.25				
Hugh Wiley—Trail Guide	16.00	8.00	24.00	(=11)
William Steinkraus				
—Night Owl	20.00	8.00	28.00	(=15)
Frank Chapot—Belair	36.25	16.00	52.25	(=27)

6 Spain 117.25				
Carlos Lopez Quesada				
—Tapatio	27.00	0.75	27.75	(14)
Francisco Goyoaga				
—Fahnenkönig	20.00	8.00	28.00	(=15)
Carlos Figueroa				
—Gracieux	33.50	28.00	61.50	(36)
7 Ireland 131.25				
Kevin Barry—Ballyneety	23.00	12.00	35.00	(18)
William Ringrose				
—Liffey Vale	24.00	20.00	44.00	(23)
Patrick Kiernan				
—Ballynonty	19.00	33.25	52.25	(=27)
8 France 154.50				
Pierre Jonquères d'Oriola				
—Voulette	7.00	8.00	15.00	(6)
Bernard de Fombelle				
—Doria	12.00	40.75	52.75	(29)
Georges Calmon				
—Virtuoso	54.75	32.00	86.75	(44)
9 Switzerland 159.50				
William de Rham				
—Va Vite	20.00	16.00	36.00	(=19)
Alexander Stoffel				
—Bricole	27.00	32.00	59.00	(=34)
Marc Büchler—Duroc	28.50	36.00	64.50	(37)
10 Brazil 228.50				
Nelson Pessoa				
—Relincho	32.00	26.00	58.00	(33)
Eloy Massey Oliveira de				
Menezes—Biguá	56.25	28.75	85.00	(41)
Renyldo Guimarães				
Ferreira—Bibelot	29.25	56.25	85.50	(42)

Eliminated: Austria, Belgium, Egypt, Finland, Hungary, Portugal, Sweden, Turkey, USSR, Venezuela.

Number of teams: 20

The injured Hans Günter Winkler, flanked by the d'Inzeo brothers, Raimondo (left) and Piero, rides into the Stockholm stadium for the 1956 medal presentation. (Popperfoto)

Individual

(No separate competition)

	Round		
	One	Two	Total
1 Hans Günter Winkler (Ger)			
—Halla	4.00	0.00	4.00
2 Raimondo d'Inzeo (Ita)			
—Merano	8.00	0.00	8.00
3 Piero d'Inzeo (Ita)—Uruguay	8.00	3.00	11.00
=4 Fritz Thiedemann (Ger)			
—Meteor	8.00	4.00	12.00
Wilf White (GB)—Nizefela	8.00	4.00	12.00
6 Pierre Jonquères d'Oriola (Fra)			
—Voulette	7.00	8.00	15.00
7 Henrique Callado (Por)			
—Martingil	12.00	4.00	16.00
8 Carlos Delia (Arg)—Discutido	15.00	4.00	19.00
9 Mohamed Selim Zaki (Egy)			
—Insh Allah	16.00	4.00	20.00
10 Pat Smythe (GB)—Flanagan	8.00	13.00	21.00
=11 Hugh Wiley (USA)—Trail Guide	16.00	8.00	24.00
Alfons Lütke-Westhues (Ger)			
—Ala	16.00	8.00	24.00
Albert Szatola (Hun)			
—Aranyos	16.00	8.00	24.00
14 Carlos Lopez Quesada (Spa)			
—Tapatio	27.00	0.75	27.75
=15 William Steinkraus (USA)			
—Night Owl	20.00	8.00	28.00
Francisco Goyoaga (Spa)			
—Fahnenkönig	20.00	8.00	28.00
17 Pedro Mayorga (Arg)			
—Coriolano	16.00	16.00	32.00
18 Kevin Barry (Ire)—Ballyneety	23.00	12.00	35.00
=19 William de Rham (Switz)			
—Va Vite	20.00	16.00	36.00
Peter Robeson (GB)			
—Scorchin	16.00	20.00	36.00
=21 Andrei Favorsky (USSR)			
—Manevr	20.00	20.00	40.00
Gamal El Din Haress (Egy)			
—Nefertiti II	20.00	20.00	40.00
23 William Ringrose (Ire)			
—Liffey Vale	24.00	20.00	44.00
24 Salvatore Oppes (Ita)—Pagoro	23.00	24.00	47.00
25 Naldo Dasso (Arg)—Ramito	16.00	32.50	48.50
26 Koichi Kawaguchi (Jap)—Fuji	28.00	24.00	52.00
=27 Frank Chapot (USA)—Belair	36.25	16.00	52.25
Patrick Kiernan (Ire)			
—Ballynonty	19.00	33.25	52.25
29 Bernard de Fombelle (Fra)			
—Doria	12.00	40.75	52.75
30 Salih Koç (Tur)—Basak	24.00	29.25	53.25
31 Kunihiro Ohta (Jap)—Eforegiot	20.00	34.25	54.25
32 Anders Gernandt (Swe)			
—Röhäll	32.00	23.00	55.00
33 Nelson Pessoa (Bra)			
—Relincho	32.00	26.00	58.00
=34 Alexander Stoffel (Switz)			
—Bricole	27.00	32.00	59.00
Brigitte Schockaert (Bel)			
—Muscadin	32.00	27.00	59.00
36 Carlos Figueroa (Spa)			
—Gracieux	33.50	28.00	61.50
37 Marc Büchler (Switz)—Duroc	28.50	36.00	64.50
38 Arslan Günes (Tur)			
—Esmer Altin	33.25	32.00	65.25
39 Vladimir Raspopov (USSR)			
—Kodeks	32.00	44.50	76.50
40 Rolf Stewen (Fin)—Lojal	47.00	36.00	83.00
41 Eloy Massey Oliveira			
de Menezes (Bra)—Biguá	56.25	28.75	85.00
42 Renyldo Guimarães Ferreira			
(Bra)—Bibelot	29.25	56.25	85.50
43 Raymond Lombard (Bel)			
—Dandy	50.50	36.00	86.50
44 Georges Calmon (Fra)			
—Virtuoso	54.75	32.00	86.75
45 Tor Burman (Swe)—Rouquade	43.25	57.75	101.00

Eliminated: Georges Poffé (Bel)—Hicamboy; Omar el Hadary (Egy)—Auer; Kauko Paananen (Fin)—Lassi; Arvi Tervalampi (Fin)—Marras; Lajos Somlay (Hun)—Dobos; István Szondy (Hun)—Higany; Boris Lilov (USSR)—Boston; Bedri Böke (Tur)—Domino; Victor Molina-Vargas (Ven)—Tamanaco; Jesus Rivas-Moncado (Ven)—Murachi; Roberto Moll (Ven)—Soro-caima; Peter Lichtner-Hoyer (Aut)—Rienzi; Adolf Lauda (Aut)—Schönbrunn; Romuald Halm (Aut)—Bianka; Rodrigo da Silveira (Por)—Limerick; João Azevedo (Por)—Licorne; Albert Jacobs (Aus)—Dumbell; Pen Saing (Cam)—Pompon; Isoup Ghanty (Cam)—Flatteur II; Birck Elgaaen (Nor)—Osira; Douglas Wijkander (Swe)—Bimbo.

Number of riders: 66

Number of nations represented: 24

1960 Rome

Nations Cup

(2 rounds, teams of 3, all 3 scores to count)

		Faults		
		Round		
	One	Two	Total	
1 **FRG** 46.50				
Hans Günter Winkler				
—Halla	9.25	4.00	13.25	(2)
Fritz Thiedemann				
—Meteor	8.00	8.00	16.00	(=3)
Alwin Shockemöhle				
—Ferdl	8.50	8.75	17.25	(5)
2 **USA** 66.00				
Frank Chapot—Trail Guide	8.00	12.00	20.00	(6)
William Steinkraus				
—Ksar d'Esprit	12.50	9.00	21.50	(7)
George Morris—Sinjon	8.50	16.00	24.50	(10)
3 **Italy** 80.50				
Raimondo d'Inzeo				
—Posillipo	4.00	4.00	8.00	(1)
Piero d'Inzeo—The Rock	24.00	8.00	32.00	(=12)
Antonio Oppes				
—The Scholar	24.50	16.00	40.50	(18)

4 **UAR (Egypt)**   135.50

Gamal El Din Haress				
—Nefertiti II	16.00	8.00	24.00	(=8)
Mohamed Selim Zaki				
—Artos	20.00	28.00	48.00	(=21)
Elwi Gazi—Mabrouk	31.50	32.00	63.50	(28)

5 **France**   168.75

Bernard de Fombelle				
—Buffalo B	18.50	14.00	32.50	(14)
Max Fresson				
—Grand Veneur	24.00	26.25	50.25	(23)
Pierre Jonquères d'Oriola				
—Eclaire au Chocolat	39.75	46.25	86.00	(35)

6 **Rumania**   175.00

Vasile Pinciu—Birsan	25.50	16.00	41.50	(19)
Virgil Barbuceanu—Robot	25.50	32.25	57.75	(26)
Gheorghe Langa—Rubin	31.75	44.00	75.75	(32)

Eliminated:

Great Britain

David Broome—Sunsalve	12.00	4.00	16.00	(=3)
Pat Smythe—Flanagan	12.00	16.00	28.00	(11)
C. David Barker—Franco	E	24.00	—	

USSR

Andrei Favorsky—Manevr	8.00	16.00	24.00	(=8)
Vladimir Raspopov				
—Kodeks	50.75	31.00	81.75	(33)
Ernst Shabailo—Boston	56.50	E	—	

Argentina

Jorge Lucardi—Stromboli	12.00	20.00	32.00	(=12)
Carlos Delia—Huipil	29.50	26.00	55.50	(24)
Naldo Dasso—Final	E	20.75	—	

Uruguay

German Mailhos—Julian	16.00	20.00	36.00	(=15)
Rafael Paullier—Arapey	28.00	34.25	62.25	(27)
Carlos Colombino				
—Guanaco	39.75	E	—	

Spain

Juan Martinez de Vallejo				
—Charmeuse	12.00	32.00	44.00	(20)
Alfredo Goyeneche				
—Duncan	28.00	20.00	48.00	(=21)
Hernando Espinosa de los				
Monteros—Frantillack	E	E	—	

Ireland

William Ringrose				
—Loch an Easpaig	24.00	16.00	40.00	(17)
John Daly—Loch Garman	25.75	40.75	66.50	(31)
Edward O'Donohoe				
—Cluain Meala	E	E	—	

Portugal

Antonio Pereira				
de Almeida—Palpite	21.25	34.75	56.00	(25)
Henrique Callado				
—Martingil	16.25	E	—	
João Craveiro Lopes				
—Rovuma II	40.75	NP	—	

Japan

Yugo Araki—Fuji	28.00	36.00	64.00	(=29)
Kunihiro Ohta—Facey	36.00	28.00	64.00	(=29)
Yuzo Kageyama				
—Eforegiot	E	E	—	

Individual gold medallists in Rome, Italy's Raimondo d'Inzeo and Posillipo. (The Photo Source)

Hungary

Istvan Suti—Szepleany	32.50	50.25	82.75	(34)
Imre Karcsu—Aranyos	E	E	—	
László Móra—Szertelen	E	NP	—	

Sweden

Anders Gernandt—Valor	16.00	20.00	36.00	(=15)
Gustaf de Geer—Ugly	34.00	53.50	87.50	(36)
Peer Fresk—Jabal	E	E	—	

Turkey

Cevdet Sumer—Isma	33.00	NP	—	
Salih Koç—Eskimo	48.75	NP	—	
Nail Gönenli—Domino	E	NP	—	

Brazil

Renyldo Guimarães Ferreira—Marengo	27.25	NP	—	
Francisco Rabelo Leite —Sultao	E	NP	—	
Oscar Sotero da Silva —Cerrito	E	NP	—	

Number of teams: 18

Individual

(Separate competition, 2 rounds)

	Faults Round		
	One	Two	Total
1 Raimondo d'Inzeo (Ita) —Posillipo	0.00	12.00	12.00
2 Piero d'Inzeo (Ita)—The Rock	8.00	8.00	16.00
3 David Broome (GB)—Sunsalve	16.00	7.00	23.00
4 George Morris (USA)—Sinjon	12.00	12.00	24.00
5 Hans Günter Winkler (FRG) —Halla	17.00	8.00	25.00
6 Fritz Thiedemann (FRG) —Meteor	13.50	12.00	25.50
=7 Naldo Dasso (Arg)—Final	4.00	24.00	28.00
Hugh Wiley (USA) —Master William	12.00	16.00	28.00
Bernard de Fombelle (Fra) —Buffalo B	12.00	16.00	28.00
10 Istvan Suti (Hun)—Szepleany	12.00	16.50	28.50
=11 Pat Smythe (GB)—Flanagan	20.00	12.00	32.00
Henrique Callado (Por) —Martingil	16.00	16.00	32.00
13 Carlos Delia (Arg)—Stromboli	16.00	20.00	36.00

14 Max Fresson (Fra) —Grand Veneur	8.00	29.25	37.25
=15 Cevdet Sumer (Tur)—Zambak	20.00	17.50	37.50
William Steinkraus (USA) —Riviera Wonder	24.00	13.50	37.50
17 Francisco Goyoaga (Spa) —Desirée	20.50	20.75	41.25
18 Pierre Jonquères d'Oriola (Fra) —Eclair au Chocolat	16.00	25.50	41.50
19 Ernesto Hartkopf (Arg) —Baltasar	19.25	24.25	43.50
=20 Dawn Wofford (GB)—Hollandia	16.00	28.00	44.00
German Mailhos (Uru)—Julian	24.00	20.00	44.00
22 Hans Möhr (Switz)—Lausbub III	23.00	21.75	44.75
23 Adrian White (NZ)—Telebrae	33.25	12.00	45.25
=24 Juan Martinez de Vallejo (Spa) —Charmeuse	23.00	24.00	47.00
Rafael Paullier (Uru)—Arapey	32.00	15.00	47.00
=26 Mohamed Selim Zaki (UAR) —Artos	16.00	32.00	48.00
Alwin Schockemöhle (FRG) —Ferdl	35.75	12.25	48.00
28 Gamal El Din Haress (UAR) —Nefertiti II	20.00	32.00	52.00
29 Kunihiro Ohta (Jap)—Facey	28.00	28.00	56.00
30 Carlos Colombino (Uru) —Guanaco	16.00	43.50	59.50
31 Nail Gönenli (Tur)—Inka	32.50	30.75	63.25
32 Vassile Pinciu (Rum)—Birsan	37.00	28.00	65.00
33 Virgil Barbuceanu (Rum) —Robot	43.75	27.50	71.25
34 Georges Hernalsteens (Bel) —Hipparque	66.00	36.00	102.00

Eliminated: Elwi Gazi (UAR)—Mabrouk; Edward O'Donohoe (Ire)—Cluain Meala; Gheorge Langa (Rum)—Rubin; Fedor Meteljkov (USSR)—Kover; Kim Donghyu (Kor)—Gracia; Imre Karcsu (Hun)—Aranyos; Salih Koç (Tur)—Rolat; Lajos Somlay (Hun)—Okulj; Hernando Espinosa de los Monteros (Spa)—Frantillack; Dag Nätterkvist (Swe)—Good Luck XX; Yuzo Kageyama (Jap)—Eforegiot; Ernst Shabailo (USSR)—Boston; Pyung Minn (Kor)—Domfee; Brigitte Schockaert (Bel)—Muscadin; Eduard Budil (Aut)—Feldherr; Peer Fresk (Swe)—Kaskad.

Did not take part in second round: Francisco Rabelo Leite (Bra)—Sultao; William Ringrose (Ire)—Loch an Easpaig; João Craveiro Lopes (Por)—Rovuma II; Paul Weier (Switz)—Centurion; Anders Gernandt (Swe)—Valor; Andrei Favorsky (USSR)—Manevr; John Daly (Ire)—Loch Garman; Renyldo Guimarães Ferreira (Bra)—Marengo; Oscar Sotero da Silva (Bra)—Cerrito; Antonio Pereira de Almeida (Por)—Palpite.

Number of riders: 60

Number of nations represented: 23

1964 Tokyo

Nations Cup

(2 rounds, teams of 3, all 3 scores to count)

	Faults Round		
	One	Two	Total
1 FRG 68.50			
Hermann Schridde —Dozent II	12.50	1.25	13.75	(2)
Kurt Jarasinski—Torro	9.75	12.50	22.25	(8)
Hans Günter Winkler —Fidelitas	17.50	15.00	32.50	(16)

2 France 77.75				
Pierre Jonquères d'Oriola —Lutteur B	9.00	0.00	9.00	(1)
Janou Lefèbvre —Kenavo D	16.00	16.00	32.00	(=14)
Guy Lefrant—M. de Littry	20.00	16.75	36.75	(20)
3 Italy 88.50				
Piero d'Inzeo—Sunbeam	12.00	12.50	24.50	(9)
Raimondo d'Inzeo —Posillipo	16.00	12.00	28.00	(11)

Graziano Mancinelli —Rockette	16.00	20.00	36.00	(19)

4 Great Britain   97.25

Peter Robeson —Firecrest	8.00	8.00	16.00	(3)
David Broome—Jacopo	16.00	21.00	37.00	(21)
David Boston Barker —North Flight	28.25	16.00	44.25	(27)

5 Argentina   101.00

Jorge Antonio Canaves —Confinado	18.75	10.75	29.50	(12)
Hugo Miguel Arrambide —Chimbote	17.50	16.75	34.25	(17)
Carlos Delia—Popin	17.25	20.00	37.25	(22)

6 USA   107.00

Frank Chapot —San Lucas	12.50	8.00	20.50	(7)
Kathy Kusner —Untouchable	13.75	16.00	29.75	(13)
Mary Mairs—Tomboy	44.50	12.25	56.75	(33)

7 Australia   109.00

John Fahey—Bonvale	8.00	8.00	16.00	(4)
Bridget McIntyre —Coronation	16.00	23.50	39.50	(24)
Kevin Bacon —Ocean Foam	29.50	24.00	53.50	(30)

8 Spain   118.75

Francisco Goyoaga —Kif Kif B	19.00	16.00	35.00	(18)
Enrique Martinez de Vallejo—Eolo IV	24.00	16.00	40.00	(25)
Alfonso Queipo de Llano —Infernal	20.00	23.75	43.75	(26)

9 Switzerland   140.75

Max Hauri—Millview	13.25	12.25	25.50	(10)
Paul Weier—Satan III	20.00	12.00	32.00	(=14)
Hans Möhr—Troll	32.00	51.25	83.25	(39)

10 New Zealand   156.25

Graeme Hansen —Saba Sam	12.75	25.00	37.75	(23)
Richard Hansen—Tide	24.00	32.00	56.00	(=31)
Adrian White—El Dorado	37.25	25.25	62.50	(35)

Eliminated: USSR, Mexico, Japan, South Korea

Number of teams: 14

Individual gold again for d'Oriola (centre) in Tokyo. Team gold medallist Hermann Schridde (left) won the individual silver and Peter Robeson the bronze. (Popperfoto)

Individual

(No separate competition)

		Faults			
		Round			Jump-off
		One	Two	Total	F/Time
1	Pierre Jonquères d'Oriola (Fra)—Lutteur B	9.00	0.00	9.00	
2	Hermann Schridde (FRG)—Dozent II	12.50	1.25	13.75	
3	Peter Robeson (GB)—Firecrest	8.00	8.00	16.00	0/1.01
4	John Fahey (Aus)—Bonvale	8.00	8.00	16.00	8/1.09
=5	Joaquim Duarte Silva (Por)—Jeune France	8.00	12.00	20.00	
	Nelson Pessoa (Bra)—Huipil	12.00	8.00	20.00	
7	Frank Chapot (USA)—San Lucas	12.50	8.00	20.50	
8	Kurt Jarasinski (FRG)—Torro	9.75	12.50	22.25	
9	Piero d'Inzeo (Ita)—Sunbeam	12.00	12.50	24.50	
10	Max Hauri (Switz)—Millview	13.25	12.25	25.50	
11	Raimondo d'Inzeo (Ita)—Posillipo	16.00	12.00	28.00	
12	Jorge Antonio Canaves (Arg)—Confinado	18.75	10.75	29.50	
13	Kathy Kusner (USA)—Untouchable	13.75	16.00	29.75	
=14	Janou Lefèbvre (Fra)—Kenavo D	16.00	16.00	32.00	
	Paul Weier (Switz)—Satan III	20.00	12.00	32.00	
16	Hans Günter Winkler (FRG)—Fidelitas	17.50	15.00	32.50	
17	Hugo Miguel Arrambide (Arg)—Chimbote	17.50	16.75	34.25	
18	Francisco Goyoaga (Spa)—Kif Kif B	19.00	16.00	35.00	
19	Graziano Mancinelli (Ita)—Rockette	16.00	20.00	36.00	
20	Guy Lefrant (Fra)—M. de Littry	20.00	16.75	36.75	
21	David Broome (GB)—Jacopo	16.00	21.00	37.00	
22	Carlos Delia (Arg)—Popin	17.25	20.00	37.25	

The first woman to win an individual jumping medal at the Olympic Games was Marion Coakes (Great Britain) riding Stroller, winner of the individual silver at Mexico in 1968.

	Faults Round One	Two	Total
23 Graeme Hansen (NZ)—Saba Sam	12.75	25.00	37.75
24 Bridget McIntyre (Aus)—Coronation	16.00	23.50	39.50
25 Enrique Martinez de Vallejo (Spa)—Eolo IV	24.00	16.00	40.00
26 Alfonso Queipo de Llano (Spa)—Infernal	20.00	23.75	43.75
27 David Boston Barker (GB)—North Flight	28.25	16.00	44.25
28 Ivan Semenov (USSR)—Sibiryak	24.50	27.00	51.50
29 Americo Simonetti (Chi)—Trago Amargo	32.25	20.00	52.25
30 Kevin Bacon (Aus)—Ocean Foam	29.50	24.00	53.50
=31 Richard Hansen (NZ)—Tide	24.00	32.00	56.00
Il Kyu Lee (Kor)—Rebel	28.00	28.00	56.00
33 Mary Mairs (USA)—Tomboy	44.50	12.25	56.75
34 Henrique Callado (Por)—Joc de l'Ile	42.00	16.25	58.25
35 Adrian White (NZ)—El Dorado	37.25	25.25	62.50
36 Alexander Purtov (USSR)—Svecha	56.25	12.50	68.75
37 Ricardo Guasch (Mex)—Huracan	33.75	36.00	69.75
38 Shinzo Sasa (Jap)—Snaefell	46.75	24.00	70.75
39 Hans Möhr (Switz)—Troll	32.00	51.25	83.25
40 Hiroshi Hoketsu (Jap)—Raro	63.75	48.00	111.75

Eliminated: Andrei Favorsky (USSR)—Manevr; Hector Zatarain Romano (Mex)—Nube; Joaquin Hermida Torres (Mex)—Porfirio; Yuzo Kageyama (Jap)—Tokinoarashi; Chul Kyu Kim (Kor)—Gothic; Duk Kee Ahn (Kor)—Ivan.

Number of riders: 46

Number of nations represented: 17

> Debbie Johnsey was the only lady rider and the youngest competitor in the 1976 Olympic Show Jumping contest. On the day of the individual competition, in which she jumped off for the silver and bronze medals, finally finishing fourth, she was 19 years and 24 days old. She was the highest placed British rider in the Nations Cup.

1968 Mexico

Nations Cup

(2 rounds, teams of 3, all 3 scores to count)

	Faults Round One	Two	Total	
1 Canada 102.75				
Jim Elder				
—The Immigrant	9.25	18.00	27.25	(5)
Jim Day—Canadian Club	18.00	18.00	36.00	(9)
Tom Gayford—Big Dee	22.25	17.25	39.50	(12)

The 1968 champions in Mexico, William Steinkraus and Snowbound. (Ed Lacey Associated Sports Photography)

	Faults Round One	Two	Total	
2 France 110.25				
Janou Lefèbvre—Rocket	17.25	12.50	29.75	(7)
Marcel Rozier —Quo Vadis	21.50	12.00	33.50	(8)
Pierre Jonquères d'Oriola —Nagir	17.75	29.25	47.00	(18)
3 FRG 117.25				
Alwin Schockemöhle —Donald Rex	13.00	5.75	18.75	(1)
Hans Günter Winkler —Enigk	11.50	16.75	28.25	(6)
Hermann Schridde —Dozent II	33.75	36.50	70.25	(33)
4 USA 117.50				
Frank Chapot —San Lucas	11.00	14.00	25.00	(4)
Kathy Kusner —Untouchable	25.00	19.50	44.50	(15)
Mary Chapot —White Lightning	27.00	21.00	48.00	(20)
5 Italy 129.25				
Raimondo d'Inzeo —Bellevue	12.00	12.25	24.25	(3)
Piero d'Inzeo—Fidux	28.50	19.00	47.50	(19)
Graziano Mancinelli —Doneraile	23.50	34.00	57.50	(25)
6 Switzerland 136.75				
Paul Weier—Satan III	23.50	13.25	36.75	(10)
Monica Bachmann —Erbach	23.00	26.50	49.50	(21)
Arthur Blickenstorfer —Marianka	21.75	28.75	50.50	(=22)

7 **Brazil**   138.00

Nelson Pessoa				
—Pass Op	28.50	10.25	38.75	(11)
Lucia Faria				
—Rush du Camp	24.75	20.00	44.75	(16)
José Reynoso Fernandez				
—Cantal	27.75	26.75	54.50	(24)

8 **Great Britain**   159.50

David Broome				
—Mister Softee	8.00	12.00	20.00	(2)
Harvey Smith				
—Madison Time	18.25	26.75	45.00	(17)
Marion Coakes—Stroller	21.75	*72.75E	94.50	(38)

9 **Australia**   166.50

John Fahey—Bonvale	21.25	21.50	42.75	(14)
Sam Campbell				
—April Love	23.75	26.75	50.50	(=22)
Kevin Bacon				
—Chichester	25.50	47.75	73.25	(34)

10 **Mexico**   209.50

Fernando Hernández				
—Churintzio	27.50	32.25	59.75	(27)
Joaquin Pérez de las				
Heras—Nancel	31.00	32.00	63.00	(29)
Ricardo Guasch				
—Mixteco	56.00	30.75	86.75	(36)

11 **Poland**   223.25

Piotr Wawryniuk				
—Poprad	37.00	23.25	60.25	(28)
Jan Kowalczyk—Braz	45.25	23.75	69.00	(32)
Antoni Pacynski—Cyrrus	41.25	52.75	94.00	(37)

12 **USSR**   230.50

Victor Matveev				
—Krokhotny	23.75	17.75	41.50	(13)
Gennadi Samosedenko				
—Aeron	25.25	42.75	68.00	(30)
Evgeny Kuzin—Figlyar	*76.00E	45.00	121.00	(41)

13 **Argentina**   275.00

Carlos Delia—Scandale	27.25	41.25	68.50	(31)
Roberto Tagle				
—Ojo Chico	54.50	47.50	102.00	(39)
Argentino Molinuevo				
—Don Gustavo	31.75	*72.75E	104.50	(40)

14 **Japan**   283.25

Masayasu Sugitani				
—Ringo	21.50	37.25	58.75	(26)
Tadashi Fukushima				
—Queen	38.50	37.25	75.75	(35)
Yugo Araki—Fokker	*76.00E	*72.75	148.75	(42)

Eliminated: Ireland (Diana Connolly-Carew—Barrymore, Ada Matheson—San Pedro, Edward Campion—Liathdruim).

Number of teams: 15

Individual

(Separate competition, 2 rounds)

	Faults			Jump-off
	Round			
	One	Two	Total	F/Time
1 William Steinkraus (USA)—Snowbound	0.00	4.00	4.00	
2 Marion Coakes (GB)—Stroller	0.00	8.00	8.00	
3 David Broome (GB)—Mister Softee	4.00	8.00	12.00	0/35.30
4 Frank Chapot (USA)—San Lucas	4.00	8.00	12.00	0/36.80
5 Hans Günter Winkler (FRG)—Enigk	8.00	4.00	12.00	0/37.50
6 Jim Elder (Can)—The Immigrant	8.00	4.00	12.00	0/39.20
=7 Alwin Schockemöhle (FRG)—Donald Rex	8.00	8.00	16.00	
Argentino Molinuevo (Arg)—Don Gustavo	8.00	8.00	16.00	
Piero d'Inzeo (Ita)—Fidux	4.00	12.00	16.00	
Monica Bachmann (Switz)—Erbach	8.00	8.00	16.00	
11 Harvey Smith (GB)—Madison Time	8.00	8.25	16.25	
12 Lucia Faria (Bra)—Rush du Camp	7.25	12.00	19.25	
=13 Carlos Delia (Arg)—Scandale	8.00	12.00	20.00	
Arthur Blickenstorfer (Switz)—Marianka	8.00	12.00	20.00	
Jim Day (Can)—Canadian Club	4.00	16.00	20.00	
16 Nelson Pessoa (Bra)—Pass Op	8.00	16.00	24.00	
17 Pierre Jonquères d'Oriola (Fra)—Nagir	8.00	20.50	28.50	
18 Kevin Bacon (Aus)—Chichester	4.00	24.75	28.75	
19 Fernando Hernández (Mex)—Churintzio	10.75			
20 Marcel Rozier (Fra)—Quo Vadis	11.00			
=21 Paul Weier (Switz)—Wildfeuer	12.00			
Kathy Kusner (USA)—Untouchable	12.00			
Graziano Mancinelli (Ita)—Doneraile	12.00			
Ricardo Guasch (Mex)—Mixteco	12.00			
John Fahey (Aus)—Bonvale	12.00			
=26 Tadashi Fukushima (Jap)—Queen	16.00			
Hartwig Steenken (FRG)—Simona	16.00			
Raimondo d'Inzeo (Ita)—Bellevue	16.00			

*To prevent total elimination of a team, a rider who was eliminated was awarded the worst score for that round plus 20, i.e. round one 56.00 plus 20.00=76.00, round two 52.75 plus 20.00=72.75.

The first women to win gold medals for show jumping at the Olympic Games were Leslie Burr riding Albany and Melanie Smith riding Calypso, both members of the winning United States team at Los Angeles in 1984.

The first all-woman team to win an official Nations Cup was the United States quartet of Anne Kursinski, Katharine Burdsall, Lisa Tarnapol and Katie Monahan at Washington in 1986.

	Faults Round One
Viktor Matveev (USSR)—Krokhotny	16.00
Sam Campbell (Aus)—April Love	16.00
Masayasu Sugitani (Jap)—Ringo	16.00
32 Janou Lefèbvre (Fra)—Rocket	20.00
33 José Reynoso Fernandez (Bra)—Cantal	23.25
34 Roberto Nielsen-Reyes (Bol)—Ukamau	24.00
35 Marian Kozicki (Pol)—Braz	28.00
36 Terrance Millar (Can)—Beefeater	31.50
37 Joaquin Pérez de las Heras (Mex)—Romeo	36.50
38 Antoni Pacynski (Pol)—Cyrrus	37.25
39 Piotr Wawryniuk (Pol)—Farys	52.75

Eliminated: Jorge Amaya (Arg)—Gemelo; Evgeny Kuzin (USSR)—Figlyar; Yugo Araki (Jap)—Far East.

Number of riders: 42 (Riders with eight faults or less in the first round qualified for the second round.)

Number of nations represented: 15

> The first civilian to represent Ireland with the Irish Army Jumping Team was a woman: Iris Kellett, who was chosen to compete for her country at London's White City in 1949.

1972 Munich

Nations Cup

(2 rounds, teams of 4, best 3 scores in each round to count)

1 FRG 32.00

	Faults Round			
	One	Two	Total	
Fritz Ligges—Robin	4.00	4.00	8.00	(=2)
Hartwig Steenken —Simona	4.00	8.00	12.00	(=6)
Gerd Wiltfang—Askan	8.00	4.00	12.00	(=6)
Hans Günter Winkler —Torphy	(8.00)	(8.00)	16.00	(=9)
	16.00	16.00		

2 USA 32.25

William Steinkraus —Main Spring	0.00	4.00	4.00	(1)
Neal Shapiro—Sloopy	8.25	0.00	8.25	(5)
Frank Chapot —White Lightning	8.00	(28.00)	36.00	(25)
Kathy Kusner —Fleet Apple	(20.00)	12.00	32.00	(=22)
	16.25	16.00		

Italy's Graziano Mancinelli and Ambassador, who got the better of Britain's Ann Moore and the United States' Neal Shapiro in a jump-off for the individual gold medal in 1972. (Ed Lacey Associated Sports Photography)

3 Italy 48.00

Vittorio Orlandi				
—Fulmer Feather Duster	4.00	4.00	8.00	(=2)
Raimondo d'Inzeo				
—Fiorello	8.00	4.00	12.00	(=6)
Graziano Mancinelli				
—Ambassador	20.00	8.00	28.00	(=20)
Piero d'Inzeo				
—Easter Light	(87.25)	(48.00)	135.25	(=30)
	32.00	16.00		

4 Great Britain 51.00

David Broome				
—Manhattan	4.00	16.00	20.00	(=14)
Michael Saywell				
—Hideaway	8.00	8.00	16.00	(=9)
Harvey Smith				
—Summertime	(16.00)	4.00	20.00	(=14)
Anne Moore—Psalm	11.00	(21.00)	32.00	(=22)
	23.00	28.00		

5 Switzerland 61.25

Monica Weier—Erbach	9.75	8.00	17.75	(11)
Paul Weier—Wulf	8.00	12.00	20.00	(=14)
Max Hauri—Haiti	15.50	8.00	23.50	(17)
Hermann von Siebenthal				
—Havana Royal	(87.25)	(48.00)	135.25	(=30)
	33.25	28.00		

6 Canada 64.00

Jim Elder—Houdini	4.00	4.00	8.00	(=2)
Jim Day—Happy Fellow	12.00	12.00	24.00	(18)
Terrance Millar				
—Le Dauphin	(23.00)	12.00	35.00	(24)
Ian Millar—Shoeman	20.00	(24.00)	44.00	(26)
	36.00	28.00		

7 Spain 66.00

Alfonso Segovia—Tic Tac	4.00	15.00	19.00	(=12)
Enrique Martinez de				
Vallejo—Val de Loire	7.00	12.00	19.00	(=12)
Luis Alvarez Cervera				
—Acorne	12.00	16.00	28.00	(=20)
Jaime de Aveyro				
—Sunday Beau	(67.25)	(48.00)	115.25	(29)
	23.00	43.00		

8 Argentina 121.00

Hugo Arrambide				
—Camalote	15.00	12.00	27.00	(19)
Roberto Tagle—Simple	26.00	20.00	46.00	(27)
Jorge Llambi				
—Okey Amigo	0.00	48.00	48.00	(28)
Argentino Molinuevo				
—Abracadabra	(87.25)	(48.00)	135.25	(=30)
	41.00	80.00		

Did not start in second round: 9 Chile (Barbara Pokorny—Quintral, 13.00; Americo Simonetti—Ataulfo, 28.00; René Varas—Anahi, 35.25, total 76.25); 10 France (Hubert Parot—Tic, 18.00; Pierre Durand—Varin, 30.25; Marc Deuquet—Ulpienne, 32.00; Marcel Rozier—Sans Souci, 87.25, total 80.25); 11 Belgium (François Mathy—Talisman, 8.00; Eric Wauters—Markies, 8.00; Françoise Thiry—Hillpark, 87.25; Jean Damman—Vasco da Gama, 87.25, total 103.25); 12 Poland (Marian Kozicki—Bronz, 4.00; Stefan Grodzicki—Biszka, 16.00; Piotr Wawryniuk—Poprad, 87.25; Jan Kowalczyk—Jastarnia, 87.25, total 107.25); 13 Portugal (Vasco Ramirez—Sir du Brossais, 16.00; Carlos Campos—Ulla de Lancôme, 25.75; Francisco Caldeira—Flipper, 65.75, total 107.50); 14 USSR (Alexander Nebogov—Equador, 12.00; Viktor Matveev—Krokhotny, 28.00; Juri Zyabrov—Grim, 87.25, total 127.25); 15 Mexico (Fernando Hernández—Dorian, 24.25; Eduardo Higareda—Biene, 45.75; Joaquin Pérez de las Heras—Savando, 87.25; Elisa Pérez de las Heras—Askari, 87.25, total 157.25); 16 Japan (Masayasu Sugitani—Seraphina, 43.75; Teruchiyo Takamiya—Alladin, 53.25; Tadashi Fukushima—Anke, 87.25; Tsunekazu Takeda—Josephine, 87.25, total 184.25); 17 Hungary (Ajtony Akos—Ozike, 12; Sándor Bognár—Faklyas, 87.25; László Móra—Betty, 87.25, total186.50).

The USSR and Hungary did not start their fourth riders.

Number of teams: 17 (The eight best-placed teams in the first round qualified for the second round.)

Individual

(Separate competition, 2 rounds)

	Faults Round			Jump-off
	One	Two	Total	F/Time
1 Graziano Mancinelli (Ita)—Ambassador	0.00	8.00	8.00	0/45.00
2 Ann Moore (GB)—Psalm	0.00	8.00	8.00	3/53.90
3 Neal Shapiro (USA)—Sloopy	4.00	4.00	8.00	8/46.00
=4 Jim Day (Can)—Steelmaster	0.00	8.75	8.75	
Hugo Simon (Aut)—Lavendel	4.75	4.00	8.75	
Hartwig Steenken (FRG)—Simona	4.00	4.75	8.75	
7 Marcel Rozier (Fra)—Sans Souci	4.00	8.00	12.00	
=8 Alfonso Segovia (Spa)—Tic Tac	4.00	12.00	16.00	
Fritz Ligges (FRG)—Robin	4.00	12.00	16.00	
=10 Kathy Kusner (USA)—Fleet Apple	4.00	16.00	20.00	
René Varas (Chi)—Quintral	8.00	12.00	20.00	
Enrique Martinez de Vallejo (Spa)—Val de Loire	8.00	12.00	20.00	
13 Carlos Campos (Por)—Ulla de Lancôme	4.00	16.50	20.50	
14 David Broome (GB)—Manhattan	8.00	13.25	21.25	
15 Michael Saywell (GB)—Hideaway	8.00	16.25	24.25	
16 Gerd Wiltfang (FRG)—Askan	4.00	28.75	32.75	
=17 Stefan Grodzicki (Pol)—Biszka	8.00	R		
Åke Hultberg (Swe)—El Vis	8.00	R		
=19 Joaquin Pérez de las Heras (Mex)—Savando	8.25	R		
Elisa Pérez de las Heras (Mex)—Askari	8.25	R		

	Faults Round One
21 Marian Kozicki (Pol)—Bronz	8.50
=22 Piero d'Inzeo (Ita)—Easter Light	12.00
Hugo Arrambide (Arg)—Camalote	12.00
Roberto Nielsen-Reyes (Bol)—Conquistador	12.00
Raimondo d'Inzeo (Ita)—Fiorello	12.00
Paul Weier (Switz)—Wulf	12.00
Jorge Llambi (Arg)—Okey Amigo	12.00
William Steinkraus (USA)—Snowbound	12.00
29 Carlos Delia (Arg)—Cardon	12.25
30 Max Hauri (Switz)—Haiti	12.50
=31 Hubert Parot (Fra)—Tic	16.00
François Mathy (Bel)—Talisman	16.00
Terrance Millar (Can)—Le Dauphin	16.00
Francisco Caldeira (Por)—Can-Can	16.00
Antonio Alegria-Simões (Bra)—Bon Soir	16.00
Viktor Matveev (USSR)—Krokhotny	16.00
=37 Vasco Ramires (Por)—Sir du Brossais	20.00
Janou Lefèbvre (Fra)—Rocket	20.00
39 Nelson Pessoa (Bra)—Nagir	21.00
40 Jean Damman (Bel)—Vasco da Gama	21.25
41 Alexander Nebogov (USSR)—Equador	22.00
42 Tsunekazu Takeda (Jap)—Josephine	23.00
=43 Masayasu Sugitani (Jap)—Seraphina	24.00
Luis Alvarez Cervera (Spa)—Appell	24.00
Jim Elder (Can)—Shoeman	24.00
Tadashi Fukushima (Jap)—Anke	24.00
=47 Kurt Maeder (Switz)—Abraxon	28.00
Pál Széplaki (Hun)—Kemal	28.00
=49 Ajtony Akos (Hun)—Ozike	29.00
Eric Wauters (Bel)—Markies	29.00
51 Eduardo Higareda-Usi (Mex)—Biene	30.75

> Prior to the 1920 Olympics, a member of the United States Army team, knowing that the available horses were not of a high enough standard, obtained permission to go to Virginia and buy himself a suitable mount from his private funds. The horse he bought cost $3 000, but became ill when he reached New York and was unable to participate in the Games.
>
> In September 1984 Ryan's Son, ridden by John Whitaker, became the first horse in Britain to pass the £200 000 winnings mark.

Eliminated: László Móra (Hun)—Antaryl; Viktor Lisitsyn (USSR)—Piniatelli; Americo Simonetti (Chi)—Altue.

Number of riders: 54 (The 20 best-placed riders in the first round qualified for the second round.)

Number of nations represented: 21

1976 Montreal

Nations Cup

(2 rounds, teams of 4, best 3 scores in each round to count)

	Faults Round One	Two	Total	
1 **France** 40.00				
Hubert Parot—Rivage	8.00	4.00	12.00	(=1)
Marcel Rozier				
—Bayard de Maupas	8.00	4.00	12.00	(=1)
Marc Roguet				
—Belle de Mars	8.00	(16.00)	24.00	(=14)
Michel Roche—Un Espoir	(24.00)	8.00	32.00	(=24)
	24.00	16.00		
2 **FRG** 44.00				
Alwin Schockemöhle				
—Warwick Rex	4.00	8.00	12.00	(=1)
Hans Günter Winkler				
—Torphy	12.00	4.00	16.00	(=5)
Sonke Sönksen—Kwept	8.00	(12.00)	20.00	(=8)
Paul Schockemöhle				
—Agent	(16.00)	8.00	24.00	(=14)
	24.00	20.00		
3 **Belgium** 63.00				
Eric Wauters—Gute Sitte	8.00	7.00	15.00	(4)
François Mathy				
—Gai Luron	12.00	8.00	20.00	(=8)
Edgar-Henri Cuepper				
—Le Champion	12.00	16.00	28.00	(=20)
Stanny van Paesschen				
—Porsche	(16.00)	(20.00)	36.00	(=26)
	32.00	31.00		
4 **USA** 64.00				
Frank Chapot—Viscount	12.00	4.00	16.00	(=5)
Robert Ridland				
—Southside	16.00	4.00	20.00	(=8)
Buddy Brown				
—Sandsablaze	12.00	16.00	28.00	(=20)
Michael Matz—Grande	(16.00)	(24.00)	40.00	(32)
	40.00	24.00		
5 **Canada** 64.50				
Jim Day—Sympatico	4.00	16.00	20.00	(=8)
Michel Vaillancourt				
—Branch County	8.00	12.50	20.50	(12)
Ian Millar—Countdown	(19.50)	8.00	27.50	(19)
Jim Elder—Raffles II	16.00	(20.00)	36.00	(=26)
	28.00	36.50		

6 Spain 71.00

Luis Alvarez Cervera —Acorne	8.00	8.00	16.00	(=5)
Alfonso Segovia —Val de Loire	11.00	12.00	23.00	(13)
José Miguel Rosillo —Agamemnon	(16.00)	20.00	36.00	(=26)
Eduardo Amoros —Limited Edition	12.00	(27.00)	39.00	(31)
	31.00	40.00		

7 Great Britain 76.00

Debbie Johnsey—Moxy	8.00	16.00	24.00	(=14)
Rowland Fernyhough —Bouncer	(27.00)	4.00	31.00	(23)
Peter Robeson —Law Court	20.00	12.00	32.00	(=24)
Graham Fletcher —Hideaway	16.00	(20.00)	36.00	(=26)
	44.00	32.00		

8 Mexico 76.25

Fernando Hernández —Fascination	(16.00)	8.00	24.00	(=14)
Fernando Senderos —Jet Run	8.00	16.00	24.00	(=14)
Luis Razo—Pueblo	8.00	20.50	28.50	(22)
Carlos Aguirre —Consejero	15.75	(22.50)	38.25	(30)
	31.75	44.50		

Did not take part in second round: =9 Italy (Piero d'Inzeo—Easter Light, 8.00; Graziano Mancinelli—Bel Oiseau, 20.00; Raimondo d'Inzeo—Bellevue, 20.00; Giorgio Nuti—Springtime, 20.00, total 48.00); =9 Australia (Guy Creighton—Mr Dennis, 12.00; Barry Roycroft—Four Corners, 16.00; Kevin Bacon—Chichester, 20.00, total 48.00); 11 Austria (Hugo Simon—Lavendel, 12.00; Thomas Frühmann—Star Favorit, 16.00; Henk Hulzebos—d'Accord, 24.00; Rüdiger Wassibauer—Sulgrave, 36.00, total 52.00); 12 Netherlands (Rob Eras—Iwan F, 8.00; Anton Ebben—Jumbo Design, 24.00; Henk Nooren—Pluto, 28.00; Johan Heins—Jagermeester, 28.00, total 60.00); 13 Japan (Massyasu Sugitani—Mary Mary, 20.00; Hirokaza Higashira—Second Mate, 20.00; Tsunekazu Takeda—Fink, 27.25; Ryuichi Obata—Manhattan, 28.00, total 67.25). Withdrew: Argentina (Roberto Tagle—Simple, 20.00; Argentino Molinuevo—Marsupial, E; Jorge Llambi—Chimborazo, did not start).

Number of teams: 14 (The eight best-placed teams in the first round qualified for the second round.)

A double clear round gave Alwin Schockemöhle and Warwick Rex a convincing victory in the individual contest at the Montreal Games in 1976. (Ed Lacey Associated Sports Photography)

Individual

(Separate competition, 2 rounds)

		Round One	Round Two	Total	Jump-off
1	Alwin Schockemöhle (FRG)—Warwick Rex	0.00	0.00	0.00	
2	Michel Vaillancourt (Can)—Branch County	4.00	8.00	12.00	4.00
3	François Mathy (Bel)—Gai Luron	8.00	4.00	12.00	8.00
4	Debbie Johnsey (GB)—Moxy	4.00	8.00	12.00	15.25
=5	Guy Creighton (Aus)—Mr Dennis	4.00	12.00	16.00	
	Marcel Rozier (Fra)—Bayard de Maupas	4.00	12.00	16.00	
	Frank Chapot (USA)—Viscount	4.00	12.00	16.00	
	Hugo Simon (Aut)—Lavendel	8.00	8.00	16.00	
9	Luis Alvarez Cervera (Spa)—Acorne	8.00	9.50	17.50	
=10	Eduardo Amoros (Spa)—Limited Edition	8.00	12.00	20.00	
	Hans Günter Winkler (FRG)—Torphy	4.00	16.00	20.00	
12	Raimondo d'Inzeo (Ita)—Bellevue	8.00	16.00	24.00	
13	Henk Nooren (NL)—Jagermeester	8.00	18.00	26.00	
14	Peter Robeson (GB)—Law Court	4.00	23.75	27.75	
=15	Jim Elder (Can)—Raffles II	8.00	20.00	28.00	
	Jim Day (Can)—Sympatico	8.00	20.00	28.00	
17	Hubert Parot (Fra)—Rivage	8.00	20.25	28.25	
18	Argentino Molinuevo (Arg)—Marsupial	8.00	27.50	35.50	
19	Carlos Aguirre (Mex)—Consejero	6.00	E		
20	Juan Rieckehoff (PR)—Don Juan	8.00	E		
21	Fernando Senderos (Mex)—Jet Run	11.75			
=22	Dennis Murphy (USA)—Do Right	12.00			
	Roberto Tagle (Arg)—Simple	12.00			
	Oswaldo Mendez (Gua)—Gray Flight	12.00			
=25	Graziano Mancinelli (Ita)—Bel Oiseau	16.00			
	Piero d'Inzeo (Ita)—The Avenger	16.00			
	Bruno Candrian (Switz)—Golden Shuttle	16.00			
	Anton Ebben (NL)—Jumbo Design	16.00			
29	Buddy Brown (USA)—A Little Bit	16.50			
=30	Joe Yorke (NZ)—Big Red	20.00			
	Rob Eras (NL)—Iwan F	20.00			
	Hirokaza Higashira (Jap)—Second Mate	20.00			
	Stanny van Paesschen (Bel)—Porsche	20.00			
	Graham Fletcher (GB)—Hideaway	20.00			
	Jan Olaf Wannius (Swe)—Kil Kellen	20.00			
36	Paul Schockemöhle (FRG)—Talisman	24.00			
37	Kevin Bacon (Aus)—Chichester	25.50			
38	Thomas Frühmann (Aut)—Star Favorit	28.00			
39	Tsunekazu Takeda (Jap)—Fink	33.00			
40	Luis Razo (Mex)—Pueblo	33.50			
41	Marc Roguet (Fra)—Belle de Mars	36.00			
42	Ryuichi Obata (Jap)—Manhattan	47.00			
43	Eric Wauters (Bel)—Gute Sitte	47.50			

Eliminated: Barry Roycroft (Aus)—Four Corners; Henk Hulzebos (Aut)—Prokat; Roberto Nielsen-Reyes (Bol)—Concorde; Alfonso Segovia (Spa)—Val de Loire.

Number of riders: 47 (The 20 best-placed riders in the first round qualified for the second round.)

Number of nations represented: 20

In 1912 the Canadian Nations Cup team which finished fifth at Olympia consisted of three brothers: John, Winfield and Clifford Sifton. The United States team which finished sixth in the Lucerne Nations Cup in 1982 was also made up of three brothers (there was no fourth member): Peter, Mark and Armand Leone.

In 1948 the United States was unable to compete in the Nations Cup at the National Horse Show, New York, because the competition was still The International Military Perpetual Challenge Trophy, and the US Army team had been disbanded following that year's Dublin Horse Show.

Sunsalve is the only horse to have won both the King George V Gold Cup (open only to men) and the Queen Elizabeth II Cup (women only). He won the Queen's Cup in 1957 when ridden by his owner's daughter, Elizabeth Anderson, and the King's Cup in 1960, ridden by David Broome.

1980 Moscow

Nations Cup

(2 rounds, teams of 4, best 3 scores in each round to count)

	Faults Round		
	One	Two	Total

1 USSR   20.25

	One	Two	Total	
Viateslav Chukanov —Gepatit	4.00	0.00	4.00	(1)
Viktor Poganovsky —Topky	8.00	0.25	8.25	(2)
Viktor Asmaev—Reis	4.00	(7.25)	11.25	(3)
Nikolai Korolkov —Espadron	(8.00)	4.00	12.00	(=4)
	16.00	4.25		

2 Poland   56.00

	One	Two	Total	
Jan Kowalczyk—Artemor	4.00	8.00	12.00	(=4)
Wieslaw Hartmann —Norton	12.00	12.00	24.00	(8)
Marian Kozicki—Bremen	(33.50)	4.00	37.50	(13)
Janusz Bobik—Szampan	16.00	(24.00)	40.00	(14)
	32.00	24.00		

3 Mexico   59.75

	One	Two	Total	
Joaquin Pérez de las Heras—Alimony	8.00	4.00	12.00	(=4)
Alberto Valdes Lacarra —Lady Mirka	8.00	(12.75)	20.75	(7)
Gerardo Tazzer Valencia —Caribe	23.25	8.50	31.75	(10)
Jesus Gómez Portugal —Massacre	(27.25)	8.00	35.25	(12)
	39.25	20.50		

4 Hungary   124.00

	One	Two	Total	
Barnabás Hevesi—Bohem	16.00	12.00	28.00	(9)
Ferenc Krucsó—Vadrozsa	16.00	16.00	32.00	(11)
József Varró—Gambrinus	36.00	(61.75)	97.75	(23)
András Balogi—Artemis	(73.75)	28.00	101.75	(24)
	68.00	56.00		

5 Rumania   150.50

	One	Two	Total	
Alexandru Bozan —Prejmer	12.00	31.75	43.75	(15)
Dumitru Velea—Fudul	12.00	(61.75)	73.75	(21)
Dania Popescu—Sonor	20.25	32.75	53.00	(17)
Ion Popa—Licurici	(53.75)	41.75	95.50	(22)
	44.25	106.25		

6 Bulgaria   159.50

	One	Two	Total	
Nikola Dimitrov—Vals	17.75	29.00	46.75	(16)
Dimitar Guenov—Makbet	30.00	26.00	56.00	(18)
Boris Pavlov—Montblanc	28.75	(32.00)	60.75	(19)
Hristo Katchov—Povod	(45.00)	28.00	73.00	(20)
	76.50	83.00		

Number of teams: 6

Poland's Jan Kowalczyk and Artemor, pictured here at the European Championships in Rotterdam in 1979, went on to win the individual gold medal and a team silver in the Moscow Games of 1980. (Findlay Davidson)

Individual

(Separate competition, 2 rounds)

		Round One	Round Two	Total	Jump-off F/Time
1	Jan Kowalczyk (Pol)—Artemor	4.00	4.00	8.00	
2	Nikolai Korolkov (USSR)—Espadron	4.00	5.50	9.50	
3	Joaquin Pérez de las Heras (Mex)—Alimony	8.00	4.00	12.00	4/43.23
4	Oswaldo Mendez Herbruger (Gua)—Pampa	8.00	4.00	12.00	4/43.59
5	Viktor Poganovsky (USSR)—Topky	4.00	11.50	15.50	
6	Wieslaw Hartmann (Pol)—Norton	4.00	12.00	16.00	
7	Barnabás Hevesi (Hun)—Bohem	16.00	8.00	24.00	
8	Marian Kozicki (Pol)—Bremen	12.00	12.50	24.50	
9	Viateslav Chukanov (USSR)—Gepatit	12.00	12.75	24.75	
10	Boris Pavlov (Bul)—Montblanc	16.00	10.50	26.50	
11	Alberto Valdes Lacarra (Mex)—Lady Mirka	12.00	16.00	28.00	
12	Christopher Wegelius (Fin)—Monday Morning	16.00	14.25	30.25	
13	Nikola Dimitrov (Bul)—Vals	24.00	12.25	36.25	
14	Ferenc Krucsó (Hun)—Vadrozsa	16.00	24.25	40.25	

Retired: Jesus Gómez Portugal (Mex)—Massacre. Eliminated: Dimitar Guenov (Bul)—Makbet.

Number of riders: 16

Number of nations represented: 7

1984 Los Angeles

Nations Cup

(2 rounds, teams of 4, best 3 scores in each round to count)

		Round One	Two	Total	
1	**USA** 12.00				
	Joe Fargis —Touch of Class	0.00	0.00	0.00	(1)
	Conrad Homfeld —Abdullah	(8.00)	0.00	8.00	(=3)
	Leslie Burr—Albany	4.00	8.00	12.00	(=8)
	Melanie Smith—Calypso	0.00	—	—	—
		4.00	8.00		
2	**Great Britain** 36.75				
	Michael Whitaker —Overton Amanda	8.00	0.00	8.00	(=3)
	John Whitaker —Ryan's Son	16.00	4.75	20.75	(19)
	Steven Smith —Shining Example	(19.00)	8.00	27.00	(23)
	Tim Grubb—Linky	0.00	(28.25)	28.25	(25)
		24.00	12.75		
3	**FRG** 39.25				
	Paul Schockemöhle —Deister	4.00	4.00	8.00	(=3)
	Peter Luther—Livius	8.00	4.00	12.00	(=8)
	Franke Sloothaak —Farmer	8.00	11.25	19.25	(14)
	Fritz Ligges—Ramzes	(17.00)	(12.00)	29.00	(26)
		20.00	19.25		
4	**Canada** 40.00				
	Ian Millar—Big Ben	8.00	4.00	12.00	(=8)
	Hugh Graham—Elrond	(16.00)	0.00	16.00	(=12)
	Jim Elder—Shawline	8.00	12.00	20.00	(=15)
	Mario Deslauriers —Aramis	8.00	(16.50)	24.50	(22)
		24.00	16.00		
5	**Switzerland** 41.00				
	Heidi Robbiani —Jessica V	0.00	5.00	5.00	(2)
	Bruno Candrian—Slygof	8.00	4.00	12.00	(=8)
	Willi Melliger—Van Gogh	(24.00)	8.00	32.00	(=27)
	Philippe Guerdat —Pybalia	16.00	(16.00)	32.00	(=27)
		24.00	17.00		
6	**France** 49.75				
	Frédéric Cottier —Flambeau C	8.00	12.00	20.00	(=15)
	Eric Navet—Je t'Adore	9.75	12.00	21.75	(20)
	Philippe Rozier—Jiva	(20.00)	0.00	20.00	(=15)
	Pierre Durand —Jappeloup	8.00	E	—	
		25.75	24.00		
7	**Spain** 52.00				
	Alberto Honrubia —Kaoua	8.00	0.00	8.00	(=3)
	Luis Alvarez Cervera —Jexico du Parc	1.50	9.50	11.00	(7)
	Rutherford Latham —Idaho E	12.00	21.00	33.00	(29)
	Luis Astolfi —Feinschnitt Z	(32.50)	(24.00)	56.50	(40)
		21.50	30.50		
8	**Italy** 75.25				
	Giorgio Nuti—Impedoumi	12.00	4.00	16.00	(=12)
	Graziano Mancinelli —Ideal de la Haye	12.00	8.00	20.00	(=15)

Individual and team gold medallists in Los Angeles, 1984, Joe Fargis and Touch of Class. The mare jumped a double clear round in the Nations Cup, the first horse ever to do so in Olympic competition. (Kit Houghton)

Bruno Scolari				
—Joyau d'Or	35.25	4.00	39.25	(32)
Filippo Moyersoen				
—Adam II	E	(16.00)	—	
	59.25	16.00		

9 Australia 92.00

Greg Eurell				
—Mr Shrimpton	16.00	8.00	24.00	(21)
George Sanna—Kite	12.00	16.00	28.00	(24)
Jeff McVean				
—King Omega	(28.25)	12.00	40.25	(33)
Guy Creighton				
—Conclusion	28.00	(28.00)	56.00	(=38)
	56.00	36.00		

10 Brazil 133.50

Jorge Carneiro				
—Testarudo	16.75	17.25	34.00	(=30)
Caio Sergio Carvalho				
—Virtuoso	21.75	21.75	43.50	(34)
Marcelo Blessman				
—Alpes	28.00	28.00	56.00	(=38)
Vitor Teixeira—Natural	(28.25)	(29.25)	57.50	(41)
	66.50	67.00		

11 Japan 137.25

Shuichi Toki—The Shinto	8.50	25.50	34.00	(=30)
Takashi Tomura				
—Purplex	21.00	(31.25)	52.25	(35)
Yoshihiro Nakano				
—Colman	24.00	28.50	52.50	(36)
Ryuichi Obata				
—Goldfinder	(25.00)	29.75	54.75	(37)
	53.50	83.75		

12 Mexico 52.75
(first round)

Fernando Senderos			
—Massacre	8.00	NP	—
Raul Nieto—Riskatek	20.50	NP	—
Gerardo Tazzer Valencia			
—Magod	24.25	NP	—
Federico Garza			
—Olympus	(46.50)	E	—

Not allowed to compete in the second round:

13 Belgium 80.25

Hermann van den Broeck	
—Wellington	8.00
Ferdi Tyteca—'t Soulaiky	32.00
Axel Verlooy—Vrijheid	40.25

14 Chile 80.50

Americo Simonetti	
—Amaranto	8.00
Alfredo Sone—Trumao	30.25
Victor Contador—Tostao	42.25
Alfonso Bobadilla	
—Soplito	E

15 Argentina 89.75

Justo Albarracin	
—Collon Cura de Tatu	19.25
Eduardo Zone—Cardal	28.25
Martin Mallo—Gonzo	42.25
Adrian Melosi—Britanica	E

Number of teams: 15 (The 12 best-placed teams in the first round qualified for the second round.)

Individual

(Separate competition, 2 rounds)

		Faults			Jump-off
		Round			
		One	Two	Total	F/Time
1	Joe Fargis (USA)—Touch of Class	0.00	4.00	4.00	0/58.06
2	Conrad Homfeld (USA)—Adbullah	4.00	0.00	4.00	8/51.03
3	Heidi Robbiani (Switz)—Jessica V	4.00	4.00	8.00	0/53.39
4	Mario Deslauriers (Can)—Aramis	4.00	4.00	8.00	4/57.07
5	Bruno Candrian (Switz)—Slygof	4.00	4.00	8.00	8/58.10
6	Luis Alvarez Cervera (Spa)—Jexico du Parc	4.25	4.25	8.50	
=7	Frédéric Cottier (Fra)—Flambeau C	8.00	4.00	12.00	
	Paul Schockemöhle (FRG)—Deister	8.00	4.00	12.00	
	Melanie Smith (USA)—Calypso	4.00	8.00	12.00	
10	Luis Astolfi (Spa)—Feinschnitt Z	5.25	8.50	13.75	
=11	Peter Luther (FRG)—Livius	12.00	4.00	16.00	
	Franke Sloothaak (FRG)—Farmer	8.00	8.00	16.00	
13	Tim Grubb (GB)—Linky	8.25	9.00	17.25	
=14	John Whitaker (GB)—Ryan's Son	12.00	8.00	20.00	
	Gerardo Tazzer Valencia (Mex)—Magod	12.00	8.00	20.00	
	Ian Millar (Can)—Big Ben	12.00	8.00	20.00	
	Pierre Durand (Fra)—Jappeloup	12.00	8.00	20.00	
18	Fernando Senderos (Mex)—Massacre	12.75	8.00	20.75	
19	Hugh Graham (Can)—Elrond	13.00	8.00	21.00	
=20	Philippe Rozier (Fra)—Jiva	16.00	8.00	24.00	
	Giorgio Nuti (Ita)—Impedoumi	12.00	12.00	24.00	
=22	Bruno Scolari (Ita)—Joyau d'Or	16.00	12.00	28.00	
	Hugo Simon (Aut)—The Freak	12.00	16.00	28.00	
24	Michael Whitaker (GB)—Overton Amanda	0.00	28.50	28.50	
25	Hermann van den Broeck (Bel)—Wellington	16.00	16.25	32.25	
26	Jeff McVean (Aus)—King Omega	12.50	24.25	36.75	
27	Shuichi Toki (Jap)—The Shinto	10.50	E		

Not allowed to compete in second round:

28	Gerry Mullins (Ire)—Rockbarton	16.25
=29	Ove Hansen (Nor)—Sancerre	16.50
	Greg Eurell (Aus)—Mr Shrimpton	16.50
31	Jaime Azcarraga (Mex)—Royal Today	18.00
32	Jorge Carneiro (Bra)—Testarudo	21.25
33	Caio Sergio Carvalho (Bra)—Virtuoso	23.25
34	Yoshihiro Nakano (Jap)—Colman	24.00
35	Alfredo Sone (Chi)—Trumao	24.25
=36	George Sanna (Aus)—Kite	24.50
	Graziano Mancinelli (Ita)—Ideal de la Haye	24.50
38	Willi Melliger (Switz)—Van Gogh	24.75
39	Peter Eriksson (Swe)—Imperator	25.75
40	Justo Albarracin (Arg)—Collon Cura de Tatu	26.50
41	Alberto Honrubia (Spa)—Kaoua	27.00
=42	Americo Simonetti (Chi)—Amaranto	28.25
	Ferdi Tyteca (Bel)—'t Soulaiky	28.25
44	Victor Contador (Chi)—Tostao	40.00
45	Marcelo Blessman (Bra)—Alpes	44.00
=46	Takashi Tomura (Jap)—Purplex	48.25
	Eduardo Zone (Arg)—Cardal	48.25
	Martin Mallo (Arg)—Gonzo	R
	Axel Verlooy (Bel)—Vrijheid	R
	Oswaldo Mendez (Gua)—Love Forever	E
	John Cottle (NZ)—Arturo	E

Number of riders: 51 (The 25 best-placed riders in the first round, including all those in equal 25th place, qualified for the second round.)

Number of nations represented: 21

Austria's top rider Hugo Simon was in the Federal Republic of Germany's winning Nations Cup team at Rotterdam in 1971. He claimed dual nationality and later opted to ride for Austria. Other riders who have changed nationality include former Dutchman Franke Sloothaak, who now rides for the Federal Republic of Germany, and Edgar-Henri Cuepper, who used to ride for Belgium and in 1985 decided to represent Luxemburg.

The first time a British civilian team competed for a Nations Cup was at Nice in April 1947.

In 1949 Eire was the only country to insist that its Nations Cup be competed for by teams composed only of military riders.

The first combined civilian/military team to represent Ireland won the Aga Khan Cup (Nations Cup) at Dublin in 1963.

In 1929 Nations Cups restricted to lady riders were staged at Budapest and Aachen. Similar events were held at Stresa in 1930 and at Düsseldorf in 1932.

International Show Jumping Festival

(Organized for those countries which did not compete in the Moscow Olympics.)

1980 Rotterdam

Nations Cup

(2 rounds, teams of 4, best 3 scores in each round to count)

	Faults Round			
	One	Two	Total	
1 Canada 16.50				
Mark Laskin—Damuraz	0.00	0.00	0.00	(=1)
Ian Millar—Brother Sam	0.25	4.25	4.50	(9)
Michel Vaillancourt				
—Chivaz	(8.00)	4.00	12.00	(=15)
Jim Elder—Volunteer	8.00	(8.00)	16.00	(=19)
	8.25	8.25		
2 Great Britain 18.50				
Nick Skelton—Maybe	0.00	0.00	0.00	(=1)
John Whitaker				
—Ryan's Son	0.00	4.00	4.00	(=4)
Graham Fletcher				
—Preachan	8.00	(8.00)	16.00	(=19)
Tim Grubb				
—Night Murmur	(14.25)	6.50	20.75	(32)
	8.00	10.50		
3 Austria 20.00				
Thomas Frühmann				
—Donau	0.00	0.00	0.00	(=1)
Hugo Simon				
—Gladstone	0.00	8.00	8.00	(=10)
Georg Riedl—Weekend	(20.00)	0.00	20.00	(30)
Roland Fischer—Icarus	12.00	(20.00)	32.00	(39)
	12.00	8.00		

Hugo Simon and Gladstone, winners of the individual gold medal at the International Festival in Rotterdam, 1980, staged for those riders who did not go to the Moscow Games. (Jim Bennett)

	Faults Round			
	One	Two	Total	
4 FRG 24.00				
Paul Schockemöhle				
—Deister	0.00	4.00	4.00	(=4)
Peter Luther—Livius	4.00	4.00	8.00	(=10)
Ulrich Meyer zu Bexten				
—Magister	4.00	(12.00)	16.00	(=19)
Gerd Wiltfang—Roman	(8.00)	8.00	16.00	(=19)
	8.00	16.00		
=5 USA 28.00				
Melanie Smith				
—Calypso	4.00	0.00	4.00	(=4)
Norman Dello Joio				
—Allegro	4.00	8.00	12.00	(=15)
Terry Rudd				
—Semi Tough	4.00	8.00	12.00	(=15)
Katie Monahan				
—Silver Exchange	(4.00)	(12.00)	16.00	(=19)
	12.00	16.00		
=5 Switzerland 28.00				
Willi Melliger				
—Trumpf Buur	0.00	4.00	4.00	(=4)
Thomas Fuchs				
—Tullis Lass	4.00	4.00	8.00	(=10)
Walter Gabathuler				
—Harley	8.00	8.00	16.00	(=19)
Max Hauri—Beethoven	(8.25)	(16.00)	24.25	(36)
	12.00	16.00		
7 France 32.00				
Gilles Bertran de				
Balanda—Galoubet A	4.00	0.00	4.00	(=4)
Frédéric Cottier				
—Flambeau C	4.00	4.00	8.00	(=10)
Jean-Marc Nicolas				
—Mador	(8.25)	12.00	20.25	(31)
Hervé Godignon				
—Faro de Biolay	8.00	(43.25)	51.25	(40)
	16.00	16.00		
8 Australia 40.00				
Mariane Gilchrist				
—Goldray	4.00	8.00	12.00	(=15)
Jeff McVean—Claret	4.00	(12.00)	16.00	(=19)
Kevin Bacon				
—Billsborough	8.00	8.00	16.00	(=19)
Chris Smith—Sanskrit	(8.00)	8.00	16.00	(=19)
	16.00	24.00		
9 Netherlands 55.00				
Rob Ehrens				
—Koh-I-Noor	4.50	4.00	8.50	(14)
Henk Nooren				
—Opstalan's Shoreline	4.00	18.75	22.75	(33)
Johan Heins—Larramy	8.00	15.75	23.75	(34)
Piet Raymakers				
—Isocratus Eurotex	E	E	—	
	16.50	38.50		

10 **Belgium**   56.00

Edgar-Henri Cuepper —Cyrano	8.00	8.00	16.00	(=19)
Christian Huysegoms —Talky	12.00	4.00	16.00	(=19)
Eric Wauters —Winnetou	(12.00)	16.00	28.00	(37)
Stanny van Paesschen —Porsche	8.00 28.00	(22.75) 28.00	30.75	(38)

11 **Mexico**   58.00

Gerardo Tazzer Valencia—Caribe	8.00	16.00	24.00	(35)
Alberto Valdez Lacarra —Lady Mirka	38.00	17.25	55.25	(41)
Joaquin Pérez de las Heras—Alimony	12.00	NP	—	

Jesus Gómez Portugal —Massacre	R	NP	—

12 **Sweden**   74.75

Royne Zetterman —Young Diamond	8.00	NP
Jan-Olaf Wannius —Tredje Mannen	8.75	NP
Leif Holgersson —Juvelin	*58.00E	NP
Leif Nilsson—Fayer Rex	E	NP

13 **Denmark**   106.25

Niels Hansen —Nighttimes Playboy	13.50	NP
Hasse Hoffman—Parco	34.75	NP
Henrik Carlsen—Lurifax	*58.00E	NP

Number of teams: 13

Individual

(Separate competition, 2 rounds)

	Faults Round			Jump-off
	One	Two	Total	F/Time
1 Hugo Simon (Aut)—Gladstone	4.00	0.00	4.00	0.75/58.60
2 John Whitaker (GB)—Ryan's Son	4.00	0.00	4.00	4.00/40.00
3 Melanie Smith (USA)—Calypso	4.00	0.00	4.00	4.00/42.40
4 Paul Schockemöhle (FRG)—Deister	4.25	0.00	4.25	
5 Jeff McVean (Aus)—Autograph	2.25	4.25	6.50	
6 Walter Gabathuler (Switz)—Harley	4.00	4.00	8.00	
7 Willi Melliger (Switz)—Trumpf-Buur	8.00	0.00	8.00	
8 Gilles Bertran de Balanda (Fra)—Galoubet A	1.00	8.00	9.00	
9 Joaquin Pérez de las Heras (Mex)—Alimony	8.00	4.00	12.00	
10 Terry Rudd (USA)—Semi Tough	8.50	4.00	12.50	
11 Jim Elder (Can)—Volunteer	5.00	8.00	13.00	
12 Peter Luther (FRG)—Livius	9.50	4.00	13.50	
13 Henk Nooren (NL)—Opstalan's Shoreline	12.50	4.00	16.50	
14 Mariane Gilchrist (Aus)—Goldray	9.00	8.00	17.00	/69.70
15 Kristian Maunula (Fin)—Kingsize	9.00	8.00	17.00	/73.10
16 Juan Antonio de Wit Guzman (Spa)—Olimpico	13.00	4.25	17.25	
17 Eric Wauters (Bel)—Winnetou	4.00	16.25	20.25	
18 Royne Zetterman (Swe)—Young Diamond	12.00	12.00	24.00	
19 Oswaldo Mendez Herbruger (Gua)—Pampa	14.00	10.25	24.25	
20 Alfonso Sevogia (Spa)—Agamenon	12.50	16.00	28.50	
21 Jan-Olaf Wannius (Swe)—Tredje Mannen	15.50	16.75	32.25	
=22 Mark Laskin (Can)—Damuraz	5.25	R		
Norman Dello Joio (USA)—Allegro	13.00	R		
Christian Huysegoms (Bel)—Talky	18.50	R		
25 Nick Skelton (GB)—Maybe	9.50	NP		
26 Jorge Carneiro (Bra)—Highland Mist	20.00	—		
27 Chris Smith (Aus)—Sanskrit	20.25	—		
28 Georg Riedl (Aut)—Weekend	21.00	—		
29 Niels Hansen (Den)—Nighttimes Playboy	22.25	—		
30 Frédéric Cottier (Fra)—Flambeau C	25.75	—		
31 Jean-René Dechamps (CRC)—Don Juan	26.00	—		
32 Thomas Fuchs (Switz)—Snow King	40.50	—		
=33 Gerd Wiltfang (FRG)—Roman	E	—		
Jean-Marc Nicolas (Fra)—Seaman	E	—		
Thomas Frühmann (Aut)—Donau	E	—		
=36 Graham Fletcher (GB)—Preachan	R	—		
Ian Millar (Can)—Brother Sam	R	—		
Rob Ehrens (NL)—Koh-I-Noor	R	—		

Number of riders: 38 (The 25 best-placed riders in the first round qualified for the second round.)

Number of nations represented: 18

---

*To prevent total elimination of a team, a rider who was eliminated was awarded the worst score for that round plus 20, i.e. 38.00 plus 20.00=58.00.

Medal Tables*

1912–1984 (Teams)

Country	Gold	Silver	Bronze
FRG/Germany	5	1	3
Sweden	3	—	1
France	1	3	—
USA	1	2	1
Great Britain	1	1	2
Spain	1	1	—
Mexico	1	—	1
Canada	1	—	—
USSR	1	—	—
Poland	—	2	—
Italy	—	1	4
Belgium	—	1	1
Chile	—	1	—
Netherlands	—	1	—
Switzerland	—	1	—
Portugal	—	—	2

*Not including International Festival 1980.

1912–1984 (Individual)

Country	Gold	Silver	Bronze
Italy	3	4	1
FRG/Germany	3	2	1
France	3	1	1
USA	2	2	1
Mexico	1	1	1
Switzerland	1	—	2
Poland	1	—	1
Czechoslovakia	1	—	—
Japan	1	—	—
Great Britain	—	2	3
Canada	—	1	—
Chile	—	1	—
Rumania	—	1	—
USSR	—	1	—
Belgium	—	—	2
Sweden	—	—	2
Hungary	—	—	1

1912–1984 (Combined Teams/Individual)

Country	Gold	Silver	Bronze
FRG/Germany	8	3	4
France	4	4	1
Italy	3	5	5
USA	3	4	2
Sweden	3	—	3
Mexico	2	1	2
Great Britain	1	3	5
Poland	1	2	1
Switzerland	1	1	2
Canada	1	1	—
Spain	1	1	—
USSR	1	1	—
Czechoslovakia	1	—	—
Japan	1	—	—
Chile	—	2	—
Belgium	—	1	3
Netherlands	—	1	—
Rumania	—	1	—
Portugal	—	—	2
Hungary	—	—	1

Number of riders per country participating in Olympic Games 1912–84

	'12	'20	'24	'28	'32	'36	'48	'52	'56	'60	'64	'68	'72	'76	'80	'84	No. of Games
USA	3	7	4	3	3	3	3	3	3	4	3	4	4	5	—	4	15
Fra	4	7	4	3	—	3	3	3	3	3	3	3	5	4	—	4	14
Ita	—	10	4	3	—	3	3	3	3	3	3	3	4	4	—	4	13
Swe	9	10	4	3	3	3	3	3	3	4	—	—	1	1	—	1	13
GB	3	—	4	—	—	3	3	3	3	4	3	3	4	4	—	4	12
Ger/FRG	6	—	—	3	—	3	—	3	3	3	3	4	4	4	—	4	11
Jap	—	—	—	1	2	3	—	1	2	3	3	3	4	4	—	4	11
Switz	—	—	4	3	—	3	—	1	3	2	3	3	5	1	—	4	11
Arg	—	—	—	3	—	—	3	3	3	4	3	4	5	3	—	4	10
Bel	4	9	4	3	—	3	—	—	3	2	—	—	4	4	—	3	10
Spa	—	—	4	3	—	—	3	3	3	4	3	—	4	4	—	4	10
Mex	—	—	—	—	3	3	3	—	—	3	3	4	4	4	—	5	9
Por	—	—	4	3	—	3	3	3	3	3	2	—	3	—	—	—	9
Bra	—	—	—	—	—	3	3	3	3	1	3	2	—	—	—	4	8
Rus/USSR	6	—	—	—	—	—	3	3	4	3	3	4	—	—	4	—	8
Nor	3	2	—	3	—	3	—	1	1	—	—	—	—	—	—	1	7
Aut	—	—	—	—	—	3	—	—	3	1	—	—	1	4	—	1	6
Hun	—	—	—	3	—	3	—	—	3	4	—	—	4	—	4	—	6
Pol	—	—	4	3	—	3	—	—	—	—	—	4	4	—	4	—	6
Aus	—	—	—	—	—	—	—	1	—	—	3	3	—	3	—	4	5
Chi	2	—	—	—	—	—	3	—	—	1	—	3	—	—	—	4	5
Ire	—	—	—	—	—	—	3	—	3	3	—	3	—	—	—	1	5
Can	—	—	—	—	—	—	—	—	—	—	—	4	4	4	—	4	4
Fin	—	—	—	—	—	—	2	3	3	—	—	—	—	—	1	—	4
NZ	—	—	—	—	—	—	—	—	—	1	3	—	—	1	—	1	4
NL	—	—	—	3	—	3	3	—	—	—	—	—	4	—	—	—	4
Rum	—	—	—	—	—	3	—	3	—	3	—	—	—	4	—	—	4
Tur	—	—	—	—	—	3	3	—	3	3	—	—	—	—	—	—	4
Bol	—	—	—	—	—	—	—	—	—	—	—	1	1	1	—	—	3
Cze	—	—	3	3	—	3	—	—	—	—	—	—	—	—	—	—	3
Egy/UAR	—	—	—	—	—	—	3	3	3	—	—	—	—	—	—	—	3
Gua	—	—	—	—	—	—	—	—	—	—	—	—	—	1	1	1	3
Kor/SKor	—	—	—	—	—	—	1	—	2	3	—	—	—	—	—	—	3
Bul	—	—	—	—	—	—	—	—	—	—	—	—	—	—	4	—	1
Cam	—	—	—	—	—	—	—	2	—	—	—	—	—	—	—	—	1
Den	—	—	—	—	—	3	—	—	—	—	—	—	—	—	—	—	1
PR	—	—	—	—	—	—	—	—	—	—	—	—	—	1	—	—	1
URU	—	—	—	—	—	—	—	—	—	3	—	—	—	—	—	—	1
Ven	—	—	—	—	—	—	3	—	—	—	—	—	—	—	—	—	1
No. of Nations	9	6	11	16	4	18	15	20	24	23	17	16	21	20	8	21	

Records: Riders

Most Medals

5 Gold, 1 Silver, 1 Bronze

Hans Günter Winkler (FRG)
Team gold 1956
Individual gold 1956
Team gold 1960
Team gold 1964
Team gold 1972
Team silver 1976
Team bronze 1968

2 Gold, 2 Silver

Pierre Jonquères d'Oriola (Fra)
Individual gold 1952
Individual gold 1964
Team silver 1964
Team silver 1968

2 Gold, 1 Silver, 1 Bronze

Alwin Schockemöhle (FRG)
Team gold 1960
Individual gold 1976
Team silver 1976
Team bronze 1968

2 Gold, 1 Bronze

Fritz Thiedemann (FRG)
Team gold 1956
Team gold 1960
Individual bronze 1952

2 Gold

Hans von Rosen (Swe)
Team gold 1912
Team gold 1920

Kurt Hasse (Ger)
Team gold 1936
Individual gold 1936

Humberto Mariles Cortés (Mex)
Team gold 1948
Individual gold 1948

Joe Fargis (USA)
Team gold 1984
Individual gold 1984

1 Gold, 2 Silver, 3 Bronze

Raimondo d'Inzeo (Ita)
Individual gold 1960
Team silver 1956
Individual silver 1956
Team bronze 1960
Team bronze 1964
Team bronze 1972

1 Gold, 2 Silver, 1 Bronze

William Steinkraus (USA)
Individual gold 1968
Team silver 1960
Team silver 1972
Team bronze 1952

1 Gold, 1 Silver, 1 Bronze

Hermann Schridde (FRG)
Team gold 1964
Individual silver 1964
Team bronze 1968

1 Gold, 1 Silver

Jean Cariou (Fra)
Individual gold 1912
Team silver 1912

Tommaso Lequio di Assaba (Ita)
Individual gold 1920
Individual silver 1924

Alphonse Gemuseus (Switz)
Individual gold 1924
Team silver 1924

Rubén Uriza Castro (Mex)
Team gold 1948
Individual silver 1948

Marcel Rozier (Fra)
Team gold 1976
Team silver 1968

Nikolai Korolkov (USSR)
Team gold 1980
Individual silver 1980

Jan Kowalczyk (Pol)
Individual gold 1980
Team silver 1980

Conrad Homfeld (USA)
Team gold 1984
Individual silver 1984

1 Gold, 2 Bronze

Graziano Mancinelli (Ita)
Individual gold 1972
Team bronze 1964
Team bronze 1972

1 Gold, 1 Bronze

Carl Gustav Lewenhaupt (Swe)
Team gold 1912
Individual bronze 1920

Harry Llewellyn (GB)
Team gold 1952
Team bronze 1948

Wilf White (GB)
Team gold 1952
Team bronze 1956

Fritz Ligges (FRG)
Team gold 1972
Team bronze 1984

2 Silver, 4 bronze

Piero d'Inzeo (Ita)
Team silver 1956
Individual silver 1960
Individual bronze 1956
Team bronze 1960
Team bronze 1964
Team bronze 1972

2 Silver

Oscar Cristi (Chi)
Team silver 1952
Individual silver 1952

Frank Chapot (USA)
Team silver 1960
Team silver 1972

Janou Lefèbvre (Fra)
Team silver 1964
Team silver 1968

1 Silver, 1 Bronze

Neal Shapiro (USA)
Team silver 1972
Individual bronze 1972

Paul Schockemöhle (FRG)
Team silver 1976
Team bronze 1984

2 Bronze

David Broome (GB)
Individual bronze 1960
Individual bronze 1968

François Mathy (Bel)
Team bronze 1976
Individual bronze 1976

Joaquin Pérez de las Heras (Mex)
Team bronze 1980
Individual bronze 1980

Peter Robeson (GB)
Team bronze 1956
Individual bronze 1964

Most Olympic Appearances

8 Piero d'Inzeo (Ita)—1948–1976 inclusive
7 Raimondo d'Inzeo (Ita)—1952–1976 inclusive
6 Hans Günter Winkler (FRG)—1956–1976 inclusive

Hans Günter Winkler is the only rider to have won a medal at six consecutive Olympic Games.

First Lady Riders

Show jumping at the Olympics was open to women for the first time in 1956. Pat Smythe (Great Britain) and Brigitte Schockaert (Bel) were the only women riders to take part. Pat Smythe was a member of the bronze medal winning British team and thus the first woman to win a show jumping medal. She finished 10th individually. Brigitte Schockaert finished =34 and was the best placed of the three Belgian riders.

First Civilian Medal Winner

Chevalier Jean d'Orgeix (Fra) who won the individual bronze in London, 1948.

Best Score

Alwin Schockemöhle (FRG) is the only rider to have won the individual gold medal outright with a zero score and no jump-off (Montreal, 1976).

František Ventura (Czech) finished with a zero score after two jump-offs for the gold medal (Amsterdam, 1928).

Youngest Winner of the Individual Gold Medal*

Alphonse Gemuseus (Switz), who was 26 years and 80 days old when he won in Paris in 1924.

Oldest Winner of the Individual Gold Medal*

Pierre Jonquères d'Oriola (France), who was 44 years and 266 days old when he won in Tokyo in 1964.

Pat Smythe, the first woman to win an Olympic show jumping medal, in a spot of trouble with Flanagan during the 1956 Stockholm Nations Cup. Nevertheless their performance was good enough to give them a team bronze medal and 10th place overall. (The Photo Source)

Riders who have won medals in more than one sport in the same Games

1912 Stockholm

Jean Cariou (Fra)
 Individual gold and Team silver, Show Jumping
 Individual bronze, Three-Day Event

1920 Antwerp

Giulio Cacciandra (Ita)
 Team bronze, Show Jumping
 Team silver, Three-Day Event

Ettore Caffaratti (Ita)
 Team bronze, Show Jumping
 Individual bronze and Team silver, Three-Day Event

Hans von Rosen (Swe)
 Team gold, Show Jumping
 Individual bronze, Dressage

1928 Amsterdam

Michael Antoniewicz (Pol)
 Team silver, Show Jumping
 Team bronze, Three-Day Event

1932 Los Angeles

Harry D. Chamberlin (USA)
 Individual silver, Show Jumping
 Team gold, Three-Day Event

Clarence von Rosen (Swe)
 Individual bronze, Show Jumping
 Individual bronze, Three-Day Event

1948 London

Humberto Mariles Cortés (Mex)
 Individual and Team gold, Show Jumping
 Team bronze, Three-Day Event

1952 Helsinki

Fritz Thiedemann (FRG)
 Individual bronze, Show Jumping
 Team bronze, Dressage

*Not including the winner at the 1912 Games, Jean Cariou, whose exact date of birth could not be ascertained.

Records: Horses

Most Medals

3 Gold

Halla (Hans Günter Winkler, FRG)
Team gold 1956
Individual gold 1956
Team gold 1960

2 Gold, 1 Bronze

Meteor (Fritz Thiedemann, FRG)
Team gold 1956
Team gold 1960
Individual bronze 1952

2 Gold

Tora (Kurt Hasse, Ger)
Team gold 1936
Individual gold 1936

Arete (Humberto Mariles Cortés, Mex)
Team gold 1948
Individual gold 1948

Touch of Class (Joe Fargis, USA)
Team gold 1984
Individual gold 1984

1 Gold, 1 Silver, 1 Bronze

Dozent II (Hermann Schridde, FRG)
Team gold 1964
Individual silver 1964
Team bronze 1968

1 Gold, 1 Silver

Mignon (Jean Cariou, Fra)
Individual gold 1912
Team silver 1912

Trebecco (Tommaso Lequio di Assaba, Ita)
Individual gold 1920
Individual silver 1924

Lucette (Alphonse Gemuseus, Switz)
Individual gold 1924
Team silver 1924

Hatuey (Rubén Uriza Castro, Mex)
Team gold 1948
Individual silver 1948

Lutteur B
Individual gold 1964
Team silver 1964

Torphy (Hans Günter Winkler, FRG)
Team gold 1972
Team silver 1976

Warwick Rex (Alwin Schockemöhle, FRG)
Individual gold 1976
Team silver 1976

Espadron (Nikolai Korolkov, USSR)
Team gold 1980
Individual silver 1980

Artemor (Jan Kowalczyk, Pol)
Individual gold 1980
Team silver 1980

Abdullah (Conrad Homfeld, USA)
Team gold 1984
Individual silver 1984

1 Gold, 2 Bronze

Posillipo (Raimondo d'Inzeo, Ita)
Individual gold 1960
Team bronze 1960
Team bronze 1964

1 Gold, 1 Bronze

Loke (Åke Thelning, Ernst Hallberg*, Swe)
Team gold 1924
Team bronze 1928*

Foxhunter (Harry Llewellyn, GB)
Team gold 1952
Team bronze 1948

Nizefela (Wilf White, GB)
Team gold 1952
Team bronze 1956

Ambassador (Graziano Mancinelli, Ita)
Individual gold 1972
Team bronze 1972

2 Silver

Bambi (Oscar Cristi, Chi)
Team silver 1952
Individual silver 1952

Merano (Raimondo d'Inzeo, Ita)
Team silver 1956
Individual silver 1956

1 Silver, 1 Bronze

Uruguay (Piero d'Inzeo, Ita)
Team silver 1956
Individual bronze 1956

The Rock (Piero d'Inzeo, Ita)
Individual silver 1960
Team bronze 1960

Sloopy (Neal Shapiro, USA)
Team silver 1972
Individual bronze 1972

2 Bronze

Gai Luron (François Mathy, Bel)
Team bronze 1976
Individual bronze 1976

Alimony (Joaquin Pérez de las Heras, Mex)
Team bronze 1980
Individual bronze 1980

Most Gold Medals

3 Halla (Hans Günter Winkler, FRG)
1956 Team and Individual gold
1960 Team gold

Most Medal-Winning Appearances

3 Meteor (Fritz Thiedemann, FRG)
The only show jumper to win a medal at three consecutive Games
1952 Individual bronze
1956 Team gold
1960 Team gold

Most Medals Won

3 Halla 3 gold
Meteor 2 gold, 1 bronze
Dozent II 1 gold, 1 silver, 1 bronze
Posillipo 1 gold, 2 bronze

Biggest winning margin

Teams

35.75 faults: 1980 (USSR beat Poland)

Individual

12.00 faults: 1976 (Alwin Schockemöhle finished on 0.00; three with 12.00 faults jumped off for the silver and bronze medals.)

Smallest winning margin

Teams

0.25 faults: 1972 (FRG beat USA)

Individual

13.60 seconds: 1936 (Kurt Hasse and Henri Rang had equal faults in the jump-off but Hasse had the faster time. This is the only occasion on which the gold medal has been decided on time, as opposed to faults.)

Highest number of starters

Teams

20: 1956 Stockholm

Individual

66: 1956 Stockholm

Highest number of nations represented

24: 1956 Stockholm

Smallest number of starters

Teams

3: 1932 Los Angeles

Individual

11: 1932 Los Angeles

Smallest number of nations represented

4: 1932 Los Angeles

Highest number of clear rounds

Teams

4: gold medal winning USA team, 1984 Los Angeles

Joe Fargis and Touch of Class are the only rider and horse to have jumped a double clear round in the Olympic Nations Cup (1984 Los Angeles)

Individual

3: František Ventura and Eliot, who had clear rounds in the one-round Nations Cup and in two jump-offs for the individual gold medal (1928 Amsterdam).

Melanie Smith and Calypso, who were members of the gold medal winning USA team at Los Angeles in 1984, are the only rider and horse to have won a medal without taking part in the entire competition. After their first three riders had jumped their second rounds in the Nations Cup, the United States team was so far ahead that no other team could beat them. In this situation the rules permit the fourth rider not to start in the second round.

Meteor

In common with his compatriot and comtemporary, Halla, the German horse Meteor is the holder of a unique Olympic record: he is the only show jumper to have won a medal at three Olympic Games. It is given to few horses to reach Olympic standard—for one to maintain that level of achievement over a period of eight years is truly remarkable.

Meteor was bred by Otto Dreessen in Nindorf and was foaled on 12 May 1943. He was a Holsteiner produced from old-established bloodlines, being by Diskus out of Konkurrentin. The big bay gelding was ridden for a while by Elke Brandt, daughter of Willi Brandt, but the rider who took him to the top of the international show jumping tree was the great Fritz Thiedemann, who rode the horse for his joint-owners, Herr Brandt and the German Olympic Committee, from 1951 to 1961.

Meteor's record in the testing Hamburg Jumping Derby is testimony to his toughness and consistency: winner in 1951 with the only clear round; fifth in 1954; seventh in 1955; sixth in 1957; third in 1958 with a clear round followed by 4 faults in the jump-off; fifth in 1959, again with a clear round, and 8 faults in the jump-off; third in 1960 and sixth in 1961, both times with 4 faults.

In his first Olympic Games in 1952 he was the only horse to go clear in the first round, finally winning the individual bronze medal after a five-sided jump-off. Four year later he was a member of the victorious German team at Stockholm and finished in fourth place individually, just 1 fault behind the bronze medallist, Uruguay. Then in Rome in 1960, at the age of 17, he finished sixth in the individual contest and, in the separate Nations Cup, won his second team gold, recording the third best score of the competition.

Meteor's other major victories included the Men's European Championship in 1958, the Grand Prix of Aachen, Berlin, Dortmund and New York, and, in 1954, the King George V Gold Cup in London. He took part in 18 Nations Cups and was in the winning team on four occasions, at Aachen in 1955 and 1957, Geneva in 1957 and Lucerne in 1958. He was retired after the Aachen show of 1961, with

Meteor, the only show jumper to have won a medal at three consecutive Olympics. Fritz Thiedemann is in the saddle. (Sport and General)

150 wins to his credit and prize money totalling DM177 112. He had been placed in the first three on 292 occasions and in the first five 380 times.

Much of Meteor's success can be attributed to the artistry of Fritz Thiedemann, a slightly built rider whose fine horsemanship enabled him to get the best out of the big, powerful Holstein horses which he favoured. Legend has it that at the Helsinki Olympics, where Thiedemann was representing Germany in both the dressage and the show jumping, the other dressage riders watched him in a practice session performing flying changes on a straight line and expressed the opinion that he would not be too much trouble to them in the dressage competition. What they did not know was that the horse on whom he was performing advanced dressage movements was his show jumper, Meteor, not his dressage horse. He went on to win a bronze medal in both disciplines.

Meteor died in 1966 and is buried in the grounds of the Reit- und Fahrschule at Elmshorn, headquarters of the Holsteiner breed society in the Federal Republic of Germany.

World Championships

A World Championship was held for the first time in June 1953 at the Parc des Princes, in Paris. Formerly, the highlight of a CHIO had always been the Nations Cup. On this occasion the team contest was replaced by an individual championship for men, comprising two qualifying competitions (a Table A and a Puissance) followed by a semi-final (a Nations Cup-type competition, with two rounds over the same course) and a final for the top four riders. In the final each rider had to jump not only his own horse but also those of each of the other finalists.

This formula was not, in fact, original—the famous French rider Comte Roland de Maillé had come up with the idea in 1949 and tried it out at the international show at Vichy—nor was it universally popular. Some riders objected to their horses having to be ridden by several other competitors, and it was this that prompted one or two of the leading nations to stay away. Some people felt the Championship followed on too quickly after the Olympic Games, while others believed only the Olympics could truly be classed as a World Championship. Nevertheless, the event went ahead and some 35 000 people watched the final.

Initially the Championship was run annually but, because of the problems and expense of travelling from one continent to another, it was in danger of degenerating into a European, not a World Championship. As a result it was decided to stage the Championship once every four years, and to begin with it was run in the same years as the Olympics. Since 1966 it has been held in the even years between one Olympic Games and the next. A separate ladies' Championship was held on three occasions but in 1978 the two events were amalgamated, and a team championship added, and this is the formula used today.

The Championships consist of three competitions: a speed class, a Nations Cup and a Grand Prix. The Team Championship is decided on the combined results of the first two classes. The four leading individual riders at the end of all three classes go into the change-horse final.

Team Championship

1978 Aachen		Nations Cup	
	Table C	Round One	Round Two
1 Great Britain 26.60			
Derek Ricketts			
—Hydrophane Coldstream	6.25	0.00	(8.00)
Caroline Bradley—Tigre	(12.35)	0.25	0.00
Malcolm Pyrah—Law Court	2.85	(8.25)	8.00
David Broome—Philco	1.25	4.00	4.00
2 Netherlands 31.30			
Dick Wieken—Sil Z	(10.15)	4.00	(8.00)
Anton Ebben—Jumbo Design	5.50	(8.00)	4.00
Henk Nooren—Pluco	2.25	4.00	0.00
Johan Heins—Pandur Z	3.55	4.00	4.00
3 USA 42.40			
Conrad Homfeld—Balbuco	2.45	12.00	0.00
Dennis Murphy—Tuscaloosa	(12.65)	8.25	16.00
Buddy Brown—Viscount	1.55	(19.75)	NP
Michael Matz—Jet Run	2.15	0.00	0.00

Caroline Bradley on Tigre at Aachen in 1978. The only woman in that year's World Championships, she won a team gold and narrowly missed qualifying for the change-horse individual final. (Bob Langrish)

4 Canada, 48.65; 5 FRG, 52.20; 6 Belgium, 74.30; 7 Switzerland, 77.60; 8 France, 98.80; 9 Ireland, 100.55; 10 Austria, 130.45; 11 Spain, 214.25; 12 USSR, 251.20.

The introduction of the Team Championship coincided with the introduction of one open Individual Championship, which replaced the separate events for men and women. The format is three preliminary competitions, a Table C speed class, a Nations Cup and a two-round Grand Prix-type competition. Each country may enter up to four riders. Each rider may enter only one horse and must ride that same horse in all three competitions. Times scored in the speed class are converted into penalties. The Team Championship is decided by adding these penalties to the faults incurred in the Nations Cup. Each country counts only its best three scores in each round. The top 20 individuals after the Nations Cup go forward into the third class, after which the four with the least total penalties contest the change-horse final.

Number of teams: 12

1982 Dublin

| | | Nations Cup | |
| | | Round | Round |
	Table C	One	Two
1 France 19.48			
Michel Robert—Idéal de la Haye	6.360	4.00	0.00
Patrick Caron—Eole IV-Malesan	(21.305)	(22.50)	R
Frédéric Cottier—Flambeau C	3.545	0.00	0.00
Gilles Bertran de Balanda —Galoubet Malesan	1.075	4.00	0.50
2 FRG 30.91			
Norbert Koof—Fire	1.340	8.50	0.00
Peter Luther—Livius	5.045	(20.00)	0.00
Gerd Wiltfang—Roman	(8.890)	0.75	(12.00)
Paul Schockemöhle—Deister	3.275	8.00	4.00

3 Great Britain 34.79			
John Whitaker—Ryan's Son	9.865	1.00	4.75
Nick Skelton—Everest If Ever	(14.405)	(56.75)	4.00
Malcolm Pyrah —Towerlands Anglerzarke	0.705	4.00	0.00
David Broome—Mr Ross	6.470	4.00	(12.00)

4 USA, 41.39; 5 Canada, 49.80; 6 Italy, 54.19; 7 Brazil, 54.25; 8 Ireland, 61.32; 9 Switzerland, 64.62; 10 Australia, 89.67; 11 Austria, 103.87; 12 Mexico, 185.01.

Number of teams: 12

1986 Aachen

| | | Nations Cup | |
| | | Round | Round |
	Table C	One	Two
1 USA 23.63			
Katie Monahan—Amadia	3.92	8.00	(9.00)
Katharine Burdsall—The Natural	(6.96)	4.50	0.00
Michael Matz—Chef	2.07	(8.00)	0.25
Conrad Homfeld—Abdullah	0.89	0.00	4.00
2 Great Britain 31.19			
Nick Skelton—Raffles Apollo	3.88	1.00	1.00
Michael Whitaker —Next Warren Point	6.67	8.00	4.00
Malcom Pyrah —Towerlands Anglezarke	2.14	4.50	0.00
John Whitaker—Next Hopscotch	(8.00)	(39.75)	NP
3 France 44.32			
Frédéric Cottier—Flambeau C	6.07	(12.00)	4.00
Michel Robert—La Fayette	9.44	4.00	(13.75)
Patrice Delaveau—Laeken	(17.87)	4.00	12.00
Pierre Durand—Jappeloup de Luze	4.31	0.50	0.00

4 Canada, 45.13; 5 FRG, 52.27; 6 Mexico, 72.30; 7 Italy, 80.47; 8 The Netherlands, 83.09; 9 Switzerland, 109.42; 10 Austria, 111.03; 11 Belgium, 116.09; 12 Spain, 120.14; 13 Argentina, 123.89; 14 Brazil, 154.74; 15 USSR, 199.39.

Number of teams: 15

Men's Individual Championship

*Indicates best placing was obtained with second horse.

1953 Paris

	Quorum	Diamant	Ali-Baba	Uruguay	Total
1 Francisco Goyoaga (Spa)	0.00	4.00	0.00	4.00	8.00
2 Fritz Thiedemann (FRG)	4.25	0.00	0.00	4.00	8.25
3 Pierre Jonquères d'Oriola (Fra)	0.00	4.00	0.00	12.00	16.00
4 Piero d'Inzeo (Ita)	0.00	4.00	8.00	12.00	24.00
	4.25	12.00	8.00	32.00	

Finalists' placings in qualifying competitions

	1st comp.	2nd comp.	3rd comp.
Francisco Goyoaga—Quorum	8	7	3
Fritz Thiedemann—Diamant	5	=1	4
Pierre Jonquères d'Oriola—Ali-Baba	2	=1	1
Piero d'Inzeo—Uruguay	7	5	2

The format for the Individual Men's Championship was three qualifying competitions: a speed class, a puissance and a two-round Nations Cup-type class.

At the end of the three competitions the four highest placed riders overall went into the final in which they each rode not only their own horse but also the horses of the other finalists. Each rider could enter two horses. Regardless of the overall placings, the rules permitted only one rider per country to go forward to the third competition and thus have a chance of qualifying for the final. The Italian equestrian federation nominated the more experienced Piero d'Inzeo to compete, in preference to his brother, Raimondo, who had in fact been more successful in the first two preliminary competitions, finishing 3rd and 1st on Merano, as opposed to Piero's 7th and 5th with Uruguay.

Number of riders: 20

Number of nations represented: 11

1954 Madrid

	Halla	Arlequin D	Baden	Pagoro	Quoniam	Total
1 Hans Günter Winkler (FRG)	0.00	0.00	—	4.00	0.00	4.00
2 Pierre Jonquères d'Oriola (Fra)	4.00	0.00	—	4.00	0.00	8.00
3 Francisco Goyoaga (Spa)	0.00	8.00	4.00	0.00	—	12.00
4 Salvatore Oppes (Ita)	4.00	4.00	—	0.00	8.00	16.00
5 Jaime Garcia Cruz (Spa)	26.00	4.00	—	0.00	0.00	30.00
	34.00	16.00	—	8.00	—	

Finalists' placings in qualifying competitions

	1st comp.	2nd comp.	3rd comp.
Hans Günter Winkler —Halla/Alpenjäger*	4*	3	1
Pierre Jonquères d'Oriola —Arlequin D	1	2	2
Salvatore Oppes—Pagoro/Somalo*	8*	1	3
Jaime Garcia Cruz—Quoniam/Eolo*	5	4*	4

In 1954 the rules permitted the holder of the title, Francisco Goyoaga, to compete in the final without taking part in the qualifying competitions. To avoid giving an advantage to the two Spanish riders involved in the final, by allowing them to ride two Spanish-trained horses, each was required to ride the horses of the other finalists plus his own horse, but not that of his compatriot. Thus, although there were five finalists, each rode only four rounds.

Number of riders: 14

Number of nations represented: 7

1955 Aachen

	Orient	Merano	Bones	Voulette	Total
1 Hans Günter Winkler (FRG)	4.00	0.00	4.00	0.00	8.00
2 Raimondo d'Inzeo (Ita)	0.00	0.00	4.00	4.00	8.00
3 Ronnie Dallas (GB)	16.00	0.00	8.00	8.00	32.00
4 Pierre Jonquères d'Oriola (Fra)	4.00	0.00	R	4.00	—
	24.00	0.00	—	16.00	

Jump-off

	Halla	Nadir	Total
1 Hans Günter Winkler	4.00	0.00	4.00
2 Raimondo d'Inzeo	4.00	4.00	8.00

Finalists' placings in qualifying competitions

	1st comp.	2nd comp.	3rd comp.
Hans Günter Winkler—Halla	1	=1	=1
Raimondo d'Inzeo—Merano	10	=1	=1
Ronnie Dallas—Marmion	5	=7	=4
Pierre Jonquères d'Oriola —Voulette/Charleston*	2*	=4	3

In 1955 the rules permitted riders to nominate a different horse for the final from that on whom they had qualified. Thus Winkler chose to ride Orient in the change-horse final, reverting to Halla for the jump-off. Dallas put Bones into the final, having qualified with Marmion.

Number of riders: 18

Number of nations represented: 11

Hans Günter Winkler is one of only two riders (Raimondo d'Inzeo being the other) who have twice been Men's World Champion. Here he is riding the great mare Halla. (Oscar Cornaz)

1956 Aachen

	Merano	Fahnenkönig	Meteor	Discutido	Total
1 Raimondo d'Inzeo (Ita)	0.50	1.25	0.00	0.00	1.75
2 Francisco Goyoaga (Spa)	3.00	0.00	0.00	0.00	3.00
3 Fritz Thiedemann (FRG)	0.00	4.00	0.00	0.00	4.00
4 Carlos Delia (Arg)	4.00	8.00	4.00	9.00	25.00
	7.50	13.25	4.00	9.00	

Finalists' placings in qualifying competitions

	1st comp.	2nd comp.	3rd comp.
Raimondo d'Inzeo —Merano/The Quiet Man*	2	=1*	=1
Francisco Goyoaga —Fahnenkönig/Toscanella*	1	=8*	4
Fritz Thiedemann—Meteor	3	=4	=1
Carlos Delia—Discutido/Oleander*	6*	=8	3

In 1956 the rules stipulated that in the final riders must ride the horse on whom they had gained the most points in the preliminary competitions, in which they could ride two horses. The rule which restricted each country to only one finalist was deleted.

Number of riders: 19

Number of countries represented: 12

1960 Venice

	Gowran Girl	Huipil	Sunsalve	Ksar d'Esprit	Total
1 Raimondo d'Inzeo (Ita)	4.00	0.00	4.00	0.00	8.00
2 Carlos Delia (Arg)	12.00	0.00	4.00	8.00	24.00
3 David Broome (GB)	16.00	4.00	4.00	4.00	28.00
4 William Steinkraus (USA)	16.00	0.00	E	4.00	—
	48.00	4.00	—	16.00	

Finalists' placings in qualifying competitions

	1st comp.	2nd comp.	3rd comp.
Raimondo d'Inzeo—Gowran Girl	1	=10	=1
Carlos Delia—Huipil	7	=2	5
David Broome—Sunsalve	4	=4	=1
William Steinkraus—Ksar d'Esprit	2	1	3

Number of riders: 22

Number of nations represented: 12

1966 Buenos Aires

	Pomone B	Quizas	Bowjak	Huipil	Total
1 Pierre Jonquères d'Oriola (Fra)	0.00	4.00	8.00	4.00	16.00
2 José Alvarez de Bohorques (Spa)	4.00	15.00	0.00	0.00	19.00
3 Raimondo d'Inzeo (Ita)	8.00	8.00	10.00	4.00	30.00
4 Nelson Pessoa (Bra)	10.50	14.75	0.00	10.00	35.25
	22.50	41.75	18.00	18.00	

Pierre Jonquères d'Oriola on the bay French-bred mare Pomone B, World Champions in Buenos Aires in 1966, the only occasion on which the Championship has been held outside Europe. (Ed Lacey Associated Sports Photography)

Finalists' placings in qualifying competitions

	1st comp.	2nd comp.	3rd comp.
Pierre Jonquères d'Oriola —Pomone B	7	1	3
José Alvarez de Bohorques—Quizas	4	2	=5
Raimondo d'Inzeo—Bowjak	=5	=10	1
Nelson Pessoa—Huipil	=5	=4	4

A new rule came into operation this year: in the final, faults incurred by a rider with his own horse were raised by 25 per cent. Had this not been the case, there would have been a jump-off for the gold and silver medals between d'Oriola and Bohorques, who each had four fences down.

Number of riders: 14

Number of nations represented: 8

1970 La Baule

	Beethoven	Fidux	Mattie Brown	Donald Rex	Total
1 David Broome (GB)	0.00	0.00	0.00	4.00	4.00
2 Graziano Mancinelli (Ita)	4.00	0.00	4.00	0.00	8.00
3 Harvey Smith (GB)	4.00	4.00	5.00	0.75	13.75
4 Alwin Schockemöhle (FRG)	4.00	4.00	8.00	0.00	16.00
	12.00	8.00	17.00	4.75	

Finalists' placings in qualifying competitions

	1st comp.	2nd comp.	3rd comp.
David Broome—Beethoven	3	=11	1
Graziano Mancinelli—Fidux	7	=1	4
Harvey Smith—Mattie Brown	1	=1	=7
Alwin Schockemöhle—Donald Rex	2	=4	=7

Number of riders: 27

Number of nations represented: 14

1974 Hickstead

	Simona	Pele	Lavendel	Main Spring	Total
1 Hartwig Steenken (FRG)	0.00	0.00	0.00	4.00	4.00
2 Eddie Macken (Ire)	0.00	0.00	0.00	4.00	4.00
=3 Hugo Simon (Aut)	4.00	4.00	0.00	0.00	8.00
Frank Chapot (USA)	0.00	4.00	4.00	0.00	8.00
	4.00	8.00	4.00	8.00	

Jump-off

	Faults/Time
1 Hartwig Steenken (FRG)—Simona	4.00/65.40
2 Eddie Macken (Ire)—Pele	8.00/45.60

Finalists' placings in qualifying competitions

	1st comp.	2nd comp.	3rd comp.
Hartwig Steenken—Simona	3	=1	1
Eddie Macken—Pele	1	=1	=2
Hugo Simon—Lavendel	2	=1	=2
Frank Chapot—Main Spring	9	9	4

Number of riders: 29

Number of nations represented: 16

Another great mare, Simona, ridden by Hartwig Steenken, winners of the World title at Hickstead in 1974. Tragically, Steenken died on 10 January 1978, aged 36, from injuries sustained in a car crash the previous year. (Ed Lacey Associated Sports Photography)

Individual Championship Open to Men and Women

1978 Aachen

	Roman	Boomerang	Jet Run	Pandur Z	Total
1 Gerd Wiltfang (FRG)	0.00	0.00	0.00	0.00	0.00
2 Eddie Macken (Ire)	0.00	0.00	0.00	0.25	0.25
3 Michael Matz (USA)	0.00	0.00	4.00	0.50	4.50
4 Johan Heins (NL)	0.00	0.00	4.00	4.00	8.00
	0.00	0.00	8.00	4.75	

Finalists' placings in qualifying competitions

	1st comp.	2nd comp.	3rd comp.	
Gerd Wiltfang—Roman	1	=3	=6	Number of riders: 53
Eddie Macken—Boomerang	4	=3	2	Number of women riders: 1
Michael Matz—Jet Run	5	1	3	Number of nations represented: 17
Johan Heins—Pandur Z	12	=7	4	

1982 Dublin

	Fire	Towerlands Anglezarke	Idéal de la Haye	Rockbarton	Total
1 Norbert Koof (FRG)	0.00	0.00	0.00	0.00	0.00
2 Malcom Pyrah (GB)	4.00	0.00	8.00	0.00	12.00
3 Michel Robert (Fra)	4.00	4.00	4.00	0.00	12.00
4 Gerry Mullins (Ire)	4.00	4.00	4.00	4.00	16.00
	12.00	8.00	16.00	4.00	

Jump-off

	Faults/Time
2 Malcom Pyrah (GB) —Towerlands Anglezarke	0.00/50.01
3 Michel Robert—Idéal de la Haye	retired after 2 knockdowns

Finalists' placings in qualifying competitions

	1st comp.	2nd comp.	3rd comp.
Norbert Koof—Fire	6	13	5
Malcom Pyrah —Towerlands Angelzarke	4	=3	=6
Michel Robert—Idéal de la Haye	21	=3	4
Gerry Mullins—Rockbarton	20	=9	=1

Number of riders: 53

Number of women riders: 2

Number of nations represented: 16

The youngest man to become World Champion, Norbert Koof, seen here with Fire during the victory ceremony in Dublin in 1982. He is one of only three riders to have jumped four clear rounds in the change-horse final. (Bob Langrish)

1986 Aachen

	Mr T	Abdullah	Raffles Apollo	Jappeloup de Luze	Total
1 Gail Greenough (Can)	0.00	0.00	0.00	0.00	0.00
2 Conrad Homfeld (USA)	0.00	0.00	4.00	4.00	8.00
3 Nick Skelton (GB)	10.00	0.00	0.00	0.00	10.00
4 Pierre Durand (Fra)	12.00	4.00	8.00	8.00	32.00
	22.00	4.00	12.00	12.00	

Finalists' placings in qualifying competitions

	1st comp.	2nd comp.	3rd comp.
Gail Greenough—Mr T	24	1	2
Conrad Homfeld—Abdullah	2	4	=3
Nick Skelton—Raffles Apollo	5	3	13
Pierre Durand—Jappeloup de Luze	9	2	1

Number of riders: 72

Number of women riders: 7

Number of nations represented: 25

Gail Greenough, the first woman to win the championship open to men and women, pictured with runner-up Conrad Holmfeld in Aachen in 1986. (Jan Gyllensten)

Ladies' Individual Championship

*Indicates best placing was obtained with second horse.

1965 Hickstead

	Points/(Placings) Competition			Total
	One	Two	Three	Points
1 Marion Coakes (GB) —Stroller	1(1)	1(1)	2(2)	4
2 Kathy Kusner (USA) —Untouchable	3(4)	2(3)	1(1)	6
3 Alison Westwood (GB) —The Maverick	2(2)	3(4)	3(3)	8
4 Monica Bachmann (Switz) —Sandro	4(5)	5(6)	5(5)	14
5 The Hon Diana Conolly-Carew (Ire) —Barrymore/Fairy Story*	7(10)*	4(5)	4(4)	15
6 Janou Lefèbvre (Fra) —Kenavo D	5(6)	6(7)	—	—
7 Arline Givaudan (Bra) —Huipil/Caribe*	8(11)*	7(9)	—	—
8 Marion McDowell (Ire) —Sweet Control	6(9)	—	—	—

The format for the Ladies' World Championship was three competitions: a speed class, a two-round Nations Cup-type competition and a two-round Grand Prix-type class. Points were awarded for each class and totalled to give the final placings. The rules allowed two riders per country, each with two horses; each rider could only count points earned by one horse in each competition. Unlike in the men's—now the open—championship, there was no 'change-horse' final.

Number of riders: 8

Number of nations represented: 6

1970 Copenhagen

	Competition Placings			Total
	One	Two	Three	Points
1 Janou Lefèbvre (Fra) —Rocket	1	=2	1	5
=2 Marion Mould (GB) —Stroller	3	1	4	8
Anneli Drummond-Hay (GB)—Merely-a-Monarch	2	=2	3	8
4 Elisa Pérez de las Heras (Mex)—Eleanora	12	5	2	15
5 Lucia Faria (Bra) —Rush du Camp	15	=2	5	19
6 Marianne Leffler (Swe) —Lamona	4	8	10	21
=7 Rita Mello (Bra) —Pasha B	13	7	7	22
Barbara Simpson (Can) —Australis/Magnor*	6*	13	6	22
9 Monica Bachmann (Switz)—Erbach	16	9	8	28
10 Ada Matheson (Ire) —Ballyking	14	14	9	31
11 Juliet Jobling-Purser (Ire)—Tiki	10	10	E	35
12 Pilar Cepeda (Per) —Malibu	11	12	R	37
13 Lisbeth Krogsgaard (Den)—Flax II	19	15	E	47
14 Jennifer Holroyd (Por) —Don Juan	17	E	NP	53

Number of riders: 16

Number of nations represented: 11

(Only 14 horses went forward to the third round to receive overall placings.)

1974 La Baule

	Competition Placings			Total
	One	Two	Three	Points
1 Janou (Lefèbvre) Tissot (Fra)—Rocket/Alterline*	2	=1*	2	5.50
2 Michele McEvoy (USA) —Mr Muskie	6	=1	3	8.50
3 Barbara (Simpson) Kerr (Can)—Magnor/Australis*	1*	6	4	10.00†
4 Caroline Bradley (GB) —True Lass/Middle Road*	7	5*	1	10.00†
5 Armelle Lovati (Fra) —Turf du Lude/Djebel*	9	4*	5	15.50
6 Eva van Paesschen (Bel) —Echo/Country Square*	8*	16	6	22.00
7 Françoise Thiry (Bel) —Valse de Vienne	15	=9	7	24.00
8 Patrizia Pousieux (Fra) —Bouton d'Or	10	17	8	26.50
9 Madeleine Gervais (Swe) —Flax II	16	=13	9	29.00

Number of riders: 12

Number of nations represented: 8

†Where riders finished with equal points, final placings were decided by the best placings in the three qualifying competitions.

Janou Tissot (née Lefèbvre) of France, with Rocket, twice winner of the Ladies' World Championship. (Findlay Davidson)

Medal Tables

Team Championship 1978–86

Country	Gold	Silver	Bronze
GB	1	1	1
France	1	—	1
USA	1	—	1
FRG	—	1	—
Netherlands	—	1	—

Men's and Open Individual Championship 1953–86

Country	Gold	Silver	Bronze
FRG	5	1	1
Italy	2	2	1
Spain	1	2	1
GB	1	1	4
France	1	1	2
Canada	1	—	—
Ireland	—	2	—
USA	—	1	2
Argentina	—	1	—
Austria	—	—	1

Ladies' Individual Championship 1965–74

Country	Gold	Silver	Bronze
France	2	—	—
GB	1	2	1
USA	—	2	—
Canada	—	—	1

Open, Men's and Ladies' Individual Championship 1953–86

Country	Gold	Silver	Bronze
FRG	5	1	1
France	3	1	2
GB	2	3	5
Italy	2	2	1
Spain	1	2	1
Canada	1	—	1
USA	—	3	2
Ireland	—	2	—
Argentina	—	1	—
Austria	—	—	1

Team and all Individual Championships 1953–86

Country	Gold	Silver	Bronze
FRG	5	2	1
France	4	1	3
GB	3	4	6
Italy	2	2	1
USA	1	3	3
Spain	1	2	1
Canada	1	—	1
Ireland	—	2	—
Argentina	—	1	—
Netherlands	—	1	—
Austria	—	—	1

Records: Riders

Most wins

Two riders have won the men's Individual Championship twice: Hans Günter Winkler (FRG), in 1954 and 1955; Raimondo d'Inzeo (Italy) in 1956 and 1960. An injury sustained during the Olympic Games at Stockholm in 1956 prevented Winkler from defending his title that year.

Janou Lefèbvre won the women's Individual Championship in 1970 and again, after her marriage, as Janou Tissot, in 1974.

Youngest winners

The youngest rider to win a World Championship is Marion Coakes (now Marion Mould), who was 18 when she won the first Ladies' Individual Championship at Hickstead in 1965. Norbert Koof, aged 26 years and 273, days is the youngest man to have become World Champion (at Dublin in 1982). Canada's Gail Greenough, the first woman to win the open Championship (first contested in 1978), is the youngest person to win the 'change-horse' final. She was 26 years and 128 days when she won at Aachen in 1986, and was the first Canadian and the first non-European to win a World title. The youngest winner of the men's Championship, which was held from 1953 to 1974, was Hans Günter Winkler, who was 27 when he won his first title in 1954.

Oldest winner

France's Pierre Jonquères d'Oriola, who won the title in Buenos Aires in 1966, at the age of 46.

Biggest winning margin

Teams

11.43 faults: 1982 (France beat West Germany)

Open Individual

12.00 faults: 1982 (Norbert Koof beat Malcom Pyrah)

Men's Individual

16 faults: 1960 (Raimondo d'Inzeo beat Carlos Delia)

Ladies' Individual

3.00 points: 1970 (Janou Lefèbvre beat Marion Mould and Anneli Drummond-Hay)
1974 (Janou [Lefèbvre] Tissot beat Michele McEvoy)

Smallest winning margin

Teams

4.70 faults: 1978 (Great Britain beat The Netherlands)

Open Individual

0.25 faults: 1978 (Gerd Wiltfang beat Eddie Macken)

Men's Individual

0.25 faults: 1953 (Francisco Goyoaga beat Fritz Thiedemann)

Ladies' Individual

2 points: 1965 (Marion Coakes beat Kathy Kusner)

Highest number of starters

Teams

15: 1986 Aachen

Open Individual

72: 1986 Aachen

Men's Individual

29: 1974 Hickstead

Ladies' Individual

16: 1970 Copenhagen

Highest number of nations represented

Open Individual

25: 1986 Aachen

Men's Individual

16: 1974 Hickstead

Ladies' Individual

11: 1970 Copenhagen

Smallest number of starters

Teams

12: 1978 Aachen
1982 Dublin

Open Individual

53: 1978 Aachen
1982 Dublin

Men's Individual

14: 1954 Madrid
1966 Buenos Aires

Ladies' Individual

8: 1965 Hickstead

Smallest number of nations represented

Open Individual

16: 1982 Dublin

Men's Individual

7: 1954 Madrid

Ladies' Individual

6: 1965 Hickstead

Jump-offs

There has been a jump-off for the individual gold medal on two occasions: between Hans Günter Winkler and Raimondo d'Inzeo in 1955 (Winkler won) and between Hartwig Steenken and Eddie Macken in 1974 (Steenken won). The introduction of the rule which gave riders 25 per cent more penalties for faults incurred in the final with their own horse prevented a jump-off in 1966 between Pierre Jonquères d'Oriola and José Alvarez de Bohorques. (This rule no longer applies.)

There was a jump-off for the individual silver medal in 1982 between Malcolm Pyrah and Michel Robert, which Pyrah won.

Men/women ratio

Since the introduction, in 1978, of championships open to both men and women only 10 women have taken part, as opposed to 168 men. In 1978 the late Caroline Bradley, the only female rider in the competition, finished fifth overall, 0.30 faults behind the fourth qualifier for the final. She won a team gold medal after putting up the best performance of the British quartette in the Nations Cup.

In 1986 the individual title was won by Gail Greenough, one of seven ladies in the championships.

Country with longest winning sequence in individual championship

Federal Republic of Germany, 3:
  1974, Hartwig Steenken;
  1978, Gerd Wiltfang;
  1982, Norbert Koof.

Change-horse final

More than one appearance

4—Raimondo d'Inzeo, 1955 (2nd), 1956 (1st), 1960 (1st), 1966 (3rd).

Pierre Jonquères d'Oriola, 1953 (3rd), 1954 (2nd), 1955 (4th), 1966 (1st).
3—Francisco Goyoaga, 1953 (1st), 1954 (3rd), 1956 (2nd).
2—Hans Günter Winkler, 1954 (1st), 1955 (1st).
  David Broome, 1960 (3rd), 1970 (1st).
  Eddie Macken, 1974 (2nd), 1978 (2nd).
  Fritz Thiedemann, 1953 (2nd), 1956 (3rd).
  Carlos Delia, 1956 (4th), 1960 (2nd).
Hans Günter Winkler is the only rider to have won each time he qualified for the final.

Best score

Only three riders have ridden clear rounds on all four horses in the final:
Gerd Wiltfang (FRG) in 1978
Norbert Koof (FRG) in 1982
Gail Greenough (Canada) in 1986

More than one rider from one country

Since the rule restricting nations to one rider in the final was waived in 1956, only one country has in fact produced two finalists: Great Britain in 1970, when David Broome won the gold medal and Harvey Smith won the bronze.

Countries most often represented

West Germany—8 times
Italy—7 times
France—6 times
Great Britain—5 times
Spain and USA—4 times

World and Olympic Champion

Raimondo d'Inzeo is the only rider to have become Olympic and World Champion in the same year (1960).

Records: Horses

Change-horse final

More than one appearance

2—Merano, 1955, 1956
  Huipil, 1960, 1966 (on both occasions had the best or equal best score in the final)

Best score

Only three horses have jumped clear rounds with all four riders in the change-horse final:
Merano (Ita) 1955
Roman (FRG) 1978
Boomerang (Ire) 1978

Three horses have jumped double clear rounds in the Team Championship Nations Cup:
Jet Run, 1978
Flambeau C, 1982
Mr T, 1986

Federico Caprilli

For several thousand years mankind's history has been inextricably interwoven with that of the horse. Ever since he first learnt to tame this most amenable of animals, man has depended upon him for transportation, a dependence which has only declined during the last few decades. During those thousands of years a few great innovators have come and gone, their names unrecorded for posterity. Who first nailed a shoe on to a horse's foot? Who devised the collar for draught work? Who invented the stirrup, that wonderfully simple piece of equipment which so greatly improved a rider's stability and comfort in the saddle? Each of them, whoever they were, had a profound effect upon the way in which man was able to use the horse to serve his needs.

Just such another great innovator was Federico Caprilli, an Italian cavalry officer who, in his short life, brought about a profound change in man's approach to riding. As the horse's usefulness as a means of transport began to wane, so his value as a form of sport and recreation grew, and it is largely thanks to the teaching of Caprilli that horsemen have been able to achieve such remarkable results in the sports of show jumping and horse trials.

Born in Leghorn in 1868, Caprilli joined the Pinerolo Cavalry School, near Turin, as a student officer. To begin with he was described as 'a less than moderate horseman', an assessment which, in the light of later events, could hardly have been more wide of the mark. In due course, however, he did impress his superiors enough to be allowed to complete a second course at Pinerolo, vindicating himself by passing second in the whole class. From Pinerolo Caprilli went to Tor di Quinto, near Rome, a sort of finishing school for students of military equitation, where work consisted primarily of cross-country riding, hunting and steeplechasing.

While at Pinerolo he had already begun to put into practice his own ideas regarding the training of horses. At Tor di Quinto he became convinced that he was right and that the old methods of instruction—based on the classical school of the Renaissance—were not applicable to the soldier of the late 19th/early 20th centuries. There is neither space nor necessity to include a detailed exposition of his complete system of horsemanship in this book. In the context of show jumping, in simple terms Caprilli's teachings were to enable horse and rider to negotiate obstacles much more easily. Up until his time, the cavalry had been taught to adopt a backward seat over a fence—as the horse took off, the rider threw his weight back, usually holding his hands high. This put the rider's weight in the very worst place from the point of view of the horse, forcing him to jump with his head high in the air and his back hollow, and all too often resulted in a painful jab in the mouth as well.

When a horse jumps without a rider he uses his head and neck extensively, adopting a rounded outline from head to tail. It was Caprilli who realized that the rider could best assist the horse to achieve this natural position by sitting *forward* in the saddle. Such a position freed the loins (the weakest part of the horse's back) of weight, enabled him to stretch out his neck and head, and kept the rider as much as possible in balance with the horse. It was a totally new concept of riding both over fences and on the flat.

Of course, as a cavalry instructor, a position which he took up in the early 1890s, first at Tor di Quinto and then at Pinerolo, Caprilli was not concerned with training the sporting horse. Of

Federico Caprilli demonstrating the forward seat in 1904.

prime importance was the need to get the military safely and expeditiously across any type of country, with the least amount of wear and tear to horse and man alike. Nevertheless, the changes which he instigated were to have more far-reaching effects. Show jumping, then in its infancy, was to become a major military and civilian sport, and Caprilli himself was able to demonstrate his techniques to a wide audience when competing (which he did with notable success) at some of the earliest international shows.

But although he proved the efficacy of his ideas both in the show ring and on the racecourse, old habits die hard, and the cavalry was in no hurry to abandon its traditional form of horsemanship, based on the extreme collection prescribed by the 16th-century Neapolitan masters. Not until 1904 was Caprilli allowed to teach his ideas to his fellow countrymen and to the many foreign officers who came to both Pinerolo and Tor di Quinto. The results he obtained were so good, and his own record as a competitor so distinguished, that in the course of time his concepts were finally accepted, and he had the satisfaction of seeing them adopted as the official, approved system (*Il sistema*) of equitation for the Italian cavalry.

Ironically, not long afterwards the 'father of modern riding' was dead. Perhaps, as his pupil and friend Piero Santini suggests in his English translation of Caprilli's brief writings on equitation, *The Caprilli Papers*, the many accidents which he suffered while developing his ideas contributed to his early death. Be that as it may, while out riding in Turin one day in December 1907, Caprilli was seen to sway in the saddle at the walk and to fall to the ground. He did not regain consciousness, and died the following day from head injuries.

In the years that followed, his *sistema* was to influence riders throughout the world. A glance through the list of foreign officers who attended courses at Pinerolo and Tor di Quinto in the 1920s and 1930s shows that they came from virtually all the top equestrian nations of Europe; from Russia, Eastern Europe and the Balkan countries; from the far east and from North, Central and South America. They included men who became heads of renowned cavalry schools, and others who won fame on the international show circuit. Thus, in a few short years, Federico Caprilli completely changed the course of horsemanship, amongst other things laying the foundations of the sport of show jumping as we know it today.

World Cup

The World Cup, introduced in 1979, is primarily a series of indoor competitions held between October and April and open to all competitors qualified by a formula assessed by computer. Outside Europe competitions may also, with the authorization of the FEI, be held during other months of the year.

The World Cup is run in a series of continental leagues, with an annual final for the leading riders. Each league consists of a number of preliminary, or qualifying, competitions, which take the form of a Grand Prix (at some shows the World Cup Qualifier and the Grand Prix are one and the same). Riders are awarded points according to their placings in these qualifying rounds and the points are totalled at the end of the league series to give the final league standings for each area.

The rules allow for a certain number of riders

Hugo Simon of Austria, in the first nine runnings of the World Cup, the only European to win the final. (Jan Gyllensten)

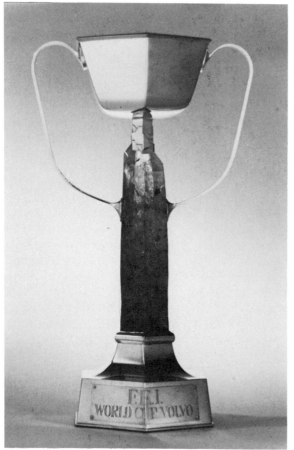

The World Cup, competed for annually by riders from four continents.

from the top of each league to compete in the final. If for any reason a rider declines to attend the final, the invitation is extended to the rider who is next in order of merit in the league points table.

The final is run in three legs (the only exception having been the first final in 1979 which comprised two competitions). The first leg is a speed class and the second a Table A consisting of one round and two jump-offs, the second against the clock. Points are awarded to the competitors in each class according to their placings. After the second class the points are converted into penalties, the competitor with the highest number of points being given 0 penalties. The other riders are given penalties calculated by multiplying with the coefficient of 0.50 the difference between their points and the points of the leading competitor after the first two classes. The third competition is a two-round Grand Prix. Faults accrued in this event are added to the penalties brought forward from the first two classes to give a final total, the rider with the lowest score being the winner. Competitors may ride two different horses in the final, provided that they have each completed at least one preliminary competition, but they may ride only one horse in each leg.

League points are not carried forward: all competitors start the final on a zero score.

World Cup Final

1979 Gothenburg

		Placings		Points		Total	Jump-off
		Day 1	Day 2	Day 1	Day 2	Points	(F./Time)
1	Hugo Simon (Aut)—Gladstone	1	2	10	8	18	0/24.50
2	Katie Monahan (USA)—The Jones Boy	2	1	8	10	18	4/25.40
=3	Norman Dello Joio (USA)—Allegro	3	11	6	0	6	
	Eddie Macken (Ire)—Carrolls of Dundalk	26	3	0	6	6	
=5	Lionel Dunning (GB)—Jungle Bunny	4	12	5	0	5	
	John Whitaker (GB)—Ryan's Son	21	4	0	5	5	
=7	Dennis Murphy (USA)—Tuscaloosa	5	21	4	0	4	
	Nick Skelton (GB)—Lastic	21	5	0	4	4	
=9	Caroline Bradley (GB)—Tigre	6	21	3	0	3	
	Peter Luther (FRG)—Livius	13	6	0	3	3	
=11	Con Power (Ire)—Loughcrew	7	15	2	0	2	
	Conrad Homfeld (USA)—Balbuco	18	7	0	2	2	
=13	Melanie Smith (USA)—Val de Loire	8	16	1	0	1	
	Bernie Traurig (USA)—The Cardinal	15	8	0	1	1	
15	David Broome (GB)—Philco	9	9	0	0	0	
16	Scott Nederlander (USA)—Southside	11	10	0	0	0	
17	Edgar-Henri Cuepper (Bel)—Le Champion	10	21	0	0	0	
18	Terrance Millar (Can)—Eaden Vale	11	14	0	0	0	
19	Derek Ricketts (GB)—Hydrophane Coldstream	18	13	0	0	0	
20	Nelson Pessoa (Bra)—Moët et Chandon Faon Rouge	14	24	0	0	0	
21	Hendrick Snoek (FRG)—Gaylord	21	16	0	0	0	
22	Gerd Wiltfang (FRG)—Roman	16	27	0	0	0	
23	Christian Huysegoms (Bel)—Katapulte	17	19	0	0	0	
24	Paul Schockemöhle (FRG)—El Paso	18	19	0	0	0	
25	Harvey Smith (GB)—Sanyo Sanmar	21	18	0	0	0	
26	Lutz Merkel (FRG)—Salvaro	25	25	0	0	0	
27	Johan Heins (NL)—Romeo Z	27	26	0	0	0	

Number of nations represented: 10

1980 Baltimore

		Placings			Points			Total
		Day 1	Day 2	Day 3	Day 1	Day 2	Day 3	Points
1	Conrad Homfeld (USA)—Balbuco	7	3	3	10	15	22.50	47.50
2	Melanie Smith (USA)—Calypso	1	2	12	20	17	7.50	44.50
3	Paul Schockemöhle (FRG)—El Paso/	6	4		11	13		42
	—Deister			5			18	
4	Hugo Simon (Aut)—Answer/	8	17		9	0		39
	—Gladstone			1			30	
5	Michael Matz (USA)—Jet Run	3	6	9	15	11	12	38
6	Rodney Jenkins (USA)—Third Man	10	8	8	7	9	13.50	29.50
7	Heinrich-Wilhelm Johannsmann (FRG)—Sarto	5	22	6	12	0	16.50	28.50
8	Gilles Bertran de Balanda (Fra)—Galoubet A	17	5	7	0	12	15	27
9	Leslie Burr (USA)—Chase the Clouds	24	21	2	0	0	25.50	25.50
10	Terry Rudd (USA)—Fat City	4	23	10	13	0	10.50	23.50
11	Lutz Merkel (FRG)—Salvaro	2	11	19	17	6	0	23
12	John Whitaker (GB)—Ryan's Son	16	18	4	1	0	19.50	20.50
13	Piet Raymakers (NL)—Isocratus S	20	1	20	0	20	0	20
14	Ian Millar (Can)—Bandit	22	7	13	0	10	5.25	15.25
15	Thomas Frühmann (Aut)—Donau	12	9	18	5	8	0	13
16	David Broome (GB)—Queensway Sportsman	9	13	NP	8	4	—	12
17	Caroline Bradley (GB)—Tigre	23	16	11	0	1	9	10
18	Nelson Pessoa (Bra)—Moët et Chandon Fil d'Argent	18	10	16	0	7	1.50	8.50
19	Mariane Gilchrist (Aus)—Goldray	21	12	15	0	5	3	8
20	Dennis Murphy (USA)—Tuscaloosa/	19			0			
	—Lyrical Lou		15	13		2	5.25	7.25
21	Fritz Ligges (FRG)—Goya	11	24	17	6	0	0	6
22	Mark Laskin (Can)—Damuraz	15	14	21	2	3	0	5
23	Derek Ricketts (GB)—Coldstream	13	20	22	4	0	0	4
24	Bernie Traurig (USA)—Eaden Vale	14	19	23	3	0	0	3
25	Noel Vanososte (Ven)—Rio IV	26	26	24	0	0	0	0
26	Paddy McMahon (GB)—Husky Gollanite	28	25	25	0	0	0	0
27	John Fahey (Aus)—The Fall	25	27	NP	0	0	—	0
28	Ricardo Goncalves (Bra)—Damn Yankee	27	28	NP	0	0	—	0

Number of nations represented: 10

1981 Birmingham

	Placings Day 1	Day 2	Day 3	Points Day 1	Day 2	Day 3	Final Points
1 Michael Matz (USA)—Jet Run	11	3	5	6	15	18	39
2 Donald Cheska (USA)—Southside	9	1	11	8	20	9	37
3 Hugo Simon (Aut)—Gladstone	10	11	3	7	6	22.50	35.50
4 Gilles Bertran de Balanda (Fra)—Galoubet Malesan	4	2	14	13	17	4.50	34.50
5 Leslie Burr (USA)—Chase the Clouds	18	9	2	0	8	25.50	33.50
6 Melanie Smith (USA)—Calypso	3	14	7	15	3	15	33
7 Harvey Smith (GB)—Sanyo Sanmar	6	5	12	11	12	7.50	30.50
8 Malcolm Pyrah (GB)—Towerlands Anglezarke	19	19	1	0	0	30	30
9 Norman Dello Joio (USA)—Allegro	7	22	4	10	0	19.50	29.50
10 Jamie Mann (USA)—Signal Point	21	7	6	0	10	16.50	26.50
11 Franke Sloothaak (FRG)—Argonaut	1	26	27	20	0	0	20
12 Buddy Brown (USA)—Felton	8	8	16	9	9	1.50	19.50
13 Johan Heins (NL)—Larramy	12	17	8	5	0	13.50	18.50
14 Nick Skelton (GB)—Maybe/	2	28		17	0		17
—If Ever			26			0	
15 Bernie Traurig (USA)—Eaden Vale	13	6	21	3.50	11	0	14.50
=16 Walter Gabathuler (Switz)—Harley	5	16	18	12	1	0	13
Hervé Godignon (Fra)—Gitan P	27	4	23	0	13	0	13
18 Derek Ricketts (GB)—Coldstream	32	21	9	0	0	12	12
19 David Broome (GB)—Queensway Philco/	20	25		0	0		
—Mr Ross			10			10.50	10.50
20 Fritz Ligges (FRG)—Goya	15	12	15	2	5	3	10
21 Thomas Frühmann (Aut)—Donau	13	20	13	3.50	0	6	9.50
22 Guy Creighton (Aus)—Spring Melody/	31			0			
—Mikneil		10	30		7	0	7
23 John Whitaker (GB)—Ryan's Son	28	13	19	0	4	0	4
24 Frédéric Cottier (Fra)—Flambeau C	25	15	17	0	2	0	2
25 Gerd Wiltfang (FRG)—Goldika/	16		NP	1		—	1
—Roman		E			0		
26 Caroline Bradley (GB)—Tricentrol Manuel/	17	24		0	0		0
—Landmine			25			0	
27 Dennis Murphy (USA)—Lyrical Lou	28	18	29	0	0	0	0
28 Kevin Bourke (Aus)—Touraliady	22	23	20	0	0	0	0
29 Robert Ridland (USA)—Island Discovery	24	R	22	0	0	0	0
30 Paul Darragh (Ire)—Carroll's Young Diamond	23	29	24	0	0	0	0
31 Roberto Tagle (Arg)—Estio	E	27	R	0	0	0	0
32 Ricardo Goncalves (Bra)—Dos Banderas	29	31	28	0	0	0	0
33 Daniel Walker (Chi)—Antillanca	30	30	R	0	0	0	0
34 Nelson Pessoa (Bra)—Moët et Chandon Fil d'Argent/	R		NP	0		—	0
—Moët et Chandon Electre		R			0		

Number of nations represented: 12

1982 Gothenburg

	Placings Day 1	Day 2	Day 3	Points Day 1	Day 2	=Total	Converted into Penalties	Penalties Day 3 A	B	Total Penalties
1 Melanie Smith (USA)—Calypso	1	2	1	31	31	62	0	0	0	0
2 Paul Schockemöhle (FRG) —Akrobat	1	4	1	31	29	60	1	0	0	1
=3 Hugo Simon (Aut)—Gladstone	10	6	4	23	27	50	6	0	4	10
John Whitaker (GB) —Ryan's Son	24	1	1	9	33	42	10	0	0	10
5 Peter Leone (USA)—Ardennes	6	8	4	27	22	49	6.50	0	4	10.50
6 Liz Edgar (GB)—Everest Forever	5	6	6	28	27	55	3.50	0	8	11.50
7 Thomas Fuchs (Switz) —Willora Carpet	9	8	6	24	22	46	8	0	8	16
8 Nick Skelton (GB) —Everest Carat/ —Copenhagen	4	17	6	29	13	42	10	4	4	18
9 Mark Leone (USA)—Tim	15	17	6	18	13	31	15.50	0	8	23.50
10 Rob Ehrens (NL)—Oscar Drum	11	25	6	22	8	30	16	0	8	24
11 Donald Cheska (USA) —Southside	19	17	6	14	13	27	17.50	0	8	25.50
12 Gerd Wiltfang (FRG) —Boyfriend/ —Gordon	21 / 8		12	12 / 22		34	14	4	8	26

	Placings Day 1	Placings Day 2	Placings Day 3	Points Day 1	Points Day 2	=Total	Points Converted into Penalties	Penalties Day 3 A	Penalties Day 3 B	Total Penalties
13 Fritz Ligges (FRG)—Goya	16	17	13	17	13	30	16	8	8	32
14 Norbert Koof (FRG)—Fire II	18	17	13	15	13	28	17	8	8	33
15 Hap Hansen (USA)										
—Faon Rouge/	26			7						
—High Karate		8	16		22	29	16.50	7.75	12	36.25
16 Norman Dello Joio (USA)										
—Allegro	14	8	18	19	22	41	10.50	0	28.75	39.25
17 Anne Kursinski (USA)—Livius	30	30	13	3	3	6	28	8	8	44
18 Thomas Fruhmann (Aut)										
—Donau/	29			4						
—Bandit		17	17		13	17	22.50	8	16	46.50
19 Willi Melliger (Switz)										
—Trumpf Buur	19	3	19	14	30	44	9	4	37	50
20 Allen Williams (Aus)—Tyzak	7	17	21	26	13	39	11.50	18.25	R	29.75
21 Oscar Pachenco (Ven)—Bambu	28	28	20	5	5	10	26	13.25	R	39.25
22 Malcolm Pyrah (GB)										
—Towerlands Anglezarke	22	5	22	11	28	39	11.50	4	NP	15.50
23 David Broome (GB)—Mr Ross	12	8	23	21	22	43	9.50	8	NP	17.50
24 Armand Leone (USA)—Loecky	12	16	25	21	17	38	12	12	NP	24
25 Edgar-Henri Cuepper (Bel)										
—Cyrano	E	8	23	0	22	22	20	8	NP	28
26 Jean Germany (GB)										
—Whistling Song	8	29	26	25	4	29	16.50	16	NP	32.50
27 Harry de Leyer (USA)										
—Dutch Crown	1	31	27	31	2	33	14.50	22.25	NP	36.75
28 Jan-Olaf Wannius (Swe)										
—V65 Mannen	27	8	—	6	22	28	17	R	NP	17
29 Bernie Traurig (USA)										
—Eaden Vale	16	17	—	17	13	30	16	NP	—	16
30 Mark Laskin (Can)—Damuraz	23	25	—	10	8	18	22	NP	—	22
31 Henk Nooren (NL)—Opstalan 3	25	27	—	8	6	14	24	NP	—	24
32 Cece Younger (USA)—Henley	31	NP	—	2	—	2	—	—	—	—

Number of nations represented: 11

1983 Vienna

	Placings Day 1	Placings Day 2	Placings Day 3	Points Day 1	Points Day 2	=Total	Points Converted into Penalties	Penalties Day 3 A	Penalties Day 3 B	Total Penalties
1 Norman Dello Joio (USA)										
—I Love You	3	3	1	30	30	60	0	0	0	0
2 Hugo Simon (Aut)—Gladstone	2	4	5	31	29	60	0	4	0	4
3 Melanie Smith (USA)—Calypso	8	10	1	25	20	45	7.50	0	0	7.50
4 Conrad Homfeld (USA)										
—Touch of Class	9	7	5	24	26	50	5	4	0	9
5 Paul Schockemöhle (FRG)										
—Deister	1	17	5	33	13	46	7	4	0	11
=6 Barney Ward (USA)										
—Eclair de l'Ille	15	6	5	18	27	45	7.50	0	4	11.50
Malcolm Pyrah (GB)										
—Towerlands Anglezarke	5	8	14	28	25	53	3.50	0	8	11.50
8 Donald Cheska (USA)										
—Southside	6	8	14	27	25	52	4	4	4	12
9 Katie Monahan (USA)—Noren	13	10	5	20	20	40	10	4	0	14
10 John Whitaker (GB)										
—Ryan's Son	16	10	5	17	20	37	11.50	0	4	15.50
11 Michael Matz (USA)—Jet Run	23	1	14	10	33	43	8.50	8	0	16.50
=12 David Asimus (Aus)										
—Golden Grand	14	17	5	19	13	32	14	4	0	18
Anne Kursinski (USA)—Livius	21	5	14	12	28	40	10	4	4	18
14 Michael Rüping (FRG)										
—Silbersee	10	25	5	23	6	29	15.50	4	0	19.50
15 Liz Edgar (GB)										
—Everest Forever	17	10	14	16	20	36	12	4	4	20
=16 Stephen Hadley (GB)—Sunorra	7	17	23	26	13	39	10.50	4	8	22.50
Nick Skelton (GB)—St James/	31			2						
—Everest If Ever		17	1		13	15	22.50	0	0	22.50
18 John Cottle (NZ)—Arturo	26	31	1	7	2	9	25.50	0	0	25.50
19 Ferdi Tyteca (Bel)—Ransome	22	17	14	11	13	24	18	4	4	26
20 Hendrik Snoek (FRG)										
—Palma Nova	19	32	5	14	1	15	22.50	0	4	26.50

	Day 1	Placings Day 2	Day 3	Day 1	Points Day 2	=Total	Points Converted into Penalties	Penalties Day 3 A	B	Total Penalties
=21 Mark Leone (USA)—Tim/	18	25		15	6					
—Loecky			14			21	19.50	4	4	27.50
Thomas Frühmann (Aut)										
—Bandit	25	17	14	8	13	21	19.50	4	4	27.50
23 Fritz Ligges (FRG)—Goya	12	10	25	21	20	41	9.50	12	8	29.50
24 Debbie Schaffer (USA)										
—Abdullah	4	17	27	29	13	42	9	8	16	33
25 Rob Ehrens (NL)—Surprise	28			5						
—Reinolvio		10	24		20	25	17.50	12	4	33.50
26 Hap Hansen (USA)										
—Fil d'Argent	32	25	14	1	6	7	26.50	4	4	34.50
27 Luiz Azevedo (Bra)										
—Tambo Nuevo	30	10	25	3	20	23	18.50	12	8	38.50
28 Kevin Maloney (USA)—Turf Fire	27	2	28	6	31	37	11.50	28.75	4	44.25
29 Gavin Chester (USA)—Hengist	11	25	29	22	6	28	16	24	NP	—
30 Hervé Godignon (Fra)										
—Je t'Adore Moët et Chandon	24	17	NP	9	13	22	19	NP	—	—
31 Robert Gage (USA)										
—Dutch Harry/	20			13						
—Sage		25	NP		6	19	20.50	NP	—	—
32 Gerry Mullins (Ire)—Rockbarton	29	25	NP	4	6	10	25	NP	—	—

Number of nations represented: 12

1984 Gothenburg

	Day 1	Placings Day 2	Day 3	Day 1	Points Day 2	=Total	Points Converted into Penalties	Penalties Day 3 A	B	Total Penalties
1 Mario Deslauriers (Can)										
—Aramis	8	1	7	32	40	72	0	4	0	4
=2 Norman Dello Joio (USA)										
—I Love You	13	5	1	27	35	62	5	0	0	5
Nelson Pessoa (Bra)										
—Moët et Chandon Larramy	2	6	7	38	32	70	1	4	0	5
4 Michael Rüping (FRG)										
—Silbersee	4	12	1	36	23	59	6.50	0	0	6.50
=5 Malcolm Pyrah (GB)										
—Towerlands Anglezarke	21	2	1	19	38	57	7.50	0	0	7.50
Michael Matz (USA)—Chef	6	12	1	34	23	57	7.50	0	0	7.50
7 Nick Skelton (GB)—St James	17	6	1	23	32	55	8.50	0	0	8.50
8 Donald Cheska (USA)										
—Southside	14	4	7	26	36	62	5	4	0	9
9 Michael Whitaker (GB)										
—Red Flight	3	6	14	37	32	69	1.50	8	0	9.50
10 Leslie Burr (USA)—Corsair/	1			40						
—Boing		11	19		29	69	1.50	4	8	13.50
11 Robert Gage (USA)— Fürst Z	19	12	1	21	23	44	14	0	0	14
12 Barney Ward (USA)—Pico	5	23	7	35	14	49	11.50	0	4	15.50
13 Anne Kursinski (USA)										
—Insolvent	15	12	7	25	23	48	12	0	4	16
=14 John Whitaker (GB)										
—Clonee Temple/	33			7						
—Ryan's Son		3	7		37	44	14	0	4	18
Gerry Mullins (Ire)—Rockbarton	11	12	14	29	23	52	10	4	4	18
16 Hugh Graham (Can)—Elrond	22	6	14	18	32	50	11	8	0	19
17 Peter Leone (USA)—Jonker	7	23	14	33	14	47	12.50	8	0	20.50
18 Ian Millar (Can)—Wotan	9	12	19	31	23	54	9	12	0	21
19 Tim Grubb (GB)—Linky	18	12	18	22	23	45	13.50	4.25	4	21.75
20 Thomas Frühmann (Aut)										
—Bandit	29	12	7	11	23	34	19	0	4	23
21 Fritz Ligges (FRG)—Ramzes	10	31	19	30	8	38	17	4	8	29
22 Hugo Simon (Aut)—Gladstone/	20			20						
—The Freak		23	19		14	34	19	4	8	31
23 David Broome (GB)										
—Last Resort	26	23	19	14	14	28	22	4	8	34
24 Hervé Godignon (Fra)										
—Moët et Chandon Je t'Adore	25	34	24	15	6	21	25.50	8	8	41.50
25 Greg Eurell (Aus)—Johnny Mac	32	23	25	8	14	22	25	10.25	8	43.50
26 Lisa Jacquin (USA)										
—For the Moment	31	E	26	9	0	9	31.50	24.75	0	56.25

	Placings Day 1	Day 2	Day 3	Points Day 1	Day 2	=Total	Points Converted into Penalties	Penalties Day 3 A	B	Total Penalties
27 Jeffrey Welles (USA)										
—Easter Jubilee	30	23	27	10	14	24	24	29.25	28	81.25
28 Harvey Smith (GB)										
—Sanyo Olympic Video	23	6	28	17	32	49	11.50	16	NP	—
29 Lennart Lindelöw (Swe)										
—Romeo	36	23	28	4	14	18	27	16	NP	—
30 Mark Leone (USA)—Arizona	16	12	30	24	23	47	12.50	R	—	—
31 Hans Lundbäck (Swe)										
—Sudden Change	34	12	30	6	23	29	21.50	E	—	—
32 Eddie Macken (Ire)										
—Carroll's El Paso/	39			1						
—Carroll's Royal Lion		12	30		23	24	24	R	—	—
33 George Sanna (Aus)										
—King Omega	28	31	30	12	8	20	26	R	—	—
34 Luis Alvarez Cervera (Spa)										
—Jexico du Parc	12	23	NP	28	14	42	15	—	—	—
35 Albert Voorn (NL)—Nimmerdor	24	NP	NP	16	—	16	28	—	—	—
36 Kevin Maloney (USA)—Turf Fire	35	31	NP	5	8	13	29.50	—	—	—
37 Willi Melliger (Switz)										
—Van Gogh	27	NP	NP	13	—	13	29.50	—	—	—
38 Conrad Homfeld (USA)										
—Abdullah	37	E	NP	3	0	3	34.50	—	—	—
39 Mauricio Morillo (Ecu)—Date Up	38	R	NP	2	0	2	35	—	—	—

Number of nations represented: 14

1985 Berlin

	Placings Day 1	Day 2	Day 3	Points Day 1	Day 2	=Total	Points Converted into Penalties	Penalties Day 3 A	B	Total Penalties
1 Conrad Homfeld (USA)										
—Abdullah	5	7	1	41	39	80	3	0	0	3
2 Nick Skelton (GB)										
—Everest St James	6	1	4	40	46	86	0	0	4	4
3 Pierre Durand (Fra)										
—Jappeloup	12	3	4	34	43	77	4.50	0	4	8.50
4 Malcolm Pyrah (GB)										
—Towerlands Anglezarke	7	2	8	39	44	83	1.50	4	4	9.50
5 Hugo Simon (Aut)—The Freak	2	8	8	44	38	82	2	4	4	10
=6 Michael Whitaker (GB)										
—Warren Point	1	17	4	46	23	69	8.50	0	4	12.50
Hap Hansen (USA)—May Be	3	11	8	43	34	77	4.50	0	8	12.50
8 Ian Millar (Can)—Big Ben	12	17	1	34	23	57	14.50	0	0	14.50
9 Stefan Schewe (FRG)										
—Wilster	14	17	1	32	23	55	15.50	0	0	15.50
10 Michael Rüping (FRG)										
—Silbersee/	8		4	38		61	12.50	4	0	16.50
—Caletto		17			23					
11 Armand Leone (USA)—Jonker	4	17	8	42	23	65	10.50	4	4	18.50
12 Lisa Tarnapol (USA)—Adam	25	5	8	21	41	62	12	4	4	20
13 Michael Matz (USA)—Chef	16	10	18	30	36	66	10	4	12	26
=14 Philippe Rozier (Fra)—Jiva	31	11	8	15	34	49	18.50	0	8	26.50
Peter Leone (USA)—Oxo	26	9	15	20	37	57	14.50	4	8	26.50
16 Joe Fargis (USA)										
—Touch of Class	23	17	8	23	23	46	20	0	8	28
17 Willi Melliger (Switz)										
—Beethoven/	34		15	12		43	21.50	4	8	33.50
—Van Gogh		15			31					
18 Franke Sloothaak (FRG)									8	
—Warkant	21	17	18	25	23	48	19	4	12	35
19 Rob Ehrens (NL)—Oscar Drum	10	31	20	36	12	48	19	8	12	39
20 Anne Kursinski (USA)										
—Medrano	24	6	24	22	40	62	12	0	27.75	39.75
21 Hugh Graham (Can)										
—Don't Look Back/	17			29						
—Elrond		17	22		23	52	17	8	16	41
22 Christian Currey (USA)										
—Manuel	18	17	23	28	23	51	17.50	9.50	16	43
23 Mario Deslauriers (Can)										
—Aramis	45	17	17	1	23	24	31	0	12.25	43.25

	Placings			Points			Points Converted into Penalties	Penalties Day 3		Total
	Day 1	Day 2	Day 3	Day 1	Day 2	=Total		A	B	Penalties
24 Jeff McVean (Aus)—Fürst Z	19	31	20	27	12	39	23.50	4	16	43.50
25 Peter Eriksson (Swe)										
—JFB Zorro	11	31	25	35	12	47	19.50	12	31.75	63.25
26 Diego Deriu (Ita)—Fanando	27	40	26	19	5	24	31	4	E	—
27 John Whitaker (GB)										
—Clonee Temple	33	31	27	13	12	25	30.50	8	NP	—
28 Mark Leone (USA)—Arizona	35	40	27	11	5	16	35	8	NP	—
29 Thomas Frühmann (Aut)										
—Furist	20	40	29	26	5	31	27.50	9	NP	—
30 Peter Luther (FRG)—Lasall/	37			9						
—Lucky		4	30		42	51	17.50	12	NP	—
31 Melanie Smith (USA)—Monroe	15	31	31	31	12	43	21.50	15.75	NP	—
32 Fritz Ligges (FRG)—Ramzes	36	17	32	10	23	33	26.50	16	NP	—
33 Laura Tidball–Balisky (Can)										
—Lavendel	30	31	33	16	12	28	29	E	NP	—
34 Leslie Burr-Lenehan (USA)										
—Boing	29	11	NP	17	34	51	17.50	—	—	—
35 Nelson Pessoa (Bra)										
—Moët et Chandon Larramy	9	31	NP	37	12	49	18.50	—	—	—
36 Lisa Jacquin (USA)										
—For the Moment	22	17	NP	24	23	47	19.50	—	—	—
37 Robert Smith (GB)										
—Sanyo Olympic Video	40	15	NP	6	31	37	24.50	—	—	—
38 Paul Schockemöhle (FRG)										
—Deister/	44			2						
—So Long		14	NP		32	34	26	—	—	—
39 Harvey Smith (GB)										
—Sanyo Galaxi	38		NP	8				—	—	—
—Sanyo Technology		17			23	31	27.50	—	—	—
40 Frédéric Cottier (Fra)										
—Flambeau C	42	17	NP	4	23	27	20.50	—	—	—
41 Graeme Thomas (NZ)										
—Jane Eyre	28	40	NP	18	5	23	31.50	—	—	—
42 Norman Dello Joio (USA)										
—Ardennes	32	39	NP	14	7	21	32.50	—	—	—
43 Allan Goodall (NZ)										
—Double Brown Skud	43	38	NP	3	8	11	37.50	—	—	—
44 Louis Jacobs (USA)										
—Janus de Ver	39	E	NP	7	0	7	39.50	—	—	—
45 Katharine Burdsall (USA)										
—Pot Luck	41	NP	NP	5	—	5	40.50	—	—	—

Number of nations represented: 13

1986 Gothenburg

	Placings			Points			Points Converted into Penalties	Penalties Day 3		Total
	Day 1	Day 2	Day 3	Day 1	Day 2	=Total		A	B	Penalties
1 Leslie Burr-Lenehan (USA)										
—McLain	4	1	1	36	40	76	0.00	0.00	0.00	0.00
2 Ian Millar (Can)—Big Ben	3	6	3	37	29	66	5.00	0.00	8.00	13.00
3 Conrad Homfeld (USA)—Maybe	10	3	10	30	37	67	4.50	4.00	8.00	16.50
4 Malcolm Pyrah (GB)										
—Towerlands Anglezarke	2	18	3	38	19	57	9.50	4.00	4.00	17.50
5 Georgio Nuti (Ita)—Larry 2/	15			25						
—Baltimore		2	10		38	63	6.50	0.00	12.00	18.50
6 Hugo Simon (Aut)—The Freak	14	18	2	26	19	45	15.50	0.00	4.00	19.50
7 Jeff McVean (Aus)—Fürst Z	1	6	14	40	29	69	3.50	12.00	4.25	19.75
8 Lisa Tarnapol (USA)—Adam	9	18	3	31	19	50	13.00	0.00	8.00	21.00
9 Klaus Reinacher (FRG)—Desirée	11	18	3	29	19	48	14.00	4.00	4.00	22.00
10 Lynne Little (USA)—Ommen	28	6	3	12	29	41	17.50	0.00	8.00	25.50
11 Pierre Durand (Fra)										
—Jappeloup de Luze	12	26	3	28	12	40	18.00	0.00	8.00	26.00
12 Jay Land (USA)—Leapy Lad	33	6	3	7	29	36	20.00	0.00	8.00	28.00
13 Jürgen Kenn (FRG)—Feuergeist	16	18	10	24	19	43	16.50	4.00	8.00	28.50
14 Peter Leone (USA)—Joe II/	20			20						
—Oxo		6	13		29	49	13.50	4.00	12.00	29.50
15 Franke Sloothaake (FRG)										
—Aviata/	8			32						
—Sandro		26	15		12	44	16.00	8.00	12.00	36.00

	Placings Day 1	Day 2	Day 3	Points Day 1	Day 2	=Total	Points Converted into Penalties	Penalties Day 3 A	B	Total Penalties
16 Stanny van Paesschen (Bel) —Intermezzo	7	32	15	33	8	41	17.50	8.00	12.00	37.50
17 George Lindemann (USA) —Sans Pardon	21	6	18	19	29	48	14.00	0.00	24.00	38.00
18 Christian Currey (USA)—Manuel	26	6	18	14	29	43	16.50	8.00	16.00	40.50
19 John Anderson (Can)—Goby	35	6	15	5	29	34	21.00	0.00	20.00	41.00
20 Lynn Witte (USA)—Hawkeye	36	6	18	4	29	33	21.50	8.00	16.00	45.50
21 Gail Greenough (Can)—Mr T	34	18	21	6	19	25	25.50	12.00	16.00	53.50
22 Peter Eriksson (Swe)—V65 Shoot	22	18	22	18	19	37	19.50	16.00	20.25	55.75
23 Hugh Graham (Can)—Wellington	18	4	23	22	36	58	9.00	31.75	20.00	60.75
24 Paul Schockemöhle (FRG) —Deister	24	5	24	16	35	51	12.50	8.00	NP	—
25 John Whitaker (GB)—Hopscotch	6	31	24	34	9	43	16.50	8.00	NP	—
26 Katie Monahan (USA)—Bean Bag	30	6	26	10	29	39	18.50	12.00	NP	—
27 Kurt Gravemeier (FRG) —Wembley	37	6	26	3	29	32	22.00	12.00	NP	—
28 Nick Skelton (GB) —Raffles St James	5	26	NP	35	12	47	14.50	—	—	—
29 Eddie Macken (Ire) —Carroll's Flight	25	6	NP	15	29	44	16.00	—	—	—
30 Diane Shaw (USA)—Logo	17	26	NP	23	12	35	20.50	—	—	—
31 Jeffery Welles (USA) —The Girlfriend	13	33	NP	27	7	34	21.00	—	—	—
32 Eric Wauters (Bel) —Malesan Bordeaux Gotthard	31	18	NP	9	19	28	24.00	—	—	—
33 Michael Whitaker (GB) —Warren Point	19	34	NP	21	6	27	24.50	—	—	—
34 Peter Weinberg (FRG)—Gaylord	32	26	NP	8	12	20	28.00	—	—	—
35 Thomas Fuchs (Switz)—El Lute	23	NP	NP	17	—	17	29.50	—	—	—
36 Helena Dickinson (GB) —Raffles Just Malone	27	R	NP	13	0	13	31.50	—	—	—
37 Michal Rüping (FRG)—Silbersee	29	NP	NP	11	—	11	32.50	—	—	—
38 Deborah Dolan (USA) —San Marco	38	35	NP	2	5	7	34.50	—	—	—
39 Hap Hansen (USA)—Gambrinus	R	NP	NP	0	—	0	38.00	—	—	—

Number of nations represented: 12

1987 Paris

	Placings Day 1	Day 2	Day 3	Points Day 1	Day 2	=Total	Points Converted into Penalties	Penalties Day 3 A	B	Total Penalties
1 Katharine Burdsall (USA) —The Natural	1	2	8	44	42	86	0.00	4.50	0.00	4.50
2 Philippe Rozier (Fra) —Malesan Jiva	9	1	2	35	44	79	3.50	0.00	4.00	7.50
3 Lisa Jacquin (USA) —For The Moment	5	5	2	39	39	78	4.00	4.00	0.00	8.00
4 Paul Schockemöhle (FRG) —Next Deister	6	7	2	38	34	72	7.00	0.00	4.00	11.00
=5 Ian Millar (Can)—Big Ben	8	7	2	36	34	70	8.00	0.00	4.00	12.00
John Whitaker (GB) —Next Milton	16	7	1	28	34	62	12.00	0.00	0.00	12.00
7 Pierre Durand (Fra) —Jappeloup de Luze	13	6	2	31	38	69	8.50	0.00	4.00	12.50
8 John McConnell (USA) —So Dark	7	17	7	37	25	62	12.00	4.25	0.00	16.25
9 Hugo Simon (Aut)—Winzer	3	3	14	41	41	82	2.00	16.00	0.00	18.00
10 Michael Whitaker (GB) —Next Warren Point	4	17	11	40	25	65	10.50	4.75	4.00	19.25
11 Vicky Roycroft (Aus)—Apache	11	7	13	33	34	67	9.50	4.00	8.00	21.50
12 Nick Skelton (GB) —Raffles J. Nick/ —Raffles Airborne	17	15	12	27	29	56	15.00	8.50	0.50	24.00
13 Franke Sloothaak (FRG) —Farmer	26	7	9	18	34	52	17.00	4.00	4.00	25.00
14 Wout-Jan van der Schans (NL) —Olympic Treffer	2	7	18	42	34	76	5.50	12.00	8.25	25.75
15 Katie Monahan-Prudent (USA) —Special Envoy	22	22	9	22	19	41	22.50	8.00	0.00	30.50

	Placings Day 1	Day 2	Day 3	Points Day 1	Day 2	=Total	Points Converted into Penalties	Penalties Day 3 A	B	Total Penalties
16 George Lindemann (USA) —Sans Pardon	28	7	15	16	34	50	18.00	8.00	12.00	38.00
17 Anne Kursinki (USA) —Kino d'Andelou	19	17	20	25	25	50	18.00	12.00	12.00	42.00
18 Beezie Patton (USA)—Medrano	24	22	15	20	19	39	23.50	16.00	4.00	43.50
19 Bernhard Kamps (FRG) —Argonaut	25	22	15	19	19	38	24.00	8.00	12.00	44.00
20 Leslie Burr-Lenehan (USA) —McLain/	33		19	11		25	30.50	4.50	16.00	51.00
—Siriska		30			14					
21 Jeff McVean (Aus)—Furst Z	37	22	21	7	19	26	30.00	8.25	NP	—
22 Deborah Dolan (USA)—VIP	34	22	21	10	19	29	28.50	16.75	NP	—
23 Michel Robert (Fra) —Pequignet La Fayette	21	4	—	23	40	63	11.50	—	—	—
24 Rodney Jenkins (USA) —Play Back	14	22	—	30	19	49	18.50	—	—	—
25 Robert Smith (GB) —Sanyo Bal Harbour	10	31	—	34	13	47	19.50	—	—	—
26 Susan Hutchinson (USA) —Livius	32	7	—	12	34	46	20.00	—	—	—
27 Vitor Teixeira (Bra) —Larramy Marcolab	20	22	—	24	19	43	21.50	—	—	—
28 Malcolm Pyrah (GB) —Towerlands Diamond —Seeker/	29		—	15				—	—	—
—Towerlands Anglezarke		17	—		25	40	23.00	—	—	—
29 Laura Tidball-Balisky (Can) —Lavendel	36	16	—	8	28	36	25.00	—	—	—
=30 Norbert Koof (FRG)—Well Done	12	36	—	32	0	32	27.00	—	—	—
Peter Charles (GB)—April Sun	31	22	—	13	19	32	27.00	—	—	—
=32 Joe Fargis (USA) —Touch of Class	40	17	—	4	25	29	28.50	—	—	—
Mario Deslauriers (Can) —Boxcar Willie	15	36	—	29	0	29	28.50	—	—	—
=34 Stanny van Paesschen (Bel) —Intermezzo	27	34	—	17	10	27	29.50	—	—	—
Lisa Tarnopol (USA) —Revlon Adam	30	31	—	14	13	27	29.50	—	—	—
36 Thomas Frühmann (Aut) —Porter	18	36	—	26	0	26	30.00	—	—	—
37 Hubert Bourdy (Fra) —Milou de Subligny/	23		—	21		21	32.50	—	—	—
—Lichen V		36			0					
38 Hap Hansen (USA)—Juniperus	39	33	—	5	11	16	35.00	—	—	—
39 Kim Kirton (Can)—Lorbas	42	35	—	2	9	11	37.50	—	—	—
40 Edgar-Henri Cuepper (Lux) —Calando/	35		—	9	0	9	38.50	—	—	—
—Dino		NP								
41 Hervé Godignon (Fra) —Moët et Chandon La Belletière	38	36	—	6	0	6	40.00	—	—	—
42 Jean-Marc Nicolas (Fra) —Midway St Paer	41	NP	—	3	0	3	41.50	—	—	—
43 Chris Chugg (Aus) —Denby Park Skyhigh	43	NP	—	0	0	0	43.50	—	—	—

Number of nations represented: 11

World Cup League Standings

*Denotes most wins

European League

		Points
1978–79	1 Paul Schockemöhle (FRG)	39
	2 Hugo Simon (Aut)	37
	3 David Broome (GB)	31
1979–80	1 David Broome (GB)	54
	2 Hugo Simon (Aut)	37
	3 Caroline Bradley (GB)	34
1980–81	1 Gilles Bertran de Balanda (Fra)	98
	2 Thomas Frühmann (Aut)	76
	=3 Frédéric Cottier (Fra)	66
	Caroline Bradley (GB)	66
1981–82	1 Thomas Fuchs (Switz)	87
	2 David Broome (GB)	84
	3 Thomas Frühmann (Aut)	72
1982–83	1 John Whitaker (GB)	88
	2 Nick Skelton (GB)	80
	3 Gerry Mullins (Ire)	67
1983–84	1 Nick Skelton (GB)	76
	2 Eddie Macken (Ire)	69
	3 Nelson Pessoa (Bra)	66
1984–85	1 Frédéric Cottier (Fra)	94*
	2 Paul Schockemöhle (FRG)	94
	3 Willi Melliger (Switz)	86
1985–86	1 Nick Skelton (GB)	86
	2 Pierre Durand (Fra)	85
	3 John Whitaker (GB)	82
1986–87	1 Paul Schockemöhle (FRG)	82
	2 John Whitaker (GB)	70
	3 Thomas Frühmann (Aut)	67

North American League

1978–79	1 Conrad Homfeld (USA)	25
	2 Norman Dello Joio (USA)	21
	3 Katie Monahan (USA)	20
1979–80	1 Bernie Traurig (USA)	42
	2 Leslie Burr (USA)	27
	3 Terry Rudd (USA)	25
1980–81	1 Melanie Smith (USA)	101
	2 Buddy Brown (USA)	92
	3 Michael Matz (USA)	85

North American League—East Coast

1981–82	1 Bernie Traurig (USA)	95
	2 Mark Laskin (Can)	87
	3 Anne Kursinski (USA)	82
1982–83	1 Katie Monahan (USA)	89
	2 Conrad Homfeld (USA)	73
	3 Mark Leone (USA)	69

North American League—East Coast USA

1983–84	1 Joe Fargis (USA)	58
	=2 Donald Cheska (USA)	57
	Michael Matz (USA)	57
1984–85	1 Joe Fargis (USA)	84
	2 Conrad Homfeld (USA)	80
	3 Leslie Burr (USA)	74
1985–86	1 Rodney Jenkins (USA)	78
	2 Katie Monahan (USA)	75
	3 Tim Grubb (GB)	70
1986–87	1 Katharine Burdsall (USA)	80
	2 Joe Fargis (USA)	76
	3 Rodney Jenkins (USA)	74

North American League—West Coast

1981–82	1 Hap Hansen (USA)	44
	2 Cece Younger (USA)	42
	3 Frank Selinger (Can)	34
1982–83	1 Hap Hansen (USA)	53
	2 Robert Gage (USA)	50
	3 Robert Ridland (USA)	43

North American League—West Coast USA

1983–84	1 Robert Gage (USA)	45
	2 Lisa Jacquin (USA)	43
	3 Robert Ridland (USA)	42
1984–85	1 Hap Hansen (USA)	71
	2 Graeme Thomas (NZ)	62
	3 Lisa Jacquin (USA)	60
1985–86	1 Hap Hansen (USA)	73
	2 Lisa Jacquin (USA)	61
	3 Lynne Witte (USA)	60
1986–87	1 Hap Hansen (USA)	71
	2 Lisa Jacquin (USA)	64
	3 Susan Hutchinson (USA)	58

North American League—Canada

1983–84	1 Ian Millar (Can)	70
	2 Hugh Graham (Can)	63
	3 Mario Deslauriers (Can)	48
1984–85	1 Ian Millar (Can)	74
	2 Hugh Graham (Can)	68
	3 Laura Tidball (Can)	57
1985–86	1 Ian Millar (Can)	95
	2 Mario Deslauriers (Can)	77
	3 John Anderson (Can)	72
1986–87	1 Ian Millar (Can)	80
	2 Gail Greenough (Can)	63
	3 Laura Tidball-Balisky (Can)	59

Pacific League

1979–80	1 Mariane Gilchrist (Aus)	20
	2 John Fahey (Aus)	15
	3 Gavin Chester (Aus)	12
1980–81	1 Guy Creighton (Aus)	78
	2 Greg Eurell (Aus)	66
	3 Kevin Bourke (Aus)	60
1981–82	1 Mariane Gilchrist (Aus)	106
	2 Greg Eurell (Aus)	94
	3 Peter Mullins (Aus)	77
1982–83	1 David Asimus (Aus)	93
	2 Guy Creighton (Aus)	91
	3 Gavin Chester (Aus)	76
1983–84	1 Greg Eurell (Aus)	122
	2 George Sanna (Aus)	114
	3 David Asimus (Aus)	92
1984–85	1 Kevin Bourke (Aus)	90
	2 Sean Squire (Aus)	76
	3 Chris Chugg (Aus)	66
1985–86	1 Kevin Bourke (Aus)	101
	2 Chris Chugg (Aus)	89
	3 Greg Eurell (Aus)	88
1986–87	1 Vicky Roycroft (Aus)	115
	2 Chris Chugg (Aus)	112
	3 Guy Creighton (Aus)	105

Pacific League—New Zealand Division

1982–83	1 John Cottle (NZ)	76
	2 Colin McIntosh (NZ)	39
	3 Chris Hansen (NZ)	35
1983–84	1 Harvey Wilson (NZ)	63
	2 Chris Hansen (NZ)	56
	3 Stuart Mitchell (NZ)	50
1984–85	1 Allan Goodall (NZ)	49
	2 Vaughan Jefferis (NZ)	48
	3 Chris Hansen (NZ)	46
1985–86	1 Greg Jamieson (NZ)	56
	2 Glen Pearce (NZ)	51
	3 Colin McIntosh (NZ)	43

1986–87	1 Tony Webb (NZ)	27
	2 John Gray (NZ)	26
	3 John Cottle (NZ)	22

South American League

1980–81	1 Roberto Tagle (Arg)	46
	2 Daniel Walker (Chi)	45
	3 Ricardo Goncalves (Bra)	41

South American League—Southern Part

1981–82	1 Americo Simonetti (Chi)	49*
	2 Daniel Walker (Chi)	49
	3 Justo Albarracin (Bra)	46
1982–83	1 Luiz F. de Azevedo (Bra)	32
	2 Juan Carlos Goncalves (Bra)	31
	3 Americo Simonetti (Chi)	26
1983–84	1 Sergio Caio de Carvalho (Bra)	35
	2 Alfredo Sone (Chi)	32
	3 Gustavo Calvo (Uru)	30
1984–85	1 André Johannpeter (Bra)	40
	2 Vitor Teixeira (Bra)	29
	=3 Sergio Caio de Carvalho (Bra)	28
	Paulo Stewart (Bra)	28
1985–86	1 Vitor Teixeira (Bra)	41
	2 João Aragão (Bra)	32
	=3 Jorge Carneiro (Bra)	29
	Elizabeth Menezes (Bra)	29

South American League—Northern Part

1981–82	1 Oscar Pacheco (Ven)	54
	2 Jorge Machado (Ven)	41
	3 Roberto Teran (Col)	39
1983–84	1 Mauricio Morillo (Ecu)	33
	2 Noel Vanososte (Ven)	29
	3 Oswaldo Mendez (Gua)	28

Records: Riders

Most Wins

Conrad Homfeld (USA): the only rider who has won two finals (1980, Baltimore, on Balbuco; 1985, Berlin, on Abdullah).

Most Appearances

Two riders competed in all nine finals 1979–1987: Hugo Simon (Aut) and John Whitaker (GB).

Most Successful Riders

Conrad Homfeld (USA): winner 1980, winner 1985, 3rd 1986, 4th 1983.

Hugo Simon (Aut): winner 1979, 2nd 1983, 3rd 1981 and 1982, 4th 1980, 5th 1985, 6th 1986, 9th 1987.

Melanie Smith (USA): winner 1982, 2nd 1980, 3rd 1983, 6th 1981.

Norman Dello Joio (USA): winner 1983, 2nd 1984, 3rd 1979, 9th 1981.

Best Winning Score

In 1982 Melanie Smith (USA) on Calypso, and in 1983 Norman Dello Joio (USA) on I Love You finished with no jumping penalties.

Biggest Winning Margin

In 1986 Leslie Burr-Lenehan (USA) on McLain won by a margin of 13 penalty points.

Closest Finish

There has been one tie for first place, in the only two-leg final (Gothenburg, 1979). Hugo Simon (Aut) on Gladstone and Katie Monahan (USA) on The Jones Boy each achieved one win and one second place in the two legs, resulting in a tie on points. In the jump-off Gladstone was clear and The Jones Boy had one fence down for 4 faults.

On three occasions the World Cup has been won by the narrow margin of 1 penalty point—in 1982 by Melanie Smith, in 1984 by Mario Deslauriers and in 1985 by Conrad Homfeld.

Youngest Winner

Mario Deslauriers (Can) in 1984. At 19 years of age he was also the youngest rider to compete in any final.

Oldest Winner

Hugo Simon (Aut) in 1979, aged 36.

Oldest Competitor in Final

Harry de Leyer (USA), who was 55 when he took part in the 1982 final. He finished equal 1st in the first leg.

Siblings

At Gothenburg in 1982, for the first time in a major equestrian championship, three brothers competed. Armand, Peter and Mark Leone (USA) finished 24th, 5th and 9th, respectively.

In 1985, in Berlin, the three Leone brothers again took part. Armand finished 11th, Peter equal 14th and Mark 28th.

The Whitaker brothers, John and Michael, competed at Gothenburg in 1984, in Berlin in 1985, again in Gothenburg in 1986 and in Paris in 1987. John and Michael finished equal 14th and 9th, respectively, in 1984; 27th and equal 6th in 1985; 25th and 33rd in 1986, and equal fifth and tenth in 1987.

Riders who have won the Final without winning one of the legs

Conrad Homfeld (USA) on Balbuco won the 1980 final, finishing 7th, 3rd and 3rd in the three legs.

Michael Matz (USA) on Jet Run won the 1981 final, finishing 11th, 3rd and 5th in the three legs.

Highest number of Starters

45 (Berlin, 1985)

Highest Number of Nations Represented

14 (Gothenburg, 1984)

Records: Horses

Youngest Winning Horse

The 1984 winner, Aramis, who was a seven-year-old.

Oldest Winning Horse

The 15-year-old Balbuco in 1980.

Sex of Winners

Two stallions have won the World Cup, the French-bred Selle Français, I Love You, in 1983, and the West German-bred Trakehner, Abdullah, in 1985. The other winners in the years 1979–87 were all geldings.

Winning Colours

Bay, six: Balbuco, 1980; Jet Run, 1981; Calypso, 1982; I Love You, 1983; Aramis, 1984; The Natural, 1987.

Chestnut, one: Gladstone, 1979.

Grey, one: Abdullah, 1985.

Dark Brown, one: McLain, 1986.

Breeders of Winners

West Germany, five: Gladstone (Hannoverian); Aramis (Hannoverian); Abdullah* (Trakehner); McLain (Oldenburg); The Natural (Hannoverian).

Argentina, one: Balbuco (TB).

France, one: I Love You (Selle Français).

The Netherlands, one: Calypso (Westfalian).

USA, one: Jet Run (TB).

* Abdullah was conceived in West Germany, was exported *in utero* and was foaled in the USA.

Hans-Heinrich Brinckmann

Asked to which trainer or trainers he considers himself most indebted, five-times Olympic gold medallist Hans Günter Winkler has a ready answer: Hans-Heinrich Brinckmann. Winkler is one of many riders, both in Germany and elsewhere, to have benefited from the teaching of this man of diverse talents. Brinckmann was the stylist par excellence among the crack German riders of the thirties, all products of the renowned Hanover Cavalry School. The perfect style which he and his horses showed in all phases of the jump is a handsome tribute to the correct teaching traditions which had been handed down at Hanover.

While there is nothing especially unusual about great riders becoming trainers, great riders turned great course builders are exceedingly scarce and Brinckmann is a rare example of a man who has embraced all three aspects of show jumping—riding, training and course building—with unqualified success.

Born on 14 November, 1911 at Ratzeburg, near Lübeck, he learnt to ride as a child. His interest in music led him to entertain ambitions of becoming a conductor. However, since his father was a cavalry officer and his riding instructor an ex-cavalry man, it is hardly surprising that Brinckmann decided, while still in his early teens, to make the army his career. In 1929 he joined the 14th German Cavalry Regiment and in 1932 graduated as a second lieutenant. He was to stay with the army until 1945, by which time he held the rank of Colonel.

A born horseman, he competed with success at national shows before being invited, in 1935, to join the German jumping team. From then until the outbreak of the Second World War he competed at top level with notable success. His first Nations Cup win came at Berlin in 1937 and was followed by further successes at Paris and Vienna in the same year. Riding alongside such luminaries as the 1936 Olympic gold medalist Kurt Hasse and the redoubtable Harald Momm, Brinckmann found himself in one of the most powerful Nations Cup teams of all time. In 1938 victories were achieved at Geneva, Brussels and Amsterdam, and in 1939 at Berlin, Amsterdam again and Aachen. At the latter show the German team showed its superiority by finishing 78 faults ahead of its nearest rival. The one European Nations Cup of 1940, which took place in Rome and which also fell to the Germans, saw Brinckmann's last success in that genre of competition. As the war gained momentum, equestrian sport ground to a halt.

Like most pre-war army officers, Brinckmann was a most accomplished all-round rider, having competed not only in show jumping but also in horse trials and steeplechasing. Sadly, he was never able to achieve the Olympic honours which were undoubtedly within his capabilities; he was reserve rider for Germany in the Berlin Games of 1936, and the 1940 Tokyo Games, for which he was selected for the team, had of course to be cancelled.

As a trainer and rider of horses, Brinckmann was somewhat unusual in that he favoured stallions, finding them to be particularly intelligent and brave. Entire horses with whom he competed with great success at the very highest level included Oberst II, Wotansbruder and Baron IV. With Wotansbruder he won the Rome Grand Prix in 1937; with Oberst II the 1938 Amsterdam Grand Prix, and with Baron IV the Grand Prix of Vienna and Berlin in 1939.

When the war finished, Brinckmann was instrumental in re-starting show jumping in Germany. He continued to compete himself, and did not retire from international riding until 1953. From 1954 until 1956 he was trainer to the Egyptian jumping team in Cairo—by 1960 the Egyptian riders had progressed so far that they finished fourth in the Olympic

Nations Cup at the Rome Games, behind the world's best riders from The Federal Republic of Germany, the United States and Italy. Their mounts were the German-bred horses Artos, Mabrouk and Nefertiti on whom they had been schooled by Brinckmann.

On his return home he began to train both horses and riders at Warendorf, the German national training centre, later becoming a member of the German Olympic Committee. And in the years that followed his talents as a course builder were to put him among the very top ranks of that difficult and specialized profession. For many years, during the sixties and seventies, he was the resident designer at Aachen, one of the world's foremost show-grounds. Here he incorporated into his courses the natural elements which he considers so important to show jumping and which can be found at very few shows—Hickstead being a notable exception. Brinckmann's fences tended to be big, but they were always so beautifully designed and constructed that they encouraged horses to jump boldly. The courses which he designed for the 1972 Olympic Games at Munich were universally described as 'big

but fair', and those which he provided at the 1978 World Championships at Aachen were considered by many onlookers to be nothing short of masterly.

Now officially retired, 'Micky' Brinckmann has been able to hand over the reins to erstwhile students of the highest calibre. Winkler, who back in the thirties named his first pony after the man who was later to become his teacher, is now in charge of training the German jumping team. Dr Arno Gego, a talented all-round rider who became a student of Brinckmann's in 1961, was his assistant at Aachen for many years, and worked with him on the Munich Olympics project, is now one of the world's leading designers: he provided the courses at the 1986 World Championships.

Hans-Heinrich Brinckmann represents a unique link with the days of the cavalry schools, those establishments which produced such great riders and great trainers—Brinckmann has been both—and which were largely responsible for putting the sport of show jumping on the map. The contribution which he has made to the sport is incalculable.

Brinckmann in 1939, the year in which he won the Grand Prix of Vienna and Berlin and was a member of the winning German Nations Cup teams at Berlin, Amsterdam and Aachen. (Max E. Ammann)

Nations Cups

Team competitions, known as Nations Cups, are among the most important events in the equestrian calendar. A team comprises four different riders (countries unable to field four may enter three), each of whom jumps the same course twice. The running order for the teams is drawn, and the first rider from the first country is followed by the first rider from the next country and so on until all four riders from each country have jumped. Up until the mid-1980s it was customary for the whole process to be repeated in the second round, but in 1986 amendments to the rules were proposed, designed to prevent Nations Cups from becoming too long drawn out and to generate a little more excitement for spectators. These amendments involve limiting the number of teams taking part in the second round, thus eliminating the 'no-hopers' from proceedings, and running the teams in reverse order of merit, the country with the best score in the first round jumping last in the second.

Each country discards its worst score in each round. Except for very large countries, such as the United States, each nation may stage only one Nations Cup per season, and at least three teams must take part for the competition to be recognized as a Nations Cup. The competitions are open to amateurs and professionals, men and women, civilian and military riders.

Nations Cups date from June 1909, when the first such contest was staged during London's International Horse Show at Olympia. A gold international challenge cup worth £500 was presented by King Edward VII for jumping the course by a team of three officers of the same nationality and riding in uniform.

The trophy for the first ever Nations Cup, competed for at the 1909 International Horse Show at Olympia: the King Edward VII Gold Cup, which was manufactured by the Goldsmiths and Silversmiths Company of Regent Street, London. Won outright by the Russians in 1914, and never seen thereafter, it was replaced by the Edward Prince of Wales Cup. (The Illustrated London News)

Rules for Judging the First Nations Cup

The First Nations Cup took place at the afternoon performance of the Horse Show, Olympia, on Tuesday, 8 June 1909. It was Class 107, which began at 4 pm, and was described as follows in the official schedule:

King Edward VII Gold Cup for Jumping over the Course by Teams of three Officers of the same Nationality in Uniform.

Only 1 team of 3 from each country can compete in any one year. Officers' and Government horses only to be ridden.

A souvenir will be presented to each member of the winning team. This Cup to be held for One Year by the Winning Nation, and to be returned to the International Horse Show, London, by 1 June, 1910.

The winning group will be that which has the least number of faults, adding together the faults of the three officers of the same nationality. In the case of an equality of faults, the Directors will require competitors to jump again.

Refusing or Bolting: 1st   2 faults
                         2nd   3 faults
                         3rd   Debarred

Horse or Rider, or Horse and Rider,
fall   4 faults
Horse touches fence without knocking
it down   ½ fault
Horse upsets fence—with fore limbs   4 faults
                    with hind limbs   2 faults

2 minutes to complete the course.

Cup value £500
Reserve Ribbon

The competition, which attracted teams from three continents, aroused great interest and it was not long before other major international shows began to hold similar contests. Although the scoring system for jumping competitions differed quite considerably from those we know today, that first Nations Cup was, broadly speaking, run along similar lines to those of the present time. Each horse and rider was required to jump the same course twice, the winning team being the one with the lowest total score for the six rounds. The chief differences from the modern Nations Cup were that teams were limited to three riders, all three scores counted in each round, and each team jumped as a unit, the three riders from one country going one after another, followed by the three riders from the next country, and so on.

Because of the lack of standardized rules, shows could and did devise their own methods of judging their Nations Cups, with the result that the competitions which proliferated in the years before the Second World War followed a variety of different formats. Some were over one round only, others permitted four or even five riders per team. Some were scored, as today, on faults, others were decided on plus points. It was common practice to award a prize to the individual horse and rider putting up the best performance, which frequently necessitated a jump-off after the Nations Cup itself had finished. A country with insufficient riders to make up a team could start the same rider twice, on two different horses. After the concept of the discard score was adopted (each team being allowed to enter four riders and count only their three best scores) it was usual to discount the horse and rider with the worst total score for the two rounds, not the worst in each round as is the case today. Also there was nothing to prevent a country from staging a Nations Cup at more than one show during the same season.

The one thing which all those early Nations Cups did have in common was that they were very much the preserve of officers and gentlemen riders—indeed some were for military teams only. Lady riders were, therefore, excluded (in the late twenties and early thirties one or two European shows made up for this by running unofficial Nations Cups for ladies only). However, when show jumping resumed after the Second World War it became clear that all Nations Cups had to be opened up to civilian riders, since the widespread mechanization of the armies made it impossible for teams to be made up solely of cavalry officers. It was only a matter of time before women were allowed to compete, too. By 1949 Ireland was the only country still insisting on military teams for their Nations Cup. It was not until the early fifties that the FEI finally ironed out all the anomalies and formulated the rules we know today.

Since that prototype competition took place at Olympia in 1909, more than 800 Nations Cups have been contested. The results included in this book are of those Nations Cups officially sanctioned by the FEI and, in the case of pre-FEI contests, those which correspond most closely to the modern concept of a Nations Cup. Research reveals a number of 'grey area' competitions and since these do not follow the accepted pattern, they have been excluded. In all cases where there is any doubt, the author has followed the leading authority on equestrian records, Max E. Ammann. The Nations Cups are listed in chronological order and, wherever possible, results are given for all the teams taking part in each event.

1909

London

France 20.50
Jean Cariou—Doomsday
Jean Broudehoux—Heroide
Capt. Bérille—Jubilee

2 Italy, 23.50; 3 Great Britain, 30.50;
4 Canada, 34.00; 5 Belgium, 44.50;
6 Argentina, 45.50.

San Sebastián

Italy
Francesco Amalfi—Mab
Georgio Bianchetti—Marghéreby
Giacomo Antonelli—Tristano
Prince Giovanni Capece
    Zurlo—St Hubert II
Gaspare Bolla—Ornella

2 Spain; 3 Argentina; 4 Belgium;
5 France; 6 Portugal; 7 Great Britain.

The winning French Team at Olympia in 1909, Captain Bérille, Captain Cariou, who was to become Olympic champion in 1912, and Lt. Broudehoux. (The Illustrated London News)

The second Nations Cup was held at the San Sebastián Horse Show in 1909. Here a competitor is seen tackling the complicated water jump and bridge climb. (The Illustrated London News)

1910

Brussels

Belgium 4.00
Maurice Lancksweert
Léon Ripet
Ernest Picard

2 France, 12.00; 3 Portugal, 16.00; 4 Sweden, 32.00; 5 Netherlands, 35.00.

London

Belgium
Léon Ripet—Miss Kitty
Maurice Lancksweert—Speranza
Desiré Landrain—Armide

2 France; 3 Great Britain.

1911

Brussels

Belgium
Léon Ripet
Baron Henry d'Oldenneel
Paul Convert

2 France.

Turin

France 471
M. Chavanne de Dalmassy—Lutin
Lt Gonnet-Thomas—Erion

Lt Dufort d'Astafort—Castibalza
Lt Costa—Joyeux
Lt Horment—Cocotte

2 Italy, 463.

Rome

Italy
Alberto Acerbo
Francesco Amalfi
Giacomo Antonelli
Vittorio Fenoglio
Leone Tappi

London

France
Vicomte François de Malherbe
—Blé d'Or
J. M. Pinczon Du Sel—L'Ami II
Bernard Meyer—Ursule

2 Russia; 3 Great Britain; also ran: Belgium, Canada, Germany, USA.

New York

Netherlands*
Baron Herman van Voorst tot Voorst
—Black Paddy
Charles Labouchère—Dreadnought
Fritz Trapman—Fox

2 Canada; 3 USA; 4 Great Britain, eliminated.

1912

Brussels

Belgium
Edouard Bary
Baron Gaston de Trannoy—Speranza
Léon Ripet

2 France.

London

Russia 15.50
Dimitri Ivanenko—Barin
Dimitri d'Exe—Epir
Paul Rodzianko—Extra

2 France, 19.50; 3 Great Britain, 35.00; 4 Netherlands, 43.00; 5 Canada, 47.50; 6 Belgium, 48.50.

The Hague

Netherlands 16.00
Charles Labouchère—Dreadnought
A. N. Coblijn—Black Paddy
Baron Herman van Voorst tot Voorst
—Powerful
2 Canada, 20.00.

Spa

Belgium
Albert de Selliers de Moranville—Zulu
Baron Emmanuel de Blommaert
—Clonmore
Léon Ripet—Speranza

2 France.

*The teams from The Netherlands and Canada finished equal first with 0.00 faults. The Dutch riders were judged to have ridden with the best style and were awarded first prize.

New York

Netherlands 2.50
Charles Labouchère—Dreadnought
A. N. Coblijn—Black Paddy
Johannes van Gellicum—Powerful

2 Great Britain; 3 Canada, 4.50;
4 Belgium; 5 USA.

1913

Brussels

France
Capt. d'Auzac de Lamartinie—Djali
J. M. Pinczon du Sel—L'Ami II
Baron de Meslon—Amazone

2 Belgium; 3 Sweden.

London

Russia 12.25
Michael Plechkoff—Epir
Paul Rodzianko—Jilly
Dimitri d'Exe—Argoust

2 France, 14.50; 3 Great Britain, 20.50;
4 Sweden, 32.50; 5 Belgium, 37.00;
6 Italy, 42.00; 7 Canada, 43.00.

The Hague

Netherlands 4 fences,
4 minutes 33 seconds
Charles Labouchère—Spes
Joshua de Kruijff—Croquette
A. N. Coblijn—Black Paddy

2 Belgium, 4 fences,
5 minutes 1 second.

New York

France 3.00
François de Thonel, Marquis d'Orgeix
—Sarah Gosse
Auguste de Laissardière—Othello
Baron de Meslon—Amazone

2 Great Britain, 4.00; 3 Canada; 4 USA;
5 Belgium.

1914

Brussels

France 5.00
Baron de Meslon—Amazone
Auguste de Laissardière—Othello
J. M. Pinczon du Sel—L'Ami II

2 Belgium.

London

Russia 5.00
Dimitri d'Exe—Che-Bella
Michael Plechkoff—Pacha
Paul Rodzianko—Macgillicuddy Reeks

2 France, 8.50; 3 Great Britain 24.50;
4 Belgium, 25.00.

The Hague

Netherlands
Joshua de Kruijff
Anton Colenbrander
Charles Labouchère

1920

London

Sweden
Count Hans von Rosen—Koks
Gustav Kilman—Irving
Count Clarence von Rosen—Poor Boy

2 Great Britain; 3 Belgium; 4 Spain
5 France; 6 Netherlands.

1921

Nice

Italy 2.00
Alessandro Alvisi—Raggio di Sole
Ettore Caffaratti—Traditor
Alessandro Valerio—Cento

Members of the crack Russian team of the pre-First World War days (from left),
Dimitri Ivanenko, Dimitri d'Exe and Paul Rodzianko, who later became trainer
to the Irish Army team. (W. W. Rouch)

=2 Belgium, France; 4 Switzerland;
5 Sweden.

London

Great Britain
Geoffrey Brooke—Combined Training
Malise Graham—Broncho
H. G. Morrison—Corinthe

2 Italy; 3 Sweden; 4 Spain; 5 France;
6 Belgium, eliminated.

1922

Nice

Italy
Ettore Caffaratti—Trebecco
Conte Carlo Calvi di Bergolo—Sbruffo
Alessandro Alvisi—Raggio di Sole

Rome

Italy
Eugenio Cerboneschi—Sterlina
Alessandro Alvisi—Raggio di Sole
Santorre de Rossi di Santa Rosa
—Queen

2 Belgium.

London

Great Britain
Malise Graham—Broncho
C. T. 'Taffy' Walwyn—Mrs Green
J. H. Gibbon—Sirdar

2 Belgium; 3 France; 4 Italy;
5 Netherlands.

1923

Nice

Italy
Tommaso Lequio di Assaba
—Trebecco
Ettore Caffaratti—Tresor
Leone Valle—Sbruffo

2 Poland; 3 Belgium; 4 France;
5 Netherlands.

Rome

Italy 53.00
Tommaso Lequio di Assaba—Ombrello
Francesco Formigli—Ulano
Ettore Caffaratti—Candy

=2 Belgium, Poland, 57.00.

Brussels

Italy
Ettore Caffaratti—Neruccio
Francesco Formigli—Porto III
Leone Valle—Camoscino

2 France; 3 Belgium.

London

Italy
Tommaso Lequio di Assaba
—Trebecco
Conte Giulio Borsarelli di Riffredo
—Don Chisciotte
Conte Carlo Calvi di Bergolo
—Sbruffo

2 Great Britain; 3 France; 4 Belgium.

1924

Nice

France
Pierre Clavé—Sans Doute
Xavier Bizard—Billou
Georges de Briolle—Herseur
Pierre Le Moyne—Manitoba

2 Switzerland; 3 Belgium; 4 Italy;
5 Poland; 6 Netherlands.

London

Great Britain   11.50
Geoffrey Brooke—Daddy Longlegs
Edward de Fonblanque—War Baby
Capel Brunker—Woodcat

2 Italy, 14.00; 3 USA, 19.50;
4 France, 32.00; 5 Switzerland, 41.00.

1925

Nice

Poland
Karol von Rommel—Revcliff
Adam Krolikiewicz—Picador
Kazimierz Szosland—Cezar
Henryk Dobrzansky—Mumm Extra Dry

Also ran: Belgium, France
Czechoslovakia, Portugal.

Stresa

Italy
Conte Alessandro Bettoni-Cazzago
—Scoiattolo
Conte Giulio Borsarelli di Riffredo
—Don Chisciotte
Giorgio Pacini—Zanghera

The Hague

Netherlands   12.00
Gerard de Kruijff
Charles Labouchère
Gerard Willen Le Heux
Anton Colenbrander

London

Italy   11.00
Tommaso Lequio di Assaba—Trebecco
Carlo Tappi—Nunzia
Giuseppe Cacciandra—Fragola

=2 Great Britain, Poland, 16.00.

Toronto

Belgium
Gaston Mesmaekers
J. Baudouin de Brabandère
Jean Breuls

New York

France
Auguste de Laissardière—Flirt
Xavier Bizard—Pantin
Pierre Clavé—The Doctor

2 Belgium; 3 USA; 4 Canada.

*The Edward, Prince of Wales Cup,
which in 1920 replaced the lost King
Edward VII Gold Cup. It is still
competed for today as Britain's Nations
Cup. (Steve Yarnell)*

1926

Nice

Belgium
Jean Breuls—Acrobate
J. Baudouin de Brabandère
—Miss America
Georges van Derton—Sneta
Raymond Leurquin—Funny Boy

Rome

Italy   0.00
Tommaso Lequio di Assaba—Trebecco
Conte Alessandro Bettoni-Cazzago
—Scoiattolo
Giorgio Pacini—Zanghera

2 France, 4.00; 3 Poland; 4 Belgium;
also ran: Switzerland, Portugal, Spain.

Naples

Italy   38.00
Tommaso Lequio di Assaba—Trebecco
Carlo Kechler—Garoso
Giorgio Pacini—Zanghera

2 France, 40.00; 3 Poland, 60.00;
4 Portugal; 5 Spain.

Milan

Italy   16.00
Conte Alessandro Bettoni-Cazzago
—Scoiatollo
Francesco Formigli—San Quintino
Giorgio Pacini—Zanghera

2 France, 28.00; 3 Portugal, 30.00;
4 Spain, 72.00; retired, Poland.

*Italy fielded some tremendously successful teams in the years between the wars and in
1923 won all four Nations Cups (Nice, Rome, Brussels and London). Pictured here
are (from left), Lt. Tommaso Lequio di Assaba, Captain Conte Carlo Calvi di Bergolo
and Captain Conte Giulio Borsarelli di Riffredo. (The Illustrated London News)*

Broncho

Although horses commonly live well into their twenties, it is unusual to find them competing when they are out of their teens, and even more rare for them to go on winning in top level competition. A horse who broke all the rules in this respect was Broncho, a British cavalry remount who acquired his name because of his habit, as a youngster, of putting in a buck and taking his unfortunate rider totally unawares.

As a jumper Broncho was, to put it mildly, a late developer. Although he was not lacking in jumping ability, he would stubbornly refuse at any obstacle which he had not seen before. As a result it was not until he was in his late teens, by which time he was familiar with virtually every type of fence ever encountered in the show ring at that time, that he could be relied upon.

In 1921 at Olympia, the British team scored its first success in a Nations Cup. Broncho, at the age of 18—a time when most horses would be in semi-retirement—was a member of that team. From then on his career went from strength to strength. When he was 22 he won no less a competition than the King George V Gold Cup, and in the years 1926 to 1929 inclusive he was a member of Britain's winning Nations Cup team at Olympia. In 1929, when he was 26, he put up the best performance of the three British horses, collecting only 1 fault in the two rounds.

His regular rider in those days was Brigadier

Broncho and Colonel Malise Graham pictured in 1925, the year they won the King George V Gold Cup at Olympia. (The Illustrated London News)

Malise Graham, a gifted and much admired horseman who had the unfortunate and rare distinction of meeting his death in the show jumping arena. At Dublin in 1929, not long after the International Horse Show at Olympia, he had a fall from a young horse, during which his foot became caught in the stirrup and he was kicked on the head. He suffered a compound fracture of the skull and died in a Dublin nursing home shortly afterwards. Broncho, whose talent had blossomed so late in life, did not long outlive him—some said it was because the old horse missed his former partner and pined away.

London

Great Britain   22.00
Malise Graham—Broncho
Geoffrey Brooke—Daddy Longlegs
W. G. E. Heath—Whisper

2 USA, 16.00; 3 France, 20.00;
4 Sweden, 22.00; 5 Belgium, 30.50.

Dublin

Switzerland   85.50
Henri von der Weid—Royal Gris
Hans E. Bühler—Vladimir
Charles Kuhn—Novello

2 France, 84.00; 3 Belgium, 83.00;
4 Ireland, 82.00; 5 Great Britain, 79.00;
6 Netherlands, 79.00.

Strasbourg

Great Britain
William Muir
John Moreton
John Holmes
Alan Hopkins

2 France; 3 Netherlands; 4 Belgium.

Toronto

France   8.00
Pierre Clavé
Yves de Fréminville
Jacques de Fonlongue

2 Belgium, 18.00; 3 Canada, 22.50.

New York

Poland   21.50
Michael Toczek—Hamlet
Adam Krolikiewicz—Jacek
Kazimierz Szosland—Readgledt

2 France, 28.00; 3 Belgium, 31.50.

The winning British team at Olympia in 1926, W. G. E. Heath (left), Geoffrey Brooke (centre) and Malise Graham. It was Geoffrey Brooke's wife, Dorothy, who founded the Old War House Memorial Hospital, now the Brooke Hospital for Animals, Cairo. (The Illustrated London News).

1927

Nice

Great Britain
Edward de Fonblanque
The Hon Arthur Baillie
Douglas Stirling
Aylmer Cameron

Rome

France   28.00
Pierre Bertran de Balanda
—Papillon XIV
Xavier Bizard—Moïse
Maurice Gudin de Vallerin—Nocelle

2 Italy, 42.00; 3 Great Britain, 74.00.

Madrid

Spain
José de Bohorques,
Marqués de los Trujillos—Zalamero
José Cavanillas Prosper—Barrote
Nemesio Martinez Hombre
—Zapatillero
Manuel Serrano—Acalorado

2 Portugal, 42.00; 3 France, 52.00.

Warsaw

Poland   48.00
Michael Toczek—Hamlet
Adam Krolikiewicz—Jacek
Kazimierz Szosland—Alli
Stefan Starniawski—Hannibal

2 France, 61.00; 3 Hungary, retired.

London

Great Britain   5.00
Edward de Fonblanque—War Baby
William Muir—Sea Count
Malise Graham—Broncho

2 France, 10.50; 3 Italy, 20.50;
4 Poland, 26.50; 5 Belgium, 31.50;
6 Sweden, 38.50; 7 Ireland, 75.50.

Lucerne

France   27.25
Théophile Carbon—Cantal
Xavier Bizard—Quinine
Camille de Montergon

2 Switzerland, 32.25; 3 Belgium, 36.00;
4 Hungary, 70.50.

Dublin

Switzerland   262.00
Henri von der Weid—Royal Gris
Heinrich Hersche—Esperance
Alphonse Gemuseus—Notas

2 Great Britain, 256.00;
3 Belgium, 241.00; 4 Ireland, 227.00.

The Hague

Germany
Eduard Pulvermann
Marten von Barnekow
Herbert Fick

Geneva

Switzerland
Max Thommen—Peptia
Pierre de Muralt—Notas
Alphonse Gemuseus—Lucette

2 France; 3 Belgium; 4 Germany.

New York

Poland   1.50
Michael Antoniewicz—Readgledt
Karol von Rommel—Fagas
Stefan Starniawski—Jacek

2 USA, 3.50; 3 Canada, 5.00;
4 France, 14.00.

1928

Nice

Poland
Karol von Rommel—Donneuse
Adam Krolikiewicz—Readgledt
Kazimierz Szosland—Alli
Kazimierz Gzowsky—Mylord

2 Belgium; 3 France. (7 ran)

Rome

France
Pierre Bertran de Balanda
—Papillon XIV
Maurice Gudin de Vallerin—Nacelle
Xavier Bizard—Pantin

2 Italy.

Madrid

Spain   16.50
José de Bohorques, Marqués de los
Trujillos—Zalamero
José Navarro Morenes—Bilbaina
Angel Somalo Paricio—Royal
Julio Garcia Fernandez—Revistada

2 Portugal, 17.00; retired, Chile.

Brussels

Great Britain   22.00
Edward de Fonblanque
—Daddy Longlegs
Aylmer Cameron—Lynz
Douglas Stirling—Nancy

=2 Poland, Switzerland, 24.00;
4 France, 24.00; 5 Belgium.

Warsaw

Poland   58.50
Michael Antoniewicz—Banzaj
Henryk Roycewicz—Black Boy
Wladyslaw Zgorzelski—Ladna
Kazimierz Gzowsky—Mylord

2 France, 103.00;
3 Czechoslovakia, 134.00;
4 Italy, 148.50; 5 Finland, retired.

London

Great Britain   7.00
Edward de Fonblanque—War Baby
William Muir—Sea Count
Malise Graham—Broncho

2 France, 19.00; 3 Belgium, 32.50.

Biarritz

Belgium
J. Baudouin de Brabandère
Jacques Misonne
Henry de Menten de Horne
Georges van Derton

Lucerne

Italy   10.00
Tommaso Lequio di Assaba—Trebecco
Francesco Forquet—Capinera
Conte Alessandro Bettoni-Cazzago
—Aladino

2 France, 22.75; 3 Switzerland, 33.25;
4 Belgium, 44.50.

Dublin

Ireland   227.00
Dan Corry—Finghlin
Jed O'Dwyer—Cuchulain
Cyril Harty—Craobh Ruadh

2 Great Britain, 272.00;
3 France, 265.00; 4 Belgium, 264.00.

Geneva

Italy   42.00
Tommaso Barbantini—Grey Fox
Enrico Raguzzi—Falconière
Riccardo d'Angelo—Primula

2 France, 44.00; 3 Switzerland, 52.50;
4 Belgium, 75.00; 5 Germany, 77.00;
6 Chile, 91.00.

New York

Germany   9.00
Hermann von Nagel—Wotan
Marten von Barnekow—Derby
Wilhelm Schmalz—Hochmeisterin

2 USA, 9.50, 7.00 in jump-off;
3 Poland, 9.50, 12.00 in jump-off;
4 Canada, 11.00; 5 Belgium, 11.50;
6 Netherlands, 12.50.

1929

Naples

France
Xavier Bizard
Maurice Gudin de Vallerin
Pierre Bertran de Balanda

2 Italy.

Nice

Italy   12.00
Francesco Forquet—Capinera
Conte Giulio Borsarelli di Riffredo
—Crispa

International
Horse Show

Olympia
June 6 -16 1910.

Cataloque – One Shilling.

The cover illustration for the catalogue of the 4th International Horse Show at Olympia in 1910. As well as being one of the highlights of the social year in London, Olympia was responsible for establishing show jumping as an international sport in Great Britain.

Raimondo d'Inzeo, who made his debut with the Italian team in 1947, competing on Stranger at the Dublin Show 32 years later. (Kit Houghton)

David Broome, World Champion in 1970 and winner of two Olympic bronze medals, jumping the ex-American racehorse Philco. (Bob Langrish)

Pierre Jonquères d'Oriola of France is the only rider to have won the individual Olympic title twice, first in 1952 with Ali-Baba and then again on Lutteur B in 1964. In 1966 he added to his remarkable score by winning the World Championship in Buenos Aires riding this French-bred mare Pomone B. (Findlay Davidson)

Two former European Champions, Alwin Schockemöhle (left) and Johan Heins. Schockemöhle, who won the amateurs only title in 1975, is the only person to have won the individual Olympic gold medal with a double clear round and no jump-off. Johan Heins, European Champion in 1977, is the first Dutchman to win a senior championship. (Bob Langrish)

Nick Skelton and Everest Lastic setting a new British high jump record of 7 ft 7⁵/₁₆ in (2.32 metres) at Olympia in 1978. (Bob Langrish)

Norbert Koof and Fire winning the 1982 World Championship in Dublin. At 26, Koof was the youngest man to hold the World title. (Kit Houghton)

Conte Alessandro Bettoni-Cazzago
—Aladino
Francesco Formigli—Suello

2 Belgium, 16.00; 3 Spain, 22.00;
also ran: Czechoslovakia, Poland,
Ireland, France.

Rome

Italy 20.00
Francesco Forquet—Capinera
Conte Giulio Borsarelli di Riffredo
—Crispa
Conte Alessandro Bettoni-Cazzago
—Aladino

2 Spain, 32.00; 3 France, 36.00;
4 Poland, retired.

Brussels

Italy
Conte Alessandro Bettoni-Cazzago
—Aladino
Giorgio Pacini—Boby
Tommaso Barbantini—Primula
Alberto Lombardi—Roccabruna

2 France; 3 Ireland; 4 Belgium.

Lisbon

Portugal 2.00
José Mousinho de Albuquerque
—Hebraico
Luis Mena e Silva—Bethulie
José Beltrão—Basquaise
João Froes de Almeida—Gaillard

2 Spain, 9.00; 3 Chile, 13.00.

Madrid

Portugal 14.00
José Mousinho de Albuquerque
—Hebraico
Luis Mena e Silva—Whisky

José Beltrão—Basquaise
Luiz Ivens Ferraz—Marco Visconti

2 Spain, 16.00; 3 Italy, 30.50;
4 Chile, 31.50.

Warsaw

Italy 17.00
Francesco Forquet—Capinera
Conte Giulio Borsarelli di Riffredo
—Crispa
Tommaso Lequio di Assaba—Urosky
Mario Lombardo di Cumia—Bacce

2 Poland, 39.50; 3 Rumania, 53.75;
4 France, 64.50; 5 USA, 115.50.

Budapest

Italy
Mario Lombardo di Cumia—Bacce
Francesco Formigli—Capinera
Tommaso Lequio di Assaba—Galatin

London

Great Britain 12.50
Malise Graham—Broncho
D. A. Stirling—Nancy
W. H. Muir—Sea Count

2 France, 13.00; 3 Ireland, 19.00;
4 Belgium, 22.00.

Cologne

Germany
Marten von Barnekow
Hans Joachim Andreae
Hanns Koerfer

Le Touquet

France
Auguste de Laissardière
—Sherry Golden

Pierre Clavé—Le Trouvère
Maurice Gudin de Vallerin—Pair II

2 Belgium; 3 Chile.

Lucerne

Switzerland 14.00
Pierre de Muralt—Notas
Alphonse Gemuseus—Lucette
Charles Kuhn—Falaisa
Jean Haecky—Severina

2 Italy, 26.00; 3 Germany, 34.50;
4 Netherlands, retired.

Aachen

Sweden
Rolf Örn—Loke
Ernst Hallberg—Mefisto
Arne Franke—Urfé

2 Italy.

Dublin

France 277.00, 140.00 in jump-off
Pierre Clavé—Volant III
Lt de Rolland—Scouissant III
Xavier Bizard—Perigord

2 Ireland, 277.00, 139.00 in jump-off;
3 Sweden, 274.00;
4 Switzerland, 273.00; 5 USA, 270.00;
6 Great Britain, 267.00;
7 Belgium, 263.00.

Boston

USA
Harry D. Chamberlin
Earl F. Thomson—Tan Bark
William B. Bradford

2 Canada; 3 Ireland.

New York

Poland 2.50
Stefan Starniawski—Pegas
Wladyslaw Zgorzelski—Leharo
Kazimierz Gzowski—Hamlet

2 Italy, 6.50; 3 USA, 8.00;
4 Ireland, 13.00; 5 Canada, 20.50.

Geneva

Germany 28.00
Hanns Koerfer—Baron III
Richard Sahla—Ninon
Rudolf Lippert—Hartmannsdorf
Ernst Hasse—Derby

2 France, 30.00; =3 Belgium,
Switzerland, 44.00.

*Three members of the great pre-war Irish
Army team which in the years 1928 to
1939 won 23 Nations Cups (from left),
Captain John Lewis on Tramore Bay,
Cdt Jed O'Dwyer on Limerick Lace
and Captain Dan Corry on Red Hugh.
(The Illustrated London News)*

1930

Berlin

Germany
Ernst Hasse—Derby
Wilhelm Schmalz—Benno
Richard Sahla—Schwabensohn
Hanns Koerfer—Baron III

2 Spain; 3 Czechoslovakia.

Nice

Italy
Conte Giulio Borsarelli di Riffredo
—Crispa
Francesco Forquet—Capinera
Conte Alessandro Bettoni-Cazzago
—Aladino
Fernando Filipponi—Nasello

2 France; 3 Belgium; 4 Chile;
5 Czechoslovakia; 6 Portugal;
7 Poland; 8 Rumania.

Rome

Italy
Francesco Forquet—Capinera
Conte Giulio Borsarelli di Riffredo
—Crispa
Conte Alessandro Bettoni-Cazzago
—Aladino

2 Switzerland; 3 Belgium; 4 Rumania;
also ran: Poland, Czechoslovakia,
France.

Brussels

Switzerland
Louis Dégallier—Ecriture
Charley Stoffel—Corona
Jean Haecky—Severina
Pierre de Muralt—Notas

2 Italy; 3 Ireland; 4 Belgium.

Lisbon

Spain
Manuel Sillio Galan—Vaguedad
Abdon Lopez Turrion—Zapatazo
Angel Somalo Paricio—Royal
Julio Garcia Fernandez—Revistada

2 Portugal; 3 France.

Warsaw

Italy
Fernando Filipponi—Nasello
Francesco Formigli—Montebello
Mario Lombardo di Cumia—Bufalina
Ettore Bocchini—Brick

2 Poland; 3 France.

London

Great Britain 4.00
Jack Talbot-Ponsonby—Chelsea
Aylmer Cameron—Irish Eagle
William Muir—Sea Count

2 Germany, 11.00; 3 Ireland, 13.00;
4 France, 18.50; 5 Chile, 27.50.

Lucerne

Italy 14.00
Conte Alessandro Bettoni-Cazzago
—Aladino
Francesco Formigli—Montebello
Mario Lombardo di Cumia—Bufalina
Fernando Filipponi—Nasello

=2 France, Belgium, 32.50;
4 Ireland, 35.50; 5 Switzerland, 42.50.

Aachen

Italy 19.00
Mario Lombardo di Cumia—Bufalina
Francesco Formigli—Montebello
Fernando Filipponi—Nasello

2 Sweden, 24.00; 3 Switzerland, 27.00;
also ran: Germany.

Dublin

Switzerland 17.00
Hans Daetwiler—Turgi
Louis Dégallier—Notas
Charles Kuhn—Corona

2 Italy, 21.00; 3 Great Britain, 22.00;
4 Ireland, 26.00;
=5 Belgium, France, 36.00.

Boston

Germany 0.00
Harald Momm—Kampfgesell
Ernst Hasse—Derby
Hermann von Nagel—Dedo

2 USA; 3 Ireland; 4 Sweden; 5 Canada.

New York

Germany 5.50
Harald Momm—Kampfgesell
Ernst Hasse—Derby
Hermann von Nagel—Dedo

2 USA, 10.00; 3 Hungary, 16.00;
4 Ireland, 17.50;
=5 Canada, Sweden, 21.00.

Toronto

USA 0.00
Harry D. Chamberlin—Tan Bark
William B. Bradford—Suzanne
John W. Wofford—Geraldyn

2 Germany, 1.50; 3 Ireland, 5.50;
4 Canada, 10.50; 5 Sweden;
6 Hungary.

Geneva

Italy 6.00
Mario Lombardo di Cumia—Bufalina
Francesco Formigli—Suello
Conte Alessandro Bettoni-Cazzago
—Aladino
Fernando Fillipponi—Nasello

2 Belgium, 12.00; 3 Switzerland, 28.00;
4 France, 30.00.

1931

Berlin

Italy 33.00
Conte Giulio Borsarelli di Riffredo
—Crispa
Francesco Formigli—Montebello
Tommaso Lequio di Assaba—Suello
Mario Lombardo di Cumia—Bacce

2 Germany, 35.50;
3 Netherlands, 82.50;
4 Sweden, 94.50.

Nice

Switzerland
Charley Stoffel—Corona
Jean Haecky—Severina
Arnold Mettler—Séretaire
Louis Dégallier—Notas

2 France; 3 Spain; 4 Portugal; 5 Italy;
6 Poland; 7 Belgium; 8 Ireland;
9 Rumania.

Rome

Germany 8.75
Richard Sahla—Wotan
Ernst Hasse—Derby
Harald Momm—Tora

2 Italy, 15.00; 3 Belgium, 26.00;
retired, France, Rumania.

Brussels

Italy
Aldo Bacca—Lettera d'Amore
Conte Giulio Borsarelli di Riffredo
—Crispa
Francesco Formigli—Suello
Mario Lombardo di Cumia—Bufalina

2 Ireland; 3 Belgium; 4 Spain; 5 France.

Lisbon

Spain
Manuel Serrano—Cliché II
Manuel Sillio Galan—Vaguedad
Fernando Artalejo Campos—Desalino
Diego Torres Santiago—Janito

2 France; 3 Portugal.

Vienna

Switzerland 8.00, 0.00 in jump-off
Hans Simmen
Charles Kuhn
Jean Haecky
Pierre de Muralt

2 Hungary, 8.00, 4.00 in jump-off;
3 Germany, 9.25; 4 Hungary, team 2;
5 Austria.

Warsaw

Poland 32.25
Zygmunt Rucinski—Roksana
Jan Salega—Nela
Josef Trenkwald—Madzia
Kazimierz Szosland—Alli

2 France, 91.00; 3 Rumania, 118.25;
4 Switzerland, retired.

Madrid

Spain
de la Macorra—Vaguedad
José Cavanillas Prosper—Arlésienne
Nemesio Martinez Hombre—Caida
Julio Garcia Fernandez—Revistada

2 Portugal; 3 France; 4 Belgium.

London

France 13.50
Hubert Gibault—Mandarin
Auguste de Laissardière—Wednesday
Xavier Bizard—Pair

2 Netherlands, 19.00;
3 Great Britain, 21.00; 4 Ireland, 23.00;
5 Belgium, 30.00; 6 Canada, 36.50.

Lucerne

Ireland 24.00
Thomas Finlay—Moonstruck
Cyril Harty—Kilmallock
Jed O'Dwyer—Rosnaree
Dan Corry

2 Switzerland, 28.00; 3 Italy, 32.00;
4 Belgium, 62.00; retired, France,
Hungary.

Aachen

Italy
Conte Giulio Borsarelli di Riffredo
—Crispa
Conte Alessandro Bettoni-Cazzago
—Aladino
Fernando Filipponi—Nasello
Mario Lombardo di Cumia—Bufalina

2 Germany; 3 Hungary.

Dublin

Great Britain 16.00
Joe Hume Dudgeon—Standard
W. H. Muir—Sea Count
Jack Talbot-Ponsonby—Irish Eagle

2 Sweden, 21.00; 3 Ireland, 23.00;
4 Belgium, 27.00; 5 Switzerland, 30.00;
6 France, 32.00; 7 Italy, 33.00;
8 Germany, 39.00; 9 Canada, retired.

Riga

Poland 28.00
Josef Trenkwald—Madzia
Henryk Roycewicz—The Hoop
Jan Strzalkowski—Yvette
Kazimierz Szosland—Sterling

2 Estonia, 42.00; 3 Latvia, retired.

Boston

Great Britain 4.00
Jack Talbot-Ponsonby—Blue Dun
Aylmer Cameron—Irish Eagle
Mike Ansell—Standard

2 USA, 6.50; 3 Canada, 7.00;
4 France, 9.00; 5 Ireland, 9.50.

New York

USA 0.00
Carl W. Raguse—Ugly
William B. Bradford—Suzanne
Harry D. Chamberlin—Tan Bark

2 France, 3.00; 3 Canada, 6.00;
4 Great Britain, 9.00; 5 Ireland, 12.50.

Toronto

Ireland 2.00
Fred Ahern—Blarney Castle
Dan Corry—Shannon Power
Jed O'Dwyer—Turoe

2 Great Britain, 5.00; 3 USA, 6.00;
4 France, 10.50; 5 Canada, 14.00.

1932

Berlin

Germany 32.00
Ernst Hasse—Derby
Hermann von Nagel—Wotan
Gustav von Nostitz-Wallwitz
—Chinese II
Heinz Brandt—Tora

2 Netherlands, 36.00;
3 Czechoslovakia, 56.50; (4 ran).

Nice

Italy 16.50 in jump-off
Tommaso Lequio di Assaba—Ardrath
Fernando Filipponi—Nasello
Bruno Bruni—Nereide
Antonio Gutierrez—Coran

2 Portugal, retired in jump-off;
3 Belgium, 44.00; 4 France, 44.50;
5 Czechoslovakia, 49.00;
6 Spain, 61.75; 7 Turkey, 156.75;
8 Ireland, 271.00.

Rome

Germany 14.50
Heinz Brandt—Tora
Gustav von Nostitz-Wallwitz
—Chinese II
Richard Sahla—Wotan
Hermann von Nagel—Benno

2 France, 20.00; 3 Italy, 24.00.

Brussels

Italy 21.00
Conte Giulio Borsarelli di Riffredo
—Crispa
Fernando Filipponi—Nasello
Alberto Guzzinati—Ripa
Bruno Bruni—Nereide

=2 Belgium, Ireland, 28.00.
4 Switzerland, 32.00; 5 France, 33.75.

Madrid

Portugal 52.00
Luis Ivens Ferraz—Marco Visconti
Marquês do Funchal—Capucho

José Beltrão—Basquaise
Luis Mena e Silva—Whisky

2 Spain, 56.00; 3 France, 60.00.

London

France 20.00
Xavier Bizard—Arcachon
Antoine Nobili—Chérubin
Auguste de Laissardière
—Wednesday

2 Great Britain, 28.00; 3 Ireland, 40.00;
4 Belgium, 55.00.

Aachen

Germany 16.00
Harald Momm—Baccarat II
Hermann, Baron von Nagel—Benno
Richard Sahla—Wotan
Siegfried von Sydow—Abendglanz

2 Italy, 22.00; 3 Switzerland, 35.00.

Dublin

Ireland 17.00
Jed O'Dwyer—Limerick Lace
Fred Ahern—Ireland's Own
Daniel Leonard—Miss Ireland

2 France, 19.00; 3 Belgium, 31.00.

Riga

Poland 36.00
Jan Salega—Nela
Kazimierz Szosland—Donneuse
Henryk Roycewicz—The Hoop
Zygmunt Rucinski—Roksana

2 Germany, 58.00; 3 Latvia, 70.00;
4 Estonia, 88.00.

Vienna

Germany
Heinz Brandt—Tora
Ernst Hasse—Der Aar
Harald Momm—Baccarat II
Hermann, Baron von Nagel—Wotan

2 Hungary; 3 Czechoslovakia.

Boston

Ireland 4.00, 24.00 in second round
Fred Ahern—Gallow Glass
James Neylon—Kilmallock
Dan Corry—Shannon Power

2 France, 4.00, 26.00 in second round;
3 USA, 16.00; 4 Canada, eliminated.

New York

USA 4.00
Earl F. Thomson—Tan Bark
Carl W. Raguse—Ugly
John Tupper Cole—Joe Aleshire

2 France, 8.00; 3 Canada, 20.00;
4 Ireland, 24.00.

Toronto

Canada 7.00
Reginald Timmis—Red Prophet

Lawrence Hammond—Red Plume
Churchill Mann—Michael

2 USA, 10.00; 3 France; 4 Ireland.

1933

Berlin

Germany   24.00
Harald Momm—Baccarat II
Victor von Salviati—Grossfürst
Heinz Brandt—Chef
Wolfgang, Freiherr von Waldenfels
—Winzige

2 Ireland, 28.75;
3 Czechoslovakia, 48.25.

Nice

France   12.00 in jump-off
Pierre Clavé—Judex
Xavier Bizard—Arcachon
Henry Pernot du Breuil—Royal
Pierre Cavaillé—Olivette

2 Portugal, 20.00 in jump-off;
3 Spain, 24.00; 4 Ireland, 61.25;
5 Switzerland, 63.25; 6 Italy, 66.75;
7 Belgium, 80.00; 8 Poland, 92.00.

Rome

Germany   8.00
Hermann, Freiherr von Nagel—Olaf
Heinz Brandt—Tora
Richard Sahla—Wotan
Harald Momm—Baccarat II

2 Italy, 35.00; 3 Spain, 20.00;
4 Poland, 40.50; 5 Belgium, 48.00;
6 Portugal, 51.00; 7 Ireland, 68.50.

Brussels

Italy   20.00
Conte Alessandro Bettoni-Cazzago
—Nereide
Fernando Filipponi—Nasello
Ettore Bocchini—Brick
Bruno Bruni—Bufalina

2 France, 28.00; 3 Netherlands, 32.00;
4 Belgium (military team), 36.00;
5 Belgium (civilian team), 44.00;
6 Ireland, 44.00.

Warsaw

Poland   78.00
Zygmunt Rucinski—Roksana
Kazimierz Szosland—Alli
Wilhelm Lewicki—Kikimora
Severyn Kulesza—Regent

2 France, 119.50;
3 Czechoslovakia, 121.00.

Lucerne

Germany   9.50
Harald Momm—Baccarat II
Gustav von Nostitz-Wallwitz—Olaf
Heinz Brandt—Tora
Gustav Grosskreutz—Benno

2 Switzerland, 31.50;
=3 Italy, France, 32.00;
5 Ireland, 42.75; 6 Belgium, retired.

Aachen

Germany   0.00
Harald Momm—Baccarat II
Ernst Hasse—Derby
Heinz Brandt—Tora
Gustav Grosskreutz—Benno

2 Hungary, 4.00; 3 Bulgaria, retired.

Dublin

France   3.00
Jean de Tillière—Papillon XIV
Pierre Cavaillé—Olivette
Henry Pernot du Breuil—Exercice

2 Ireland, 12.00; 3 Switzerland, 43.00;
4 Netherlands, 46.00;
5 Czechoslovakia, 58.00;
6 Belgium, 113.00.

Riga

Poland   4.00
Wojciech Bilinski—Rabus
Roman Pohorecki—Olaf
Zygmunt Rucinski—Roksana
Stanislaw Czerniawski—Rezska

2 Germany, 12.00; 3 Latvia, 49.00;
4 Estonia, 74.00.

Vienna

Italy   26.00
Carlo Olivieri—Eglantine
Tommaso Lequio di Assaba—Nereide
Carlo Kechler—Coclite
Fernando Filipponi—Nasello

2 Hungary, 36.00;
3 Netherlands, 44.00.

Geneva

France   20.00
Maurice de Bartillat—Royal
Pierre Clavé—Judex
Hubert de Maupeou d'Ableiges—Saïda
Christian de Castries

2 Belgium, 24.00;
3 Netherlands, 32.00;
4 Switzerland, 48.75; 5 Italy, retired.

New York

Sweden   0.00
Ernst Hallberg—Aida
Count Gustaf von Rosen—Kornett
Herbert Sachs—Orient

2 USA, 4.00; 3 Ireland, 15.00;
4 Czechoslovakia, 41.00;
5 Canada, 43.00.

Toronto

Ireland   14.00
Dan Corry—Shannon Power
Cyril Harty—Limerick Lace
Fred Ahern—Blarney Castle

2 Sweden*, 18.00; 3 USA*, 18.00.

*Tossed a coin for second place.

1934

Berlin

Germany   24.00
Harald Momm—Baccarat II
Ernst Hasse—Derby
Heinz Brandt—Tora
Axel Holst—Egly

2 France, 36.00; 3 Ireland, 64.00.

Nice

Switzerland   8.00 in second jump-off
Pierre de Muralt—Notas
Louis Dégallier—Corona
Jean Haecky—Wexford
Hans R. Schwarzenbach
—E. Chantecler

2 Germany, 16.00 in second jump-off;
3 France, 48.00; 4 Spain, 67.00;
5 Italy, 79.25; 6 Poland, 90.75;
7 Portugal, 140.75.

Rome

Italy   35.50
Carlo Kechler—Coclite
Fernando Filipponi—Nasello
Tommaso Lequio di Assaba—Nereide
Conte Alessandro Bettoni-Cazzago
—Judex

2 Germany, 37.75;
3 Switzerland, 42.25; 4 France, 65.25;
5 Poland, eliminated;
6 Portugal, eliminated.

Madrid

France   21.00
Capt Durand—Henri IV
Pierre Clavé—Volant III
Jean de Tillière—Wednesday
Christian de Castries—Tenace

2 Spain, 29.75; 3 Portugal, retired.

Warsaw

Germany   36.00
Kurt Hasse—Olaf
Axel Holst—Egly
Heinz Brandt—Tora
Harald Momm—Baccarat II

=2 France, Poland, 75.00;
4 Latvia, 148.25.

Lisbon

Spain   52.75
José Cavanillas Prosper—Arlésienne
Fernando Artalejo Campos—Desalino
Eduardo Luiz—Desairado
Abdon Lopez Turrion—Le Cabanon

2 Portugal, 88.00; 3 France, 116.50.

London

France 3.00
Auguste de Laissardière—Espiatz
Xavier Bizard—Arcachon
Hubert de Maupeou d'Ableiges—Saïda

2 Ireland, 16.00; 3 Sweden, 19.00;
4 Great Britain, 20.00.

Amsterdam

Italy 74.75
Conte Giulio Borsarelli di Riffredo
—Crispa
Conte Alessandro Bettoni-Cazzago
—Judex
Fernando Filipponi—Nasello
Carlo Kechler—Coclite

2 Belgium, 92.00;
3 Netherlands, 172.25.

Aachen

Italy 22.00
Conte Alessandro Bettoni-Cazzago
—Judex
Mario Lombardo di Cumia—Bufalina
Carlo Kechler—Coclite
Francesco Forquet—Nereide

2 Germany, 37.75; 3 Poland, 48.50;
4 Hungary, retired.

Lucerne

France 40.00
Pierre Clavé—Volant III
Xavier Bizard—Arcachon
Christian de Castries—Tenace
Maurice de Bartillat—Welcome

2 Ireland, 55.25; 3 Italy, 58.00;
4 Switzerland, 73.75;
5 Belgium, retired.

Spa

Belgium 81.75
Edouard de la Court—Fakir
Chevalier Henry de Menten de Horne
—Musaphiki
Georges van Derton—Gigolo
Raymond Leurquin—Gulden Vlies

2 Netherlands, 94.75;
3 France, 113.75.

Dublin

Germany 31.00
Marten von Barnekow—Nicoline
Victor von Salviati—Senator
Goerdt Schlickum—Dedo

2 France, 55.00; 3 Ireland, 60.00;
4 Belgium, 72.00; also ran: Sweden,
Netherlands, Switzerland.

Riga

Poland 8.75
Stanislaw Czerniawski—Dion
Janusz Komorowski—Owoc
Zygmunt Rucinski—Reszka
Wilhelm Lewicki—Kikimora

2 Latvia, 24.00; 3 Germany, 28.00;
4 Sweden, retired; 5 Estonia, retired.

Vienna

France 4.00
Pierre Clavé—Volant III
Xavier Bizard—Arcachon
Maurice Gudin de Vallerin—Exercice
Christian de Castries—Wednesday

2 Italy, 19.25; 3 Netherlands, 32.00;
4 Hungary, 45.00; 5 Turkey, 46.00;
6 Austria, 89.25;
7 Czechoslovakia, 94.00.

Geneva

Belgium 16.00
Chevalier Henry de Menten de Horne
—Musaphiki
Georges van Derton—Gigolo
Georges Ganshof van der Meersch
—St Georges
Yves van Strydonck—Ramona

2 Italy, 19.75; 3 Switzerland, 28.00;
4 Netherlands, 36.00;
5 France, eliminated.

New York

France 4.00
Maurice de Bartillat—Saïda
Christian de Castries—Henri IV
Pierre Clavé—Welcome

2 USA, 8.00; 3 Canada, 11.00;
4 Chile, 12.00; 5 Ireland, 15.00.

Toronto

USA 9.00
William B. Bradford—Dan
Cornelius C. Jadwin—Tan Bark
Carl W. Raguse—Ugly

2 Ireland, 13.00; 3 Chile, 15.00;
4 France, 21.00; 5 Canada, 28.00.

1935

Berlin

Germany 19.00
Goerdt Schlickum—Dedo
Harald Momm—Baccarat II
Kurt Hasse—Tora
Heinz Brandt—Baron IV

2 France, 24.00.

Nice

Germany 5.50
Harald Momm—Baccarat II
Kurt Hasse—Olaf
Goerdt Schlickum—Wange
Heinz Brandt—Tora

2 Ireland, 12.00; 3 Portugal, 17.00;
4 Turkey, 26.75; 5 Italy, 28.00;
6 Belgium, 28.00; 7 Netherlands, 36.00;
8 France, 52.00; 9 Spain, 55.50;
10 Rumania, 68.00;
11 Switzerland, 97.75.

Rome

France 56.00
Xavier Bizard—Gobe Mouche
Pierre Cavaillé—Anousta
Amador de Busnel—Champagne
Maurice de Bartillat—Welcome

2 Italy, 58.50; 3 Ireland, 66.50;
4 Rumania, 67.25;
5 Netherlands, 71.50; 6 Spain, 74.00;
7 Portugal, 90.25.

Brussels

Italy 15.50
Conte Alessandro Bettoni-Cazzago
—Juno
Fernando Filipponi—Nasello
Renzo Bonivento—Ronco
Antonio Gutierrez—Intrepida

2 Belgium, 19.00; 3 Ireland, 34.00;
4 France, 36.00; 5 Switzerland, 40.00;
6 Netherlands, 40.00.

Aachen

Germany 14.00
Hermann, Freiherr von Nagel—Wotan
Gustav Grosskreutz—Harras
Ernst Hasse—Nemo
Karlo Schunck—Nelke

2 Rumania, 20.00;
3 Netherlands, 21.00; 4 Turkey, 32.00;
5 Hungary, 36.00.

Amsterdam

Germany 12.75
Heinz Brandt—Tora
Goerdt Schlickum—Fanfare
Kurt Hasse—Olaf
Harald Momm—Baccarat II

2 Ireland, 36.00;
3 Netherlands, 68.00; 4 France, 68.50;
5 Belgium, 107.25.

Budapest

Italy 19.00
Renzo Bonivento—Ronco
Antonio Gutierrez—Intrepida
Carlo Kechler—Coclite
Conte Alessandro Bettoni-Cazzago
—Judex

2 Germany, 28.00; 3 Hungary, 48.00;
4 Turkey, 102.00.

London

Great Britain 12.00
Joe Hume-Dudgeon—Goblet
Alex Cleeve—Kineton
Alec Tod—Blue Dun

2 Germany, 15.00; 3 Ireland, 16.00;
4 France, 24.00; 5 Belgium, 28.00.

Vienna

Italy 16.00
Conte Alessandro Bettoni-Cazzago
—Judex
Renzo Bonivento—Ronco   ▶

Humberto Mariles Cortés

From the mid-forties to the mid-fifties the Mexican Army jumping team was one of the most successful in the world, with wins at the 1948 Olympic Games, plus 17 Nations Cups in North America and Europe, to its credit. Much of that success can be attributed to one man: Humberto Mariles Cortés. The brilliance of his riding career was equalled only by the turbulance of his private life, which reads like a latter-day screen scenario.

Born in Chihuahua in 1913, the son of a cavalry officer, he too joined the cavalry and while still a young man was appointed riding instructor. A gifted horseman, he became increasingly influential in all equestrian matters in Mexico during the thirties and forties, taking charge of the Military Academy in 1938 and contributing to the formation of the National Riding Association for civilians in 1941. He began competing internationally before the Second World War, and was appointed captain of the Mexican Olympic team, leading his country to a resounding win at the first post-war Games in London.

The show jumping competition at those 1948 Games consisted of a one-round Nations Cup, which was also used to determine the individual medals. Rain prior to the event had rendered the going deep and slippery and the 16 obstacles, which included a double and a treble and therefore required 19 jumping efforts, caused a great deal of grief. To add to the problems, the water supply to the arena had been turned off for the weekend and could not be reconnected during the competition. The water level in the water jump and water ditches began to go down as more and more horses failed to clear them, and it was impossible to top them up again for the benefit of the competitors who were drawn towards the end. Of the 44 starters, 21 were eliminated, and only seven managed to clear the 4.50-metre water jump. This fence, number 15, was all the more problematical because it was followed by a big vertical—a classic test of controlled jumping.

When Mariles, last to go, entered the arena

he knew that he could afford just one fence down to win the individual gold medal outright. Before him only three competitors had completed the course with single-figure scores: his team-mate Rubén Uriza Castro, the Frenchman Jean d'Orgeix and Franklin F. Wing of the United States, who had all finished on 8 faults. Seemingly undeterred by the complexities of the course and the dramas and eliminations which had preceded him, Mariles rode his one-eyed horse Arete coolly and calmly round the course—so calmly in fact that it soon became apparent to the 82 000-strong crowd that he was going to incur time faults. It also became clear that this was a deliberate tactic, and one which was paying off, for he cleared the first 14 fences—including the difficult treble— with nonchalant ease. Coming to the troublesome water jump, Mariles still showed no signs of changing gear and, to the astonishment of onlookers, simply allowed Arete to pop over the little fence and splash straight into the water at the same steady canter. Because of this strategy Arete was perfectly balanced as he approached the big wall at the end of the course. He cleared it without problem and, with 2¼ time faults to add to his 4 jumping faults, finished on 6¼, thus winning the individual gold and giving the Mexican team a convincing victory over Spain and Great Britain. With this inspired piece of riding Colonel Mariles became the first—and remains the only—Mexican to win the Olympic title.

Earlier in the Games, Mariles had demonstrated his all-round horsemanship by competing in the three-day event, in which he finished 12th individually—the best performance by a member of the bronze-medal winning Mexican team.

With Mariles at its head, the Mexican team had burst upon the post-war jumping scene with wins in two of the three Nations Cups run in 1946, those at New York and Toronto. They repeated their New York success in 1947 and then, prior to the Olympics in 1948, had travelled to Europe and carried off the prestigious Rome Nations Cup, ahead of France, Italy, Ireland and Switzerland. Except for 1953, the team won one or more of the North American Nations Cups every year from 1946 to 1956. Mariles himself won the New York Grand Prix on three occasions, in 1948 and 1951 with Arete and again in 1955 riding Chihuahua II, and was four times victorious in the Toronto Championship, in 1947 on Resorte, in 1949 on Arete, in 1950 on Alteno and in 1955 on Chihuahua II. Also in 1955 he won a team gold medal in the second running of the Pan American Games, again riding Chihuahua.

Mariles' successes may well have continued for many years, had it not been for a change in his personal fortunes. The year 1955 saw the death of his friend, Manuel Avila Camacho, the former President of Mexico, whose backing had enabled Mariles to have whatever he wanted in the way of horses, staff, equipment and financial assistance. After Camacho's death the new regimes closed the equestrian schools operated by Mariles and disbanded the cavalry and thereafter Mexico's most successful rider began to drop from sight.

In 1964 came a dramatic turn of events. Mariles, by now a General, was arrested in Mexico City and charged with shooting a man fatally during a traffic dispute. He pleaded self-defence—but fled the country before he could be sentenced. In 1966 he returned to Mexico to face a 20-year prison term, though

this was later reduced to 10, and he was released in 1971. Rumour had it that he would start training international riders after his release, but events took a quite different and tragic course.

In the winter of 1972 he was arrested in France with a number of other men and charged with carrying four suitcases containing heroin. General Mariles said that he was working for the Mexican Tourist Board and denied that he knew the suitcases contained heroin. Two weeks later he was found dead in his Paris prison cell. The cause of death was given variously as a heart attack and an overdose of drugs.

Reporting his death, *The New York Times* of 17 December, 1972 said of this controversial figure of the show jumping world, 'There is no doubt that Mariles made many enemies during his lifetime. His temper was explosive and he was willing to go to almost any lengths to win.

'Still his talent was to be admired. When he was pushed into the background Mexico's fortunes began to fall in the international equestrian world. It is interesting to note that since Mariles last appeared at the National Horse Show [New York] in 1956, Mexico has won the Nations Cup just once, in 1960.'

In the years from 1961 to 1986 Mexico did not win another Nations Cup.

Colonel Humberto Mariles Cortés and the one-eyed Arete en route to victory in the 1948 Olympic Games.

Carlo Kechler—Coclite
Tommaso Lequio di Assaba—Nereide

2 France, 39.00; 3 Hungary, 64.00;
4 Turkey, 71.00; 5 Austria, 102.50.

Lucerne

Ireland   0.00
John Lewis—Limerick Lace
Fred Ahern—Ireland's Own
Jed O'Dwyer—Blarney Castle
Dan Corry—Gallowglass

2 Switzerland, 24.00;
3 Belgium, 35.00; 4 Poland, 39.00;
5 Italy, retired.

Spa

Poland   4.00
Kazimierz Szosland—Mylord
Michael Gutowski—Warszawianka
Janusz Komorowski—Wizja
Jan Mossakowski—Wenecja

2 Belgium, 20.25;
3 Netherlands, 48.50.

Dublin

Ireland   15.00
Jed O'Dwyer—Limerick Lace
Fred Ahern—Blarney Castle
Dan Corry—Miss Ireland

2 Germany, 59.00; 3 Sweden, 86.00;
4 Netherlands, 143.00.

Riga

Latvia   47.00
Ludwigs Ozols—Etimologija
Robert Jostons—Mikelis
Teodors Broks—Klaips
Gustaw Insbergs—Perkonis

2 Poland, 57.25; 3 Germany, 93.75.

Warsaw

Italy   12.00
Fernando Filipponi—Nasello
Renzo Bonivento—Ronco
Tommaso Lequio di Assaba—Bufalina
Conte Giulio Borsarelli di Riffredo
—Crispa

2 Germany, 16.00; 3 Hungary, 30.25;
4 Latvia, 32.00; 5 Poland, 34.00.

New York

Ireland   0.00, 4.00 in jump-off
Jed O'Dwyer—Limerick Lace
Dan Corry—Red Hugh
Fred Ahern—Blarney Castle
John Lewis—Glendalough

2 USA, 0.00, 12.00 in jump-off;
3 Chile, 8.00; 4 Canada, 16.00;
5 France, 16.00; 6 Netherlands, 19.00.

Toronto

Ireland   7.00
John Lewis—Glendalough
Fred Ahern—Gallow Glass

Jed O'Dwyer—Blarney Castle

2 Netherlands, 12.00; 3 Canada, 14.00;
=4 France, USA, 16.00; 6 Chile, 21.00.

1936

Berlin

Germany   8.00
Harald Momm—Baccarat II
Kurt Hasse—Tora
Marten von Barnekow—Olaf
Heinz Brandt—Baron IV

2 Poland, 33.00; 3 Italy, 50.00.

Nice

Ireland   32.50
Fred Ahern—Blarney Castle
James Neylon—Kilmallock
Dan Corry—Red Hugh
Jed O'Dwyer—Limerick Lace

2 Spain, 39.25; 3 Portugal, 49.50;
4 Poland, 53.75; 5 France, 56.00;
6 Switzerland, 88.25;
7 Czechoslovakia, 89.50.

Brussels

Netherlands   20.00
Baron I. L. D. Sirtema van
   Grovestins—Godard
Johan Greter—Trixie
Henri van Schaik—Santa Bell
Jan de Bruine—Ernica

2 Ireland, 31.00; 3 Portugal, 44.00;
4 France, 49.75; 5 Belgium, 52.00.

London

France   24.00
Capt Durand—Nelson
Xavier Bizard—Fière et Brune
Amador de Busnel—Saïda

2 Ireland, 27.00; 3 Belgium, 28.00;
4 Great Britain, 32.00.

Warsaw

Germany   16.00
Harald Momm—Baccarat II
Marten von Barnekow—Olaf
Kurt Hasse—Tora
Ernst Hasse—Derby

2 Rumania 18.25; 3 Poland, 20.00;
4 France, 24.00; 5 Latvia, 48.00.

Amsterdam

Ireland   16.00
Jed O'Dwyer—Blarney Castle
James Neylon—Miss Ireland
John Lewis—Kilmallock
Dan Corry—Limerick Lace

2 Belgium, 19.00; 3 France, 27.00;
4 Japan, 64.00; 5 Netherlands, 73.50.

Lucerne

Ireland   59.75
Jed O'Dwyer—Blarney Castle
James Neylon—Limerick Lace
Dan Corry—Red Hugh
John Lewis—Glendalough

2 France, 59.75; 3 USA, 82.50;
4 Switzerland, 95.50.

Dublin

Ireland   37.00
Jed O'Dwyer—Clontarf
John Lewis—Glendalough
Dan Corry—Red Hugh

2 Great Britain, 38.00; 3 France, 41.00;
4 Belgium, 63.00;
5 Netherlands, 135.00.

Aachen

Germany   12.00
Harald Momm—Baccarat II
Marten von Barnekow—Olaf
Kurt Hasse—Tora
Heinz Brandt—Alchimist

2 USA, 26.00; 3 Hungary, 27.00;
4 Netherlands, 36.00;
5 Rumania, 38.50; 6 Turkey, 40.00;
7 Italy, 51.75; 8 Czechoslovakia, 60.00;
9 Austria, 79.50; 10 Sweden, retired.

Riga

Poland   48.00
Janusz Komorowski—Dunkan
Severyn Kulesza—Zephir
Michael Gutowski—Warszawianka
Tadeusz Sokolowski—Zbieg

2 Latvia, 101.50; 3 Norway, retired.

Vienna

Germany   24.00
Harald Momm—Baccarat II
Kurt Hasse—Tora
Heinz Brandt—Alchimist
Marten von Barnekow—Olaf

2 Rumania, 39.75; 3 Italy, 41.50;
4 Turkey, 42.00; 5 Austria, 48.00;
6 Hungary, 59.75.

New York

Great Britain   0.00, 8.00 in first
jump-off, 3.00 in second jump-off
Sir Peter Grant-Lawson—Baby
Jack Talbot-Ponsonby—Kineton
Richard Fanshawe—Norah
Aylmer Cameron—Blue Dun

2 Ireland, 0.00, 8.00 in first jump-off,
4.00 in second jump-off; 3 USA, 0.00,
8.00 in first jump-off,
7.00 in second jump-off; 4 Chile, 0.00,
15.00 in first jump-off; 5 Canada, 4.00;
6 France, 4.00; 7 Sweden, 4.00.

Toronto

Canada   0.00, 0.00 in jump-off
Stuart Bate—Squire

Reginald Timmis—Lady Jane
Marshall Cleland—Roxana
Douglas Cleland—Dunadry

2 Great Britain, 0.00, 4.00 in jump-off;
3 USA, 0.00, 11.00 in jump-off.

1937

Berlin

Germany 4.00
Marten von Barnekow—Olaf
Kurt Hasse—Tora
Hans-Heinrich Brinckmann
—Alchimist
Harald Momm—Baccarat II

2 France, 28.75; 3 Hungary, 36.25;
4 Netherlands, 56.75.

Rome

Italy 12.25
F. Frassetto—Torno
Gerardo Conforti—Babà
Count Alessandro Bettoni-Cazzago
—Judex
Ranieri di Campello—Ronco

2 Germany, 16.25;
3 Switzerland, 53.75; 4 France, 56.00;
5 Turkey, 81.00; 6 Austria, 84.75;
7 Netherlands, retired.

Paris

Germany 33.00
Kurt Hasse—Tora
Hans-Heinrich Brinckmann
—Alchimist
Marten von Barnekow—Olaf
Harald Momm—Baccarat II

2 Ireland, 56.00; 3 France, 59.50;
4 Rumania, 68.00;
5 Switzerland, 83.00;
6 Netherlands, 96.00;
7 Turkey, 100.00; 8 Belgium, 149.50;
9 Austria, retired.

Brussels

Belgium 34.50
Henry, Chevalier de Menten de Horne
—Whisky
Raymond Leurquin—Gulden Vlies
Jean 'tSerstevens—Bilboquet
Jean Gonze—Ali Baba

2 Ireland, 45.50; 3 Rumania, 48.00;
4 France, 51.75; 5 Netherlands, 64.00.

Warsaw

Rumania 27.75
Constantin Zahei—Hunter
Constantin Apostol—Dracustie
Henri Rang—Delfis
Toma Tudoran—Pyr

2 Poland, 36.00; 3 Lavtia, 48.00.

London

Ireland 12.00
Jed O'Dwyer—Limerick Lace
Dan Corry—Red Hugh
John Lewis—Tramore Bay

=2 Germany, Belgium, 28.00;
4 Great Britain, 44.00; 5 USA, 48.00;
6 Rumania, 68.00; 7 Turkey, 85.00.

Amsterdam

France 24.00, 16.00 in jump-off
Jacques Chevallier—D'Huis
Maurice de Bartillat—Français
Jean des Roches de Chassay
—Batailleuse
André Broussaud—Epreuve

2 Ireland, 24.00, 19.00 in jump-off;
3 Netherlands, 40.00;
4 Belgium, 86.75.

Lucerne

Ireland 13.50
James Neylon—Duhallow
Fred Ahern—Ireland's Own
John Lewis—Limerick Lace
Dan Corry—Red Hugh

2 France, 17.00; 3 Italy, 29.00;
4 Switzerland, 36.25;
5 Belgium, retired.

Dublin

Ireland 17.00
Fred Ahern—Duhallow
Dan Corry—Red Hugh
Jed O'Dwyer—Limerick Lace

2 France, 41.00; 3 USA, 51.00;
4 Netherlands, 54.00;
5 Switzerland, 57.00;
6 Great Britain, eliminated.
7 Belgium, eliminated.

Aachen

Ireland 24.00
John Lewis—Limerick Lace
Fred Ahern—Ireland's Own
John Stack—Red Hugh
George Heffernan—Duhallow

2 Germany, 32.00; 3 USA, 36.75;
4 Rumania, 44.00; 5 Italy, 52.00;
6 Hungary, 68.50; 7 Belgium, 86.00;
8 Austria, retired.

Riga

France 44.00
Xavier Bizard—Apollon
André Broussaud—Galopin
Jacques Chevallier—Castagnette
Amador de Busnel—Choquine

2 Poland, 44.00 (Poland declined a
jump-off); 3 Sweden, 51.00;
4 Latvia, 52.50.

Vienna

Germany 8.00
Harald Momm—Alchimist
Kurt Hasse—Tora

Hans-Heinrich Brinckmann—Baron IV
Marten von Barnekow—Olaf

2 Italy, 23.00; 3 Hungary, 60.00.

New York

Canada 12.00
Marshall Cleland—Roxana
Reginald Timmis—Lady Jane
Douglas Cleland—Flying Poet
Stuart Bate—Squire

2 Belgium, 15.00; 3 Ireland, 20.00*;
4 USA, 20.00*: 5 Netherlands, 28.00.

*Third place decided by tossing a coin.

Toronto

Netherlands 0.00
Baron I. L. D. Sirtema van Grovestins
—Isard
Charles Pahud de Mortanges
—Madel Wie Du
Baron I. L. D. Sirtema van Grovestins
—Juno
Charles Pahud de Mortanges—Godard

2 Canada, 3.00; 3 USA, 4.00;
=4 Ireland, Belgium, 8.00.

1938

Geneva

Germany 6.75
Harald Momm—Alchimist
Max Huck—Olaf
Hans-Heinrich Brinckmann—Oberst II
Kurt Hasse—Tora

2 France, 48.00; 3 Belgium, 66.50;
4 Switzerland, 83.00.

Nice

Ireland 32.25
John Stack—Red Hugh
Dan Corry—Duhallow
John Lewis—Limerick Lace
Fred Ahern—Ireland's Own

2 France, 47.00; 3 Netherlands, 60.00;
4 Poland, 72.00; 5 Rumania, 82.75;
6 Turkey, 95.00; 7 Portugal, 104.00.

Rome

Turkey 35.75
Cevat Kula—Gutchlu
Cevat Gürkan—Yildiz
Saim Polatkan—Tchakal
Eyup Oncü—Unal

2 Germany, 36.75; 3 Ireland, 42.00;
4 Italy, 43.50; 5 Rumania, 61.50.

Brussels

Germany 20.50
Harald Momm—Alchimist
Max Huck—Olaf
Hans-Heinrich Brinckmann—Oberst II
Kurt Hasse—Tora

2 Belgium, 52.50;
3 Netherlands, 76.00;
4 Ireland, 144.25.

Warsaw

Poland 22.75
Janusz Komorowski—Zbieg II
Bronislaw Skulicz—Dunkan
Roman Pohorecki—Abd-El-Krim
Aleksander Rylke—Bimbus

2 Germany, 32.00; 3 Turkey, 54.00;
4 Belgium, 58.00; 5 France, 59.00;
6 Rumania, 60.75.

Bucharest

Belgium 22.25
Ferdinand Poswick—Acrobate
Yves van Strydonck—Ramona
Jean Gonze—Ali Baba
Henry, Chevalier de Menten de Horne
—Whisky

2 France, 27.00; 3 Rumania, 36.75;
4 Poland, 40.00; 5 Italy, 42.00;
6 Germany, 48.00.

London

Great Britain 12.00
John Friedberger—Derek
Jack Talbot-Ponsonby—Big Sweep
Richard Sheppard—Blue Steel

2 Ireland, 28.00; 3 France, 52.00;
4 Belgium, 56.00; 5 Portugal, 64.00.

Lucerne

France 4.00
Pierre de Maupeou d'Ableiges
—Vindex
Jacques Chevallier—D'Huis
Amador de Busnel—Apollon
Maurice de Bartillat—Castagnette

2 Ireland, 11.25; 3 Switzerland, 33.50;
4 Czechoslovakia, 63.25.

Amsterdam

Germany 16.00
Harald Momm—Alchimist
Hans-Heinrich Brinckmann—Baron IV
Kurt Hasse—Tora
Fritz Weidemann—Olaf

2 Netherlands, 20.00; 3 Ireland, 24.00;
4 Belgium, 214.75.

Dublin

Ireland 16.00
Fred Ahern—Blarney Castle
Dan Corry—Duhallow
Jed O'Dwyer—Limerick Lace

2 Germany, 24.00; 3 France, 29.00;
4 Great Britain, 37.00;
5 Netherlands, 59.00; 6 Canada, 93.00.

Aachen

Rumania 20.00
Ioan Epure—Delfis
Felix Topescu—Fulger

Constantin Zahei—Hunter
Toma Tudoran—Pyr

2 Germany, 28.00; 3 Belgium, 41.50;
4 Ireland, 48.00; 5 Netherlands, 71.50;
6 Italy, 132.75; 7 Hungary, 136.75;
8 Canada, retired.

New York

Ireland 0.00
Dan Corry—Duhallow
John Stack—Blarney Castle
James Neylon—Clontarf
Dan Corry—Tramore Bay

2 Mexico, 4.00*; 3 USA, 4.00*;
4 Canada, 8.00; 5 Chile, 20.00;
6 Cuba, 57.00.

*Placing decided by a jump-off.

Toronto

Ireland 9.00
John Stack—Blarney Castle
Dan Corry—Duhallow
James Neylon—Owen Roe
Dan Corry—Tramore Bay

2 USA, 11.00; 3 Chile; also ran:
Mexico, Brazil, Canada.

1939

Berlin

Germany 18.00
Harald Momm—Alchimist
Kurt Hasse—Tora
Hans-Heinrich Brinckmann—Baron IV
Max Huck—Artur

2 Italy, 24.50; 3 Poland, 25.25;
4 France, 40.00; 5 Belgium, 56.50;
6 Sweden, 131.50.

Nice

France 36.00, 0.00 in jump-off
Jacques Chevallier—Halte Là
Lt de Vries—Honduras
Maurice de Bartillat—Cambronne
Pierre de Maupeou d'Ableiges—Idylle

2 Great Britain, 36.00, 4.00 in jump-off;
3 Belgium, 43.25; 4 Ireland, 47.00;
5 Turkey, 54.50; 6 Poland, 56.00;
7 Latvia; 8 Portugal, 76.00;
9 Rumania, 78.00.

Rome

Italy 20.00
Conte Alessandro Bettoni-Cazzago
—Adigrat
Fernando Filipponi—Nasello
Gerardo Conforti—Ronco
Antonio Gutierrez—Torno

2 Germany, 28.00; 3 Poland, 40.00;
4 Rumania, 69.75; 5 Turkey, 80.00;
6 Great Britain, 84.25;
7 Belgium, 84.75; 8 Portugal, 91.00.

Brussels

Belgium 8.00
Jean 'tSerstevens—Bilboquet
Ferdinand Poswick—Acrobate
Henry, Chevalier de Menten de Horne
—Whisky
Jean Gonze

2 Ireland, 19.00; 3 Italy, 29.00;
4 France, 31.00.

Warsaw

Rumania 20.25
Felix Topescu—Jolca
Constantin Zahei—Graur
Alex Purcherea—Haiduc
Ioan Epure—Carpen

2 Poland, 24.00; 3 Sweden, 46.00.

Bucharest

Rumania 19.00
Felix Topescu—Fulger
Constantin Zahei—Dracul Stie
Alex Purcherea—Haiduc
Ioan Epure—Carpen

2 Poland, 24.00; 3 Sweden, 46.00.

London

Great Britain 12.00
Nat Kindersley—Maguire
Capel Brunker—Cark Clever Vixen
W. F. Butler—Big Sweep

2 France, 20.00; 3 Italy, 27.00;
4 Ireland, 28.00; 5 Belgium, 44.00.

Amsterdam

Germany
Fritz Weidemann—Alant
Kurt Hasse—Tora
Hans-Heinrich Brinckmann—Oberst II
Max Huck—Artur

Lucerne

Ireland 16.50
Jed O'Dwyer—Limerick Lace
Fred Ahern—Ireland's Own
James Neylon—Duhallow
John Lewis—Kilmallock

2 Germany, 25.75; 3 France, 36.25;
4 Switzerland, 46.50; 5 Belgium, 64.50;
retired, Italy, Hungary.

Dublin

France 16.00
Jacques Chevallier—Jacynthe
Max Fresson—Homlette
Maurice de Bartillat—Cambronne

2 Ireland, 19.00; 3 Germany, 21.00;
4 Great Britain, 31.00;
5 Switzerland, 35.00; 6 Belgium, 66.00.

Aachen

Germany 9.00
Harald Momm—Alchimist
Fritz Weidemann—Alant
Max Huck—Artur

Largely through the influence of one man, Humberto Mariles Cortés (right) Mexico became a force to be reckoned with on the international circuit in the 1940s and 1950s. He is pictured here with Captain Ramiro Palafox (left) and Major Armando Villareal Mayo at the National Horse Show, New York, in 1940. (The Illustrated London News)

Hans-Heinrich Brinckmann—Oberst II

2 Rumania, 87.00;
3 Switzerland, 96.50; 4 Hungary;
5 Belgium; 6 Latvia.

New York

USA 12.00
Frank S. Henry—Renzo
Franklin F. Wing—Sir Conrad
Royce Drake—Dinger
Carl W. Raguse—Dakota

2 Chile, 16.00; 3 Mexico, 24.00.

1940

Rome

Germany 8.00
Harald Momm—Alchimist
Hans-Heinrich Brinckmann—Oberst II
Ernst Hasse—Notar
Fritz Weidemann—Alant

2 Italy, 12.00; 3 Rumania, 32.00;
4 Switzerland, 41.50; 5 Hungary, 71.00.

New York

USA 0.00
Marshall W. Frame—Dinger
Frank S. Henry—Dakota
Franklin F. Wing—Democrat
Royce Drake—King-Hi

2 Mexico, 16.00; 3 Cuba, 36.50;
4 Chile, 40.00.

1941

New York

USA 0.00, 8.00 in jump-off
Frank S. Henry—Louisita
Henri A. Luebbermann—Smacko
Franklin F. Wing—Democrat

Marshall W. Frame

2 Cuba, 0.00, 16.00 in jump-off;
3 Peru, eliminated.

1946

Dublin

Ireland 29.00
Dan Corry—Antrim Glens
John Stack—Tramore Bay
John Lewis—Clontibret

2 France, 36.00; 3 Sweden, eliminated.

New York

Mexico 0.00, 4.00 in jump-off
Humberto Mariles Cortés—Resorte
Raoul Campero—Hatuey
Victor Saucedo Carrillo—Michoacano
Alberto Valdés Ramos—Chihuahua

2 USA, 0.00, 15.00 in jump-off;
3 Peru, eliminated.

Toronto

Mexico
Humberto Mariles Cortés
Raoul Campero
Alberto Valdés Ramos
Victor Saucedo Carrillo

2 USA; 3 Peru.

1947

Nice

France 32.00
Jean de Tillière—Nankin
Pierre Jonquères d'Oriola—Marquis III
Max Fresson—Saboulard
Comte Pierre de Maupeou d'Ableiges
—Sagitta

=2 Switzerland, Ireland, 64.00;
4 Great Britain, 87.75;
5 Czechoslovakia, eliminated.

Rome

Italy 39.75
Conte Alessandro Bettoni-Cazzago
—Uranio
Gerardo Conforti—Fabro
Alessandro Perrone—Bambi
Piero d'Inzeo—Tulipano

2 Ireland, 67.50; 3 Great Britain, 75.50;
4 USA, 153.00.

Lucerne

France 12.00
Max Fresson—Décamètre
Comte Pierre de Maupeou d'Ableiges
—Sagitta
Pierre Jonquères d'Oriola—Marquis III
Maurice Gudin de Vallerin—Nankin

2 Ireland, 24.00; 3 Switzerland, 40.25;
4 Italy, 79.25.

London

France 31.00
Pierre Jonquères d'Oriola
—Marquis III
Jean de Tillière—Nankin
Comte Pierre de Maupeou d'Ableiges
—Sagitta
Chevalier Jean d'Orgeix—Kama

=2 Ireland, Italy 36.00;
4 Great Britain, 40.00;
5 Belgium.

Ostend

France 31.00
Pierre Jonquères d'Oriola—Marquis III
Max Fresson—Nankin
Comte Pierre de Maupeou d'Ableiges
—Sagitta
Chevalier Jean d'Orgeix
—Sucre de Pomme

=2 Great Britain, Switzerland, 48.00;
4 Belgium, 58.00.

Dublin

Great Britain 19.00
Arthur Carr—Notar
Henry Nicoll—Pepper Pot
Alec Scott—Lucky Dip

2 Ireland, 34.00; 3 France, 37.00;
4 Switzerland, 39.00; 5 Sweden, 56.00;
6 Italy, 72.00.

Blackpool

Sweden 52.00
Karl-Åke Hultberg—Ismed
Stig Holm—Grim
Tor Eliasson—Grand Prix
Greger Lewenhaupt—Orkan

2 Great Britain, 80.50; 3 Italy, 92.00;
4 Ireland, 99.00.

New York

Mexico 4.75 in jump-off
Alberto Valdés Ramos—Arete
Rubén Uriza Castro—Hatuey
Humberto Mariles Cortés—Resorte
Victor Saucedo Carrillo—Poblano

=2 USA, Ireland, 8.00 in jump-off;
4 Canada.

Toronto

USA
Franklin F. Wing—Democrat
Frank S. Henry—Roll-on
Charles Symroski—Swizzlestick
Jonathan Burton—Totilla

Geneva

Italy 17.75
Gerardo Conforti—Encomiabile
Raimondo d'Inzeo—Magnifico
Alessandro Perrone—Marco IV
Piero d'Inzeo—Furore

2 France, 28.00; 3 Switzerland, 78.25;
4 Belgium, 231.50.

1948

Rome

Mexico 22.50
Alberto Valdés Ramos—Chihuahua
Raoul Campero—Jarocho
Rubén Uriza Castro—Hatuey
Humberto Mariles Cortés—Arete

2 France, 36.75; 3 Italy, 39.25;
retired, Ireland, Switzerland.

Lisbon

Portugal 28.00
Helder de Souza Martins—Optus
João E. Correia Barrento—Alcoa
José Carvalhosa—Tete
Henrique Callado—Xerez

2 Spain, 40.00; 3 France, 56.00.

Courtrai

France
Pierre Cavaillé—Marquis III
Comte Pierre de Maupeou d'Ableiges
—La Ferté
Pierre Boulangeat—Nasilleur
Max Fresson—Saboulard

2 Belgium; 3 Netherlands;
4 Great Britain.

Lucerne

USA 26.50
Franklin F. Wing—Democrat
John Russell—Air Mail
Charles Symroski—Swizzlestick
Andrew Frierson—Rascal

2 Mexico, 28.00; 3 Great Britain, 36.00;
4 Switzerland, 48.25; 5 Italy, 49.25;
6 Ireland, 88.00.

Vichy

France 21.00
Pierre Jonquères d'Oriola—Marquis III
Comte Pierre de Maupeou d'Ableiges
—Nankin
Chevalier Jean d'Orgeix
—Sucre de Pomme
Max Fresson—Sagitta

2 Mexico, 31.50; 3 Netherlands, 96.50;
4 Italy, retired.

London

USA 7.00
Andrew Frierson—Rascal
Charles Symroski—Nipper
John Russell—Air Mail
Franklin F. Wing—Totilla

2 Spain, 8.00; 3 Great Britain, 12.00;
4 France, 20.00; 5 Sweden, 23.25;
6 Italy, 40.75; 7 Turkey, 64.50.

Dublin

USA 32.00
John Russell—Air Mail
Charles Anderson—Riem
Charles Symroski—Nipper
Franklin F. Wing—Democrat

=2 Great Britain, France, 48.00;
4 Sweden, 55.00; 5 Ireland, 60.00.

Rotterdam

Netherlands
Joachim Joseph Gruppelaar
—Random Harvest
Ernest van Loon—Michou
Jacob Rijks—Romanichel
J. Piet Vos—Franklin D

2 Belgium; 3 Great Britain; 4 Turkey.

Harrisburg

Mexico 0.00
Humberto Mariles Cortés—Arete
Rubén Uriza Castro—Hatuey
Raoul Campero—Chihuahua

2 France, 3.75; 3 Canada, 12.50.

New York

Mexico 0.00, 0.00 in jump-off
Humberto Mariles Cortés—Arete
Rubén Uriza Castro—Hatuey
Victor Saucedo Carrillo—Poblano
Alberto Valdés Ramos—Chihuahua

2 France, 0.00, 12.00 in jump-off;
3 Canada,

Toronto

France 3.00
Pierre Cavaillé—Marquis III
Comte Pierre de Maupeou d'Ableiges
—La Ferté
Guy Lefrant—Sagitta
Max Fresson—Décamètre

2 Mexico, 4.00; 3 Canada, 8.00.

1949

Cairo

France
Bernard Chevallier
Max Fresson
Pierre de Maupeou d'Ableiges

Nice

Spain 52.00
José Navarro Morenes—Quorum
Jaime Garcia Cruz—Bizarro
Marcelino Gavilán y Ponce de Léon
—Foragido
Joaquin Nogueras Marquez—Frizar

2 Great Britain, 84.75;
3 France, 103.75; 4 Sweden, 115.00.

Rome

France 36.00
Chevalier Jean d'Orgeix
—Sucre de Pomme
Max Fresson—Nankin
Pierre de Maupeou d'Ableiges
—The Rat d'Asturies
Pierre Jonquères d'Oriola—Marquis III

2 Italy, 44.00; 3 Sweden, 48.00;
4 Great Britain, 52.00; 5 Spain, 63.50;
6 Ireland, 73.00.

Lisbon

Spain 60.00
José Navarro Morenes—Quorum
Pedro Dominguez Manjon—Bohemio
Marcelino Gavilán y Ponce de Léon
—Foragido
Joaquin Nogueras Marquez—Frizar

2 Portugal, 64.00; 3 France, 80.00.

Paris

France 39.00
Chevalier Jean d'Orgeix
—Sucre de Pomme
Max Fresson—Nankin
Bernard Chevallier—Riloo
Pierre Jonquères d'Oriola—Marquis III

2 Great Britain, 43.75; 3 USA, 44.50;
4 Portugal, 74.75; 5 Belgium, retired.

London

Great Britain 23.00
Harry Llewellyn—Foxhunter
Duggie Stewart—Kilgeddin
Wilf White—Talisman

Brian Butler—Tankard

2 Ireland, 32.00; 3 Netherlands, 95.00;
4 France, retired.

Dublin

Ireland 37.00
Michael Tubridy—Lough Neagh
Colin O'Shea—Rostrevor
William Mullins—Bruree
Dan Corry—Clonakilty

2 France, 47.00; 3 Great Britain, 53.00;
4 USA, 67.00.

Ostend

France
Chevalier Jean d'Orgeix—Marquis III
Max Fresson—Nankin
Bernard Chevallier—Tourbillon
Fortuné de la Sayette
—Princess d'Eternes

2 Belgium; 3 Netherlands;
4 Great Britain.

Le Zoute

France 24.00
Pierre Cavaillé—Marquis III
Max Fresson—Nankin
Bernard Chevallier—Tourbillon
Fortuné de la Sayette
—Princess d'Eternes

2 Great Britain, 27.50;
3 Belgium, 59.00;
4 Netherlands, 108.00.

Rotterdam

France 20.00
Pierre Cavaillé—Marquis III
Max Fresson
Bernard Chevallier—Tourbillon
Fortuné de la Sayette

2 Netherlands, 36.00;
3 Sweden, 55.25;
4 Great Britain, 84.50.

Harrisburg

Ireland 12.00
Michael Tubridy—Bruree
Colin O'Shea—Rostrevor
Dan Corry—Clare
William Mullins—Lough Neagh

2 Chile, 16.00; 3 Mexico, 17.50;
4 Canada, 24.00.

New York

Mexico 3.25
Humberto Mariles Cortés—Arete
Rubén Uriza Castro—Hatuey
Alberto Valdés Ramos—Chihuahua
Joaquin d'Harcourt—Jarocho

2 Ireland, 4.00; 3 Canada, 8.00;
4 Chile, 16.00.

Toronto

Mexico 0.00
Humberto Mariles Cortés—Arete

Rubén Uriza Castro—Hatuey
Alberto Valdés Ramos—Chihuahua
Joaquin d'Harcourt—Resorte

2 Ireland, 4.00; 3 Canada, 8.00.

Geneva

Great Britain 20.50
Wilf White—Nizefela
Harry Llewellyn—Kilgeddin
Brian Butler—Tankard
Harry Llewellyn—Foxhunter

2 France, 28.00; 3 Italy, 41.50;
4 Switzerland, 59.75; 5 Sweden, 66.25;
6 Belgium, 116.50.

1950

Cairo

France 24.25
Pierre Cavaillé—Marquis III
Bertrand du Breuil—Tourbillon
Charles de Couët de Lory—Ukase
Pierre de Maupeou d'Ableiges
—Rat d'Asturies

2 Italy, 42.25; 3 Egypt, 52.50.

Nice

Ireland 41.75
Michael Tubridy—Bruree
Louis Magee—Clontibret
Colin O'Shea—Ormonde
William Mullins—Lough Neagh

2 Spain, 45.50;
=3 France, Netherlands, 56.00;
5 Switzerland, 80.00; 6 Italy, 84.25.

Rome

Italy 24.25
Raimondo d'Inzeo—Uranio II
Piero d'Inzeo—Destino
Alessandro Perrone—Oriur
Luciano Ambrosio—Furore

2 France, 27.25; 3 Chile, 29.50;
4 Ireland, 42.00; 5 Switzerland, 45.75.

Madrid

Chile 30.50
Hernan Vigil-Simpson—Chileno
Alberto Larraguibel—Cacique
Ricardo Echeverria—Cueca
Pelayo Izurieta—Allipen

2 Spain, 34.25; 3 Portugal, 44.00.

Lucerne

Great Britain 8.00
Guy Wathen—Strathmore
Peter Robeson—Craven A
Brian Butler—Tankard
Harry Llewellyn—Foxhunter

2 France, 12.25; 3 Ireland, 13.50;
4 Chile, 24.00; 5 Italy, 36.00;
6 Switzerland, 36.75.

Vichy

France 20.00
Bertrand du Breuil—Tourbillon
Chevalier Jean d'Orgeix
—Sucre de Pomme
Pierre Jonquères d'Oriola—Marquis III
Bertrand du Breuil—Nankin

2 Great Britain, 44.00; 3 Chile, 56.00.

London

Great Britain 15.00
Guy Wathen—Strathmore
Wilf White—Nizefela
Brian Butler—Tankard
Harry Llewellyn—Foxhunter

2 Ireland, 27.00; 3 Spain, 28.00;
4 France, 36.00; 5 Sweden, 44.00.

Dublin

Great Britain 17.00
Michael Weber—Night Bird
Peter Robeson—Craven A
Henry Nicoll—Pepper Pot
Harry Llewellyn—Foxhunter

2 France, 27.00; 3 Spain, 31.00;
4 Italy, 40.00; 5 Ireland, 42.00;
6 Sweden, 51.00;
7 Switzerland, retired.

Rotterdam

Belgium 33.00
Guy du Bois—Billericay
Raymond Moonens—Dolly
R. Nève de Mévergnies—Samba
Charles de Selliers de Moranville
—Sea Prince

2 Netherlands, 50.00;
3 Great Britain, 51.50;
4 Denmark, 68.50; 5 Sweden, retired.

Bilbao

Spain
Jaime Garcia Cruz—Quoniam
Joaquin Nogueras Marquez—Frizar
Marcelino Gavilán y Ponce de Léon
—Bizarro
José Navarro Morenes—Quorum

2 France; 3 Portugal.

Harrisburg

Mexico 1.00
Joaquin d'Harcourt—Jalisco
Roberto Vinals Contreras—Alteno
Eva Valdes—Arete

2 USA, 1.25; 3 Great Britain, 9.00;
4 Ireland, 10.25; 5 Chile, 12.75;
6 Canada, 37.50.

New York

USA 8.00
Arthur McCashin—Paleface
Norma Matthews—Country Boy
Carol Durand—Reno Kirk

2 Mexico, 11.00; 3 Great Britain, 12.00;
4 Ireland, 20.00.

Toronto

USA 0.00, 4.00 in jump-off
Arthur McCashin—Paleface
Norma Matthews—Country Boy
Carol Durand—Reno Kirk

=2 Great Britain, Mexico, 0.00,
12.00 in jump-off; 4 Ireland; 5 Canada;
6 Chile.

1951

Cairo

France 8.50
Pierre Jonquères d'Oriola—Marquis III
Bertrand du Breuil—Tourbillon
Charles de Couët de Lory—Ukase
Comte Pierre de Maupeou d'Ableiges
—Rat d'Asturies

2 Egypt, 21.25; 3 Italy, 37.00;
4 Belgium, 54.00; 5 Turkey, 70.00.

Nice

Spain 32.00
Joaquin Nogueras Marquez—Frizar
Manuel Ordovas Gonzales—Bohemio
Jaime Garcia Cruz—Quoniam
José Navarro Morenes—Quorum

2 Great Britain, 44.25; 3 France, 52.00;
4 Portugal, 60.00; 5 Ireland, 84.00;
6 Netherlands, 99.00.

Rome

Italy 15.00
Gianni Serpi—Giua
Piero d'Inzeo—Brando
Raimondo d'Inzeo—Destino
Alessandro Perrone—Oriur

=2 France, Great Britain, 16.00;
4 Spain, 23.00; 5 Ireland, 43.00;
6 Netherlands, 49.50; 7 Egypt, 51.00.

Madrid

Spain 12.00
Manuel Ordovas Gonzales—Bohemio
Jaime Garcia Cruz—Quoniam
Joaquin Nogueras Marquez—Frizar
Manuel Ordovas Gonzales—Quorum

2 France, 20.00;
=3 Great Britain, Portugal, 26.00.

Vichy

France
Pierre Jonquères d'Oriola—Aiglonne
Bertrand du Breuil—Tourbillon
Charles de Couët de Lory—Nankin
Chevalier Jean d'Orgeix—Arlequin D

2 Italy; 3 Belgium.

London

Great Britain 0.00
Alan Oliver—Red Star II
Edward Holland-Martin—Aherlow
Wilf White—Nizefela
Harry Llewellyn—Foxhunter

2 Italy, 12.00; 3 Spain, 31.00;
4 Ireland, 39.25.

Dublin

Great Britain 30.00
Andrew Massarella—The Monarch
Edward Holland-Martin—Aherlow
Peter Robeson—Craven A
Harry Llewellyn—Foxhunter

2 Ireland, 44.00; 3 Spain, 50.00;
4 Italy, 54.00.

Le Zoute

Netherlands 36.25
Jacob, Baron van Lynden
—Compétente
Tony Timmer—Zwarte Piet
Wiel Hendrickx—Bijou
Jacob Rijks—Romanichel

2 Great Britain, 36.75; 3 France, 41.25;
4 Belgium, eliminated.

Rotterdam

Great Britain 24.00
Andrew Massarella—The Monarch
Duggie Stewart—Bones
Henry Nicoll—Pepper Pot
Harry Llewellyn—Foxhunter

2 France, 26.25; 3 Netherlands, 48.00;
4 Switzerland, 68.00.

Harrisburg

Canada 12.00
Thomas Gayford—Skip Across
Robert Ballard—Reject
Charles Baker—Star Clift

2 USA, 16.00; 3 Mexico, 21.75;
4 Brazil, 23.00; 5 Ireland, 34.50.

New York

Mexico 8.00
Humberto Mariles Cortés—Cordoves
Victor Saucedo Carrillo—Resorte II
Rubén Uriza Castro—Arete

2 Ireland, 12.00; 3 USA, 16.00;
4 Canada, 20.00; 5 Brazil, 36.00.

Toronto

Ireland 0.00
Michael Tubridy—Glandore
Louis Magee—Red Castle
Kevin Barry—Ballyneety

2 USA, 4.50; 3 Mexico, 5.00;
4 Brazil, 10.75; 5 Canada, 15.25.

Geneva

France 12.00
Guy Lefrant—Marquis III
Chevalier Jean d'Orgeix—Arlequin D
Bertrand du Breuil—Tourbillon
Pierre Jonquères d'Oriola—Aiglonne

2 Italy, 27.00; 3 Switzerland, 32.00;
4 Spain, 48.00; 5 Great Britain, 59.00;
6 Sweden, 74.50; 7 Ireland, 148.00.

1952

Nice

France 4.25
Chevalier Jean d'Orgeix—Arlequin D
Guy Lefrant—Vézelise
Pierre Jonquères d'Oriola—Aiglonne
Bertrand du Breuil—Tourbillon

2 Spain, 24.00; 3 Ireland, 32.00;
4 Chile, 36.75; 5 Portugal, 64.00.

The British team which won the Prince of Wales Cup at White City in 1951 (from left), Harry Llewellyn on Foxhunter, Wilf White on Nizefela, 'Ruby' Holland-Martin on Aherlow and Alan Oliver on Red Star II. (BBC Hulton Picture Library)

Rome

Italy 8.00
Raimondo d'Inzeo—Litargirio
Antonio Gutierrez—Serena
Salvatore Oppes—Leila de Samassi
Piero d'Inzeo—Uruguay

2 France, 15.00; 3 Spain, 20.00;
4 Mexico, 20.25; 5 Ireland, 20.50;
6 Argentina, 21.25; 7 Chile, 24.25;
8 Switzerland, 64.25; 9 Belgium, 66.25;
10 Germany, retired.

Madrid

Mexico 8.00
Mario Becerril—Tamaulipas
Roberto Vinals Contreras—Alteno
Victor Saucedo Carrillo—Resorte II
Humberto Mariles Cortés—Petrolero

2 Portugal, 31.00; 3 Italy, 39.00;
4 Chile, 43.00; 5 Spain, 44.00;
6 Ireland, 48.00.

Lucerne

Argentina 00.50
Orfilio Bertiller—Mi Moro
Jorge Canaves—Discutido
Argentino Molinuevo, Sen.—Ramito
Julio Sagasta—Don Juan

2 Great Britain, 4.00; 3 Ireland, 8.00;
4 Italy, 16.25; 5 Switzerland, 20.00;
6 Egypt, 60.00.

Vichy

France 27.75
Guy Lefrant—Vézelise
Chevalier Jean d'Orgeix—Arlequin D
Bertrand du Breuil—Tourbillon
Pierre Jonquères d'Oriola—Ali Baba

2 Mexico, 58.50; 3 Brazil, 61.50;
4 Egypt, 93.25; 5 Belgium, 159.50.

Stockholm

Argentina 28.00
Argentino Molinuevo, Sen.—Discutido
Sergio Dellacha—Santa Fe
Julio Sagasta—Bon Vin
Jorge Canaves—Ramito

2 FRG, 31.00; 3 France, 32.00;
4 Mexico, 36.00; 5 Italy, 39.00;
6 Brazil, 70.00; 7 Sweden, 96.00.

Aachen

Italy 40.00, 8.00 in jump-off
Piero d'Inzeo—Brando
Salvatore Oppes—Macezio
Raimondo d'Inzeo—Litargirio
Piero d'Inzeo—Uruguay

2 FRG, 40.00, 12.00 in jump-off;
3 Mexico, 43.50; 4 Argentina, 44.25;
5 Netherlands, retired.

London

Great Britain 4.00
Pat Smythe—Tosca
Harry Llewellyn—Foxhunter

Wilf White—Nizefela
Peter Robeson—Craven A

2 USA, 29.00; 3 Ireland, 48.00.

Ostend

Argentina 24.00
Sergio Dellacha—Bon Vin
Orfilio Bertiller—Discutido
Argentino Molinuevo, Sen.—Santa Fe
Julio Sagasta—Ramito

2 Italy, 36.00; 3 France, 44.00;
4 Mexico, 57.75; 5 Belgium, 58.00.

Rotterdam

Argentina 30.00
Sergio Dellacha—Bon Vin
Orfilio Bertiller—Discutido
Argentino Molinuevo, Sen.—Santa Fe
Julio Sagasta—Ramito

2 Mexico, 36.50; 3 Belgium, 44.00;
4 Netherlands, 49.00;
5 Great Britain, 49.50.

Bilbao

Spain 28.00
Joaquin Nogueras Marquez
—Mister B
Pedro Dominguez Manjon—Vitamen
Manuel Ordovas Gonzales—Bohemio
Jaime Garcia Cruz—Quorum

2 France, 28.75; 3 Germany, 36.00.

Harrisburg

Mexico 8.00
Joaquin d'Harcourt—Cordoves
Humberto Mariles Cortés—Petrolero
Victor Saucedo Carrillo—Acapulco

2 USA, 23.00; 3 France, 27.50;
4 Ireland, 60.75.

New York

Mexico 4.00
Joaquin d'Harcourt—Cordoves
Humberto Mariles Cortés—Petrolero
Victor Saucedo Carrillo—Acapulco

2 France, 7.00; 3 USA, 8.00;
4 Ireland, 12.00; 5 Canada, 20.25.

Toronto

France
Bertrand du Breuil—Tourbillon
Guy Lefrant—Ukase
Pierre Jonquères d'Oriola—Ali-Baba

2 Ireland; 3 USA; 4 Canada.

1953

Nice

France 12.00
Guy Lefrant—Ali-Baba
Georges Calmon—Bienvenue
Bertrand du Breuil—Tourbillon

Pierre Jonquères d'Oriola—Voulette

=2 Spain, Great Britain, 28.00;
4 Portugal, 48.00; 5 Italy, 60.00.

Rome

Italy 20.50
Salvatore Oppes—Nangis
Natalie Perrone—Voltigeur
Piero d'Inzeo—Uruguay
Raimondo d'Inzeo—Merano

2 FRG, 40.25; 3 France, 44.50;
4 Great Britain, 87.00.

Madrid

Portugal 20.50
Eduardo Netto de Almeida
—Impecavel
José Carvalhosa—Licorme
João Cruz-Azevedo—Rama
Henrique Callado—Caramulo

2 FRG, 24.00; 3 Spain, 38.00.

Lisbon

Portugal 20.00
Eduardo Netto de Almeida
—Impecavel
Antonio Pereira de Almeida
—Florentina
Henrique Callado—Caramulo
José Fernando Cavaleiro—Cara Linda

2 Spain, 60.75; 3 France, 89.25.

Spa

Belgium 51.75
Charles de Selliers de Moranville
—Cambridge
R. Nève de Mévergnies—Samba
Georges Poffé—Hicamboy
Georges van Derton—Roland

2 France, 103.00;
3 Netherlands, 107.75; 4 FRG, 171.25;
5 Great Britain, retired.

Aachen

Spain 47.75
Angelo Alonso Martin—Brise Brise
Manuel Ordovas Gonzales—Bohemio
Joaquin Nogueras Marquez—Frizar
Francisco Goyoaga—Quorum

2 FRG, 56.25; 3 Italy, 67.00;
4 Sweden, 68.75;
5 Netherlands, 92.00.

London

Great Britain 32.00
Peter Robeson—Craven A
Pat Smythe—Tosca
Wilf White—Nizefela
Harry Llewellyn—Foxhunter

2 Ireland, 48.50; 3 France, 53.25;
4 Italy, 56.00.

Dublin

Great Britain 25.50
William Hanson—The Monarch

Peter Robeson—Craven A
Wilf White—Nizefela
Harry Llewellyn—Foxhunter

2 France, 39.00; 3 Ireland, 54.75;
4 Sweden, 93.50;
5 Switzerland, 122.00.

Le Zoute

France 56.00
Guy Lefrant—Ali-Baba
Bertrand du Breuil—Ukase
G. Favre de Thierrens—Azur
Pierre Jonquères d'Oriola—Arlequin D

2 Great Britain, 56.25;
3 Netherlands, 61.00; 4 Switzerland;
5 Italy; 6 Belgium, 106.25.

Rotterdam

Great Britain 12.00
Jeremy Beale—Bones
Lady Mary Rose Williams—Grey Skies
Ronnie Dallas—Marmion
Geoffrey Gibbon—Blue Lady

2 Italy, 16.00; 3 France, 19.00;
4 Netherlands, 20.00; 5 FRG, 24.00;
6 Switzerland, 36.00.

Pinerolo

Switzerland
Mario Mylius—Nundina
Frank Lombard—Vol-au-Vent
William de Rham—Va Vite
Alexander Stoffel—Sirius

2 Italy; 3 France.

Buenos Aires

Argentina
Argentino Molinuevo, Sen.
Carlos Ruchti
Pedro Mayorga
Rafael Deyheralde

Harrisburg

USA 8.00
Arthur McCashin—Rusty
Ronnie Mutch—Briar Lad
Carol Durand—Reno Kirk

2 Canada, 20.00; 3 Ireland, 61.50;
4 Great Britain, eliminated.

New York

Ireland 23.75
Kevin Barry—Kilcarne
Colin O'Shea—Clonsilla
Michael Tubridy—Ballynonty

2 Great Britain, 28.75;
3 Canada, 36.00; 4 USA, 40.00.

Toronto

Great Britain 8.00
Pat Smythe—Prince Hal
William Hanson—The Monarch
Harry Llewellyn—Foxhunter

2 USA, 17.00;
=3 Canada, Ireland, 27.00.

Geneva

France 4.00
Guy Lefrant—Ali-Baba
Bertrand du Breuil—Azur
Georges Calmon—Camelia IV
Pierre Jonquères d'Oriola—Voulette

2 Spain, 16.00; 3 FRG, 19.50;
4 Italy, 31.00; 5 Switzerland, 46.75;
6 Sweden, 72.75;
7 Netherlands, eliminated.

1954

Dortmund

FRG 10.50
Hans Günter Winkler—Halla
Helga Köhler—Armalva
Gunter Rodenberg—Hanna
Magnus von Buchwaldt—Jaspis

2 Sweden, 52.00;
3 Great Britain, 64.75.

Nice

Portugal 15.00
Eduardo Netto de Almeida
—Impecavel
Fernando Marques Cavaleiro
—Cara Linda
Antonio Pereira de Almeida
—Florentina
Henrique Callado—Caramulo

2 France, 16.00; 3 Spain, 23.00;
4 Switzerland, 31.50; 5 Italy, 32.00;
6 Turkey, 79.00; 7 Egypt, 84.00.

Rome

Spain 23.00
Jaime Garcia Cruz—Quoniam
Francisco Goyoaga—Baden
Angelo Alonso Martin—Brise Brise
Manuel Ordovas Gonzales—Bohemio

2 FRG, 28.25; 3 France, 40.00;
4 Egypt, 53.00; 5 Turkey, 53.25;
6 Italy, 55.50; 7 Belgium, 76.50;
8 Sweden, 130.75.

Lucerne

FRG 44.50
Gunter Rodenberg—Hanna
Helga Köhler—Armalva
Magnus von Buchwaldt—Jaspis
Hans Günter Winkler—Halla

2 Ireland, 53.25; 3 France, 55.00;
4 Turkey, 61.00; 5 Switzerland, 94.25.

Lisbon

Portugal 20.00
Eduardo Netto de Almeida
—Impecavel
Fernando Marques Cavaleiro—Febus
Antonio Pereira de Almeida
—Florentina
Henrique Callado—Caramulo

2 Spain, 32.00; 3 Italy, 49.75;
4 Ireland, 55.25; 5 Great Britain, 56.00;
6 Egypt, eliminated.

Madrid

Spain 8.00
Angelo Alonso Martin—Brise Brise
Manuel Ordovas Gonzales—Bohemio
Francisco Goyoaga—Baden
Jaime Garcia Cruz—Quoniam

2 France, 15.75; 3 Portugal, 21.75;
4 Italy, 32.25; 5 FRG, 49.25;
6 Great Britain, 63.25.

Aachen

Spain 26.75
Jaime Garcia Cruz—Quoniam
Carlos Figueroa—Gracieux
Manuel Ordovas Gonzales—Bohemio
Francisco Goyoaga—Baden

=2 FRG, Italy, 28.00;
4 Denmark, 48.00;
5 Switzerland, 55.50; 6 Sweden, 56.00.

Spa

Belgium 32.00
Frank Lombard—Dandy
Monique de Moerkerke—Calino
Georges Poffé—Inès
Georges van Derton—Roland

2 Italy, 60.00; 3 France, 73.00;
4 FRG, 124.50; 5 Sweden, 217.00.

London

Great Britain 16.00
Peter Robeson—Craven A
Donald Beard—Costa
Alan Oliver—Red Admiral
Wilf White—Nizefela

2 FRG, 20.00; 3 France, 24.00;
4 Ireland, 56.00; 5 Canada, 105.25;
6 Portugal, 110.00.

Blackpool

Great Britain
Duggie Stewart—The Monarch
Peter Robeson—Craven A
Alan Oliver—Galway Boy
Wilf White—Nizefela

2 Ireland; 3 Canada; 4 Sweden.

Dublin

Great Britain 21.00
Henry Nicoll—Pepper Pot
Donald Beard—Costa
Duggie Stewart—The Monarch
Peter Robeson—Craven A

2 FRG, 31.75; 3 Portugal, 39.75;
4 Ireland, 41.75; 5 France, 72.25;
6 Canada, 106.25.

Ostend

Italy 8.00
Salvatore Oppes—Somalo
Marchese Lorenzo de Medici—Dick
Fabrizio Finesi—Oceano IV
Salvatore Oppes—Cluain Meala

2 Great Britain, 12.00; 3 FRG, 24.00;
=4 Canada, Belgium, 36.00.

Captain Antonio Pereira de Almeida on Florentina, members of Portugal's winning Nations Cup teams at the Nice and Lisbon shows in 1954. (The Illustrated London News)

Rotterdam

Ireland   24.00
Kevin Barry—Ballycotton
Brendan Cullinan—Ballynonty
William Ringrose—Liffey Vale
Patrick Kiernan—Glenamaddy

2 Netherlands, 25.00;
3 Great Britain, 26.25; 4 FRG, 36.00;
5 Canada, 46.25; 6 Belgium, retired.

Harrisburg

Mexico   13.00
Humberto Mariles Cortés
—Chihuahua II
Joaquin d'Harcourt—Cordoves
Roberto Vinals Contreras—Acapulco

2 Spain, 20.25; 3 USA, 21.25;
4 FRG, 31.25.

New York

Mexico   0.00
Humberto Mariles Cortés
—Chihuahua II
Joaquin d'Harcourt—Petrolero
Roberto Vinals Contreras—Cordoves

=2 USA, Canada, 8.00; 4 Spain, 12.00;
5 FRG, 16.25.

Toronto

Spain   0.00
Manuel Ordovas Gonzales—Asar
Jaime Garcia Cruz—Quoniam
Francisco Goyoaga—Bayamo

2 Mexico, 4.00; 3 FRG, 8.00;
4 USA, 19.00; 5 Canada, 20.00.

1955

Nice

Spain   16.00
Francisco Goyoaga—Baden
Angelo Alonso Martin—Brise Brise
Manuel Ordovas Gonzales—Bohemio
Jaime Garcia Cruz—Quoniam

2 Portugal, 19.00; 3 FRG, 23.00;
4 France, 24.00; 5 Ireland, 43.00.

Rome

Italy   4.00
Fabrizio Finesi—Oceano IV
Salvatore Oppes—Pagoro
Raimondo d'Inzeo—Merano
Piero d'Inzeo—Uruguay

2 Spain, 20.00; 3 France, 28.00;
4 FRG, 43.25; 5 Ireland, 48.75;
6 Great Britain, retired.

Lisbon

Spain   21.25
Pedro Dominguez Manjon—Jawohl
Juan Nardiz Bernaldo—Sad Prince
Carlos Lopez Quesada—Tapatio
Marcelino Gavilán y Ponce de Léon
—Very Hot

2 Portugal, 40.00; 3 France, 60.00.

Madrid

Portugal   29.25
D. J. Semedo de Albuquerque
—Febus
Rodrigo da Silveira—Florentina
Eduardo Netto de Almeida—Limerick
Henrique Callado—Caramulo

2 Spain, 40.00; 3 Switzerland, 84.50.

Paris

Italy   8.00
Natalie Perrone—Voltigeur
Salvatore Oppes—Pagoro
Raimondo d'Inzeo—Merano
Piero d'Inzeo—Uruguay

2 Great Britain, 14.25; 3 France, 16.75;
4 Portugal, 20.50; 5 Belgium, 86.00.

Aachen

FRG   0.00
Alfons Lütke-Westhues—Ala
Hans Günter Winkler—Halla
Walter Schmidt—Kiel
Fritz Thiedemann—Meteor

=2 Italy, Spain, 12.00; 4 France, 16.00;
5 Great Britain, 20.00;
6 Belgium, 27.00; 7 Sweden, 39.00;
8 Denmark, 101.00.

London

Italy   8.00
Luigi Cartasegna—Brando
Salvatore Oppes—Pagoro
Raimondo d'Inzeo—Merano
Piero d'Inzeo—Uruguay

2 Great Britain, 24.00; 3 Ireland, 48.00;
4 USA, 55.00; 5 Sweden, 88.00.

Dublin

Italy   16.00
Salvatore Oppes—Pagoro
Luigi Cartasegna—Brando
Raimondo d'Inzeo—Merano
Salvatore Oppes—The Quiet Man

2 Great Britain, 20.00; 3 Ireland, 51.25;
4 Sweden, 83.50; 5 USA, 96.25.

Le Zoute

France   15.00
Guy Lefrant—Vézelise
Charles Moreau—Urgel
Bertrand du Breuil—Dark Noé
Bernard de Fombelle—Buffalo B

2 Great Britain, 16.50;
3 Belgium, 32.00; 4 USA, 33.25.

Rotterdam

Netherlands   16.00, 8.00 in jump-off
Jacob, Baron van Lynden—Master
Benny Arts—Tatjana
M. M. Koster—Tarahumara
Wiel Hendrickx—Bijou

2 Great Britain, 16.00, 12.00
in jump-off; 3 Spain, 20.00;
4 Ireland, 32.00; 5 FRG, 36.00;
6 France, 38.25.

Halla

Opinions will always differ as to who was the greatest show jumping horse but if the Olympic Games are taken as the supreme achievement in the sport, then Halla's claims to the title of 'the greatest' are indisputable: for she is the only show jumper to have won three Olympic gold medals.

Foaled on 16 May 1945, Halla was by a trotting stallion, and was in training for two seasons as a steeplechaser. In 15 starts she was placed five times and won once, at Frankfurt over 3400 metres on 12 December 1948. Her speed and jumping ability impressed the German Olympic selectors, who at that time were looking for potential three-day event horses. So it was that her owner-breeder Gustav Vierling, from Darmstadt, was invited to send her to the state stud at Dillenburg where the Germans were endeavouring to put together a team of horses with the 1952 Olympics in mind.

The experiment was not a success. Halla gained the reputation of being a difficult horse: undisciplined and nervous, she was not interested in the dressage training which she had to undergo and was, moreover, a shy feeder and a weaver (weaving is a so-called stable 'vice' in which a horse swings its head from side to side while standing in the stable, and is usually attributable to boredom). After a while Herr Vierling was politely asked to take her home again. Thinking that perhaps she was 'only' going to make a show jumper, he offered her to Hans Günter Winkler, who had at that time recently been invited to move to Warendorf to train for the Olympic team.

The partnership which these two struck up has become legendary. Realizing that the mare was still wound up from racing, Winkler gave her a chance to adjust. She rewarded him by becoming the horse of a lifetime. Her 125 wins included those three Olympic gold medals, two World Championships, eight Nations Cups, a Hamburg Derby, the German National Championship, the Aachen Championship and Grand Prix, and the Grand Prix of Rome. She was equally at home jumping a puissance wall or against the clock in a jump-off and could always be relied upon to bring out that something special on the big occasion.

Her first two Olympic gold medals were won in extraordinary circumstances at the 1956 Stockholm Games. In the first round, the mare was one of the very few horses to come successfully through the difficult treble at 12, but the effort perhaps left her and her rider unbalanced for the next fence.

Halla, the only show jumper to have won three Olympic Gold medals, with her devoted pilot, Hans Günter Winkler. (Sport and General)

Although she cleared it, Winkler returned somewhat heavily into the saddle, tearing a muscle and sustaining a groin injury. Racked with pain he was unable to help Halla at the 14th and final fence where she made her only mistake. Winkler left the ring doubled up with pain but to an ovation—Halla was the only horse to have negotiated the course with just 4 faults which put her in the lead at the halfway mark of the competition.

It was evident when Winkler went in to ride his second round that he was still in great pain. Eye witnesses reported that all he could do was to point the mare in the right direction, sit as still as he could and leave the rest to her—riding as such being quite out of the question. Incredibly the mare, seeming to understand her rider's plight, simply carried him round, jumping the entire course without error. She was the first horse to go clear and one of only two to do so in the entire competition, and as a result won both individual and team gold medals. Amazingly, she was still on top form four years later at the Rome Games where she finished fifth in the individual competition and went even better in the Nations Cup, the second best horse overall, to win a second team gold.

She jumped for the last time on 25 October 1960 in the Brussels Grand Prix—and won it—before being retired to stud. She died in 1979, not long after her 34th birthday.

Belgrade

Italy 48.50
Vicenzo Bettoni—Pooka
Fabrizio Finesi—Oceano IV
Duccio Marzichi—Ventuno
Marchese Lorenzo de Medici—Dick

2 France, 56.00; 3 Turkey, 69.25;
4 Rumania, 80.50; 5 Hungary, 88.25;
6 Yugoslavia, 99.75.

Pinerolo

Italy 11.25
Luigi Cartasegna—Brando
Salvatore Oppes—Pagoro
Raimondo d'Inzeo—Merano
Piero d'Inzeo—Uruguay

2 Turkey, 29.00; 3 Switzerland, 73.25.

Harrisburg

Ireland 16.00
Kevin Barry—Ballyneety
Patrick Kiernan—Ballynonty
William Ringrose—Hollyford

2 Mexico, 17.75; 3 Canada, 19.00;
4 USA, 32.00.

New York

Mexico 12.00, 4.00 in jump-off
Eva Valdes—Mexicano
Roberto Vinals Contreras—Illusion
Humberto Mariles Cortés
—Chihuahua II

2 Ireland, 12.00, 16.00 in jump-off;
3 USA, 12.50; 4 Canada, 42.50.

Toronto

Ireland 8.00, 12.00 in jump-off
Kevin Barry—Ballyneety
Patrick Kiernan—Ballynonty
William Ringrose—Glencree

2 USA, 8.00; 20.00 in jump-off;
3 Mexico, 16.00.

Geneva

Italy 26.00
Vicenzo Bettoni—Pooka
Marchese Lorenzo de Medici—Dick
Raimondo d'Inzeo—The Quiet Man
Piero d'Inzeo—Nadir

2 Belgium, 28.25; 3 France, 30.75;
4 Spain, 37.00; 5 Switzerland, 42.50;
6 FRG, 49.00; 7 Netherlands, 84.25;
8 Australia, 101.50.

1956

Nice

France 24.00
Georges Calmon—Virtuoso
Guy Lefrant—Far West
Pierre Jonquères d'Oriola—Dark Noé
Georges Calmon—Camelia IV

2 Spain, 28.00; 3 Switzerland, 43.00;

4 Netherlands, 48.00; 5 Italy, 50.50;
6 Belgium, 52.00

Rome

Italy 32.00
Vicenzo Bettoni—Pooka
Salvatore Oppes—Pagoro
Piero d'Inzeo—Somalo
Raimondo d'Inzeo—Merano

2 France, 42.00; 3 Belgium, 70.25;
4 Argentina, 76.00;
5 Switzerland, 96.75;
6 Netherlands, retired.

Lucerne

Great Britain 5.00
Dawn Palethorpe—Earlsrath Rambler
Peter Robeson—Scorchin
Pat Smythe—Flanagan
Wilf White—Nizefela

2 Switzerland, 16.00;
3 Argentina, 20.00;
4 Netherlands, 26.25; 5 Egypt, 29.00;
=6 Belgium, Ireland, 36.00;
8 Italy, 40.00.

Stockholm

Great Britain 12.00, 0.00 in jump-off
Dawn Palethorpe—Earlsrath Rambler
Peter Robeson—Scorchin
Pat Smythe—Flanagan
Wilf White—Nizefela

2 Italy, 12.00, 4.00 in jump-off;
=3 Spain, Portugal, 20.00;
5 FRG, 30.00; 6 USA, 32.00;
7 Argentina, 35.00; 8 Turkey, 56.00;
9 Ireland, 60.00; 10 Switzerland, 67.00;
11 Sweden, 140.75; 12 GDR, 143.00;
13 Venezuela, 152.50;
14 Austria, 326.50;
retired, Brazil, Hungary.

Aachen

Brazil 22.25
Eloy Massey Oliveira de Menezes
—Salvatico
Renyldo Pedro Guimaraes Ferreira
—Travessura
Nelson Pessoa—Relincho
Eloy Massey Oliveira de Menezes
—Caramelo

2 FRG, 24.00; 3 Spain, 28.00;
4 Portugal, 35.00; 5 USA, 36.00;
6 Belgium, 49.50; 7 Turkey, 125.00;
retired, Argentina, Egypt.

London

Great Britain 20.00
Dawn Palethorpe—Earlsrath Rambler
Alan Oliver—Red Admiral
Pat Smythe—Flanagan
Wilf White—Nizefela

2 Brazil, 24.00; 3 Turkey, 48.00;
4 Ireland, 52.00; 5 USA, 64.00.

Dublin

Great Britain 31.50
Dawn Palethorpe—Earlsrath Rambler
John Lanni—Huntsman VI
Mary (Whitehead) Marshall—Nobbler
Harry Llewellyn—Aherlow

2 Turkey, 44.00; 3 Ireland, 48.00;
4 USA, 60.00; 5 Brazil, retired.

Ostend

Italy 20.00
Marchese Lorenzo de Medici
—Irish Rover
Luciano Ambrosio—Brando
Piero d'Inzeo—Uruguay
Raimondo d'Inzeo—Merano

2 Great Britain, 22.75;
3 Belgium, 32.00;
4 Netherlands, 62.00.

Rotterdam

Great Britain 5.75
Tom Barnes—Sudden
Dawn Palethorpe—Earlsrath Rambler
Alan Oliver—Red Admiral
Pat Smythe—Flanagan

2 Italy, 8.00; 3 FRG, 16.00;
4 Netherlands, 20.00;
5 Belgium, 50.25.

Harrisburg

Canada 24.00
Tom Gayford—Blue Beau
Douglas Cudney—Flash Gordon
Douglas Hood—Oregon Duke

2 USA, 37.25; 3 Ireland,
22.00; 4 Chile, 28.00.

New York

Mexico 4.00
Julio Herrera—Acapulco
Samuel Soberon—14 de Agosto
Humberto Mariles Cortés—
Chihuahua II

2 Ireland, 4.25; =3 Canada, USA, 8.00;
5 Chile, 12.00.

Toronto

USA 18.25
Frank Chapot—Defense
Hugh Wiley—Nautical
William Steinkraus—First Boy

2 Chile, 21.25; 3 Ireland, 34.00;
4 Canada, 35.25; 5 Mexico, eliminated.

1957

Rome

Italy 16.00
Marchese Fabio di Mangilli—Hack On
Salvatore Oppes—Pagoro
Raimondo d'Inzeo—Merano
Piero d'Inzeo—The Rock

2 Great Britain, 42.75; 3 France, 45.50;
4 Portugal, 64.75; 5 Ireland, 92.50;
6 Netherlands, 136.00;
retired, Poland, Belgium.

Lisbon

FRG   11.00
Alfons Lütke-Westhues—Ala
Hans Günter Winkler—Fahnenjunker
Magnus von Buchwaldt—Tabitha
Fritz Thiedemann—Finale

2 Spain, 20.00; 3 Portugal, 25.00;
4 Brazil, 52.00.

Madrid

Spain   24.00, 0.00 in jump-off
Francisco Goyoaga—Fahnenkönig
Angelo Alonso Martin—Brise Brise
Carlos Lopez Quesada—Tapatio
Carlos Figueroa—Gracieux

2 Portugal, 24.00; 11.00 in jump-off;
3 Brazil, 35.50; 4 FRG, 49.00;
5 France, retired.

Paris

Italy   17.00
Salvatore Oppes—Pagoro

Luciano Ambrosio—Brando
Raimondo d'Inzeo—Merano
Piero d'Inzeo—The Rock

2 France, 18.00; 3 Brazil, 20.50;
4 Spain, 20.75; 5 FRG, 33.25;
6 Turkey, 74.75.

Aachen

FRG   8.00
Alfons Lütke-Westhues—Ala
Alwin Schockemöhle—Bachus
Fritz Thiedemann—Meteor
Hans Günter Winkler—Fahnenjunker

The Rock

In 13 years as a show jumper, The Rock totted up more victories in international and national events than any horse had ever done before: 172 wins, 95 second places, 44 thirds and 156 other placings. In 1958 alone he won 44 classes. One of the best-loved horses in the history of the sport, he was foaled in Ireland in 1948, out of a daughter of Sandyman by Water Serpent. A handsome, upstanding grey gelding, he was imported into Italy in 1953 as a hunter. In the event, he was never used in that capacity but was trained instead for jumping.

During his long competitive career he was ridden with success by Carlo d'Angelo, Graziano Mancinelli, Gualtiero Castellini, Adriano Capuzzo and, most memorably, by Piero d'Inzeo, who described him as 'willing and generous in all he did'. The Rock made his debut in 1954, in which season he was

ridden by d'Angelo and Mancinelli, and it was Mancinelli who resumed riding him towards the end of his career.

The Rock's major wins included the individual silver medal and a team bronze at the 1960 Olympic Games; the silver medal in the 1958 European Championships, and the King George V Gold Cup in 1961 and 1962—all achieved with Piero d'Inzeo in the saddle. This brilliant and consistent horse took part in numerous Nations Cups, in Rome, Aachen, London, Dublin, Nice, Geneva, Paris, Lucerne and Barcelona, and won some of the sport's most important Grand Prix, including Aachen, Dortmund, Dublin, Lucerne and Rome.

He was working right up to his death—caused by intestine trouble—at the age of 19, on 20 September 1967.

The Rock, ridden by Piero d'Inzeo, jumping at the White City in London, where he twice won the King George V Gold Cup. (Leslie Lane)

2 Brazil, 28.00; 3 Switzerland, 64.00;
4 Spain, 68.00; 5 Turkey, 100.00;
retired, Belgium, Denmark, Poland.

London

Great Britain 12.00
Dawn Palethorpe—Earlsrath Rambler
Ted Williams—Dumbell
Pat Smythe—Flanagan
Wilf White—Nizefela

2 Italy, 20.00; 3 France, 32.00;
4 Ireland, 64.00.

Dublin

France 11.00
Guy Lefrant—Caballero
Bernard de Fombelle—Grand Veneur
Chevalier Jean d'Orgeix
—Topinambour
Bernard de Fombelle—Bucephale

2 FRG, 12.00; 3 Italy, 16.00;
4 Great Britain, 16.75; 5 Ireland, 28.00;

Le Zoute

Switzerland 19.00
Victor Morf—Duroc
Rolf Ruff—Attila IV
Werner Brenzikofer—Falko IV
Frank Lombard—Bissada

=2 Netherlands, Belgium, 20.00;
4 Great Britain, 27.00.

Rotterdam

Great Britain 11.75
Elizabeth Anderson—Sunsalve
Dawn Palethorpe—Earlsrath Rambler
Jean Harper—Eckey
Ted Edgar—Jane Summers

2 FRG, 12.00; 3 Netherlands, 27.75;
4 Italy, 36.00; 5 Belgium, retired.

Harrisburg

Great Britain 13.00
Dawn Palethorpe—Earlsrath Rambler
Ted Williams—Pegasus
Pat Smythe—Flanagan

=2 USA, Mexico, 16.00;
4 Ireland, 20.00; 5 Argentina, 28.00;
6 Canada, 28.50.

New York

USA 0.00, 0.00 in jump-off
Frank Chapot—Pill Box
William Steinkraus—First Boy
Hugh Wiley—Nautical

2 Great Britain, 0.00, 4.00 in jump-off
(retired after two rounds);
3 Ireland, 4.00;
=4 Argentina, Canada, 8.00.

Toronto

USA 12.00
Charles Dennehy—Pill Box
William Steinkraus—Night Owl
Hugh Wiley—Nautical

2 Great Britain, 16.00;
=3 Ireland, Argentina, 20.00;
=5 Mexico, Chile, 24.00.

Geneva

FRG 35.75
Alfons Lütke-Westhues—Ala
Hermann Schridde—Flagrant
Fritz Thiedemann—Meteor
Hans Günter Winkler—Halla

2 Spain, 36.00; 3 France, 43.00;
4 Switzerland, 80.00;
5 Great Britain, 81.00;
6 Netherlands, 102.50;
7 Belgium, retired.

1958

Nice

France 24.25
Guy Lefrant—Caballero II
Claude Roy—Dark Noé
Max Fresson—Grand Veneur
Bernard de Fombelle—Buffalo B

2 Spain, 28.25; 3 Italy, 32.00;
4 Turkey, 34.00; 5 Chile, 35.00;
6 Poland, 39.25.

Rome

FRG 12.00
Walter Günther—Asta
Anna Clement—Delphin
Magnus von Buchwaldt—Flugwind
Peter Stackfleth—Frechdachs

2 Italy, 16.00; 3 Chile, 41.75;
4 France, 47.00; 5 UAR, 48.25;
6 Spain, 62.50; 7 Switzerland, 69.75;
8 Poland, 84.00; 9 Rumania, 86.50.

Lucerne

FRG 28.00
Alfons Lütke-Westhues—Ala
Hermann Schridde—Fugosa
Fritz Thiedemann—Meteor
Hans Günter Winkler—Halla

2 Ireland, 32.50; 3 Chile, 40.25;
4 Italy, 41.25; 5 Switzerland, 48.00;
6 UAR, 62.25; 7 Poland, 86.00;
8 Netherlands, 130.00;
retired, Belgium, France.

Madrid

Spain 27.00
Francisco Goyoaga—Fahnenkönig
Angelo Alonso Martin—Incierto
Carlos Lopez Quesada—Tapatio
Hernando Espinosa de los Monteros
—Frantillack

2 France, 50.25; 3 Portugal, 52.00;
4 FRG, 81.50; retired, Italy.

Lisbon

Spain 29.50
Angelo Alonso Martin—Brise Brise

Hernando Espinosa de los Monteros
—Mister B
Fernando Lopez del Hierro
—Amado Mio
Carlos Lopez Quesada—Tapatio

2 Portugal, 35.75; 3 France, 40.00.

Aachen

Spain 20.00, 8.00 in jump-off
Hernando Espinosa de los Monteros
—Mister B
Carlos Figueroa—Brûle Tout
Francisco Goyoaga—Toscanella
Hernando Espinosa de los Monteros
—Frantillack

2 USA, 20.00, 16.00 in jump-off;
3 FRG, 20.00, 28.00 in jump-off;
4 Italy, 35.00; 5 Netherlands, 51.50;
6 Great Britain, 52.00; 7 Chile, 60.00;
8 Sweden, 78.50; 9 USSR, 84.00;
retired, Belgium, Denmark, Norway.

London

USA 4.00
George Morris—Night Owl
Frank Chapot—Diamant
Hugh Wiley—Nautical
William Steinkraus—Ksar d'Esprit

2 Great Britain, 8.00; 3 Ireland, 24.00;
4 Portugal, 31.00.

Dublin

Great Britain 12.00
Marshall Charlesworth—Smokey Bob
Jill Banks—Earlsrath Rambler
Harvey Smith—Farmer's Boy
George Hobbs—Royal Lord

2 USA, 21.75; 3 Portugal, 32.00;
4 France, 36.00; 5 Ireland, 36.50.

Ostend

France 27.00
Guy Lefrant—Caballero
Renaud Dubuisson—Radis
Max Fresson—Dark Noé
Bernard de Fombelle—Topinambour

2 USA, 32.25; 3 FRG, 53.50;
4 Great Britain, 68.00;
5 Netherlands, 72.75,
6 Belgium, 93.25.

Rotterdam

France 21.00
Guy Lefrant—Caballero
Renaud Dubuisson—Radis
Max Fresson—Dark Noé
Bernard de Fombelle—Topinambour

2 FRG, 24.25; 3 Ireland, 36.00;
4 USA, 37.50; 5 Netherlands, 46.00;
6 Great Britain, 48.75.

Harrisburg

FRG 26.00
Fritz Thiedemann—Retina
Alfons Lütke-Westhues—Ala
Hans Günter Winkler—Halla

2 Canada, 55.75; 3 USA, 78.00;
4 Cuba, 104.75; 5 Mexico, eliminated.

New York

FRG 24.00
Alfons Lütke-Westhues—Ala
Fritz Thiedemann—Finale
Hans Günter Winkler—Halla

2 USA, 62.50; 3 Mexico, 75.00;
4 Canada, 91.75; 5 Cuba, retired.

Toronto

FRG 1.25
Alfons Lütke-Westhues—Ala
Fritz Thiedemann—Finale
Hans Günter Winkler—Halla

2 Canada, 21.00; 3 USA, 28.50;
4 Mexico, 86.75; 5 Cuba, eliminated.

1959

Rome

USA 12.00, 0.00 in jump-off
George Morris—Sinjon
Frank Chapot—Diamant
William Steinkraus—Ksar d'Esprit
Hugh Wiley—Nautical

2 Italy, 12.00, 8.00 in jump-off;
3 France, 15.00; 4 FRG, 19.00;
=5 Spain, Hungary, 56.00;
7 Rumania, 69.50; 8 Poland, 114.00;
9 Portugal, 120.50;
10 Belgium, 121.50; 11 Turkey, 127.00;
12 Netherlands, 129.75.

Lisbon

Spain 20.25
Hernando Espinosa de los Monteros
—Frantillack
Alfonso Queipo de Llano—Celtibero
Juan Martinez de Vallejo—Charmeuse
Manuel, Conde de Velle—Baden

2 Great Britain, 28.00;
3 Portugal, 44.00.

Madrid

Great Britain 32.00
Marshall Charlesworth—Smokey Bob
Dawn (Palethorpe) Wofford
—Hollandia
Cecil Blacker—Workboy
Pat Smythe—Flanagan

2 Spain, 39.00; 3 FRG, 52.00;
4 Portugal, 78.00; 5 France, 79.25;
6 Switzerland, 103.00.

Paris

USSR 4.50
Andrei Favorski—Manevr
Boris Lilov—Diagramma
Vladimir Raspopov—Sed
Ernst Shabailo—Plastun

2 FRG, 8.25; 3 USA, 16.00;
4 Italy, 20.00; 5 Great Britain, 24.75;
6 Spain, 27.25; 7 France, 28.00;
8 Sweden, 66.25.

Aachen

Italy 7.00
Antonio Oppes—The Scholar
Adriano Capuzzo—Pioneer
Raimondo d'Inzeo—Gowran Girl
Piero d'Inzeo—The Quiet Man

2 USA, 16.00; 3 FRG, 20.00;
=4 Rumania, Sweden, 32.00;
6 France, 32.25; 7 Belgium, 36.25;
8 Hungary, 51.00; 9 Poland, 54.25;
10 Denmark, 69.50;
retired, Netherlands.

London

USA 20.00
George Morris—Night Owl
Frank Chapot—Tally Ho
William Steinkraus—Riviera Wonder
Hugh Wiley—Nautical

2 Spain, 23.00; 3 Great Britain, 24.00;
4 Ireland, 27.00.

Dublin

Great Britain 32.00
Jill Banks—Earlsrath Rambler
Susan Cohen—Clare Castle
Dawn (Palethorpe) Wofford
—Hollandia
Douglas Bunn—Coady

2 Spain, 44.00; 3 Ireland, 51.00;
4 S. Africa, retired.

Le Zoute

Great Britain 12.00
C. David Barker—Franco
Marshall Charlesworth—Smokey Bob
David Boston Barker—Red Port
Ann Townsend—Bandit IV

2 FRG, 27.50; 3 Belgium, 38.25;
4 Netherlands, 43.00; 5 Ireland, 50.25.

Rotterdam

Great Britain 16.00
C. David Barker—Franco
David Broome—Wildfire III
Ann Townsend—Bandit IV
Pat Smythe—Flanagan

2 Netherlands, 28.00;
=3 Ireland, Belgium, 36.00;
5 FRG, 56.00.

Harrisburg

USA 8.00
George Morris—Sinjon
Frank Chapot—Springboard
William Steinkraus—Trail Guide

2 Brazil, 16.25; 3 Canada, 20.00;
4 Argentina, 31.00; 5 Mexico, 52.00.

New York

Canada 19.50
Jim Elder—Isguilda
Douglas Cudney—Blarney Castle
Thomas Gayford—Blue Beau

2 USA, 22.25; 3 Argentina, 28.50;
4 Brazil, 33.75.

Toronto

USA 33.75
George Morris—Sinjon
Frank Chapot—Springboard
William Steinkraus—Trail Guide

2 Canada, 43.00; 3 Mexico, 46.00;
4 Brazil, 53.50.

Geneva

Italy 20.00
Antonio Oppes—The Scholar
Adriano Capuzzo—Pioneer
Piero d'Inzeo—The Quiet Man
Raimondo d'Inzeo—Gowran Girl

2 France, 25.50; 3 FRG, 28.25;
4 Great Britain, 35.75;
5 Switzerland, 41.25;
retired, Netherlands.

1960

Nice

Italy 18.00
Mario Maini—Shepherd's Bush
Gualtiero Castellini—Ventuno
Graziano Mancinelli—Kildare Lass
Fabrizio Finesi—Furio

2 Portugal, 55.50; 3 France, 57.50;
4 Ireland, 59.25;
5 Netherlands, 151.25; retired, Spain.

Madrid

Spain 40.00
Hernando Espinosa de los Monteros
—Frantillack
José Alvarez de Bohorques
—Descosido
Juan Martinez de Vallejo—Charmeuse
Francisco Goyoaga—Desirée

2 FRG, 54.00; 3 Portugal, 60.00;
retired, France.

Lucerne

USA 20.00
George Morris—Sinjon
Frank Chapot—Tally Ho
Hugh Wiley—Nautical
William Steinkraus—Riviera Wonder

2 Great Britain, 24.00; 3 Italy, 44.00;
4 FRG, 56.00; 5 Switzerland, 59.50;
6 Rumania, 91.25.

Turin

Italy 28.00
Graziano Mancinelli—Rockette

Gualtiero Castellini—Ventuno
Piero d'Inzeo—The Rock
Raimondo d'Inzeo—Posillipo

2 FRG, 44.00; 3 Hungary, 67.50;
4 Spain, 89.75; 5 France, 129.75.

Copenhagen

FRG   12.00
Anna Clement—Danina
Helga Köhler—Armalva
Magnus von Buchwaldt—Servus
Peter Wandschneider—Fels

2 Sweden, 20.00; 3 Denmark, 47.25.

Aachen

FRG   16.00
Klaus Pade—Fröhlich
Hermann Schridde—Flagrant
Hans Günter Winkler—Laila
Alwin Schockemöhle—Bachus

2 USA, 32.00; 3 Spain, 43.00;
4 Rumania, 64.00; 5 Belgium, 85.00;
6 Poland, 131.00.

London

USA   27.00
George Morris—Sinjon
Frank Chapot—Tally Ho
Hugh Wiley—Master William
William Steinkraus—Riviera Wonder

2 Great Britain, 40.00;
3 Argentina, 62.50; 4 Ireland, 72.00;
5 Japan, 132.50.

Ostend

France   16.00, 4.00 in jump-off
Bertrand du Breuil—Caballero II
Max Fresson—Grand Veneur
Pierre Jonquères d'Oriola
—Eclair au Chocolat
Bernard de Fombelle—Buffalo B

2 USA, 16.00, 8.00 in jump-off;
3 Belgium, 48.00; 4 Turkey, 64.00;
retired, Netherlands.

Dublin

Argentina   60.00
Naldo Dasso—Final
Jorge Lucardi—Stromboli
Ernesto Hartkopf—Baltasar
Carlos Delia—Huipil

2 Great Britain, 67.00; 3 Ireland, 92.00;
4 Denmark, retired.

Rotterdam

Turkey   15.25
Nail Gönenli—Domino
Cevdet Sumer—Izma
Salih Koc—Eskimo

2 Hungary, 32.75;
3 Netherlands, 36.00; 4 FRG, 40.75;
5 France, 47.00; 6 Belgium, 56.00.

Harrisburg

Venezuela   30.25
Jesus Palacios—Polichinela

Carola Behrens—Mio Topo
Josue Rivas—Quezanne

2 USA, 33.00; 3 Canada, 49.00;
4 Ireland, 64.00; 5 Mexico, 64.75.

New York

Mexico   13.75
Joaquin Perez de las Heras—Perico
Enrique Ladron de Guevara
—Traga Leguas
Ricardo Guasch—Comodoro

2 USA, 22.00; 3 Canada, 22.50;
4 Venezuela, 36.50; 5 Ireland, 51.00.

Toronto

USA   4.00
George Morris—Sinjon
Frank Chapot—Ksar d'Esprit
Hugh Wiley—Master William

=2 Canada, Ireland; 4 Mexico;
5 Venezuela.

1961

Nice

Ireland   20.00
Sean Daly—Lough Gorman
Edward O'Donohoe—Cill an Fhail
William Ringrose—Loch an Easpaig
Edward Campion—Cluain Meala

2 Spain, 27.00; 3 Italy, 32.00;
4 France, 51.25.

Rome

Italy   12.00
Raimondo d'Inzeo—Posillipo
Piero d'Inzeo—The Rock
Giulia Serventi—Doly
Graziano Mancinelli—Rockette

2 Great Britain, 54.75; 3 Ireland, 67.75.

Madrid

Spain   23.25
Francisco Goyoaga—Kif Kif
Juan Martinez de Vallejo—Charmeuse
José Alvarez de Bohorques
—Descosido
Enrique Martinez de Vallejo—Ixion

=2 Italy, France, 52.00; 4 FRG, 71.00;
5 Portugal, retired.

Copenhagen

Sweden   24.00, 0.00 in jump-off
Christer Roswall—Valör
Knut-Åke Nordenbelt—Orchidé
Gustaf de Geer—Ugly
Folke Stenbom—Sisu II

2 FRG, 24.00, 8.00 in jump-off;
3 Denmark, 99.50.

Aachen

FRG   6.25
Fritz Thiedemann—Godewind
Hermann Schridde—Ferdl
Hans Günter Winkler—Romanus
Alwin Schockemöhle—Bachus

2 Italy, 8.50; 3 Great Britain, 12.00;
4 Portugal, 49.50; 5 USSR, 64.00;
6 Poland, 65.00; 7 Belgium, 74.25;
8 Ireland, 81.25; 9 Hungary, 136.50;
10 Rumania, 187.25; 11 Spain, retired.

London

Italy   8.00
Giulia Serventi—Doly
Graziano Mancinelli—Rockette
Raimondo d'Inzeo—Merano
Piero d'Inzeo—The Rock

2 Great Britain, 12.00; 3 FRG, 47.25;
4 Ireland, 48.25; 5 Sweden, 70.00.

Dublin

FRG   8.00
Thomas Bagusat—Bajazzo
Hermann Schridde—Fugosa
Alwin Schockemöhle—Ferdl
Hans Günter Winkler—Feuerdorn

2 Italy, 19.00; 3 Ireland, 23.00;
4 Great Britain, 24.00; 5 Sweden, 43.25;
6 Switzerland, 47.00.

Ostend

FRG   20.00
Lutz Merkel—Fidelitas
Klaus Pade—Fröhlich
Hermann Schridde—Fugosa
Hans Günter Winkler—Feuerdorn

2 Ireland, 24.00; 3 Belgium, 47.00;
4 Italy, 93.25.

Rotterdam

Great Britain   16.00
Peter Robeson—Firecrest
Lady Sarah FitzAlan-Howard
—Oorskiet
Valerie Clark—Atalanta
David Broome—Sunsalve

2 FRG, 17.25; 3 Italy, 24.00;
4 Ireland, 24.50; 5 Netherlands, 32.00;
6 Belgium, retired.

Harrisburg

USA   23.50
Frank Chapot—Night Owl
Kathy Kusner—Sinjon
William Steinkraus—Ksar d'Esprit

2 Canada, 24.00; 3 Argentina, 25.00;
4 Mexico, 36.00; 5 Ireland, 68.00.

New York

Argentina   12.25
Hugo Arrambide—S'll Vous Plait
Eduardo Castaing—Don Costa
Carlos Damm—Sheriff

2 Canada, 17.50; 3 Mexico, 44.25;
4 Ireland, 115.25; 5 USA, retired.

Toronto

USA   8.00
Frank Chapot—San Lucas
Kathy Kusner—Sinjon

William Steinkraus—Ksar d'Esprit

2 Argentina, 27.50; 3 Mexico, 40.00;
4 Ireland, 56.50; 5 Canada, retired.

Geneva

FRG   28.00
Hermann Schridde—Fugosa
Kurt Jarasinski—Raffaela
Alwin Schockemöhle—Ferdl
Hans Günter Winkler—Feuerdorn

2 Italy, 29.50; 3 Spain, 31.25;
4 Ireland, 40.00; 5 Switzerland, 44.25;
6 France, 67.25; 7 Poland, 128.75.

1962

Nice

Italy   12.00
Ugo d'Amelio—Fancy Socks
Graziano Mancinelli—Rockette
Piero d'Inzeo—Sunbeam
Adriano Capuzzo—The Scholar

2 Great Britain, 16.00;
3 Rumania, 21.25; 4 France, 28.00.

Rome

Italy   4.00
Graziano Mancinelli—Rockette
Ugo d'Amelio—Fancy Socks
Piero d'Inzeo—The Rock
Raimondo d'Inzeo—Gowran Girl

2 Great Britain, 12.00;
3 Rumania, 28.00.

Lucerne

Great Britain   16.00, 8.00
in 159.10 secs in jump-off
Pat Smythe—Scorchin
Valerie Clark—Franco
C. David Barker—Mister Softee
Peter Robeson—Firecrest

2 FRG, 16.00, 8.00
in 164.00 secs in jump-off;
3 Ireland, 48.75; 4 Switzerland, 51.75.

Barcelona

Great Britain   12.00
Pat Smythe—Scorchin
Carole Beard—Mayfly XVI
Fred Welch—Brûle Tout
David Broome—Grand Manan

2 Spain, 16.00; 3 Portugal, 19.50;
4 Ireland, 83.75; 5 Italy, 135.00.

Aachen

USA   4.00
William Robertson—The Sheriff
Mary Mairs—Tomboy
Frank Chapot—San Lucas
William Steinkraus—Sinjon

2 FRG, 8.00; 3 Spain, 12.50;
4 Sweden, 20.00; 5 Rumania, 94.75;
6 Belgium, 122.00.

London

FRG   8.50
Hermann Schridde—Ilona
Kurt Jarasinski—Godewind
Hans Günter Winkler—Romanus
Alwin Schockemöhle—Ferdl

=2 Italy, USA, 16.00;
4 Great Britain, 32.00; 5 USSR, 48.50;
6 Ireland, 82.00; 7 Spain, retired.

Dublin

Italy   3.00
Ugo d'Amelio—Fancy Socks
Graziano Mancinelli—Rockette
Raimondo d'Inzeo—Posillipo
Piero d'Inzeo—The Rock

2 USA, 4.00; 3 Great Britain, 20.00;
4 Ireland, 28.75; 5 Spain, 52.00.

Copenhagen

FRG   13.50
Kurt Jarasinski—Raffaela
Helga Köhler—Pesgö
Alwin Schockemöhle—Freiherr
Hans Günter Winkler—Romanus

2 Switzerland, 32.00; 3 Sweden, 36.00;
4 Denmark, 90.75.

Ostend

FRG   38.00
Thomas Bagusat—Bajazzo
Lutz Merkel—Fidelitas
Kurt Jarasinski—Raffaela
Hermann Schridde—Ilona

2 Switzerland, 52.00; 3 Belgium, 72.00;
4 Netherlands, 139.00.

Rotterdam

FRG   9.25
Hermann Schridde—Ilona
Kurt Jarasinski—Godewind
Alwin Schockemöhle—Ferdl
Hans Günter Winkler—Romanus

2 Great Britain, 12.50;
3 Switzerland, 44.25; 4 Ireland, 46.75;
5 Belgium, 89.00;
6 Netherlands, 96.00.

Budapest

USSR   16.00
Ivan Semenov—Sibiryak
Boris Lilov—Plastun
Fedor Metelkov—Kover
Andrej Favorski—Manevr

2 GDR, 23.00; 3 Poland, 40.50;
4 Rumania, 44.25; 5 Hungary, 58.00;
6 Czechoslovakia, 60.00;
7 Bulgaria, 76.00.

Harrisburg

USA   8.00
William Steinkraus—Sinjon
Mary Mairs—Tomboy
Frank Chapot—San Lucas

2 Ireland, 32.00;
=3 Canada, Mexico, 40.00.

New York

USA   11.00
William Steinkraus—Sinjon
Mary Mairs—Tomboy
Frank Chapot—San Lucas

2 Canada, 24.00; 3 Mexico, 36.00;
4 Ireland, 78.50.

Toronto

USA   16.00
William Robertson—Master William
Mary Mairs—Tomboy
Frank Chapot—San Lucas

2 Mexico, 20.00; 3 Canada, 45.00;
4 Ireland, 47.00.

1963

Nice

Italy   20.00
Ugo d'Amelio—Fancy Socks
Gualtiero Castellini—Lausbub
Lalla Novo—Rahin
Graziano Mancinelli—Rockette

2 France, 27.00; 3 Spain, 30.00;
4 Ireland, 48.00; 5 Rumania, 90.00;
6 Netherlands, 139.75.

Rome

Great Britain   16.00
Peter Robeson—Firecrest
Anneli Drummond-Hay
—Merely-a-Monarch
C. David Barker—Mister Softee
Harvey Smith—Warpaint

2 FRG, 20.00; 3 Italy, 24.00;
4 USSR, 47.75; 5 France, 48.50;
6 Ireland, 76.50; 7 Spain, 78.50;
8 Rumania, 84.00.

Madrid

Spain   25.25
Alfonso Queipo de Llano—Eolo IV
Alfredo Goyeneche—Jaseur
Enrique Martinez de Vallejo
—Grande de Espana
Francesco Goyoaga—Rififi

2 Italy, 28.00; 3 Portugal, 36.00;
4 France, 39.50;
5 Netherlands, 222.50.

Aachen

FRG   8.00
Kurt Jarasinski—Godewind
Hermann Schridde—Ilona
Alwin Schockemöhle—Ferdl
Hans Günter Winkler—Romanus

2 Italy, 23.50; 3 Switzerland, 36.00;
4 Ireland, 40.00; 5 Poland, 42.00;
6 Sweden, 53.50; 7 Rumania, 77.00.

London

Great Britain   12.00
Anneli Drummond-Hay
—Merely-a-Monarch
Ann Townsend—Dunboyne III
C. David Barker—Mister Softee
Harvey Smith—Warpaint

2 Ireland, 24.00; 3 Italy, 32.00;
4 France, 35.25; 5 Switzerland, 56.00.

Dublin

Ireland   4.00
Seamus Hayes—Goodbye III
The Hon Diana Conolly-Carew
—Barrymore
William Ringrose—Loch an Easpaig
Tommy Wade—Dundrum

2 FRG, 8.00; 3 Switzerland, 8.25;
4 Italy, 16.00; 5 Great Britain, 23.25.

Ostend

Great Britain   24.00
Liz Broome—Bess X
Michael Cresswell—Moonlight IX
Douglas Bunn—Beethoven
C. David Barker—Mister Softee

2 FRG, 28.00; 3 Hungary, 56.75;
4 Belgium, 84.00; 5 Poland, 97.75;
6 Ireland, 138.00.

Rotterdam

Great Britain   8.00
Liz Broome—Bess X
Michael Cresswell—Moonlight IX
Ann Townsend—Dunboyne III
C. David Barker—Mister Softee

2 FRG, 32.00; 3 Poland, 36.00;
4 Switzerland, 39.00; 5 Ireland, 41.00;
6 Netherlands, 55.00;
7 Hungary, 76.00.

Harrisburg

USA   49.25
Mary Mairs—Tomboy
Frank Chapot—Manon
William Steinkraus—Fire One

2 Canada, 61.00; 3 Ireland, 95.00;
4 Argentina, retired.

New York

USA   8.00, 0.00 in jump-off
Mary Mairs—Tomboy
Frank Chapot—San Lucas
William Steinkraus—Sinjon

2 Canada, 8.00, 8.00 in jump-off;
3 FRG, 11.00; 4 Ireland, 31.00;
5 Argentina, 36.00.

Toronto

USA   16.00
Mary Mairs—Tomboy
Frank Chapot—San Lucas
William Steinkraus—Unusual

2 FRG, 20.00; 3 Ireland, 55.00;
4 Canada, 62.00.

Geneva

Switzerland   12.00
Hans Möhr—Troll
Max Hauri—Millview
Arthur Blickenstorfer—Posillipo
Frank Lombard—Japonais

2 France, 15.25; 3 Spain, 23.50;
4 Great Britain, 24.75;
5 Portugal, 25.50; 6 FRG, 36.50;
7 Italy, 47.25; 8 Ireland, 54.25;
9 Sweden, 69.75; 10 Jugoslavia, 91.75.

1964

Nice

France   8.50
Guy Lefrant—Monsieur de Littry
Alain Navet—Luma
Bernard de Fombelle—Incroyable
Pierre Jonquères d'Oriola—Lutteur B

2 Italy, 16.00; 3 Portugal, 20.00;
4 FRG, 77.75; 5 Spain, 80.00.

Rome

Italy   16.00
Graziano Mancinelli—Turvey
Piero d'Inzeo—Rahin
Stefano Angioni—Canio
Raimondo d'Inzeo—Posillipo

=2 Portugal, Switzerland, 32.50;
4 FRG, 48.00; 5 France, 48.25;
6 Spain, 94.00; 7 Turkey, 207.00;
8 Poland, 229.75.

Madrid

Spain   37.25
Alfonso Queipo de Llano—Infernal
José Alvarez de Bohorques—Quizas
Francisco Goyoaga—Kif Kif
Enrique Martinez de Vallejo—Ixion

=2 France, Portugal, 40.00;
4 Ireland, 96.25.

Lucerne

Switzerland   28.00
Hans Möhr—Troll
Arthur Blickenstorfer—Florenz II
Max Hauri—Millview
Paul Weier—Junker

2 France, 48.00; 3 Italy, 64.25;
4 FRG, 68.50.

Lisbon

Portugal   19.00
Antonio Pimenta da Gama
—Castico
Joaquim Duarte Silva—Jeune France
Antonio Ramires—Labrador
Henrique Callado—Joc de l'Ile

2 Spain, 26.00; 3 Ireland, 52.00.

Lourenço Marques

South Africa   20.00
Ernest Hayward—Boldhearted

Michael Louw—Jurigo
E. Guthrie—Boldfinish
Bob Grayston—Sabre

2 S. Rhodesia, 23.00;
3 Portugal, 53.00.

Olsztyn

Poland   44.25
Marian Kozicki—Tyras
Antoni Pacynski—Don Hubertus
Andrzej Kubiak—Fis
Wladyslaw Byszewski—Isandra

2 Czechoslovakia, 54.50;
3 GDR, 72.00; 4 Hungary, 89.00.

Buenos Aires

Chile   31.00
Americo Simonetti—El Gitano
Alejandro Perez—Trago Amargo
Luis Labbe—Entorchado
Manuel Rodriquez—Aysen

2 Argentina, 32.00; 3 Brazil, 45.00;
4 Uruguay, 52.00; 5 Bolivia, 124.00.

Aachen

Italy   23.00
Graziano Mancinelli—Rockette
Adriano Capuzzo—Rubicon
Stefano Angioni—Canio
Raimondo d'Inzeo—Bells of Clonmell

2 FRG, 28.00; 3 Spain, 31.00;
4 France, 32.00; 5 Great Britain, 39.00;
6 Switzerland, 55.00; 7 USSR, 158.25;
8 Belgium, retired.

London

Great Britain   0.00
Peter Robeson—Firecrest
Liz Broome—Jacopo
David Boston Barker—North Riding
Harvey Smith—O'Malley

2 Italy, 15.00; 3 USA, 16.00;
4 Ireland, 24.00.

Dublin

USA   8.00
Mary Mairs—Tomboy
Kathy Kusner—Untouchable
Frank Chapot—Manon
William Steinkraus—Sinjon

2 Great Britain, 16.00;
3 Portugal, 24.00; 4 Ireland, 24.25.

Ostend

USA   16.00
Kathy Kusner—Untouchable
Carol Hofmann—San Pedro
Frank Chapot—San Lucas
William Steinkraus—Sinjon

2 Great Britain, 23.00;
=3 Ireland, Belgium, 44.00;
5 Netherlands, 52.00.

Rotterdam

FRG 6.75
Hermann Schridde—Ilona
Kurt Jarasinski—Torro
Alwin Schockemöhle—Zukunft
Hans Günter Winkler—Cornelia

2 USA, 7.50; 3 Great Britain, 16.50;
4 Netherlands, 41.75;
5 Belgium, 44.75;
6 Ireland, 46.50; 7 Poland, 70.75.

New York

USA 4.00
Neal Shapiro—Jacks or Better
Kathy Kusner—Untouchable
Frank Chapot—Manon
William Steinkraus—Sinjon

2 Canada, 16.00;
=3 Brazil, Argentina, 28.00;
5 Mexico, 67.00.

Toronto

USA 12.00
Mary Mairs—Tomboy
Kathy Kusner—Untouchable
William Steinkraus—Sinjon

=2 Canada, Mexico, 16.00;
4 Brazil, 30.00; 5 Argentina, 42.00.

1965

Nice

Italy 8.00
Piero d'Inzeo—Ballyblack
Lalla Novo—Rahin
Graziano Mancinelli—The Rock
Stefano Angioni—Canio

2 Spain, 24.00; 3 Argentina, 29.00;
4 Ireland, 32.25; 5 France, 33.00;
6 Portugal, 40.50.

Rome

Italy 16.00
Piero d'Inzeo—Ballyblack
Lalla Novo—Rahin
Graziano Mancinelli—The Rock
Stefano Angioni—Canio

2 France, 24.00; 3 FRG, 44.00;
4 Argentina, 56.00; 5 Spain, 68.00;
6 Ireland, 80.00.

Madrid

Great Britain 24.00
Harvey Smith—Harvester VI
Fred Welch—Brûle Tout
Andrew Fielder—Vibart
Peter Robeson—Firecrest

2 FRG, 36.00; 3 Spain, 39.00;
4 Portugal, 48.00; 5 Italy, 103.25.

Lisbon

Portugal 20.00
Antonio Pimenta da Gama—Mazarino

Manuel Malta da Costa—Palpite
Artur Brito da Cruz—Foxglove
Jorge Mathias—Joc de l'Ile

2 Spain, 32.50; 3 Great Britain, 33.00.

Lourenço Marques

South Africa 0.00 in 93.00 seconds
in jump-off
Ernest Hayward—Flash
Peter Levor—Shaza
George Myburg—Moby Dick
William Angus—Foxfire

2 Portugal, 0.00 in 95.00 seconds in
jump-off; 3 Rhodesia, 21.00.

Olsztyn

Great Britain 28.00
Marion Coakes—Stroller
David Boston Barker—North Riding
George Hobbs—Brandy Soda
Douglas Bunn—Beethoven

2 GDR, 32.00; 3 USSR, 48.00;
4 Sweden, 64.00; 5 Poland, 68.00;
6 Czechoslovakia, 83.00;
7 Bulgaria, 136.00; 8 Denmark, 182.00.

Aachen

Italy 28.25
Piero d'Inzeo—Ballyblack
Graziano Mancinelli—The Rock
Stefano Angioni—Canio
Lalla Novo—Sunbeam

2 FRG, 33.00; 3 France, 52.00;
4 Ireland, 53.25; 5 USSR, 80.75;
6 Czechoslovakia, 187.00.

London

Italy 24.00
Piero d'Inzeo—Ballyblack
Stefano Angioni—Canio
Graziano Mancinelli—The Rock
Lalla Novo—Rahin

2 Ireland, 25.25; 3 Australia, 44.00;
4 Great Britain, 56.00; 5 FRG, 67.25.

Dublin

Great Britain 20.00
C. David Barker—O'Malley
Marion Coakes—Stroller
Valerie (Clark) Barker—Atalanta
Harvey Smith—Harvester VI

2 Ireland, 28.75; 3 Australia, 32.00;
4 Netherlands, 43.00; 5 Italy, 48.00.

Copenhagen

Great Britain 3.50
Ted Williams—Carnaval
Alison Westwood—The Maverick VII
Marion Coakes—Stroller
Andrew Fielder—Vibart

2 FRG, 4.00; 3 Sweden, 30.00;
4 Poland, 44.00; 5 USSR, 59.50;
6 Czechoslovakia, 113.50;
7 Denmark, retired.

Ostend

Great Britain 24.00
Althea Roger Smith—Havana Royal
Andrew Fielder—Vibart
John Kidd—Bali H'ai II
Douglas Bunn—Beethoven

2 FRG, 26.00; 3 Poland, 52.50;
4 France, 100.75; 5 Belgium, 129.25.

Rotterdam

Great Britain 20.00
Harvey Smith—Harvester VI
Judy Crago—Spring Fever
William Barker—North Flight
Alison Westwood—The Maverick VII

2 FRG, 36.00; 3 Switzerland, 40.25;
4 France, 60.00; 5 Netherlands, 74.50.

Harrisburg

USA 4.00
Mary (Mairs) Chapot—Tomboy
Kathy Kusner—Untouchable
Frank Chapot—San Lucas
William Steinkraus—Snowbound

2 Canada, 6.50; 3 Mexico, 27.50;
4 Ireland, 34.50.

New York

USA 0.00
Mary (Mairs) Chapot—Tomboy
Kathy Kusner—Fire One
Frank Chapot—San Lucas
William Steinkraus—Sinjon

2 Canada, 4.00; 3 Mexico, 11.00;
4 Argentina, 35.00; 5 Ireland, 40.00.

Toronto

USA 8.00
Carol Hofmann—San Pedro
Kathy Kusner—Unusual
Mary (Mairs) Chapot—Tomboy
Frank Chapot—San Lucas

=2 Ireland, Mexico, 32.00;
4 Canada, 36.00

Geneva

Spain 15.75
José Alvarez de Bohorques—Quizas
Alfonso Queipo de Llano—Infernal
Francisco Goyoaga—Kif Kif
Enrique Martinez de Vallejo—Opium

2 Italy, 16.00; 3 FRG, 23.00;
4 Brazil, 28.75; 5 Switzerland, 29.25;
6 Great Britain, 30.00; 7 France, 33.75.

1966

Paris

Great Britain 17.00
Harvey Smith—Warpaint
Ted Williams—Carnaval

Alison Westwood—O'Malley
George Hobbs—Brandy Soda

2 France, 22.25; 3 Spain, 29.25;
4 FRG, 33.75; 5 Italy, 40.25;
6 Netherlands, 57.75.

Rome

Italy   16.00
Graziano Mancinelli—The Rock
Lalla Novo—Rahin
Adriano Capuzzo—Rubicon
Stefano Angioni—Canio

2 Great Britain, 20.00; 3 FRG, 24.00;
4 Switzerland, 31.50; 5 France, 48.00.

Lisbon

Portugal   31.00
Jennifer Holroyd—Zawenda
Antonio Pimenta da Gama—Mistral
Artur Brito da Cruz—Foxglove
Eduardo Netto de Almeida—Joc de l'Ile

2 France, 36.00; 3 Spain, 52.75.

Barcelona

Spain   16.00
Enrique Martinez de Vallejo—Opium
José Alvarez de Bohorques—Quizas
Alfonso Queipo de Llano—Infernal
Francisco Goyoaga—Kif Kif

2 France, 24.00; 3 Italy, 54.75;
4 Portugal, 84.75.

Olsztyn

GDR   16.00
Reinhold Schierle—Kasbek
Rudolf Beerbohm—Domos
Helmut Gille—Sandor
Werner Hakus—Koran

2 Poland, 28.25; 3 Hungary, 32.00;
4 USSR, 40.00; 5 Italy, 61.50.

Lucerne

USA   24.00
Mary (Mairs) Chapot—Tomboy
Kathy Kusner—Untouchable
Frank Chapot—San Lucas
William Steinkraus—Sinjon

2 France, 35.00; 3 Switzerland, 47.00;
4 Hungary, 59.25; 5 Spain, 61.00;
6 FRG, 63.00; 7 USSR, 108.25;
8 Italy, retired.

Leipzig

Poland   12.25
Franciszek Ciebielski
Jan Kowalczyk—Ronceval
Marian Kozicki—Tyras
Antoni Pacynski—Chrenowska

2 GDR, 16.00;
3 Czechoslovakia, 43.50;
4 Hungary, 63.00.

Lourenço Marques

South Africa   16.00
William Angus—Foxfire
Peter Levor—Shaza
Yvonne Johnson—Gay Lord
George Myburg—Moby Dick

2 Rhodesia, 56.75; 3 Portugal, 67.00.

Aachen

Italy   20.00
Graziano Mancinelli—Turvey
Adriano Capuzzo—Rubicon
Stefano Angioni—Canio
Raimondo d'Inzeo—Posillipo

2 USA, 22.00; 3 FRG, 32.00;
4 Spain, 60.00; 5 Poland, 61.75;
6 Hungary, 142.50.

Ostend

Brazil   7.00
Antonio Alegria Simoes—Samurai
José Reynoso Fernandez—Cantal
Nelson Pessoa—Caribe

2 Spain, 12.00; 3 Belgium, 13.00;
4 Netherlands, 36.50.

Rotterdam

Spain   17.50
Alfredo Goyeneche—Jasseur
Jaime, Duque de Aveyro
—Pascha du Bourg
Manuel Ordovas Gonzales
—Naughty Girl
Eduardo Amoros—Rabanito

=2 Belgium, Netherlands, 28.25;
4 Brazil, 36.00; 5 Sweden, 44.75;
6 Poland, 60.50; 7 Denmark, 90.25.

Harrisburg

USA   0.00
Mary (Mairs) Chapot—Tomboy
Chrystine Jones—Fru
Frank Chapot—San Lucas
William Steinkraus—Snowbound

2 Canada, 22.75; 3 Chile, 62.25;
4 Ireland, 102.50.

New York

USA   4.00
Mary (Mairs) Chapot—Tomboy
William Steinkraus—Bold Minstrel
Frank Chapot—San Lucas
Kathy Kusner—Untouchable

2 Canada, 8.00; 3 Ireland, 24.00;
4 Chile, 36.00.

Toronto

Canada   12.00
Moffat Dunlap—Grand Nouvel
Tom Gayford—Canadiana
Gail Ross Amdan—The Hood
Jim Day—Canadian Club

2 USA, 24.00; 3 Ireland, 75.75;
4 Chile, 106.00.

1967

Nice

Great Britain   0.00
Harvey Smith—O'Malley
Anneli Drummond-Hay
—Merely-a-Monarch
Douglas Bunn—Beethoven
Peter Robeson—Firecrest

2 Brazil, 12.75; 3 France, 16.00;
4 Italy, 32.00; 5 FRG, 47.50.

Rome

Switzerland   16.75
Arthur Blickenstorfer—Marianka V
Frank Lombard—Page
Monica Bachmann—Erbach
Paul Weier—Satan III

2 Great Britain, 19.50; 3 FRG, 20.25;
4 Brazil, 22.25; 5 Italy, 24.00;
6 France, 34.75.

Olsztyn

Great Britain   16.00
John Kidd—Mill Street
Simon Rodgerson—Nearberry
Caroline Bradley—Franco
John Baillie—Dominic IV

2 FRG, 20.00; 3 Poland, 24.00;
4 USSR, 27.00; 5 GDR, 32.00;
6 Japan, 43.00;
7 Czechoslovakia, 48.50;
8 Hungary, 68.00.

Leipzig

Great Britain   15.00
John Kidd—Mill Street
Robin Leyland—Ebony X
Caroline Bradley—Franco
John Baillie—Dominic IV

2 GDR, 32.00; 3 USSR, 49.25;
4 Czechoslovakia, 66.75;
5 Hungary, 84.00; 6 Poland, 99.75.

Lourenço Marques

South Africa   8.00
André Ferreira—Knight's Gambit
George Myburg—The Laird
Peter Levor—Shaza
William Angus—Foxfire

2 Portugal, 109.00;
3 Rhodesia, 117.00.

Aachen

Great Britain   4.25
Andrew Fielder—Vibart
Althea Roger Smith—Havana Royal
John Baillie—Dominic IV
Ted Williams—Carnaval

2 Italy, 4.75; 3 USA, 17.00;
4 France, 28.00; 5 FRG, 28.25;
6 Brazil, 33.75; 7 Poland, 41.25;
8 Belgium, 43.50; 9 Sweden, 58.75;
10 Japan, 62.00.   ▶

Pat Koechlin-Smythe

Ever since the earliest days of the sport there has been no shortage of fine women show jumpers. However, because of the dominant part played by the military up until the Second World War, the international side of the sport was, to a large extent, restricted to men. Until the mechanization of the armies forced a change in the rules, Nations Cups were very much the preserve of cavalry officers, and despite Germany's requests, as long ago as the early 1930s, for women to be given a chance to compete (in their own competition) in the Olympic Games, the doors of the latter remained firmly closed to them for another 20 years.

When at Stockholm in 1956 countries were at last allowed to include women in their teams, only two did so. And it was given to Pat Smythe to prove once and for all that women were capable of competing against men on equal terms at the very highest level.

Patricia Rosemary Smythe was born on 22 November, 1928 in East Sheen, not far from London. Her early riding experience was gained in the nearby Richmond Park, first on the lead rein on her older brother's pony, Bubbles, later on her own mare, Pixie, a real character of a pony by an Arab stallion out of a Dartmoor mare. Pat was taught to ride by her mother, an accomplished horsewoman who broke in and schooled polo ponies imported from Argentina. It was with Pixie that Pat learned to jump, practising over benches and natural obstacles such as tree trunks in Richmond Park—an exercise fraught with danger, since it was greatly disapproved of by the park keepers!

Her first competition with Pixie, at the age of eight, was a Pony Club hunter trials, in which she ended up on the floor at the first fence. But Pixie also gave her first taste of success. In 1939 the mare lost the sight of an eye—the result of being kicked by another pony. Inexplicably, her jumping prowess improved rather than diminished thereafter, so much so that not long afterwards she was entered for the children's jumping class at the Richmond Royal Horse Show, at that time one of the major events in the equestrian calendar. Pixie jumped four clear rounds to finish in equal first place.

More ponies followed and then, during the war, the polo player for whom her mother had schooled so many ponies, sent them a youngster by a Thoroughbred stallion out of a milk-float mare. She was christened Finality, and it was this bottle-reared, accident-prone mare who brought the name Pat Smythe to the attention of both the public and the British team selectors. By the time she was 18, Pat had already jumped Finality with success in open classes, and in 1947 she performed to such good effect at the International Show at the White City that an invitation came to make her debut with the British team in Belgium that summer. Then, in June 1948, just as Pat and Finality looked to have an exciting career ahead of them, the mare was sold to a new owner. Finality and her devoted rider had one last outing together—at the White City where they qualified for the final of the King George V Gold Cup in the last year that women were allowed to compete in that event—before going their separate ways. Reunited briefly in 1949, they triumphed in the Leading Show Jumper of the Year class at Harringay, and the following year at the same show survived a memorable duel with Harry Llewellyn and Foxhunter to finish equal first in the puissance.

Invited once again to go abroad with the British team, Pat won her first major international event, the 1949 Brussels Grand Prix, with Mary Whitehead's Nobbler. Then, thanks to her consummate horsemanship, she was able in the early 1950s to turn two new purchases, the excitable ex-racehorse Prince Hal and the difficult grey mare Tosca, into top-class jumpers. Her international career blossomed. She became a regular member of the British team during the fifties and early sixties. She was in 13 winning Nations Cup teams, two with Tosca, one with Prince Hal, eight with Flanagan and two with Scorchin. She was four times Ladies'

Pat Smythe relaxing at home in Gloucestershire in 1958 with Flanagan (right) and Brigadoon.

European Champion and won the British National Championship a record eight times between 1952 and 1962. In 1954, riding Prince Hal, she set a European Ladies' high jump record when clearing 7 ft 3½ in (2.22 metres) at Brussels.

Like all great riders, Pat Smythe achieved success not just with one brilliant horse but on a number of quite different animals. With her own Tosca and Prince Hal and later, Scorchin, Robert Hanson's Flanagan and John King's Mr Pollard, she won Grand Prix and other major events in Madrid, Paris, Aachen, Lisbon, Lucerne, Palermo, London and many other international venues. She became a source of inspiration to a whole generation of young girls wanting to show jump seriously—and nowhere more so than at Stockholm in 1956.

The course at those Olympic Games produced only two clear rounds, one each by the individual gold and silver medalists. In the first round the best score, by the winner, was 4 faults. With just two fences down for 8 faults, Pat Smythe and Flanagan had the distinction of finishing in equal second place (out of 66 starters) after the first round. Thirteen faults in

the second round was still good enough to give them 17th place for that round, and 10th place overall. Having put up the second best performance of the British trio, Pat was rewarded with a team bronze medal and so became the first woman to stand on the Olympic victory podium following the Nations Cup. It was a historic moment, and Pat was subsequently awarded the OBE for her services to show jumping. Four years later, at the Rome Olympics, she and Flanagan were just as effective, finishing equal eleventh individually.

In the autumn of 1963 jumping's first lady married the Swiss horse trials rider Sam Koechlin, and thereafter devoted more time to her family and less to competing. However, she has never relinquished her ties with the sport. For a number of years she was a member of the executive committee of the British Show Jumping Association and from 1983 to 1986 was president of that organization. A prolific author—her first book, *Jump for Joy*, was published before those memorable Stockholm Olympics—she has written several entertaining books about the show jumping world, as well as some very successful children's fiction.

London

Great Britain 8.00
Harvey Smith—O'Malley
Althea Roger Smith—Havana Royal
Andrew Fielder—Vibart
David Broome—Mister Softee

2 Italy, 23.00;
=3 Ireland, Poland, 40.00.

Dublin

Ireland 20.25
Seamus Hayes—Goodbye III
Ned Campion—Liathdruim
Tommy Wade—Dundrum
William Ringrose
—Loch an Easpaig

2 Great Britain, 24.50;
3 Italy, 61.75.

Ostend

FRG 8.00
Heinrich Meyer—Deichgraf
Michael Gockel—Enzi
Fritz Ligges—Alk
Kurt Jarasinski—Revale

2 Ireland, 12.00; 3 France, 20.00;
4 Belgium, 32.00;
5 Netherlands, 40.75; 6 Japan, 50.25.

Rotterdam

Great Britain 12.00
Harvey Smith—Harvester VI
Marion Coakes—Stroller
Peter Robeson—Firecrest
David Broome—Mister Softee

2 FRG, 20.00;
=3 France, Switzerland, 24.00;
5 Ireland, 34.00; 6 Poland, 46.00;
7 Netherlands, 53.75;
8 Belgium, 56.25; 9 USSR, 63.75.

Budapest

USSR 41.75
Victor Durkot—Dissacharia
Victor Nenakhov—Zaur
Victor Matveev—Krokhotny
Boris Konkov—Gerach

2 GDR, 56.75; 3 Austria, 69.50;
6 Poland, 95.75; 5 Hungary, 104.75;
6 Czechoslovakia, 112.25.

New York

USA 0.00, 4.00 in jump-off
Neal Shapiro—Night Spree
Carol Hofmann—Salem
Kathy Kusner—Untouchable
William Steinkraus—Snowbound

2 Great Britain, 0.00, 16.00 in jump-off;
3 Canada, 8.00.

Toronto

USA 12.00
Neal Shapiro—Night Spree
Chrystine Jones—Trick Track

Mary (Mairs) Chapot—Anakonda
Kathy Kusner—Untouchable

2 Great Britain, 16.00;
3 Canada, 32.50.

Geneva

Brazil 13.75
Antonio Algeria Simoes—Necochea
José Reynoso Fernandez—Cantal
Nelson Pessoa—Gran Geste

=2 Italy, Switzerland, 20.00;
4 Ireland, 25.75; 5 France, 26.75.

1968

Nice

Italy 20.50
Piero d'Inzeo—Fidux
Gualtiero Castellini—King's Coin
Ugo d'Amelio—Sensation
Vittorio Orlandi
—Fulmer Feather Duster

2 Spain, 29.25; 3 FRG, 30.50;
4 France, 35.50; 5 Brazil, 39.25;
6 Mexico, 39.50;
=7 Switzerland, Poland, 76.00;
9 Chile, eliminated.

Rome

Italy 12.00
Piero d'Inzeo—Fidux
Vittorio Orlandi
—Fulmer Feather Duster
Giulia Serventi—Gay Monarch
Graziano Mancinelli—Petter Patter

2 Great Britain, 27.00;
3 Switzerland, 39.00; 4 France, 40.00;
5 Mexico, 80.00; 6 Poland, 132.75.

Lucerne

Switzerland 29.75
Arthur Blickenstorfer—Marianka
Monica Bachmann—Erbach
Max Hauri—Telstar
Paul Weier—Satan III

2 Mexico, 38.25; 3 Great Britain, 48.00;
4 France, 51.00; 5 FRG, 68.75;
6 Ireland, 122.00.

Madrid

Portugal 32.00
Antonio Pimenta da Gama—Castico
Vasco Ramires—Namur du Payre
Artur Brito da Cruz—Marau
Henrique Callado—Joc de l'Ile

2 Spain, 59.00; 3 Chile, 83.25.

Lisbon

Portugal 32.50
Antonio Pimenta da Gama—Castico
Vasco Ramires—Namur du Payre
Artur Brito da Cruz—Marau
Henrique Callado—Joc de l'Ile

2 Spain, 72.25; 3 Chile, 76.00.

Olsztyn

Poland 15.00
Jan Kowalczyk—Drobnica
Stefan Grodzicki—Biszka
Piotr Wawryniuk—Poprad
Marian Kozicki—Berry

2 USSR, 33.50;
=3 Czechoslovakia, GDR, 44.00;
5 Hungary, 51.00; 6 Austria, 63.00.

Leipzig

USSR 13.00
Gennadi Samosedenko—Aeron
Eugeni Kuzin—Figlar
Victor Nenakhov—Zaur
Vjateslav Kartavski—Vaterpass

2 GDR, 16.00;
3 Czechoslovakia, 96.50;
4 Hungary, 144.00.

Aachen

Italy 0.00
Graziano Mancinelli—Doneraile
Raimondo d'Inzeo—Bellevue
Gualtiero Castellini—King's Coin
Piero d'Inzeo—Fidux

2 Switzerland, 12.00; 3 FRG, 16.00;
4 USSR, 20.00; 5 France, 36.00;
6 Poland, 44.25; 7 Spain, 50.50;
8 Brazil, 51.00; 9 Mexico, 65.00;
10 Sweden, 97.75.

Lourenço Marques

South Africa 4.00
George Myburg—Moby Dick
Michael Louw—Esprit
Janie Myburg—Mastrap
Peter Levor—Shaza

2 Rhodesia, 7.25; 3 Portugal, 32.00.

London

USA 12.00
Mary (Mairs) Chapot
—White Lightning
Kathy Kusner—Untouchable
Frank Chapot—San Lucas
William Steinkraus—Snowbound

2 Great Britain, 28.00; 3 FRG, 36.00;
4 Italy, 51.00; 5 Ireland, 55.50.

Dublin

USA 4.25
Mary (Mairs) Chapot
—White Lightning
Kathy Kusner—Fru
Frank Chapot—San Lucas
William Steinkraus—Snowbound

2 Great Britain, 8.00; 3 Ireland, 20.25;
4 Sweden, 27.50; 5 Italy, 27.75;
6 Belgium, 100.75.

Copenhagen

FRG 17.75
Kurt Jarasinski—Pirat
Manfred Kloess—Anthea

Lutz Merkel—Sir
Fritz Ligges—Zuckerpuppe

2 Sweden, 23.00; 3 Denmark, 72.00;
4 Japan, 152.75.

Ostend

USA   20.00
Mary (Mairs) Chapot
—White Lightning
Carol Hofmann—Out Late
Kathy Kusner—Untouchable
Frank Chapot—San Lucas

2 Spain, 36.00; 3 France, 36.00;
4 Belgium, 60.00; 5 Portugal, 70.50.

Rotterdam

USA   4.00
Mary (Mairs) Chapot
—White Lightning
Carol Hofmann—Out Late
Kathy Kusner—Untouchable
Frank Chapot—San Lucas

2 Brazil, 13.00; 3 France, 20.00;
4 FRG, 20.75; 5 Great Britain, 24.25;
6 Sweden, 36.00; 7 Japan, 68.00;
8 Denmark, 69.50;
9 Netherlands, 81.75;
10 Belgium, 157.25.

New York

USA   12.00
Carol Hofmann—Salem
Frank Chapot—San Lucas
Mary (Mairs) Chapot
—White Lightning
William Steinkraus—Bold Minstrel

2 Great Britain, 32.00;
3 Canada, 36.00; 4 Australia, 44.00;
5 Brazil, 71.75.

Toronto

USA   16.50
Mary (Mairs) Chapot
—White Lightning
Neal Shapiro—Trick Track
Carol Hofmann—Salem
Frank Chapot—San Lucas

2 Canada, 27.25;
3 Great Britain, 44.75;
4 Australia, 56.25; 5 Brazil, 96.00.

1969

Nice

France   16.00
Marcel Rozier—Quo Vadis
Janou Lefèbvre—Rocket
Gilles Bertran de Balanda—Sigurd
Philippe Jouy—Prélude de Palustra

2 FRG, 20.00; 3 Italy, 28.00;
4 Great Britain, 32.00; 5 Brazil, 37.25;
6 Belgium, 66.50.

Rome

FRG   16.50
Gerd Wiltfang—Domjunge
Manfred Kloess—Der Lord
Fritz Ligges—Zuckerpuppe
Hartwig Steenken—Simona

2 Great Britain, 20.00; 3 Italy, 23.25;
4 France, 40.00.

Barcelona

Great Britain   0.00
Alan Oliver—Sweep III
Paddy McMahon—Hideaway
George Hobbs—War Lord
David Broome—Top of the Morning II

2 France, 4.75; 3 FRG, 5.25;
4 Portugal, 39.50; 5 Spain, retired.

Lourenço Marques

South Africa   0.00
Michael Louw—Clowshorse
Gonda Butters—Ratification
Peter Levor—Esprit
George Myburg—The Laird

2 Portugal, 18.00; 3 Rhodesia, 32.00.

Olsztyn

Poland   4.00
Marian Kozicki—Bronz
Henryk Hucz—Deptak
Jan Kowalczyk—Brzeszczot
Piotr Wawryniuk—Poprad

2 USSR, 8.00; 3 GDR, 28.00;
4 France, 40.00; 5 Hungary, 120.00.

Leipzig

USSR   35.75
Victor Nenakhov—Zaur
Vjateslav Kartavski—Epigraf
S. Chodyrev—Arsenal
Victor Durkot—Dissacharia

2 GDR, 36.75; 3 Poland, 40.00;
4 Hungary, 80.75.

Aachen

FRG   24.00
Gerd Wiltfang—Extra
Hartwig Steenken—Simona
Hans Günter Winkler—Torphy
Alwin Schockemöhle—Donald Rex

2 Great Britain, 39.25;
3 Switzerland, 43.00; 4 Italy, 52.00;
5 Netherlands, 83.25; 6 Poland, 88.75;
7 France, retired; 8 Belgium, retired.

London

FRG   0.00
Lutz Merkel—Anmut
Hartwig Steenken—Simona
Hans Günter Winkler—Torphy
Alwin Schockemöhle—Donald Rex

2 Great Britain, 12.00; 3 Italy, 16.00;
4 France, 20.00; 5 Sweden, 36.00;
6 Ireland, 52.00; 7 Australia, 121.00.

Dublin

FRG   4.00, 0.00 in jump-off
Lutz Merkel—Sir
Hartwig Steenken—Simona
Hans Günter Winkler—Torphy
Alwin Schockemöhle—Donald Rex

2 Great Britain, 4.00, 4.00 in jump-off;
3 Italy, 12.00; 4 Switzerland, 40.25;
5 Australia, 40.75; 6 Ireland, 41.50;
7 Belgium, 116.25.

Ostend

FRG   4.00
Hendrik Snoek—Feiner Kerl
Manfred Kloess—Der Lord
Fritz Ligges—Zuckerpuppe
Lutz Merkel—Sir

2 Great Britain, 12.00;
3 Belgium, 16.50; 4 France, 41.25;
5 Ireland, 44.00; 6 Netherlands, 61.25.

Rotterdam

Great Britain   12.25
Ann (Townsend) Backhouse
—Cardinal II
Stephen Pritchard—Telstar XI
Aileen Ross—Trevarrion
George Hobbs—Battling Pedulas

2 Poland, 14.50; 3 Netherlands, 16.00;
4 FRG, 16.50; 5 Belgium, 20.00;
6 Denmark, 28.00; 7 France, 39.00;
8 Ireland, 39.25.

Lisbon

Switzerland   12.00
Monica Bachmann—Erbach
Ernst Eglin—Carver Doon
Mario Baumgartner—Waldersee
Paul Weier—Wildfeuer

2 Italy, 16.00; 3 Belgium, 24.00;
=4 Spain, Portugal, 40.25;
6 France, 42.00.

Harrisburg

USA   0.25
Neal Shapiro—Trick Track
Jared Brinsmade—Triple Crown
Frank Chapot—San Lucas
William Steinkraus—Bold Minstrel

2 Canada, 8.00; 3 Mexico, 35.25;
4 Argentina, 37.25.

New York

USA   16.00
Kathy Kusner—Wicked City
Jared Brinsmade—Triple Crown
Frank Chapot—San Lucas
William Steinkraus—Bold Minstrel

2 Canada, 40.00; 3 Mexico, 58.00;
4 Argentina, eliminated.

Toronto

Canada   8.00
Moffat Dunlap—Grand Nouvel
Tom Gayford—Big Dee

Jim Day—Canadian Club
Jim Elder—The Immigrant

2 USA, 23.00; 3 Argentina, 59.50;
4 Mexico, 75.00.

Geneva

FRG 8.25
Lutz Merkel—Sir
Hartwig Steenken—Simona
Hermann Schridde—Heureka
Alwin Schockemöhle—Donald Rex

2 Italy, 12.00;
=3 France, Great Britain, 16.00;
5 Ireland, 41.50; 6 Switzerland, 46.25;
7 Netherlands, 60.25;
8 Brazil, eliminated.

1970

Rome

Great Britain 20.50
Anneli Drummond-Hay
—Merely-a-Monarch
Harvey Smith—Ten to Twelve
David Broome—Top of the Morning II
George Hobbs—Battling Pedulas

2 FRG, 24.25; 3 Italy, 47.00;
4 France, 58.50; 5 Spain, 92.00.

Madrid

FRG 12.25
Hauke Schmidt—Wolfdieter
Bernd Kuwertz—Sieno
Sönke Sönksen—Palisander
Hans Günter Winkler—Torphy

=2 France, Spain, 16.00;
4 Great Britain, 31.25.

Lucerne

USA 8.00
Neal Shapiro—San Lucas
Joe Fargis—Bonte II
Kathy Kusner—Silver Scot
William Steinkraus—Snowbound

2 Great Britain, 12.00; 3 FRG, 16.00;
4 Switzerland, 16.75; 5 Ireland, 45.75.

Lourenço Marques

South Africa 3.00
Peter Levor—Format
Theo Laros—Goya
Wendy Grayston—King Canute
Michael Louw—Torch Sign

2 Rhodesia, 36.00; 3 Portugal, 80.00.

Olsztyn

USSR 23.75
Victor Durkot—Abzac
Victor Poganovsky—Gejzer
Victor Lisitsyn—Peneteli
Yuri Zyabrev—Grim

2 FRG, 28.00; 3 GDR, 32.25;
4 Poland, 44.00; 5 Hungary, 48.00;
6 Italy, 110.25; 7 Bulgaria, eliminated.

Aachen

FRG 4.00
Hendrik Snoek—Dorina
Gerd Wiltfang—Goldika
Lutz Merkel—Sir
Hartwig Steenken—Simona

2 Great Britain, 12.00; 3 USA, 16.25;
4 Brazil, 33.50; 5 Italy, 36.00;
6 Argentina, 40.50;
7 Netherlands, eliminated.

La Baule

Canada 12.00, 0.00 in jump-off
Tom Gayford—Big Dee
Jim Day—Canadian Club
Moffat Dunlap—Argyll
Jim Elder—Shoeman

2 France, 12.00; 4.00 in jump-off;
=3 USA, Great Britain, 16.00;
5 Brazil, 32.25; 6 Italy, 38.25;
7 Belgium, 40.00; 8 Argentina, 42.25;
9 Mexico, 117.50; 10 Chile, eliminated.

London

Great Britain 12.00
Michael Saywell—Hideaway
Marion (Coakes) Mould—Stroller
Harvey Smith—Mattie Brown
David Broome—Beethoven

2 Italy, 20.75; 3 Canada, 28.25;
4 Argentina, 63.00; 5 Mexico, 92.00;
6 Sweden, retired.

Dublin

Great Britain 8.00
Harvey Smith—Mattie Brown
Michael Saywell—Hideaway
George Hobbs—Battling Pedulas
David Broome—Manhattan

2 Italy, 11.25; 3 FRG, 14.50;
4 France, 29.00; 5 Canada, 37.75;
6 Ireland, 44.50; 7 Sweden, 61.00.

Ostend

Great Britain 18.50
Ray Howe—Balmain
Ann Moore—Psalm
Stephen Hadley—Prospero
Anneli Drummond-Hay—Xanthos II

2 FRG, 20.50; 3 France, 31.00;
4 Belgium, 41.75; 5 Spain, 58.00;
6 Netherlands, 85.25.

Rotterdam

FRG 12.25
Bernd Kuwertz—Sieno
Willibert Mehlkopf—Fidelus
Hartwig Steenken—Tasso
Gerd Wiltfang—Goldika

2 Great Britain, 20.00;
3 Belgium, 49.75; 4 Spain, 64.50;
5 Netherlands, 73.50; 6 France, 82.75;
7 Mexico, 89.00; 8 Italy, 95.00;
9 Poland, 112.75.

Budapest

GDR 40.50
Fredo Kasten—Orkus
Manfred Nietzschmann—Fermor
Siegfried Hohloch—Freier
Heinz Schulenburg—Fakir

2 USSR, 56.00; 3 Poland, 73.00;
4 Hungary, 75.00;
5 Czechoslovakia, 118.50.

Libson

Switzerland 4.00
Monica Bachmann—Erbach
Mario Baumgartner—Waldersee
Ernst Eglin—Carver Doon
Paul Weier—Wildfeuer

2 Portugal, 24.25; 3 Spain, 33.75;
4 Italy, 36.25.

Harrisburg

FRG 0.00
Lutz Merkel—Sir
Gerd Wiltfang—Goldika
Hartwig Steenken—Simona
Hans Günter Winkler—Torphy

2 USA, 12.25; 3 Canada, 16.00;
4 Ireland, 37.75; 5 Mexico, retired.

New York

FRG 0.00
Lutz Merkel—Sir
Gerd Wiltfang—Goldika
Hartwig Steenken—Simona
Hans Günter Winkler—Torphy

2 USA, 4.00; 3 Ireland, 12.00;
4 Mexico, 20.00; 5 Canada, 48.25.

Toronto

FRG 4.50
Lutz Merkel—Sir
Gerd Wiltfang—Goldika
Hartwig Steenken—Simona
Hans Günter Winkler—Torphy

2 USA, 8.00; 3 Canada, 32.50;
4 Mexico, 40.75; 5 Ireland, 44.00.

1971

Rome

FRG 16.00
Lutz Merkel—Gonzales
Paul Schockemöhle—Askan
Hartwig Steenken—Simona
Hans Günter Winkler—Torphy

2 Great Britain, 20.00; 3 France, 24.00;
4 Italy, 28.00.

Barcelona

Spain 8.00
Jaime, Duque de Aveyro
—Sunday Beau

Alfonso Segovia—Sableuse
Luis Alvarez Cervera—Acorne
Enrique Martinez de Vallejo
—Romantico

=2 FRG, Great Britain,
12.00; 4 Portugal, 89.00.

Fontainebleau

FRG   5.25
Paul Schockemöhle—Askan
Hartwig Steenken—Simona
Alwin Schockemöhle—Donald Rex
Hans Günter Winkler—Torphy

2 Italy, 13.00; 3 Great Britain, 16.75;
4 USA, 25.75; 5 Switzerland, 36.25;
6 France, 40.00; 7 Belgium, 53.00.

Lourenço Marques

South Africa   24.00
Anthony Lewis—Take a Chance
Gonda Butters—BP Superblend
Peter Levor—Format
Wendy Grayston—King Canute

2 Rhodesia, 46.00;
3 Portugal, eliminated.

Olsztyn

Poland   40.00
Marian Kozicki—Bronz
Jan Kowalczyk—Via Vitae
Norbert Wieja—Aral
Piotr Wawryniuk—Poprad

2 GDR, 56.00; 3 Hungary, 74.50;
4 Czechoslovakia, 84.00;
5 USSR, 107.00.

Aachen

USA   16.00, 0.00 in jump-off
Joe Fargis—Bonte II
Conrad Homfeld—Triple Crown
Neal Shapiro—Sloopy
William Steinkraus—Fleet Apple

2 Great Britain, 16.00, 12.00 in
jump-off; 3 FRG, 23.50;
4 France, 32.00; 5 Italy, 48.00;
6 USSR, 54.25; 7 Spain, 56.00;
8 Switzerland, 60.00; 9 Poland, 64.00;
10 Belgium, 72.25;
11 Netherlands, 124.50;
12 Hungary, retired.

Dublin

FRG   33.25
Hendrik Snoek—Faustus
Gerd Wiltfang—Askan
Hans Günter Winkler—Torphy
Hartwig Steenken—Simona

2 Great Britain, 33.50; 3 Italy, 37.50;
4 USA, 47.00; 5 Spain, 50.25;
6 France, 57.25; 7 Ireland, 92.50;
retired, Poland, Denmark.

Ostend

Ireland   8.25
Ned Campion—Garrai Eoin

Eddie Macken—Oatfield Hills
Larry Kiely—Inis Cara

2 Great Britain, 13.25; 3 France, 24.25;
4 Belgium, 28.00.

Rotterdam

FRG   0.00
Hendrik Snoek—Faustus
Hugo Simon—Fair Lady
Fritz Ligges—Robin
Hans Günter Winkler—Torphy

2 Great Britain, 11.00;
3 Belgium, 25.50;
4 Netherlands, 33.00; 5 Ireland, 40.50;
6 Denmark, eliminated.

Budapest

FRG   28.00, 13.50 in jump-off
Lutz Gössing—Frappant
Bernd Kuwertz—Wartburg
Sönke Sönksen—Palisander
Kurt Jarasinski—Revale

2 Poland, 28.00, 34.25 in jump-off;
3 Italy, 37.00; 4 Switzerland, 41.25;
5 Hungary, 50.75; 6 Japan, 57.75;
7 USSR, 67.00;
8 Czechoslovakia, 133.25.

Lisbon

Great Britain   16.00
Peter Robeson—Grebe
Faith Panton—Alcatraz
Caroline Bradley—Wood Nymph
Alison (Westwood) Dawes
—The Maverick VII

=2 France, Italy, 24.00;
4 Switzerland, 24.75; 5 Belgium, 32.75;
6 Portugal, 41.00; 7 Spain, 52.00.

Harrisburg

USA   4.25
Joe Fargis—Bonte II
Neal Shapiro—Sloopy
Frank Chapot—San Lucas
William Steinkraus—Fleet Apple

2 Canada, 8.25; 3 Argentina, 32.50.

New York

Canada   7.00
Eleanor MacCowan—Hombre
Barbara Simpson Kerr—Catbird
Terrance Millar—Le Dauphin
Jim Day—Sun Dancer

2 USA, 12.00; 3 Argentina, 31.75.

Toronto

Canada   4.00, 4.00 in 108.00 secs
in jump-off
Moffatt Dunlap—Intrepid
Barabra Simpson Kerr—Magnor
Terrance Millar—Le Dauphin
Jim Day—Sun Dancer

2 USA, 4.00, 4.00 in 118.10 secs
in jump-off; 3 Argentina, 48.00.

Geneva

FRG   8.25
Fritz Ligges—Robin
Lutz Merkel—Sir
Gerd Wiltfang—Dorian Gray
Hans Günter Winkler—Torphy

2 Great Britain, 12.25; 3 Spain, 31.25;
4 Switzerland, 32.25; 5 Italy, 32.50.

1972

Nice

Great Britain   10.00
Lionel Dunning—Arran Blaze
Simon Rodgerson—Savannah III
Stephen Hadley—Freeman IV
Peter Robeson—Grebe

2 France, 19.25; 3 Spain, 20.00;
4 Portugal, 22.75; 5 Belgium, 29.00;
6 Italy, 70.00.

Rome

Italy   12.00
Graziano Mancinelli—Ambassador
Vittorio Orlandi—Valetta
Raimondo d'Inzeo—Fiorello
Piero d'Inzeo—Red Fox

2 Great Britain, 24.00; 3 FRG, 28.00;
4 Brazil, 48.00; 5 Portugal, 69.50;
6 France, 77.75; 7 Belgium, retired.

Madrid

Great Britain   0.00, 9.00 in jump-off
Peter Robeson—Grebe
Ann (Townsend) Backhouse
—Cardinal III
Lionel Dunning—Arran Blaze
Alison (Westwood) Dawes
—The Maverick VII

2 France, 0.00, 61.75 in jump-off;
3 Italy, 8.00; 4 Spain, 12.00;
5 Portugal, 43.50.

Lucerne

FRG   33.00
Lutz Merkel—Gonzales
Michael Gockel—Bonanza
Haucke Schmidt—Trumpf IV
Sönke Sönksen—Kwept

2 Switzerland, 35.00; 3 USA, 71.25;
4 USSR, 135.00; 5 Japan, 151.25.

Lourenço Marques

South Africa   20.25
Wendy Grayston—King Cole
Peter Levor—Esprit
Gonda Butters—Havoc
Anthony Lewis—Take a Chance

2 Portugal, 52.00; 3 Rhodesia, 66.00.

Olsztyn

Great Britain   36.00, 4.00 in jump-off
John Greenwood—Mr Punch II

Stephen Pritchard—Telstar
Derek Ricketts—Dakota

2 Poland, 36.00, 8.00 in jump-off;
3 Hungary, 40.00; 4 USSR, 44.00;
5 Czechoslovakia, 52.00;
6 GDR, 94.25; 7 Rumania, 112.25.

Ostend

FRG   24.00
Achaz von Buchwaldt—Askari
Peter Schmitz—Panama
Manfred Kloess—Nadir
Lutz Merkel—Sir

2 France, 25.00; 3 Great Britain, 50.75;
4 Belgium, 51.00.

Aachen

FRG   20.00
Fritz Ligges—Robin
Hermann Schridde—Kadett
Gerd Wiltfang—Dorian Gray
Hartwig Steenken—Kosmos

2 Argentina, 36.00; 3 USA, 44.00;
4 Switzerland, 48.00; 5 France, 51.75;
6 Poland, 52.50; 7 Netherlands, 77.25;
8 Austria, 88.00; 9 Belgium, 120.75;
10 Chile, 125.75; 11 Japan, retired.

London

Great Britain   4.00
Alan Oliver—Sweep III
Paddy McMahon
  —Pennwood Forge Mill
Harvey Smith—Mattie Brown
David Broome—Sportsman

2 Italy, 28.00; 3 Belgium, 70.75.

Dublin

FRG   8.00
Hendrik Snoek—Faustus
Karl-Heinz Giebmanns—The Saint
Lutz Merkel—Gonzales
Alwin Schockemöhle—The Robber

2 Ireland, 32.00; 3 Italy, 58.75;
4 Switzerland, 85.50.

Rotterdam

FRG   8.00
Fritz Ligges—Robin
Gerd Wiltfang—Askan
Alwin Schockemöhle—The Robber
Hartwig Steenken—Simona

2 Great Britain, 8.25;
3 Netherlands, 34.00;
4 Belgium, 45.50.

Lisbon

Switzerland   16.00
Monica (Bachmann) Weier—Vassal
Paul Weier—Fink
Mario Baumgartner—Frustra
Kurt Maeder—Abraxon

2 Portugal, 18.00; 3 Spain, 52.75.

Harrisburg

USA   5.00
Neal Shapiro—Duke's Honor
Kathy Kusner—Triple Crown
Frank Chapot—Good Twist
William Steinkraus—Main Spring

2 Canada, 46.75; 3 Mexico, 63.75.

New York

USA   8.00, 0.00 in 97.70 secs
in jump-off
Neal Shapiro—Duke's Honor
Kathy Kusner—Triple Crown
Frank Chapot—Good Twist
William Steinkraus—Main Spring

2 Canada, 8.00, 0.00 in 103.70 secs
in jump-off; 3 Mexico, 24.25.

Toronto

USA   0.00
Neal Shapiro—Trick Track
Kathy Kusner—Triple Crown
William Steinkraus—Main Spring
Frank Chapot—Good Twist

2 Canada, 11.00; 3 Mexico, 36.50.

1973

Nice

Great Britain   20.75
John Greenwood—Mr Punch II
Caroline Bradley—True Lass
Lionel Dunning—Arran Blaze
Ted Edgar—Everest Peak

2 Italy, 25.50; 3 France, 33.50;
4 Netherlands, 33.75; 5 FRG, 34.25.

Rome

Great Britain   16.00
Harvey Smith—Summertime
Ann Moore—April Love
Lionel Dunning—Arran Blaze
Peter Robeson—Grebe

2 Italy, 24.00; 3 Netherlands, 48.50;
4 FRG, 56.00; 5 Belgium, 68.00.

Madrid

Great Britain   20.00
Ray Howe—Fanta
Ann Backhouse—Cardinal III
Malcolm Pyrah—Trevarrion
Paddy McMahon
  —Pennwood Forge Mill

2 Spain, 28.00; 3 Portugal, 103.00.

Olsztyn

FRG   20.00
Peter Schmitz—Panama
Bernd Kuwertz—Girl
Hartmut Röder—Rebell
Manfred Kloess—Nadir

2 Poland, 28.00; 3 Hungary, 36.00.

Lourenço Marques

South Africa   8.00
Gonda (Butters) Betrix—Esprit
Anthony Lewis—Red Gambit
Wendy Grayston—King Cole
Michael Louw—Torch Sign

2 Rhodesia, 52.00; 3 Portugal, 60.00.

Aachen

FRG   8.00
Gerd Wiltfang—Askan
Hartwig Steenken—Kosmos
Hans Günter Winkler—Torphy
Alwin Schockemöhle—Rex the Robber

2 Great Britain, 24.00;
3 Switzerland, 28.00; 4 Italy, 48.00;
5 Belgium, 60.25;
6 Netherlands, 69.00.

London

FRG   0.00
Fritz Ligges—Genius
Paul Schockemöhle—Abadir
Hans Günter Winkler—Torphy
Alwin Schockemöhle—Rex the Robber

2 Great Britain, 16.00;
3 Belgium, 48.00.

Buenos Aires

Argentina
Carlos Marcelli—Chopin
Hugo Arrambide—Camalote
Carlos Delia—Cardon
Jorge Llambi—Okey Amigo

Dublin

Great Britain   0.00
Anne Moore—Psalm
Paddy McMahon
  —Pennwood Forge Mill
David Broome—Manhattan
Peter Robeson—Grebe

2 FRG, 16.25; 3 Netherlands, 24.25;
4 Ireland, 36.50; 5 France, 41.75.

Rotterdam

FRG   9.00
Hermann Schridde—Kadett
Fritz Ligges—Genius
Hartwig Steenken—Kosmos
Alwin Schockemöhle—Rex the Robber

2 Great Britain, 12.00;
3 Netherlands, 21.75; 4 France, 50.25;
5 Switzerland, 51.75; 6 Sweden, 84.75;
7 Austria, 130.25; 8 Italy, 146.75;
9 Belgium, 185.75.

Ostend

Great Britain   12.00
Derek Ricketts—Beau Supreme
Tony Newbery—Warwick III
Rowland Fernyhough—Automatic
Ann Moore—Psalm

2 Switzerland, 28.75; 3 Italy, 29.25;
4 Belgium, 35.00; 5 France, 39.50;
6 FRG, 56.50.

Lisbon

Switzerland   31.50
Monica (Bachmann) Weier—Vassal II
Peter Reid—Casanova
Jürg Friedli—Rocket
Paul Weier—Fink

2 Portugal, 32.50; 3 Spain, 44.75;
4 Great Britain, 51.00;
5 Belgium, 67.50.

São Paulo

Chile   15.00
René Varas—Quintral
Victor Contador—Bony
Américo Simonetti—Ataulfo

2 Argentina, 16.00; 3 Brazil, 20.00.

Washington

USA   8.00, 0.00 in jump-off
Frank Chapot—Main Spring
Mac Cone—Triple Crown
Michael Matz—Snow Flurry
Rodney Jenkins—Idle Dice

2 Great Britain, 8.00, 4.00 in jump-off;
3 FRG, 23.75; 4 Canada, 24.00.

New York

Great Britain   8.00
Harvey Smith—Salvador
Graham Fletcher—Buttevant Boy
Derek Ricketts—Beau Supreme
David Broome—Sportsman

=2 USA, FRG, 12.00; 4 Canada, 24.00.

Toronto

USA   8.25
Mac Cone—Triple Crown
Michael Matz—Mighty Ruler
Rodney Jenkins—Idle Dice
Frank Chapot—Main Spring

2 FRG, 15.25; 3 Canada, 16.75;
4 Great Britain, 20.00.

Geneva

FRG   16.00
Gerd Wiltfang—Frederikus Rex
Hendrik Snoek—Rasputin
Lutz Merkel—Humphrey
Hartwig Steenken—Simona

2 Switzerland, 20.00;
3 Great Britain, 24.00;
4 France, 28.00; 5 Belgium, 52.00;
6 Italy, 76.00.

1974

Rome

Italy   12.00, 4.00 in jump-off
Adriano Capuzzo—Beau Regard
Vittorio Orlandi
—Fulmer Feather Duster
Graziano Mancinelli—Bel Oiseau

Piero d'Inzeo—Easter Light

2 France, 12.00, 12.00 in jump-off;
3 Great Britain, 17.25;
=4 Spain, Belgium, 24.25.

Barcelona

Italy   4.00, 0.00 in jump-off
Stefano Angioni—Puckoon
Stefano Lupis—Drummage
Graziano Mancinelli—Ambassador
Piero d'Inzeo—Easter Light

2 Spain; 3 FRG; 4 Portugal, retired.

Lucerne

Great Britain   20.00
Malcolm Pyrah—Law Court
Rowland Fernyhough—Autumatic
Judy Cargo—Brevitt Bouncer
Paddy McMahon
—Pennwood Forge Mill

2 FRG, 36.00; 3 Switzerland, 38.25;
4 USA, 39.75; 5 Ireland, 44.75;
6 Netherlands 74.25; 7 Austria, 88.25;
8 Argentina, retired.

Olsztyn

Poland   28.00
Stefan Migdalski—Balsam
Rudolf Mrugala—Farsa
Henryk Hucz—Bertyn
Jan Kowalczyk—Blekot

2 Great Britain, 32.00;
3 Belgium, 48.00; 4 FRG, 50.25;
5 USSR, 56.25; 6 Rumania, 64.75;
7 GDR, 66.75;
8 Czechoslovakia, 105.75.

Trinwillershagen

Poland   24.00
Wojciech Dabrowski—Babinicz
Stefan Migdalski—Balsam
Franciszek Ciebielski—Tenor
Henryk Hucz—Bertyn

2 GDR, 28.75; 3 Rumania, 31.50;
4 Czechoslovakia, eliminated.

La Baule

FRG   12.50
Paul Schockemöhle—Agent
Hans Günter Winkler—Torphy
Alwin Schockemöhle—Rex the Robber
Hartwig Steenken—Simona

2 USA, 18.25; 3 Great Britain, 32.00;
4 France, 40.00; 5 Italy, 43.75;
6 Spain, 56.00; 7 Belgium, 83.00;
8 Portugal, 149.25; 9 Argentina, retired.

London

Great Britain   0.00
Harvey Smith—Salvador
Graham Fletcher—Buttevant Boy
Malcolm Pyrah—Trevarrion
David Broome—Sportsman

2 USA, 8.00; 3 Netherlands, 20.00;
4 FRG, 24.00; 5 Argentina, 31.00;
6 Spain, 31.75; 7 Italy, 58.25.

Buenos Aires

Argentina
(No details available.)

Dublin

Great Britain   0.75
Harvey Smith—Salvador
Tony Newbery—Warwick III
David Broome—Sportsman
Peter Robeson—Grebe

2 FRG, 4.00; 3 USA, 7.25;
4 Ireland, 24.00.

Rotterdam

Great Britain   4.00
Harvey Smith—Salvador
Derek Ricketts—Beau Supreme
David Broome—Manhattan
Peter Robeson—Grebe

2 France, 12.00; =3 FRG, Italy, 16.00;
5 Belgium, 26.00;
6 Netherlands, 27.00;
7 Switzerland, 36.00; 8 Ireland, 48.75.

Ostend

France   8.75
Pierre Durand—Varin
Laurent Persyn—Boulzicourt
Daniel Constant—Vicomte d'Aubinier
Michel Roche—Un Espoir

2 Belgium, 17.50;
3 Great Britain, 18.00;
4 Sweden, 79.50.

Aachen

FRG   12.00
Gerd Wiltfang—Firlefanz
Paul Schockemöhle—Talisman
Hartwig Steenken—Erle
Alwin Schockemöhle—Rex the Robber

2 Great Britain, 28.00;
3 Switzerland, 40.00;
4 Netherlands, 50.75; 5 Austria, 72.50;
6 Sweden, 93.25.

Lisbon

France   8.00
Hubert Parot—Rivage
Philippe Henry—Bamby
Daniel Constant—Vicomte d'Aubinier
Pierre Durand—Varin

2 Spain, 11.00; 3 FRG, 16.00;
4 Great Britain, 16.25;
5 Portugal, 28.00; 6 Switzerland, 31.50;
7 Belgium, 32.00.

Laxenburg

FRG   8.00
Gerd Wiltfang—Firlefanz
Hermann Schridde—Kadett
Fritz Ligges—Thronfolger
Hans Günter Winkler—Torphy

2 Great Britain, 9.25;
3 Switzerland, 16.00; 4 Austria, 16.50;
5 Poland, 47.25.

Washington

USA 12.00
Buddy Brown—Sandsablaze
Thom Hardy—Coming Attraction
Dennis Murphy—Do Right
Rodney Jenkins—Number One Spy

2 France, 12.50;
3 Great Britain, 19.00;
4 Canada, 48.25.

New York

USA 0.00
Buddy Brown—Sandsablaze
Thom Hardy—Coming Attraction
Dennis Murphy—Do Right
Frank Chapot—Main Spring

2 France, 3.00; 3 Great Britain, 8.00;
4 Canada, 11.00.

Toronto

France 12.00, 0.00 in jump-off
Hubert Parot—Rivage
Michel Roche—Un Espoir
Pierre Durand—Varin
Janou (Lefèbvre) Tissot—Rocket

2 Canada, 12.00, 4.00 in jump-off;
3 Great Britain, 15.00; 4 USA, 24.00.

1975

Geneva

FRG 4.00
Hendrik Snoek—Rasputin
Gerd Wiltfang—Galipolis
Paul Schockemöhle—Talisman
Hartwig Steenken—Kosmos

2 Great Britain, 4.25; 3 Belgium, 16.25;
4 Switzerland, 19.75; 5 Ireland, 26.00;
6 Netherlands, 44.75; 7 France, 49.00.

Rome

Italy 8.00
Graziano Mancinelli—Lydican
Stefano Angioni—Puckoon
Vittorio Orlandi—Fiorello
Piero d'Inzeo—Easter Light

2 Great Britain, 12.00; 3 FRG, 12.50;
4 Ireland, 28.00; 5 France, 48.00;
6 Belgium, 68.50.

Barcelona

Italy 4.50
Graziano Mancinelli—Bel Oiseau
Georgio Nuti—Try Over
Stefano Angioni—Puckoon
Piero d'Inzeo—Easter Light

2 Spain, 8.00; 3 Portugal, 12.00;
4 Great Britain.

Olsztyn

FRG 12.00
Hendrik Schultze-Siehoff—Dömitz
Paul Kronenberger—Flint

Axel Wöckener—Glasgow
Lutz Merkel—Salvaro

2 France, 24.00; 3 Great Britain, 40.00;
4 Netherlands, 45.00; 5 GDR;
6 Rumania; 7 USSR; 8 Poland.

Trinwillershagen

GDR 16.00
Volker Tonn—Pflicht
Heinz Schulenburg—Kardinal
Reinhold Schierle—San Remo
Wolfgang Gshwandter—Dukat

2 Rumania, 19.00; 3 Poland, 24.00.

Fontainebleau

Italy 18.50
Piero d'Inzeo—Easter Light
Stefano Angioni—Puckoon
Vittorio Orlandi—Fiorello
Graziano Mancinelli—Bel Oiseau

2 Belgium, 25.00; 3 France, 30.25;
4 FRG, 31.50;
=5 Great Britain, Brazil, 32.00;
7 Switzerland, 42.25;
8 Netherlands, 51.25.

Aachen

FRG 16.00, 16.00 in jump-off
Hendrik Snoek—Rasputin
Gerd Wiltfang—Galipolis
Hartwig Steenken—Erle
Alwin Schockemöhle—Warwick

2 Great Britain, 16.00, retired
in jump-off; 3 Switzerland, 24.00;
4 Belgium, 32.00; 5 France, 32.75;
6 Italy, 48.00; 7 Austria, 64.50;
8 Netherlands, 97.50;
9 Rumania, eliminated.

Hickstead

Great Britain 8.00
Harvey Smith—Salvador
Graham Fletcher—Tauna Dora
Paddy McMahon—Penwood Forge Mill
David Broome—Heatwave

2 FRG, 9.00; 3 Ireland, 12.00;
4 Switzerland, 40.00;
5 Australia, 52.75; 6 Belgium, 57.25;
7 Netherlands, retired.

Dublin

Great Britain 16.00
Harvey Smith—Salvador
Paddy McMahon—Penwood Forge Mill
Graham Fletcher—Tauna Dora
David Broome—Heatwave

2 Ireland, 29.00; 3 FRG, 33.25;
4 Belgium, 73.25; 5 Australia, 101.00.

Rotterdam

FRG 8.00
Hendrik Snoek—Gaylord
Sönke Sönksen—Kwept
Hartwig Steenken—Erle
Alwin Schockemöhle—Warwick

2 Great Britain, 12.00;

3 Netherlands, 12.50; 4 France, 23.50;
5 Switzerland, 27.00; 6 Belgium, 28.00;
7 Sweden, 101.25.

Ostend

FRG 25.50
Jürgen Ernst—Gerry
Lutz Merkel—Salvaro
Hermann Schridde—West Point
Hans Günter Winkler—Grande Giso

2 Great Britain, 28.00;
3 Belgium, 32.00; 4 Italy, 40.75.

Washington

USA 20.00
Conrad Homfeld—Old English
Melanie Smith—Radnor II
Neal Shapiro—Jury Duster
Rodney Jenkins—Idle Dice

2 France, 27.25; 3 Canada, 48.25;
4 Poland, 67.25.

New York

USA 4.00
Buddy Brown—Sandsablaze
Michael Matz—Grande
Dennis Murphy—Do Right
Rodney Jenkins—Idle Dice

2 Canada, 16.00; 3 France, 20.00;
4 Poland, 24.00.

Toronto

USA 7.00
Buddy Brown—Sandsablaze
Robert Ridland—Southside
Dennis Murphy—Do Right
Rodney Jenkins—Idle Dice

2 France, 15.00; 3 Canada, 24.00;
4 Poland, 28.00.

1976

Hickstead

FRG 24.00
Gerd Wiltfang—Duell
Fritz Ligges—Wapiti
Hartwig Steenken—Kosmos
Paul Schockemöhle—Talisman

2 Great Britain, 32.00;
3 Netherlands, 32.75; 4 France, 37.50;
5 Austria, 44.00; 6 Ireland, 55.00;
7 Sweden, retired.

Rome

Italy 29.00
Graziano Mancinelli—La Bella
Vittorio Orlandi—Creme de la Coeur
Raimondo d'Inzeo—Talky
Piero d'Inzeo—Easter Light

2 France, 36.00; 3 Ireland, 52.00;
4 Belgium; 5 Switzerland; 6 Spain.

Madrid

Italy   19.00
Robledo Rossi—Coolahune
Emilio Puricelli—April Whisper
Giorgio Nuti—Springtime
Graziano Mancinelli—Lydican

2 France, 20.25; 3 Spain, 24.00.

Aachen

Italy   12.00
Graziano Mancinelli—Bel Oiseau
Giorgio Nuti—Springtime
Vittorio Orlandi—Creme de la Coeur
Raimondo d'Inzeo—Hermes

2 France, 23.00; 3 Netherlands, 29.00;
4 Great Britain, 32.00;
=5 FRG, USA, 36.00;
7 Switzerland, 44.00; 8 Spain, 45.25;
9 Austria, 52.50; 10 Belgium, 72.00;
11 Poland, 93.25.

The most successful rider in the 828 Nations Cups that were run between 1909 and 1986, Frank Chapot, seen riding Main Spring. He was a member of the winning USA team on 46 occasions. (Ed Lacey Associated Sports Photography)

Lucerne

USA   33.00
Dennis Murphy—Hummer
Michael Maz—Grande
Robert Ridland—Almost Persuaded
Buddy Brown—Viscount

2 Ireland, 48.75; 3 Austria, 54.75;
4 FRG, 57.00; 5 France, 58.00;
6 Switzerland, 93.50;
7 Great Britain, 102.75; 8 Italy, retired.

Olsztyn

FRG   24.00
Gustav Bauer—Baroud
Achaz von Buchwaldt—Pims
Hartmut Röder—Ducat
Lutz Merkel—Salvaro

=2 Switzerland, USSR, 36.00;
4 Great Britain, 40.00; 5 Poland, 91.00;
6 Czechoslovakia, 158.00.

Trinwillershagen

GDR   24.00
Rudolf Beerbohm—Ingolf
Heinz Schulenburg—Kardinal
Reinhard Austerhoff—Udo
Volker Tonn—Pflicht

2 Poland, 56.50; 3 USSR, 68.00.

Dublin

FRG   8.00
Willibert Mehlkopf—Fantast
Lutz Merkel—Salvaro
Fritz Ligges—Genius
Hartwig Steenken—Erle

2 Ireland, 12.00; 3 Great Britain, 16.00;
4 Italy, 20.00; 5 Belgium, 60.00.

Rotterdam

France   16.00, 0.00 in jump-off
Hubert Parot—Rivage
Marc Roguet—Belle de Mars
Michel Roche—Un Espoir
Marcel Rozier—Brin d'Honneur

2 Ireland, 16.00, 1.25 in jump-off;
3 FRG, 16.75; 4 Great Britain, 21.00;
=5 Netherlands, Belgium, 33.00;
7 Switzerland, 90.25.

Ostend

Ireland   21.75
James Kernan—Spring Trout
Larry Kiely—Inis Cara
Con Power—Coolronan
Ned Campion—Sliabh na mBan

2 Belgium, 23.25; 3 FRG, 35.00;
4 France, 42.00; 5 Great Britain, 51.00.

Laxenburg

Switzerland   36.00
Bruno Candrian—Golden Shuttle
Thomas Fuchs—Unimatic
Walter Gabathuler—Harley
Jurg Friedli—Volontaire II

2 FRG, 44.00; 3 France, 48.25;
4 Austria, 51.25; 5 Belgium, 100.00;
6 Hungary, 120.00.

Washington

USA   20.00
Michael Matz—Grande
Buddy Brown—Flying John
Dennis Murphy—Do Right
Frank Chapot—Coach Stop

2 Belgium, 25.00; 3 Canada, 28.00;
4 Ireland, 48.00.

New York

USA   4.00
Michael Matz—Grande
Buddy Brown—Flying John
Dennis Murphy—Tuscaloosa
Frank Chapot—Coach Stop

2 Canada, 4.25; 3 Ireland, 16.25;
4 Belgium, 28.25.

Toronto

USA   8.00, 4.00 in jump-off
Michael Matz—Grande
Buddy Brown—Flying John
Dennis Murphy—Tuscaloosa
Frank Chapot—Coach Stop

2 Canada, 8.00, 8.00 in jump-off;
3 Ireland, 35.00; 4 Belgium, eliminated.

Paris

Great Britain   8.00
Harvey Smith—Olympic Star
Caroline Bradley—Marius
Debbie Johnsey—Moxy
David Broome—Philco

=2 Belgium, Italy, 12.00; 4 FRG, 20.00;
5 Spain, 29.75; 6 France, 40.00;
7 Morocco, retired.

1977

Geneva

Great Britain   4.25
Derek Ricketts
—Hydrophane Coldstream
Caroline Bradley—Marius
Debbie Johnsey—Moxy
Harvey Smith—Upton

2 Belgium, 5.00; 3 France, 6.50;
4 Spain, 9.25; 5 FRG, 9.75;
6 Switzerland, 21.25.

Rome

Italy   24.00
Piero d'Inzeo—The Avenger
Vittorio Orlandi—Creme de la Coeur
Graziano Mancinelli—Ursus de Lasco
Raimondo d'Inzeo—Stranger

2 Great Britain, 32.50; 3 Ireland, 40.00;
4 France, 40.50; 5 FRG, 52.50;
6 Switzerland, 67.75;
7 Rumania, retired.

Barcelona

Italy   4.50
Piero d'Inzeo—Easter Light
Georgio Nuti—Springtime
Graziano Mancinelli—Ursus de Lasco
Raimondo d'Inzeo—Stranger

2 France, 12.00; 3 Great Britain, 16.25.

Olsztyn

FRG   24.00
Jürgen Ernst—Saloniki
Lutz Gössing—Gaurer
Hans Quellen—Arco
Hans-Ulrich Mucha—Gerry

2 GDR, 36.00; 3 USSR, 44.50;
4 Czechoslovakia, 70.00.

Trinwillershagen

GDR   8.00
Reinhard Austerhoff—Kardinal

Rudolf Beerbohm—Ingolf
Günter Till—Fakt II
Volker Tonn—Fantasie

2 Poland, 12.00; 3 USSR, 32.00.

Aachen

FRG   0.00, 0.00 in 140.50 secs
in jump-off
Fritz Ligges—Genius
Norbert Koof—Minister
Paul Schockemöhle—Agent
Gerd Wiltfang—Davos

2 Great Britain, 0.00, 0.00
in 150.80 secs in jump-off;
3 Ireland, 20.00; 4 Switzerland, 32.00;
=5 Spain, Netherlands, 36.00;
7 Belgium, 44.00; 8 Italy, 50.25;
9 USSR, 101.25.

La Baule

FRG   20.00
Peter Weinberg—Uhland
Hauke Schmidt—Sirio
Karsten Huck—Alvaro
Sönke Sönksen—Kwept

2 Ireland, 28.25; 3 France, 31.75;
4 Belgium, 35.75;
5 Great Britain, 38.00; 6 Italy, 90.75.

Hickstead

Great Britain   19.00
John Whitaker—Ryan's Son
Tony Newbery—Warwick III
Caroline Bradley—Marius
Derek Ricketts
—Hydrophane Coldstream

2 Netherlands, 35.75; 3 Ireland, 36.00;
4 FRG, 44.00; 5 Belgium, retired.

Dublin

Ireland   8.00, 0.00 in jump-off
Paul Darragh—Heather Honey
James Kernan—Condy
Con Power—Coolronan
Eddie Macken—Boomerang

2 FRG, 8.00, retired in jump-off;
3 Great Britain, 16.00; 4 Italy, 39.00;
5 Belgium, 52.00.

Bratislava

FRG   8.00
Hans-Ulrich Mucha—Excellent
Peter Sünkel—Graciosa
Norbert Koof—Advent
Lutz Merkel—Golden Gate

2 Czechoslovakia, 20.25;
3 GDR, 22.00; 4 Hungary, 46.00;
5 Poland, 93.00; 6 Austria, retired.

Rotterdam

Ireland   16.00
Larry Kiely—Lough Sheelin
Con Power—Look Out
James Kernan—Condy
Paul Darragh—Heather Honey

=2 Great Britain, Netherlands, 28.00;
4 Belgium, 28.75; 5 FRG, 52.75;
6 France, 53.00; 7 Australia, 60.75.

Ostend

Belgium   8.00
Jules Cuelemans—Grey Mist
Stanny van Paesschen—Porsche
Edgar-Henri Cuepper—Le Champion
Ferdi Tyteca—Passe Partout

2 Ireland, 12.00; 3 France, 31.75.

Calgary

USA   12.00
Joe Fargis—Pueblo
Melanie Smith—Radnor II
Michele McEvoy—Night Murmur
Conrad Homfeld—Balbuco

2 FRG, 16.50;
=3 Great Britain, Canada, 36.00;
5 Mexico, 41.50.

Washington

USA   12.00, 0.00 in jump-off
Conrad Homfeld—Balbuco
Joe Fargis—Pueblo
Michael Matz—Jet Run
Buddy Brown—Sandsablaze

2 Canada, 12.00, 4.00 in jump-off;
3 Great Britain, 16.00; 4 FRG, 24.00.

New York

USA   4.00, 0.00 in jump-off
Conrad Homfeld—Balbuco
Michael Matz—Jet Run
Buddy Brown—Sandsablaze
Rodney Jenkins—Idle Dice

2 Great Britain, 4.00, 12.00 in jump-off;
3 Canada, 13.00; 4 FRG, 15.75.

Toronto

Canada   0.00, 0.00 in jump-off
John Simpson—Texas
Terry Leibel—Merchant of Venice
Ian Millar—Brother Sam
Jim Elder—Scotch Valley

2 USA, 0.00, 3.00 in jump-off;
=3 FRG, Great Britain, 8.00.

1978

Nice

FRG   12.00, 0.00 in 90 secs
in jump-off
Hans-Ulrich Mucha—Leon
Paul Schockemöhle—El Paso
Gerd Wiltfang—Duell
Fritz Ligges—Goya

2 Great Britain, 12.00, 0.00 in
94.20 secs in jump-off; 3 France, 13.00;
4 Netherlands, 20.00;
5 Belgium, 27.75; 6 Ireland, 35.75;
7 Italy, 36.00.

Rome

France   28.00, 0.00 in jump-off
Manuel Henry—Derby VI
Hervé Godignon—Electre II
Frédéric Cottier—Babette XVII
Christophe Cuyer—Bambi

2 Ireland, 28.00, retired in jump-off;
3 Great Britain, 33.00; 4 Italy, 46.50;
5 FRG, 58.25; 6 Belgium, 72.50.

Madrid

Belgium   8.00
Stanny van Paesschen—Porsche
Eva van Paesschen—Esbrouffe
Hervé Daout—Zerra
Ferdi Tyteca—Ransome

2 France, 11.00; 3 Spain, 12.00;
4 Portugal, 20.00.

St Gallen

FRG   35.50
Jürgen Ernst—Lustig
Ulrich Meyer zu Bexten—Ralf
Norbert Koof—Minister
Lutz Merkel—Salvaro

2 Great Britain, 36.25;
=3 Austria, Netherlands, 44.00;
5 France, 60.00; 6 Switzerland, 80.00;
7 Belgium, 80.25; 8 Italy, 90.25.

Olsztyn

FRG   12.00
Heinrich-Wilhelm Johannsmann
—Sarto
Peter Weinberg—Patras
Julius Schulze-Hesselmann
—Fernando
Hans-Ulrich Mucha—Leon

2 USSR, 17.00; 3 Poland, 20.00;
4 Hungary, 25.00;
5 Finland, eliminated.

Aachen

FRG   9.00
Peter Sünkel—Graziosa
Hendrik Snoek—Gaylord
Gerd Wiltfang—Roman
Paul Schockemöhle—El Paso

2 Great Britain, 16.00; 3 Ireland, 20.00;
=4 France, Belgium, 24.00;
6 Switzerland, 28.00;
7 Netherlands, 32.00; 8 USA, 36.00;
9 Austria, 40.25.

Bratislava

FRG   28.00
Axel Wöckener—Gilbert
Thomas Bartels—Brabek
Julius Schulze-Hesselmann—McMato
Hans-Ulrich Mucha—Lucifer

2 Czechoslovakia, 42.75;
3 USSR, 64.00; 4 Austria, 67.00.

Hickstead

Great Britain   0.00
Derek Ricketts
—Hydrophane Coldstream
Caroline Bradley—Tigre
Malcolm Pyrah—Law Court
David Broome—Philco

2 USA, 20.00; 3 FRG, 24.00;
4 Canada, 28.25; 5 Ireland, 36.00;
6 France, 40.00; 7 Belgium, 50.50.

Dublin

Ireland   0.00, 0.00 in 130 secs
in jump-off
Con Power—Castle Park
James Kernan—Condy
Paul Darragh—Heather Honey
Eddie Macken—Boomerang

2 France, 0.00, 0.00 in 134.30 secs
in jump-off; 3 Canada, 4.00;
=4 FRG, Great Britain, 8.00;
6 Switzerland, 28.00.

Rotterdam

USA   8.00
Conrad Homfeld—Balbuco
Dennis Murphy—Tuscaloosa
Robert Ridland—Nazarius
Michael Matz—Sandor

2 Great Britain, 15.00;
=3 Canada, Netherlands, 20.00;
5 Ireland, 32.00; 6 Belgium, 37.00;
7 FRG, 44.00; 8 Poland, 94.50.

Ekeren

Great Britain   4.00
John Whitaker—Ryan's Son
Rowland Fernyhough—Bouncer
Fred Welch—Rossmore II
Harvey Smith—Sanyo Sanmar

=2 France, Netherlands, 12.00;
4 Ireland, 16.00; 5 Belgium, 20.00;
6 Switzerland, 23.00; 7 Sweden, 32.25;
8 Australia, 36.25; 9 FRG, 51.25;
10 Poland, 57.75.

Calgary

Great Britain   24.00
Graham Fletcher—Buttevant Boy
Mark Phillips—Hideaway
Caroline Bradley—Tigre
Mike Saywell—Chainbridge

2 Canada, 28.75; 3 USA, 36.00;
4 Mexico, 43.00; 5 FRG, 56.00;
6 New Zealand, 170.50.

Laxenburg

Switzerland   16.00
Thomas Fuchs—Snowking
Kurt Maeder—Top of the Morning II
Jürg Friedli—Volontaire II
Walter Gabathuler—Harley

2 Great Britain, 20.00; 3 FRG, 24.50;
4 Netherlands, 29.25; 5 Austria, 52.00;
6 Czechoslovakia, 75.00;
7 Poland, 88.00.

Washington

Canada   10.00
Terrance Millar—Eaden Vale
Terry Leibel—Merchant of Venice
John Simpson—Texas
Ian Millar—Bandit

2 USA, 12.00; 3 Ireland, 36.00;
4 Belgium, 44.00.

New York

USA   37.50
Dennis Murphy—Tuscaloosa
Buddy Brown—Flying John
Melanie Smith—Val de Loire
Bernie Traurig—Gucci

2 Ireland, 40,00; 3 Belgium, 45.50;
4 Canada, 62.00.

Toronto

USA   0.00
Robert Ridland—Nazarius
Scott Nederlander—Southside
Dennis Murphy—Tuscaloosa
Michael Matz—Sandor

2 Canada, 12.00; 3 Ireland, 16.00;
4 Belgium, 20.00.

1979

Geneva

Great Britain   8.00
John Whitaker—Ryan's Son
Lionel Dunning—Jungle Bunny
Caroline Bradley—Marius
David Broome—Queensway Big Q

2 FRG, 12.00; 3 Ireland, 16.00;
4 France, 28.00; 5 Switzerland, 32.00;
6 Belgium, 52.00; 7 Spain, 84.75.

Rome

France   12.00
Gilles Bertran de Balanda—Danoso
Eric Leroyer—Bayart du Peray
Hervé Godignon—Electre II
Patrick Caron—Eole IV

2 FRG, 27.75; 3 Spain, 31.75;
4 Belgium, 32.75; 5 Italy, 34.25;
6 Switzerland, 76.25; 7 Poland, 132.25.

Olsztyn

USSR   19.75
Nikolai Korolkov—Eskadron
Victor Durkot—Bakien
Oleg Oganesov—Topkyj
Victor Poganovsky—Fazan

2 FRG, 33.00; 3 Hungary, 37.75;
4 Poland, 49.50; 5 GDR, 81.50;
6 Czechoslovakia, 151.50.

Barcelona

Spain   17.75
Alfonso Sevogia—Agamenon
Jaime de Aveyro—Constant

Antonio de Wit—Alerta
Luis Alvarez Cervera—Romeo

2 France, 24.00; 3 Belgium, 33.50;
4 Portugal, retired.

Aachen

Ireland 16.00
Paul Darragh
—Carroll's Heather Honey
Con Power—Rockbarton
John Roche—Maigh Cullins
Eddie Macken—Carroll's Boomerang

2 FRG, 16.75; 3 Great Britain, 20.00;
4 France, 32.00; 5 Austria, 36.00;
6 Spain, 37.00; 7 Belgium, 40.00;
8 USSR, 42.50; 9 Switzerland, 44.00;
10 Italy, 51.25; 11 Netherlands, 65.00;
12 Poland, 97.00.

Paris

Great Britain 16.00, 8.25 in jump-off
Derek Ricketts
—Hydrophane Coldstream
Lionel Dunning—Jungle Bunny
Caroline Bradley—Tigre
Malcolm Pyrah—Law Court

2 Belgium, 16.00, 12.00 in jump-off;
=3 FRG, France, 24.00;
=5 Switzerland, Sweden, 32.00;
7 Italy, 36.00; 8 Ireland, 40.50;
9 Netherlands, 48.00;
10 Spain, 105.50.

Bratislava

GDR 4.00
Volker Tonn—Pflicht
Günter Till—Stompflug
Bernd Peters—Grand Geste
Ralf Deutschmann—Dorit

2 Poland, 8.00; 3 Switzerland, 16.00;
4 FRG, 20.00; 5 Austria, 20.75;
6 Bulgaria, 35.00; 7 Hungary, 48.00;
8 Czechoslovakia, 60.00.

Hickstead

Great Britain 16.00
Derek Ricketts
—Hydrophane Coldstream
Caroline Bradley—Tigre
Malcolm Pyrah—Law Court
David Broome—Queensway Big Q

2 France, 28.25;
3 Netherlands, 40.25; 4 FRG, 44.50;
5 Ireland, 48.00; 6 Belgium, 69.50;
7 Australia, 200.00.

Dublin

Ireland 8.00
Paul Darragh
—Carroll's Heather Honey
James Kernan—Condy
Con Power—Rockbarton
Eddie Macken—Carroll's Boomerang

=2 Great Britain, FRG, 16.00;
4 Belgium, 32.50.

Ekeren

Great Britain 12.00
Liz Edgar—Forever
Mark Fuller—Channel Five
Robert Smith—Video
John Whitaker—Ryan's Son

2 Netherlands, 16.00; 3 France, 23.00;
4 Sweden, 32.50; 5 Belgium, 43.25;
6 Poland, 44.00.

Calgary

Great Britain 13.75
Lionel Dunning—Jungle Bunny
Tim Grubb—Night Murmur
Caroline Bradley—Marius
Malcolm Pyrah—Law Court

2 USA, 24.00; 3 FRG, 40.75;
4 Ireland, 43.50; 5 Canada, 73.50;
6 Japan, 152.25.

Lisbon

France 12.75
Manuel Henry—Gold Rose
Claude Merrien—Giralda
Laurent Persyn—Guendalina
Jerôme Chabrol—Feu Follet

2 Spain, 30.75; 3 Portugal, 32.50;
4 Italy, retired.

Washington

USA 8.00
Norman Dello Joio—Allegro
Peter Leone—Semi Pro
Melanie Smith—Calypso
Michael Matz—Jet Run

2 Canada, 20.00; 3 Switzerland, 24.00;
4 Great Britain, 31.25.

New York

USA 4.00
Melanie Smith—Val de Loire
Terry Rudd—Fat City
Norman Dello Joio—Allegro
Michael Matz—Jet Run

2 Canada, 8.00; 3 Great Britain, 11.00;
4 Switzerland, 16.00.

Toronto

Canada 0.00
Michel Vaillancourt—Wrong Number
Ian Millar—Bandit
Terry Leibel—Merchant of Venice
John Simpson—Texas

=2 Great Britain, USA, 4.00;
4 Switzerland, 8.00.

Zuidlaren

Great Britain 0.00
Lionel Dunning—Jungle Bunny
Mark Fuller—Channel Five
Nick Skelton—Maybe
John Whitaker—Ryan's Son

2 FRG, 12.00; 3 Netherlands, 12.50;
4 Switzerland, 20.00; 5 Austria, 32.25;
6 France, 36.00; 7 Belgium, 44.00.

1980

Rome

France 20.00
Frédéric Cottier—Flambeau C
Hervé Godignon—Gitan P
Etienne Laboute—Fidélité A
Patrick Caron—Eole IV

2 Spain, 24.00; 3 Switzerland, 32.00;
4 Austria, 40.00;
=5 Belgium, Italy, 48.00;
7 Poland, 71.00.

Lucerne

Great Britain 8.00
Lionel Dunning—Jungle Bunny
Graham Fletcher—Preachan
Tim Grubb—Night Murmur
Malcolm Pyrah—Charles Fox

=2 Switzerland, Austria, 12.00;
4 France, 16.50; 5 Belgium, 24.25;
6 Poland, 27.50; 7 Italy, 28.00;
8 FRG, 29.75; 9 Ireland, 36.00.

Hickstead

Great Britain 8.00
Lionel Dunning—Jungle Bunny
Liz Edgar—Forever
Robert Smith—Video
John Whitaker—Ryan's Son

2 France, 16.00; 3 Netherlands, 31.00;
4 Australia, 42.25; 5 Ireland, 52.00;
6 FRG, 56.25; 7 Sweden, retired.

Madrid

Belgium 20.00
Christian Huysegoms—Katapulte
Pierre Delcourt—Samy
Eva van Paesschen—Red River
Stanny van Paesschen—Porsche

2 Spain, 28.00; 3 Portugal, 36.50;
4 Morocco, 52.00.

Aachen

France 8.00
Frédéric Cottier—Flambeau C
Hervé Godignon—Faola d'Escla
Jean-Marc Nicolas—Mador
Gilles Bertran de Balanda—Galoubet A

=2 Netherlands, Switzerland,
FRG, 12.00; 5 Great Britain, 16.00;
6 Belgium, 20.00;
=7 Ireland, Poland, 24.00;
9 Mexico, 26.75; 10 Spain, 44.00;
11 Brazil, 45.75; 12 Austria, 65.25;
13 Japan, 99.00.

Prague

Switzerland 12.00
Bruno Candrian—Domingo
Anne Laubscher—Black Eagle
Jürg Notz—Sunrick
Markus Mändli—Lionel

2 FRG, 16.00; 3 Poland, 20.25;
4 GDR, 44.00; 5 Hungary, 65.25;

6 Rumania, 69.00;
7 Czechoslovakia, 75.25;
8 Austria, 103.25; 9 Bulgaria, retired.

Liège

France 0.75
Frédéric Cottier—Flambeau C
Hervé Godignon—Faola d'Escla
Jean-Marc Nicolas—Mador
Gilles Bertran de Balanda—Galoubet A

2 FRG, 8.00; 3 Great Britain, 15.00;
4 Belgium, 18.00; 5 Mexico, 29.25;
6 Netherlands, 60.00.

Paris

France 12.50
Frédéric Cottier—Flambeau C
Etienne Laboute—Fidélité A
Jean-Marc Nicolas—Mador
Gilles Bertran de Balanda—Galoubet A

2 Switzerland, 16.25; 3 USA, 18.00;
4 Belgium, 19.50; =5 Italy, FRG, 24.00;
7 Great Britain, 24.75;
8 Australia, 25.50; 9 Austria, 76.00;
10 Brazil, 117.50.

Dublin

USA 1.00
Armand Leone—Wallenstein
Katie Monahan—Silver Exchange
Norman Dello Joio—Allegro
Melanie Smith—Calypso

2 Great Britain, 4.25;
=3 Ireland, France, 8.00;
5 FRG, 29.25; 6 Australia, 53.25.

Rotterdam

Canada 16.50
Michel Vaillancourt—Chivaz
Mark Laskin—Damuraz
Ian Millar—Brother Sam
Jim Elder—Volunteer

2 Great Britain, 18.50; 3 Austria, 20.00;
4 FRG, 24.00;
=5 USA, Switzerland, 28.00;
7 France, 32.00; 8 Australia, 40.00;
9 Netherlands, 55.00;
10 Belgium, 56.00; 11 Mexico, retired;
12 Sweden, retired;
13 Denmark, retired.

Calgary

Great Britain 8.00
Graham Fletcher—Preachan
Jean Germany—Whistling Song
John Whitaker—Ryan's Son
Malcolm Pyrah—Charles Fox

2 Netherlands, 16.00; 3 Canada, 32.00;
4 Switzerland, 36.00; 5 USA, 40.00;
6 Ireland, 56.00.

Lipica

FRG 12.50
André Heller—Akrobat
Norbert Koof—Wanderer

Julius Schulze-Hesselmann—Sir
Peter Weinberg—Lemur

2 Italy, 20.50; 3 USSR, 31.00;
4 Switzerland, 51.00;
5 Czechoslovakia, 80.00;
6 Bulgaria, 107.00;
7 Yugoslavia, 369.50.

Lisbon

Spain 36.75
Antonio de Wit—Olimpico
Alberto Mingo—Notaire
Luis Alvarez Cervera—Ferryman
Alfonso Segovia—Agamenon

2 Portugal, 49.00; 3 Morocco, 49.75.

Washington

USA 4.00
Peter Leone—Semi Pro
Leslie Burr—Chase the Clouds
Norman Dello Joio—Allegro
Melanie Smith—Calypso

2 France, 20.00; 3 Canada, 32.00.

New York

USA 0.00
Armand Leone—Wallenstein
Leslie Burr—Chase the Clouds
Norman Dello Joio—Allegro
Melanie Smith—Calypso

2 Canada, 4.00; 3 France, 9.00;
4 FRG, 21.00.

Toronto

France 0.00, 0.00 in 111.20 secs
in jump-off
Marcel Rozier—Echo de Cavron
Frédéric Cottier—Flambeau C
Christophe Cuyer—Faola d'Escla
Gilles Bertran de Balanda—Galoubet A

2 USA, 0.00, 0.00 in 112.57 secs
in jump-off;
3 Canada, 0.00, 4.00 in jump-off;
4 FRG, 0.00, 12.00 in jump-off.

1981

Geneva

Great Britain 0.00, 12.00 in jump-off
Harvey Smith—Sanyo Sanmar
John Whitaker—Ryan's Son
Malcolm Pyrah
—Towerlands Anglezarke
David Broome—Mr Ross

2 Spain, 0.00, 13.75 in jump-off;
3 Ireland, 0.00, 40.50 in jump-off;
=4 France, Netherlands, 4.00;
6 Switzerland, 8.00; 7 Belgium, 27.25;
8 FRG, 36.00.

Rome

France 16.25
Christophe Cuyer—Faolo d'Escla
Jean-Marc Nicolas—Mador

Patrick Caron—Eole IV
Frédéric Cottier—Flambeau C

2 Switzerland, 24.00; 3 Italy, 38.50;
4 Belgium, 39.75;
5 Great Britain, 41.25.

Barcelona

Spain 13.00
Antonio de Wit—Alerta
Alejandro Zambrano—Hering
Alfonso Segovia—Agamenon
Luis Alvarez Cervera—Romeo

2 Italy, 16.00; 3 France, 16.50;
4 Switzerland, 37.50; 5 Belgium, 40.00;
6 Portugal, 167.25.

Paris

Netherlands 4.00, 0.00 in jump-off
Emiel Hendrix—Livius
Rob Ehrens—Koh-I-Noor
Henk Nooren—Opstalan's Orpheus
Johan Heins—Larramy

2 Switzerland, 4.00, 4.00 in jump-off;
3 Great Britain, 7.75; 4 France, 20.50;
5 FRG, 24.00; 6 Ireland, 28.25;
7 Belgium, 32.00; 8 Italy, 56.75.

Olsztyn

FRG 12.50
Klaus Reinacher—Furry
Iris Bayer—Lester
André Heller—Akrobat
Wolfgang Brinkmann—Jamiro

2 Poland, 16.00; 3 GDR, 41.50.

Liège

FRG 8.00, 1.00 in jump-off
Ulrich Meyer zu Bexten—Magister
Franke Sloothaak—Argonaut
Fritz Ligges—Goya
Paul Schockemöhle—Deister

2 GDR, 8.00, 9.00 in jump-off;
3 Belgium, 12.25; 4 Spain, 20.50;
5 France, 40.00; 6 Netherlands, 62.50.

Aachen

Great Britain 8.00
Nick Skelton—Maybe
Liz Edgar—Everest Forever
Fred Welch—Norbain Norstar
Malcolm Pyrah
—Towerlands Anglezarke

2 Ireland, 20.00;
=3 Netherlands, France, FRG, 24.00;
6 Switzerland, 28.75; 7 Poland, 63.00;
8 Spain, 81.75; 9 Austria, 131.50;
10 Belgium, retired.

Helsinki

FRG 20.00
Kurt Gravemeier—Saint Tropez
Iris Bayer—Lester
Sönke Sönksen—Rangpur
Achaz von Buchwaldt—Pims

2 Sweden, 36.00; 3 Poland, 40.00;
4 Finland, 56.00; 5 Norway, 73.25.

Hickstead

France 20.00
Frédéric Cottier—Flambeau C
Patrick Pierre—Flon Flon
Patrick Caron—Eole IV
Jean-Marc Nicolas—Mador

2 Great Britain, 24.00;
3 Switzerland, 31.00; 4 FRG, 32.00;
5 Mexico, 44.00; 6 Ireland, 44.25;
7 Australia, 55.00; 8 Italy, 78.75.

Dublin

FRG 0.00
Franke Sloothaak—Argonaut
Norbert Koof—Fire
Peter Luther—Livius
Paul Schockemöhle—Deister

2 Switzerland, 4.00;
3 Great Britain, 8.00; 4 Ireland, 20.00;
5 Italy, 32.50; 6 Australia, 36.00;
7 Belgium, 77.00; 8 Mexico, retired.

Bratislava

FRG 12.00
Klaus Reinacher—Furry
Peter Nagel-Tornau—Platon
Iris Bayer—Lester
Wolfgang Brinkmann—Jomiro

2 Poland, 16.00; 3 Austria, 27.50;
4 GDR, 39.25;
5 Czechoslovakia, 46.50;
6 USSR, 50.50; 7 Hungary, 58.25.

Rotterdam

France 4.00, 0.00 in 104.70 secs
in jump-off
Frédéric Cottier—Flambeau C
Patrick Pierre—Flon Flon
Patrick Caron—Eole IV
Gilles Bertran de Balanda
—Galoubet Malesan

2 FRG, 4.00, 0.00 in 105.90 secs
in jump-off;
3 Great Britain, 4.00, 0.00 in
120.40 secs in jump-off;
4 Belgium, 4.00, 8.00 in jump-off;
5 Netherlands, 12.00;
6 Sweden, 24.75; 7 Switzerland, 49.75;
8 Mexico, retired.

Lisbon

France 6.25
Catherine Bonnafous—I Love You
Jerôme Thomas—Gargantua
Laurent Elias—Guenour
Manuel Henry—Gold Rose

2 Spain, 20.00; 3 Belgium, 30.50;
4 Portugal, 128.50.

Calgary

Netherlands 20.00, 0.00 in jump-off
Anton Ebben—Jumbo Design
Rob Ehrens—Koh-I-Noor
Henk Nooren—Opstalan
Johan Heins—Larramy

2 France, 20.00, 8.00 in jump-off;

3 Great Britain, 20.25; 4 USA, 28.00;
5 Canada, 36.75; 6 Switzerland, 52.00.

Washington

USA 13.00
Melanie Smith—Calypso
Rodney Jenkins—Coastline
Michael Matz—Jet Run
Norman Dello Joio—Johnny's Pocket

2 Canada, 56.00; 3 Italy, 91.75.

New York

USA 11.25
Melanie Smith—Calypso
Rodney Jenkins—Coastline
Michael Matz—Jet Run
Norman Dello Joio—Johnny's Pocket

2 Italy, 20.00; 3 Great Britain, 24.25;
4 Canada, 48.00.

Toronto

USA 0.00, 0.00 in jump-off
Norman Dello Joio—Johnny's Pocket
Donald Cheska—Southside
Anne Kursinski—Third Man
Melanie Smith—Calypso

2 Great Britain, 0.00, 16.00 in jump-off;
3 Canada, 18.75; 4 Italy, 28.00.

1982

Rome

France 12.75
Michel Robert—Ideal de la Haye
Frédéric Cottier—Flambeau C
Patrick Caron—Eole IV
Gilles Bertran de Balanda
—Galoubet Malesan

2 Great Britain, 16.00;
3 Switzerland, 33.00; 4 Italy, 33.25;
5 FRG, 36.25; 6 Ireland, 56.75;
7 Brazil, 65.50; 8 Belgium, 109.50;
9 Austria, 144.00.

Madrid

Great Britain 12.00
Lionel Dunning—San Francisco
Sally Mapleson—Con Brio
Pam Dunning—Ona Promise
Fred Welch—Rossmore II

=2 FRG, France, 16.00;
4 Spain, 24.25; 5 Belgium, 32.00;
6 Portugal, 36.25; 7 Morocco, 37.50.

Lucerne

Great Britain 20.75
Nick Skelton—Everest If Ever
Liz Edgar—Everest Forever
Pam Dunning—Roscoe
Malcolm Pyrah
—Towerlands Chainbridge

2 Switzerland, 24.00; 3 France, 28.00;
4 FRG, 33.00; 5 Italy, 45.25;

6 USA, 46.00; 7 Brazil, 50.25;
8 Poland, 52.00; 9 Ireland, 55.00;
10 Belgium, 68.75.

Aachen

FRG 4.00
Norbert Koof—Fire
Ulrich Meyer zu Bexten—Magister
Gerd Wiltfang—Goldika
Paul Schockemöhle—Deister

2 Great Britain, 4.25; 3 USA, 11.00;
4 Netherlands, 13.25;
5 Switzerland, 17.00; 6 France, 30.50;
7 Belgium, 53.00; 8 Mexico, 65.25;
9 Australia, 141.25.

Paris

FRG 4.00
Fritz Ligges—Goya
Ulrich Meyer zu Bexten—Magister
Gerd Wiltfang—Roman
Paul Schockemöhle—Deister

=2 France, Great Britain,
Switzerland, 8.00; 5 USA, 20.00;
6 Italy, 24.00;
=7 Belgium, Netherlands, 44.00;
9 Mexico, 51.00; 10 Australia, 52.00.

Hickstead

FRG 4.00
Norbert Koof—Fire
Peter Luther—Livius
Gerd Wiltfang—Goldika
Paul Schockemöhle—Deister

2 Great Britain, 8.00; 3 France, 22.25;
4 Italy, 24.00; 5 Ireland, 44.00;
6 Australia, 64.00.

Dublin

Great Britain 0.00
Harvey Smith—Sanyo Olympic Video
John Whitaker—Ryan's Son
Malcolm Pyrah
—Towerlands Chainbridge
David Broome—Mr Ross

2 FRG, 16.00; 3 Italy, 28.00;
4 Ireland, 28.25; 5 Australia, 32.00.

Bratislava

FRG 8.00, 4.00 in jump-off
Klaus Reinacher—Little Joe
Willibert Mehlkopf—Salut
Michael Fervers—Santa Claus
Julius Schulze-Hesselmann—Sir

2 Switzerland, 8.00, 8.00 in jump-off;
=3 Austria, Poland, 20.00;
5 GDR, 35.00;
6 Czechoslovakia, 38.50;
7 Hungary, 48.75.

Rotterdam

FRG 4.00
Norbert Koof—Fire
Peter Luther—Livius
Fritz Ligges—Goya
Paul Schockemöhle—Deister

2 Great Britain, 12.00;
3 Belgium, 20.50;
4 Netherlands, 21.00;
5 Sweden, 23.25; 6 France, 45.50.

Liège

FRG   4.00
Peter Schmitz—Lotus
Achaz von Buchwaldt—Wendy
Julius Schulze-Hesselmann—Sir
Ulrich Meyer zu Bexten—Marco

2 Belgium, 12.00; 3 France, 16.00;
=4 Great Britain, Netherlands, 24.00;
6 Italy, 32.00; 7 Sweden, 40.00.

Calgary

Great Britain   12.00
Harvey Smith—Sanyo Olympic Video
John Whitaker—Ryan's Son
Malcolm Pyrah
—Towerlands Anglezarke
David Broome—Mr Ross

2 USA, 13.25; 3 FRG, 16.00;
4 Canada, 29.00; 5 France, 30.50;
6 Netherlands, 44.00.

Lisbon

Spain   9.00
Antonio de Wit—Alerta
Alejandro Zambrano—Hering
Luis Alvarez Cervera—Pico
Alfonso Segovia—Agamenon

2 Belgium, 16.00; 3 Switzerland, 16.75;
4 Portugal, 29.50.

Washington

USA   4.00
Katie Monahan—Noren
Norman Dello Joio—I Love You
Donald Cheska—Southside
Melanie Smith—Calypso

2 Canada, 8.00; 3 France, 16.25;
4 Switzerland, 36.75.

New York

USA   0.00
Katie Monahan—Noren
Donald Cheska—Southside
Rodney Jenkins—Coastline
Melanie Smith—Calypso

2 France, 8.75; 3 Canada, 9.25;
4 Switzerland, 28.00.

Toronto

Switzerland   0.00
Markus Fuchs—Insolvent
Philippe Guerdat—Liberty
Walter Gabathuler—Beethoven
Thomas Fuchs—Willora Carpets

2 USA, 4.00; 3 France, 8.00;
4 Canada, 12.00.

1983

Geneva

Switzerland   0.00
Walter Gabathuler—Typhoon
Heidi Robbiani—Jessica V
Thomas Fuchs—Willora Swiss
Bruno Candrian—Van Gogh

2 FRG, 8.00; 3 France, 12.00;
4 Great Britain, 16.50; 5 Austria, 32.50;
6 Italy, 35.00; 7 Netherlands, 49.25;
8 Belgium, 94.75.

Rome

USA   8.00
Anne Kursinski—Livius
Joe Fargis—Touch of Class
Katie Monahan—Noren
Melanie Smith—Calypso

2 France, 15.00; 3 Switzerland, 16.00;
4 Austria, 29.50; 5 Italy, 33.25;
6 FRG, 36.00; 7 Belgium, 49.00;
8 Libya, 55.50.

Barcelona

Great Britain   8.00
Peter Richardson—Rye Hill
Gary Gillespie—Goldfink
Kelly Brown—Foxlight
Michael Whitaker—Overton Amanda

2 Spain, 16.50; 3 Italy, 17.00;
4 France, 28.25; 5 Morocco, 33.75;
6 Belgium, 36.75; 7 Portugal, 65.00;
8 Switzerland, 93.00.

Hickstead

France   19.75
André Chenu—Impedoumi
Philippe Rozier—Jiva
Patrick Caron—Eole IV
Pierre Durand—Jappeloup

2 Netherlands, 28.00;
=3 FRG, Australia,
Great Britain, 32.00; 6 Ireland, 39.75;
7 Italy, 51.00; 8 Sweden, 60.25.

Sopot

FRG   20.00
Klaus Reinacher—Little Joe
Klaus Brinkmann—Sumatra
Julius Schulze-Hesselmann—McMato
Wolfgang Brinkmann—Wilstar

2 Poland, 25.25; 3 Italy, 28.25;
4 Denmark, 37.50; 5 GDR, 40.00;
6 Bulgaria, eliminated.

Paris

Great Britain   8.00
Nick Skelton—St James
Harvey Smith—Sanyo Technology
Malcolm Pyrah
—Towerlands Anglezarke
David Broome—Last Resort

2 France, 8.25; 3 Switzerland, 16.00;
4 Ireland, 30.50; 5 Spain, 32.75;
6 Italy, 62.75; 7 Austria, 64.00.

Aachen

Switzerland   12.00, 4.00 in jump-off
Walter Gabathuler—Beethoven
Heidi Robbiani—Jessica V
Willi Melliger—Van Gogh
Thomas Fuchs—Willora Carpets

2 Great Britain, 12.00, 8.00 in
113.64 secs in jump-off;
3 FRG, 12.00, 8.00 in 115.11 secs
in jump-off; 4 Ireland, 36.25;
5 Poland, 61.00; 6 Austria, 71.00;
7 Netherlands, 75.75.

Dublin

Switzerland   4.00
Walter Gabathuler—Beethoven
Heidi Robbiani—Jessica V
Willi Melliger—Van Gogh
Thomas Fuchs—Willora Carpets

2 Ireland, 4.25; 3 FRG, 8.75;
4 Italy, 11.50; 5 Great Britain, 24.00.

Bratislava

FRG   4.00, 0.00 in 137.48 secs in
jump-off
Klaus Reinacher—Little Joe
Willibert Mehlkopf—Salut
Hauke Schmidt—Lafayette
Peter Weinberg—Lemur

2 Great Britain, 4.00, 0.00 in
142.40 secs in jump-off; 3 Poland, 8.00;
4 Switzerland, 12.00; 5 Austria, 24.00;
6 Czechoslovakia, 36.00;
7 GDR, 51.75; 8 Hungary, 64.50;
9 Bulgaria, 109.50.

Rotterdam

Great Britain   0.00
Michael Whitaker—Overton Amanda
Derek Ricketts—Money Market
Pam Dunning—Boysie
Malcolm Pyrah
—Towerlands Anglezarke

2 Switzerland, 0.25; 3 FRG, 4.00;
4 France, 8.00; 5 Netherlands, 12.00;
6 Sweden, 20.00; 7 Belgium, 28.00.

Liège

France   4.00, 4.00 in jump-off
Xavier Leredde—Jalisco B
Hubert Bourdy—Juniperus
André Chenu—Krichna
Patrick Caron—Eole IV

2 Belgium, 4.00, 12.00 in jump-off;
3 FRG, 15.50; 4 Great Britain, 20.00.

São Paulo

Brazil
Details not available.

2 Argentina; 3 Chile.

Calgary

USA   0.25
Joe Fargis—Touch of Class
Norman Dello Joio—I Love You

Katie Monahan—Noren
Melanie Smith—Calypso

=2 Great Britain, FRG, 4.00;
4 Canada, 32.50; 5 France, 48.50;
6 Netherlands, 61.00.

Lisbon

Great Britain 8.00
Michael Mac—Snowking
Jane Sargent—Packers Hill
David Bowen—Don Quixote
Tony Newbery—Maguire Esq

2 Spain, 20.50; 3 Portugal, 33.75;
4 Belgium, 38.50.

Plovdiv

FRG 5.50
Bernhard Kamps—Saloniki
Heinrich-Wilhelm Johannsmann
—Karthago
Reiner Supan—Kemenate
Lutz Gössing—Miss G

2 Czechoslovakia, 25.50;
3 GDR, 35.25; 4 Poland, 36.75;
5 Bulgaria, 55.25.

Washington

USA 0.00
Katie Monahan—Noren
Norman Dello Joio—I Love You
Joe Fargis—Touch of Class
Michael Matz—Jet Run

2 FRG, 12.00; 3 Canada, 12.25.

New York

USA 4.00
Katie Monahan—Noren
Conrad Homfeld—Corsair
Joe Fargis—Touch of Class
Norman Dello Joio—I Love You

2 Canada, 8.00; 3 FRG, 11.75.

Toronto

USA 0.00, 0.00 in jump-off
Anne Kursinski—Insolvent
Donald Cheska—Eaden Vale
Michael Matz—Chef
Norman Dello Joio—I Love You

2 Canada, 0.00, 4.00 in jump-off;
3 FRG, retired.

1984

Rome

France 8.00
Frédéric Cottier—Flambeau C
Philippe Rozier—Jiva
Hubert Bourdy—Juniperus
Pierre Durand—Jappeloup

2 Switzerland, 12.00;
3 Great Britain, 16.00; 4 Italy, 16.50;
5 Belgium, 24.00; 6 FRG, 36.00;
7 Libya, 58.50; 8 Ireland, 72.50.

Paris

Great Britain 7.00
Derek Ricketts—Money Market
Harvey Smith—Sanyo Technology
Robert Smith
—Sanyo Shining Example
Nick Skelton—St James

2 FRG, 28.00; 3 France, 32.00;
4 Switzerland, 32.50; 5 Austria, 40.00;
6 Belgium, 44.00; 7 Australia, 48.00;
8 Ireland, 56.00; 9 Italy, 58.75;
10 Netherlands, 61.25.

Barcelona

Belgium 4.00
François Mathy—Wally
Evelyne Blaton—Wilfried
Hervé Daout—Quelle Avenir
Ferdi Tyteca—'tSoulaiky

2 Spain, 5.00; 3 Switzerland, 17.50;
4 FRG, 18.50; 5 Australia, 24.50;
6 Italy, 28.50; 7 France, 32.25;
8 Great Britain, 32.50;
9 Morocco, 35.75; 10 Portugal, 54.25;
11 Argentina, 64.25; 12 Brazil, retired.

Lucerne

FRG 12.00
Fritz Ligges—Ramzes
Ulrich Meyer zu Bexten—Merano
Franke Sloothaak—Farmer
Gerd Wiltfang—Saloniki

2 Netherlands, 12.50;
3 Australia, 16.00;
4 Switzerland, 20.00;
=5 Italy, France, 24.00;
7 Austria, 48.00; 8 Sweden, 60.00;
9 Great Britain, 65.00.

Sopot

FRG 24.00
Tjark Nagel—Fregula
Stefan Schewe—Otto
Eberhard Saul—Goby
Kurt Gravemeier—Sylvester

2 Italy, 47.00; =3 Poland, GDR, 60.00;
5 Belgium, 69.00; 6 USSR, 78.75;
7 Finland, 100.25; 8 Bulgaria, 107.50;
9 Czechoslovakia, retired.

Aachen

Switzerland 0.00
Philippe Guerdat—Pybalia
Heidi Robbiani—Jessica V
Bruno Candrian—Slygof
Willi Melliger—Van Gogh

2 Great Britain, 4.00; 3 France, 12.00;
4 FRG, 19.00; 5 Italy, 20.00;
6 Australia, 24.00;
7 Netherlands, 24.50; 8 Ireland, 32.00;
9 Spain, 32.25; 10 Belgium, 36.00;
11 Mexico, 39.50; 12 Austria, 40.00;
13 Poland, 45.50; 14 Brazil, 68.75.

Hickstead

FRG 8.00
Peter Luther—Livius
Franke Sloothaak—Farmer
Ulrich Meyer zu Bexten—Merano
Paul Schockemöhle—Deister

2 France, 8.50; 3 Australia, 16.00;
4 Great Britain, 20.00; 5 Ireland, 68.00.

Falsterbo

FRG 4.25
Karsten Huck—Calando
Bernhard Kamps—Saloniki
Peter Weinberg—Lemur
Michael Rüping—Silbersee

2 Austria, 25.25; 3 Sweden, 29.00;
4 Netherlands, 32.25;
5 Denmark, 79.75.

Dublin

Ireland 14.00
John Ledingham—Gabhran
George Stewart—Leapy Lad
Jack Doyle—Kerrygold Island
Eddie Macken—Carroll's El Paso

2 FRG, 16.00; 3 Great Britain, 20.00;
4 Netherlands, 34.25.

Bratislava

Poland 8.00, 0.00 in 142.42 secs
in jump-off
Krzysztof Ferenstein—Dynamit
Wieslaw Hartmann—Hart
Bogdan Sas-Jaworski—Bremen
Rudolf Mrugala—Gaudeamus

2 Great Britain, 8.00, 0.00 in
151.47 secs in jump-off;
3 FRG, 8.00, 4.00 in jump-off;
4 GDR, 32.00;
5 Czechoslovakia, 48.00;
6 Hungary, 60.00; 7 Austria, 95.50.

Rotterdam

France 4.00
Hubert Bourdy—Juniperus
Philippe Rozier—Janus de Ver
Gilles Bertran de Balanda
—Loripierre Malesan
Frédéric Cottier—Flambeau C

2 Great Britain, 8.25; 3 FRG, 9.25;
=4 Switzerland, Ireland, 16.00;
6 Netherlands, 41.25;
7 Sweden, 52.50; 8 Poland, 83.25.

Calgary

FRG 8.25
Karsten Huck—Calando
Peter Luther—Livius
Franke Sloothaak—Farmer
Paul Schockemöhle—Deister

2 Switzerland, 12.00; 3 Canada, 16.00;
4 USA, 20.00; 5 Great Britain, 24.00;
6 Ireland, 30.00

Chaudfontaine

Great Britain   0.00
Nick Skelton—Apollo II
Helena Dickinson—Just Malone
David Broome—Last Resort
Malcolm Pyrah
—Towerlands Anglezarke

2 FRG, 0.25; 3 France, 0.75;
4 Italy, 8.00; 5 Sweden, 12.00;
6 Belgium, 16.00.

Plovdiv

FRG   4.00
Julius Schulze-Hesslemann—Dublin
Thomas Dietz—Flagrantus
Ralf Runge—Fair Lady
Lutz Gössing—Liberal

2 Poland, 23.00; 3 GDR, 28.00;
4 Hungary, 49.00; 5 Rumania, 76.25;
6 Bulgaria, 80.25.

Lisbon

Great Britain   0.25
Michael Mac—Packers Hill
Gary Gillespie—Lorenzo
Janet Hunter—Lisnamarrow
Lionel Dunning—Spirit of Lee

2 Spain, 3.25; 3 Portugal, 18.00;
4 Belgium, 20.75.

Washington

USA   12.00
Joe Fargis—Touch of Class
Leslie Burr—Albany
Conrad Homfeld—Abdullah
Melanie Smith—Calypso

2 Great Britain, 18.50;
3 Canada, 22.50.

New York

Canada   9.25
Mario Deslauriers—Aramis
Gail Greenough—Mr T
Ian Millar—Big Ben
Hugh Graham—Abraxas

2 Great Britain, 16.25; 3 USA, 27.75.

Toronto

USA   0.00, 0.00 in jump-off
Katie Monahan—Amadia
Jeffrey Welles—Ardennes
Michael Matz—Chef
Norman Dello Joio—I Love You

2 Great Britain, 0.00, retired in jump-off;
3 Canada, 4.00.

1985

Rome

Italy   5.25
Graziano Mancinelli—Karata
Emilio Puricelli—Impedoumi
Bruno Scolari—Joyau d'Or

Giorgio Nuti—Silvano

2 Switzerland, 11.00; 3 France, 16.00;
4 Brazil, 29.25; 5 Great Britain, 40.50;
6 Belgium, 48.50.

Madrid

Great Britain   0.00, 4.00 in jump-off
Michael Whitaker—Overton Amanda
Helena Dickinson—Just Malone
Malcolm Pyrah
—Towerlands Diamond Seeker
John Whitaker—Hopscotch

2 FRG, 0.00, retired in jump-off;
3 France, 4.00; 4 Spain, 24.00;
5 Belgium, 33.25; 6 Brazil, 36.00;
7 Portugal, 44.25; 8 Morocco, 50.00;
9 Ireland, retired.

Hickstead

Great Britain   4.00
Nick Skelton—Everest Apollo
Liz Edgar—Everest Forever
Malcolm Pyrah
—Towerlands Anglezarke
John Whitaker—Hopscotch

=2 FRG, Netherlands, 12.00;
4 France, 25.00; 5 Sweden, 52.00.

Aachen

USA   12.25
Joe Fargis—Touch of Class
Louis Jacobs—Janus de Ver
Christian Currey—Manuel
Conrad Homfeld—Abdullah

2 Great Britain, 20.25;
3 Netherlands, 24.00;
=4 France, FRG, 28.00;
6 Argentina, 32.75;
=7 Switzerland, Italy, 36.00;
9 Brazil, 43.50; 10 Sweden, 59.25;
11 Belgium, 72.00; 12 Mexico, 85.25;
13 Poland, 136.00;
14 Austria, retired.

Sopot

Poland   24.00, 5.00 in jump-off
Rudolf Mrugala—Gaudeamus
Marian Kozicki—Festyn
Bogdan Kubiak—Gabon
Wieslaw Hartmann—Markus

2 FRG, 24.00, 8.00 in jump-off;
3 Sweden, 28.00; 4 Switzerland, 36.00;
5 GDR, 60.00; 6 Bulgaria, 150.00.

Falsterbo

USA   12.00
Lisa Tarnapol—Adam
Joan Scharffenberger—Nataal
Michaela Murphy—Ramzes
George Morris—Rio

2 Great Britain, 20.50; 3 FRG, 24.50;
4 Poland, 38.00; 5 Belgium, 41.00;
=6 Sweden, Austria, 48.25;
8 Netherlands, retired.

Dinard

Great Britain   21.56
Nick Skelton—Everest St James
Michael Whitaker—Warren Point
Malcolm Pyrah
—Towerlands Anglezarke
John Whitaker—Hopscotch

2 Switzerland, 42.08; 3 FRG, 44.75;
4 France, 55.61; 5 Netherlands, 81.34;
6 Italy, 109.93; 7 USSR, 116.75;
8 Austria, 128.34.

Dublin

Great Britain   8.00
Nick Skelton—Everest Apollo
Liz Edgar—Everest Forever
Robert Smith—Sanyo Olympic Video
John Whitaker—Ryan's Son

2 Ireland, 17.75; =3 FRG, USA, 20.00;
5 France, 24.00.

Rotterdam

France   8.00
Roger-Yves Bost—Jorphée de Prieur
Philippe Rozier—Jiva
Patrice Delaveau—Laeken
Hubert Bourdy—Juniperus

2 FRG, 13.25; 3 Austria, 15.00;
4 Italy, 23.75; 5 Netherlands, 24.00;
6 Great Britain, 28.50;
7 Belgium, 33.00.

Chaudfontaine

Netherlands   4.00
Jan Tops—Furist
Eric van der Vleuten—Expo Graphic
Henk Nooren—Glenn
Emiel Hendrix—Optiebeurs Een

2 Belgium, 8.00; 3 Great Britain, 12.00;
4 France, 23.00; 5 FRG, 24.00;
6 Italy, 29.25; 7 Switzerland, 48.00.

Prague

FRG   9.50
Karl-Heinz Schwab—Winnipeg
Frank Müller—Baroness
Julius Schulze-Hesselmann—Dublin
Hauke Schmidt—Lafayette

2 Great Britain, 12.00; 3 Austria, 24.00;
4 GDR, 28.00;
5 Czechoslovakia, 33.00;
6 Poland, 45.25; 7 Bulgaria, 111.00.

St Gallen

FRG   0.00
Jürgen Kenn—Feuergeist
Ludger Beerbaum—Saloniki
Gerd Wiltfang—Walido
Paul Schockemöhle—So Long

2 Great Britain, 4.00;
3 Switzerland, 8.00; 4 France, 16.00;
5 Ireland, 20.00; 6 Poland, 36.00;
7 Italy, 72.00.

1986

Calgary

Great Britain 8.00
Nick Skelton—Everest Apollo
Michael Whitaker—Warren Point
Malcolm Pyrah
—Towerlands Anglezarke
John Whitaker—Hopscotch

2 Switzerland, 8.25; 3 Canada, 14.25;
4 France, 21.75; =5 USA, FRG, 24.00.

Plovdiv

FRG 12.00
Lutz Gössing—Liberal
Dirk Hafemeister—Borodin
Frank Müller—Baroness
Julius Schulze-Hesselmann—Dublin

2 USSR, 23.75; 3 GDR, 25.25;
4 Bulgaria, 48.00; 5 Poland, 49.50;
6 Czechoslovakia, retired.

Wiesenhof-Salzburg

FRG 4.00
Jürgen Ernst—Lustig
Werner Peters—Romantika
Stefan Schewe—Wilster
Fritz Ligges—Rodney

2 Great Britain, 8.00; 3 Austria, 12.00;
4 Poland, 28.00; 5 Sweden, 36.00;
6 Belgium, 40.00.

Lisbon

Great Britain 4.00
Geoff Luckett—For Sure
Annette Lewis—Tutein
Kelly Brown—Foxlight
Derek Ricketts—Master Guy

2 Spain, 8.00; 3 Portugal, 12.00;
4 France, 23.50;
=5 Switzerland, Belgium, 40.75;
7 Morocco, 90.25.

Washington

USA 4.00
Michael Matz—Bon Retour
Louis Jacobs—Janus de Ver
Katie Monahan—The Governor
Joe Fargis—Touch of Class

2 FRG, 10.25; 3 Canada, 71.25.

New York

USA 4.00
Katie Monahan—The Governor
Lisa Tarnapol—Adam
Michael Matz—Chef
Joe Fargis—Touch of Class

2 Canada, 11.50; 3 FRG, 14.25.

Toronto

FRG 4.00
Stefan Schewe—Wilster
Werner Peters—Romantika
Klaus Reinacher—Windus
Ludger Beerbaum—Saloniki

2 Canada, 8.25; 3 USA, 8.50.

Rome

France 4.00
Frédéric Cottier—Flambeau C
Philippe Rozier—Jiva
Patrice Delaveau—Laeken
Pierre Durand—Jappeloup de Luze

2 Great Britain, 9.75; 3 Austria, 15.75;
4 Switzerland, 16.25; 5 Belgium, 17.50;
6 Brazil, 21.25; 7 Italy, 27.75;
8 Spain, 32.00; 9 Argentina, 44.00;
10 FRG, 46.00; 11 Chile, 88.00.

Lucerne

France 8.25
Frédéric Cottier—Flambeau C
Philippe Rozier—Jiva
Patrice Delaveau—Laeken
Pierre Durand—Jappeloup de Luze

2 FRG, 14.00; 3 Great Britain, 17.00;
4 Argentina, 30.00; 5 Italy, 30.50;
6 Switzerland, 32.50;
7 Netherlands, 37.00; 8 Brazil, 58.00.

Jerez de la Frontera

Great Britain 8.00. 0.00 in jump-off
Nick Skelton—Raffles Apollo
Michael Whitaker—Next Amanda
Malcolm Pyrah
—Towerlands Diamond Seeker
John Whitaker—Hopscotch

2 Belgium, 8.00, 4.00 in jump-off;
3 FRG, 8.00, 12.00 in jump-off;
=4 Switzerland, Argentina, Chile,
Spain, Portugal, 28.00;
9 Morocco, 67.75.

Hickstead

France 24.75
Frédéric Cottier—Flambeau C
Philippe Rozier—Jiva
Michel Robert—Lafayette
Pierre Durand—Jappeloup de Luze

2 Great Britain, 30.50; 3 FRG, 32.25;
4 Italy, 41.25; 5 Netherlands, 46.75;
6 Ireland, retired.

Fontainebleau

France 11.75
Frédéric Cottier—Flambeau C
Michel Robert—Lafayette
Patrice Delaveau—Laeken
Pierre Durand—Jappeloup de Luze

2 Great Britain, 12.00;
3 Switzerland, 12.50; 4 Italy, 16.50;
5 Austria, 25.00; 6 FRG, 25.25;
7 Brazil, 28.25; 8 Spain, 32.00;
9 Belgium, 38.25; 10 Argentina, 49.50;
11 Chile, 68.25.

Sopot

FRG 12.00
Lutz Gössing—Liberal
Peter Nagel-Tornau—Carossa

Tjark Nagel—Gotthard Ass
Wolfang Brinkmann—Pedro

2 Belgium, 48.25; 3 Poland, 48.50;
4 GDR, 57.50; 5 USSR, 112.00;
6 Bulgaria, 168.75.

Falsterbo

Great Britain 18.50
Harvey Smith—Sanyo Cadnica
Joe Turi—Vital
Gillian Greenwood—Monsanta
David Broome—Royale

2 FRG, 49.00; 3 Sweden, 50.50;
4 Belgium, 70.25; 5 Denmark, 76.50;
6 Poland, 139.25.

Dublin

Great Britain 5.50
Nick Skelton—Raffles Apollo
Michael Whitaker—Next Warren Point
Peter Charles—April Sun
John Whitaker—Next Ryan's Son

2 USA, 8.00; 3 Ireland, 16.00;
4 FRG, 28.00.

Bratislava

FRG 4.00
Frank Müller—Baroness
Andre Heller—Aviata
Ernst Hofschroer—Société
Dirk Schroder—Lacros

2 Great Britain, 16.00;
3 Switzerland, 20.00; 4 GDR, 32.00;
5 Hungary, 56.00;
6 Czechoslovakia, 79.00;
7 Bulgaria, retired.

Rotterdam

Great Britain 8.75
Nick Skelton—Raffles Airborne
Michael Whitaker—Next Amanda
Janet Hunter—Everest Lisnamarrow
John Whitaker—Next Milton

2 Switzerland, 16.00; 3 FRG, 20.25;
4 Austria, 21.50; 5 France, 24.25;
6 Netherlands, 28.25; 7 Spain, 18.75*;
8 USA, 24.00*; 9 Brazil, 28.50*;
10 Belgium, 42.75*.

*First-round scores (teams did not take
part in second round).

Chaudfontaine

= **Netherlands** 20.00
Emiel Hendrix—Optibeurs Een
Wiljan Laarakkers—Up To Date
Wout-Jan van der Schans
—Olympic Treffer
Rob Ehrens—Oscar Drum

= **Brazil** 20.00
João Arago—Miss Globo
Luis Azevedo
—Moët et Chandon Lassall
Vitor Teixeira
—Moët et Chandon Tipiton
Nelson Pessoa
—Moët et Chandon Wellington

3 FRG, 24.00; 4 USA, 28.00;
5 Great Britain, 31.00*;
6 France, 39.00;
7 Switzerland, 40.00;
8 Belgium, 53.75.

*Great Britain won the Nations Cup but one of the team members, Peter Charles, was later disqualified following a positive medication control test on his horse, April Sun. April Sun's score of 4.00/0.00 had to be discounted, which dropped the team to 5th place.

Donaueschingen

FRG   8.00
Kurt Gravemeier—Wembley
Franke Sloothaak—Farmer
Gerd Wiltfang—Wieland
Paul Schockemöhle—Next Deister

2 USA, 12.00; 3 Great Britain, 16.00;
4 France, 17.00; 5 Ireland, 20.00;
6 Austria, 24.00; 7 Netherlands, 32.00;
8 Belgium, 40.00; 9 Switzerland, 49.00.

Plovdiv

FRG   0.00
Detlef Brüggemann—Inshallahboy

Norbert Nuxoll—Santana
Dirk Hafemeister—Valido
Julius Schulze-Hesselmann—Gondolo

2 GDR, 24.50; 3 USSR, 28.25;
4 Czechoslovakia, 41.00;
5 Bulgaria, 80.75.

Calgary

USA   4.00, 4.00 in 103.38 in jump-off
Robert Ridland—Mon Bambi
Jennifer Newell—Nero
Joan Scharffenberger—Winnipeg
Hap Hansen—Juniperus

2 Great Britain, 4.00, 4.00 in 103.47 secs in jump-off;
=3 Canada, Netherlands, 12.00;
5 Switzerland, 12.25; 6 France, 28.00.

Lisbon

FRG   8.00
Frank Müller—Baroness
Marion Henkel—Dixato
Jürgen Ernst—Prinz Charming
Achaz von Buchwaldt—Ricarda

=2 Portugal, Spain, 12.00;
4 Belgium, 16.00.

Washington

USA   8.00
Anne Kursinski—Montreal
Katharine Burdsall—The Natural
Lisa Tarnapol—Adam
Katie Monahan—The Bean Bag

2 Great Britain, 16.00;
3 Canada, 20.75.

New York

Canada   12.00, 4.00 in jump-off
Mario Deslauriers—Box Car Willie
John Anderson—Scirocco
Ian Millar—Big Ben
Laura Tidball-Balisky—Lavendel

2 USA, 12.00, 8.00 in jump-off;
3 Great Britain, 20.25; 4 France, retired.

Toronto

Great Britain   4.00
Nick Skelton—Raffles Apollo
Michael Whitaker—Next Heliopolis
Peter Charles—April Sun
Malcolm Pyrah—Towerlands Anglezarke

=2 Canada, USA, 8.00;
4 France, 12.50.

Records

Nations Cups 1909–1986

Winning Countries

FRG/Germany	142
Great Britain	130
USA	100
Italy	95
France	91
Ireland	43
Spain	36
Switzerland	27
Poland	25
Belgium	20
Mexico	18
Canada	17
Netherlands	15
Portugal	14
South Africa	10
USSR/Russia	10
Argentina	9
DDR	6
Brazil	5
Sweden	5
Rumania	4
Chile	3
Turkey	2
Latvia	1
Venezuela	1
	829*

*828 Nations Cups, of which one (in 1986) had two teams placed equal first.

With 37 winning appearances, Hans Günter Winkler, here riding Enigk, is the German rider with the best tally in Nations Cups and fourth overall behind Frank Chapot (46), Piero d'Inzeo (41) and William Steinkraus (39). (Ed Lacey Associated Sports Photography)

Country with most wins in one season

Italy—7 (1955)

Nations Cups 1909–1986 —Most Successful Riders

Up to the end of 1986 some 850 riders had made at least one appearance in a winning Nations Cup team. Listed below are the most successful riders—those who have been in 10 or more winning teams.

Hungarian-born Bertalan de Nemethy, for 25 years trainer of the United States Equestrian Team's show jumpers and the man responsible for turning them into one of the strongest teams in the world. Up to the end of 1986 the United States had won 100 Nations Cups, only bettered by Germany (142) and Great Britain (130). (Bob Langrish)

No. of wins		
46 Frank Chapot (USA)		
41 Piero d'Inzeo (Ita)		
39 William Steinkraus (USA)		
37 Hans Günter Winkler (FRG)		
32 Raimondo d'Inzeo (Ita)		
31 Harvey Smith (Great Britain)		
30 Graziano Mancinelli (Ita)		
27 David Broome (Great Britain)		
27 Harald Momm (Ger)		
26 Gerd Wiltfang (FRG)		
25 Peter Robeson (Great Britain)		
25 Hartwig Steenken (FRG)		
24 Alwin Schockemöhle (FRG)		
23 Lutz Merkel (FRG)		
23 Malcolm Pyrah (Great Britain)		
22 Conte Alessandro Bettoni-Cazzago (Ita)	15 Fernando Filipponi (Ita)	12 Ernst Hasse (Ger)
22 Dan Corry (Ire)	15 Francesco Goyoaga (Spa)	12 John Lewis (Ire)
22 Kathy Kusner (USA)	15 Guy Lefrant (Fra)	12 Salvatore Oppes (Ita)
22 Mary (Mairs) Chapot (USA)	15 Tommaso Lequio di Assaba (Ita)	12 Derek Ricketts (Great Britain)
20 Pierre Jonquères d'Oriola (Fra)	15 Melanie Smith (USA)	12 Neal Shapiro (USA)
20 Fritz Ligges (FRG)	14 Norman Dello Joio (USA)	11 Buddy Brown (USA)
20 Michael Matz (USA)	14 Nick Skelton (Great Britain)	11 Pierre Clavé (Fra)
20 Paul Schockemöhle (FRG)	13 Giulio Borsarelli di Riffredo (Ita)	11 Francesco Formigli (Ita)
18 John Whitaker (Great Britain)	13 Caroline Bradley (Great Britain)	11 Dennis Murphy (USA)
17 Max Fresson (Fra)	13 Pierre de Maupeou d'Ableiges (Fra)	11 Marten von Barnekow (Ger)
17 Hermann Schridde (FRG)	13 Bertrand du Breuil (Fra)	10 Hans-Heinrich Brinckmann (Ger)
16 Xavier Bizard (Fra)	13 Harry Llewellyn (Great Britain)	10 Jaime Garcia Cruz (Spa)
16 Frédéric Cottier (Fra)	13 Pat Smythe (Great Britain)	10 Kurt Jarasinski (FRG)
16 Kurt Hasse (Ger)	13 Wilf White (Great Britain)	10 Rodney Jenkins (USA)
16 Humberto Mariles Cortés (Mex)	12 Stefano Angioni (Ita)	10 Mario Lombardo di Cumia (Ita)
16 Jed O'Dwyer (Ire)	12 Chevalier Jean d'Orgeix (Fra)	10 Dawn Palethorpe (Great Britain)
15 Fred Ahern (Ire)	12 Lionel Dunning (Great Britain)	10 Julius Schulze-Hesselmann (FRG)
15 Heinz Brandt (Ger)	12 Joe Fargis (USA)	10 Hendrik Snoek (FRG)

The high jump competition at the International Horse Show, Olympia, in 1909 ran, without intermission, from 9.30 pm to 2.00 am. The winner was France's Captain Bérille riding Jubilee, who cleared 7 ft 4 in to beat the previous British record of 7 ft 2 in.

At London's Horse of the Year Show in 1984 Nick Skelton (Great Britain) won 10 competitions, three on Monday, one on Tuesday, four on Friday and two on Saturday. Eight were international classes, the other two were national championships.

In 1963 Britain's Ted Edgar rode Jacopo round the British Jumping Derby course at Hickstead one-handed. He had broken his left arm a few days before and rode with it in a sling. He collected only 8 faults.

Stroller

If complete and accurate records of every horse who has competed in international show jumping were available—which, regrettably, they are not—it is doubtful whether there would be a more serious contender for the title 'smallest' than Mr Ralph Coakes' remarkable little Stroller. Standing only 14.2hh, this bay, Irish-bred gelding was officially a pony, and was registered as such with the BSJA for Mr Coakes' daughter Marion (now Mrs David Mould) to jump as a junior. Marion's achievements with him in that capacity included a team gold medal in the 1962 Junior European Championships in Berlin, where Stroller jumped a double clear round, and a team silver medal in the same Championships two years later in Budapest.

When Marion graduated to the senior ranks, she decided to take Stroller with her instead of letting him be sold to another junior rider as is usual with jumping ponies. Competing against the world's best horses, the majority of whom were some 6 to 8 inches taller than he was, Stroller became a legend in his own lifetime. In 1965 he carried Marion to victory in the first Ladies' World Championship, at Hickstead, and the same year won his first Queen Elizabeth II Cup at the Royal International Horse Show. He excelled at Hickstead where he three times jumped a clear round in the Derby (1964, 1967 and 1968), winning that marathon contest in 1967. His victories in 1968 included the BSJA National Championship and the John Player Trophy (Grand Prix) at the Royal International. But that year will be remembered above all for his amazing performance in the Mexico Olympics. In the individual contest he was one of only two horses to jump a clear round, the other being Snowbound, who won the gold medal. In the second round he had just two fences down as against Snowbound's one, a performance which clinched the individual silver medal.

Sadly, he came to grief in the team contest when the toothache which had plagued him throughout the Games finally took its toll. But the pony had proved himself in the highest company. He was back at his best when he won the gruelling Hamburg Derby in 1970 with a clear round, the first ridden by a woman. That same year he was equal second in the Ladies' World Championship at Copenhagen, again

Stroller, the diminutive pony who won an Olympic silver medal, pictured at home with Marion Coakes in 1969. (Popperfoto)

won the John Player Trophy, and rounded off a wonderful season by taking the Leading Show Jumper of the Year title at the Horse of the Year Show, Wembley. In 1971 he won his second Queen's Cup and National Championship.

He was in five of Britain's winning Nations Cup teams: at Olsztyn, Dublin and Copenhagen, all in 1965; Rotterdam in 1967; and London in 1970. His last victory came in the *Country Life* and *Riding* Cup at the 1971 Horse of the Year Show, after which he retired to his owner's farm. He died on 24 March, 1986 at the age of 36.

The President's Cup

This trophy was introduced by the FEI in 1965, to be awarded annually to the most successful country in the season's series of Nations Cups. Each country taking part in a Nations Cup is awarded points on a sliding scale according to their placing and the number of teams taking part. At the end of the season each country totals the points earned for its six best performances and the trophy goes to the nation at the head of the points table. To mark HRH Prince Philip's 21st year in office as President of the FEI in 1985, the award was renamed the Prince Philip Trophy. Following his retirement at the end of 1986, and to coincide with a new sponsorship agreement for the Nations Cup series between the FEI and the fashion company, Gucci, the Prince Philip Trophy was replaced by the Gucci Trophy.

Top Ten Nations, 1965–86

*Denotes most wins

1965

		Points
1	Great Britain	34.00
2	FRG	31.00
3	Italy	30.00
4	Ireland	19.50
5	France	16.00
6	Portugal	12.00
=7	Poland	11.00
	USSR	11.00
9	Argentina	10.00
10	Switzerland	6.00

1966

1	USA	26.00*
2	Spain	26.00
3	France	20.00
4	Italy	18.00
=5	Canada	13.00
	Poland	13.00
7	FRG	12.00
=8	Great Britain	10.00
	Portugal	10.00
	Hungary	10.00

1967

1	Great Britain	37.00
2	FRG	26.00

3	Italy	20.50
=4	Ireland	17.50
	France	17.50
=6	USA	15.00
	USSR	15.00
8	Poland	14.50
=9	Czechoslovakia	5.00
	Belgium	5.00
	Hungary	5.00

1968

1	USA	33.00
2	Great Britain	25.00
=3	Italy	24.00
	FRG	24.00
5	France	21.50
6	Spain	18.50
7	Switzerland	17.00
=8	Portugal	14.00
	USSR	14.00
=10	Poland	10.00
	Sweden	10.00

1969

1	FRG	39.00
2	Great Britain	35.00
3	Italy	29.00
4	France	23.50
5	Switzerland	17.00
6	Poland	16.00
=7	Belgium	14.00
	USA	14.00
9	Canada	13.00
=10	Netherlands	10.00
	Ireland	10.00

1970

1	Great Britain	36.00
2	FRG	35.00
3	USA	26.50
4	France	21.50
=5	Canada	21.00
	Italy	21.00
7	Spain	13.50
8	USSR	11.00
9	GDR	10.00
=10	Mexico	9.00
	Ireland	9.00

The most successful nation in the President's Cup 1965–86 was Great Britain, with 12 wins compared with the Federal Republic of Germany's seven. One of the Nations Cup successes which helped Britain to retain the trophy in 1986 came at Rotterdam, where the team comprised (from left) Janet Hunter on Everest Lisnamarrow, Nick Skelton on Raffles Airborne, Michael Whitaker on Next Amanda and John Whitaker on Next Milton. (Elizabeth Furth)

1971

1	**FRG**	37.00
2	Great Britain	33.00
3	USA	28.00
4	Italy	26.50
5	France	19.50
=6	Canada	14.00
	Switzerland	14.00
8	Belgium	11.00
=9	Portugal	7.00
	Hungary	7.00

1972

1	**Great Britain**	33.00
2	FRG	32.00
=3	Italy	18.00
	France	18.00
=5	Switzerland	15.00
	Portugal	15.00
7	Canada	12.00
8	Belgium	11.00
9	Spain	9.00
10	USSR	6.00

1973

1	**Great Britain**	34.00
2	FRG	33.00
3	Switzerland	22.00
4	Italy	19.00
5	Netherlands	16.00
6	France	15.00
7	Belgium	13.00
8	Portugal	10.00
9	Chile	9.00
10	Brazil	8.00

1974

1	**Great Britain**	37.00
2	FRG	33.50
3	France	31.00
4	USA	29.00
5	Italy	18.50
=6	Spain	15.00
	Belgium	15.00
	Switzerland	15.00
9	Poland	13.00
10	Netherlands	12.00

1975

1	**FRG**	39.00
2	Great Britain	35.00
3	France	26.00
=4	Italy	22.00
	Belgium	22.00
6	Switzerland	17.00
=7	Ireland	15.00
	USA	15.00
9	Netherlands	14.00
=10	Poland	10.00
	Canada	10.00

1976

1	**FRG**	32.00
2	France	31.00
3	Ireland	28.00
4	Italy	22.00
5	Great Britain	21.00
6	Belgium	17.50
7	Switzerland	16.50
8	Netherlands	12.50
9	Austria	12.00
10	Canada	11.00

1977

1	**Great Britain**	35.50
2	FRG	32.00
3	Ireland	31.00
4	Belgium	23.50
5	France	23.00
6	Italy	22.50
7	USA	19.00
8	Canada	14.50
9	Netherlands	12.00
10	Czechoslovakia	8.00

1978

1	**Great Britain**	38.00
2	FRG	36.00
3	USA	31.00
4	France	29.00
5	Ireland	27.00
6	Canada	26.50
7	Netherlands	23.50
8	Belgium	19.50
9	Switzerland	14.00
10	Austria	10.50

1979

1	**Great Britain**	40.00
2	FRG	33.50
3	France	30.50
4	Ireland	28.00
5	Belgium	19.00
=6	Switzerland	18.50
	USA	18.50
8	Spain	18.00
9	Netherlands	16.00
10	Canada	14.00

1980

1	**France**	38.00
2	Great Britain	35.00
3	Switzerland	32.50
4	FRG	29.50
5	USA	27.50
6	Canada	21.00
7	Belgium	19.50
8	Austria	17.50
9	Netherlands	17.00
10	Spain	16.00

1981

1	**FRG**	36.00
2	Great Britain	35.00
3	France	33.00
4	Switzerland	26.00
5	Netherlands	24.50
6	Italy	20.00
7	Ireland	19.00
8	USA	18.00
9	Belgium	16.00
10	Poland	14.00

1982

1	**FRG**	40.00
2	Great Britain	37.00
3	France	31.50
4	Switzerland	30.00
5	USA	27.00
6	Belgium	19.00
7	Italy	17.00
8	Netherlands	12.50
9	Canada	12.00
10	Ireland	7.00

1983

1	**Great Britain**	38.00
2	Switzerland	35.00
3	FRG	34.00
4	France	33.00
5	USA	28.00
6	Italy	18.00
7	Poland	15.00
8	Canada	14.00
9	Austria	13.00
=10	Netherlands	12.00
	Belgium	12.00

1984

1	**FRG**	37.00
2	Great Britain	36.00
3	France	32.00
4	Switzerland	31.00
5	Italy	20.50
6	Poland	18.50
7	Belgium	18.00
8	USA	16.00
9	Canada	15.00
10	Netherlands	14.00

1985

1	**Great Britain**	39.00
2	FRG	38.00
3	USA	29.50
4	France	28.00
5	Switzerland	26.50
6	Netherlands	22.50
7	Poland	19.00
8	Austria	17.50
9	Belgium	16.50
10	Italy	16.00

1986

1	**Great Britain**	38.00
2	FRG	36.00
3	France	34.00
4	USA	29.00
5	Switzerland	24.20
6	Belgium	20.00
7	Netherlands	16.00
8	Canada	15.00
9	Austria	14.00
10	Italy	11.50

Winning nations 1965–86

Great Britain	12
FRG	7
USA	2
France	1

Highest and Widest

The high jump used to be a very popular event, particularly in the early days of show jumping, but it is rarely seen nowadays. There is no course as such, just one fence, which must comply exactly with the regulations laid down by the FEI. The fence is designed to ensure maximum jumpability—it is sloped, and has a good groundline—and minimum risk of injury in the event of a fall. The light wooden poles which are used must be covered with a binding of straw or nylon, and the clearance between the bottom pole and the ground has to be filled with suitable material, such as a brush fence, to give an appearance of solidity. High wings are used and the finished obstacle must be at least 6 metres (19 ft 8¼ in) wide. The organizing committee decides at what height the competition should commence, and each horse and rider is allowed three attempts at each height. Faults are awarded differently from other competitions: 2 penalties for a knock-down, 3 penalties for a refusal, run-out or resistance, with elimination following the third of such faults during the same attempt. Faults are only incurred when the horse, with the rider aboard, is actually in the penalty zone, that is an area extending 15 metres (49 ft 2½ in) in front of the obstacle, and bound on each side by red and white flags. If, after clearing the obstacle successfully, either horse or rider falls, no penalties are awarded.

The winner is the competitor who clears the greatest height without penalties, regardless of faults collected during previous attempts. In the event of two or more horses clearing the same height they must try the next height. If there is still no outright winner, competitors are placed according to the number of penalties accrued, either in the final jump-off or, in the case of further equality, in the preceding round or rounds.

The long jump is even more rare these days than the high jump. It is judged under the same rules as the high jump and again a special obstacle must be provided. The inclined hurdle which marks the base of the jump is moved back progressively as the spread is increased. The shallow water jump must end in a gradual slope covered with matting. As the hurdle is moved back, the free space between it and the water is covered by other hurdles set at a more acute angle. Low wide wings are provided, forming a passageway in front of the jump.

Competitors may attempt to beat the existing world records either by jumping the necessary height or spread straight away or by progressive jumps. A competitor is allowed only three attempts at the height or spread which will constitute a record, and a refusal counts as an attempt. In order to beat a record the horse must clear a height of at least 2 cm (0.79 in) or a spread of 10 cm (3.94 in) more than the existing record.

Occasionally a competition is run as an amalgam of high jump and puissance, the fence being a wall, as in a puissance, but the contest being judged under high jump rules—the current West German high jump record was achieved in this type of competition (see the National Championships section).

World High Jump Record

5 February, 1949, Chile
At the official international show at Santiago, Captain Alberto Larraguibel Morales (Chile), riding the 15-year-old Thoroughbred **Huaso** (ex-Faithful), cleared **2.47 Metres (8 ft 1¼ in)** at the third attempt. This record, which was ratified on 28 May, 1949, by the FEI Committee of Records, still stands. At least 2.49 metres (8 ft 2 in) must be cleared to beat it.

Previous Records ratified by the FEI

27 October, 1938, Italy
At the National Championships in Rome, the Irish-bred horse **Osoppo,** owned by the Italian Government and ridden by Captain Antonio Gutierrez (Italy), cleared **2.44 metres (8 ft).**

10 April, 1933, France
At the Grand Palais in Paris, the Vicomte de Salignac-Fénelon's horse **Vol-au-Vent,** ridden by Lt Christian de Castries (France), cleared **2.38 metres (7 ft 9¾ in).**

17 August, 1912, France
At Vittel, Messrs de Mumm and Loewenstein's **Biskra,** ridden by François de Juge Montespieu (France), and Messrs de Rovira and René Ricard's

Howard Willett's Thoroughbred Heatherbloom, ridden by Dick Donnelly, jumping 2.49 metres (8 ft 2 in) in 1902.

Montjoie III, ridden by René Ricard (France), both jumped **2.36 metres (7 ft 9 in).**

12 April, 1906, France
At the Grand Palais, Paris, M. de Mumm's Canadian-bred **Conspirateur,** ridden by Captain Crousse (France), jumped **2.35 metres (7 ft 8½ in).**

North American Records (not ratified by the FEI)

8 June, 1923, USA
In Chicago, **Great Heart,** ridden by Fred Vesey (USA), jumped **2.46 metres (8 ft ⅞ in).**

14 September, 1912, Canada
At the Central Canadian Exhibition in Ottawa, Clifford Sifton's part-bred Hackney **Confidence,** ridden by Jack Hamilton (Canada), cleared **2.45 metres (8 ft ½ in).**

1902, USA
At Richmond, Virginia, Howard Willett's Thoroughbred **Heatherbloom,** ridden by Dick Donnelly (USA), jumped **2.40 metres (7 ft 10½ in).**

Unofficial Records

18 September, 1904, Spain
At San Sebastian, **Conspirateur,** ridden by Captain Crousse, jumped **2.23 metres (7 ft 3¾ in).**

1902, USA
At two public demonstrations at his owner's farm in Richmond, Virginia, **Heatherbloom,** ridden by Dick Donnelly, jumped **2.49 metres (8 ft 2 in)** and **2.515 metres (8 ft 3 in).**

15 June, 1902, Italy
At Turin, **Meloppo,** ridden by Federico Caprilli (Italy), cleared **2.08 metres (6 ft 9⅞ in)** though not without a certain amount of outside assistance: Caprilli's fellow cavalry officers hooked shovels over the top rail to prevent it from falling!

World Long Jump Record

26 April, 1975, South Africa
At the Rand Show in Johannesburg, Mrs I. G. van de Merwe's **Something,** ridden by André Ferreira, cleared a width of **8.40 metres (27 ft 6¾ in).** In September 1975 during the FEI Bureau meeting in Rabat, Morocco, the Committee of Records confirmed this new record, which still stands.

Previous Records ratified by the FEI

August, 1951, Spain
At the Barcelona CSIO, the seven-year-old Anglo-Arab **Amado Mio,** ridden by Fernando del Hierro (Spain), cleared a water jump of **8.30 metres (27 ft 2¾ in)** at the third attempt.

2 September, 1950, Spain
At the Bilbao CSIO, **Balcamo,** ridden by Lt-Colonel Nogueras Marquez (Spain), jumped **8.20 metres (26 ft 10¾ in).**

14 August, 1949, The Netherlands
At The Hague national show, the 11-year-old German-bred **Coeur Joli,** owned by D.-H. Pasman and ridden by B. van der Woort, jnr (Netherlands), cleared **8.10 metres (26 ft 6⅞ in)** at the first attempt.

12 September, 1948, Spain
On the last day of the CSIO at Bilbao, **Balcamo,** ridden by Commandant Nogueras Marquez, jumped **7.80 metres (25 ft 7 in)** at his first attempt, and **Faun,** ridden by Captain Maestre Salinas, did likewise at his second attempt. The two competitors then attempted to clear **8.00 metres (26 ft 3 in).** Faun failed at all three attempts, but **Balcamo** cleared this width at his first try.

1 December, 1946, Argentina
At the Buenos Aires CSIO, **Guarana,** ridden by Jorge Fraga Patrao (Argentina), cleared a water jump of **7.70 metres (25 ft 3⅛ in).**

18 July, 1935, Belgium
At the Spa CSIO, the 16-year-old French-bred **Tenace,** ridden by Lt Christian de Castries (France), cleared a water jump of **7.60 metres (24 ft 11¼ in).**

1913, France
At Le Touquet, **Saint-Jacques,** owned by M. Santa Victoria and ridden by Henry de Royer (France), cleared **7.50 metres (24 ft 7¼ in).**

1912, France
At Le Touquet, **Pick me up,** owned by J. Delesalle and ridden by Henry de Royer, jumped **7.50 metres (24 ft 7¼ in).**

Mrs I. G. van der Merwe's Something, ridden by André Ferreira, setting the world record long jump of 8.40 metres (27 ft 6¾ in) in Johannesburg in 1975.

Puissance Records

The puissance is an old-established competition which aims to demonstrate the ability of a horse to jump a limited number of large obstacles, the most spectacular being the wall. The competition begins over four to six fences which for jump-off purposes are reduced in number to two, a wall and a spread. Up to four jump-offs are permitted, after which the competition is stopped.

Listed here are the greatest heights known to have been cleared over a puissance wall.

7 ft 7¾ in (2.33 metres)
Jumped by Nelson Pessoa (Bra) riding Miss Moët at the outdoor Paris CSIO in June, 1983.

7 ft 7½ in (2.325 metres)
Jumped by Anthony d'Ambrosio (USA) riding Sweet n' Love at the indoor Washington CSIO in October, 1983.

7 ft 7⁵⁄₁₆ in (2.32 metres)
Jumped by Willi Melliger (Switz) and Beethoven at the outdoor St Gallen CSIO in August, 1985.

7 ft 7¼ in (2.31 metres)
Jumped by Gavin Chester (Aus) and Rockefella at the outdoor Warrnambool (Australia) show in November, 1978.

7 ft 6¾ in (2.305 metres)
Jumped by Barney Ward (USA) riding Glandor Akai at the indoor Washington CSIO in October, 1982.

7 ft 6½ in (2.30 metres)
Jumped by Willibert Mehlkopf (FRG) riding Hennessy Wabbs and Boris Boor (Aut) riding Vancouver at the outdoor Rome CSIO in May, 1987; by Nelson Pessoa (Bra) riding Miss Möet at the outdoor Lucerne CSIO in May, 1986; by Willibert Mehlkopf riding Wabbs and Markus Fuchs (Switz) riding Puschkin at the outdoor Madrid CSI in May, 1986; by Diego Deriu (Ita) riding Fanando and Willi Melliger (Switz) riding Beethoven at the outdoor Rome CSIO in May, 1985; by Wabbs and Beethoven at the outdoor Aachen CSIO in June, 1985; by Emilio Puricelli (Ita) riding Pentagon at the outdoor Rome CSIO in May, 1983; by Willi Melliger (Switz) riding David at the outdoor Paris CSIO in July, 1981; and by Eric Wauters (Bel) riding Pomme d'Api at the outdoor Le Touquet CSA in July, 1975.

7 ft 6 in (2.286 metres)
Jumped by Walter Gabathuler (Switz) riding Beethoven, by Rodney Jenkins (USA) riding Arbitrage, and by Michel Robert (Fra) riding Janus de Ver at the indoor New York CSIO in November, 1982; and by Filippo Moyersoen (Ita) riding Adam at the indoor Washington CSIO in October, 1981.

7 ft 5½ in (2.27 metres)
Jumped by Walter Gabathuler riding Beethoven at the indoor Dortmund CSI in March, 1983.

7 ft 5¼ in (2.266 metres)
Jumped by Patrick Caron (Fra) riding Gai Sarda at the Olympia (London) CSI in December, 1980.

Merely-a-Monarch

Before the Second World War, when equestrian sports were dominated by the cavalry, which demanded high standards of general all-round horsemanship, it was not unusual for both horses and riders to compete in more than one discipline. In the different climate of the post-war years, specialization has been very much the order of the day. Horses tend to be switched from one discipline to another only if they fail at the first, so a horse such as Merely-a-Monarch was rare indeed. He was a strapping gelding by the Thoroughbred stallion Happy Monarch, winner of eight races, and out of the Hunters' Improvement Society registered mare, Dalemain Butterfly, later known as Highland Fling. This mare traced back to a pure-bred Fell pony. Merely-a-Monarch (originally named Highland Monarch) was bought as a youngster by event rider Anneli Drummond-Hay for £300.

In 1961 he was a most impressive winner of the first running of the Burghley Horse Trials, performing an outstanding dressage test and going clear both across country and in the show jumping. The following year at Badminton, Merely-a-Monarch again put up an impressive dressage performance to win that phase, and thereafter, despite having a fence down in the show jumping, never looked like being headed, winning by the huge margin of 42 marks.

His rider's desire to try for the British Olympic team led her to switch to show jumping, since at that time women were not permitted to compete in the three-day event at the Games. Merely-a-Monarch made the transition without difficulty. He was in two winning Nations Cup teams in 1963, at Rome and London, and was short-listed for the 1964 Games. There followed a period of physical problems, but when he had overcome them he went right to the top of the jumping tree. In 1967 he was in the British team which won the Nice Nations Cup and the following year he helped Anneli to win the Ladies' European Championship, winning the second leg and finishing fourth in the third. Thus Merely-a-Monarch became the only horse to win Badminton and Burghley and a European Jumping title. Other successes included another Nations Cup win at Rome in 1970 and that year's Queen Elizabeth II Cup at London's Royal International Horse Show.

Merely-a-Monarch was retired in 1971 and although his rider, who married that winter, went to live in South Africa, the horse remained in his native land and lived to be 25, dying in 1980.

Great eventer turned show jumper, Merely-a-Monarch with his regular rider Anneli Drummond-Hay, now Mrs Wucherpfenning.

European Championships

Separate championships for men and women were first held in 1957. Initially they were held annually and run along the same lines as the World Championship, with a change-horse final, though this format was soon abandoned. Subsequent championships comprised three or four qualifying rounds, in which the faults, or points, were generally cumulative. In 1975 the FEI introduced a new format, comprising a team event and an individual championship open to both men and women. Complicated new rules for judging the team championship were devised for 1977, but were replaced in 1979 by the now familiar system (for description of rules, see the Team Championship and Individual Championship results). European Championships are held once every two years, in the year between the Olympic Games and the World Championships.

Team Championship

1975 Munich (Amateurs only)

	Leg 1 Time	Leg 2 Faults	Leg 3 Faults	Final Points
1 **West Germany** 35.50				
Alwin Schockemöhle —Warwick	95.80	4.00	16.75	4.50
Hartwig Steenken—Erle	90.10	16.00	24.75	15.50
Sönke Sönksen—Kwept	100.30	16.00	17.00	15.50
Hendrik Snoek —Rasputin	128.90	W	—	—
2 **Switzerland** 94.00				
Paul Weier—Wulf	112.60	8.25	25.50	27.00
Walter Gabathuler —Butterfly	109.30	13.00	36.00	30.00
Bruno Candrian —Golden Shuttle	97.50	24.00	40.00	37.00
Jurg Friedli—Firebird	132.30	62.25	35.00	(58.00)
3 **France** 97.00				
Marcel Rozier —Bayard de Maupas	99.90	29.25	21.25	26.00
Gilles Bertran de Balanda —Bearn	107.50	9.00	43.75	30.00
Michel Roche—Un Espoir	99.20	38.00	55.75	41.00
Hubert Parot—Rivage	109.10	16.00	R	(50.50)

4 Belgium, 104.00; 5 Italy, 114.50; 6 Spain, E.

This year, the first in which a team competition was held, the Championships were restricted to amateur riders, each being allowed to ride only one horse throughout. The format was the same as that used in the former men's individual event: a speed class followed by a Nations Cup-type competition and a two-round Grand Prix-type competition. Points were awarded according to placings and totalled to give the final results in both Individual and Team Championships.

Number of teams: 6

From 1977 onwards open to amateurs and professionals

1977 Vienna

	Table C Faults	Nations Cup One Faults	Two Faults
1 **Netherlands** 20.00			
Johan Heins—Seven Valleys	0.00	4.00	0.00
Henk Nooren—Pluco	0.00	0.00	4.00
Anton Ebben—Jumbo Design	0.00	8.00	4.00
Harry Wouters van der Oudenweyer—Salerno	(12.00)	(20.00)	(20.00)
2 **Great Britain** 20.25			
David Broome—Philco	(4.00)	0.00	0.00
Debbie Johnsey—Moxy	0.25	0.00	(8.00)
Derek Ricketts —Hydrophane Coldstream	0.00	4.00	8.00
Harvey Smith—Olympic Star	0.00	(4.00)	8.00
3 **FRG** 36.00			
Paul Schockemöhle—Agent	0.00	0.00	8.00
Paul Schockemöhle—Talisman	0.00	—	—
Norbert Koof—Minister	4.00	0.00	12.00
Gerd Wiltfang—Davos	0.00	8.00	W
Lutz Merkel—Salvaro	(4.75)	(16.00)	4.00

4 France, 52.00; 5 Belgium, 58.75; 6 Switzerland, 60.00; 7 Ireland, 64.00; 8 Spain, 69.25; 9 Austria, 110.00.

There were significant changes to the rules this year. The Team Championship was decided by adding together the faults accrued in the first leg—the speed class—and in the Nations Cup on the final day. Faults in the two-round second leg of the Individual Championship did not count towards the Team Championship. Although riders were restricted to one horse for the Individual Championship they were allowed to bring in a reserve horse for the Nations Cup. All reserve horses had to compete in the first leg of the Individual Championship where their scores did not count. The total score for a rider who chose to jump a reserve horse in the Nations Cup was this horse's total faults for those two rounds plus the faults earned by the other horse in the first leg.

Number of teams: 9

1979 Rotterdam

	Table C Faults	Nations Cup One Faults	Nations Cup Two Faults
1 Great Britain 24.70			
Derek Ricketts			
—Hydrophane Coldstream	4.65	0.00	0.00
Caroline Bradley—Tigre	5.05	0.00	(8.00)
David Broome—Queensway Big Q	7.00	8.00	0.00
Malcolm Pyrah—Law Court	(12.05)	(8.00)	0.00
2 FRG 30.95			
Gerd Wiltfang—Roman	4.95	0.00	4.00
Paul Schockemöhle—Deister	1.10	4.00	4.00
Peter Luther—Livius	(6.00)	8.00	0.00
Heinrich-Wilhelm Johannsmann			
—Sarto	4.90	(8.25)	(12.00)
3 Ireland 34.10			
Eddie Macken			
—Carroll's Boomerang	0.00	0.00	3.75
Con Power—Rockbarton	1.85	4.00	8.00
Gerry Mullins—Ballinderry	7.00	4.00	(16.00)
John Roche—Maigh Cuillin	(29.80)	(29.50)	5.50

4 Netherlands, 46.80; 5 Switzerland, 59.25; 6 France, 73.30; 7 Belgium, 86.25; 8 Sweden, 113.50; 9 Poland, 152.50; 10 USSR, 157.70.

The format for the Championships was revised this year and the new format has been used at all Championships since. The event begins with a Table C class; then comes a Nations Cup and lastly a two-round Grand Prix, with only the top 20 riders

The victorious British team in 1985 (from left), Nick Skelton, John Whitaker, team manager Ronnie Massarella, Malcolm Pyrah and Michael Whitaker. (Bob Langrish)

competing in the second round. The scores obtained by each competitor in the Table C class are converted into penalties: this is done by multiplying the time of each competitor by the co-efficient 0.50; after this conversion the competitor with the lowest number of points is given a score of 0.00, the others being credited with the number of faults representing the difference in points between each of them and the leading rider. The Team Championship is decided by adding together the scores in the Table C class and those in the Nations Cup, each country counting only its best three scores in each round. For the individual awards the scores in all three competitions count.

Number of teams: 10

The arena at Dinard, venue for the 1985 Championships. (Bob Langrish)

1981 Munich

	Table C Faults	Nations Cup One Faults	Two Faults
2 FRG 11.86			
Paul Schockemöhle—Deister	0.00	0.00	0.00
Peter Luther—Livius	3.21	0.00	(4.00)
Gerd Wiltfang—Roman	4.65	(8.00)	0.00
Norbert Koof—Fire	(14.89)	4.00	0.00
2 Switzerland 21.86			
Bruno Candrian—Van Gogh	1.24	0.00	0.00
Walter Gabathuler—Harley	1.60	0.00	8.00
Thomas Fuchs—Willora Carpets	(9.48)	4.00	0.00
Willi Melliger—Trumpf Buur	7.02	(4.00)	(24.50)
3 Netherlands 26.35			
Emiel Hendrix—Livius	5.58	0.00	0.00
Johan Heins—Larramy	3.12	4.00	4.00
Henk Nooren—Opstalan II	1.65	(8.00)	4.00
Rob Ehrens—Koh-I-Noor	(5.91)	4.00	(8.00)

4 Great Britain, 28.63; 5 France, 35.34; 6 Ireland, 55.53;
7 Austria, 55.75; 8 Poland, 111.16; 9 USSR, 165.67.

Number of teams: 9

1983 Hickstead

	Table C Faults	Nations Cup One Faults	Two Faults
1 Switzerland 12.19			
Walter Gabathuler—Beethoven II	0.00	0.00	4.00
Willi Melliger—Van Gogh	0.57	4.00	0.00
Thomas Fuchs—Willora Swiss	3.62	(4.00)	0.00
Heidi Robbiani—Jessica V	(6.87)	0.00	(8.00)
2 Great Britain 21.89			
Malcolm Pyrah —Towerlands Anglezarke	4.89	0.00	4.00
John Whitaker—Ryan's Son	5.27	4.00	0.00
David Broome—Mr Ross	3.73	0.00	(8.00)
Harvey Smith —Sanyo Olympic Video	(10.56)	(20.00)	0.00

Three times Men's European Champion, David Broome won his first title in 1961. His partner on that occasion was Sunsalve, pictured here during a schooling session. (Peter Roberts)

3 FRG 24.32			
Paul Schockemöhle—Deister	1.24	0.00	0.00
Michael Rüping—Caletto	8.00	0.00	0.00
Achaz von Buchwaldt—Wendy	7.08	8.00	0.00
Gerd Wiltfang—Goldika	(10.56)	(16.00)	0.00

4 Netherlands, 40.14; 5 France, 48.47; 6 Austria, 50.44;
7 Italy, 69.69; 8 Ireland, 71.53; 9 Sweden, 72.84;
10 Poland, 108.75; 11 USSR, 147.90.

Number of teams: 11

1985 Dinard

	Table C Faults	Nations Cup One Faults	Two Faults
1 Great Britain 21.56			
John Whitaker—Hopscotch	1.71	0.00	0.00
Michael Whitaker—Warren Point	2.45	4.00	0.00
Nick Skelton—Everest St James	1.40	8.00	4.00
Malcolm Pyrah —Towerlands Anglezarke	(8.53)	(8.00)	(4.00)
2 Switzerland 42.08			
Heidi Robbiani—Jessica V	4.29	4.00	0.00
Willi Melliger—Beethoven II	0.18	12.00	4.00
Philippe Guerdat—Pybalia	(12.26)	4.00	8.00
Walter Gabathuler—The Swan	5.61	(12.00)	(8.00)
3 FRG 44.75			
Paul Schockemöhle—Deister	3.06	8.00	0.00
Peter Luther—Livius	4.86	0.00	8.00
Michael Rüping—Silbersee	8.33	8.50	4.00
Franke Sloothaak—Walido	(11.54)	(12.00)	(8.00)

4 France, 55.61; 5 Netherlands, 81.34; 6 Italy, 109.93;
7 USSR, 116.75; 8 Austria, 128.34.

Number of teams: 8

Men's Individual Championship

*Indicates second horse

1957 Rotterdam

	Sonnenglanz	Bucéphale	Pagoro	Sea Leopard	Total
1 Hans Günter Winkler (FRG)	4.00	0.00	0.00	4.00	8.00
2 Bernard de Fombelle (Fra)	7.00	0.00	0.00	4.00	11.00
3 Salvatore Oppes—(Ita)	16.00	4.00	0.00	4.00	24.00
4 Marquis Lorenzo de Medici—(Ita)	24.00	R	0.00	0.00	—
	51.00	—	0.00	12.00	

Finalists' placings in qualifying competitions

	1st comp.	2nd comp.	3rd comp.
Hans Günter Winkler—Sonnenglanz/ Halla*	3*	=1	5
Bernard de Fombelle—Bucéphale/ Buffalo B*	2	=1*	6
Salvatore Oppes—Pagoro	1	=1	=2
Marquis Lorenzo de Medici —Sea Leopard/Irish Rover*	4	=1*	1

This first Men's Individual European Championship was run along the same lines as the early World Championships. Riders could compete with two different horses in the three qualifying competitions, a speed class, a puissance and a two-round competition; the four leading riders at the end of all three classes went into the final, where each was required to ride his own horse and those of the other finalists.

Number of riders: 8

Number of nations represented: 5

1958 Aachen

	Total Points	Competition Placings			
		One	Two	Three	Four
1 Fritz Thiedemann (FRG)—Meteor	106.00	1	2	=4	1
2 Piero d'Inzeo (Ita)—The Rock	98.30		1	=1	
3 Hans Günter Winkler (FRG)—Halla	98.00	2	3	=4	2

New rules applied this year. The change-horse final was abandoned. Competitors rode only one horse in each of four legs, a speed class, a parcours de chasse, a puissance and a Nations Cup-type class, the winner being the rider with the highest number of points at the end of the four competitions.

Number of nations represented: 13

1959 Paris

	Uruguay	Virtuoso	Godewind	Halla	Total
1 Piero d'Inzeo (Ita)	0.00	0.00	4.00	4.00	8.00
2 Pierre Jonquères d'Oriola (Fra)	8.50	0.00	4.00	4.00	16.50
3 Fritz Thiedemann (FRG)	4.00	0.00	4.00	16.00	24.00
4 Hans Günter Winkler (FRG)	12.00	4.00	4.50	4.00	24.50
	24.50	4.00	16.50	28.00	

Finalists' placings in qualifying competitions

	1st comp.	2nd comp.	3rd comp.
Piero d'Inzeo (Ita)—Uruguay/ The Quiet Man*	4	=1	=4
Pierre Jonquères d'Oriola (Fra) —Virtuoso/Isofelt*	3		1
Fritz Thiedemann (FRG)—Godewind/ Retina*	5*	=1	2
Hans Günter Winkler (FRG)—Halla	2	=1	3

This Championship reverted to three qualifying competitions—a speed class, a puissance and a Nations Cup-type competition—plus a change-horse final.

Number of riders: 18

Number of nations represented: 9

1961 Aachen

	Points	Competition Placings			
		One	Two	Three	Four
1 David Broome (GB)—Sunsalve/Ballan Silver Knight*	181.70	2	=1	2	1
2 Piero d'Inzeo (Ita)—Pioneer/The Rock*	177.45	1	=1	1	5
3 Hans Günter Winkler (FRG)—Romanus/Feuerdorn*	156.00	3			4

Four competitions, speed, puissance, parcours de chasse, Nations Cup-type. There was no change-horse final this year and in fact it was never again used in the European Championships.

Number of riders: 27

Number of nations represented: 13

1962 London

	Faults in Final	Competition Placings One	Two	Three
1 C. David Barker (GB)—Mister Softee/Franco*	4.00	2*	=1	2*
=2 Hans Günter Winkler (FRG)—Romanus/Feuerdorn*	8.00	1	=1	11
Piero d'Inzeo (Ita)—The Rock	8.00	6		10

Three qualifying competitions, a Table A, a puissance and a speed class, followed by a two-round final. Riders were allowed two horses in the qualifiers, but could ride only one in the final.

Number of riders: 7

Number of nations represented: 4

1963 Rome

	Points	Competition Placings One	Two	Three
1 Graziano Mancinelli (Ita)—Rockette/The Rock*	6.00	3	=1*	1
2 Alwin Schockemöhle (FRG)—Freiherr/Ferdl*	8.00	2	=1*	4
3 Harvey Smith (GB)—O'Malley/Warpaint*	16.00	4*	=1*	

This year saw the introduction of a new format which comprised three competitions, a Table C or speed class, a Nations Cup-type competition and a two-round final competition, the points for all three classes being cumulative.

Number of riders: 18

Number of nations represented: 10

1965 Aachen

	Points	Competition Placings One	Two	Three
1 Hermann Schridde (FRG)—Kamerad/Dozent II*	11.00	4	=5*	1*
2 Nelson Pessoa (Bra)—Huipil/Gran Geste*	14.00	1	=5	7*
3 Alwin Schockemöhle (FRG)—Exakt/Freiherr*	15.50	3	=9	3

Number of riders: 21

Number of nations represented: 12

1966 Lucerne

	Points	Competition Placings One	Two	Three
1 Nelson Pessoa (Bra)—Huipil/Gran Geste*	6.00	2*	1	3
2 Frank Chapot (USA)—Good Twist/San Lucas*	9.50	1	3	4*
3 Hugo Arrambide (Arg)—Chimbote	11.00		3	2

Number of riders: 19

Number of nations represented: 11

1967 Rotterdam

	Points	Competition Placings One	Two	Three	Four
1 David Broome (GB)—Mister Softee/Top of the Morning*	15.50	5	=1	3	1
2 Harvey Smith (GB)—Harvester	20.50	11	=1	2	4
3 Alwin Schockemöhle (FRG)—Pesgo/Donald Rex*	22.00	2*	=1	=6	

Four competitions, speed, puissance, Nations Cup-type, two-round.

Number of riders: 23

Number of nations represented: 13

1969 Hickstead

	Points	Competition Placings		
		One	Two	Three
1 David Broome (GB)—Mister Softee/Top of the Morning*	6.00†	1	4	1
2 Alwin Schockemöhle (FRG)—Donald Rex/Wimpel*	6.00†	2*	=1	2
3 Hans Günter Winkler (FRG)—Enigk/Torphy*	8.00	4	=1	3

†Broome took first place in view of his better placings in the three competitions.

Three competitions, speed, Nations Cup-type, two-round.

Number of riders: 11

Number of nations represented: 6

1971 Aachen

	Points	Competition Placings		
		One	Two	Three
1 Hartwig Steenken (FRG)—Simona/Kosmos*	11.50	2	=4	6
2 Harvey Smith (GB)—Evan Jones/Mattie Brown*	13.50	4	=1	8
3 Paul Weier (Switz)—Wulf/Donauschwalbe*	14.00	1	=10*	4

Three competitions, speed, Nations Cup-type, two-round.

Number of riders: 24

Number of nations represented: 13

1973 Hickstead

	Points	Competition Placings		
		One	Two	Three
1 Paddy McMahon (GB)—Pennwood Forge Mill	7.50	1	=2	2
2 Alwin Schockemöhle (FRG)—The Robber/Weiler*	14.00	2*		1
3 Hubert Parot (Fra)—Tic/Port Royal*	15.00		1	4

Three competitions, speed, Nations Cup-type, two-round.

Number of riders: 17

Number of nations represented: 11

Individual Championship (open to men and women)

1975 Munich (Amateurs only)

	Points	Competition Placings		
		One	Two	Three
1 Alwin Schockemöhle (FRG)—Warwick	4.50	2	1	1
2 Hartwig Steenken (FRG)—Erle	15.50**	1	=6	7
3 Sönke Sönksen (FRG)—Kwept	15.50	6	=6	2

The Championship, which was restricted to amateurs in 1975, was open to both men and women and replaced the two separate events held in previous years. There were three competitions, a speed class, a Nations Cup-type competition and a two-round Grand Prix-type class. Riders were allowed only one horse throughout, points being awarded according to placings and totalled to give the final result.

Number of riders: 26

Number of nations represented: 8

**Win on first day earned him overall second place.

1977 Vienna

	Faults	Jump-off F./Time	Competition Placings One	Two-A	Two-B
1 Johan Heins (NL)—Seven Valleys	8.00	4.00/51.40	7	=3	3
2 Eddie Macken (Ire)—Kerrygold	8.00	4.00/51.50	23	=3	1
3 Anton Ebben (NL)—Jumbo Design	9.00		15	=11	2

The championships were reopened to professionals this year. The individual comprised two legs, a speed class followed by a two-round competition, with only the top 20 horses after the first leg and the first round of the second leg going through to the second round. Unlike in the majority of previous individual championships, in which points were awarded, one for a win, two for a second and so on, this year faults were carried forward from each class, the riders being classified according to their total number of faults over the three rounds.

Number of riders: 39

Number of nations represented: 11

1979 Rotterdam

	Faults	Competition Placings One	Two	Three
1 Gerd Wiltfang (FRG)—Roman	8.95	14	5	=1
2 Paul Schockemöhle (FRG)—Deister	9.10	3	=6	=1
3 Hugo Simon (Aut)—Gladstone	10.85	6	=1	10

(New format: three competitions, Table C, Nations Cup, Grand Prix-type.)

Number of riders: 47

Number of nations represented: 15

1981 Munich

	Faults	Competition Placings One	Two	Three
1 Paul Schockemöhle (FRG)—Deister	0.00	1	=1	=1
2 Malcolm Pyrah (GB)—Towerlands Anglezarke	2.03	7	=1	=1
3 Bruno Candrian (Switz)—Van Gogh	5.24	4	=1	10

Number of riders: 41

Number of nations represented: 13

1983 Hickstead

	Faults	Competition Placings One	Two	Three
1 Paul Schockemöhle (FRG)—Deister	2.49	3	=1	2
2 John Whitaker (GB)—Ryan's Son	9.27	13	=4	1
3 Frédéric Cottier (Fra)—Flambeau C	13.18	=11	=4	=3

Number of riders: 46

Number of nations represented: 12

1985 Dinard

	Faults	Competition Placings One	Two	Three
1 Paul Schockemöhle (FRG)—Deister	15.06	7	=6	=1
2 Heidi Robbiani (Switz)—Jessica V	16.29	8	=2	=6
3 John Whitaker (GB)—Hopscotch	17.71	5	1	14

Number of riders: 39

Number of nations represented: 14

At Lucerne, in 1956, Britain's Pat Smythe and Italy's Giulia Serventi finished first and second in the Grand Prix Militaire. The 'winner's' name inscribed on the trophy is Captain Bernard de Fombelle—having finished third, he was the highest placed military rider.

The first woman to ride in the World Championships open to men and women was Caroline Bradley in 1978. She was also the first woman to win a medal, a team gold.

The first lady rider to win the Hamburg Jumping Derby was Irmgard von Opel (Germany) riding Nanuk. In 1934 she was one of three riders to finish on 4 faults and in the jump-off won with a clear round, beating her compatriots Harald Momm on Baccarat and Heinz Brandt on Baron IV.

The first lady rider to jump a clear round to win the Hamburg Derby was Marion (Coakes) Mould (Great Britain) with Stroller in 1970.

At Aachen in 1958 the second competition finished so late that it was too dark for a jump-off, and the jump-off had to be held at 8 am the following morning. It was won by Anna Clement (FRG) riding Nico.

Ladies' Individual Championship

*Indicates second horse

1957 Spa

	Flanagan	Doly	Océane	Nico	Total
1 Pat Smythe (GB)	0.00	12.00	0.00	0.00	12.00
2 Giulia Serventi (Ita)	4.00	0.00	0.00	8.00	12.00
3 Michèle d'Orgeix-Cancre (Fra)	8.00	4.00	8.00	16.00	36.00
4 Anna Clement (FRG)	8.75	31.50	12.25	0.00	52.50
	20.75	47.50	20.25	24.00	

Jump-off

	Prince Hal	Perseo	Total
1 Pat Smythe	0.00	16.00	16.00
2 Giulia Serventi	18.50	4.00	22.50

Finalists' placings in qualifying competitions

	1st comp.	2nd comp.	3rd comp.
Pat Smythe (GB)—Flanagan/Prince Hal*	2*	=1	1
Giulia Serventi (Ita)—Doly/Perseo*	4*	=1	6
Michèle d'Orgeix-Cancre (Fra)—Océane/Hector*	3	=5*	3
Anna Clement (FRG)—Nico	1	=5	4

This was the only occasion on which the Ladies' Championship was decided by a change-horse final.

Number of riders: 9

Number of nations represented: 6

1958 Palermo

	Points
1 Giulia Serventi (Ita)—Doly	50.50†
2 Anna Clement (FRG)—Nico	50.50
3 Irene Jansen (NL)—Adelboom	48.50

Four competitions

Number of riders: 13

Number of nations represented: 7

1959 Rotterdam

		Competition Placings		
	Points	One	Two	Three
1 Ann Townsend (GB)—Bandit IV	30.00	2		1
2 Pat Smythe (GB)—Flanagan	29.33	3	=1	3
=3 Giulia Serventi (Ita)—Doly	23.83		=1	2
Anna Clement (FRG)—Nico	23.83	=4	=1	=4

Three competitions, speed, puissance, Nations Cup.

Number of riders: 10

Number of nations represented: 5

1960 Copenhagen

		Competition Placings		
	Points	One	Two	Three
1 Susan Cohen (GB)—Clare Castle	41.750	1	2	
2 Dawn (Palethorpe) Wofford (GB)—Hollandia	39.125		1	=2
3 Anna Clement (FRG)—Nico	38.125			=2

Three competitions, speed, puissance, Nations Cup.

Number of riders: 10

Number of nations represented: 6

†*Better second round in fourth competition.*

Four-times Ladies' Champion Pat Smythe (left) with Iris Kellett, up to 1986 the oldest rider ever to have won a European title. (Popperfoto)

The first woman to act as chef d'équipe (team manager) to an official Nations Cup team was Britain's Pat Koechlin-Smythe at Aachen in 1967.

The first Nations Cup to have a lady rider in every team was Rome 1953. The winners, Italy, fielded Natalie Perrone; The Federal Republic of Germany, Helga Köhler; France, Josée Bonnaud; and Great Britain, Pat Smythe.

1961 Deauville

| | Points | Competition | | |
		One	Two	Three
1 Pat Smythe (GB)—Scorchin/Flanagan*	45.950	1	=1	1*
2 Irene Jansen (NL)—Kairouan/Icare F*	35.845		=1	=3*
3 Michèle Cancre (Fra)—Océane/Jimmy B*	35.250	3		2

Three competitions, Table A on time, puissance, Nations Cup-type.

Number of riders: 12

Number of nations represented: 7

1962 Madrid

| | Points | Competition Placings | | |
		One	Two	Three
1 Pat Smythe (GB)—Flanagan	26.33	4	=1	2
2 Helga Köhler (FRG)—Cremona	25.50	3	=5	1
3 Paola Goyoaga-Elizalde (Spa)—Kif Kif	25.33	1	=1	6

Three competitions, speed, puissance, Nations Cup.

Number of riders: 9

Number of nations represented: 5

1963 Hickstead

| | Points | Competition Placings | | |
		One	Two	Three
1 Pat Smythe (GB)—Flanagan/Scorchin*	5.50	1	=1	3
2 Arline Givaudan (Bra)—Huipil/Caribe*	7.50	2*	3	2
3 Anneli Drummond-Hay (GB)—Merely-a-Monarch/ O'Malley's Tango*	8.50	6	=1	1

A new format came into effect this year, comprising three competitions: a Table C, a Nations Cup-type competition and a two-round final competition.

Number of riders: 10

Number of nations represented: 6

1966 Gijon

	Points
1 Janou Lefèbvre (Fra)—Kenavo/Or Pailleur*	3.00
2 Monica Bachmann (Switz)—Sandro/Ibrahim*	10.00
3 Lalla Novo (Ita)—Oxo Bob/Rahin*	10.50

Number of riders: 8

Number of nations represented: 5

1967 Fontainebleau

| | Points | Competition Placings | | |
		One	Two	Three
1 Kathy Kusner (USA)—Untouchable/Aberali*	5.00	1	2*	2
2 Lalla Novo (Ita)—Prédestiné	11.50	=8	3	1
3 Monica Bachmann (Switz)—Erbach/Dax*	13.50	4*	=5*	3

Number of riders: 14

Number of nations represented: 8

Up to the beginning of 1987, the biggest prize for a jumping competition was that offered for the du Maurier Grand Prix at the 1986 Calgary CSIO in Canada. The first prize, won by Next Milton, ridden by John Whitaker (Great Britain), was worth £39 000. The richest single show jumping event in Europe in 1987 was the Silk Cut Derby at Hickstead, with prize money totalling £75 000 (down to 15th place), and worth £25 000 to the winner, plus a £5 000 bonus, should the winner go clear in both the first round and the jump-off.

The highest known price paid for a show jumper is $1 million. In the 1980s the brown Hannoverian gelding The Natural changed hands for this sum in the United States. Ridden by Katharine Burdsall, he was in the winning team at the 1986 World Championships in Aachen. One or two horses are reputed to have changed hands for six-figure sums, among them the French-bred stallion I Love You, who went on to win the 1983 World Cup final when ridden by Norman Dello Joio (USA). Some years ago a then world record £56 000 was paid for the grey Hannoverian gelding Askan, whom Gerd Wiltfang (FRG) rode in the victorious team at the 1972 Munich Olympics.

In Switzerland the first horses to win more than 100 000 Swiss francs were Jessica V and Van Gogh. In 1984 the mare Jessica V won a total of 138 677 Swiss francs and Van Gogh won 101 220 francs.

British team manager Ronnie Massarella holding the Aga Khan Trophy, the Irish Nations Cup, after the 1986 victory of (from left) Peter Charles, Michael Whitaker, Nick Skelton, and John Whitaker. (Mike Roberts)

Team gold medallists in the Los Angeles Olympics and individual bronze medallists at the 'alternative' Olympics in 1980, Melanie Smith (USA) and the Dutch-bred Calypso prepare for take-off at Hickstead. (Bob Langrish)

Hats off for two great champions: Deister and Paul Schockemöhle celebrate their third consecutive European Championship at Dinard in 1985. (Bob Langrish)

One of the most successful lady riders of the 1980s, Switzerland's Heidi Robbiani with Jessica V. Before injury halted her career, this mare had won an Olympic bronze medal, and a gold and two silvers in the European Championships. (Kit Houghton)

The Junior European Championship has the distinction of being the oldest of the FEI championships. Pictured here is the 1983 individual winner Iain Morgan with the British chef d'équipe Ann Newbery, herself a former international rider. (Bob Langrish)

Champion of the Soviet Union in 1983, Zigmanta Sharka, seen tackling the Aachen lake on Fort Post during the 1986 World Championships meeting. (Elizabeth Furth)

Jappeloup de Luze is one of the best recommendations for France's competition horse breeding programme. This Selle Français gelding was third in the World Cup in 1985 and the following year put up the best performance by any horse in the World Championships prior to the change-horse final, in which his rider, Pierre Durand, finished fourth. (Elizabeth Furth)

The Trakehner stallion Abdullah, who was conceived in Germany but foaled in the USA, carried Conrad Homfeld to victory in the Nations Cup at the Los Angeles Olympics, collected individual silver medals both there and at the 1986 World Championships, and won the World Cup in 1985. (Elizabeth Furth)

Ann Moore with her Olympic silver medal winner Psalm, winners of the Ladies' European Championship in 1971 and again in 1973, after which the separate events for men and women were amalgamated. (Ed Lacey Associated Sports Photography)

1968 Rome

		Competition Placings		
	Points	One	Two	Three
1 Anneli Drummond-Hay (GB) —Merely-a-Monarch/Xanthos*	6.50	1*	=1	4
2 Giulia Serventi (Ita)—Gay Monarch	11.50	9	=1	1
=3 Marion Coakes (GB)—Stroller	12.00	3	=7	2
Janou Lefèbvre (Fra)—Rocket/Quitus*	12.00	2	=7	3

Number of riders: 10

Number of nations represented: 6

1969 Dublin

		Competition Placings		
	Points	One	Two	Three
1 Iris Kellett (Ire)—Morning Light	4.00	2	1	1
2 Anneli Drummond-Hay (GB)—Xanthos/ Merely-a-Monarch*	6.00	1	2	3
3 Alison Westwood (GB)—The Maverick VII	8.00	3	3	2

Number of riders: 6

Number of nations represented: 4

1971 St Gallen

		Competition Placings		
	Points	One	Two	Three
1 Ann Moore (GB)—Psalm/April Love*	4.00	1	2	1
2 Alison (Westwood) Dawes (GB) —The Maverick VII/Meridian*	5.00	2	1	2
3 Monika Leitenberger (Aut) —Limbara de Porto Conte/Gioiosa de Nora*	16.00	8	8	3

Number of riders: 10

Number of nations represented: 6

1973 Vienna

		Competition Placings		
	Points	One	Two	Three
1 Ann Moore (GB)—Psalm/April Love*	4.50	1	=2	1
2 Caroline Bradley (GB)—True Lass/New Yorker*	7.00	5	1	2
3 Monica (Bachmann) Weier (Switz) —Erbach/Vasall*	10.50	3	=2	5

Number of riders: 9

Number of nations represented: 6

Reporting the running of the first Nations Cup, at Olympia, *Horse and Hound* of 12 June 1909 records: 'The novelty of a troop of dummy infantry about the height of the average Laplander was one of the fences, but most of the horses knocked the dummies' heads off, and some galloped through them like a charge of cavalry. The spectators exclaimed, "Killed two more men". Taking the jump altogether, it was highly commendable considering the height and trappy nature of the fences, and when a horse did well the applause was deafening.'

Prior to the standardization of the rules, fence judges did not have an easy time, particularly in Ireland. *Horse and Hound* of 17 August 1946 has this to say about the Dublin Show: 'In Military competitions 4 faults are counted if the obstacle is knocked with either front or hind legs, except in the case of the wall, where one fault is recorded if up to three stones are dislodged by the hind legs, and two if dislodged by the front legs. There are further penalties if more stones are dislodged. . . . Six different mistakes can be penalized over the single bank, including changing leg on the top. There are six for the double bank, too, and in this case the horse is faulted if he does *not* change!'

Medal Tables

Team Championship 1975–1985

Country	Gold	Silver	Bronze
Great Britain	2	2	—
FRG	2	1	3
Switzerland	1	3	—
Netherlands	1	—	1
France	—	—	1
Ireland	—	—	1

Men's and Open Individual Championship 1957–1985

Country	Gold	Silver	Bronze
FRG	9	6	7
Great Britain	5	4	2
Italy	2	2	2
Brazil	1	1	—
Netherlands	1	—	1
France	—	2	2
Switzerland	—	1	2
Ireland	—	1	—
USA	—	1	—
Austria	—	—	1
Argentina	—	—	1

C. David Barker with Mister Softee, heading for victory in 1962. Mister Softee was later ridden by David Broome and became the only horse to win a European Championship with two different riders. (The Photo Source)

Ladies' Individual Championship, 1957–1973

Country	Gold	Silver	Bronze
Great Britain	9	5	3
Italy	1	3	2
France	1	—	3
Ireland	1	—	—
USA	1	—	—
FRG	—	2	2
Switzerland	—	1	2
Netherlands	—	1	1
Brazil	—	1	—
Austria	—	—	1
Spain	—	—	1

Open, Men's and Ladies' Individual Championship 1957–1985

Country	Gold	Silver	Bronze
Great Britain	14	9	5
FRG	9	8	9
Italy	3	5	4
France	1	2	5
Brazil	1	2	—
Netherlands	1	1	2
Ireland	1	1	—
USA	1	1	—
Switzerland	—	2	4
Austria	—	—	2
Argentina	—	—	1
Spain	—	—	1

Team and all Individual Championships 1957–1985

Country	Gold	Silver	Bronze
Great Britain	16	11	5
FRG	11	9	12
Italy	3	5	4
Netherlands	2	1	3
Switzerland	1	5	4
France	1	2	6
Brazil	1	2	—
Ireland	1	1	1
USA	1	1	—
Austria	—	—	2
Argentina	—	—	1
Spain	—	—	1

Records: Riders

One rider has won the open Individual Championship three times: Paul Schockemöhle (FRG), in 1981, 1983 and 1985. He is the only male rider with three consecutive wins in a European Championship.

One rider won the Men's Individual Championship three times: David Broome (Great Britain), in 1961, 1967 and 1969.

One rider has won four Individual Championships: Pat Smythe (Great Britain), who was successful in the Ladies' Championship in 1957, 1961, 1962 and 1963.

Youngest winners

Ann (Townsend) Backhouse is the youngest rider to have won a European Championship. She was 19 when she won the Ladies' title in 1959.

The youngest man to win a Championship is David Broome, who was 21 when he won the Men's title in 1961.

Oldest winners

Iris Kellett (Ire) is the oldest rider to have won a

European Championship. She was 43 when she won the Ladies' Individual title in 1969.

Paddy McMahon (Great Britain) is the oldest rider to win the Men's, and the oldest man to win any European title. He was 40 years and 157 days when he won in 1973.

Two other 40-year-olds have won Championships: Fritz Thiedemann (FRG), who was 40 years and 125 days when he won the Men's Championship in 1958. Paul Schockemöhle (FRG), who was 40 years and 135 days when he won the Championship open to men and women in 1985.

Biggest winning margin

Teams

58.50 faults: 1975 (West Germany beat Switzerland)

Open Individual

11.00 points: 1975 (Alwin Schockemöhle beat Hartwig Steenken)

Men's Individual

8.50 faults: 1959 (Piero d'Inzeo beat Pierre Jonquères d'Oriola)

Ladies' Individual

10.105 points: 1961 (Pat Smythe beat Irene Jansen)

Smallest winning margin

Teams

0.25 faults: 1977 (The Netherlands beat Great Britain)

Open Individual

0.10 seconds in a jump-off: 1977 (Johan Heins beat Eddie Macken)

Men's Individual

In 1969 David Broome and Alwin Schockemöhle finished with 6 points apiece. In the event of a tie the rules stated that the rider with the best placings in the three competitions which made up the Championship would be the winner. Thus Broome, with two wins to his credit (as against Schockemöhle's one equal first) was awarded the title.

Ladies' Individual

There have been two ties for first place in the Ladies' Championship. In 1957 Pat Smythe and Giulia Serventi finished the change-horse final with 12.00 faults each. In the jump-off Pat Smythe, with 16.00 faults, beat Guilia Serventi, who finished on 22.50.

In 1958 Giulia Serventi and Anna Clement tied with 50.50 points apiece. Giulia Serventi was awarded the title in view of her better second round in the fourth competition of the Championship.

Highest number of starters

Teams

11: 1983 Hickstead

Open Individual

47: 1979 Rotterdam

Men's Individual

27: 1961 Aachen

Ladies' Individual

14: 1967 Fontainebleau

Highest number of nations represented

Open Individual

15: 1979 Rotterdam

Men's Individual

13: 1958 Aachen
    1961 Aachen
    1967 Rotterdam
    1971 Aachen

Ladies' Individual

8: 1967 Fontainebleau

Smallest number of starters

Teams

6: 1975 Munich

Open Individual

26: 1975 Munich

Men's Individual

7: 1962 London

Ladies' Individual

6: 1969 Dublin

Smallest number of nations represented

Open Individual

8: 1975 Munich

Men's Individual

4: 1962 London

Ladies' Individual

4: 1969 Dublin

Jump-offs

There has been a jump-off for the individual gold medal on two occasions: between Pat Smythe and Giulia Serventi in the Ladies' Individual Championship in 1957 (Pat Smythe won) and between Johan Heins and Eddie Macken in the Championship open to men and women in 1977 (Heins won).

Men/women ration

Since the introduction, in 1975, of championships open to both men and women, only six women have taken part (one of them, Heidi Robbiani, in two consecutive championships) as opposed to 231 men.

The first woman to contest the open championships was Denmark's Connie Holm in 1975 but she was eliminated in the first competition.

In 1977 Debbie Johnsey (the only woman rider) was a member of the silver-medal winning British team, but was unplaced individually.

In 1979 Caroline Bradley (the only woman rider) won a team gold, and finished 6th individually.

In 1981 Britain's Liz Edgar (the only woman rider) finished 21st individually.

In 1983 Heidi Robbiani (the only woman rider) won a team gold, and was 8th in the Individual Championship.

In 1985 Heidi Robbiani, one of two women in the championships, won the individual silver medal and a team silver. The other woman rider was Belgium's Evelyne Blaton, who finished 26th.

Country with longest winning sequence in individual championship

Federal Republic of Germany, 4:
   1979 Gerd Wiltfang
   1981 Paul Schockemöhle
   1983 Paul Schockemöhle
   1985 Paul Schockemöhle

The Federal Republic of Germany is also the only country whose riders have won all three individual medals in the same championships, in 1975 at Munich, when Alwin Schockemöhle won the gold, Hartwig Steenken the silver and Sönke Sönksen the bronze.

Best winning score

0.00 faults, achieved by Paul Schockemöhle in 1981 when he won the first competition and was equal first in the other two.

Records: Horses

Most wins

Flanagan is the only horse to have won four European Championships. Ridden by Pat Smythe, he was successful in the Ladies' Individual Championship in 1957 (jointly with Prince Hal), in 1961 (jointly with Scorchin), in 1962, and in 1963 (jointly with Scorchin).

Two horses have won three European titles: Deister, who won the Individual Championship open to men and women riders in 1981, 1983 and 1985, and is the only horse other than Flanagan with three consecutive wins to his credit; Mister Softee, who won the Men's title in 1962 (jointly with Franco) when ridden by C. David Barker, and in 1967 and 1969 when ridden by David Broome. Mister Softee is the only horse to have won the European title with two different riders.

Best score

One horse has completed a European Championship with a zero score: Paul Schockemöhle's Deister in 1981.

One horse jumped clear rounds with all four riders in the men's change-horse final: Salvatore Oppes' Pagoro in 1957.

David Broome and Mister Softee, winners of the Men's title in 1967 and 1969. (Ed Lacey Associated Sports Photography)

Eventer turned show jumper

Merely-a-Monarch is the only horse to have won the Badminton and Burghley international three-day events and a European Show Jumping Championship. He won Burghley in 1961 and Badminton in 1962 before being switched to show jumping, in which he won the ladies' European title in 1968. His regular rider in both sports was Anneli Drummond-Hay.

Pan American Games

The first Pan American Games, open to countries in North, Central and South America, took place in Buenos Aires, Argentina, in 1951. To begin with the jumping consisted only of a Nations Cup, individual awards being made on the basis of the performance of the riders over the two rounds. Later a separate individual competition was introduced, and since 1979 the format has been the same as for other regional championships: a speed class and a Nations Cup (the combined scores of which are used to decide the team championship), followed by a two-round competition, all three classes counting for the individual classifications. The Games are held once every four years, in the year prior to the Olympics.

1951 Buenos Aires

Details of some scores and team horses not available.

Nations Cup

1 **Chile** 64.00

Alberto Larraguibel—Julepe
Joaquin Larrain—Pillan
Ricardo Echeverria—Bambi
Cesar Mendoza—Van Dyck

2 **Argentina** 100.25

Carlos Delia—El Linyera
Rafael Campos
Argentino Molinuevo, Snr—Ramito
Carlos Ruchti—Mineral

3 **Mexico** 109.00

Roberto Vinals Contreras—Alteno
Manuel Rodriguez—Mexico
Joaquin d'Harcourt—Malisco
Alberto Valdes—Arete

Number of teams: 4

Individual

		F./Time
1	Alberto Larraguibel (Chi)—Jalepe	16.00
2	Carlos Delia (Arg)—El Linyera	24.00/1:58,00
=3	Joaquin Larrain (Chi)—Pillan	24.00/2:02,80
	Ricardo Echeverria (Chi)—Bambi	24.00/2:02,80

Number of riders: 16

Number of nations represented: 4

1955 Mexico City

Details of some scores and team horses not available.

Nations Cup

1 **Mexico** 71.25

Roberto Vinals Contreras—Acapulco
Jaime de la Garza—14 de Agosto
Joaquin d'Harcourt—Petrolero
Humberto Mariles Cortés—Chihuahua

2 **Argentina** 89.75

Jorge Lucardi—Banturro
Argentino Molinuevo, Snr—Ramito
Carlos Ruchti—Discutido
Pedro Mayorga—Desengano

3 **Chile** 122.50

Mario Leuenberg—Baranco
Leopoldo Rojas—
Guillermo Arrenda—Maiten
Oscar Cristi—Bambi

Number of teams: 4

Individual

		Faults
1	Roberto Vinals Contreras (Mex)—Acapulco	10.75
2	Jorge Lucardi (Arg)—Baturro	18.00
3	Jaime de la Garza (Mex)—14 de Agosto	27.25

Number of riders: 16

Number of nations represented: 4

1959 Chicago

Nations Cup

		Faults	
		One	Two
1	**USA** 32.00		
	George Morris—Night Owl	E	(4.00)
	Frank Chapot—Tally Ho	8.00	4.00
	Hugh Wiley—Nautical	8.00	0.00
	William Steinkraus—Riviera Wonder	8.00	4.00
2	**Brazil** 59.00		
	Antonio Carvalho—Relincho	12.00	4.00
	Francisco Leite Rabelo—Sultao	11.00	8.00
	Renyldo Ferreira—Marengo	12.00	12.00
	Nelson Pessoa—Copacabana	E	NP

3 **Chile** 80.75

Oscar Cristi—Cordoves	(45.75)	(16.00)
Americo Simonetti—Chanaval	19.75	16.00
Joaquin Larrain—Pillán	12.00	12.00
Gastón Zúñiga—Maitén	9.00	12.00

4 Argentina, 93.75; 5 Venezuela, 125.25.

Number of teams: 5

Only Clear Round

Hugh Wiley (USA)—Nautical.

No Individual competition

1963 São Paulo

Nations Cup

	Faults	
	One	Two
1 **USA** 44.25		
Mary Mairs—Tomboy	5.75	4.00
Kathy Kusner—Unusual	(29.00)	14.00
Frank Chapot—San Lucas	12.50	4.00
William Steinkraus—Sinjon	4.00	NP
2 **Argentina** 52.50		
Jorge Amaya—Escipion	13.00	4.50
Carlos Damm—Swing	13.75	8.75
Jorge Osacar—Santiago	E	(18.75)
Carlos Delia—Popin	4.25	8.25

Mary Mairs was the first woman to win a gold medal at the Pan American Games. Riding Tomboy she won team and individual golds in 1963. With White Lightning, pictured here, she won a team silver in 1967, by which time she had become Mrs Frank Chapot. (Ed Lacey Associated Sports Photography)

3 **Chile** 69.00

Alejandro Perez—Trago Amargo	10.75	9.50
Sergio Arredondo—Choir Boy	23.25	(17.50)
Americo Simonetti—El Gitano	9.50	4.00
Gastón Zúñiga—Maitén	(24.00)	12.00

4 Mexico, 87.75; 5 Brazil, 99.50; Eliminated: Uruguay.

Number of teams: 6

Only Clear Round

Antonio Alegria-Simoes (Brazil)—Rei Negro (second round)

Individual

	Faults
1 Mary Mairs (USA)—Tomboy	9.75
2 Carlos Delia (Argentina)—Popin	12.50
3 Americo Simonetti (Chile)—El Gitano	13.50

Number of riders: 24

Number of nations represented: 6

1967 Winnipeg

Nations Cup

	Faults	
	One	Two
1 **Brazil** 8.00		
Renyldo Ferreira—Shannon Shamrock	(16.00)	(12.00)
Antonio Alegria-Simoes—Samusai	4.00	0.00
José Fernandez—Cantal	0.00	4.00
Nelson Pessoa—Gran Geste	0.00	0.00
2 **USA** 16.00		
Mary Chapot—White Lightning	4.00	4.00
Kathy Kusner—Untouchable	0.00	4.00
Frank Chapot—San Lucas	0.00	(8.00)
William Steinkraus—Bold Minstrel	(8.00)	4.00
3 **Canada** 24.00		
Tom Gayford—Big Dee	(11.50)	4.00
Moffat Dunlap—Argyll	8.00	(8.00)
Jim Day—Canadian Club	0.00	0.00
Jim Elder—Pieces of Eight	8.00	4.00

4 Mexico, 52.00; 5 Chile, 60.00; 6 Argentina, 92.00.

Number of teams: 6

Double Clear Rounds

Jim Day (Can)—Canadian Club
Nelson Pessoa (Bra)—Gran Geste

Individual

	Faults	Jump-off F./Time
1 Jim Day (Canada)—Canadian Club	0.00	8.00/38.70
2 Nelson Pessoa (Brazil)—Gran Geste	0.00	8.00/39.80
3 Manuel Mendivil (Mexico)—Veracruz	4.00	0.00/42.80

Number of riders: 25

Number of nations represented: 7

1971 Cali

Nations Cup
No details of scores available.

1 **Canada** 8.00

Tom Gayford—Big Dee
Barbara Simpson—Magnor
Terrance Millar—Le Dauphin
Jim Elder—Shoeman

2 **Mexico** 16.00

Joaquin Pérez de las Heras—Nangel
Carlos Salinas—Agualeguas
Edouardo Higareda—Acapulco
Elisa Pérez de las Heras—Eleanora

3 **Chile** 36.00

Rene Varas—Llanero
Eugenio Lavin—Copihue
Barbara Barone—Anahi
Guido Larrondo—Quintral

4 Venezuela, 40.00; 5 Argentina, 60.25; 6 Colombia, 208.25.

Number of teams: 6

Individual

		Jump-off F./Time
1 Elisa Pérez de las Heras (Mexico)—Eleanora		0.00/34.80
2 Jorge Llambi (Argentina)—Always		0.00/35.20
3 Terrance Millar (Canada)—Le Dauphin		0.00/35.90

Number of riders: 24

Number of nations represented: 6

1975 Mexico City

Nations Cup

		Faults	
		One	Two
1 **USA** 44.25			
Michael Matz—Grande		12.00	(16.00)
Dennis Murphy—Do Right		(13.25)	4.00
Joe Fargis—Caesar		12.00	4.25
Buddy Brown—Sandsablaze		8.00	4.00
2 **Mexico** 46.50			
Luis Razo—Pueblo		14.50	8.00
Carlos Aguirre—Consejero		16.00	(10.25)
Fernando Senderos—Jet Run		4.00	0.00
Fernando Hernandez-Izquierdo —Fascination		(19.50)	4.00
3 **Canada** 76.75			
Norma Chornawaka—Rest Assured		20.00	(16.00)
Frank Sellinger—Go Jamie		20.00	16.00
Michel Vaillancourt—UFO		(42.50)	12.75
Jim Elder—Count Down		0.00	8.00

4 Brazil, 88.00; 5 Venezuela, 143.75; 6 Guatemala, 298.50; eliminated, El Salvador.

Number of teams: 7

Individual

		Jump-off F./Time
1 Fernando Senderos (Mex)—Jet Run	4.00	
2 Buddy Brown (USA)—A Little Bit	8.00	
3 Michael Matz (USA)—Grande	12.00	4.00/45.70

Number of riders: 22

Number of nations represented: 8

1979 Puerto Rico

Teams

	Speed Class	Faults Nations Cup One	Two
1 **USA** 39.545			
Buddy Brown—Sandsablaze	7.250	8.250	(12.000)
Norman Dello Joio—Allegro	(10.290)	(8.250)	4.000
Michael Matz—Jet Run	5.015	0.250	8.000
Melanie Smith—Val de Loire	2.780	0.000	4.000
2 **Canada** 66.045			
Terry Leibel—Sympatico	0.000	12.250	12.000
Ian Millar—Brother Sam	10.005	5.500	5.250
John Simpson—Texas	(41.255)	E	—
Michel Vaillancourt —Crimson Tide	11.040	5.500	4.500
3 **Mexico** 100.245			
Carlos Aguirre —War Supreme	10.850	16.500	34.750
Ricardo Guasch—Rafina	11.065	(23.000)	7.500
Fernando Senderos —Kleen Sweep	(64.465)	12.250	E
Gerardo Tazzer —Butch Cassidy	4.330	1.500	1.500

4 Venezuela, 147.315; 5 Puerto Rico, 244.245; 6 Colombia, 276.850; 7 Brazil, 281.400.

Number of teams: 7

Individual

	Team Comp.	Individual One	Two	Total
1 Michael Matz (USA) —Jet Run	13.265	0.000	0.000	13.265
2 Gerardo Tazzer (Mex) —Butch Cassidy	7.330	0.000	8.000	15.330
3 Ian Millar (Can) —Brother Sam	20.755	0.000	0.250	21.005

Number of riders: 16

Number of nations represented: 9

1983 Caracas

Teams

	Speed Class	Faults Nations Cup One	Two
1 USA 16.92			
Michael Matz—Chef	1.60	0.00	4.00
Leslie Burr—Boing	4.77	0.25	4.00
Donald Cheska—Southside	2.30	(8.00)	(4.50)
Anne Kursinski—Livius	(6.72)	0.00	0.00
2 Canada 21.23			
Ian Millar—Foresight	(5.85)	0.00	4.00
Hugh Graham—Abraxas	1.57	5.25	4.00
Jim Elder—Shawline	0.00	4.00	0.00
Terrance Millar—Concord	2.41	(99.99)	(99.99)
3 Mexico 28.94			
Raul Nieto—First Time	4.16	4.00	(12.00)
Jaime Ascarraga—Huizachal	(7.32)	0.00	0.25
Alberto Rivera—Rey A	5.69	0.00	8.00
Gerardo Tazzer—Magod	6.84	(8.00)	0.00

4 Chile, 46.33; 5 Argentina, 56.84; 6 Brazil, 65.29; 7 Venezuela, 89.85; 8 Colombia, 168.60.

Number of teams: 8

Only Double Clear in Nations Cup

Anne Kursinski (USA)—Livius

Individual

	Team Comp.	Individual One	Two	Total
1 Anne Kursinski (USA) —Livius	6.72	4.00	0.00	10.72
2 Jim Elder (Can) —Shawline	4.00	4.00	4.00	12.00
3 Michael Matz (USA) —Chef	5.60	0.00	8.00	13.60

Number of riders: 20

Number of nations represented: 12

Medal Tables

Team Championship 1951–83

Country	Gold	Silver	Bronze
USA	5	1	—
Mexico	1	2	3
Canada	1	2	2
Brazil	1	1	—
Chile	1	—	4
Argentina	—	3	—

Individual Championship 1951–83

Country	Gold	Silver	Bronze
Mexico	3	1	2
USA	3	1	2
Canada	1	1	2
Chile	1	—	3
Argentina	—	4	—
Brazil	—	1	—

Team and Individual Championships 1951–83

Country	Gold	Silver	Bronze
USA	8	2	2
Mexico	4	3	5
Canada	2	3	4
Chile	2	—	7
Brazil	1	2	—
Argentina	—	7	—

Records: Riders

Most Successful Riders

Michael Matz (USA) is the only rider to have won 4 gold medals (1975 team, 1979 team and individual, 1983 team). He is also the only rider to have won a total of 6 medals at the Games (4 gold plus 1975 individual bronze and 1983 individual bronze).

Jim Elder (Can) is the only rider to have won a medal at 4 Games (1967 team bronze, 1971 team gold, 1975 team bronze, 1983 team and individual silver).

5 riders have won team and individual gold medals in the same year:

Alberto Larraguibel (Chi), 1951
Roberto Vinals Contreras (Mex), 1955
Mary Mairs (USA), 1963
Michael Matz (USA), 1979
Anne Kursinski (USA), 1983

1 rider has won team gold medals in 3 consecutive Games:
Michael Matz (USA), 1975, 1979, 1983

3 riders have won team gold medals in 2 consecutive Games:
Frank Chapot (USA), 1959, 1963
William Steinkraus (USA), 1959, 1963
Buddy Brown (USA), 1975, 1979

Boomerang

The toast of Ireland, Boomerang, four times winner of the Hickstead Derby and victorious in numerous Grand Prix, always with Eddie Macken.

Like Hans Günter Winkler's Halla, Eddie Macken's Boomerang was a horse in a lifetime. When he retired in 1980, his money winnings were in the region of a quarter of a million pounds, which at that time no other horse had achieved. To this day no one has come near his record four consecutive victories in the British Jumping Derby at Hickstead, and he was, in addition, one of the most consistent Grand Prix horses of all time.

As is so often the case, it was pure chance which brought Eddie Macken and Boomerang together. Macken had ridden him as a youngster in Ireland and found him a difficult horse: he had mouth problems and a tendency to stop. The County Tipperary-bred gelding, by the Thoroughbred stallion Battleburn, passed through several yards before Paul Schockemöhle bought him for £15 000, a big sum in the seventies for a horse with his problems. It was during the mid-seventies, when Macken was based at Schockemöhle's yard in Germany, that he came to be given the ride on Boomerang. At that stage the gelding filled the role of Schockemöhle's speed horse. Macken was responsible for schooling him, and his wife, Suzanne, did much to sweeten the horse's temperament by taking him out hacking away from the work environment.

Just before the Wiesbaden Show of 1975 Macken, who found himself without a good horse of his own, took over the ride on Boomerang thanks to Schockemöhle, who told him to keep him 'until you get a better horse'. The new partnership won the Grand Prix at that show and for the next five years proved to be one of the hardest to beat on the international circuit.

The highlights of Boomerang's career included those four Hickstead Derby victories, in 1976, 1977, 1978 and 1979 (in 1976 and 1978 he jumped a clear round); a near miss in the 1978 World Championships, when Macken lost the change-horse final by only a quarter of a time fault, and in which Boomerang became only the third horse in the history of the championships to go clear with all four riders; and another near miss in the 1979 European Championships, when a controversial 4 faults at the water left him in fourth place. Grand Prix wins included London, St Gallen, New York, La Baule, Brussels, Gothenburg, Nice, Rome, Aachen and Calgary.

Retired in 1980, he had to be put down on 20 May 1983 through ill-health and was buried at Eddie Macken's stud in Kells.

Boomerang's fame and popularity are well portrayed in a story related by a member of the equestrian press. Because of the horse's mouth problems, Eddie Macken habitually rode him in a hackamore, a bitless bridle. On one occasion at a big English show, when another horse came into the arena sporting an identical bridle, a young spectator was heard to say to her companion, 'Oh look, he's wearing a Boomerang!

Balkan Championships

Usually held annually, the Balkan Championships were first run in 1968 and are open to Bulgaria, Greece, Rumania, Turkey and Yugoslavia.

1968 Istanbul (Turkey)

Seniors, Teams

	Faults Round One	Faults Round Two
1 Turkey 11.25		
Nail Gönenli—Sim	(8.00)	(12.00)
Engin Mirel—Uvava	0.00	0.00
Ibrahim Murat—Yüksel	0.00	4.00
Levin Okcuoğlu—Casanova	3.25	4.00
2 Bulgaria 12.00		
Milio Kisseuv—Elen	(4.00)	8.00
Stefan Shopov—Feri	0.00	(16.00)
Boris Pavlov—Krater	0.00	0.00
Dimitar Guenov—Baven	0.00	4.00
3 Rumania 62.00		
Vasile Pincius—Gratis	4.00	NP
Aurelian Stoica—Blond	4.00	4.00
Anghel Danescu—Gind	4.00	23.00
Dumitru Velea—Simplon	(29.50)	23.00

Number of teams: 3

Seniors, Individual

	Faults
1 Engin Mirel (Tur)—Uvava	3.00
2 Ibrahim Murat (Tur)—Yüksel	5.00
3 Levin Okcuoğlu (Tur)—Casanova	9.00

Number of riders: 16

Number of nations represented: 3

Juniors, Teams

	Faults Round One	Faults Round Two
1 Turkey 39.00		
Bülent Bora—Afak	4.00	4.00
Atif Kamcil—Galia	8.00	8.00
Toufan Alanyali—Tita	E	7.00
Ferhan Yucel—Ringo	8.00	(12.00)
2 Bulgaria 40.00		
Miltcho Mitovski—Europa	E	E
Dzenko Sabev—Formoza	8.00	4.00
Todor Ratchev—Esmeralda	8.00	8.00
Mitko Vassilev—Eugana	12.00	0.00
3 Rumania 48.00		
Gabriela Ionescu—Ghidran	8.00	4.00
Simion Marian—Stok	8.00	12.00
Dan Athanassiu—Paunas	(8.00)	12.00
Camelia Verdes—Saghia	4.00	(12.00)

Number of teams: 3

Juniors, Individual

	Faults
1 Todor Ratchev (Bul)—Esmeralda	0.00/67.40
2 Bülent Bora (Tur)—Afak	0.00/67.90
3 Ferhan Yucel (Tur)—Ringo	4.00/62.10

Number of riders: 16

Number of nations represented: 3

1969 Sofia (Bulgaria)

Seniors, Teams

	Faults Round One	Faults Round Two
1 Rumania 27.00		
Cornelu Ilin—Vitiaz	0.00	(12.00)
Dumitru Velea—Altai	(22.50)	4.00
Alexandru Bozan—Pick Up	8.00	8.00
G. Ionescu—Rival	7.00	0.00
2 Bulgaria 37.50		
Boris Pavlov—Ekvator	0.00	0.00
Dimitur Guenov—Baven	4.00	E
Stefan Shopov—Feri	7.00	8.00
Milio Kisseuv—Elen	(19.00)	18.50
3 Turkey 39.00		
Engin Mirel—Uvava	(17.00)	11.00
Ibrahim Murat—Yüksel	8.00	(12.00)
A. Innoolou—Ien	0.00	4.00
A. Daaleu—Oulach	4.00	12.00

4 Yugoslavia, 108.50.

Number of teams: 4

Individual

	Faults
1 Stefan Shopov (Bul)—Feri	7.00
2 Alexandru Bozan (Rum)—Pick Up	10.00
3 Valentin Katchev—Laska	10.00

Number of riders: 20

Number of nations represented: 4

Juniors, Teams

	Faults Round One	Round Two
1 **Bulgaria** 24.00		
Milan Tenev—Grousia	(16.00)	(8.00)
Oleg Goranov—Filko	8.00	0.00
Mitko Vassilev—Pelikan	4.00	4.00
Petar Yankov—Mageusnik	8.00	0.00
2 **Yugoslavia** 36.00		
Milan Miloutinovic—Vestnik	8.00	4.00
Eva Zaveustnik—Zuria	8.00	8.00
Rodmilo Spasojevic—Mirote	4.00	4.00
Vlad Ranchigataï—Kobra	(8.00)	(12.00)
3 **Turkey** 43.00		
Oouzlouztu—Mistrel	E	11.00
Fercham Utgel—Atom	8.00	(12.00)
Feyzi Atabek—Peter Pan	4.00	8.00
Volkan Ozan—Chanelle	4.00	8.00

4 Rumania, 82.50.

Number of teams: 4

Juniors, Individual

	Faults
1 Petar Yankov (Bul)—Mageusnik	4.00
2 Vlad Ranchigataï (Yug)—Kobra	4.00
3 Milan Miloutinovic (Yug)—Vestnik	13.00

Number of nations represented: 4

1970 Craiova (Rumania)

Seniors, Teams

	Faults Round One	Round Two
1 **Turkey** 13.00		
Salih Koc—Silvester	10.00	3.00
Engin Mirel—Uvava	(25.00)	0.00
Ateş Dagli—Ulas	0.00	0.00
Nurettin Yaran—Tunca	0.00	(4.00)
2 **Bulgaria** 17.00		
Kroum Rashkov—Polet	9.00	0.00
Boris Pavlov—Feri	E	E
Dimitar Guenov—Gloria	4.00	0.00
Nikolaï Tihomirov—Gasela	0.00	4.00
3 **Rumania** 28.00		
Cornelu Ilin—Vitiaz	0.00	4.00
Alexandru Bozan—Rival	(16.00)	E
Aurelian Stoïka—Pick Up	4.00	8.00
Oskar Rätscher—Vifor	4.00	8.00

4 Yugoslavia, 82.75.

Number of teams: 4

Individual

	Faults
1 Aurelian Stoica (Rum)—Pick Up	3.00
2 Cornel Ilin (Rum)—Vitiaz	4.00
3 Nurettin Yaran (Tur)—Tunca	9.00

Number of riders: 30

Number of nations represented: 4

Juniors, Teams

	Faults Round One	Round Two
1 **Bulgaria** 4.00		
Stephan Augustinov—Gater	(8.00)	4.00
Mitko Vassilev—Eugana	0.00	0.00
Oleg Goranov—Filko	0.00	0.00
Margarit Spassov—Krater	0.00	E
2 **Turkey** 12.00		
Volkan Ozan—Somak	4.00	0.00
Hayal Gönenli—Çapkin	(8.00)	(8.00)
Metin Kalmik—Leyla	4.00	0.00
Feyzi Atabek—Peter Pan	4.00	0.00
3 **Rumania** 16.00		
George Popescu—Titan	4.00	4.00
Marius Vourtea—Gika	0.00	0.00
George Nikolae—Aprod	4.00	4.00
Cornel Hvioru—Electric	(14.00)	(11.00)

4 Yugoslavia, 104.00.

Number of teams: 4

Juniors, Individual

	Faults
1 Rodmilo Spasojevic (Yug)—Mirote	3.00
2 Oleg Goranov (Bul)—Filko	10.00
3 Marius Vourtea (Rum)—Gika	10.00

Number of riders: 16

Number of nations represented: 4

1971 Belgrade (Yugoslavia)

Seniors, Teams

Details of scores not available.

1 **Turkey** 60.25

Ateş Dagli—Ulas
Nurettin Yaran—Tunca
Tunc Capa—Colibri
Ibrahim Murat—Yüksel

2 **Yugoslavia** 82.50

Milan Miloutinovic—Vestnik
Z. Kavur—Bambarder
Jovan Blagojevic—Polaris
R. Dokic—Srecko

3 Bulgaria   91.00

Ivan Adzemov—Goblen
Nikolaï Tihomirov—Gazela
Stephan Augustinov—Gater
Dimitar Guenov—Gloria

4 Rumania, 138.00; 5 Greece, 218.00.

Number of teams: 5

Individual

	Faults
1 Jovan Blagojevic (Yug)—Polaris	11.00
2 Cornelu Ilin (Rum)—Vitiaz	12.00
3 Milan Miloutinovic (Yug)—Vestnik	12.00

Juniors, Teams
Details of scores not available.

1 Bulgaria   24.00

Liuben Georgiev—Malina
Oleg Goranov—Emisia
Margarit Spassov—Feri
Petar Jankov—Mageusnik

2 Yugoslavia   29.25

Rodmilo Spasojevic—Mirote
V. Mladenovic—Satelit
B. Speglie—Ibar
E. Saversnik—Kobra

3 Turkey   58.50

Metin Kalmik—Atom
Hayal Gönenli—Leyla
Halim Seyalloğlu—Çapkin
Feyzi Atabek—Peter Pan

4 Rumania, 72.75; 5 Greece, 83.00.

Number of teams: 5

Juniors, Individual

	Faults
1 N. Vlad (Rum)—Sondor	5.00
2 Petar Jankov (Bul)—Mageusnik	6.00
3 Liuben Georgiev (Bul)—Malina	7.00

1973 Athens (Greece)

Seniors, Teams

	Faults Round One	Round Two
1 Greece 32.00		
F. Serpieris—Brule Parfum	12.00	4.00
Aris Kipreos—Arames	4.00	4.00
Georges Fragogiannis—Venesmes	4.00	4.00
Patsarikas—Melisanthe	(16.50)	(12.00)
2 Bulgaria 43.50		
Dimitar Guenov—Gloria	8.00	12.00
Dimo Christov—Avtomat	7.50	4.00
Liuben Krastev—Molnar	(16.00)	(16.00)
Boris Pavlov—Eleonora	4.00	8.00

3 Rumania   44.75

Dumitru Velea—Sondor	8.00	8.00
Constantin Vlad—Sondor	8.00	0.00
Oskar Rätscher—Jak	12.00	8.75
Aurelian Stoïka—Jul	(34.50)	(12.00)

4 Turkey, 61.00; 5 Yugoslavia, 79.00.

Number of teams: 5

Individual

	Faults
1 Fotis Bravos (Gre)—Va Ma Belle	0.00–4.00
2 Feyzi Atabek (Tur)—Peter Pan	0.00–7.00
3 Boris Pavlov (Bul)—Eleonora	8.00–0.00

Number of nations represented: 5

Juniors, Teams

	Faults Round One	Round Two
1 Rumania 24.00		
George Popescu—Piersic	4.00	4.00
George Nicolae—Aprod	(12.00)	4.00
Soveza—Spiridus	4.00	4.00
Mazilu—Argint	4.00	(4.00)
2 Turkey 31.00		
Volkan Ozan—Somak	0.00	(12.00)
Metin Kalmik—Pinar	4.00	4.00
Hulki Karagülle—Hayat	0.00	12.00
Emine Silan—Leyla	E	11.00
3 Greece 36.25		
Sotiriou—Renoza	(20.00)	4.00
Teologlou—Paddy	4.00	0.00
Sergopoulo—Flica	11.00	(34.25)
Lila Liappi—My Boy	0.00	17.25

4 Bulgaria, 40.00; 5 Yugoslavia, 42.00.

Number of teams: 5

Juniors, Individual

	Faults
1 George Nicolae (Rum)—Aprod	3.00
2 Mazilu (Rum)—Argint	10.00
3 Emine Silan (Tur)—Leyla	12.00

Number of nations represented: 5

1975 Istanbul (Turkey)

Seniors, Teams

	Faults Round One	Round Two
1 Rumania 8.75		
Alexandru Bozan—Calin	0.25	0.00
Dumitru Velea—Albinita	4.00	4.50
Oskar Rätscher—Begonia	(12.00)	0.00
Constantin Vlad—Sondor	0.00	NP

2 Bulgaria 24.00

Dimitar Guenov—Gloria	4.00	(4.50)
Mitko Vassilev—Stroga	8.00	0.00
Boris Pavlov—Gymnastik	12.00	0.00
Dimo Christov—Avtomat	(17.50)	0.00

3 Turkey 43.50

Reşit Özlen—Kimo	(12.50)	4.00
Kemal Öncü—Alaettïn	4.00	4.00
Levin Okçuoğlu—Colombo	11.75	15.75
Feyzi Atabek—Peter Pan	4.00	NP

4 Yugoslavia, 56.75.

Number of teams: 4

Individual

1 Constantin Vlad (Rum)—Sondor
2†Dimo Christov (Bul)—Avtomat
3 Reşit Ozlen (Tur)—Kimo

Number of riders: 20

Number of nations represented: 4

Juniors, Teams

	Faults	
	Round One	Round Two
1 Bulgaria 4.00		
Jachar Totzev—Goblen	0.00	0.00
Mihail Iliev—Lebed	0.00	0.00
Jivko Borisov—Ribka	(8.00)	0.00
Gueorgui Yankov—Elborous	4.00	NP
2 Rumania 16.00		
Radu Crisan—Vals	0.00	8.00
Gerhard Schneider—Cerbu	(12.00)	4.00
Monica Ranghianu—Beladona	0.00	0.00
George Nicolae—Argint	4.00	NP
3 Turkey 27.00		
Emine Silan—Neyzen	(8.75)	(12.75)
Mehmet Berker—Capriccio	8.00	11.00
Bülent Kaplangi—Britania	0.00	0.00
Levent Erdoğan—Twiggy	0.00	8.00

4 Yugoslavia.

Number of teams: 4

Juniors, Individual
Details of scores not available.

1 Jivko Borisov (Bul)—Ribka
2 Levent Erdoğan (Tur)—Twiggy
3 Gueorgui Yankov (Bul)—Elborous

Number of riders: 20

Number of nations represented: 4

1977 Sibiu (Rumania)

Seniors, Teams

	Faults	
	Round One	Round Two
1 Rumania 12.50*		
Alexandru Bozan—Calin	4.50*	0.00
Ion Popa—Piersic	4.00	4.00
Oskar Rätscher—Begonia	0.00	0.00
Constantin Vlad—Prejmer	(8.00)	(4.00)
2 Bulgaria 38.00		
Gueorgui Yankov—Ametis	5.25	(29.00)
Dimitar Guenov—Gloria	(13.00)	8.00
Boris Pavlov—Gymnastik	8.75	4.00
Nicola Dimitrov—Vals	6.75	5.25
3 Greece 49.00		
Aris Kipreos—Arames	4.00	4.00
Georges Fragogiannis—Venesmes	14.25	(20.00)
Fotis Bravos—Grimaux	(53.25)	14.50
Nikolas Skenther—Little Jimmy	4.00	8.25

4 Yugoslavia, 52.50**; 5 Turkey, 94.75.

Number of teams: 5

Seniors, Individual

	Faults
1 Dumitru Velea (Rum)—Sonor	7.00
2 Oskar Rätscher (Rum)—Begonia	7.00
3 Constantin Vlad (Rum)—Prejmer	8.00

Number of riders: 24

Number of nations represented: 5

Juniors, Teams

	Faults	
	Round One	Round Two
1 Bulgaria 4.00		
Jivko Borisov—Ribka	0.00	0.00
Plamen Peinov—Effort	0.00	0.00
Juri Dinev—Fidra	4.00	0.00
Peter Nedeltav—Matador	(12.00)	(12.00)†
2 Rumania 8.00		
Liviu Matran—Beladona	(8.00)	4.00
Peter Fleischer—Bolid	0.00	0.00
Gruia Deac—Nazdravan	4.00	0.00
Mircea Neagu—Caprioara	0.00	(4.00)
3 Greece 19.75		
Helene Papakonstantinou—Zarnocyn	0.00	4.00

▶

---

†Bulgarian records show the winner of the silver medal to be Boris Pavlov (Bul)—Gymnastik.

*Bulgarian records show these scores to be 12.00/4.00.
**Bulgarian records=54.00.
†Turkish records=16.00.

Pierre Jonquères d'Oriola

On 24 October, 1964, in the somewhat unlikely equestrian setting of Tokyo, Frenchman Pierre Jonquères d'Oriola earned himself a unique place in the record books by winning his second individual Olympic gold medal. He was the first show jumping rider to achieve this feat since equestrian events were introduced into the Games in 1900, and when the 1984 Games drew to a conclusion his record remained unbeaten. It was, by any standards, a remarkable achievement; the manner of his victory only served to underline his superb mastery of the art of horsemanship.

With only six horses still to go in the second round of the Nations Cup (there was no separate individual contest that year) no one had jumped a clear round. Dozent II, ridden by Hermann Schridde for Germany, had jumped all the fences but had incurred 1.25 time faults; d'Oriola himself had had a time fault, and two fences down, in the first round. But his second attempt was to be the highlight of the competition.

Riding with that combination of élan and perfect control which were always a hallmark of

Voulette, one of the many successful mares ridden by d'Oriola, jumping off the bank at Dublin in 1954. (The Illustrated London News)

his style, he conjured a brilliant clear round, within the time limit, from his nine-year-old French-bred bay gelding Lutteur B, to finish with more than a fence in hand over Schridde, and to claim that unique second gold medal. The performances of his compatriots Janou Lefèbvre and Guy Lefrant were good enough to ensure that France also took the team silver.

Born on 1 February 1920, d'Oriola was taught to ride when still a small child by his father, himself a distinguished horseman. He made his debut with the French team in his country's first post-war Nations Cup at Nice, in April 1947. It was an impressive one: France won the competition and d'Oriola took the prize for the best individual performance. The same year he subsequently appeared in the winning team in the Nations Cups at Lucerne, London and Ostend, and also won the King George V Gold Cup at the London show and the Grand Prix in Ostend. On each occasion his partner was the brilliant little Anglo-Arab gelding Marquis III.

His partner for his first Olympic Games at Helsinki in 1952 was another Anglo-Arab, the chestnut gelding Ali-Baba. Two fences down in the first round (in which only Fritz Thiedemann for Germany went clear) put him in equal 12th place, but a faultless second round, an achievement equalled by only two other riders, pulled him up to equal first. In the jump-off for the medals d'Oriola jumped a masterly clear, the only one of the five finalists to do so, to win his first major international title. The following year he and Ali-Baba won the bronze medal in the first World Championship and in 1954 d'Oriola, this time riding Arlequin D, went one better when finishing runner-up to Winkler.

Undoubtedly one of the greatest post-war riders, d'Oriola rode with a marked lack of 'gadgetry', his horses always going with tremendous impulsion but in complete control in the simplest bridles. In some 25 years of top-level international competition he took nearly a dozen different animals to the top of the jumping tree, including several mares, with whom he established a sympathetic rapport. The grey Voulette, and the two Anglo-Arabs, L'Historiette and Aiglonne, were all big winners. And it was on yet another mare, Pomone B, that he achieved his second most prestigious win of the 1960s, the World Championship of 1966.

The competition was held that year in

With Pomone after winning the 1966 World Championship in Buenos Aires. (Popperfoto)

Buenos Aires and, because of the travelling difficulties, attracted only a small field. However, with riders such as Raimondo d'Inzeo, Graziano Mancinelli, José Alvarez de Bohorques, Alfonso Queipo de Llano and Nelson Pessoa present, it was by no means a walk-over, and d'Oriola's victory was well-earned. He was 46 when he won the title and is by far the oldest rider to have done so.

His other major victories include the silver medal in the 1959 European Championships and a team silver in the 1968 Olympics. He rode in more than 100 Nations Cups and was in the winning team on 20 occasions, with Marquis III (9), Aiglonne (3), Ali-Baba (2), Voulette (2), Arlequin (1), Dark Noë (1), Eclair au Chocolat (1) and Lutteur B (1). He won numerous Grand Prix, his last major victory being in the Aachen Championship in 1971. D'Oriola nominates Lutteur, Pomone, Ali-Baba, Voulette, L'Historiette, Charleston, Aiglonne, Arlequin, Virtuoso and Marquis III as the best horses he has ridden, and among his own achievements values most his Olympic medals, his World title and his Grand Prix successes.

A farmer and wine grower by profession, d'Oriola enjoys travel and sport, which naturally includes horses: no longer in the competitive limelight, he still rides daily for pleasure at his home in the French Pyrenees.

*Cristian Filis—Jessy	7.75	(10.75)
Lila Liappi—My Boy	(8.00)	4.00
**Aris Milonas—Brules Parfum	4.00	0.00

4 Turkey, 20.00; 5 Yugoslavia, 31.75†.

Number of teams: 5

Juniors, Individual

	Faults
1 Peter Fleischer (Rum)—Bolid	4.00
2 Liviu Matran (Rum)—Beladona	6.00
3 Mircea Neagu (Rum)—Caprioara	8.00

Number of nations represented: 5

1978 Zagreb (Yugoslavia)

Seniors, Teams

	Faults	
	Round One	Round Two
1 Bulgaria 19.50		
Dimitar Guenov—Gloria	(8.75)	(4.25)
Nikola Dimitrov—Vals	4.50	4.00
Hristo Katchov—Eden	3.00	4.00
Boris Pavlov—Gymnastik	0.00	4.00
2 Rumania 21.25		
Alexandru Bozan—Calin	0.00	(8.00)
Constantin Vlad—Sondor	4.00	0.00
Ion Popa—Rondel	13.25	4.00
Oskar Rätscher—Rebell	(17.25)	0.00
3 Greece 32.00		
Aris Kipreos—Arames	(10.75)	4.00
Georges Fragogiannis—Venesmes	4.00	8.00
Nikola Meimarides—Mack Douey	0.00	8.00
Nikolas Skenther—Carnkoe	8.00	(12.00)

4 Yugoslavia, 50.50; 5 Turkey, retired.

Number of teams: 5

Seniors, Individual

	Faults
1 Alexandru Bozan (Rum)—Calin	3.00
2 Boris Pavlov (Bul)—Gymnastik	6.00
3 Nikola Meimarides (Gre)—Mack Douey	8.00

1979 Athens (Greece)

Seniors, Teams

	Faults	
	Round One	Round Two
1 Rumania 30.25		
Alexandru Bozan—Calin	(16.00)	8.00
Ion Popa—Ficus	0.00	8.00

*Turkish records=Cristian Filis—Brules Parfum.
**Turkish records=Aris Milonas—Pilote.
†Turkish records=21.75.

Cornelu Ilin—Fudul	1.25	5.00
Dania Popescu—Sonor	8.00	NP

2 Greece 51.25		
Dimitri Lambadarios—Winotu	6.75	8.75
Christine Dimitriadu—Quincy Jones	(20.25)	(28.00)
Georges Fragogiannis—Fleur du Valon	14.00	9.75
Costis Meimarides—Mack Douey	0.00	12.00
3 Bulgaria 59.25		
Dimitar Guenov—Gloria	22.75	13.50
Plamen Peinov—Matador	(23.50)	(29.00)
Boris Pavlov—Gymnastik	8.00	4.00
Nikola Dimitrov—Vals	6.00	5.00

4 Turkey, 86.50; 5 Yugoslavia, 150.00.

Number of teams: 5

Seniors, Individual

	Faults
1 Costis Meimarides (Gre)—Mack Douey	6.00
2 Kaya Oktayuren (Tur)—Ronsard	9.00
3 Dimitri Lambadarios (Gre)—Winotu	11.00

Number of nations represented: 5

Ladies, Teams

	Faults	
	Round One	Round Two
1 Rumania 28.00, 4.00 in jump-off		
Mariana Moisei—Beladona	0.00	12.00
Ioana David—Gruia	16.00	0.00
Dania Popescu—Piersic	(59.00)	(12.00)
2 Greece 28.00, 8.00 in jump-off		
Carina Guertsou—Question	(11.00)	12.00
Christina Dimitriadu—Mastermind	4.00	(16.50)
Elizabeth Logotheti—Sweet Caroline	8.00	4.00
3 Yugoslavia 43.25		
Eva Rancigaj—Eclan de Salant	23.25	12.00
Tania Marusic—Angelo	0.00	8.00

4 Turkey, 52.00; 5 Bulgaria, 62.00.

Number of teams: 5

Ladies, Individual

	Faults
1 Tania Marusic (Yug)—Angelo	5.00
2 Mariana Moisei (Rum)—Beladona	6.00
3 Elizabeth Logotheti (Gre)—Sweet Caroline	8.00

Number of nations represented: 5

Juniors, Teams

	Faults	
	Round One	Round Two
1 Rumania 39.50		
Gruia Deac—Glorios	8.50	0.00
Georg Pasarin—Sturion	(16.00)	8.00
Mircea Preda—Palermo	7.00	(16.00)
Mircea Neagu—Neva	12.00	4.00

2 **Turkey** 47.00

Hakan Özkan—Plevne	7.00	12.00
Ali Ersin—Hermes	0.00	4.00
Ata Zorlu—Nilhan	8.00	(20.00)
Hulki Karagülle—Bonanza	(12.00)	16.00

3 **Greece** 60.00

Theodorakis Dallas—Entertainer	(30.25)	(20.00)
Georges Grazios—Franco	4.00	16.00
Constantin Grazios—Ferns Hill	12.00	16.00
N. Apostolopoulos—Zarnocyn	4.00	8.00

4 Bulgaria, 66.25; 5 Yugoslavia, 103.50.

Number of teams: 5

Juniors, Individual

	Faults
1 Hulki Karagülle (Tur)—Bonanza	6.00
2 Theodorakis Dallas (Gre)—Entertainer	6.00
3 Constantin Grazios (Gre)—Ferns Hill	8.00

Number of riders: 23

Number of nations represented: 5

1980 Ankara (Turkey)

Seniors, Teams

	Faults	
	Round One	Round Two
1 **Rumania** 16.50		
Alexandru Bozan—Calin	0.00	4.00
Ion Popa—Ficus	0.00	0.00
Dumitru Velea—Fudul	(9.00)	8.00
Dania Popescu—Sonor	4.50	(13.25)
2 **Bulgaria** 17.50		
Nikola Dimitrov—Vals	(13.25)	4.00
Boris Pavlov—Gymnastik	1.00	0.00
Hristo Katchov—Povod	0.50	0.00
Jivko Borisov—Gaer	12.00	(4.00)
3 **Turkey** 49.75		
Reşit Özlen—Kimo	17.75	4.25
Rafet Can—Meric	12.75	(8.50)
Ata Zorlu—Alkim	2.25	8.00
Feyzi Atabek—Rainlover	(20.00)	4.75

4 Yugoslavia, 75.50.

Number of teams: 4

Individual

	Points
1 Dumitru Velea (Rum)—Fudul	41.00
2 Boris Pavlov (Bul)—Gymnastik	37.00
3 Feyzi Atabek (Tur)—Ares	35.00

Number of riders: 20

Number of nations represented: 4

Ladies, Teams

	Faults	
	Round One	Round Two
1 **Rumania** 0.00		
Ruxandra Badulescu—Pardon	(0.50)	0.00
Ioana David—Gruia	0.00	(4.75)
Mariana Moisei—Beladona	0.00	0.00
2 **Yugoslavia** 8.25		
Tania Marisci—Luxor	(18.75)	0.00
Alenka Kersic—Paraon	8.00	(4.00)
Rajka Jurici—Parade	0.25	0.00
3 **Turkey** 34.50		
Barbara Buldanlioğlu—Neyzen	10.50	(32.00)
Esin Zembilci—Scapen	12.00	0.00
Neylan Etiman—Fitz-Royal	(13.50)	12.00

4 Bulgaria, 44.00.

Number of teams: 4

Ladies, Individual

	F./Time
1 Ioana David (Rum)—Gruia	3.00–0.00/52.80
2 Rajka Jurici (Yug)—Parade	3.00–0.00/53.10
3 Ruxandra Badulescu (Rum)—Pardon	0.00–4.00/55.90

Number of riders: 12

Number of nations represented: 4

Juniors, Teams

	Faults		
	Round One	Round Two	Jump-off
1 **Rumania** 16.00, 4.00 in jump-off			
Horatiu Marchis—Enva	(12.00)	8.00	0.00
Florin Stoica—Nehoiv	0.00	0.00	4.00
Otto Fabich—Stindard	0.00	0.00	0.00
Theodor Panca—Spulber	8.00	(8.00)	(8.00)
2 **Bulgaria** 16.00, 8.00 in jump-off			
Kamen Gentchev—Pisarka	0.00	(12.00)	4.00
Marian Nikolov—Morena	4.00	0.00	0.00
Ivo Marinov—Velmir	8.00	0.00	4.00
Tzvetana Atanossova—Socrat	(9.25)	4.00	(4.00)
3 **Turkey** 23.00			
Murat Batur—Vauban	7.00	4.00	
Murat Dizioğlu—Derby Day	E	4.00	
Ali Ersin—Hermes	4.00	(4.50)	
Hulki Karagülle—Bonanza	0.00	4.00	

4 Yugoslavia, 24.25.

Number of teams: 4

Juniors, Individual

	Points
1 Ivo Marinov (Bul)—Velmir	41.00
2 Marian Nikolov (Bul)—Morena	38.00
3 Hulki Karagülle (Tur)—Bonanza	37.00

Number of riders: 20

Number of nations represented: 4

1981 Plovdiv (Bulgaria)

Seniors, Teams

	Faults	
	Round One	Round Two
1 Bulgaria 28.00		
Boris Pavlov—Montblanc	8.00	0.00
Dobrin Gramtchev—Neoumolim	8.00	4.00
Nikola Dimitrov—Molnar	4.00	4.00
Mehmed Aliev—Gabarit	(11.00)	R
2 Greece 32.00		
Aris Milonas—Wenderlin	(12.00)	4.00
Christine Dimitriadu—Quincy Jones	0.00	8.00
Dimitri Voulgarakis—Tusko Jack	8.00	(8.00)
Fotis Bravos—Constellation	8.00	4.00
3 Rumania 36.00		
Dumitru Velea—Fudul	8.00	4.00
Alexandru Bozan—Calin	(12.00)	4.00
Ion Popa—Licurici	12.00	(8.00)
Mircea Neagu—Ecou	4.00	4.00

4 Turkey, 48.50; 5 Yugoslavia, 59.75.

Number of teams: 5

Individual

	Points
1 Dumitru Velea (Rum)—Fudul	68.00
2 Dobrin Gramtchev (Bul)—Neoumolim	64.00
3 Alexandru Bozan (Rum)—Calin	63.00

Ladies, Teams
Details of team members not available.

1 **Greece** 19.00
2 **Rumania** 24.50
3 **Bulgaria** 28.00

4 Yugoslavia, 32.00; 5 Turkey, 82.75.

Number of teams: 5

Ladies, Individual

	Points
1 Dania Popescu (Rum)—Ficus	36.00
2 Emanuela Athanassiades (Gre)—Sweet Caroline	30.00
3 Ruxandra Badulescu (Rum)—Pardon	28.50

Number of nations represented: 5

Juniors, Teams
Details of team members not available.

1 **Bulgaria** 16.00
2 **Greece** 20.00
3 **Turkey** 28.00

4 Rumania, 51.50; 5 Yugoslavia, 61.25.

Number of teams: 5

Juniors, Individual

	Points
1 Theagenis Iliadis (Gre)—Forever	44.00
2 Georges Grazios (Gre)—Franco	43.00
3 Marian Nikolov (Bul)—Morena	41.00

1982 Sibiu (Rumania)

Seniors, Teams

	Faults	
	Round One	Round Two
1 Rumania 17.75		
Florin Stoica—Ficus	5.75	0.00
Mircea Neagu—Ecou	(16.00)	8.00
Dumitru Velea—Fudul	0.00	4.00
Ion Popa—Sonor	0.00	R
2 Greece 28.00		
Fotis Bravos—Constellation	(16.00)	4.00
Georges Fragogiannis—Donald	0.00	4.00
Dimitri Voulgarakis—Tusko Jack	12.00	4.00
Georges Rosiadis—Albrus	4.00	R
3 Turkey 46.50		
Reşit Özlen—Kimo	15.50	4.00
Ata Zorlu—Binboğa	(32.25)	(16.00)
Ali Ersin—Hermes	19.00	4.00
Feyzi Atabek—Ares	4.00	0.00

4 Bulgaria, 67.50; 5 Yugoslavia, 77.00.

Number of teams: 5

Seniors, Individual

	Points
1 Mircea Neagu (Rum)—Ecou	48.00
2 Florin Stoica (Rum)—Ficus	46.00
3 Dumitru Velea (Rum)—Fudul	44.00

Number of riders: 24

Number of nations represented: 5

Ladies, Teams

	Faults	
	Round One	Round Two
1 Bulgaria 4.00		
Galina Georgieva—Prevrat	4.00	0.00
Theodora Stoianova—Apolonia	(4.00)	0.00
Emilia Atanasova—Morena	0.00	(8.00)
2 Greece 16.00		
Marina Marinopoulou—Heather Queen	8.00	4.00
Amalia Bogdanou—Gemini	4.00	0.00
3 Turkey 24.00		
Barbara Buldanlioğlu—Napoleon	8.00	4.00
Gülay Demirci—Alberto	8.00	4.00
Emine Silan—Tuğrul Bey	(8.00)	(8.00)

4 Rumania, 28.00; 5 Yugoslavia, 31.00.

Number of teams: 5

Ladies, Individual

	Points
1 Rajka Jurici (Yug)—Parade	38.00
2 Ruxandra Badulescu (Rum)—Pardon	33.00
3 Galina Georgieva (Bul)—Prevrat	28.00

Number of riders: 17

Number of nations represented: 5

Juniors, Teams

	Faults Round One	Round Two
1 Bulgaria 24.00		
Vaselin Nikolov—Velmir	4.00	4.00
Emil Russev—Sokrat	12.00	4.00
Dimitar Vasilev—Vezma	0.00	0.00
Krassimir Kostantinov—Saigon	(16.00)	(4.00)
2 Greece 28.00		
Stelios Benakopoulos—Mack Douey	(8.00)	(12.00)
Theagenis Iliadis—Forever	4.00	8.00
Georges Grazios—Franco	4.00	4.00
Nicolas Papadopoulos—Wismar	4.00	4.00
3 Yugoslavia 36.00		
Dusko Ivanovici—Gem	(15.00)	4.00
Dragan Mudrici—Fair Play	0.00	8.00
Dejan Suvasdici—Hérodes	12.00	0.00
Vasa Ignatovici—Darling	12.00	(8.00)

4 Rumania, 40.00; 5 Turkey, 60.00.

Number of teams: 5

Juniors, Individual

	Points
1 Georges Grazios (Gre)—Franco	49.00
2 Ionel Bucur (Rum)—Calin	46.00
3 Stelios Benakopoulos (Gre)—Mack Douey	43.00

Number of riders: 24

Number of nations represented: 5

1983 Sabac (Yugoslavia)

Seniors, Teams

	Faults Round One	Round Two
1 Rumania 32.75		
Mircea Neagu—Licurici	(24.25)	4.75
Alexandru Bozan—Jan	4.00	8.00
Florin Stoica—Ficus	8.00	(8.00)
Dumitru Velea—Fudul	8.00	0.00
2 Turkey 37.00		
Cuneyt Eryildiz—Güclü	8.00	4.00
Kemal Öncü—Let's Go	(20.00)	(14.75)
Feyzi Atabek—Ares	4.00	4.00
Ata Zorlu—Binboğa	10.50	6.50

3 **Greece** 40.00

Constantin Grazios—Donald	(12.00)	8.00
Dimitri Voulgarakis—Tusko Jack	12.00	4.00
Georges Rosiadis—Albrus	4.00	(12.00)
Fotis Bravos—Sleave Na Mon	0.00	12.00

4 Yugoslavia, 43.25; 5 Bulgaria, 77.25.

Number of teams: 5

Seniors, Individual

	Points
1 Dumitru Velea (Rum)—Fudul	44.00
2 Alexandru Bozan (Rum)—Jan	42.00
3 Jivko Borisov (Bul)—Klementina	42.00

Number of riders: 24

Number of nations represented: 5

Ladies, Teams

Details of scores not available.

1 Rumania 28.00

Dania Popescu—Pacala
Ioana David—Baical
Christina Stefanescu—Calin

2 Greece 35.25

Marina Marinopoulou—Heather Queen
Helena Zacharapolou—Ira
Amalia Bogdanou—Gemini

3 Bulgaria 39.00

Velisava Lozanova—Elastik
Galina Koleva—Prevrat
Amelia Angelova—Molnar

4 Turkey, 39.75; 5 Yugoslavia, 42.00.

Number of teams: 5

Ladies, Individual

	Points
1 Amalia Bogdanou (Gre)—Gemini	35.00
2 Marina Marinopoulou (Gre)—Heather Queen	34.00
3 Galina Koleva (Bul)—Prevrat	30.00

Number of riders: 15

Number of nations represented: 5

Juniors, Teams

Details of scores not available.

1 Greece 16.00

Denis Iliades—Forever
Angelos Aspirides—Moby Dick
Stelios Benakopoulos—Mack Douey
Keli Lauda—Karamela

2 Bulgaria 31.00

Evelin Valev—Elbrus
Najdan Stojanov—Kabel
Marian Nikolov—Morena
Dimitar Vasilev—Celzius

3 Rumania 64.00

Gheorghe Claudiu—Aida
Arina Savu—Solario
Jon Tincu—Balans
Horatiu Marchis—Cocor

4 Turkey, 68.75; 5 Yugoslavia, 80.50.

Number of teams: 5

Juniors, Individual

	Points
1 Horatiu Marchis (Rum)—Cocor	46.00
2 Dimitar Vasilev (Bul)—Celzius	41.00
3 Denis Iliades (Gre)—Forever	41.00

Number of riders: 24

Number of nations represented: 5

1984 Athens (Greece)

Seniors, Teams

	Faults	
	Round One	Round Two
1 Rumania 48.00		
Florin Stoica—Ficus	8.00	8.00
Mircea Neagu—Vanadiu	0.00	8.00
Dumitru Velea—Jan	12.00	12.00
Gruia Deac—Matroz	(16.00)	(24.00)
2 Bulgaria 56.00		
Boiko Naidenov—Razin	12.00	20.00
Boris Pavlov—Montblanc	0.00	4.00
Panayotis Gudjamanis—Kadet	12.00	8.00
Jivko Borisov—Temp	(40.00)	(56.00)
3 Greece 60.00		
Fotis Bravos—Mama Kass	12.00	4.00
Michel Kazis—Fortell	12.00	8.00
Dimitri Lambadarios—Go for Gold	8.00	(32.00)
Georges Fragogiannis—What's the Point	(20.00)	16.00

4 Turkey, 68.00.

Number of teams: 4

Seniors, Individual

	Points
1 Milan Miloutinovic (Yug)—Right One	40.00
2 Georges Fragogiannis (Gre)—What's the Point	36.00
3 Michel Kazis (Gre)—Fortell	31.00

Number of riders: 19

Number of nations represented: 4

Ladies, Teams

	Faults	
	Round One	Round Two
1 Greece 48.00		
Emánuela Athanassiades—Camarade	(19.00)	(21.25)
Helene Drakatou—Pop Star	12.00	4.00
Marina Marinopoulou—Senon Garth	16.00	16.00
2 Turkey 64.00		
Neslihan Up—Boomerang	16.00	8.00
Nuray Aydin—Binboğa	20.00	20.00
Emine Silan—Tuğrul Bey	(51.75)	(41.25)
3 Rumania 83.50		
Ligia Ilin—Aida	23.50	20.00
Mariana Moisei—Baikal	20.00	20.00
Ioana David—Lastun	(51.75)	(41.25)

4 Yugoslavia, 110.25; 5 Bulgaria, 129.00.

Number of teams: 5

Ladies, Individual

	Points
1 Helene Drakatou (Gre)—Pop Star	32.00
2 Marina Marinopoulou (Gre)—Senon Garth	31.00
3 Nuray Aydin (Tur)—Binboğa	29.00

Number of riders: 17

Number of nations represented: 5

Juniors, Teams

	Faults	
	Round One	Round Two
1 Greece 28.00		
Kira Gontika—Wenderlin	0.00	4.00
Denis Iliades—Wismar	4.00	4.00
Georges Moutsis—Moby Dick	4.00	12.00
Makis Skountzos—Scarva	(20.00)	NP
2 Rumania 35.50		
Tite Raducanu—Sadic	(19.00)	(8.00)
Ilioi Radu—Spartac	7.50	4.00
Gheorghe Claudiu—Fanion	8.00	4.00
Albert Constantin—Multiubit	8.00	4.00
3 Bulgaria 56.00		
Ilian Iskarov—Karka	(27.25)	12.00
Todor Anguelov—Pisarka	8.00	12.00
Rossen Raitchev—Gortchak	8.00	12.00
Todor Todorov—Velmir	4.00	NP

4 Turkey, 71.00; 5 Yugoslavia, 123.00.

Number of teams: 5

Juniors, Individual

	Points
1 Todor Todorov (Bul)—Velmir	43.00
2 Kira Gontika (Gre)—Wenderlin	42.00
3 Panayotis Loverdos (Gre)—Franco	41.00

Number of riders: 23

Number of nations represented: 5

1985 Istanbul (Turkey)

Seniors, Teams

		Faults	
		Round One	Round Two
1 Turkey 26.75			
Bulent Bora—Ramado		7.00	3.75
Ali Ersin—Cornet		(8.00)	4.00
Tunc Capa—Fatih		0.00	8.00
Feyzi Atabek—Ares		4.00	NP
2 Greece 44.50			
Costis Meimarides—Mac Deal		12.00	8.25
Georges Katsianos—Thunder Thighs		(15.25)	12.00
Yanis Andreotis—Golden Valley		12.25	(12.00)
Fotis Bravos—Mama Kass		0.00	0.00
3 Rumania 60.00			
Mircea Neagu—Licuriçi		12.00	(12.00)
Gruia Deac—Matroz		12.00	8.00
Ionel Bucur—Lastun		(20.00)	4.00
Alexandru Bozan—Radiana		16.00	8.00

4 Yugoslavia, 63.00.

Number of teams: 4

Seniors, Individual

	Points
1 Fotis Bravos (Gre)—Mama Kass	42.00
2 Yanis Andreotis (Gre)—Golden Valley	36.00
3 Feyzi Atabek (Tur)—Ares	35.00

Number of riders: 20

Number of nations represented: 4

Ladies, Teams

		Faults	
		Round One	Round Two
1 Greece 8.00			
Emanuela Athanassiades—Camarade		0.00	(12.00)
Laura Papa—Why Not		(11.00)	4.00
Iona Lalaouni—Sharka		4.00	0.00
2 Rumania 22.00			
Ligia Ilin—Aida		(12.00)	(12.00)
Silvana Todea—Baical		0.00	8.00
Ioana David—Mentor		7.00	7.00
3 Turkey 38.75			
Şefika Pekin—Akdoğan		11.25	(28.75)
Mine Koyuncuoğlu—Pikant		(17.25)	16.00
Neslihan Up—Boomerang		0.00	11.50

4 Bulgaria, 76.75; 5 Yugoslavia, retired.

Number of teams: 5

Ladies, Individual

	Points
1 Ioana David (Rum)—Mentor	39.00
2 Alenka Kerşiç (Yug)—St Maria	36.00
3 Emanuela Athanassiades (Gre)—Camarade	36.00

Number of riders: 15

Number of nations represented: 5

Juniors, Teams

		Faults	
		Round One	Round Two
1 Greece 32.00			
Dorina Papalios—Cool Abbey		0.00	8.00
Pavlos Rizopoulos—Who Care		8.00	8.00
Panayotis Bartzoglou—Féole du Vallon		(15.75)	(11.00)
Makis Skountzos—Scarva		4.00	4.00
2 Rumania 35.25			
Ion Tincu—Stindard		(44.00)	(51.00)
Albert Constantin—Multiubit		4.00	4.00
Gheorghe Claudiu—Fanion		16.25	3.00
Tite Raducanu—Solario		4.00	4.00
3 Bulgaria 42.75			
Tichomir Mitov—Dusha		12.00	12.00
Naiden Nedkov—Raphael		18.75	(16.00)
Radomir Velitchov—Moreno		(21.75)	0.00
Todor Tzanev—Velmir		0.00	0.00

4 Yugoslavia, 52.50; 5 Turkey, 60.50.

Number of teams: 5

Juniors, Individual

	Points
1 Dorina Papalios (Gre)—Cool Abbey	47.00
2 Tite Raducanu (Rum)—Solario	45.00
3 Pavlos Rizopoulos (Gre)—Who Care	41.00

Number of riders: 23

Number of nations represented: 5

1986 Istanbul (Turkey)
Juniors only
Juniors, Teams

		Faults	
		Round One	Round Two
1 Yugoslavia 39.00			
Andrej Laufer—Atom		8.00	8.00
Zoran Piper—Right One		0.00	0.00
Milana Dragič—Lale		8.00	15.00
Majda Şnautil—Don Carlos		(28.00)	(20.00)
2 Turkey 40.00			
Alev Sarç—Şah		(16.00)	8.00
Ülgen Adigüzel—Maliska		8.00	4.00
Merve Kurttepeli—Binboğa		12.00	(12.00)
Mehmet Aksel—Laredo		0.00	8.00
3 Rumania 48.00			
Stelian Mocanu—Multiubit		0.00	12.00
Razvan Bozan—Radiana		12.00	12.00
Petre Ionescu—Bilbor		(20.00)	(16.00)
Octavian Haneş—Pamela		4.00	8.00

Number of teams: 3

Juniors, Individual

	Faults
1 Mehmet Aksel (Tur)—Laredo	8.00
2 Zoran Piper (Yug)—Right One	8.55
3 Octavian Haneş (Rum)—Pamela	26.15

Number of riders: 16

Number of nations represented: 3

Mediterranean Games

The Mediterranean Games were started in 1951 and take place every four years in the year prior to the Olympics. Equestrian events were included for the first time in 1955. However, since the Games clashed with international shows elsewhere in Europe, the FEI was not in favour of their staging equestrian events at all, and in fact gave authority for teams to be admitted to the Games that year only if they never normally took part in the International Horse Show in London. After 1959 equestrian events were dropped from the schedule for a period of 20 years. They were reintroduced in 1979. The Games are open only to countries whose National Olympic Committees are members of the Comité International des Jeux Méditerranéens and in 1987 those nations eligible to compete in the Games were Algeria, Cyprus, Egypt, France, Greece, Italy, Lebanon, Libya, Malta, Monaco, Morocco, San Marino, Spain, Syria, Tunisia, Turkey, and Yugoslavia.

1955 Barcelona (Spain)

Teams

		Faults	
		One	Two
1	**Italy** 28.25		
	Vicenzo Bettoni—Pooka	8.00	4.00
	Fabrizio Finesi—Oceano IV	4.25	4.00
	Marchese Lorenzo de Medici—Irish Rover	8.00	0.00
2	**Spain** 44.50		
	Juan Nardiz Bernaldo—Mister B	8.00	4.00
	José Alvarez de Bohorques—Michoacano	22.50	8.00
	Carlos Lopez Quesada—Tapatio	0.50	1.50
3	**France** retired		
	Guy Lefrant—Bagatelle	4.00	0.00
	Charles Moreau—Eros	45.00	—
	Bernard de Fombelle—Caballero	8.00	4.00

Number of teams competing: 3

Individual

		Faults
1	Carlos Lopez Quesada (Spa)—Tapatio	2.00
2	Guy Lefrant (Fra)—Bagatelle	4.00
3	Marchese Lorenzo di Medici (Ita)—Irish Rover	8.00

1959 Beirut (Lebanon)

Incomplete results only available for this year.

Individual

1 Capt Jalabi (UAR)
2 Kabbari Hammad (UAR)
3 Pierre Asselay (Lib)

Egypt and Syria competed together under the name of the United Arab Republic.

1979 Split (Yugoslavia)

Teams

		Faults	
		One	Two
1	**France** 4.25		
	Gilles Bertran de Balanda —Fil d'Argent	0.00	0.00
	Hubert Parot—Fukase Grimeu	(8.00)	0.25
	Patrick Caron—Eole IV	0.00	4.00
	Eric Leroyer—Flambeau	0.00	R
2	**Italy** 24.25		
	Filippo Moyersoen—Moudy	(38.75)	R
	Michele della Casa—Scartel	8.00	4.00
	Duccio Bartalucci—Delylah	0.00	4.25
	Emilio Puricelli—Bridge Ende	4.00	4.00
3	**Spain** 36.25		
	Luis Alvarez Cervera—Romeo	12.00	0.00
	Jaime de Aveyro—Constant	8.25	4.00
	Antonio de Wit—Limited Edition	(12.00)	(12.00)
	Alfonso Segovia—Agamenon	4.00	8.00

4 Morocco, 56.00; 5 Yugoslavia, 86.75; 6 Greece, 91.75; 7 Algeria, 137.25.

Number of teams: 7

Individual

		F./Time
1	Eric Leroyer (Fra)—Flambeau	0.00–0.00–0.00/42.00
2	Emilio Puricelli (Ita)—Bridge Ende	0.00–0.00–4.00/38.80
3	Alfonso Segovia (Spa)—Agamenon	0.00–0.00–4.00/41.10

Number of riders: 28

Number of nations represented: 7

1983 Rabat (Morocco)

Teams

	Faults	
	One	Two
1 Spain 8.00		
Rutherford Latham—Idaho	4.00	0.00
Alberto Honrubia—Kaoua	0.00	4.00
Luis Alvarez Cervera—Jexico du Parc	(8.00)	0.00
Alfonso Segovia—Feiner Kerl	0.00	NP
2 France 20.00, 0.00 in jump-off		
Xavier Leredde—Jalisco	8.00	0.00
Hubert Bourdy—Juniperus	4.00	4.00
Philippe Rozier—Jiva	(8.00)	4.00
Pierre Durand—Jappeloup	0.00	(4.00)
3 Morocco 20.00, 12.00 in jump-off		
Ahmed Touil—Chafik	4.00	4.00
Fikri Cherkaoui—Patriote	4.00	(8.75)
Karim Loubaris—Blazeway	(4.00)	0.00
Bachir Chaouqui—Bally Mac Duff	0.00	8.00

4 Libya, 52.00; 5 Algeria, 102.00.

Number of teams: 5

Individual

	Faults
1 Hubert Bourdy (Fra)—Juniperus	0.00–0.00
2 Rutherford Latham (Spa)—Idaho	0.00–4.00–0.00
3 Alberto Honrubia (Spa)—Kaoua	4.00–0.00–4.00

Number of riders: 20

Number of nations represented: 5

'Taps' for **Chilena**

The story of Chilena is a sad one, for she was among the few show jumpers who have been 'killed in action'. But it is also a story which admirably demonstrates the high regard in which horses are so often held by their human masters.

At the 1940 National Horse Show in New York the handsome bay 16-year-old was as usual competing as a member of the Chilean jumping team with her devoted rider, Major Eduardo Yanez. Chilena had been a regular and successful visitor to the show at Madison Square Garden over the years, and had clocked up some 60 000 miles travelling to and fro between Santiago and New York.

On the November day that was to be her last, she was being schooled by another of the Chilean riders, Captain Armanda Fernandez who put her at a warm-up fence, a triple bar. For some reason the mare failed to make the height, hit the third rail with her chest and took a crashing fall. Her rider was soon up again and she, too, struggled to her feet, but as she was led slowly in the direction of the stables, her head wobbling from side to side, it was obvious that she was gravely injured. Quite suddenly she collapsed and died. She was found to have cracked her breastbone, and had also ruptured a blood vessel.

Her body was removed to the ASPCA hospital on Avenue A and Twenty-Fourth Street and it was announced that she would be given a military burial on 14 November.

The New York Times of 15 November carried the following report:

'On a hill at Fort Wadsworth, on Staten Island, overlooking the bay, Chilena, the beloved mount of the Chilean Army horse show team that had been killed in a practice jump at Madison Square Garden on Wednesday, was buried shortly after noon yesterday.

'Ceremonies befitting the "soldier horse" were held for the mare, who had participated in the National Horse Show six times since 1934 and had become one of the most popular horses ever to compete there.

'When Major Eduardo Yanez, who had ridden to victory with Chilena many times, and his party arrived at the Army reservation, they were received by soldiers at attention under Lieut Col H. E. Dager, Commanding Officer of the fort.

'The entourage walked up the hill. In the rain the party stood beside the grave. Lieut Col Dager said a few words in praise of the horse. Major Yanez thanked him for the courtesy extended. The flag of Chile was placed over Chilena, and as the body was covered a three-volley salute was fired. "Taps" was sounded . . .

'The group adjourned to the officers' quarters, where the Consul General of Chile in New York, Anibal Jara, thanked everyone again . . .

'. . .Among the wreaths sent was one bearing a card which read "From Lucy Ann, a child, who loved to see Chilena".'

Asian Games

The Asian Games are staged every four years in the even year between the Olympic Games. An individual show jumping competition was included in the ninth running of the Games in 1982, and both team and individual events were staged in 1986.

1982 New Delhi (India)

Individual

	Faults
1 Nadia M. Al Mutawa (Kuw)—Feydan	0.00–0.00–0.00
2 Gamila M. Al Mutawa (Kuw)—Sligo Gigi	0.00–0.00–4.00
3 Barah S. Al Sabah (Kuw)—Sicca Chante	0.00–0.00–E

Number of riders: 19

Number of nations represented: 6

1986 Seoul (Korea)

Nations Cup

	Faults Round One	Faults Round Two
1 Japan 5.00		
Yoshihiro Nakano—Challenger 1	0.00	0.00
Ryuzo Okuno—Benroy	(4.50)	4.00
Shuichi Toki—Step by Step	0.00	1.00
Takashi Tomura—Ardes	0.00	(4.00)
2 Kuwait 12.25		
Sami A. Al Mudaf—Ballindine	(4.00)	(14.00)
Tariq H. Shuaib—Excite	4.00	0.00
Gamila M. Al Mutawa—Sweet Briar	0.00	4.25
Nadia M. Al Mutawa—Sligo Gigi	0.00	4.00
3 Korea 30.75		
Seong Joong Kim—Dynaris	4.00	8.00
Sung Hwan Kim—Yuhan Tiger	(12.00)	(12.25)
Jae Woong Ma—Dae Sung	4.00	9.75
Un Jin Moon—Le Purser	0.25	4.75

4 Hong Kong, 54.75; 5 Bahrain, 60.75; 6 India, 123.50; 7 Indonesia, 139.50.

Number of teams: 7

Individual

	Faults
1 Takashi Tomura (Jap)—Ardes	0.00–0.00–0.00–0.00
2 Shuichi Toki (Jap)—Step by Step	0.00–0.00–0.00–4.00
3 Ryuzo Okuno (Jap)—Challenger 1	4.00–0.00–0.00–8.00

Number of riders: 22

Number of nations represented: 7

Mare's Nest

In the 1980s mares are heavily outnumbered by geldings in top level jumping. Yet a look through the results included in this book will show that the mares lack nothing in ability. They are, and always have been, well able to compete on equal terms with their male rivals—and beat them.

All the same, many riders prefer geldings, who, because of their sexual neutrality, tend to be far less complicated creatures than mares (or, indeed, stallions). True, the female of the species can be temperamentally more troublesome, though by no means all mares are. But it is a fact that those riders who have a rapport with them have very often been the ones to reach the pinnacles of achievement.

In the days when the cavalry dominated the sport, riders were less selective—perhaps, since their respective armies were providing them with mounts, they could not choose to be otherwise. However that may be, a look at the Olympic records shows that at the 1912 Games eight of the 22 horses in the Nations Cup and 15 out of the 31 in the individual competition were mares, and that three of the six Nations Cup teams included two mares. By 1956, when there was only one competition at the

Masters Games

The first Masters Games were run in 1985. They were restricted to riders aged 45 years and over, and contested on borrowed horses drawn from a pool. The intention is to hold these Games once every four years.

1985 Toronto

		Points
1	Harry DeLeyer (USA)	33
2	Giuseppe Moretti (Ita)	28
3	Jim Elder (Can)	23
=4	Eric Ropiha (NZ)	22
	Tom Gayford (Can)	22
6	Noel Vanososte (Ven)	21
=7	Joan Tapling (Ber)	20
	Ray Skoropad (Can)	20
9	Sydney Draper (NZ)	19
=10	Gerald King (Can)	17
	Bill Rawle (USA)	17
=12	Eldon Hughes (Can)	14
	Benjamin Sutcliffe (Can)	14
14	Albert Gatrell (Can)	9
15	Colin Peace (Can)	5
16	Harold Prowse (USA)	2

Position of medallists in the two competitions

	One	Two
1 Harry DeLeyer	1	1
2 Giuseppe Moretti	3	2
3 Jim Elder	=5	=5

The winning rider, Harry DeLeyer, was 20 days short of his 58th birthday.

The 57-year-old United States rider Harry DeLeyer, here riding Dutch Crown, won the first running of the Masters Games in 1985. The Games, for riders aged 45 and upwards, are contested on borrowed horses. (Findlay Davidson)

Olympics, the number of mares entered had dropped to nine out of 66. The numbers rose slightly to 10 out of 54 in the 1960 Nations Cup, but by 1984 had dropped to a meagre three out of 51 in the individual.

Considering their lack of numbers, the batting average of the mares is extraordinarily impressive. Winners of individual Olympic medals include Lucette (gold, 1924), Tora (gold, 1936), Sellö (bronze, 1936), Halla (gold, 1956), Touch of Class (gold, 1984) and Jessica V (bronze, 1984). In the separate Nations Cup at the 1984 Los Angeles Games Touch of Class and Jessica V also recorded the two best scores of the entire competition. Halla has the added distinction of having won more gold medals than any other show jumper and of being one of only two horses to win gold at two consecutive Games. The records are just as impressive in the World Championships, where Halla, Gowran Girl, Pomone B and Simona were all ladies who made it into the winners' enclosure.

An interesting footnote to the 1984 Olympics is that in the individual event the geldings did not get a look in: the silver medallist was a stallion!

Young Riders Championships European

Championships for young riders were introduced by the FEI in 1981 in Europe and in 1982 in the Americas, where the large countries are divided into regional zones. The championships are designed to form a stepping stone between junior and senior competitions, and are for riders aged 16 to 21.

Having reached the age of 18, a rider may compete in regional and Olympic Games, but once a rider has taken part in a senior championship he cannot go back to championships for young riders in the same discipline. Similarly, having competed in a championship for young riders, he cannot revert to junior championships. Juniors aged 16 to 18 may take part in championships for young riders but may not take part in young riders and junior championships in the same year in the same discipline. Young riders below the age of 18 may not be classified as professionals.

1981 Copenhagen (Denmark)

Team Championship

		Faults	
		Round One	Round Two
1 **FRG** 0.25			
Dirk Hermesmeier—Peron		0.00	0.00
Achim Tilger—Angelino		0.00	0.25
Detlef Brüggemann—Locky		0.00	(4.00)
Sabine Knepper—Tower		(4.00)	0.00
2 **Switzerland** 4.00			
Markus Dürrer—Lord O'Connell		0.00	0.00
Pierre Nicolet—Takirou		0.00	0.00
Erich Mosset—Brown Spark		4.00	0.00
Kurt Blickenstorfer—Warrier		(4.50)	(24.00)
3 **France** 8.00			
Stephane Uzan—Jumper J		0.00	0.00
Philippe Linget—Grand Jour		0.00	4.00
Christian Hermon—Jelca d'Isigny		(18.50)	4.00
Jean Gasagrande—Eclair d'Ile		0.00	(28.50)

4 Netherlands, 8.50; 5 Denmark, 27.00; 6 Sweden, 63.75; 7 Belgium, 87.75.

Number of teams: 7

Individual Championship

	Faults
1 Jan Tops (NL)—Nargus	4.00–0.00–0.00/36.00
2 Achim Tilger (FRG)—Angelino	4.00–0.00–4.00/38.00
3 Philippe Linget (Fra)—Grand Jour	0.00–4.00–8.00/36.00

Number of riders: 33

Number of nations: 7

1982 Wolfsburg (FRG)

Team Championship

		Faults	
		Round One	Round Two
1 **Italy** 12.00			
Gian Palmizzi—Glorieux		0.00	0.00
Filippo Giannini—Dorian		0.00	8.00
Giulio Riva—Argonaut		(12.00)	4.00
Bruno Scolari—Eole		0.00	NP
2 **Netherlands** 20.00, 0.00 in jump-off			Jump-off
Sven Harmsen—Rétrial		0.00	4.00	0.00
Eric van der Vleuten—Expo Visar		4.00	4.00	0.00
Ton Klumpers—Copain du NRK		4.00	(8.00)	0.00
Jan Tops—San Marco		(12.00)	4.00	NP
3 **FRG** 20.00, 8.00 in jump-off			
Sabine Knepper—Tower		4.00	0.00	NP
Jürgen Kenn—Maestoso		4.00	4.00	0.00
Willi Weber—Aberalie		4.00	4.00	4.00
Dirk Huerkamp—Soltau		(8.00)	(4.00)	4.00

4 Switzerland, 24.00; =5 France, 36.00, Sweden, 36.00; 7 Ireland, 44.00; 8 Belgium, 112.75.

Number of teams: 8

Individual Championship

	Faults
1 Eric van der Vleuten (NL) —Expo Visar	0.00–0.00
2 Sven Harmsen (NL)—Rétrial	0.00–4.00–0.00/37.85
3 Jürgen Kenn (FRG)—Maestoso	0.00–4.00–0.00/38.32

Number of riders: 40

Number of nations represented: 10

1983 Geesteren (NL)

Team Championship

	Faults Round One	Round Two
1 Great Britain 12.00		
Carl Edwards—More Candy	0.00	0.00
Helena Dickinson—Cool Million	0.00	4.00
Jonathan Egmore—Postmark	4.00	4.00
Mark Heffer—Saucy Brown	(4.00)	NP
2 FRG 16.00		
Frank Müller—Baroness	4.00	0.00
Thiess Luther—Heros	0.00	4.00
Ralf Runge—Fair Lady	4.00	4.00
Dirk Huerkamp—Soltau	(4.00)	(12.00)
3 France 20.25		
Roger-Yves Bost —Jorphée du Prieur	0.00	4.00
Patrice Delaveau—Iena A	4.00	4.00
Eric Levallois—Graine d'Oria	8.00	0.25
Thierry Rozier—Heur du Bratand	(8.00)	(8.00)

4 Italy, 28.00; 5 Belgium, 44.00; 6 Netherlands, 48.75; 7 Sweden, 52.25; 8 Switzerland, 55.75; 9 Austria, 59.75; 10 Poland, 77.00; 11 Ireland, 92.00.

Number of teams: 11

Individual Championship

	Faults
1 Roger-Yves Bost (Fra) —Jorphée du Prieur	0.00–4.00–1.00/41.60
2 Mark Heffer (GB)—Saucy Brown	4.00–0.00–4.00/37.12
3 Helena Dickinson (GB)—Cool Million	8.00–0.00–0.00/32.94*

Number of riders: 53

Number of nations represented: 11

1984 Cervia (Italy)

Team Championship

	Faults Round One	Round Two
1 France 20.25		
Roger-Yves Bost—Jorphée du Prieur	0.00	4.00
Jean Charles Gayat—Ignace B	4.00	4.00
Eric Levallois—Le Tot de Semilly	4.25	4.00
Patrice Delaveau—Jena	(7.25)	(12.00)
2 Great Britain 22.00		
Helena Dickinson—Cool Million	0.00	4.00
Iain Morgan—Dun Topper	0.00	4.00
Mark Heffer—Saucy Brown	4.75	(10.50)
Annette Lewis—Tutein	(24.00)	9.25

*There was a jump-off for the bronze medal between six riders. Dickinson was the only one to jump a clear round.

3 FRG 36.75		
Ralf Runge—Fair Lady	0.00	4.00
Stefan Lang—Silver Girl	4.00	12.00
Kay Alberding—Tyros 3°	(14.50)	4.00
Ludger Beerbaum—Wetteifernde	12.75	(12.50)

4 Switzerland, 54.25; 5 Sweden, 57.00.

Number of teams: 10

Individual Championship

	Faults
1 Monika Hirsch (Aut)—Marathon	0.00–0.00–04.00/40.12
2 Svante Johansson (Swe) —Hydro Screen	0.00–0.00–12.00/41.41
3 Ludger Beerbaum (FRG) —Wetteifernde	0.50

Number of riders: 45

Number of nations represented: 10

1985 Donaueschingen (FRG)

Team Championship

	Faults Round One	Round Two
1 Great Britain 8.00		
Philip Heffer—View Point	0.00	0.00
Janet Hunter—Lisnamarrow	(4.00)	0.00
Gillian Greenwood—Sky Fly	0.00	8.00
Iain Morgan—Dun Topper	0.00	(16.00)
2 France 16.00		
Patrice Delaveau—Laeken	0.00	0.00
Roger-Yves Bost—Jorphée du Prieur	4.00	4.00
André Roguet—Herminette	4.00	4.00
Thierry Rozier—El Dorat	(12.00)	(8.00)
3 FRG 32.50		
Ulf Plate—Skiatos	0.00	8.00
Alois Pollman-Schweckhorst—Fulda	(21.25)	0.00
Thiess Luther—Landrätin	12.50	12.00
Hauke Luther—Lasall	0.00	NP

4 Sweden, 54.50; 5 Switzerland, 60.75; 6 Netherlands, 64.25; 7 Belgium, 66.25; 8 Austria, 69.25; 9 Spain, 72.75; 10 Norway, 96.75.

Number of teams: 10

Individual Championship

	Faults
1 Patrice Delaveau (Fra)—Laeken	0.00–0.00–0.00/35.55
2 Roger-Yves Bost (Fra) —Jorphée du Prieur	0.00–0.00–0.00/35.95
3 Janet Hunter (GB)—Lisnamarrow	0.00–0.00–8.00/36.19

Number of riders: 51

Number of nations represented: 13

Gillian Greenwood is typical of the up-and-coming internationals which the Young Riders Championships are designed to encourage. Junior European Champion in 1984, she went on to win a Young Riders' team gold medal in 1985, and became British Ladies' Champion in 1986, all with the horse she is riding here, Sky Fly. (Findlay Davidson)

1986 Reims (France)

Team Championship

		Faults Round One	Faults Round Two
1 Belgium 12.50			
Johan Lenssens—Malstriker		4.75	0.00
Freddy de Muynck—Vienna		4.00	3.75
Ben Vanwijn—Vanna		(8.00)	(4.00)
Mike van Belle—Titi's Friend		0.00	0.00
2 Great Britain 16.25			
Duncan Inglis—West End Evita		4.25	4.00
Paul Sutton—Samboy		4.00	4.00
Gillian Greenwood—Monsanta		(8.00)	(11.25)
Philip Heffer—View Point		0.00	0.00
3 France 16.75			
Jean Charles Gayat—Lord du Miral		4.25	0.50
Alain Pignolet—Natif d'Elle		4.00	0.00
Olivier Desutter—Malesan Francossette		8.00	(4.50)
Roger-Yves Bost—Jorphée du Prieur		(12.00)	0.00

=4 Sweden, Italy, 32.00; 6 FRG, 36.75; 7 USSR, 39.50; 8 Norway, 48.50; 9 Austria, 65.75; 10 Switzerland, 70.50.

Number of teams: 10

Individual Championships

	Faults
1 Hauke Luther (FRG)—Landrätin	0.00–0.00–0.00/43.90
2 Ulrich Kirchhoff (FRG)—Piquet	0.00–0.00–4.00/43.72
3 Rajmondas Udrakis (USSR) —Dekoratsia	0.00–0.75

Number of riders: 50

Number of nations represented: 12

Medal Tables

1981–1986 Team Championship

Country	Gold	Silver	Bronze
Great Britain	2	2	—
France	1	1	3
FRG	1	1	3
Belgium	1	—	—
Italy	1	—	—
Netherlands	—	1	—
Switzerland	—	1	

1981–1986 Individual Championship

Country	Gold	Silver	Bronze
France	2	1	1
Netherlands	2	1	—
FRG	1	2	2
Austria	1	—	—
Great Britain	—	1	2
Sweden	—	1	—
USSR	—	—	1

1981–1986 Team/Individual Championships

Country	Gold	Silver	Bronze
France	3	2	4
FRG	2	3	5
Great Britain	2	3	2
Netherlands	2	2	—
Austria	1	—	—
Belgium	1	—	—
Italy	1	—	—
Sweden	—	1	—
Switzerland	—	1	—
USSR	—	—	1

Biggest winning margin

Teams

8.00 faults: 1982 (Ita beat Netherlands and FRG)
1985 (Great Britain beat Fra)

Individual

(without a jump-off)
4.00 faults: 1982 (Eric van der Vleuten finished on 0.00 faults, the only rider to do so. He is the only rider to have won the individual gold medal without a jump-off)

(with a jump-off)
8.00 faults: 1984 (Monika Hirsch beat Svante Johansson)

Smallest winning margin

Teams

1.75 faults: 1984 (Fra beat Great Britain)

Individual

0.40 seconds: 1985 (Patrice Delaveau beat Roger-Yves Bost in a jump-off, the only occasion on which the gold medal has been decided on time, as opposed to faults)

Clear rounds

Nine riders have jumped double clear rounds in the team championship:

Dirk Hermesmeier (FRG)—Peron	1981
Markus Dürrer (Switz)—Lord O'Connell	1981
Pierre Nicolet (Switz)—Takirou	1981
Stephane Uzan (Fra)—Jumper J	1981
Gian Palmizzi (Ita)—Glorieux	1982
Carl Edwards (GB)—More Candy	1983
Patrice Delaveau (Fra)—Laeken	1985
Philip Heffer (GB)—View Point	1985 and 1986
Mike van Belle (Bel)—Titi's Friend	1986

Most medals

6 Roger-Yves Bost (Fra) riding Jorphée du Prieur
Individual gold 1983
Team gold 1984
Individual silver 1985
Team silver 1985
Team bronze 1983
Team bronze 1986

Young Riders Championships American

1982 Maple Ridge (Canada)

Team Championship

	Faults Round One	Round Two
1 Canada (British Columbia) 12.50		
Alex Sales—Baccarat	8.00	4.50
Tracy Madson—Outer Limits	(45.00)	NP
Laura Tidball—Cool Pool	0.00	0.00
Ann-Marie Loughran—Jack	0.00	0.00
2 Canada (Alberta) 16.00		
Kim Morrison—Jericho Hill	4.00	0.00
Margo Rayment—Quick Malo	4.00	(16.00)
Debbie Simpson—Soft Touch	0.00	8.00
Linda Southern—Hallo	(8.00)	0.00
3 USA (Area IX) 24.50		
Cathy Sigismund—Strider	0.00	4.00
Jill Lytle—Playin Hookie	12.00	4.00
Ashley Griffin—Jaywalker	(45.00)	(8.00)
Shaina Masters—William Z	0.50	4.00

Number of teams: 3 regional teams from 2 nations

Individual Championship

	Faults
1 Laura Tidball (Can)—Cool Pool	0.00–4.50
2 Shaina Masters (USA)—William Z	0.00–5.00
3 Ann-Marie Loughran (Can)—Jack	8.00–0.00

Number of riders: 17

Number of nations represented: 3

1983 Hamilton (USA)

Team Championship

	Faults Round One	Round Two
1 Mexico 4.00		
Ruben Rodriguez—Brujo	4.00	(4.00)
Gerardo Rodriguez—Dutch Uncle	0.00	0.00
Antonio Maurer—Mr Fabulous	(8.00)	0.00
Jorge Hernandez—Aldila	0.00	0.00

2 **Canada (Alberta)**   5.75

Kim Morrison—Jericho Hill	0.00	0.00
Cheryl Sagan—Ebony Buzz	4.00	(4.00)
Linda Southern—Hallo	1.50	0.25
John Carl Anderson—Marcato	(4.00)	0.00

3 **USA (Zone 2)**   24.00

Vivi Malloy—Apple Core	(33.00)	NP
Hans Richter—Sky High	4.00	4.00
Pam Sherman—Little John	4.00	4.00
Gregory Best—Valid	4.00	4.00

4 Canada (Quebec), 41.25; 5 Bahamas, 60.25;
6 USA (Zone 1), 78.25; 7 USA (Zone 5), 95.50;
8 Canada (Ontario), eliminated.

Number of teams: 8 (2 national teams and 6 regional teams from 2 nations)

Individual Championship

		Faults
1	Ann-Marie Loughran (Can)—Jack	0.00–0.00
2	John Carl Anderson (Can)—Marcato	4.00–0.00–0.00/40.28
3	Ruben Rodriguez (Mex)—Brujo	4.00–0.00–0.00/40.55

Number of riders: 40

Number of nations represented: 7

1984 Cedar Valley (Canada)

Team Championship

	Faults	
	Round One	Round Two
1 **Canada (Quebec)** 0.00		
Francis Gagnon—Nuance	0.00	(4.00)
Annie de Fresne—Who Knows Haney	0.00	0.00
Natalie Mathers—Black Mounty	0.00	0.00
Richard Lapointe—Arabelle	0.00	0.00
2 **Canada (Ontario)** 4.00		
Lisa Carlsen—Tango	0.00	0.00
Caroline Grenon—Bullit	0.00	0.00
Karen Powell—Wellington	0.00	4.00
Harold Chopping—Jackie Blue	0.00	(4.00)
3 **USA (Zones 2/3)** 8.00		
James Benedetto—Neat & Sweet	4.00	0.00
Stacy Casio—L. C. Smith	4.00	0.00
Jay Bozick—Thumbs Up	(4.25)	0.00
Gregory Best—Valid	0.00	NP

4 USA (Zone 5), 19.00; 5 Canada (Alberta), 20;
6 USA (Zone 7) 27.

Number of teams: 6 regional teams from 2 nations

Individual Championship

		Faults
1	Lisa Carlsen (Can)—Tango	0.00–0.00–0.00/38.74
2	Jennifer Bort (USA)—Cinderella	0.00–0.00–4.00/37.28
3	Chris Kappler (USA)—Bremen Star	0.00–0.00–8.00/38.88

Number of riders: 31

Number of nations represented: 4

1985 Wadsworth (USA)

Team Championship

	Faults	
	Round One	Round Two
1 **Mexico (North)** 4.00		
Jaime Guerra—Cihautl	0.00	0.00
Frederico Fernandez—Robin Hood	0.00	0.00
Ruben Rodriguez—Gentle Gene	4.00	0.00
Monica Carnejo—Nocito	(4.00)	NP
2 **Canada (Alberta)** 28.00		
Kim Morrison—Marcato	4.00	4.00
Cheryl Sagan—Don Masetto	(18.25)	4.00
Nikki Humen—Blues Boy	8.00	(12.00)
Bryan Anderson—Corniche	8.00	0.00
3 **USA (Zone 10)** 32.00		
Gigi Herman—Surge	4.00	12.00
Stacey Eurich—Along Comes Jones	8.00	(12.25)
Michael Endicott—Pantomime	0.00	4.00
Mandy Porter—Orbit	(8.00)	4.00

4 Canada (Ontario), 58.00; 5 Mexico (South), 60.00;
6 USA (Zones 2/3), 102.50; 7 Canada (Quebec), retired;
8 USA (Zone 7), retired.

Number of teams: 8 regional teams from 3 nations

Individual Championship

		Faults
1	Gregory Best (USA)—Gem Twist	0.00–0.00
2	Michael Endicott (USA) —Pantomime	0.00–4.00–0.00/42.2
3	Marsha Walters (Can)—Favorit	0.00–4.00–0.00/45.98

Number of riders: 35

Number of nations represented: 3

1986 No competition

Piero and Raimondo d'Inzeo

The annals of show jumping abound with the names of successful fathers and sons, brothers and sisters, husbands and wives. But in terms of family achievement it is doubtful if anyone will ever match the brothers d'Inzeo, who for 30 years formed the backbone of the post-war Italian jumping team.

Piero d'Inzeo, born in Rome on 4 March, 1923, and his brother Raimondo, born in Poggio Mirteto on 8 February, 1925, grew up in a world where horses still played an important role. Their father, Carlo Costante d'Inzeo, a Warrant Officer in the Cavalry of the Royal Army, was heir to the doctrine of horsemanship founded by Federico Caprilli, and a dedicated teacher of riding. His sons began to ride at an early age—though not to the exclusion of other sports—and competed with success in junior competitions. When, later, they graduated to senior international level, it was their father who remained their teacher, watching, analysing and criticizing their performances.

Piero decided to follow his father into the Army and was admitted to the Academy at Modena in 1942. Raimondo was originally more interested in engineering, but later he, too, opted for a military career. He was with the Italian cavalry until 1950, then in 1951 he joined the Carabinieri, and today holds the rank of Colonel. After the Second World War Gerardo Conforti, a successful rider in the pre-war years, began to try to resurrect what little was left of the Italian Cavalry and to put together a jumping team. In 1946 Piero was invited to become a member of that team and the following year had his first Nations Cup success, riding General Monfort's Argentinian-bred Tulipano, in Rome's renowned arena, the Piazza di Siena. Raimondo made his debut with the team that year. His first Nations Cup appearance, at Geneva in November, was a winning one.

Both brothers competed in the 1948 Olympic Games in London, Piero in the show jumping, Raimondo in the three-day event, in which he finished 30th. Piero, who was forced to ride the reserve horse, Briacone, after his own Formidabile fell sick shortly before the Games, did not have a happy time. Briacone, insufficiently trained for this level of competition, made a mistake at the first fence and although it did not fall, he dislodged a marker flag and was eliminated. Bad luck also dogged him four years later at Helsinki. He finished sixth in the three-day event riding Pagoro, but was again eliminated in the show jumping when a misunderstanding over weighing out before the competition caused him to miss his start. His mount that year was the French-bred Uruguay, whom Piero believes might well have won that Olympic contest had he been able to take part, since the course was made to measure for him. Raimondo finished equal seventh on Colonel Bettoni's bay gelding Litargirio.

In 1956 at Stockholm things went better for Piero. Uruguay was at last given his chance, and he took the individual bronze and a team silver. However, Raimondo, who is by nature the more competitive rider and who has always tended to be more successful than his brother in big championships, did even better. Apart from the winner (Hans Günter Winkler), he was the only rider to jump a clear round. Riding Merano, a horse he had brought on from a four-year-old, he won both individual and team silvers.

The previous year Raimondo had finished runner-up to Winkler in the World Championship. In 1956 he won that title, again riding Merano in the change-horse final, and in 1960 he became only the second rider (Winkler was the first) to win it a second time, on this occasion with Gowran Girl. The World Championship has been run in the same year as the Olympics on only two occasions, 1956 and

Piero d'Inzeo on Easter Light, one of the many Irish horses ridden with such success by the top Italian riders.

1960, and so it is extremely unlikely that anyone will ever be able to emulate Raimondo's unique achievement of becoming Olympic and World Champion in the same year.

The 1960 World Championship was held in Venice shortly after the Rome Olympics where, on their home ground, the brothers d'Inzeo had achieved the remarkable feat of finishing one/two in the individual jumping. Sadly, their father was not alive to see this supreme achievement: he had died in a car crash in 1957. Riding the Italian-bred Posillipo, another horse which he had trained from a youngster, Raimondo won the gold with a score of 12 faults for the second round, having jumped the only clear round of the entire competition in the first round. Piero had two 8-fault rounds with the brilliant grey Irish gelding, The Rock, to win the silver. In the team event, a separate competition that year, Raimondo again reigned supreme, his two 4-fault rounds being by far the best of the day, and ensuring that Italy won the bronze.

The brothers continued to ride at the Olympics until 1976. Piero is the only rider to have represented his country in show jumping at eight consecutive Games, while Raimondo has also been to eight Games, seven in show jumping and one in eventing. In addition to these achievements Piero was European Champion in 1959 and runner-up in 1958, 1961 and 1962. Piero has been in 41 winning Nations Cup Teams, Raimondo in 32. Both brothers have been victorious in the major European Grand Prix. Raimondo's successes include Rome (five times), Brussels (four times), Dublin, Aachen and Nice, as well as the

Raimondo d'Inzeo on the Italian-bred Merano, the horse with whom he won his first World Championship in 1956. (Leslie Lane)

Hamburg Derby; Piero is one of only four riders who have won the King George V Gold Cup on three occasions, once with Uruguay, twice with The Rock.

Universally admired for their fine horsemanship, both brothers have produced some truly great horses—not always by any means from the most promising, or particularly expensive, basic material. Piero's many successes included Uruguay, The Rock, Sunbeam (ninth at the 1964 Olympics) and Easter Light, another of the wonderful Irish-bred horses on which the Italians have had so much success over the years. Raimondo nominates as his best rides Litargirio; his own horses Merano, Posillipo, Fiorello and Stranger, all Italian bred; and the Carabinieri's Irish gelding Bellevue, a brilliant Grand Prix horse in the sixties and seventies.

The last winning Nations Cup team in which the d'Inzeos appeared was at Barcelona in 1977. Yet, even though they are no longer concerned with the cut and thrust of the international show circuit, at the time of writing (the mid-1980s) both were still producing young horses and competing (not without success) in national competitions. Show jumping will probably not see their like again.

Junior European Championships

The Junior European Championship has the distinction of being the oldest of the FEI official championships, having been held for the first time in 1952. It has been held annually ever since, and in 1974 an American Championship for junior riders was introduced. To begin with the European Championship was a team event only, but later an individual championship was added. Riders aged 14–18 may take part in these championships. Many riders who figured in the medal placings in Junior Championships have gone on to become leading internationals at senior level.

1952 Ostend (Belgium)

Team Championship
(Details of scores not available.)

1 **Belgium**

Françoise Vanderhaegen—Sybelle
George Hernalsteens—Le Conquérant
George Asselberghs—Sans Doute
André Roggemans—Squib

2 **Italy**
Alberto Riario Sforza—Malefico
Graziano Mancinelli—Falkner
Gian Piero Bembo—Sonny boy
Alberto Salvati—Ippo

Number of teams: 2

1953 Rome (Italy)

Team Championship

	Faults	
	Round One	Round Two
1 **France** 12.00		
Jean-Pierre Cancre—Sidi	0.00	4.00
Martine Refait—Yola	0.00	4.00
Yves Daudré—Zephir B	0.00	4.00
Françoise Hamel—Titi	0.00	(12.00)
2 **Italy** 32.00		
Graziano Mancinelli—Falkner	8.00	0.00
Alberto Riario Sforza—Fox Law	0.00	4.00
Sergio Albanese—Arnold	(17.00)	(16.00)
Gian Piero Bembo—Nosetto	8.00	12.00

3 **Belgium** 36.00

	E	E
George Asselberghs—Sans Doute	E	E
Marie-Luce Jamagne—Epi	9.00	4.00
Françoise Vanderhaegen—Salambo	4.00	4.00
George Hernalsteens—Le Conquérant	7.00	8.00

4 Austria, eliminated.

Number of teams: 4

1954 Rotterdam (NL)

Team Championship
(Details of scores not available.)

1 **Italy** 0.00

Mr d'Anno—Querino
Gian Piero Bembo—Zattera
Monica Rapalli—Gretel
Graziano Mancinelli—Que Quento

=2 **FRG** 4.00

Karl-Ludwig Hoffmann—Cuttu
Hermann Schridde—Norbert
Alwin Schockemöhle—Fehmarn
Gerd Hinrichsen—Wirbelwind

=2 **Netherlands** 4.00

Miss N. E. Koster—Axel
Miss N. Vortsman—Shirley
Miss Arts—Roszny
A. A. Loudon—Napoléon

4 Belgium, 8.00; 5 France, 24.00.

Number of teams: 5

1955 Bilbao (Spain)

Team Championship

	Faults	
	Round One	Round Two
1 **FRG** 15.00		
Hans-Werner Ritters—Cyrano	4.00	4.00
Klaus Pade—Finette	(12.00)	(12.00)
Gerhard Salmen—Fitina	4.00	3.00
Wolfgang Hoepner—Adola	0.00	0.00
2 **Netherlands** 20.00		
Mr Englebert—Lady Jane	(8.00)	(15.00)
Miss Arts—Roszny	4.00	4.00
Mr Heijbroek—Doesjka	0.00	4.00
Miss N. E. Koster—Axel	4.00	4.00

3 Spain   27.00

J. Goyeneche—Robert	0.00	4.00
F. Uriate—Furia	16.00	0.00
A. Goyeneche—Menorca	4.00	(8.00)
J. Argüelles—Toscanella	(49.25)	3.00

4 Italy, 31.00; 5 France, 39.00; 6 Belgium, 114.00.

Number of teams: 6

=2 Italy   12.00

Lucio Tasca—Extra Dry	(12.00)	4.00
Giuseppe Ravano—Falkonett	4.00	4.00
Stephano Angioni—Perla de Porto Conte	0.00	0.00
Alberto Stretta—Zattera	0.00	(4.00)

4 Germany, 15.00; 5 Italy, 16.00; 6 Netherlands, 32.00;
7 Belgium, 40.00.

Number of teams: 7

1956 Spa (Belgium)
Team Championship

	Faults Round One	Round Two
1 Great Britain 0.00		
Christine Middleton—Leo II	0.00	0.00
Jan White—Full Cry	0.00	0.00
Michael Freer—Billy Boy	(8.00)	(4.00)
Mary Barnes—Sonia Rumer	0.00	0.00
2 FRG 28.00		
Klaus Pade—Fröhlich	4.00	8.00
Renate Freitag—Freya	0.00	4.00
Peter Stackfleth—Frechdachs	4.00	8.00
=3 France 36.00		
Bernard Darbier—Tornade	(11.00)	4.00
Martine Refait—Calvados	8.00	4.00
Armelle Pisier—Fragonard	8.00	4.00
Philippe Jouy—Zette	8.00	(12.00)
=3 Belgium 36.00		
Béatrice Koning—Champion de la Rivière	(8.00)	8.00
Marie-Luce Jamagne—Epi	4.00	0.00
Claude du Roy de Blicquy—Amber's Folie	4.00	16.00
J. P. Delforge—Fiat	4.00	E

5 The Netherlands, 62.25; 6 Denmark, 95.00.

Number of teams: 6

1957 London (GB)
Team Championship

	Faults Round One	Round Two
1 Great Britain 8.00		
Tony Makin—Montana II	0.00	4.00
Jan White—Full Cry	4.00	0.00
Mary Barnes—Moonlight Gambler	0.00	0.00
Ann Townsend—Swift	(4.00)	(4.00)
=2 France 12.00		
Jean Ollieric—Glandor	4.00	(8.00)
Marie-Claude Bourdeleau—Sunset	4.00	0.00
Bernard Darbier—Guy d'Avril	4.00	0.00
Philippe Ollieric—Glaneur	(4.00)	0.00

1958 Hanover (FRG)
Team Championship
(Details of some team members and scores not available.)

1 Great Britain   0.00

Lady Sarah FitzAlan-Howard—Tan
Carole Beard—Corbar
Norton Brookes—Granite
Joe Ashmore—Desilu

2 South Africa   4.00

3 Italy   4.00

4 FRG, 8.00; 5 Hungary, 16.00; 6 Poland, 19.00;
7 France, 58.00; 8 Denmark, 120.25.

Number of teams: 8

1959 London (GB)
Team Championship

	Faults Round One	Round Two
1 Great Britain 8.00		
Michael Cresswell—Tally Ho XVII	4.00	4.00
Jane Kidd—Manka	0.00	(4.00)
Douglas Coakes—Catriona	(4.00)	0.00
Lady Sarah FitzAlan-Howard—Oorskiet	0.00	0.00
2 FRG 15.25		
Michael Bagusat—Bajazzo III	0.00	4.00
Hans-Michael Niemann—Hartherz	4.00	0.00
Bernd Bagusat—Listo	0.00	7.25
Renate Freitag—Freiherr	E	(11.75)
3 France 16.00		
J. L. Planchard—Touch Wood	0.00	4.00
Philippe Ollieric—Nasse	4.00	0.00
F. Fabius—Hernant	(25.00)	(8.00)
Janou Lefèbvre—Frou-Frou	4.00	4.00

=4 Poland, Italy, 20.00; 6 Ireland, 22.25; 7 Belgium, 23.00;
8 Hungary, 24.00; 9 Spain, 142.00; 10 Norway, eliminated.

Number of teams: 10

Individual Championship

=1 Lady Sarah FitzAlan-Howard (GB)—Oorskiet
    Gualtiero Castellini (Ita)—Ventuno
 3 Norbert Wieja (Pol)—Kanon

1960 Venice (Italy)

Team Championship

	Faults Round One	Round Two
1 Great Britain 8.00		
Jane Kidd—Manka	(12.00)	0.00
Douglas Coakes—Catriona	0.00	(12.00)
Michael Cresswell—Mackeson	0.00	4.00
Liz Broome—Gay Monty	0.00	4.00
2 Poland 16.00		
Antoni Pacynski—Bolgami	0.00	8.00
Tomasz Pacynski—Siekacz	0.00	4.00
Bronislaw Kaczmarek—Hilga	(20.00)	(8.00)
Norbert Wieja—Kanon	0.00	4.00
3 Italy 20.00		
Giuseppe Ravano—Prince Regent	0.00	0.00
C. Guidi—Verbena	4.00	(12.00)
F. Tavazzani—Quick Silver	4.00	4.00
S. Carli—Ulla II	(4.00)	8.00

4 Netherlands, 23.00; 5 France, 24.00;
6 Portugal, 48.00; 7 Hungary, 61.75; 8 Belgium, 74.00.
Number of teams: 8

Individual Championship

	Faults
1 Giuseppe Ravano (Ita)—Prince Regent	0.00
2 Antoni Pacynski (Pol)—Bolgami	0.50
3 José Dias de Almeida (Por)—Corsario	4.00

Number of starters: 32

1961 Hickstead (GB)

Team Championship

	Faults Round One	Round Two
1 FRG 16.00		
Rainer Buchholz—Chica	4.00	4.00
Hasso von Zychlinski—Drossel	4.00	E
Heinz von Opel—Cari	0.00	0.00
Bernd Bagusat—Listo	(15.00)	4.00

2 Netherlands 19.75		
Cees Schmal—Feldblume	4.00	0.00
Hans Brugman—An Tostel	8.00	0.00
Lan Huet—Free Lance	(8.00)	3.75
San van Spaendonck—Prinz Ayax	4.00	(4.00)
3 Great Britain 20.00		
Althea Roger Smith—Fanshaw	4.00	(8.00)
Janet Smith—Silver Toes	8.00	4.00
Sheila Barnes—Sola	(12.00)	0.00
Jabeena Maslin—Arkvar	4.00	0.00

4 Belgium, 24.00; 5 France, 32.00; 6 Poland, 39.00;
7 Hungary, 62.75; 8 Ireland, 102.50; 9 Italy, 144.50.
Number of teams: 9

Individual Championship

1 Sheila Barnes (GB)—Sola
2 Althea Roger Smith (GB)—Fanshaw
3 Jabeena Maslin (GB)—Arkvar

Number of riders: 35
Number of nations represented: 9

1962 Berlin (FRG)

Team Championship
(Details of some scores not available.)

	Faults Round One	Round Two
1 Great Britain 0.00, 0.00 in jump-off		
Vivienne Oliver—Red Mint	0.00	0.00
Marion Coakes—Stroller	0.00	0.00
Michael Kane—Lough Foyle	0.00	0.00
John Kidd—Copper Castle	(4.00)	0.00
2 FRG 0.00, 5.25 in jump-off		
Hasso von Zychlinski—Avenue II		
Karsten Huck—Frega		
Jürgen Niewald—Orinde		
Peter von Dreusche—Hartherz		
3 France 4.00		
A. Lorre—Lansquenet		
C. Nossi—Kesbere B		
Gilles Curti—Mouki		
G. Lutturgue—Hennani		

4 Italy, 8.00; 5 Portugal, 11.00; 6 Belgium, 12.00;
7 Netherlands, 19.00; 8 Denmark, 60.00.
Number of teams: 8

Individual Championship
(Details of scores not available.)

1 John Kidd (GB)—Copper Castle
2 Hasso von Zychlinkski (FRG)—Avenue II
3 Karsten Huck (FRG)—Frega

1963 Rotterdam (NL)

Team Championship

	Faults Round One	Faults Round Two
1 Great Britain 3.00		
Jackie Doney—Glenshelane	0.00	3.00
Andrew Fielder—Vibart	0.00	0.00
William Barker—North Flight	0.00	(8.00)
Marion Coakes—Spring Shandy	0.00	0.00
2 FRG 4.00		
Hubertus Destree—Federspiel	(8.00)	4.00
Karsten Huck—Aurikel	0.00	(4.00)
Michael Gockel—Wendelin	0.00	0.00
Hendrick Snoek—Achill	0.00	0.00
3 France 11.00		
Jean-Michel Cagnat—Lapidaire	(4.00)	(18.25)
Gilles Curti—Mouki	0.00	4.00
Laurent Fabius—Hugo II	0.00	3.00
Guy Laffargue—Kampanule	0.00	4.00

=4 Belgium, Poland, Netherlands, 24.00;
7 Yugoslavia, 27.00; 8 Italy, 37.50; 9 Hungary, 40.00.

Number of teams: 9

Individual Championship

	Jump-off F./Time
1 Francesca Ghedini (Ita)—Gengis Kan	0.00/48.80
=2 Vladan Marinkov (Yug)—Beladona	4.00/50.90
Jos Ernst (NL)—Blacky	4.00/54.00
Andrew Fielder (GB)—Vibart	4.00/55.80

Number of riders: 36

Number of nations represented: 9

1964 Budapest (Hungary)

Team Championship

	Faults Round One	Faults Round Two
1 Italy 16.25		
Rudolfo Castagna—It's a Pleasure	4.00	4.00
Giacinta Ulrich—Shillelag	8.00	(27.50)
Giovanna Binetti—Quaso di Ghilarza	(8.00)	0.00
Paola Baccaglini—Vallombrosa	0.25	0.00
2 Great Britain 20.00		
Sarah Roger Smith—Foxtrot	4.00	4.00
Robert Woodward—Tomboy	(12.00)	(12.00)
Lynne Raper—Keewis	4.00	0.00
Marion Coakes—Stroller	4.00	4.00
3 Belgium 23.00		
Hetty Laenens—Insarda	4.00	4.00
Thierry Storme—Willing	7.00	0.00
Thierry van der Veken—Kleber	(16.00)	4.00
Christian Maigret—Telstar	4.00	(8.00)

4 Hungary, 29.00; 5 Sweden, 30.25; 6 FRG, 35.00;
7 Denmark, 38.00; 8 Bulgaria, 45.50; 9 Rumania, 65.50;
10 Yugoslavia, 70.75; 11 Ireland, 87.75; 12 Poland, 91.00.

Number of teams: 12

Individual Championship

	Jump-off F./Time
1 Lynne Raper (GB)—Keewis	0.00/39.00
2 Thierry Storme (Bel)—Willing	0.00/41.00
3 Joseph Mitterer (FRG)—San Remo	4.00/38.60

Number of nations represented: 14

1965 Salice Terme (Italy)

Team Championship

	Faults Round One	Faults Round Two
1 Great Britain 8.00		
Lynne Raper—Keewis	0.00	4.00
Sarah Roger Smith—Foxtrot	0.00	(8.00)
Ann Moore—Kangaroo	0.00	0.00
John Baillie—Dominic IV	0.00	4.00
2 Italy 16.00		
Emanuele Castellini—Ventuno	0.00	4.00
Giorgio Rovaldi—Revelation	8.00	0.00
Giovanna Binetti—Quaso de Ghilarza	4.00	(8.00)
Rudolfo Castagna—It's a Pleasure	(12.00)	0.00
3 FRG 28.00		
Michael Gockel—Doll	8.00	4.00
Breido Graf zu Rantzau—Weintraube	0.00	4.00
Hans-Joachim Schmidt—Fiona	8.00	4.00
Hendrik Snoek—Akteur	(12.00)	(12.25)

4 USSR, 31.00; 5 France, 40.00; 6 Spain, 44.50;
7 Belgium, 58.25; 8 Sweden, 64.00; 9 Hungary, 68.50;
10 Ireland, 75.25; 11 Portugal, 75.50; 12 Yugoslavia, 112.00;
13 Netherlands, 114.00; 14 Denmark, 156.25;
15 Algeria, 219.00.

Number of teams: 15

Individual Championship

	Jump-off F./Time
1 John Baillie (GB)—Dominic IV	0.00/28.20
2 José Roberto Fernandez (Bra)—Samurai	4.00/29.30
3 Ann Moore (GB)—Kangaroo	4.00/30.20

Number of riders: 59

Number of nations represented: 17

1966 Copenhagen (Denmark)

Team Championship

	Faults Round One	Faults Round Two
1 Italy 8.00		
Francesco Ricciotti—Snow Flake	0.00	0.00
Marco Filipucci—Carabella	0.00	0.00
Andrea Bacigalupo—Magical Boy	(8.00)	(8.00)
Emanuele Castellini—King's Coin	4.00	4.00

In the first 35 runnings of the Junior European Championships British riders won the lion's share of the medals. Pictured is the winning team at Stoneleigh in 1968 (from left), Michael Hall Hall on Pablo, Michael Docherty on Government Grant, Ann Moore on Psalm and Gay Traherne on Black Fury, Ann Moore went on to win an Olympic silver medal and was twice Ladies' European Champion. (Findlay Davidson)

2 **Belgium** 12.00		
Thierry Storme—Red Bill	(8.00)	(8.00)
Marianne Monteyne—Kartolina	4.00	8.00
Myriam Thiry—Noisette	0.00	0.00
Jean Damman—Sonia	0.00	0.00

3 **Switzerland** 15.00		
Beat Röthlisberger—Marshall V	0.00	4.00
René Frei—White Wing	E	E
Frank Wettstein—Nagasaki	0.00	8.00
Brigitte Nater—Lanceur	0.00	3.00

4 USSR, 28.00; 5 Denmark, 40.00; 6 FRG, 43.00;
7 Netherlands, 47.00; 8 Czechoslovakia, 55.50.

Number of teams: 8

Individual Championship

	Jump-off F./Time
1 Rinne Möller (Den)—Anzac	0.00/39.20
2 Janos Krizan (Hun)—Zsena	8.00/40.20
3 Krzysztof Ferenstein (Pol)—Cynadra	21.00/93.20

Number of riders: 41

Number of nations represented: 11

2 **France** 5.00
Gilles Bertran de Balanda—Naika
Diane Empain—Remember
Isabella Bertran de Balanda—Turenne
Jean-Marie Nicolas—Isola Bella

3 **FRG** 8.00
Thomas Bartels—Glück
Ulrich Jünemann—Schaum
Breido Graf zu Rantzau—Weintraube
Michael Deppe—Granit

=4 Sweden, Italy, Switzerland, 16.00.

Number of teams: 14

Individual Championship

	Jump-off F./Time
1 Breido Graf zu Rantzau (FRG)—Weintraube	0.00/36.50
2 John Reid (GB)—Dunbell II	0.00/38.00
3 Diane Empain (Fra)—Remember	0.00/41.90

Number of riders: 62

Number of nations represented: 14

1967 Jesolo (Italy)

Team Championship
(Details of some scores not available.)

	Faults	
	Round One	Round Two
1 **Great Britain** 4.00		
John Reid—Dunbell II	(5.25)	0.00
Ann Moore—Hopalong Cassidy	0.00	0.00
Gay Traherne—Black Fury	0.00	(4.00)
Mallowry Spens—Meridian	4.00	0.00

1968 Stoneleigh (GB)

Team Championship
(Details of some scores not available.)

	Faults	
	Round One	Round Two
1 **Great Britain** 8.00		
Ann Moore—Psalm	4.00	0.00
Gay Traherne—Black Fury	(4.00)	0.00
Michael Hall Hall—Pablo	0.00	4.00
Michael Docherty—Government Grant	0.00	(8.00)

2 **France** 12.00

Hugues Rambaud—Quidam
Isabelle Bertran de Balanda—Sableuse
Bertrand Arles-Dufour—Mounana
Jean-Marc Nicolas—Isola Bella

=3 **FRG** 20.00

Paul Kronenberger—Morle
Sylvia Kempter—Daphne
Hendrick Schulze-Siehoff—Medea
Ulrich Jünemann—Schaum

=3 **Denmark** 20.00

Lisbeth Krogsgaard—Visir
Sten Andersen—Maybe
Ulrick Worziger—Boston
Rinne Moller—Anzac

=3 **Ireland** 20.00

Barbara Moore—Mabestown Duchess
Fiona Kinnear—Errigal
John Kyle—Ardnaree
Paul White—Molly Mayo

6 Switzerland, 23.00; 7 Italy, 28.00; 8 Hungary, 34.75;
9 Belgium, 48.00; 10 USSR, 55.00.

Number of teams: 10

Individual Championship

		Jump-off F./Time
1 Ann Moore (GB)—Psalm		0.00/34.30
2 Bertrand Arles-Dufour (Fra)—Mounana		4.00/33.20
3 Charles Grandjean (Switz)—Grandios		4.00/41.40

Number of riders: 49

Number of nations represented: 10

1969 Dinard (France)

Team Championship

		Faults	
		Round One	Round Two
1 **Switzerland**	4.00		
Brigitte Nater—Lanceur		0.00	(7.00)
Jürg Notz—Sherif		0.00	0.00
Beat Röthlisberger—Donauschwalbe		0.00	4.00
Charles Grandjean—Grandios		E	0.00
2 **France**	8.00		
Philippe Giraud—La Grisi		(18.75)	4.00
Isabelle Bertran de Balanda—Mascaret		4.00	0.00
Bertrand Arles-Dufour—Mounana		0.00	0.00
Jean-Marc Nicolas—Isola Bella		0.00	(4.00)
3 **FRG**	12.00		
Wolfgang Kun—Agent		4.00	4.00
Dietrich Riemann—Nasseur		(4.00)	0.00
Marion Snoek—Janeau		0.00	0.00
Wolfgang Knorren—Feuerland		4.00	(4.00)

4 USSR, 19.75; =5 Spain, Great Britain, 20.00; 7 Italy, 20.25;
8 Ireland, 24.75; 9 Poland, 31.00; 10 Belgium, 32.00;
11 Portugal, 62.25; 12 Hungary, 64.00; 13 Denmark, 82.25;
14 Yugoslavia, 112.50.

Number of teams: 14

Individual Championship

		Jump-off F./Time
1 Bertrand Arles-Dufour (Fra)—Mounana		0.00/39.90
2 Paul Darragh (Ire)—Errigal		0.00/40.10
3 Barbara Carlon (Ita)—Philip II		0.00/40.70

Number of riders: 75

Number of nations represented: 17

*Junior European Champion and team
silver medallist in 1970, Markus Fuchs
of Switzerland, seen here competing on
Lady Seven in the 1973 Championships,
in which he won a team gold with a
double clear round in the Nations Cup.
(Ed Lacey Associated Sports
Photography)*

1970 St Moritz (Switzerland)

Team Championship

	Faults Round One	Round Two
1 Great Britain 8.50		
John Francome—Red Paul	0.00	(8.00)
Ann Coleman—Havana Royal	0.00	0.00
Fiona Wilson-Kay—Lonely Boy II	(13.00)	4.00
Michael Hall Hall—Washington	4.00	0.50
2 Switzerland 12.00		
Markus Fuchs—Famos II	E	0.00
Kurt Mäder—Abraxon	4.00	0.00
Jürg Notz—Sherif	0.00	0.00
Charles Grandjean—Grandios	8.00	NP
3 FRG 16.00		
Klaus Bohlmann—Arnika	0.00	0.00
Dietrich Riemann—Nasseur	(8.00)	(8.00)
Stefan Thürnagel—Sentenz	4.00	4.00
Marion Snoek—Janeau	4.00	4.00

4 France, 24.00; 5 Ireland, 31.50; 6 Netherlands, 44.50;
7 Belgium, 47.50; 8 Italy, 58.75; 9 USSR, 72.25;
10 Poland, 76.00; 11 Denmark, 109.75; 12 Yugoslavia, 145.00;
13 Hungary, 145.25; 14 Czechoslovakia, 184.75.

Number of teams: 14

Individual Championship

	Second Jump-off F./Time
1 Markus Fuchs (Switz)—Famos II	0.00/35.20
2 Rob Eras (NL)—Carnaby Street	R
3 Paul Darragh (Ire)—Errigal	

Number of riders: 74

Number of nations represented: 18

A young man who was to find fame in a different equestrian sphere: John Francome, later to become the most successful jockey in National Hunt racing history, jumps Red Paul to a team gold medal at the 1970 Junior European Championships. (Findlay Davidson)

	Faults	
3 Switzerland 12.00		
Charles Grandjean—Grandios	0.00	4.00
Dany Pachoud—Czardaz II	0.00	(12.00)
Thomas Fuchs—Lady Seven	0.00	8.00
Markus Fuchs—Famos II	NP	0.00

4 Belgium, 19.25; 5 Netherlands, 22.00; 6 France, 23.00;
7 Great Britain, 23.25; 8 USSR, 28.00; 9 Italy, 39.00;
10 Denmark, 57.50; 11 Sweden, 84.00; 12 Austria.

Number of teams: 12

Individual Championship

	Jump-off F./Time
1 Marion Snoek (FRG)—Janeau	4.00/39.00
2 Paul Darragh (Ire)—Woodpecker II	4.00/40.00
3 Rebecca Richardson (GB)—Relincho	8.00/43.10

Number of nations represented: 15

1971 Hickstead (GB)

Team Championship
(Details of some scores not available.)

	Faults Round One	Round Two	Jump-off
1 Ireland 8.00, 0.25 in jump-off			
Charlie Curtis—Feltrim	0.00	0.00	0.00
Marilyn Dawson—Clare Cottage	4.00	4.00	0.00
Kevin Barry—Costo	(14.75)	(8.00)	0.50
Paul Darragh—Woodpecker II	0.00	0.00	NP
2 FRG 8.00			
Klaus Bohlmann—Arnika	4.00	0.00	
Wolfgang Kun—Palermo	0.00	4.00	
Marion Snoek—Janeau	0.00	0.00	
Peter Sunkel—Abu Hassan	(4.00)	NP	

1972 Cork (Ireland)

Team Championship

	Faults Round One	Round Two
1 Belgium 0.00		
Eva van Paesschen—Huntmaster	0.00	0.00
Ferdi Tyteca—Mitsouko	0.00	0.00
Patrick Ronge—White City	0.00	0.00
Alain Storme—Condylus	0.00	NP
2 Netherlands 8.00		
Emiel Hendrix—Palatin	0.00	0.00
Franke Sloothaak—Sarno	4.00	(12.00)
Henk Nooren—Gondolier	0.00	0.00
Rob Eras—Sleeping Partner	(4.00)	4.00

3 Ireland   12.00

Margi Lowry—Woodpecker II	4.00	0.00
Justin Carty—Little Madam	(8.00)	4.00
James Kernan—Marcella	4.00	0.00
Eimear Haughey—Feltrim	0.00	(4.00)

4 France, 20.00; 5 Italy, 24.00; 6 FRG, 28.00;
7 Switzerland, 36.00.

Number of teams: 7

Individual Championship
(Details of scores not available.)

1 Jürg Notz (Switz)—Sherif
2 Alain Storme (Bel)—Condylus
3 Lucio Manfredi (Ita)—Red Wind

Number of riders: 37

Number of nations represented: 9

1973 Ekeren (NL)

Team Championship

	Faults	
	Round One	Round Two
1 Switzerland 12.00		
Dieter Frauenfelder—Saltarim	4.00	(16.25)
Dieter Hauser—Iron Flock	(16.00)	8.00
Markus Fuchs—Lady Seven	0.00	0.00
Thomas Fuchs—Royal Can	0.00	0.00

2 France   19.50

Xavier Leredde—Ussor	4.50	0.00
Ines Fraissinet—Dusty	7.00	0.00
Eric Leroyer—Bayart de Peray	4.00	4.00
J. P. Deroullers—Soupçon	(12.00)	NP

3 FRG   26.00

Kurt Gravemeier—Rendant	14.00	4.00
Jochen Laubscher—Mario	4.00	4.00
Georg Kahny—Petra	(17.00)	(12.00)
Norbert Koof—Minister	0.00	0.00

4 Belgium, 28.00; =5 Great Britain, USSR, 35.00;
also Ireland, Spain, Netherlands, France, Czechoslovakia,
Denmark, Austria.

Number of teams competing: 16

Individual Championship
(Details of scores not available.)

1 Debbie Johnsey (GB)—Speculator
2 Stanny van Paesschen (Bel)—Smart Alec
3 Norbert Koof (FRG)—Minister

Number of riders: 79

Number of nations represented: 17

1974 Lucerne (Switzerland)

Team Championship

	Faults	
	Round One	Round Two
1 Austria 4.00		
Klaus Ott—Tommi	0.00	0.00
Andreas Nairz—Sheriff	(8.00)	0.00
Egan Blum—White Wing	4.00	0.00
Michael Göbel—Hully Hill	0.00	NP
=2 Great Britain 8.00		
Debbie Johnsey—Assam	4.00	0.00
Nick Skelton—Everest Maybe	0.00	4.00
Cheryl Walker—Wishbone III	0.00	(4.00)
Lynn Chapman—Mandalay Lass	(4.00)	0.00
=2 Netherlands 8.00		
René Kliijnee—Prins Charles	0.00	4.00
Conni Brink—Gamin	4.00	(12.00)
Heber Wiel—Golden Future	0.00	0.00
Franke Sloothaak—Polo Marco	(4.00)	0.00

4 France, 12.00; 5 Ireland, 20.00; 6 Belgium, 25.75;
7 Spain, 27.00; 8 Switzerland, 32.00; 9 FRG, 36.00;
10 Hungary, 47.00; 11 Portugal, 50.75; 12 Italy, 52.25;
13 USSR, 91.25; 14 Czechoslovakia, retired.

Number of teams: 14

*Janeau, ridden by Marion Snoek, is one of only five horses to
have won a medal at three consecutive Junior Championships.
The West German pair's tally was two team bronzes, in 1969
and 1970, team silver in 1971 and the individual gold that same
year. (The Photo Source)*

Ireland has had a good deal of success in the Junior European Championships, including the individual title in 1976, won by Brian McMahon and Heather Honey. (Findlay Davidson)

Individual Championship

	F./Time
1 James Kernan (Ire)—Marcella	0.00–0.00–0.00/47.90
2 Xavier Leredde (Fra)—Triple Sec	0.00–0.00–4.00/48.20
3 Sabina Luciani (Ita)—Garuando	0.00–0.00–4.00/50.90

Number of riders: 69

Number of nations represented: 16

5 Italy, 16.00; 6 France, 24.00; 7 Switzerland, 25.75; 8 Netherlands, 36.00; 9 Spain, 40.00; 10 Ireland, 44.00; 11 Austria, 52.00; 12 USSR, 60.00; 13 Czechoslovakia, 68.75; 14 Norway, retired.

Number of teams: 14

Individual Championship

	Jump-off F./Time
1 Nick Skelton (GB)—Everest O.K.	0.00/29.80
2 Daniella de Bruycker (Bel)—Candy	0.00/30.20
3 John Brown (GB)—Paddy Connelly	0.00/30.50

Number of riders: 67

Number of nations represented: 14

1975 Dornbirn (Austria)

Team Championship

		Faults Round One	Faults Round Two
1	**Belgium** 8.00		
	Marlene Martens—Bill	0.00	4.00
	Veronique Daems-Vastapane—Jonas	4.00	0.00
	Hilde Goris—Little Jockey	(4.00)	0.00
	Daniella de Bruycker—Candy	0.00	(11.00)
=2	**FRG** 12.00		
	Kurt Gravemeier—Axero	0.00	0.00
	Gerd Hellfrich—Grandessa	8.00	0.00
	Dirk Dahler—Mythose	(20.00)	(24.00)
	Robert Gremme—Roulette	4.00	0.00
=2	**Poland** 12.00		
	Andrzej Konieczny—Czata	E	(11.25)
	Janusz Prasek—Brok	4.00	4.00
	Stanislaw Helak—Ostrozen	0.00	4.00
	Stanislaw Jasinski—Kajtek	0.00	0.00
=2	**Great Britain** 12.00		
	Nick Skelton—Everest O.K.	0.00	(8.00)
	Marion Howard—Top Rank	0.00	4.00
	Vicky Gascoine—Extra Special	4.00	0.00
	John Brown—Paddy Connelly	(4.00)	4.00

1976 Brussels (Belgium)

Team Championship

		Faults Round One	Faults Round Two
1	**Switzerland** 12.00		
	Elisabeth Mosset—Harley	4.00	4.00
	Marc Vingerhoets—Sweety	(12.00)	4.00
	Margreth Mollet—Elsetta	0.00	0.00
	Olivier Lauffer—Ashlines	0.00	(4.00)
2	**Ireland** 16.00		
	Brian McMahon—Heather Honey	(8.00)	0.00
	Feargal Kavanagh—Warrior	8.00	(6.00)
	Margaret Tolerton—Willowdale	4.00	0.00
	Mennell Watson—Kong	4.00	0.00
3	**Great Britain** 24.00		
	Christopher Parker—Brackenhill	4.00	(12.00)
	Michael Whitaker—Bericote Capucino	4.00	0.00
	Vicky Gascoine—Extra Special	(8.00)	8.00
	John Brown—Paddy Connelly	4.00	4.00

4 Netherlands, 28.00*; 5 Austria, 28.00*; 6 Poland, 28.00*; 7 Italy, 32.00; 8 FRG, 36.00; 9 France, 46.25; 10 USSR, 53.00; 11 Norway, 76.00; 12 Belgium, eliminated; 13 Spain, retired.

Number of teams: 13

Individual Championship
(Details of scores not available.)

  1 Brian McMahon (Ire)—Heather Honey
=2 Veronique Daems-Vastapane (Bel)—Jonas
     Bruno Scolari (Ita)—Dinamiteur
     Eric Navet (Fra)—Brooklyn
     Cristine Teich (FRG)—Tambour
     Margreth Mollet (Switz)—Elsetta
     Vicky Gascoine (GB)—Extra Special
     Y. Polyakov (USSR)—Forpost
     Xavier Leredde (Fra)—Altesse N
     Franke Sloothaak (NL)—San Angelo

Number of riders: 63

1977 Geneva (Switzerland)
Team Championship

	Faults Round One	Round Two
1 Great Britain 12.00		
Jean Germany—Dark Vale	4.00	4.00
Robert Smith—Royal Rufus	(4.00)	0.00
Steven Smith—Alabama	0.00	4.00
Stephen Vallance—Moydrum	0.00	(8.00)
=2 Ireland 16.00		
John Carty—Little Madam	4.00	(8.00)
Jim McCartan—Easy Girl	4.00	0.00
Heather Gahan—Maguire	(12.00)	4.00
Mennell Watson—Exodus	0.00	4.00
=2 France 16.00		
Philippe Poulet—Clotaire	4.00	4.00
Adeline Cancre—Daisy III	(8.00)	(16.00)
Xavier Leredde—Far West	4.00	4.00
Eric Navet—Brooklyn	0.00	0.00

=4 Belgium, FRG, 20.00; =6 USSR, Poland, Italy, 24.00; 9 Switzerland, 31.75; 10 Netherlands, 45.25; 11 Austria, 54.00.

Number of teams: 11

Individual Championship

	Jump-off F./Time
1 Eric Navet (Fra)—Brooklyn	0.00/36.30
2 Veronique Daems-Vastapane (Bel)—Jonas	0.00/36.60
3 Robert Smith (GB)—Alabama	0.00/38.90

Number of riders: 64

Number of nations represented: 14

*The scores of a team's best individual riders were taken into consideration in order to place those teams which finished with equal penalties.

1978 Stannington (GB)

Team Championship

	Faults Round One	Round Two
1 Great Britain 0.00		
Michael Whitaker—Brother Scott	0.00	0.00
Jill Kelly—Pepperpot	0.00	0.00
Steven Smith—Sunningdale	0.00	0.00
Jean Germany—Leafield Lad	(4.00)	NP
2 Ireland 4.00		
Mandy Lyons—Chilon Flight	0.00	4.00
Anne Hatton—Mia	(12.00)	(4.00)
Declan McGarry—Nephin Mor	0.00	0.00
Trevor McConnell—Supermac	0.00	0.00
3 Netherlands 16.00		
Piet Jacobs—Royal Palm	4.00	(12.00)
Abe Koopmans—Miranda K	(12.00)	4.00
Irma Smulders—Tiffany	0.00	0.00
Jan Tops—Nero	0.00	8.00

4 Switzerland, 20.00; 5 Belgium, 23.50; 6 Austria, 24.00; 7 Spain, 32.00; 8 FRG, 33.25; 9 Poland, 36.00; 10 France, 38.50; 11 Italy, 53.25; 12 Norway, retired.

Number of teams: 12

Individual Championship

	Jump-off F./Time
1 Lionel Collard Bovy (Bel)—Loecky	0.00/36.90
2 Jean Germany (GB)—Leafield Lad	0.00/38.50
3 Jill Kelly (GB)—Pepperpot	0.00/40.60

Number of riders: 60

Number of nations represented: 13

1979 Gijon (Spain)
Team Championship

	Faults Round One	Round Two	
1 Switzerland 19.00			
Rolf Hegner—Victorious	0.00	4.00	
Christian Ineichen—Gregor	0.00	(28.00)	
Werner Zemp—Black Water	4.00	3.00	
Paolo Bernasconi—Mr Proofy	(4.00)	8.00	
			Jump-off
2 Great Britain 20.00, 0.00 in jump-off			
Gillian Milner—Cottage Star	(16.00)	0.00	0.00
Richard Hill—Arjay	4.00	4.00	0.00
Pamela Rayton—Wilwin	8.00	(4.00)	0.00
Vicky Gascoine—McGinty	4.00	0.00	NP

3 **FRG** 20.00, 4.00 in jump-off

Thomas Möhr—Walhalla	0.00	4.00	(12.00)
Ulla Kraus—Filia	4.00	4.00	0.00
Carsten Nagel—White Star	(4.00)	4.00	4.00
Bernd Herbert—Wladika	4.00	(4.00)	0.00

=4 Belgium, Ireland, Italy, 24.00; 7 Austria, 31.50;
8 Sweden, Netherlands, 32.00; 10 Spain, 44.00.

Number of teams: 10

Individual Championship

	Jump-off F./Time
1 Vicky Gascoine (GB)—McGinty	0.00/46.80
2 Gillian Milner (GB)—Cottage Star	0.00/47.80
3 Lisbeth Hansson (Swe)—Aluette	0.00/48.30

Number of riders: 51

Number of nations represented: 11

1980 Millstreet (Ireland)

Team Championship
(Details of jump-off scores not available.)

	Faults	
	Round One	Round Two
1 **France** 4.00		
Patrice Delaveau—Etendard du Nord	0.00	0.00
Philippe Rozier—Fetiche d'Armor	(4.00)	0.00
Eric Levallois—Graine d'Oria	0.00	0.00
Jean-Charles Gayat—Elsa III	4.00	(11.00)
2 **Netherlands** 8.00		
Erik van der Vleuten—Napoleon S	4.00	4.00
Tonko Barlagen—Santo Rosario	0.00	(4.00)
Yolanda Markslag—Nelson Balbo	0.00	0.00
Tanja van Malsen—Calypso II	(8.00)	0.00
3 **FRG** 12.00, 4.00 in jump-off		
Guido Flass—Minus	0.00	4.00
Hans-Jörn Ottens—Garant	0.00	4.00
Josef Elbers—Poseiden	(4.25)	0.00
Alfons Kloepper—Abigail	4.00	(4.00)

4 Belgium, 12.00, 8.00 in jump-off; 5 Great Britain, 12.25;
6 Spain, 12.75; 7 Ireland, 16.00; 8 Italy, 16.25;
9 Switzerland, 32.00; 10 Finland, 188.00.

Number of teams: 10

Individual Championship

	Jump-off F./Time
1 Michael Mac (GB)—Persian Shah	0.00/36.45
2 Jane Sargent (GB)—Ladiesman	0.00/39.61
3 Caterina Vacchelli (Ita)—Edelweiss	0.00/47.07

Number of riders: 49

Number of nations represented: 11

1981 Aarau (Switzerland)

Team Championship

	Faults	
	Round One	Round Two
1 **Great Britain** 16.00		
Zoë Bates—Intrepid	0.00	0.00
Michelle Lewis—Tutein	(12.00)	(9.25)
Mark Heffer—Valley View	8.00	8.00
Lesley McNaught —One More Time	0.00	0.00
2 **Belgium** 16.25		
Ludo Philippaerts—Terrible	(8.00)	(17.75)
Marcel Rombouts—Coolroe	0.00	4.00
Danny van den Bosch—Simson	4.00	8.00
Axel Verlooy—Fiasco II	0.00	0.25

3 **FRG** 20.50, 0.00 in jump-off

			Jump-off
Josef Elbers—Poseidon	4.00	4.00	0.00
Peter Jostes—Pascal	8.00	0.00	0.00
Hans-Jürgen Deuerer—Top Time	4.00	0.50	0.00
Ulf Plate—Peggy	(8.00)	(4.00)	NP

4 Spain, 20.50, 28.00 in jump-off;
=5 Netherlands, France, 24.00; =7 Poland, Switzerland, 28.00;
9 Ireland, 32.00; 10 Italy, 40.00; 11 Sweden, 53.00;
12 Austria, 68.00; 13 USSR, 92.00.

Number of teams: 13

Individual Championship

	F./Time
1 Lesley McNaught (GB) —One More Time	0.00–0.00–0.00/45.02
2 Peter Jostes (FRG)—Pascal	0.00–0.00–0.00/50.45
3 Jan Kuipers (NL)—Peu Nerveux	0.00–0.00–0.00/51.18

Number of riders: 54 (26 clear rounds went into second round on last day)

Number of nations represented: 14

1982 Le Vaudreuil (France)

Team Championship

	Faults	
	Round One	Round Two
1 **France** 0.00		
Patrice Delaveau—Iena A	(4.00)	0.00
Roger-Yves Bost—Jorphée de Prieur	0.00	0.00
André Roguet—Hygie A	0.00	0.00
Jean-Charles Gayat—Ignace B	0.00	NP

2 Belgium 8.50

Michel Smismans—Velco	0.50	0.00
Didier Labye—Tarzan	(4.00)	(8.00)
Sacha Marissen—Lavendel	0.00	4.00
Danny van den Bosch—Rapide	0.00	4.00

3 Ireland 11.25

Vincent Burke—Good Brew	0.50	0.00
Linda Courtney—Suzy	1.50	4.00
Edward Kelly—Fine Act	0.00	5.25
Vina Lyons—Onward Bound	(8.00)	(8.00)

4 FRG, 16.00; 5 Spain, 20.00; 6 Switzerland, 21.25;
7 Great Britain, 26.00; 8 Netherlands, 32.25; 9 Sweden, 38.25;
10 Austria, 60.75; 11 Finland, 129.75.

Number of teams: 11

Individual Championship

	F./Time
1 Jonathan Egmore (GB)—Postmark	0.00–0.00–0.00/37.38
2 Peter Jostes (FRG)—Pascal	0.00–0.00–0.00/37.90
3 Vincent Burke (Ire)—Good Brew	0.00–0.00–0.00/39.56

Number of riders: 53

Number of nations represented: 11

1983 Thorpe Park (GB)

Team Championship

	Faults	
	Round One	Round Two
1 France 4.00		
Yves Patron—Icare	0.00	(4.00)
Pascale Wittmer		
—Isle de Toucane	(4.75)	4.00
Olivier Desutter—Lassie du Loire	0.00	0.00
Jean Charles Gayat—Ignace B	0.00	0.00
2 Ireland 8.00		
Vina Lyons—China Doll	(8.00)	0.00
Michael Walsh—Phantom	0.00	(7.00)
Thomas Duggan—Heather Honey	4.00	0.00
Vincent Burke—Another Brew	0.00	4.00

			Jump-off
3 Belgium 16.00, 0.00 in jump-off			
Johan Lenssens—Pezewever	0.00	4.00	0.00
Stefan Vandewalle—Ipanema	(12.00)	(8.00)	0.00
Beatrice Botte—Piqueur	4.00	4.00	0.00
Michel Smismans—Velco	0.00	4.00	NP

4 Great Britain, 16.00, 8.00 in 92.42 seconds in jump-off;
5 Spain, 16.00, 8.00 in 110.73 seconds in jump-off;

6 FRG, 19.25; 7 Poland, 20.75;
=8 Switzerland, Netherlands, 28.00;
=10 Sweden, Austria, 32.00; 12 Italy, retired.

Number of teams: 12

Individual Championship

	F./Time
1 Iain Morgan (GB)—Dun Topper	0.00–0.00–0.00/32.55
2 Francisco Parra (Spain)—Jutland C	0.00–0.00–0.00/36.48
3 Michael Walsh (Ire)—Phantom	0.00–0.00–4.00/29.94

Number of riders: 61

Number of nations represented: 13

1984 Gesves (Belgium)

Team Championship

	Faults	
	Round One	Round Two
1 Belgium 12.00		
Johan Lenssens—Pezewever	4.00	4.00
Stefan Vandewalle—Affrodite	4.00	(4.00)
Ben Vanwijn—Vivaldi	(4.00)	0.00
Michel Smismans—Velco	0.00	0.00
2 Ireland 12.75		
Linda Courtney—Mahogany	0.00	0.00
Hanley Charles—Yankie	0.50	8.00
Nigel Smith—French View	0.25	(8.75)
Stephen Smith—Silveroid	(4.00)	4.00

			Jump-off
3 France 16.00, 0.00 in jump-off			
Pascale Wittmer			
—Isle de Toucane	4.00	(8.00)	E
Sylvie Parot—La Folle Envie	(4.00)	4.00	0.00
Max Thirouin—Iara	0.00	4.00	0.00
Stephane Delaveau—Iris A	0.00	4.00	0.00

4 Great Britain, 16.00; 4.00 in jump-off; 5 FRG, 29.00;
6 Spain, 32.00; 7 Italy, 36.00; 8 Austria, 42.00;
9 Netherlands, 44.00; 10 Poland, 46.50; 11 Switzerland, 52.00;
12 Sweden, 60.00; 13 Denmark, 63.50.

Number of teams: 13

Individual Championship

	F./Time
1 Gillian Greenwood (GB)—Sky Fly	0.00–0.00–0.00/37.04
2 Stefan Vandewalle (Bel)—Affrodite	0.00–0.00–4.00/33.06
3 Johan Lenssens (Bel)—Pezewever	0.00–0.00–8.00/32.10

Number of riders: 73

Number of nations represented: 17

1985 Fontainebleau (France)

Team Championship

	Faults	
	Round One	Round Two
1 Belgium 8.00		
Bernard Mathy—Max du Menilod	(8.00)	(20.00)
Stefan Vandewalle—Oskar	0.00	0.00
François Mathy—Voulez-Vous	0.00	0.00
Rik Hemerijck—Cambronne de Lauzelle	4.00	4.00
2 France 12.00		
Christophe Roguet—Herminette III	0.00	0.00
Sophie Pelissier—Mousse	4.00	(4.00)
Max Thirouin—Iara	0.00	4.00
Stephane Delaveau—Lekkak	(12.00)	4.00
3 Italy 16.00		
Gianni Govoni—Rebel	4.00	4.00
Fabrizzio Ambrosetti—Velco	0.00	(8.00)
Luca Orsini—Senator	(12.00)	4.00
Barbara Scarpa—Seaman	0.00	4.00

4 Great Britain, 20.00; 5 FRG, 24.00; 6 Netherlands, 28.00; 7 Austria, 32.00; 8 Ireland, 36.00; 9 Spain, 55.75; 10 Denmark, 57.00; 11 Sweden, 60.75; 12 Poland, 96.75; 13 Switzerland, 100.75.

Number of teams: 13

Individual Championship

	F./Time
1 Kirk Kalender (FRG)—Gigolo	0.00–0.00–0.00/44.29
2 Emma Gascoine (GB)—MacGinty	0.00–0.00–0.00/45.53
3 Anke Ense (FRG)—Wim	0.00–0.00–0.00/48.76

Number of riders: 67

Number of nations represented: 15

1986 Ennis (Ireland)

Team Championship

	Faults	
	Round One	Round Two
1 France 15.50		
Christophe Rouget—Laurentides	8.00	(8.00)
Eugenie Legrand—Kali du Moulin	0.00	0.00
Max Thirouin—Ignace B	0.50	3.00
Stephane Delaveau—Lekkak	(12.00)	4.00
2 Great Britain 20.00		
Sandra Klinkhamer—Willownook Venture	4.00	0.00
Ian Barker—Timandra	4.00	4.00
Emma Gascoine—Napoleon Zero	(8.00)	(8.00)
Julie Greenwood—Monsanta	4.00	4.00
3 FRG 20.25		
Rene Tebbel—Stardust	8.00	0.00
Thomas Mühlbauer—Gomo	(23.00)	(9.50)
Alexandra Bischoff—Maybe	8.00	0.00
Barbara Reitter—Iris d'Espoir	0.00	4.25

4 Netherlands, 22.50; 5 Austria, 32.00; 6 Italy, 44.25; 7 Belgium, 46.25; 8 Ireland, 48.75; 9 Spain, 77.00.

Number of teams: 9

Individual Championship

	F./Time
1 Javier Salvador (Spa)—Viking	0.00–0.00–4.00
2 Julie Greenwood (GB)—Monsanta	0.00–0.00–17.00
3 Eva-Maria Orthuber (Aut) —Northern Lights	0.00–0.25

Number of riders: 48

Number of nations represented: 12

Medal Tables

Team Championship 1952–1986

Country	Gold	Silver	Bronze
Great Britain	14	5	2
France	5	7	5
Belgium	5	3	4
Switzerland	4	1	2
Italy	3	4	3
FRG	2	7	10
Ireland	1	5	3
Austria	1	—	—
Netherlands	—	6	1
Poland	—	2	—
South Africa	—	1	—
Denmark	—	—	1
Spain	—	—	1

Individual Championship 1959–1986

Country	Gold	Silver	Bronze
Great Britain	14	9	6
FRG	3	4	4
Italy	3	1	4
France	2	4	1
Ireland	2	2	3
Switzerland	2	1	1
Belgium	1	7	1
Spain	1	1	—
Denmark	1	—	—
Netherlands	—	3	1
Poland	—	1	2
Brazil	—	1	—
Hungary	—	1	—
USSR	—	1	—
Yugoslavia	—	1	—
Austria	—	—	1
Portugal	—	—	1
Sweden	—	—	1

Team and Individual Championships 1952–1986

Country	Gold	Silver	Bronze
Great Britain	28	14	8
France	7	11	6
Belgium	6	10	5
Switzerland	6	2	3
Italy	6	5	7
FRG	5	11	14
Ireland	3	7	6
Spain	1	1	1
Austria	1	—	1
Denmark	1	—	1
Netherlands	—	9	2
Poland	—	3	2
Brazil	—	1	—
Hungary	—	1	—
South Africa	—	1	—
USSR	—	1	—
Yugoslavia	—	1	—
Portugal	—	—	1
Sweden	—	—	1

Records: Riders

Most Medals

4 Gold, 1 Bronze

Ann Moore (GB)
  Team gold 1965
  Team gold 1967
  Team gold 1968
  Individual gold 1968
  Individual bronze 1965

3 Gold

Lady Sarah FitzAlan-Howard (GB)
  Team gold 1958
  Team gold 1959
  Individual gold (=) 1959

Jean-Charles Gayat (Fra)
  Team gold 1980
  Team gold 1982
  Team gold 1983

2 Gold, 1 Silver, 1 Bronze

Markus Fuchs (Switz)
  Individual gold 1970
  Team gold 1973
  Team silver 1970
  Team bronze 1971

Stefan Vandewalle (Bel)
  Team gold 1985
  Team gold 1984
  Individual silver 1984
  Team bronze 1983

2 Gold, 1 Silver

Marion Coakes (GB)
  Team gold 1962
  Team gold 1963
  Team silver 1964

Jean Germany (GB)
  Team gold 1977
  Team gold 1978
  Individual silver 1978

Jürg Notz (Switz)
  Team gold 1969
  Individual gold 1972
  Team silver 1970

Lynne Raper (GB)
  Individual gold 1964
  Team gold 1965
  Team silver 1964

2 Gold

John Baillie (GB)
  Team gold 1965
  Individual gold 1965

Mary Barnes (GB)
  Team gold 1956
  Team gold 1957

Douglas Coakes (GB)
  Team gold 1959
  Team gold 1960

Michael Cresswell (GB)
  Team gold 1959
  Team gold 1960

Patrice Delaveau (Fra)
  Team gold 1980
  Team gold 1982

Michael Hall Hall (GB)
  Team gold 1968
  Team gold 1970

Jane Kidd (GB)
  Team gold 1959
  Team gold 1960

John Kidd (GB)
  Team gold 1962
  Individual gold 1962

Lesley McNaught (GB)
  Team gold 1981
  Individual gold 1981

Steven Smith (GB)
  Team gold 1977
  Team gold 1978

Gay Traherne (GB)
  Team gold 1967
  Team gold 1968

Jan White (GB)
  Team gold 1956
  Team gold 1957

1 Gold, 3 Silver, 1 Bronze

Vicky Gascoine (GB)
  Individual gold 1979
  Team silver 1975
  Individual silver 1976
  Team silver 1979
  Team bronze 1976

1 Gold, 3 Silver

Bertrand Arles-Dufour (Fra)
  Individual gold 1969
  Team silver 1968
  Individual silver 1968
  Team silver 1969

1 Gold, 2 Silver, 1 Bronze

Paul Darragh (Ire)
  Team gold 1971
  Individual silver 1969
  Individual silver 1971
  Individual bronze 1970

1 Gold, 2 Silver

Gian Piero Bembo (Ita)
  Team gold 1954
  Team silver 1952
  Team silver 1953

Veronique Daems-Vastapane (Bel)
  Team gold 1975
  Individual silver (=) 1976
  Individual silver 1977

Graziano Mancinelli (Ita)
  Team gold 1954
  Team silver 1952
  Team silver 1953

Eric Navet (Fra)
  Individual gold 1977
  Individual silver (=) 1976
  Team silver 1977

Nick Skelton (GB)
  Individual gold 1975
  Team silver 1974
  Team silver 1975

Hasso von Zychlinski (FRG)
  Team gold 1961
  Team silver 1962
  Individual silver 1962

1 Gold 1 Silver, 2 Bronze

Charles Grandjean (Switz)
  Team gold 1969
  Team silver 1970
  Individual bronze 1968
  Team bronze 1971

Marion Snoek (FRG)
  Individual gold 1971
  Team silver 1971
  Team bronze 1969
  Team bronze 1970

1 Gold, 1 Silver, 1 Bronze

Stephane Delaveau (Fra)
  Team gold 1986
  Team silver 1985
  Team bronze 1984

Giuseppe Ravano (Ita)
  Individual gold 1960
  Team silver 1957
  Team bronze 1960

Michel Smismans (Bel)
  Team gold 1984
  Team silver 1982
  Team bronze 1983

Max Thirouin (Fra)
  Team gold 1986
  Team silver 1985
  Team bronze 1984

1 Gold, 1 Silver

Bernd Bagusat (FRG)
  Team gold 1961
  Team silver 1959

Giovanna Binetti (Ita)
  Team gold 1964
  Team silver 1965

Rudolfo Castagna (Ita)
  Team gold 1964
  Team silver 1965

Emanuele Castellini (Ita)
  Team gold 1966
  Team silver 1965

Daniella de Bruycker (Bel)
  Team gold 1975
  Individual silver 1975

Andrew Fielder (GB)
  Team gold 1963
  Individual silver (=) 1963

Debbie Johnsey (GB)
  Individual gold 1973
  Team silver 1974

Brian McMahon (Ire)
  Individual gold 1976
  Team silver 1976

Margreth Mollet (Switz)
  Team gold 1976
  Individual silver (=) 1976

Klaus Pade (FRG)
  Team gold 1955
  Team silver 1956

John Reid (GB)
  Team gold 1967
  Individual silver 1967

Sarah Roger Smith (GB)
  Team gold 1965
  Team silver 1964

Christophe Roguet (Fra)
  Team gold 1986
  Team silver 1985

Alain Storme (Bel)
  Team gold 1972
  Individual silver 1972

1 Gold, 2 Bronze

Johan Lenssens (Bel)
  Team gold 1984
  Team bronze 1983
  Individual bronze 1984

Breido Graf zu Rantzau (FRG)
  Individual gold 1967
  Team bronze 1965
  Team bronze 1967

1 Gold, 1 Bronze

George Asselberghs (Bel)
  Team gold 1952
  Team bronze 1953

Sheila Barnes (GB)
  Individual gold 1961
  Team bronze 1961

Nick Skelton riding Everest O.K. wins the Junior European title at Dornbirn, Austria, in 1975 before going on to a highly successful career as a senior rider. (Findlay Davidson)

Thomas Fuchs (Switz)
  Team gold 1973
  Team bronze 1971

George Hernalsteens (Bel)
  Team gold 1952
  Team bronze 1953

Jill Kelly (GB)
  Team gold 1978
  Individual bronze 1978

James Kernan (Ire)
  Individual gold 1974
  Team bronze 1972

Rinner Möller (Den)
  Individual gold 1966
  Team bronze 1968

Brigitte Nater (Switz)
  Team gold 1969
  Team bronze 1966

1 Gold, 1 Bronze

Martine Refait (Fra)
  Team gold 1953
  Team bronze 1956

Beat Rothlisberger (Switz)
  Team gold 1969
  Team bronze 1966

Robert Smith (GB)
  Team gold 1977
  Individual bronze 1977

Françoise Vanderhaegen (Bel)
  Team gold 1952
  Team bronze 1953

Michael Whitaker (GB)
  Team gold 1978
  Team bronze 1976

Pascale Wittmer (Fra)
  Team gold 1983
  Team bronze 1984

Two riders have won three team gold medals:
  Ann Moore (GB) 1965, 1967, 1968
  Jean-Charles Gayat (Fra) 1980, 1982, 1983

Ann Moore is the only rider to have won 4 gold medals (team 1965, 1967, 1968; individual 1968).

5 riders have won a team and an individual gold medal in the same year:
  John Baillie (GB) 1965
  Lady Sarah FitzAlan-Howard (GB) 1959
  John Kidd (GB) 1962
  Lesley McNaught (GB) 1981
  Ann Moore (GB) 1968

12 riders have won team gold medals at two consecutive championships:
  Mary Barnes (GB), 1956, 1957
  Douglas Coakes (GB) 1959, 1960
  Marion Coakes (GB) 1962, 1963
  Michael Cresswell (GB) 1959, 1960
  Lady Sarah FitzAlan-Howard (GB) 1958, 1959
  Jean-Charles Gayat (Fra) 1982, 1983
  Jean Germany (GB) 1977, 1978
  Jane Kidd (GB) 1959, 1960
  Ann Moore (GB) 1967, 1968
  Steven Smith (GB) 1977, 1978
  Gay Traherne (GB) 1967, 1968
  Jan White (GB) 1956, 1957

Country with longest winning sequence

Team Championship

  GB—5: 1956, 1957, 1958, 1959, 1960

Individual Championship

  GB—6: 1979, 1980, 1981, 1982, 1983, 1984

Great Britain is also the only country whose riders have won all three individual medals in the same championships, in 1961 at Hickstead, when Sheila Barnes won the gold, Althea Roger Smith the silver, and Jabeena Maslin the bronze.

Highest number of starters

Teams
16: 1973 Ekeren
Individual
79: 1973 Ekeren

Highest number of nations represented

18: 1970 St Moritz

Smallest number of starters

Teams
2: 1952 Ostend

Smallest number of nations represented

2: 1952 Ostend

Jump-offs

There has been a jump-off for the team gold medal on two occasions: between Great Britain and FRG in 1962 (Great Britain won), and between Ireland and FRG in 1971 (Ireland won).

Best winning score in Team Championship

0.00 faults, achieved by Italy in 1954, by Great Britain in 1956, 1958, 1962 and 1978; by Belgium in 1972, and by France in 1982.

Smallest winning margin in Team Championship

0.25 faults in 1981, when Great Britain (16.00) beat Belgium (16.25).

Biggest winning margin in Team Championship

28 faults in 1956, when Great Britain beat FRG.

Records: Horses

Most gold medals

12 horses have each won two gold medals:
   Black Fury (Gay Traherne, GB), 1967, 1968
   Catriona (Douglas Coakes, GB), 1959, 1960
   Copper Castle (John Kidd, GB), 1962
   Dominic IV (John Baillie, GB), 1965
   Full Cry (Jan White, GB), 1956, 1957
   Ignace B (Jean-Charles Gayat, Fra), 1982, 1983
   Keewis (Lynne Raper, GB), 1964, 1965
   Manka (Jane Kidd, GB), 1959, 1960
   One More Time (Lesley McNaught, GB), 1981
   Oorskiet (Lady Sarah FitzAlan-Howard, GB), 1959
   Psalm (Ann Moore, GB), 1968
   Sherif (Jürg Notz, Switz), 1969, 1972

Copper Castle, Dominic IV, One More Time, Oorskiet and Psalm won team and individual golds in the same year.

Keewis and Sherif won team and individual golds in different years.

Black Fury, Catriona, Full Cry, Ignace B and Manka each won two team golds.

Most medal-winning appearances

4 Grandios (Charles Grandjean, Switz)
   The only horse to win a medal at 4 consecutive championships
      1968 Individual bronze
      1969 Team gold
      1970 Team silver
      1971 Team bronze

3 Sherif (Jürg Notz, Switz)
      1969 Team gold
      1970 Team silver
      1972 Individual gold

Jonas (Veronique Daems-Vestapane, Bel)
      1975 Team gold
      1976 Individual silver
      1977 Individual silver

Janeau (Marion Snoek, FRG)
      1969 Team bronze
      1970 Team bronze
      1971 Individual gold, Team silver

Isola Bella (Jean-Marc Nicolas, Fra)
      1967 Team silver
      1968 Team silver
      1969 Team silver

Junior American Championships

1974 Buenos Aires (Argentina)

Team Championship
(Details of team members and scores not available.)

1 **Brazil**
2 **Argentina**
3 **Uruguay**

Individual Championship
(Details of scores not available.)

```
 1 P. San Felice (Arg)
=2 G. Rosselot (Chi)
   G. C. Farias (Bra)
   José L. Lopez (Chi)
   Rafael Paullier (Uru)
```

Number of nations represented: 4

1975 Porto Allegro (Brazil)

Team Championship
(Details of team members and scores not available.)

1 **Brazil**
2 **Argentina**

Individual Championship
(Details of scores not available.)

```
 1 Rafael Fragoso Pires (Bra)
 2 Walmor Zeredo, Jnr (Bra)
=3 Françoise Isnard (Bra)
   Maria Zubiaurre (Arg)
```

Number of riders: 15
Number of nations represented: 3

1976

Team Championship
(Full details not available.)

1 **Chile**

1977 Montevideo (Uruguay)

Team Championship
(Details of scores not available.)

1 **Uruguay** 12.00

Enrique Penades—Pirata
Fernando Yoffe—Chispa
Rafael Paullier—Jacinta
Daniel Freyre—Masoller

2 **Argentina** 19.00

Federico Castaing—Notre Dame
Oswaldo Ornia—Jocoso
Alicia Estatjio—Best Seller
Estebán Brucco—Fra Angelico

3 **Chile** 26.00

Alicia Subercaseaux—Patriota
Estebán Halcartegaray—Orondo
Pablo Drapela—Canelo
Pablo Caram—Antorcha

4 Brazil, 36.00.

Individual Championship
(Details of scores not available.)

1 Claudia Itajahy (Bra)—Mar Sol
2 Alicia Estatjio (Arg)—Best Seller
3 Daniel Freyre (Uru)—Masoller

1978 Buenos Aires (Argentina)

Team Championship

	Faults Round One	Round Two
1 **Brazil** 47.75		
A. J. Azambuja—Black Fire	4.50	12.00
K. Naday—Passepartout	4.00	18.75
André Johanpeter—Imperatriz	0.50	8.00
Claudia Itajahy—Mar Sol	(5.75)	NP
2 **Argentina** 48.00		
M. Mulhall—Faunico	(16.50)	(27.00)
Hector Alvaro—Tacuba	8.00	8.00
L. Aldazabal—Premier	11.00	8.00
J. Berretta—Año Nuevo	5.00	8.00

3 **Chile** 53.75

M. Lagos Peric—Avantar	(19.50)	E
Francisco Navellán—Yacara	12.00	4.00
E. Minassian—Sierpe	12.00	12.00
Pablo Drapela—Canelo	5.75	8.00

Individual Championship
(Details of scores not available.)

1 J. Berretta (Arg)—Año Nuevo
2 Pablo Drapela (Chi)—Canelo
3 Claudia Itajahy (Bra)—Mar Sol

1979 Rio de Janeiro (Brazil)

Team Championship

	Faults		
	Round One	Round Two	Jump-off
1 **Argentina** 0.00, 0.00 in jump-off			
Hugo Dircie—Porron	(4.00)	(4.00)	0.00
Guido Sztyrle—Acheral	0.00	0.00	0.00
Oswaldo Ornia—Don Joaquin	0.00	0.00	(8.00)
Hector Alvaro—Tacuba	0.00	0.00	0.00
2 **Brazil** 0.00, 4.00 in jump-off			
André Johanpeter—Barbara	0.00	0.00	0.00
Paula Padilha—Don Luiz	(8.00)	0.00	0.00
Marcelo Blessmann—Genesis	0.00	(4.00)	4.00
Claudia Itajahy—Mar Sol	0.00	0.00	(4.00)
3 **Venezuela** 7.00			
Pablo Barrios—Don Gustavo	(9.75)	4.00	
Pablo Ceballos—Bronze Arrow	0.00	(5.50)	
Carlos Larrazabal—Que Nota	0.00	0.00	
Carolina Godoy—Gran Capitan	0.00	3.00	

4 Chile, 17.00; 5 Uruguay, 32.75.

Number of teams: 5

Individual Championship

	Faults
1 Carolina Godoy (Ven)—Gran Capitan	0.00/4.00
2 Pablo Drapela (Chi)—Canelo	0.00/4.50
3 Hugo Dircie (Arg)—Porron	4.00/4.00

1980 Caracas (Venezuela)

Team Championship

	Faults	
	Round One	Round Two
1 **Mexico** 15.00		
Antonio Maurer—Cantabrio	0.00	(8.00)
Alejandro Orozco—Casilda	4.00	4.00
Alejandro Farias—Paradise	(11.75)	4.00
Manuel Locken—Ambassador	3.00	0.00

2 **Venezuela** 25.25

Gerardo Baricelli—Gracioso	(7.00)	4.00
Carlos Larrazabal—Steemery	5.25	(16.75)
Francisco Herrera—Gift Wrapper	4.00	4.00
Pablo Barrios—Yanu	4.00	4.00

3 **Columbia** 32.00, 4.25 in jump-off

			Jump-off
Fernando San Clemente —Abolengo	4.00	4.00	0.00
Gonzalo Guevara—El Otro	(40.25)	4.00	4.00
Rene Lopez—Africa	4.00	12.00	0.25
William Escobar—Kojak	4.00	(15.00)	NP

4 Peru, 32.00, 6.00 in jump-off; 5 Guatemala, 36.00.

Number of teams: 5

Individual Championship

	F./Time
1 Alejandro Orozco (Mex)—Casilda	3.00–0.00
2 Carlos Farje (Per)—Lirio	4.00–0.00–0.00/38.71
3 Hector Quinones (Pur)—Don Fruto	0.00–4.00–8.00/35.60

Number of riders: 32

Number of nations represented: 7

1981 Buenos Aires (Argentina)

Team Championship
(Details of scores not available.)

1 **Brazil**

Luciano Blessman—Leao
Nelson Marcon—Charbon Pionero
Antonio Barros—Complicado
Pedro Mello—San Martin

2 **Argentina**

Alejandro Cash—Clarito
Hector Alvaro—Tacuba
Federico Sztyrle—Acheral
Fabio Fasciolo—Figaredo

3 **Peru**

Natalia Ugarte—Rasputin
Ricardo Canales—El Gitano
Jessica van Ginhoven—Maraton
Carlos Farje—Lirio

Individual Championship
(Details of scores not available.)

1 Alejandro Cash (Arg)—Clarito
2 Paulo Stewart (Bra)—O'Anjo
3 Alfredo Sone (Chi)—Trumac

1982 Mexico City

Team Championship

	Faults Round One	Faults Round Two
1 **Mexico** 16.00		
Ruben Rodriguez—She's a Lady	8.00	0.00
Monica Williams—Beau Geste	4.00	(20.00)
Oscar Gallegos—Raramuri	0.00	4.00
Jaime Guerra—Super Gene	(12.50)	0.00
2 **Argentina** 54.00		
Mario Guiliani—Aspersel	12.00	4.00
Roberto Madcur—Chaibu	13.00	8.00
Deborah Bogo—Studioso	(29.25)	(14.75)
Alejandro Cash—Clarito	16.00	1.00
3 **Brazil** 69.00		
Antonio Severo—Opium Junior	15.50	(50.75)
Antonio Quintella—Sigilo	(24.00)	20.00
Nelson Marcon—Charbon Pionero	16.00	12.75
Paulo Stewart—O'Anjo	0.00	4.75

4 Guatemala, 173.50; 5 USA, 317.00.

Number of teams: 5

Individual Championship

	Faults
1 Alejandro Orozco (Mex)—Casilda	0.00–0.00–0.00
2 Roberto Madcur (Arg)—Chaibu	0.00–0.00–12.00
3 Antonio Quintella (Bra)—Sigilo	0.00–0.00–25.00

Number of riders: 21

Number of nations represented: 5

1983 Rio de Janeiro (Brazil)

Team Championship

	Faults Round One	Faults Round Two
1 **Argentina** 0.00		
Sandra Koppany—Bobby Blue	(4.00)	0.00
Guillermo Valente—Mon Ami	0.00	0.00
Pablo Rolt—Cepera	0.00	0.00
Alejandro Cash—Clarito	0.00	NP
2 **Brazil** 8.00		
Rodrigo Ullmann Lima—Viking	4.00	0.00
Ricardo Guida Fernandes—Fedayn	0.00	(12.00)
Antonio Marcos Barros—Poente	0.00	0.00
Nelson Marcon—Encanto	(12.00)	4.00

Number of teams: 2

Individual Championship

	F./Time
1 Rodrigo Ullmann Lima (Bra)—Viking	0.00–0.00–0.00/41.22
2 Pablo Rolt (Arg)—Cepera	0.00–0.00–0.00/43.86
3 Ricardo Guida Fernandes (Bra) —Fedayn	0.00–4.25

Number of riders: 10

Number of nations represented: 2

1984 Buenos Aires (Argentina)

Team Championship

	Faults Round One	Faults Round Two
1 **Argentina** 4.00		
Daniela Moira Colombo—Immigrante	0.00	0.00
Gabriel Pitrola—Going	0.00	0.00
Guillermo Valente—Mon Ami	(8.00)	4.00
Roberto Madcur—Chaibu	0.00	NP
2 **Brazil** 20.75		
Roberta Sa Mota—Menino do Rio	4.00	4.00
Celso Figueira Melo—Bally Hy	(13.25)	4.75
Dalton Camargo Maia—Cigana	0.00	0.00
Rodrigo Ullmann Lima—Viking	8.00	(8.00)
3 **Peru** 36.00		
Carmen Morelli—Tobruk	4.00	8.00
Sandro Pettinari—Tanque	8.00	4.00
Manuel Aramburu—Mandolino	E	E
Juan José Mostajo—Beau Geste	8.00	4.00

4 Chile, 48.00.

Number of teams: 4

Individual Championship

	Faults
1 Guillermo Valente (Arg)—Mon Ami	0.00–0.00
2 Gabriel Pitrola (Arg)—Going	3.00–0.00
3 Carmen Morelli (Per)—Tobruk	0.00–4.00

Number of riders: 39

Number of nations represented: 9

Huaso, the horse who holds the world high jump record of 2.47 metres, was a Thoroughbred by Henry Lee out of Tamaya, tracing maternally to Desmond, a son of the great racehorse and sire St Simon. Huaso raced without success and was acquired by the Chilean Army show jumping team for £120.

1985 Lima (Peru)

Team Championship

		Faults Round One	Faults Round Two
1	**Venezuela** 12.00		
	Pedro José Rojas—Corralero	(5.50)	(16.75)
	Alfredo Luis Riviere—Goloso	4.00	0.00
	Mireya Godoy—Quilique	4.00	0.00
	Maria Luisa Luxardo—Morena	4.00	0.00
2	**Colombia** 20.00		
	Eduardo Gaytan—Obus	(10.25)	(16.00)
	Francisco Montoya—Merecumbe	4.00	0.00
	Alejandro Montana—Reina de Plata	8.00	0.00
	Juan Carlos Garcia—Pecuario	4.00	4.00
3	**Peru** 24.00		
	Manuel Diego Aramburu—Soar Neck	(8.00)	8.00
	Carmen Morelli—Tobruk	4.00	8.00
	Sandro Pettinari—Tanque	0.00	(8.00)
	Juan José Mostajo—Fuego	0.00	4.00

Number of teams: 3

Individual Championship

		Faults
1	Maria Luisa Luxardo (Ven)—Morena	0.00–4.00
2	Sandro Pettinari (Per)—Tanque	3.50–4.00
3	Francisco Montoya (Col)—Merecumbe	0.00–8.00–4.00

Number of riders: 15

Number of nations represented: 4

1986 Caracas (Venezuela)

Team Championship

		Faults Round One	Faults Round Two
1	**Venezuela** 8.00		
	Andres Sanclaudio—Serrana	0.00	0.00
	Mariana Montenegro—Chico	(4.00)	4.00
	Carlos Riviere—California	0.00	4.00
	Teodoro Gubaira—Salsifi	0.00	R
2	**Colombia** 19.50		
	Juan Garcia—Ambar	4.50	3.00
	Alejandro Montana—Reina de Plata	(8.00)	0.00
	Hernando Carrasco—Kinkivo	4.00	(8.00)
	Fernando Cardenas—Notre Dame	4.00	4.00
3	**Peru** 72.00		
	Manuel Aramburu—Scarneck	8.00	4.00
	Dieter Aranda—Firpo	11.50	12.00
	Sandro Pettinari—Tanque	20.50	16.00

4 Puerto Rico, eliminated.

Number of teams: 4

Individual Championship

		F./Time
1	Alejandro Montana (Col) —Reina de Plata	0.00–0.00
2	Ricardo Delfini (Ecu) —Rayo de Plata	4.00–0.00–8.00/49.02
3	Teodoro Gubaira (Ven)—Salsifi	0.00–4.00–15.75/62.03

Number of riders: 19

Number of nations represented: 5

Medal Tables

Team Championship 1974–1986*

Country	Gold	Silver	Bronze
Brazil	4	3	1
Argentina	3	6	—
Venezuela	2	1	1
Mexico	2	—	—
Chile	1	—	2
Uruguay	1	—	1
Colombia	—	2	1
Peru	—	—	4

*Does not include silver/bronze awards for 1976 (no results available).

Individual Championship 1974–1986*

Country	Gold	Silver	Bronze
Argentina	4	4	2
Brazil	3	3	4
Venezuela	2	—	1
Mexico	2	—	—
Colombia	1	—	1
Chile	—	4	1
Peru	—	2	1
Uruguay	—	1	1
Ecuador	—	1	—
Puerto Rica	—	—	1

*Does not include gold/silver/bronze awards for 1976 (no results available).

Team and Individual Championships 1974–1986*

Country	Gold	Silver	Bronze
Argentina	7	10	2
Brazil	7	6	5
Venezuela	4	1	2
Mexico	4	—	—
Chile	1	4	3
Uruguay	1	1	2
Colombia	1	2	2
Peru	—	2	5
Ecuador	—	1	—
Puerto Rica	—	—	1

*Does not include silver/bronze team awards or gold/silver/bronze individual awards for 1976 (no results available).

Pony European Championships

The first official European Championship for ponies took place in 1978 and the event has been held annually ever since. To the original team championship has been added an individual championship, both events open to riders aged from 12 to 17 years, and to ponies standing not more than 148 cm without shoes or 149 cm with shoes.

1978 Le Touquet (France)

Team Championship

	Faults	
	Round One	Round Two
1 Ireland 0.00		
Tom Costello—Star Trek	0.00	0.00
John Bamber—Misty Moods	0.00	0.00
Taylor Vard—Follyfoot II	0.00	0.00
Alan Irwin—You Can Do It	0.00	0.00
2 Great Britain 0.50		
Sadie Ann Burchmore—Main Line	(4.00)	(4.00)
Carole Yardley—Innerhaddon	0.50	0.00
Jane Sargent—Minnie Mouse	0.00	0.00
Michael Mac—Dunglenn III	0.00	0.00
3 Belgium 14.25		
Fabienne Daigneux—Cochise	(8.50)	2.25
Yves Vilain—Zef du Château	4.00	4.00
Evelyne Blaton—Sun Seeker	0.00	0.00
Dirk Demeersman—Merline	4.00	(8.00)

4 FRG, 21.00; 5 Netherlands, 24.00; 6 France, 44.00; 7 Sweden, 84.00; 8 Switzerland, 89.75.

Number of teams: 8

1979 Lincoln (GB)

Team Championship

	Faults	
	Round One	Round Two
1 Ireland 4.00		
Vina Lyons—Caramel Dessert	4.00	0.00
Colette Lawlor—Fair Game	(13.25)	0.00
Philip Dagg—Beau Brummel	0.00	0.00
Tom Costello—Star Trek	0.00	NP
2 Great Britain 4.25		
Keith Shore—Cogshall Powys	(1.25)	4.00
Helena Dickinson—The Welshman	0.00	0.00
Martyn Gallon—Mr Punch III	0.00	0.00
Mark Heffer—Frère Jacques	0.25	(4.00)

3 FRG 40.00		
Joachim Goffert—Zenobia	E	E
Ralf Niemann—Ole	4.00	8.00
Maren Hottendorf—Ramo	8.00	12.00
Udo Wagner—Festival Time	4.00	4.00

4 France, 47.75; 5 Sweden, 52.00; 6 Netherlands, 55.00; 7 Switzerland, 102.50; 8 Belgium, eliminated.

Number of teams: 8

1980 Groenendaal (Belgium)

Team Championship

	Faults	
	Round One	Round Two
1 Great Britain 4.00		
Keith Shore—Cogshall Powys	0.00	0.00
Amanda Gaskell—Woodnymph III	0.00	0.00
Philip Heffer—Frère Jacques	0.00	4.00
Robert Bevis—Sligo Master	0.00	(12.00)
2 Ireland 8.00		
Vina Lyons—Caramel Dessert	0.00	4.00
Dermot Costello—Star Trek	0.00	0.00
Roisin Allen—Misty Moods	(4.00)	4.00
Edward Doyle—Ashfield Bobby	0.00	(4.00)
3 France 31.50		
Eileen Travers—Captain Brown	4.00	11.00
Sylvie Parot—Warpaint	4.00	8.50
Gregoire Leman—Griby	4.00	(12.00)
Philippe Barbot—Hibis du Bec	(4.00)	0.00

4 Belgium, 32.00; 5 Sweden, 34.00; 6 Switzerland, 55.75; 7 FRG, 58.75; 8 Netherlands, 89.00; 9 Denmark, retired.

Number of teams: 9

1981 Millstreet (Ireland)

Team Championship

	Faults	
	Round One	Round Two
1 Great Britain 0.00		
Amanda Gaskell—Woodnymph III	0.00	0.00
James Edgson—Luptons Duke	0.00	0.00
Robert Bevis—Innerhaddon	0.00	0.00
Philip Heffer—Frère Jacques	0.00	0.00

2 Sweden 12.00

Agneta Dahlgren—Shona	(8.00)	4.00
Charlotte Emanuelsson—Kings Mistress	0.00	(4.00)
Patrick Svensson—Serpico	0.00	0.00
Svante Johansson—Jam Delilah	8.00	0.00

3 France 15.00

François Belvisi—Brown Beauty	(8.00)	(8.00)
Sylvie Parot—Warpaint	0.00	4.00
Isabelle Rabouan—Joli Coco	0.00	4.00
Philippe Barbot—Hibis du Bec	3.00	4.00

4 FRG, 16.00; 5 Ireland, 23.00; 6 Belgium, 40.00;
7 Netherlands, 44.00.

Number of teams: 7

1982 Copenhagen (Denmark)

Team Championship

	Faults		
	Round One	Round Two	Jump-off F./Time
1 Great Britain 8.00, 0.00 in 136.60 seconds in jump-off			
Marnie Wilson—Welshman	0.00	4.00	0.00/48.00
Clare Inglefield —Luggershall Sable	0.00	(8.00)	0.00/46.40
Beverley Rees—Hillside Lad	(4.00)	4.00	(0.00/48.40)
Matthew Lanni —Holmsley Lady	0.00	0.00	0.00/42.20
2 Sweden 8.00, 0.00 in 141.50 seconds in jump-off			
Anna Emanuelsson —Kings Mistress	0.00	0.00	0.00/51.10
Patrick Svensson—Serpico	0.00	4.00	0.00/44.80
Jessica Johansson —Highland Fling	0.00	(4.00)	0.00/45.60
Lotta Emanuelsson —Blue Double	(4.00)	4.00	(4.00/43.00)
3 France 8.00, 4.00 in jump-off			
Isabelle Rabouan—Joli Coco	0.00	4.00	(8.00/47.40)
Alexandra Lederman —Ira de Garenne	0.00	(4.00)	0.00/49.60
Marie-Christine Barbot —Hibis du Bec	4.00	0.00	0.00/48.40
Sylvie Parot—Warpaint	(8.00)	0.00	4.00/50.20

4 Belgium, 8.00, 12.00 in jump-off; 5 FRG, 12.00;
6 Ireland, 20.00; 7 Netherlands, 32.00; 8 Denmark, 37.75.

Number of teams: 8

Individual Championship

	F./Time
1 Beverley Rees (GB)—Hillside Lad	0.00–4.00/42.50
2 Clare Inglefield (GB)—Luggershall Sable	0.00–4.00/44.40
3 Alison Gemmel (GB)—Sovereign Seeker	0.00–8.00/40.70

Number of riders: 41

Number of nations represented: 9

1983 Vetlanda (Sweden)

Team Championship

(Complete details of scores not available.)

	Faults	
	Round One	Round Two
1 Great Britain 0.00		
Peter Murphy—Mr Punch	0.00	0.00
Louise Targett—Northfield Fashion	0.00	0.00
Vicky Bell—Spooky III	0.00	0.00
Camille Crow—Woodnymph III	0.00	0.00

2 Ireland 12.00, 4.00 in jump-off

Eddie Dermody—Borris High Ace
Joanne Prentice—Folyfoot II
Colin Turkington—Spur of the Moment
Beverley Anne Irwin—You Can Do It

3 Netherlands 12.00, 14.00 in jump-off
(Team consisted of four of the following)

Gerard Schulter—Blitslicht
Trudy Bom—Dynamite
Jenny Zoer—Promises
Nicolle van der Brook—Purdey
Uriel Taaken—Quicksilver

4 FRG, 16.00; 5 Sweden, 20.00; 6 Denmark, 27.00;
7 France, 28.00; 8 Belgium, 32.00; 9 Italy, 64.00.

Number of teams: 9

Individual Championship

	F./Time
1 Jessica Johansson (Swe) —Highland Fling	0.00–0.00
2 Vicky Bell (GB)—Spooky III	0.00–4.00–0.00/41.90
3 Louise Targett (GB) —Northfield Fashion	0.00–4.00–0.00/45.84

Number of riders: 50

Number of nations represented: 11

1984 Soder (FRG)

Team Championship

	Faults	
	Round One	Round Two
1 Ireland 8.00		
Peter Smith—Mr Boogie	0.00	0.00
Sinead Slattery—Dunmacreena Davy	(31.25)	(12.00)
Marcus Swail—Houdini	0.00	0.00
Marion Hughes—Bright Ruby	4.00	4.00
2 Great Britain 8.25		
Emma Gascoine—Silver King X	4.00	4.00
Camille Crow—Woodnymph III	0.25	0.00
Emma Michael—Dancing Springs	(4.00)	(4.00)
Peter Murphy—Foxlynch Little John	0.00	0.00 ▶

Hans Günter Winkler

On 13 July, 1986, a few days before his 60th birthday, Hans Günter Winkler entered an international arena for the last time, not to compete but for a presentation to mark his retirement. The scene was the famous showground at Aachen, the occasion the closing ceremony of the World Championships.

As Winkler took his final lap of honour round the vast arena he was given an impromptu 'Aachen farewell', normally reserved for the final parade of nations. Members of the huge crowd—over 45 000 strong that day—rose to their feet and waved white handkerchiefs in time to the music as a tribute to one of the greatest horsemen the sport has seen.

Winkler's extraordinarily successful career, spanning more than 30 years, can be attributed to his consummate all-round horsemanship, and particularly to his sound knowledge of dressage, that essential training of the horse on the flat which is at the basis of all successful jumping work. Germany's training principles, based on the teachings of the old cavalry schools (which in turn inherited the traditions of the classical riding masters of previous centuries) have enabled jumping riders to achieve tremendous success in international competitions. Among many glittering achievements, Winkler's record of five Olympic gold medals remains unparalleled.

Hans Günter Winkler was born on 24 July, 1926 in Wuppertal-Barmen. His father was a professional riding instructor and inevitably the young Winkler came into contact with horses at

One of the great partnerships of all time: Winkler and Halla, seen here during their winning clear round in the 1955 Hamburg Derby (Popperfoto)

an early age. However, it was not his father's intention to push his son towards a life with horses and Winkler has, in fact, pursued a successful career as a businessman. But horses were in his blood and the writing was already on the wall when, in the early thirties, the young boy would watch with fascination the great riders of the renowned Hannover Cavalry School competing in Dortmund, where Winkler spent most of his schooldays. Above all he admired the elegant horsemanship of Hans-Heinrich 'Micky' Brinckmann, who became his idol. When, at the age of six, Winkler was given his first pony, it was inevitable that he should be christened Micky.

Riding continued to be a part of Winkler's life until the war broke out. But, his father having been killed during the last few weeks of hostilities, it seemed unlikely that a career with horses would be conceivable in the difficult years that followed. Then out of the blue came the opportunity to work for Herr Eckhardt, an old friend of his father's and formerly head of the royal stables of the Landgräfin of Hesse at Kronberg. It was during the two years he spent at Kronberg, doing all kinds of administrative work, that Winkler was able to learn the finer points of dressage from Herr Eckhardt.

In 1948 came the opportunity to combine work in the textile business in Frankfurt with training horses and competing in jumping events. Hans Günter Winkler's competitive debut took place on 1 and 2 May that year at a show in Nördlingen, when he finished sixth in a novice class on a horse called Falkner. He won his first competition on 10 October with the same horse. In the following two seasons his tally of victories began to grow, and he attracted the notice of the German Olympic selectors who invited him to go to Warendorf, the headquarters of equestrian sport in West Germany, where riders selected to represent their country are given top level training. His international career was about to take off. His destiny was sealed when into his stable in the spring of 1951 there came a six-year-old mare owned by Gustav Vierling of Darmstadt. Her name was Halla and she became one of the best jumpers ever to look through a bridle.

Winkler made his international debut in Bilbao in 1952 where, with Sturmwind, he competed in his first Nations Cup. Twenty-two years later, at Laxenburg in Austria, he clocked up his century, and by the time he retired he had made 108 appearances with his country's team, 37 of them winning ones. Of those Halla accounted for 8, Fahnenjunker 2, Laila 1, Romanus 5, Feuerdorn 3, Cornelia 1 and Torphy 17.

Winkler's first major international championship win came in 1954 when, in the second running of the World Championships, he defeated the reigning champion, 'Paco' Goyoaga, in Madrid. Winkler successfully defended his title in Aachen the following year and then, in 1956, achieved what he still considers to be the highlight of his career: the individual gold medal at the Stockholm Olympics, plus his first team gold medal. An injury sustained during the Olympic event prevented him from defending his World title that year, but in 1957 he won the first Men's European Championship, an event in which he was subsequently to pick up a silver medal (1962) and three bronzes (1958, 1961 and 1969). At the Rome Olympics in 1960 he won his second team gold, again with Halla, and finished fifth individually. Four years later in Tokyo it was gold again, this time with Fidelitas. In 1968 at Mexico the team could manage only the bronze, but Winkler was once more up at the sharp end of things in the individual, finishing fifth on Enigk. At Munich in 1972, riding Frau Hagelstein's Torphy, he won his fifth gold, and in 1976 at Montreal this great Nations Cup horse carried him to a team silver.

Aside from the incomparable Halla, Winkler rates his best rides as his own Cornelia and Enigk, and four horses whom he rode for other owners: Terminus; the ill-fated Jägermeister, whose career was tragically cut short by injury; Romanus, a horse with great ability but a marked aversion to water jumps, and the ever-reliable Torphy. With this formidable array of talent, plus many other good, if not quite top-class horses, Winkler won countless Grand Prix and major international competitions throughout the world.

Although he has finally hung up his international boots, Winkler is not exactly leading a life of leisure. He still rides daily and his non-horsey interests include tennis, skiing, swimming and hunting, as well as reading and history. He continues to be professionally involved with jumping, since he is now the training director of the German Olympic committee, a job for which it would be difficult to find anyone more highly qualified.

3 Sweden 24.75

Lotta Bornudd—Vibys Dennieson	(13.25)	8.75
Linda Permbeck—Brunette	4.00	(12.00)
Jessica Johansson—Highland Fling	8.00	0.00
Robert Eskilsson—Super Tramp	4.00	0.00

4 FRG, 26.00; 5 France, 43.00; 6 Netherlands, 59.50; 7 Denmark, 90.25; 8 Italy, 111.75; 9 Belgium, eliminated.

Number of teams: 9

Individual Championship

	F./Time
1 Peter Murphy (GB)	
—Foxlynch Little John	0.00–0.00/35.81
2 Bernard Mathy (Bel)—Gobi Dust	0.00–12.00/37.60
3 Emma Gascoine (GB)—Silver King X	0.00–E

1985 Rotterdam (NL)

Team Championship

	Faults	
	Round One	Round Two
1 Great Britain 0.00		
Camille Crow—Woodnymph III	0.00	0.00
Vicki Letherbarrow—Prince Pepe	0.00	(4.00)
John Renwick—Days Topic	0.00	0.00
Peter Murphy—Foxlynch Little John	0.00	0.00
2 France 11.00		
Isabelle Rabouan—Joli Coco	(4.00)	3.00
François Leguen—Brown Beauty	0.00	(16.00)
Eric Scalabre—Irish of Sligo	0.00	8.00
Eugenie Legrand—Hibis du Bec	0.00	0.00
3 Sweden 20.00		
Anna Heed—Fandango	(4.00)	4.00
Lotta Bornudd—Another Flight	0.00	4.00
Helena Lundqvist		
—Moingegardens Napoleon	4.00	8.00
Robert Eskilsson—Super Tramp	0.00	NP

=4 Ireland, Netherlands, 28.00; 6 Denmark, 32.00; 7 FRG, 38.00; 8 Belgium, 43.00; 9 Switzerland, eliminated; 10 Norway, retired.

Number of teams: 10

Individual Championship

	F./Time
1 Vicki Letherbarrow (GB)	
—Prince Pepi	0.00–0.00–0.00/49.84
2 Peter Murphy (GB)	
—Foxlynch Little John	0.00–0.00–4.00/37.84
3 Robert Eskilsson (Swe)	
—Super Tramp	0.00–0.00–4.00/43.57

Number of riders: 50

Number of nations represented: 11

1986 San Remo (Italy)

Team Championship

	Faults	
	Round One	Round Two
1 Sweden 4.00		
Robert Eskilsson—Super Tramp	0.00	0.00
Helena Lundqvist		
—Moingegardens Napoleon	4.00	(3.00)
Linda Andersson—Glendale Ambassador	0.00	0.00
Diana Muskantor—Super Trouper	(22.00)	0.00
2 Great Britain 16.00		
Angela Bell—Golden Autumn	4.00	0.00
Alexandra Newsham—Rogerio	0.00	4.00
Vicki Letherbarrow—Prince Pepi	(4.00)	4.00
Emma Lynch—Shipton Eblana	4.00	(8.00)
3 Ireland 20.00		
Louise Daly—Hawk Eye	4.00	4.00
Philip Gaw—Spur of the Moment	0.00	8.00
Gillian Connors—Feather Duster	(4.00)	4.00
Conor Swail—Hampton Bridge	0.00	(8.00)

4 Belgium, 20.00; 5 FRG, 24.00; 6 Italy, 32.00; 7 France, 39.00; 8 Netherlands, 44.00; 9 Denmark, 52.75; 10 Switzerland, retired.

Number of teams: 10

Individual Championship

	F./Time
1 Simone Meulman (NL)	
—Daisy Brown	0.00–0.00–4.00/35.29
2 Robert Eskilsson (Swe)	
—Super Tramp	0.00–0.00–8.00/39.30
3 Diana Muskantor (Swe)	
—Super Trouper	0.00–4.00–0.00/34.41

Number of riders: 39

Number of nations represented: 10

Medal Tables

Teams, 1978–86

Country	Gold	Silver	Bronze
Great Britain	5	4	—
Ireland	3	2	1
Sweden	1	2	2
France	—	1	3
Belgium	—	—	1
FRG	—	—	1
Netherlands	—	—	1

Individual, 1982–86

Country	Gold	Silver	Bronze
Great Britain	3	3	3
Sweden	1	1	2
Netherlands	1	—	—
Belgium	—	1	—

Combined Teams, Individual 1978–86

Country	Gold	Silver	Bronze
Great Britain	8	7	3
Ireland	3	2	1
Sweden	2	3	4
Netherlands	1	—	1
France	—	1	3
Belgium	—	1	1
FRG	—	—	1

Grand Prix

A Grand Prix is a major competition for individual competitors which may be conducted in one of two ways: over one round with one or two jump-offs, the first or second being against the clock; over two rounds (identical or different courses may be used) with one jump-off against the clock.

Included in this section is a selection of some of the most prestigious Grand Prix, a number of them dating from the very earliest days of show jumping; competitions such as the King George V Gold Cup which, although they do not have the title Grand Prix, were the equivalent of such competitions before the formulation of FEI rules, and which still carry great prestige; and one or two competitions which in recent years have been merged with preliminary rounds for the World Cup and, although they may have been retitled, are in effect a continuation of old-established Grand Prix.

Aachen
(Der Grosse Preis von Aachen)

1925 Willy Spillner (Ger)—Baron III
1926 Carl Friedrich von Langen (Ger)
    —Goliath
1927 R. Lotz (Ger)—Olnad
1928 Ernest Hallberg (Swe)—Loke
1929 Ernest Hallberg (Swe)—Mephisto
1930 Mario Lombardo di Cumia (Ita)
    —Rocabruna
1931 = Fernando Filipponi (Ita)—Nasello
    Giulio Borsarelli (Ita)—Crispa
    Tommaso Lequio di Assaba (Ita)
    —Norgil
1932 Conte Alessandro
    Bettoni-Cazzago (Ita)
    —Nereide
1933 Heinz Brandt (Ger)—Coralle
1934 Axel Holst (Ger)—Bianka
1935 Tomo Tudoran (Rum)
    —Rayon de Soleil
1936 Henri Rang (Rum)—Delfis
1937 Hans-Heinrich Brinckmann (Ger)
    —Erle
1938 Paul Mondron (Bel)—Ibrahim
1939 Hans-Heinrich Brinckmann (Ger)
    —Baron IV
1947 Karl Prince zu Salm (FRG)
    —Garant
1948 Franklin F. Wing (USA)—Totilla
1949 Erich Hafemann (FRG)—Erle II
1950 Erich Hafemann (FRG)—Erle II
1951 Fritz Thiedemann (FRG)
    —Original
1952 Piero d'Inzeo (Ita)—Uruguay
1953 Fritz Thiedemann (FRG)—Aar
1954 Hans Günter Winkler (FRG)
    —Orient
1955 Fritz Thiedemann (FRG)—Meteor
1956 Francisco Goyoaga (Spa)
    —Fahnenkönig
1957 Hans Günter Winkler (FRG)
    —Halla
1958 Magnus von Buchwaldt (FRG)
    —Flugwind
1959 Piero d'Inzeo (Ita)—The Rock

1960 George Morris (USA)—Night Owl
1961 Piero d'Inzeo (Ita)—The Rock
1962 Alwin Schockemöhle (FRG)
    —Freiherr
1963 Raimondo d'Inzeo (Ita)—Posillipo
1964 Nelson Pessoa (Bra)
    —Gran Geste
1965 = Hugo Arrambide (Arg)—Chimbote
    Piero d'Inzeo (Ita)—Ballyblack
1966 Neal Shapiro (USA)
    —Jack or Better
1967 Andrew Fielder (GB)—Vibart

1968 = Alwin Schockemöhle (FRG)
    —Donald Rex
    Hendrik Snoek (FRG)—Dorina
1969 = Alwin Schockemöhle (FRG)
    —Wimpel
    Hans Günter Winkler (FRG)
    —Enigk
1970 Hermann Schridde (FRG)
    —Heureka
1971 = Neal Shapiro (USA)—Sloopy
    Marcel Rozier (FRA)
    —Sans-Souci

Alwin Schockemöhle, one of the most prolific Grand Prix winners of all time, successful in both the Grosse Preis von Aachen and the Aachen Championship. Here he is riding his 1976 Olympic gold medal horse Warwick Rex. (Findlay Davidson)

1972 Nelson Pessoa (Bra)—Nagir
1973 Paul Weier (Switz)—Fink
1974 Paul Schockemöhle (FRG)
      —Talisman
1975 Graham Fletcher (GB)
      —Buttevant Boy
1976 Gerd Wiltfang (FRG)—Davos
1977 Harvey Smith (GB)—Graffiti
1978 Eddie Macken (Ire)—Boomerang
1979 Paul Schockemöhle (FRG)
      —El Paso
1980 Liz Edgar (GB)—Forever
1981 Malcolm Pyrah (GB)
      —Towerlands Anglezarke
1982 Nick Skelton (GB)
      —Everest If Ever
1983 Willi Melliger (Switz)—Van Gogh
1984 Paul Schockemöhle (FRG)
      —Deister
1985 Michael Rüping (FRG)
      —Silbersee

Aachen
(Championship)

1957 Hans Günter Winkler (FRG)
      —Halla
1958 Fritz Thiedemann (FRG)—Meteor
1959 William Steinkraus (USA)
      —Riviera Wonder
1960 Alwin Schockemöhle (FRG)
      —Bachus
1961 David Broome (GB)—Sunsalve
1962 Nelson Pessoa (Bra)
      —Gran Geste
1963 Hermann Schridde (FRG)—Ilona
1964 Nelson Pessoa (Bra)
      —Gran Geste
1965 Hermann Schridde (FRG)
      —Dozent
1966 Graziano Mancinelli (Ita)
      —Turvey
1967 Pierre Jonquères d'Oriola (Fra)
      —Pomone B
1968 Piero d'Inzeo (Ita)—Fidux
1969 Alwin Schockemöhle (FRG)
      —Donald Rex
1970 Nelson Pessoa (Bra)—Pass Op
1971 Pierre Jonquères d'Oriola (Fra)
      —Moët et Chandon
1972 Gerd Wiltfang (FRG)—Askan
1973 Alwin Schockemöhle (FRG)
      —Rex the Robber
1974 Graham Fletcher (GB)
      —Buttevant Boy
1975 Alwin Schockemöhle (FRG)
      —Warwick
1976 Hartwig Steenken (FRG)
      —Gladstone
1977 Gerd Meier (NL)—Casimir
1978 Eddie Macken (Ire)—Boomerang
1979 Walter Gabathuler (Switz)
      —Harley
1980 Ulrich Meyer zu Bexten (FRG)
      —Magister
1981 Gerd Wiltfang (FRG)—Goldika
1982 Ulrich Meyer zu Bexten (FRG)
      —Magister
1983 Paul Schockemöhle (FRG)
      —Deister
1984 Michael Whitaker (GB)
      —Overton Amanda
1985 Franke Sloothaak (FRG)—Walido

American Gold Cup

1970 Conrad Homfeld (USA)—Act I
1971 Steve Stephens (USA)—Houdini
1972 Rodney Jenkins (USA)—Balbuco
1973 Rodney Jenkins (USA)—Idle Dice
1974 Rodney Jenkins (USA)—Idle Dice
1975 Rodney Jenkins (USA)—Idle Dice
1976 Melanie Smith (USA)—Radnor
1977 Michael Matz (USA)—Grande
1978 Michael Matz (USA)—Jet Run
1979 Michael Matz (USA)—Jet Run
1980 Buddy Brown (USA)—Felton
1981 Melanie Smith (USA)—Calypso
1982 Melanie Smith (USA)—Calypso
1983 Leslie Burr (USA)—Albany
1984 Conrad Homfeld (USA)
      —Coastline
1985 Rodney Jenkins (USA)
      —The Natural
1986 Barney Ward (USA)—Sedac

American Invitational,
Tampa

1973 Rodney Jenkins (USA)—Idle Dice
1974 Michele McEvoy (USA)
      —Sundancer
1975 Michele McEvoy (USA)
      —Sundancer
1976 Robert Ridland (USA)
      —South Side
1977 Terry Rudd (USA)—Mr Demeanor
1978 Norman Dello Joio (USA)
      —Allegro
1979 Rodney Jenkins (USA)
      —Third Man
1980 Bernie Traurig (USA)
      —Eaden Vale
1981 Buddy Brown (USA)—Felton
1982 Melanie Smith (USA)—Calypso
1983 Katie Monahan (USA)—Noren
1984 Leslie Burr (USA)—Albany
1985 Katie Monahan (USA)
      —The Governor
1986 Tim Grubb (GB)—Linky

Amsterdam

1933 Carlo Kechler (Ita)—Coclita
1934 Yves van Strydonck (Bel)
      —Ramona
1935 Heinz Brandt (Ger)—Baron IV
1936 Jean des Roches de Chassey
      (Fra)—Batailleuse
1937 George Heffernan (Ire)
      —Killmallock
1938 Hans-Heinrich Brinckmann (Ger)
      —Oberst II
1939 Jed O'Dwyer (Ire)
      —Limerick Lace
1958 Harry Wouters van den
      Oudenweijer (NL)—Leutnant
1959 Max Fresson (Fra)
      —Grand Veneur
1960 Hans Günter Winkler (FRG)
      —Atoll
1961 Piero d'Inzeo (Ita)—Sunbeam
1962 Alain Navet (Fra)—Luma
1963 Hans Günter Winkler (FRG)
      —Romanus

1964 Harvey Smith (GB)—Harvester
1965 Alwin Schockemöhle (FRG)
      —Exakt
1966 Alwin Schockemöhle (FRG)
      —Athlet
1967 Gerd Wiltfang (FRG)—Athlet
1968 Raimondo d'Inzeo (Ita)
      —Bellevue
1969 Nelson Pessoa (Bra)—Nagir
1970 Nelson Pessoa (Bra)—Nagir
1971 Alwin Schockemöhle (FRG)
      —Rex the Robber
1972 Alwin Schockemöhle (FRG)
      Rex the Robber
1973 Hartwig Steenken (FRG)
      —Simona
1974 Hartwig Steenken (FRG)—Erle
1975 Malcolm Pyrah (GB)
      —Severn Valley
1976 Sönke Sönksen (FRG)—Kwept
1977 Christian Huysegoms (Bel)
      —Katapulte
1978 Hugo Simon (Aut)—Gladstone
1979 David Broome (GB)—Sportsman
1980 Franke Sloothaak (FRG)
      —Argonaut
1981 Edgar-Henri Cuepper (Bel)
      —Cyrano
1982 Rob Ehrens (NL)—Surprice
1983 David Broome (GB)—Last Resort
1984 Willi Melliger (Switz)
      —Beethoven
1985 Thomas Fuchs (Switz)—El Lute
1986 Wiljan Laarakkers (NL)
      —Up to Date

Antwerp

1978 Fritz Ligges (FRG)—Goya
1979 Edgar-Henri Cuepper (Bel)
      —Le Champion
1980 Hugo Simon (Aut)—Answer
1981 Gilles Bertran de Balanda (Fra)
      —Galoubet Malesan
1982 Malcolm Pyrah (GB)
      —Towerlands Anglezarke
1983 Malcolm Pyrah (GB)
      —Towerlands Anglezarke
1984 John Whitaker (GB)
      —Clonee Temple
1985 Nick Skelton (GB)
      —Everest St James
1986 Albert Voorn (NL)
      —Optiebeurs Rasputin
1987 Harvey Smith (GB)
      —Sanyo Shining Example

Barcelona

1962 Piero d'Inzeo—The Rock
1963 Marc Bertran de Balanda (Fra)
      —Sultan
1964 Francisco Goyoaga (Spa)
      —Kif Kif
1965 Marc Bertran de Balanda (Fra)
      —Labrador
1966 Enrique Martinez de Vallejo (Spa)
      —Opium
1967 Alfredo Goyeneche (Spa)
      —On dit
1968 Jorge Llambi (Arg)—Maxim

1969 Gilles Bertran de Balanda (Fra)
—Sigurd
1970 Hans Günter Winkler (FRG)
—Torphy
1971 Alison Dawes (GB)
—The Maverick VII
1972 Luis Alvarez Cervera (Spa)
—Val de Loire
1973 Alfonso Segovia (Spa)—Tic Tac
1974 Hans Günter Winkler (FRG)
—Torphy
1975 Sarah Ward (GB)—Pleeman
1976 Jaime de Aveyro (Spa)
—Kurfurst
1977 Piero d'Inzeo (Ita)
—Easter Light
1978 Daniel Constant (Fra)—Danoso
1979 Luis Alvarez Cervera (Spa)
—Romeo
1980 Alejandro Zambrano (Spa)
—Speed
1981 Luis Alvarez Cervera (Spa)
—Izalco
1982 Pierre Delcourt (Bel)—Sami
1983 Michael Whitaker (GB)
—Overton Amanda
1984 John Whitaker (GB)—Hopscotch
1985 Michel Fervers (FRG)
—Santa Claus
1986 Xavier Leredde (Fra)
—Jalisco B

Berlin

(1930–33 Grand Prix der
Republik; 1934–39 Preis der
nationalsozialistischen
Erhebung; since 1950 Preis
von Deutschland)

1930 Richard Sahla (Ger)
—Schwabensohn
1931 Gerard de Kruijff (NL)—Preten
1932 Heinz Brandt (Ger)—Tora
1933=Irmgard von Opel (Ger)—Nanuk
Siegfried von Sydow (Ger)
—Bajazzo
1934=Harald Momm (Ger)—Baccarat
Axel Holst (Ger)—Egly
1935=Ernst Hasse (Ger)—Immertreu
Goerdt Schlickum (Ger)—Fanfare
Harald Momm (Ger)—Baccarat
1936 Marten von Barnekow (Ger)
—Immertreu
1937 Hans-Heinrich Brinckmann (Ger)
—Alchimist
1938 Gunter Temme (Ger)—Nordland
1939 Hans-Heinrich Brinckmann (Ger)
—Baron IV
1950 Hans Jürgen Huck (FRG)—Toni
1951 Not held
1952 Wilhelm von Cramm (FRG)
—Alstergold
1953 Magnus von Buchwaldt (FRG)
—Jaspis
1954 Günther Rodenberg (FRG)
—Hanna
1955 Walter Günther (FRG)
—Goldanger
1956 Francisco Goyoaga (Spa)
—Fahnenkönig
1957 Bernard de Fombelle (Fra)
—Ukase

1958 Francisco Goyoaga (Spa)
—Fahnenkönig
1959 Magnus von Buchwaldt (FRG)
—Flugwind
1960 Fritz Thiedemann (FRG)—Meteor
1961 Hermann Schridde (FRG)
—Flagrant
1962 Hermann Schridde (FRG)
—Fugosa
1963 Alwin Schockemöhle (FRG)
—Freiherr
1964 Kurt Jarasinski (FRG)—Torro
1965 Kurt Jarasinski (FRG)—Torro
1966 Hermann Schridde (FRG)
—Dozent
1967 Graziano Mancinelli (Ita)
—Turvey
1968 Graziano Mancinelli (Ita)
—Water Surfer
1969 Alwin Schockemöhle (Ita)
—Donald Rex
1970 Hartwig Steenken (FRG)
—Simona
1971 Hartwig Steenken (FRG)
—Fairness
1972 Gustav Bauer (FRG)—Penny
1973 Jean-Michel Gaud (Fra)
—Tango C
1974 Harvey Smith* (GB)—Volvo
1974 Hans Günter Winkler** (FRG)
—Torphy
1975 Hendrik Snoek (FRG)—Rasputin
1976 Nelson Pessoa (Bra)—Oak Burn
1977 Johan Heins (NL)—Seven Valleys
1978 Paul Schockemöhle (FRG)
—El Paso
1979 Henk Nooren (NL)—Pluco
1980 Thomas Fuchs (Switz)
—Tullis Lass
1981 Hugo Simon (Aut)—Gladstone
1982 Norbert Koof (FRG)—Fire
1983 David Broome (GB)—Last Resort
1984 Malcolm Pyrah (GB)
—Towerlands Anglezarke
1985 Hugo Simon (Aut)—The Freak
1986 Stanny van Paesschen (Bel)
—Intermezzo

Bratislava

1977 Jiri Pechacek (Czech)—Dany
1978 Jiri Pechacek (Czech)—Amor
1979 Paul Weier (Switz)—Pen Duick
1981 Jan Kowalczyk (Pol)—Artemor
1982 Julius Schulze-Hesselmann
(FRG)—Sir
1983 Gerhard Etter (Switz)—Parkgate
1984 Paul Crago (GB)—Autumn Folly
1985 Richard Funder (Aut)
—Prof. Bernardi
1986 André Heller (FRG)—Aviata

Bordeaux

1974 M. Tison (Fra)
—Amor de Courtieux
1975 Marc Roguet (Fra)
—Belle de Mars

*Spring
**Autumn

1976 Tony Newbery (GB)—Warwick
1977 Alfonso Segovia (Spa)
—Agamenon
1978 Christian Huysegoms (Bel)
—Katapulte
1979 David Broome (GB)
—Queensway Big Q
1980 Hervé Godignon (Fra)—Gitan
1981 Gerd Wiltfang (FRG)—Goldika
1982 Gerry Mullins (Ire)—Rockbarton
1983 Thomas Frühmann (Aut)
—Arizona
1984 John Whitaker (GB)
—Clonee Temple
1985 John Whitaker (GB)—Next Milton
1986 Pierre Durand (Fra)
—Jappeloup de Luze

Brussels

(Since 1983 World Cup Qualifier)

1906 Alfred Loewenstein (Bel)
—Conquérant
1907 Paul van der Velde (Bel)
1908=van Hoboken (NL)—Billy Boy
D. de la Chevalerie (Bel)
—Timber Topper
1909=Jean-Marie Brodin (Fra)—Roxane
H. Mottet (Bel)—Billy Boy
Henry Leclerc (Fra)—Lady Belle
Paul Fort (Fra)—Mascarille
1910 Alfred Loewenstein (Bel)—Pouff
1911=Henry Leclerc (Fra)—Psyché
Alfred Loewenstein (Bel)
—Marron
Roger Driard—All Right
Léon Ripet (Bel)—Miss Kitty
M. Morel—Zwanzinette
H. Mottet (Bel)—Lord Steady
1912=H. Mottet (Bel)—Biscuit
Arthur Philippot (Bel)—Petit Ami
Edouard Bary (Bel)—Yproise
1913=Henry Leclerc (Fra)—Psyché
René Ricard (Fra)—Double R
1914=Henry Leclerc (Fra)—Dan Leno
Capt d'Auzac de Lamartinie (Fra)
—Djali
1921=Henry de Royer (Fra)
—The Doctor
Auguste de Laissardière (Fra)
—Dignité
1922 Pierre Clavé (Fra)—Le Trouvère
1923 M. Jeannerod (Fra)—Isba
1924 M. Desmazières (Fra)—Rajah
1925 M. Desmazières (Fra)—Rajah
1926 M. Rolland (Fra)—Tabarin
1927 Hubert Gibault (Fra)—Mandarin
1928 Christian de Castries (Fra)
—Galatée
1929 J. Baudoin de Brabandère (Bel)
—Miss America
1930 Joseph Laame (Bel)—Caprice
1931 Francesco Formigli (Ita)
—Suello
1932 Christian de Castries (Fra)
—Tenace
1933 Pierre Clavé (Fra)—
—Robespierre
1935 Maurice Gudin de Vallerin (Fra)
Apollon
1936 Henri van Schaik (NL)
—Santa Bell

1937 Jean Gonze (Bel)—Ali Baba
1938 Pierre Clavé (Fra)—Espiatz
1939 Amador de Busnel (Fra)
       —Honduras
1949 Pat Smythe (GB)—Nobbler
1951 Chevalier Jean d'Orgeix (Fra)
       —Arlequin
1952 Pat Smythe (GB)—Tosca
1953 Georges Calmon (Fra)
       —Camelia/Virtuoso
1954 Georges Poffé (Bel)—Hicamboy
1956 Raimondo d'Inzeo (Ita)—Merano
1957 Georges Poffé (Bel)—Hicamboy
1958 Hans Günter Winkler (FRG)
       —Halla
1959 Georges Calmon (Fra)
       —Gerboise
1960 Hans Günter Winkler (FRG)
       —Halla
1961 Nelson Pessoa (Bra)
       —Gran Geste
1962 Tommy Wade (Ire)—Dundrum
1963 Hans Günter Winkler (FRG)
       —Romanus
1964 Pierre Jonquères d'Oriola (Fra)
       —Labrador
1965 Peter Schmitz (FRG)—Amsella
1966 Alain Navet (Fra)—Luma
1967 Alwin Schockemöhle (FRG)
       —Wimpel
1968 Alwin Schockemöhle (FRG)
       —Donald Rex
1969 Raimondo d'Inzeo (Ita)
       —Bellevue
1970 Nelson Pessoa (Bra)—Nagir
1971 Raimondo d'Inzeo (Ita)
       —Fiorello
1972 Hartwig Steenken (FRG)
       —Simona
1973 Nelson Pessoa (Bra)—Ali Baba
1974 Raimondo d'Inzeo (Ita)
       —Bellevue
1975 Debbie Johnsey (GB)—Moxy
1976 David Broome (GB)—Philco
1977 Eddie Macken (Ire)—Boomerang
1978 Paul Schockemöhle (FRG)
       —El Paso
1979 David Broome (GB)
       —Queensway Big Q
1980 Paul Schockemöhle (FRG)
       —Deister
1981 Fillipo Moyersoen (Ita)—Adam
1982 John Whitaker (GB)—Ryan's Son
1983 Malcolm Pyrah (GB)
       —Towerlands Anglezarke
1984 Philippe Rozier (Fra)—Jiva
1985 Peter Charles (GB)—April Sun
1986 Paul Schockemöhle (FRG)
       —Next Deister

Calgary

1976 Michel Vaillancourt (Can)
       —Branch County
1977 John Simpson (Can)—Texas
1978 Caroline Bradley (GB)—Tigre
1979 Eddie Macken (Ire)—Boomerang
1980 Rob Ehrens (NL)—Koh i Noor
1981 David Broome (GB)
       —Queensway Philco
1982 Malcolm Pyrah (GB)
       —Towerlands Anglezarke
1983 Norman Dello Joio (USA)
       —I Love You
1984 Heidi Robbiani (Switz)—Jessica V
1985 Nick Skelton (GB)
       —Everest St James
1986 John Whitaker (GB)—Next Milton

Cleveland

1965 Mary Chapot (USA)—Tomboy
1966 Carlene Blunt (USA)
       —Silver Lining
1967 Rodney Jenkins (USA)
       —Gustavus
1968 Jim Day (Can)—Canadian Club
1969 Moffat Dunlap (Can)—Lights Out
1970 Steve Stephens (USA)
       —Toy Soldier
1971 Frank Chapot (USA)
       —Grey Carrier
1972 Michael Matz (USA)
       —Rosie Report

1973 Bernie Traurig (USA)
       —Springdale
1974 Thom Hardy (USA)
       —Coming Attraction
1975 Buddy Brown (USA)
       —Sandsablaze
1976 Conrad Homfeld (USA)—Balbuco
1977 Rodney Jenkins (USA)—Idle Dice
1978 Bernie Traurig (USA)
       —The Cardinal
1979 Rodney Jenkins (USA)
       —Second Balcony
1980 Debbie Shaffner (USA)
       —Abdullah
1981 Michael Matz (USA)—Jet Run
1982 Katie Monahan (USA)—Noren
1983 Katie Monahan (USA)—Jethro
1984 George Morris (USA)—Brussels
1985 Norman Dello Joio (USA)
       —Corsair
1986 Debbie Dolan (USA)—Albany

Dortmund

(Grand Prix der
Bundesrepublik)

1955 Fritz Thiedemann (FRG)—Finale
1956 Fritz Thiedemann (FRG)—Meteor
1957 Francisco Goyoaga (Spa)
       —Fahnenkönig
1958 Francisco Goyoaga (Spa)
       —Fahnenkönig
1959 Piero d'Inzeo (Ita)—The Rock

*Calgary Grand Prix winner in 1984,
Heidi Robbiani and the Irish-bred mare
Jessica V. (Bob Langrish)*

1960	Hans Günter Winkler (FRG)—Romanus	1949	Mrs St. John Nolan (Ire)—Outdoor Girl	1983	Nick Skelton (GB)—Everest If Ever

1960 Hans Günter Winkler (FRG)
—Romanus
1961 Hermann Schridde (FRG)
—Flagrant
1962 Piero d'Inzeo (Ita)—Sunbeam
1963 Hans Günter Winkler (FRG)
—Romanus
1964 Nelson Pessoa (Bra)
—Gran Geste
1965 Kurt Jarasinski (FRG)—Torro
1966 Fritz Ligges (FRG)—Finette
1967 Nelson Pessoa (Bra)
—Gran Geste
1968 Alwin Schockemöhle (FRG)
—Donald Rex
1969 Andrew Fielder (GB)—Vibart
1970 Gualtiero Castellini (Ita)
—Fidux
1971 Hartwig Steenken (FRG)
—Simona
1972 Hartwig Steenken (FRG)
—Daniela
1973 Alwin Schockemöhle (FRG)
—Rex the Robber
1974 Harvey Smith (GB)—Volvo
1975 Derek Ricketts (GB)
—Beau Supreme
1976 Debbie Johnsey (GB)—Cruppier
1977 Peter Weinberg (FRG)—Uhland
1978 Nelson Pessoa (Bra)
—Moët et Chandon Bunny
1979 Hugo Simon (Aut)—Gladstone
1980 Hugo Simon (Aut)—Gladstone
1981 Hugo Simon (Aut)—Gladstone
1982 Edgar-Henri Cuepper (Bel)
—Cyrano
1983 Edgar-Henri Cuepper (Bel)
—Cyrano
1984 John Whitaker (GB)
—Clonee Temple
1985 John Whitaker (GB)
—Clonee Temple
1986 Hugo Simon (Aut)—The Freak

Dublin

(1934–39 International
Championship, since 1946
The Irish Trophy)

1926 Auguste de Laissardière (Fra)
—Harrio
1927 Joe Hume-Dudgeon (GB)—Chum
1928 M. de Vienne (Fra)—Quidet
1929 Pierre de Muralt (Switz)—Notas
1930 Dan Corry (Ire)—Slievenamon
1931 Joe Hume-Dudgeon (GB)
—Blue Dun
1932 Jed O'Dwyer (Ire)—Limerick Lace
1933 Pierre Cavaillé (Fra)—Olivette
1934 Jed O'Dwyer (Ire)—Limerick Lace
1935 Heinz Brandt (Ger)—Baron IV
1936 Maurice de Bartillat (Fra)
—Olivette
1937 John Bamber, Jnr (Ire)
—Silver Mist
1938 Fred Ahern (Ire)—Blarney Castle
1939 Dan Corry (Ire)—Red Hugh
1946 Michael Tubridy (Ire)—Kilkenny
1947 Stig Holm (Swe)—Grim
1948 Iris Kellett (Ire)—Rusty

1949 Mrs St. John Nolan (Ire)
—Outdoor Girl
1950 Ian Hume-Dudgeon (Ire)
—Go Lightly
1951 John Lewis (Ire)—Hack On
1952 Ian Hume-Dudgeon (Ire)
—Go Lightly
1953 Michael Tubridy (Ire)—Ballynonty
1954 Shirley Thomas (Can)
—Revlon's White Sable
1955 Patrick Kiernan—Glenamaddy
1956 Joe Hume-Dudgeon (Ire)
—Sea Spray
1957 Chevalier Jean d'Orgeix (Fra)
—Topinambour
1958 George Morris (USA)—Night Owl
1959 Seamus Hayes (Ire)—Kilrush
1960 David Broome (GB)—Sunsalve
1961 Tommy Wade (Ire)—Dundrum
1962 Piero d'Inzeo (Ita)—The Rock
1963 Tommy Wade (Ire)—Dundrum
1964 Kathy Kusner (USA)
—Untouchable
1965 Kathy Kusner (USA)
—Untouchable
1966 Diana Conolly-Carew (Ire)
Barrymore
1967 David Broome (GB)
—Mister Softee
1968 David Broome (GB)
—Mister Softee
1969 Raimondo d'Inzeo (Ita)—Bellevue
1970 Harvey Smith (GB)
—Mattie Brown
1971 Graham Fletcher (GB)
—Buttevant Boy
1972 Alwin Schockemöhle (FRG)
—Rex the Robber
1973 Johan Heins (NL)—Antrieb
1974 Buddy Brown (USA)
—Sandsablaze
1975 Raimondo d'Inzeo (Ita)—Bellevue
1976 Harvey Smith (GB)—Olympic Star
1977 David Broome (GB)—Philco
1978 Michael Saywell (GB)
—Chainbridge
1979 David Broome (GB)—Sportsman
1980 Harvey Smith (GB)
—Sanyo Sanmar
1981 David Broome (GB)
—Queensway Big Q
1982 Malcolm Pyrah (GB)
—Towerlands Chainbridge
1983 Harvey Smith (GB)
—Sanyo Technology
1984 Hendrik Snoek (FRG)
—Palma Nova
1985 Nick Skelton (GB)
—Everest Apollo
1986 Gerry Mullins (Ire)—Rockbarton

Gothenburg

1977 Gerd Wiltfang (FRG)—Duell
1978 Eddie Macken (Ire)—Boomerang
1979 Hugo Simon (Aut)—Little One
1980 Harvey Smith (GB)
—Sanyo Sanmar
1981 Fritz Ligges (FRG)—Goya
1982 Bernie Traurig (USA)
—Eaden Vale

1983 Nick Skelton (GB)
—Everest If Ever
1984 Eddie Macken (Ire)
—Carroll's El Paso
1985 Rob Ehrens (NL)—Oscar Drum
1986 Ian Millar (Can)—Lukas
1987 John Whitaker (GB)—Next Milton

Harrisburg

1948 Humberto Mariles Cortés (Mex)
—Arete
1949 Pelayo Izurieta (Chi)—Condor
1950 Roberto Vinals Contreras (Mex)
—Alteno
1951 Arthur McCashin (USA)—Totilla
1952 Pierre Jonquères d'Oriola (Fra)
—Ali-Baba
1953 Pat Smythe (GB)—Prince Hal
1954 Hans Günter Winkler (FRG)
—Halla
1955 Roberto Vinals Contreras (Mex)
—Malinche
1956 Humberto Mariles Cortés (Mex)
—Chihuahua II
1957 Ted Williams (GB)—Pegasus
1958=William Steinkraus (USA)
—Ksar d'Esprit
Hans Günter Winkler (FRG)
—Halla
1959 William Steinkraus (USA)
—Trail Guide
1960 Frank Chapot (USA)—Tally Ho
1961 William Steinkraus (USA)
—Ksar d'Esprit
1962 William Steinkraus (USA)
—Fire One
1963 William Steinkraus (USA)—Sinjon
1964 William Ringrose (Ire)
—Loch an Easpaig
1965 Mary (Mairs) Chapot (USA)
—Tomboy
1966 Mary (Mairs) Chapot (USA)
—Tomboy
1967 Mary (Mairs) Chapot (USA)
—Anakonda
1968 Jared Brinsmade (USA)
—Triple Crown
1969 Jared Brinsmade (USA)
—Triple Crown
1970 Barbara Simpson (Can)
—Australis
1971 Neal Shapiro (USA)—Sloopy
1972 Frank Chapot (USA)—Good Twist

's-Hertogenbosch

1967 Seamus Hayes (Ire)—Doneraile
1968 Harvey Smith (GB)—O'Malley
1969 Lucia Faria (Bra)—Rush du Camp
1970 Alwin Schockemöhle (FRG)
—Donald Rex
1971 Ann Backhouse (GB)—Cardinal
1972 Harvey Smith (GB)—Evan Jones
1973 Fritz Ligges (FRG)—Genius
1974 Hendrik Snoek (FRG)—Rasputin
1975 Hugo Simon (Aut)—Lavendel
1976 David Broome (GB)
—Jägermeister
1977 Johan Heins (NL)—Seven Valleys
1978 Fritz Ligges (FRG)—Goya

1979 David Broome (GB)—Philco
1980 Hugo Simon (Aut)—Gladstone
1981 Gilles Bertran de Balanda (Fra)
     —Galoubet Malesan
1982 Rob Ehrens (NL)—Oscar Drum
1983 Edgar-Henri Cuepper (Bel)
     —Cyrano
1984 Thomas Fuchs (Switz)
     —Willora Carpets
1985 Harvey Smith (GB)
     —Sanyo Technology
1986 Paul Schockemöhle (FRG)
     —Deister
1987 Nick Skelton (GB)
     —Raffles Airborne

King George V Gold Cup

(1911–83 London, since 1984 Birmingham)

(Men only except in 1947 and 1948.)

1911 Dimitri d'Exe (Rus)—Piccolo
1912 Lt Delvoie (Bel)—Murat
1913 Baron de Meslon (Fra)
     —Amazone
1914 Baron de Meslon (Fra)
     —Amazone
1920 Auguste de Laissardière (Fra)
     —Dignité
1921 Geoffrey Brooke (GB)
     —Combined Training
1922 Conte Giacomo Antonelli (Ita)
     —Bluff
1923 Auguste de Laissardière (Fra)
     —Grey Fox
1924 Conte Giulio Borsarelli di Riffredo
     (Ita)—Don Chisciotte
1925 Malise Graham (GB)—Broncho
1926 Fred Bontecou (USA)
     —Ballymacshane
1927 Xavier Bizard (Fra)—Quinine
1928 A. G. Martyr (GB)—Forty-Six
1929 Hubert Gibault (Fra)—Mandarin
1930 Jack Talbot-Ponsonby (GB)
     —Chelsea
1931 Jacques Misonne (Bel)
     —The Parson
1932 Jack Talbot-Ponsonby (GB)
     —Chelsea
1933 Not held
1934 Jack Talbot-Ponsonby (GB)
     —Best Girl
1935 John Lewis (Ire)—Tramore Bay
1936 Jed O'Dwyer (Ire)—Limerick Lace
1937 Xavier Bizard (Fra)—Honduras
1938 John Friedberger (GB)—Derek
1939 Conte Alessandro
     Bettoni-Cazzago (Ita)—Adigrat
1947 Pierre Jonquères d'Oriola (Fra)
     —Marquis III
1948 Harry Llewellyn (GB)—Foxhunter
1949 Brian Butler (GB)—Tankard
1950 Harry Llewellyn (GB)—Foxhunter
1951 Kevin Barry (Ire)—Ballyneety
1952 Carlos Figueroa (Spa)—Gracieux
1953 Harry Llewellyn (GB)—Foxhunter
1954 Fritz Thiedemann (FRG)—Meteor
1955 Luigi Cartasegna (Ita)—Brando
1956 William Steinkraus (USA)
     —First Boy

Xavier Bizard, from the French Cavalry School at Saumur, with Honduras after winning the King George V Gold Cup in 1937. During the war Honduras was captured first by the Germans and then by the Americans. Bizard identified his old partner when he saw him jumping under the name of Nipper with the victorious American team in the London Nations Cup of 1948. (Sport and General)

1957 Piero d'Inzeo (Ita)—Uruguay
1958 Hugh Wiley (USA)
     —Master William
1959 Hugh Wiley (USA)—Nautical
1960 David Broome (GB)—Sunsalve
1961 Piero d'Inzeo (Ita)—The Rock
1962 Piero d'Inzeo (Ita)—The Rock
1963 Tommy Wade (Ire)—Dundrum
1964 William Steinkraus (USA)—Sinjon
1965 Hans Günter Winkler (FRG)
     —Fortun
1966 David Broome (GB)
     —Mister Softee
1967 Peter Robeson (GB)—Firecrest
1968 Hans Günter Winkler (FRG)
     —Enigk
1969 Ted Edgar (GB)—Uncle Max
1970 Harvey Smith (GB)
     —Mattie Brown
1971 Gerd Wiltfang (FRG)—Askan
1972 David Broome (GB)—Sportsman
1973 Paddy McMahon (GB)
     —Pennwood Forge Mill
1974 Frank Chapot (USA)
     —Main Spring
1975 Alwin Schockemöhle (FRG)
     —Rex the Robber

1976 Michael Saywell (GB)
     —Chainbridge
1977 David Broome (GB)—Philco
1978 Jeff McVean (Aus)—Claret
1979 Robert Smith (GB)—Video
1980 David Bowen (GB)—Scorton
1981 David Broome (GB)—Mr Ross
1982 Michael Whitaker (GB)
     —Disney Way
1983 Paul Schockemöhle (FRG)
     Deister
1984 Nick Skelton (GB)—St James
1985 Malcolm Pyrah (GB)
     —Towerlands Anglezarke
1986 John Whitaker (GB)
     —Next Ryan's Son

Most wins—rider

5 David Broome (1960, 1966, 1972, 1977, 1981)

Most wins—horse

3 Foxhunter (1948, 1950, 1953)

Lisbon

1909 Gustavo Spencer (Spa)—Exquiss

1910	Lourenço Casal Ribeiro (Por)—Ganthois
1911	Jaime Alto Mearim (Por)—Clematite
1912	José Alverca (Por)—Atalaia
1913	Sebastião da Cunha e Silva (Por)—Farinelo
1914	Francisco Lusignan de Azevedo (Por)—Alvear
1916	Carlos Marin (Por)—Dina
1917	Octavio Duarte (Por)—Cirano
1918	Delfim Maya (Por)—Mufilo
1919	Carlos Maturana (Spa)—Delicia
1920	Anibal Borges de Almeida (Por)—Profond
1921	José Julio de Morais (Por)—Reginald
1922	José Julio de Morais (Por)—Reginald
1923	José Mousinho de Albuquerque (Por)—Hebraico
1924	Hermano Margaride (Por)—Vencedor
1925	Alfredo Morais Sarmento (Por)—Volga
1926	Luis Ivens Ferraz (Por)—Roussi
1927	Luis Ivens Ferraz (Por)—Marco Visconti
1928	Julio Garcia Fernandez (Spa)—Revistada
1929	João Froes de Almeida (Por)—Gaillard
1930	Luis Ivens Ferraz (Por)—Marco Visconti
1931	Helder Martins (Por)—Belin
1932	Abdon López Turrion (Spa)—Arlésienne
1933	Marquês do Funchal (Por)—Altivo
1934	José Beltrão (Por)—Fossette
1935	Diego Torres (Spa)—Egalite
1936	Antonino Guzman (Spa)—Batanero
1937	Helder Martins (Por)—Paloia
1938	José Costa Pina (Por)—Manfield
1939	Luigi Coccia (Ita)—Don Rodrigo
1940	Mario Machado de Faria (Por)—Chaimite
1941	Pascoal Rodrigues (Por)—Namir
1942	Antonio Reymão Nogueira (Por)—Sado
1943	Joaquin Nogueras Marquéz (Spa)—Batato
1944	Henrique Callado (Por)—Paiol
1945	Rodrigo Castro Pereira (Por)—Hopeful Don
1946	Joaquin Nogueras Marquéz (Spa)—Ranchero
1947	Helder Martins (Por)—Optus
1948	Marcelino Gavilán y Ponce de Léon (Spa)—Foragido
1949	Francisco Farrusco, Jnr (Por)—Abandonado
1950	Pedro Dominguez Manjon (Spa)—Vitamen
1951	José Carvalhosa (Por)—Mondina
1952	José Carvalhosa (Por)—Estemido
1953	Henrique Callado (Por)—Caramulo
1954	Henrique Callado (Por)—Caramulo

1955	Henrique Callado (Por)—Martingil
1956	Henrique Callado (Por)—Caramulo
1957	Fritz Thiedemann (FRG)—Finale
1958	Conde de Velle (Spa)—Llanero
1959	Pat Smythe (GB)—Flanagan
1960	Francisco Goyoaga (Spa)—Desirée
1961	Henrique Callado (Por)—Konak
1962	José Alvarez de Bohorques (Spa)—Janita
1963	José Alvarez de Bohorques (Spa)—Quizas
1964	Joaquim Duarte Silva (Por)—Jeune France
1965	Jorge Mathias (Por)—Joc de l'Ile
1966	Jean Dasque (Fra)—Prédestiné
1967	Manuel Malta de Costa (Por)—Alentejo
1968	Vasco Ramires (Por)—Namur du Payre
1969	Monica Bachmann (Switz)—Erbach
1970	Paul Weier (Switz)—Wildfeuer
1971	Paul Weier (Switz)—Wulf
1972	Paul Weier (Switz)—Wulf
1973	Paul Weier (Switz)—Wulf
1974	Alwin Schockemöhle (FRG)—Warwick
1979	Manuel Malta da Costa (Por)—Ecaussevillais
1980	Diego Porres (Spa)—Malambo
1981	Rutherford Latham (Spa)—Fidias
1982	Thomas Fuchs (Switz)—Willora Swiss
1983	Alfonso Segovia (Spa)—Feiner Kerl
1984	Michel Blaton (Bel)—Waigon
1985	Guido Dominici (Ita)—Quo Vadis
1986	Achaz von Buchwaldt (FRG)—Ricarda

Most wins—riders

6 Henrique Callado (Por) (1944, 1953, 1954, 1955, 1956, 1961)

Most wins—horses

3 Caramulo (1953, 1954, 1956)
  Wulf (1971, 1972, 1973)

London (Olympia)

1972	Hartwig Steenken (FRG)—Simona
1973	Graham Fletcher (GB)—Buttevant Boy
1974	Paul Weier (Switz)—Wulf
1975	David Broome (GB)—Philco
1976	Hartwig Steenken (FRG)—Goya
1977	David Broome (GB)—Philco
1978	David Broome (GB)—Sportsman
1979*	Gerd Wiltfang (FRG)—Goldika
1980*	Johan Heins (NL)—Larramy
1981*	David Broome (GB)—Philco
1982	Nick Skelton (GB)—St James
1983	Nick Skelton (GB)—St James
1984	Hugo Simon (GB)—The Freak

*Combined with World Cup Qualifier

1985	Malcolm Pyrah (GB)—Towerlands Anglezarke
1986	Malcolm Pyrah (GB)—Towerlands Anglezarke

Lourenço Marques

1964	Mickey Louw (SA)—Jurico
1965	A. Edward—Ranie
1966	Yvonne Johnson (SA)—Gay Lord
1967	Peter Levor (SA)—Shaza
1968	Peter Levor (SA)—Shaza
1969	George Myburg (SA)—The Laird
1970	Peter Levor (SA)—Format
1971	K. Turner (SA)—Harry Lime
1972	Wendy Grayston (SA)—Lobol King Cole
1973	Mickey Louw (SA)—Torch Sign

Lucerne

1909	Prince Giovanni Capeci Zurlo (Ita)—St Hubert
1910	Guy du Vaucelles (Fra)—Pink Paper
1911	Henry Leclerc (Fra)—Blue Moon
1912	René Ricard (Fra)—Erion
1913	Henry Leclerc (Fra)—Psyché
1914	Leone Tappi (Ita)—Don Basilio
1920	Charles Kuhn (Switz)—Gecko
1921	Hans E. Bühler (Switz)—Reck
1922	Henri Von der Weid (Switz)—Glocester
1923	Werner Stuber (Switz)—Girandole
1924	Adam Krolikiewicz (Pol)—Picador
1925	Joseph Laame (Bel)—Biscuit
1926	Jean Gailly de Taurines (Fra)—Vermouth
1927	Camille de Montergon (Fra)—Barnes
1928	Francesco Formigli (Ita)—Montebello
1929	Giulio Borsarelli (Ita)—Crispa
1930	J. Baudoin de Brabandère (Bel)—Acrobate
1931	Conte Alessandro Bettoni-Cazzago (Ita)—Aladino
1933	Nikolaus Odescalchi (Hun)—Devolé
1934	Christian de Castries (Fra)—Wednesday
1935	Tommaso Lequio di Assaba (Ita)—Nereide
1936	François Durand (Fra)—Olivette
1937	Dan Corry (Ire)—Red Hugh
1938	John Lewis (Ire)—Limerick Lace
1939	Lilian Wittmack (Den)—Mister
1947	Gerardo Conforti (Ita)—Encomiabile
1948	Victor Saucedo-Carillo (Mex)—Poblano
1950	Harry Llewellyn (GB)—Foxhunter
1952	Harry Llewellyn (GB)—Foxhunter
1954=	Pierre Jonquères d'Oriola (Fra)—Voulette
	Ferdinand Béghin (Fra)—Vengeur II

1956	Brigitte Schockaert (Bel) Muscadin	
1958=	Fritz Thiedemann (FRG) —Godewind	
	Hans Günter Winkler (FRG) —Fahnenjunker	
1960	Pat Smythe (GB)—Flanagan	
1962=	Piero d'Inzeo (Ita)—The Rock	
	Hans Günter Winkler (FRG) —Romanus	
1964	Hans Möhr (Switz)—Troll	
1966	Kathy Kusner (USA) —Untouchable	
1968	Hubert Parot (Fra)—Garant	
1970	Paul Weier (Switz)—Wildfeuer	
1972	Hugo Arrambide (Arg) —Camalote	
1974	Robert Ridland (USA) —Almost Persuaded	
1976	Willi Melliger (Switz) —Rhonas Boy	
1979	Walter Gabathuler (Switz) —Harley	
1980	Hugo Simon (Aut)—Sorry	
1982	Bruno Candrian (Switz) —Van Gogh	
1984	Willi Melliger (Switz) —Van Gogh	
1986	Pierre Durand (Fra) —Jappeloup de Luze	
1987	Katharine Burdsall (USA) —The Natural	

Madrid

1950	Joaquin Nogueras-Marquéz (Spa)—Frisar
1951	Manuel Ordovas (Spa)—Quorum
1952	Jaime Garcia Cruz (Spa) —Quorum
1953	Angel Alonso Martin (Spa) —Sainette
1954	Pat Smythe (GB)—Prince Hal
1955	Carlos Figueroa (Spa) —Gracieux
1956	Francisco Goyoaga (Spa) —Fahnenkönig
1957	Henrique Callado (Por) —Caramulo
1958	Francisco Goyoaga (Spa) —Fahnenkönig
1959	Dawn Wofford (GB)—Hollandia
1960	Henrique Callado (Por) Martingil
1961	Graziano Mancinelli (Fra) —Rockette
1962	Henrique Callado (Por) —Martingil
1963	Graziano Mancinelli (Ita) —Rockette
1964	Pierre Jonquères d'Oriola (Fra) —Lutteur B
1965	Francisco Goyoaga (Spa) —Kif-Kif
1966	Francisco Goyoaga (Spa) —Kif-Kif
1967	Eduardo Amoros (Spa) —Rabanito
1968	Eduardo Amoros (Spa) Kif-Kif
1969	Hans Günter Winkler (FRG) —Torphy

1970	Anneli Drummond-Hay (GB) —Merely-a-Monarch
1971	
1972	Vasco Ramirez (Por) —Sire de Brossais
1973	Paddy McMahon (GB) Penwood Forge Mill
1974	Hubert Parot (Fra)—Tic
1975	Graziano Mancinelli (Ita) —Bel Oiseau
1976	Graziano Mancinelli (Ita) —Bel Oiseau
1977	Luis Alvarez Cervera (Spa)—Thor
1978	Eva van Paesschen (Bel) —Esbrouffe
1979	Michel Robert (Fra)—Belle Bleu
1980	Antonio de Wit (Spa)—Olímpico
1981	Gilles Bertran de Balanda (Fra) —Grand Coeur Malesan
1982	Sönke Sönksen (FRG)—Rangpur
1983	Laurent Elias (Fra)—Guenor
1984	Kevin Bacon (Aus)—Megabit
1985	Michael Whitaker (GB) —Overton Amanda
1986	David Bowen (GB)—Hawk

New York

1910	C. T. 'Taffy' Walwyn (GB) —The Nut
1911	Winfried Sifton (Can)—Ironsides
1912	Mervyn Crawshay (GB) —Princess Charlotte
1913	Baron de Meslon (Fra) —Amazone
1925	J. Baudoin de Brabandère (Bel) —Véronique
1926	Yves de Freminville (Fra) —Pair II
1927	Karol von Rommel (Pol)—Fargas
1928	Marten von Barnekow (Ger) —Semper Avanti
1929	Earl F. Thomson (USA) —Tan Bark
1930	Hermann von Nagel (Ger)—Dedo
1931	Carl W. Raguse (USA)—Ugly
1932	Earl F. Thomson (USA) —Tan Bark
1933	Fred Ahern (Ire)—Gallow Glass
1934	Dan Corry (Ire)—Limerick Lace
1935	Raymond W. Curtis (USA)—Don
1936	Jack Talbot-Ponsonby (GB) —Kineton
1937	Joshua de Kruijff (NL)—Godard
1938	Ramiro Palafox (Mex)—Azteca
1939	Armando Fernandez (Chi) —Andina
1940	Franklin Wing (USA)—Democrat
1941	Carlos Alfaro (Per)—Ayachucho
1946	William H. S. Wright (USA) —Reno Jumper
1947	Jonathan Burton (USA)—Air Mail
1948	Humberto Mariles Cortés (Mex) —Arete
1949	Rubén Uriza Castro (Mex) —Hatuey
1950	Michael Tubridy (Ire)—Rostrevor
1951	Humberto Mariles Cortés (Mex) —Arete
1952	William Ballard (Can)—Reject
1953	Carol Durand (USA)—Reno Kirk
1954	Fritz Thiedemann (FRG)—Meteor

Prince Giovanni Capeci Zurlo and St Hubert, winners of the first Lucerne Grand Prix in 1909. (The Illustrated London News)

1955	Humberto Mariles Cortés (Mex) —Chihuahua II
1956	William Ringrose (Ire) —Ballynonty
1957	Ted Williams (GB)—Pegasus
1958	Fritz Thiedemann (FRG) —Godewind
1959	William Steinkraus (USA) —Riviera Wonder
1960	Ricardo Guasch (Mex) —Piel Canela
1961	Frank Chapot (USA)—San Lucas
1962	C. David Barker (GB) —Mister Softee
1963	Gail Ross (Can)—Thunderbird
1964	Tom Gayford (Can)—Blue Beau
1965	William Steinkraus (USA) —Snowbound
1966	Mary Chapot (USA)—Tomboy
1967	Harvey Smith (GB)—O'Malley
1968	Mary (Mairs) Chapot (USA) —White Lightning
1969	Hugo Arrambide (Arg)—Adagio
1970	Hans Günter Winkler (FRG) —Terminus
1971	Robert Ridland (USA) —Almost Persuaded
1972	Frank Chapot (USA) —Good Twist
1973	Rodney Jenkins (USA)—Idle Dice
1974	Juan Rieckehoff (PR)—Don Juan
1975	Rodney Jenkins (USA) —Number One Spy
1976	Eddie Macken (Ire)—Boomerang
1977	Liz Edgar (GB)—Everest Wallaby
1978	John Simpson (Can)—Texas
1979	Michael Matz (USA)—Jet Run

1980	Paul Schockemöhle (FRG) —El Paso
1981	Filippo Moyersoen (Ita)—Adam
1982	Thomas Fuchs (Switz) —Willora Carpets
1983	Nick Skelton (GB) —Everest Arabesque
1984	Nick Skelton (GB)—Apollo
1985	Leslie Burr Lenehan (USA) —McLain
1986	Ian Millar (Can)—Big Ben

Nice

1921=	Charles Kuhn (Switz)—Gecko
	August de Laissardière (Fra) —Flirt
1922	M. Courtecuisse (Fra) —Illuminateur
1923=	Francesco Formigli (Ita)—Novello
	Beraudo di Pralermo (Ita) —Camoscino
1924	Adam Krolikiewicz (Pol)—Kasiek
1925	Adam Krolikiewicz (Pol)—Picador
1926=	J. Baudoin de Brabandère (Bel) —Acrobate
	Pierre Clavé (Fra)—Billou
1927	Kazimierz Szosland (Pol) —Readgledt
1928	Maurice Gudin de Vallerin (Fra) —Pair II
1929	Maurice Gudin de Vallerin (Fra) —Vermouth
1930	Fernando Filipponi (Ita)—Nasello
1931	Francesco Forquet (Ita) —Capinera
1932	Antoine Nobili (Fra)—Cherubin
1933	Abdon López Turrion (Spa) —Revistada

1934	Conte Giulio Borsarelli di Riffredo (Ita)—Crispa
1935	Fred Ahern (Ire)—Ireland's Own
1936	Fernando Artalejo Campos (Spa) —Montmorency
1938	Bronislaw Skulicz (Pol)—Dunkan
1939	John Lewis (Ire)—Limerick Lace
1947	Jean de Tillière (Fra)—Marquis III
1949	Harry Llewellyn (GB)—Foxhunter
1950	Dick Gelderman (NL)—Countess
1951	Manuel Ordovas (Spa)—Bohemio
1952	Dan Corry (Ire)—Ballycotton
1953	Pedro Dominguez Manjon (Spa) —Friso
1954	Jaime Carcia Cruz (Spa) —Quoniam
1955	Patrick Kiernan (Ire)—Ballynonty
1956	Francisco Goyoaga (Spa) —Fahnenkönig
1958	Raimondo d'Inzeo (Ita)—Merano
1960	Pierre Jonquères d'Oriola (Fra) —Gerboise
1961	José Alvarez de Bohorques (Spa) —Descosido
1962	Piero d'Inzeo (Ita)—Sunbeam
1963	Graziano Mancinelli (Ita) —Rockette
1964	Graziano Mancinelli (Ita) —Turvey
1965	William Ringrose (Ire) —Loch an Easpaig
1967	Harvey Smith (GB)—O'Malley
1968	Gerson Monteiro (Bra) —Arachan
1969	Janou Lefèbvre (Fra)—Rocket
1970	Philippe Jouy (Fra)—Stella
1972	Marc Dequet (Fra)—Ulpienne
1973	Johan Heins (NL)—Antrieb
1978	Caroline Bradley (GB)—Tigre

Olsztyn

1964	Juray Hanulay (Czech)—Tosca
1965	Jan Kowalczyk (Pol)—Drobnica
1966	Marian Kozicki (Pol)—Berry
1967	John Baillie (GB)—Dominic
1968	Piotr Wawriniuk (Pol)—Poprad
1969	Rudolf Beerbohm (DDR) —Freiherr
1970	Hugo Simon (FRG)—Fair Lady
1971	Heinz Schulenburg (DDR) —Freiherr
1972	Stefan Grodzicki (Pol)—Biszka
1973	Bernd Kuwertz (FRG)—Girl
1974	Ferdi Tyteca (Bel)—Exact
1975	Gilles Royon (Fra)—Rodeo C
1976	Achaz von Buchwaldt (FRG) —El Paso
1977	Julius Schulze-Hesselmann (FRG)—Fernando
1978	Peter Weinberg (FRG)—Patras
1979	Günter Till (DDR)—Fakt
1981	Bogdan Sas-Jaworsky (Pol) —Bremen

Paris (Coupe)

1897	Marquis de Galard (Fra)—Rebel
1898	Pierre Dupray (Fra) —Jack Scarlet
1899	Georges van de Poële (Bel) —Laffitte
1900	Louis de Champsavin (Fra) —Terpsichore
1901	Henry Leclerc (Fra) —Général Dewet
1902	Louis de Champsavin (Fra) —Old Chap

The picturesque Piazzi di Siena, situated in the Villa Borghese gardens, home of the Rome Horse Show. (Findlay Davidson)

1903 Henry Leclerc (Fra)—Black Fly
1904 Georges Crousse (Fra)
—Messaoud
1905 Louis de Champsavin (Fra)
—Rayon d'Or
1906 Felix Petit (Fra)—Ratz-Fana
1907 Alfred Loewenstein (Bel)
—Conquérant
1908 Bompart (Fra)—Riquiqui
1909 Bompart (Fra)—Patrick II
1910 Jean-Marie Brodin (Fra)
—Brown Bess
1911 Prince Giovanni Capece Zurlo
(Ita)—St Hubert II
1912 d'Auzac de Lamartinie (Fra)
—Djali
1913 Jean-Marie Brodin (Fra)
—Mount Pleasant
1914=Henri Gailliard (Fra)—Gamin
Henri Horment (Fra)—Lady Sarah
1921 Marcel Rousseau (Fra)—Irène
1922 Pierre Clavé (Fra)—Le Trouvère
1923 Michel Bignon (Fra)—Psyché
1924 Pierre Clavé (Fra)—Flyer
1925 Pierre Clavé (Fra)—Flyer
1926 Joseph Laame (Bel)—Biscuit
1927 Charles Labouchère (NL)
—Gamin
1928 Théophile Carbon (Fra)—Topsin
1929 Maurice Gudin de Vallerin (Fra)
—Verdun II
1930 Henry de Royer (Fra)
—Vol-au-Vent
1931 Belle Baruch (USA)—Souriant III
1932 Jean Salmon (Fra)—Unicus
1933 J. Dogny (Fra)—Flavian
1934 Jean Avot (Fra)
—Dame de Coeur III
1935 Xavier Bizard (Fra)—Sarakako
1936 Maurice Gudin de Vallerin (Fra)
—Ecuyère
1937 Georges Briolle (Fra)
—Gobe-Mouche
1938 Maurice Gudin de Vallerin (Fra)
—Ecuyère
1939 Christian de Castries (Fra)
—Wednesday

Paris Le Jumping

1947 H. de Courtivron (Fra)
—Pervanche
1948 Piero d'Inzeo (Ita)—Destino
1949 Piero d'Inzeo (Ita)—Destino
1950 Francisco Goyoaga (Spa)
—Vergel
1951 Francisco Goyoaga (Spa)
—Vergel
1952 Josée Bonnaud (Fra)
—Charleston
1954 Pat Smythe (GB)—Prince Hal
1955 Francisco Goyoaga (Spa)
—Fahnenkönig
1958 Pierre Jonquères d'Oriola (Fra)
—Virtuoso

Paris Salon du Cheval

1974=Jean-Michel Gaud (Fra)—Salome
Ted Edgar (GB)—Everest Mylord
1975 Hartwig Steenken (FRG)
—Gladstone

1976=Walter Gabathuler (Switz)
—Harley
Kevin Bacon (Aus)—Chichester
1977 Kevin Bacon (Aus)—Jet
1979 Hendrik Snoek (FRG)—Gaylord
1980 Nelson Pessoa (Switz)
—Moët et Chandon Fil d'Argent
1981 Willi Melliger (Switz)
—Trumpf Buur
1982 Hervé Godignon (Fra)
—Moët et Chandon Je t'Adore
1983 Willi Melliger (Switz)—Van Gogh
1984 Willi Melliger (Switz)—Beethoven

Queen Elizabeth II Cup

(1949–83 London, since 1984
Birmingham)
(*Ladies only*)

1949 Iris Kellett (Ire)—Rusty
1950 Jill Palethorpe (GB)—Silver Cloud
1951 Iris Kellett (Ire)—Rusty
1952 Gill Rich (GB)—Quicksilver III
1953 Marie Delfosse (GB)
—Fanny Rosa
1954 Josée Bonnaud (Fra)
—Charleston
1955 Dawn Palethorpe (GB)
—Earlsrath Rambler
1956 Dawn Palethorpe (GB)
—Earlsrath Rambler
1957 Elizabeth Anderson (GB)
—Sunsalve
1958 Pat Smythe (GB)—Mr Pollard
1959 Anna Clement (FRG)—Nico
1960 Susan Cohen (GB)—Clare Castle
1961 Lady Sarah FitzAlan-Howard
(GB)—Oorskiet
1962 Judy Crago (GB)—Spring Fever
1963 Julie Nash (GB)—Trigger Hill
1964 Gillian Makin (GB)—Jubilant
1965 Marion Coakes (GB)—Stroller
1966 Althea Roger Smith (GB)
—Havana Royal
1967 Betty Jennaway (GB)—Grey Leg
1968 Mary (Mairs) Chapot (USA)
—White Lightning
1969 Alison (Westwood) Dawes (GB)
—The Maverick VII
1970 Anneli Drummond-Hay (GB)
—Merely-a-Monarch
1971 Marion (Coakes) Mould (GB)
—Stroller
1972 Ann Moore (GB)—Psalm
1973=Alison (Westwood) Dawes (GB)
—Mr Banbury
(ex The Maverick VII)
Ann Moore (GB)—Psalm
1974 Jean Davenport (GB)
—All Trumps
1975 Jean Davenport (GB)—Hang On
1976 Marion (Coakes) Mould (GB)
—Elizabeth Ann
1977 Liz (Broome) Edgar (GB)
—Everest Wallaby
1978 Caroline Bradley (GB)—Marius
1979 Liz (Broome) Edgar (GB)
—Forever
1980 Caroline Bradley (GB)—Tigre
1981 Liz (Broome) Edgar (GB)
—Everest Forever

1982 Liz (Broome) Edgar (GB)
—Everest Forever
1983 Jean Germany (GB)—Mandingo
1984 Veronique (Daems-Vastapane)
Whitaker (GB)—Jingo
1985 Sue Pountain (GB)—Ned Kelly VI
1986 Liz (Broome) Edgar (GB)
—Everest Rapier

Rome

1922 Morel de Westgaver (Bel)
—Miss Daisy
1923 Gaston Mesmaekers (Bel)
—Periscope
1924 Not held
1925 Not held
1926 Adam Krolikiewicz (Pol)
—Picador
1927 Conte Giulio Borsarelli di Riffredo
(Ita)—Glauco
1928 Francesco Formigli (Ita)—Grumo
1929 Conte Alessandro
Bettoni-Cazzago (Ita)—Aladino
1930 Henry Pernot du Breuil (Fra)
—Vermouth
1931 Henry Pernot du Breuil (Fra)
—Welcome
1932 Maurice Gudin de Valerin (Fra)
—Vermouth
1933 Henry Pernot du Breuil (Fra)
—Exercice
1934 Hubert de Maupeou (Fra)
—Espiatz
1935 Fernando Filipponi (Ita)—Nasello
1936 Gerardo Conforti (Ita)—Saba
1937 Hans-Heinrich Brinckmann (Ger)
—Wotansbruder
1938 John Lewis (Ire)—Limerick Lace
1939 Fernando Filipponi (Ita)
—Nasello
1940 Alessandro Perrone (Ita)—Guapo
1947 Alesandro Perrone (Ita)—Uranio
1948 Chevalier Jean d'Orgeix (Fra)
—Sucre de Pomme
1949 José Navarro Morenes (Spa)
—Quorum
1950 Bertrand du Breuil (Fra)
—Tourbillon
1951 Jaime Garcia Cruz (Spa)
—Quoniam
1952 Ricardo Echeverria (Chi)
—Lindo Peal
1953 William Hanson (GB)
—The Monarch
1954 Pierre Jonquères d'Oriola (Fra)
—Arlequin
1955 Pierre Jonquères d'Oriola (Fra)
—Charleston
1956 Raimondo d'Inzeo (Ita)—Merano
1957 Raimondo d'Inzeo (Ita)—Merano
1958 Piero d'Inzeo (Ita)—The Rock
1959 Hans Günter Winkler (FRG)
—Halla
1960 Raimondo d'Inzeo (Ita)
—Gowran Girl*
1961 William Ringrose (Ire)
—Loch an Easpaig
1962 Piero d'Inzeo (Ita)—Sunbeam
1963 Harvey Smith (GB)—O'Malley

*Turin.

1964	Alfonso Queipo de Llano (Spa) —Infernal
1965	Hugo Arrambide (Arg) —Chimbote
1966	Paul Weier (Switz)—Junker
1967	Piero d'Inzeo (Ita)—Navarette
1968	Piero d'Inzeo (Ita)—Fidux
1969	Salvatore Danno (Ita)—Kim Ando
1970	Piero d'Inzeo (Ita)—Red Fox
1971	Raimondo d'Inzeo (Ita)—Fiorello
1972	Graziano Mancinelli (Ita) —Ambassador
1973	Piero d'Inzeo (Ita)—Easter Light
1974	Raimondo d'Inzeo (Ita) —Gone Away
1975	Malcolm Pyrah (GB)—April Love
1976	Piero d'Inzeo (Ita)—Easter Light
1977	Hendrik Schulze-Siehoff (FRG) —Sarto
1978	Eddie Macken (Ire)—Boomerang
1979	Arthur Blickenstorfer (Switz) —Hendrik
1980	Frédéric Cottier (Fra) —Flambeau C
1981	Jean-Marc Nicolas (Fra)—Mador
1982	Frédéric Cottier (Fra) —Flambeau C
1983	Anne Kursinski (USA)—Livius
1984	Frédéric Cottier (Fra) —Flambeau C
1985	Michel Robert (Fra)—Lafayette
1986	Bernhard Kamps (FRG) —Argonaut
1987	Vicky Roycroft (Aus)—Apache

Rotterdam

1947	Jan de Bruine (NL)—Tabouret
1948	Zia Azak (Tur)—Rüzgar
1949	J. P. Starkey (GB)—Cascade
1950	Geoffrey Gibbon (GB)—Sarah
1951	Harry Llewellyn (GB)—Foxhunter
1952	Victor Saucedo-Carrillo (Mex) —Resorte II
1953	Magnus von Buchwaldt (FRG) —Jaspis
1954	Kevin Barry (Ire)—Hollyford
1955	Francisco Goyoaga (Spa) —Toscanella
1956	Dawn Palethorpe (GB) —Earlsrath Rambler
1957	Hans Günter Winkler (FRG) —Halla
1958	William Steinkraus (USA) —Ksar d'Esprit
1959	Klaus Pade (FRG)—Domherr
1960	Anna Clement (FRG)—Nico
1961	Valerie Clark (GB)—Atalanta
1962	Harvey Smith (GB)—O'Malley
1963	C. David Barker (GB) —Mister Softee
1964	Seamus Hayes (Ire)—Goodbye III
1965	William Barker (GB) —North Flight
1966	Nelson Pessoa (Bra)—Caribe
1967	David Broome (GB) —Mister Softee
1968	Carol Hofmann (USA)—Out Late
1969	Harry Wouters van der Oudenweyer (NL)—Abadan
1970	Hauke Schmidt (FRG)—Causa

1971	Alison Dawes (GB) —The Maverick VII
1972	Hendrik Snoek (FRG)—Faustus
1973	Alwin Schockemöhle (FRG) —Rex the Robber
1974=	Piero d'Inzeo (Ita)—Easter Light Harvey Smith (GB)—Salvador
1975	Hendrik Snoek (FRG)—Gaylord
1976	Christophe Cuyer (Fra)—Varin
1977	John Simpson (Can)—Texas
1978	Terry Leibel (Can)—Sympatico
1980	Hugo Simon (Aut)—Gladstone
1981	Gilles Bertran de Balanda (Fra) —Galoubet Malesan
1982	Paul Schockemöhle (FRG) —Deister
1983	Walter Gabathuler (Switz) —Beethoven
1984	Paul Schockemöhle (FRG) —Deister
1985	Philip Heffer (GB)—Viewpoint
1986	Bruno Candrian (Switz) —Lampire

Royal International Horse Show—London

(John Player Trophy)

1961	Pat Smythe (GB)—Scorchin
1962	Harvey Smith (GB)—O'Malley
1963	Raimondo d'Inzeo (Ita)—Posillipo
1964	Mary Mairs (USA)—Tomboy
1965	Harvey Smith (GB)—Harvester VI
1966	Harvey Smith (GB)—Harvester VI
1967	Harvey Smith (GB)—Harvester VI
1968	Marion Coakes (GB)—Stroller
1969	Alwin Schockemöhle (FRG) —Donald Rex
1970	Marion (Coakes) Mould (GB) —Stroller
1971	William Steinkraus (USA) —Fleet Apple
1972	Harvey Smith (GB) —Summertime
1973	Harvey Smith (GB)—Salvador
1974	Rodney Jenkins (USA) —Number One Spy
1975	Alwin Schockemöhle (FRG) —Rex the Robber
1976	Gerd Meier (NL)—Casimir
1977	David Broome (GB)—Philco
1978	Harvey Smith (GB) —Sanyo Sanmar
1979	Eddie Macken (Ire) —Carroll's Boomerang
1980	Terry Rudd (USA)—Semi Tough
1981	Nick Skelton (GB)—St James
1982	Michael Whitaker (GB) —Disney Way
1983	John Whitaker (GB)—Ryan's Son

Royal International Horse Show—Birmingham

(Everest Double Glazing Grand Prix)

1984	Nick Skelton (GB)—St James
1985	Peter Charles (GB)—April Sun
1986	John Whitaker (GB)—Next Milton

South Africa

(Show Jumping Grand Prix of South Africa)

1975	Mickey Louw—Ford Appraise
1976	Mickey Louw—Ford Appraise
1977	Philip Smith —Burhose Power Drive
1978	Mickey Louw—Epol Appraise
1979	Heather Hillcoat—Chev's Dual
1980	Gonda Betrix—Honey Girl
1981	Janie Myburg—Toyota Dress Suit
1982	Errol Wucherpfennig —Compass Line
1983	Not held
1984	Bryce McCall—Hamadan
1985	
1986	Anneli (Drummond-Hay) Wucherpfennig —Audi Storm Finch

South Africa

(Indoor Show Jumping Grand Prix of South Africa)

1975	Janie Myburg—Toyota Crown
1976	Gonda Betrix—Prima's Format
1977	Peter Götz—Toyota's Thales
1978	Not held
1979	Mickey Louw—Epol Appraise
1980	Klaus Degener —Wondercoats Utamara
1981	Mickey Louw—Epol Appraise
1982	Philip Smith—Linden Rock
1983	Anneli (Drummond-Hay) Wucherpfennig—Nebraska
1984–86	Not held

Toronto

1925	Auguste de Laissardière (Fra) —Flirt
1926	Jacques de Fonlongue (Fra) —Laitue
1928	Reginald Timmis (Can) —Bucephalus
1930	Ernst Hasse (Ger)—Elan
1931	Andrew A. Frierson (USA) —Show Girl
1932	Marshall W. Cleland (Can) —Roxana
1933	Carl W. Raguse (USA)—Ugly
1934	Christian de Castries (Fra) —Henry VI
1935	William B. Bradford (USA)—Don
1936	Jack Talbot-Ponsonby (GB) —Kineton
1937	Douglas Cleland (Can)—Dunady
1938	Franklin Wing (USA)—Dakota
1946	
1947	Humberto Mariles Cortés (Mex) —Resorte
1948	Rubén Uriza Castro (Mex) —Hatuey
1949	Humberto Mariles Cortés (Mex) —Arete
1950	Humberto Mariles Cortés (Mex) —Alteno
1951	Luciano Dias de Toledo (Bra)

1952 William Steinkraus (USA)
—Democrat
1953 Shirley Thomas (Can)
—Revlon's White Sable
1954 Francisco Goyoaga (Spa)
—Bayamo
1955 Humberto Mariles Cortés (Mex)
—Chihuahua II
1956
1957 Ted Williams (GB)—Pegasus
1958 William Steinkraus (USA)
—Ksar d'Esprit
1959 William Steinkraus (USA)
—Trail Guide
1960 Jim Elder (Can)—O'Malley
1961 Jim Elder (Can)—O'Malley
1962 Hector Zatarain (Mex)—Goliath
1963 Gail Ross (Can)—Thunderbird
1964 William Steinkraus (USA)—Sinjon
1965 Frank Chapot (USA)—San Lucas
1966 Jim Day (Can)—Canadian Club
1967 Kathy Kusner (USA)
—Untouchable
1968 Tom Gayford (Can)—Canadiana
1969 Jim Day (Can)—Steelmaster
1970 Hans Günter Winkler (FRG)
—Terminus
1971 Joe Fargis (USA)—San Lucas
1972 William Steinkraus (USA)
—Main Spring
1973 Frank Chapot (USA)
—Main Spring
1974 Frank Chapot (USA)
—Main Spring
1975 Robert Ridland (USA)
—Southside
1976 Jim Day (Can)—Sympatico
1977 Michael Matz (USA)—Jet Run
1978 Terrance Millar (Can)
—Eaden Vale
1979 Mark Laskin (Can)—Damuraz
1980 Frédéric Cottier (Fra)
—Flambeau C
1981 Bernie Traurig (USA)
—Eaden Vale
1982 Frédéric Cottier (Fra)
—Flambeau C
1983 Nick Skelton (GB)—St James
1984 Norman Dello Joio (USA)
—I Love You
1985 Nick Skelton (GB)
—Everest Apollo
1986 Mark Leone (USA)—Costello

Vienna

1926 Rudolf Görtz (Ger)—Henry
1927 Rudolf Görtz (Ger)—Hanepü
1928 Rudolf Popler (Czech)—Denk
1929 Sergei Rodzianko (Rus)—Roxilan
1930 Giovanni Pinna (Ita)—Gagliardo
1931 Axel Holst (Ger)—Anleihe
1932 Hermann von Nagel (Ger)
—Wotan
1933 Fernando Filipponi (Ger)
—Nasello
1934= Jozsef von Platthy (Hun)
—Gergély-Vitéz
Conte Alessandro
Bettoni-Cazzago (Ita)—Judex
1935 Conte Alessandro
Bettoni-Cazzago (Ita)—Judex

1936 Felix Topescu (Rum)—Jolka
1937 Hans-Heinrich Brinckmann (Ger)
—Baron IV
1939 Hans Gert von Baath (Ger)
—Mönch
1958 W. Kiesewetter (Aut)—Floridan
1959 Hans Günter Winkler (FRG)
—Fahnenjunker
1960 Adolf Lauda (Aut)—Schönbrunn
1961 Hans Günter Winkler (FRG)
—Feuerdorn
1962 Nelson Pessoa (Bra)
—Gran Geste
1963 Achim von Malsen (FRG)—Aali
1964 Alma Holländer (Aut)—Anisette
1965 Nelson Pessoa (Bra)—Huipil
1966 Hans Günter Winkler (FRG)
—Saila
1967 Monica Bachmann (Switz)—Apa
1968 Raimondo d'Inzeo (Ita)
—Bellevue
1969 Piero d'Inzeo (Ita)—Red Fox
1970 Piero d'Inzeo (Ita)—Red Fox
1971 Gerd Wiltfang (FRG)
—Dorian Gray
1972 Vittorio Orlandi (Ita)
—Fulmer Feather Duster
1973 Nelson Pessoa (Bra)—Ali Baba
1974 Marcel Rozier (Fra)
—Bayard de Maupas
1975 Lutz Gössing (FRG)—Festa
1976 Graziano Mancinelli (Ita)
—La Bella
1977 Kevin Bacon (Aus)—Saloniki
1978 Paul Schockemöhle (FRG)
—El Paso
1979 Not held
1980 David Broome (GB)—Philco
1981 Gerd Wiltfang (FRG)—Roman
1982 Paul Schockemöhle (FRG)
—Akrobat
1983–85 Not held
1986 Kevin Bacon (Aus)—Santex

The first Canadian to win the Toronto Grand Prix, Reginald Timmis riding Bucephalus. (The Illustrated London News)

Washington

(The President of the United States Cup)

1961 Carlos Damm (Arg)—Sheriff
1962 Kathy Kusner (USA)—Unusual
1963 Hermann Schridde (FRG)—Ilona
1965 Frank Chapot (USA)—San Lucas
1966 Chrystine Jones (USA)
—Trick Track
1967 Neal Shapiro (USA)—Night Spree
1968 Jared Brinsmade (USA)
—Triple Crown
1969 Juan Giralda (Arg)—El Ganso
1970 Rodney Jenkins (USA)—Idle Dice
1971 Rodney Jenkins (USA)—Idle Dice
1972 Elizabeth Ashton (Can)
—Scotch Valley
1973 Alwin Schockemöhle (FRG)
—Rex the Robber
1974 Janou (Lefèbvre) Tissot (Fra)
—Rocket
1975 Daniel Constant (Fra)
—Vicomte d'Aubinier
1976= Rodney Jenkins (USA)
—Number One Spy
Terry Rudd (USA)—Mr Demeanor
1977 Buddy Brown (USA)
—Sandsablaze
1978 John Simpson (Can)—Texas
1979 Bernie Traurig (USA)
—Eaden Vale
1980 Michael Matz (USA)—Jet Run
1981 Melanie Smith (USA)—Calypso
1982 Katie Monahan (USA)—Noren
1983 Rodney Jenkins (USA)
—Coastline
1984 Joe Fargis (USA)—Touch of Class
1985 Michael Matz (USA)—Brussels
1986 Katharine Burdsall (USA)
—The Natural

Derbies

The Derby is an unusual competition, taking place as it does over a course some 1300 metres long (about 500 metres longer than an Olympic Nations Cup course) and which incorporates several obstacles that riders are more likely to encounter when going across country than in the show ring: banks, ditches, water complexes and so on. The oldest show jumping event of this type is the Hamburg Derby, created by Eduard F. Pulvermann, a well-known German rider in the years after the First World War. One of the obstacles on the Hamburg course—an in-and-out comprising a set of rails, an incline down to a water ditch, followed by rising ground and another set of rails—is known to this day as 'Pulvermann's Grave', commemorating a fall which its designer sustained there during one of his earliest attempts to jump it and which caused great merriment among his fellow competitors. In 1961 Douglas Bunn introduced the British Jumping Derby at his All England Jumping Ground, Hickstead, and the popularity of both this event and its great Hamburg prototype led other countries to follow suit, among them Sweden in 1969, Finland and Portugal in 1973, the United States in 1976 and Ireland in 1979.

Falsterbo—Swedish Derby

1969 Jan-Olaf Wannius (Swe)
    —Mr Goldfinger
1970 Åke Hultberg (Swe)—El-Vis
1971 Hermann Schridde (FRG)
    —Kadett
1972 Lene Nissen-Lembke (Swe)
    —Cottage Incident
1973 Åke Hultberg (Swe)—El-Vis
1974 Åke Hultberg (Swe)—El-Vis
1975 Hermann Schridde (FRG)
    —Fredericus Rex
1976 Not held
1977 Paul Weier (Switz)—Falk
1978 Paul Weier (Switz)—Pen Duick
1979 Not held
1980 Åke Hultberg (Swe)—Rousseau
1981 Gosta Asker (Swe)—Date Up
1982 Achaz von Buchwald (FRG)
    —Wendy
1983 Niels K. Hansen (Den)
    —Nighttimes Playboy
1984 Michael Rüping (FRG)
    —Silbersee
1985 Peter Charles (GB)—April Sun
1986 Harvey Smith (GB)
    —Sanyo Shining Example
1987 Harvey Smith (GB)
    —Sanyo Shining Example

Most wins—riders

4 Åke Hultberg (1970, 1973, 1974, 1980)

Most wins—horses

3 El-Vis (1970, 1973, 1974)

Harvey Smith and Sanyo Shining Example take their lap of honour after winning the 1986 Swedish Derby in Falsterbo. (Jan Gyllensten)

Finn Derby—Finnish Jumping Derby

1973 Christopher Wegelius (Fin)
      —No Girls
1974 Per Fresk (Swe)—Ylva
1975 Christopher Wegelius (Fin)
      —Trixie
1976 Tom Gordin (Fin)—Last Change
1977 Viktor Nenakhov (USSR)
      —Imperial
1978 Kristian Maunula (Fin)—Bawian
1979 Peter Wrenke (FRG)—Daniela
1980 Veikko Heikkilä (Fin)—Amigo II
1981 Royne Zetterman (Swe)—Bugatti
1982 Dietrich Schulze (FRG)
      —Seute Dearn
1983 Juhani Eho (Fin)—Prins Fred
1984 Christopher Wegelius (Fin)
      —Monday Morning
1985 Satu Väihkönen (Fin)—Little Gold
1986 Marek Orlos (Pol)—Arion

Most wins—riders

3—Christopher Wegelius, (1973, 1975, 1984)

Hamburg—German Jumping Derby

1920 Paul Heil (Ger)—Cyrano
1921 Hans Joachim Andreae (Ger)
      —Teufel
1922 H. Martins (Ger)—Döllnitz
1923 H. Martins (Ger)—Döllnitz
1924 C.-F. von Langen (Ger)—Hanko
1925 H. C. von Wietersheim (Ger)
      —Kreon
1926 Graf Willi Hohenau (Ger)—Apoll
1927 C.-F. von Langen (Ger)—Falkner
1928 C.-F. von Langen (Ger)—Falkner
1929 Marten von Barnekow (Ger)
      —Derby
1930 Herbert Frick (Ger)
      —Morgenglanz
1931 Ernst Hasse (Ger)—Derby
1932 Marten von Barnekow (Ger)
      —General
1933 Harald Momm (Ger)—Baccarat
1934 Irmgard von Opel (Ger)—Nanuk
1935 Günter Temme (Ger)—Egly
1936 W. Nippe (Ger)—Landrat
1937 Hermann Fegelein (Ger)
      —Schorsch
1938 Günter Temme (Ger)—Nordland
1939 Waldemar Fegelein (Ger)
      —Nordtrud
1949 Käthe Schmidt-Metzger (FRG)
      —Fenek
1950 Fritz Thiedemann (FRG)—Loretto
1951 Fritz Thiedemann (FRG)—Meteor
1952 John Russell (USA)—Rattler
1953 Walter Schmidt (FRG)—Caesar
1954 Fritz Thiedemann (FRG)
      —Diamant
1955 Hans Günter Winkler (FRG)
      —Halla
1956 Carlos Delia (Arg)—Discutido
1957 Alwin Schockemöhle (FRG)
      —Bachus

1958 Fritz Thiedemann (FRG)—Finale
1959 Fritz Thiedemann (FRG)—Retina
1960 Kurt Jarasinski (FRG)—Raffaela
1961 Raimondo d'Inzeo (Ita)—Posillipo
1962 Nelson Pessoa (Bra)—Espartaco
1963 Nelson Pessoa (Bra)
      —Gran Geste
1964 Hermann Schridde (FRG)
      —Dozent II
1965 Nelson Pessoa (Bra)
      —Gran Geste
1966 Kurt Jarasinski (FRG)—Torro
1967 Andrew Fielder (GB)—Vibart
1968 Nelson Pessoa (Bra)
      —Gran Geste
1969 Alwin Schockemöhle (FRG)
      —Wimpel III
1970 Marion Mould (GB)—Stroller
1971 Alwin Schockemöhle (FRG)
      —Wimpel III
1972 Not held
1973 Hartwig Steenken (FRG)
      —Simona
1974 Hartwig Steenken (FRG)
      —Kosmos
1975 Caroline Bradley (GB)
      —New Yorker
1976 Eddie Macken (Ire)—Boomerang
1977 Hugo Simon (Aut)—Little One
1978 Eddie Macken (Ire)—Boy
1979 Gerd Wiltfang (FRG)—Roman
1980 Peter Luther (FRG)—Livius
1981 Eddie Macken (Ire)
      —Carroll's Spotlight
1982 Achaz von Buchwaldt (FRG)
      —Wendy
1983 Hugo Simon (Aut)—Gladstone
1984 Hugo Simon (Aut)—Gladstone
1985 Louis Jacobs (USA)
      —Janus de Vers
1986 David Broome (GB)—Royale

Most wins—riders

5 Fritz Thiedemann (1950, 1951, 1954, 1958, 1959)

Most wins—horses

3 Gran Geste (1963, 1965, 1968)

Most clear rounds—riders

8 Fritz Thiedemann
7 Nelson Pessoa
6 Hartwig Steenken
5 Paul Schockemöhle
  Hugo Simon

1 rider has ridden three clear rounds on different horses in the same Derby:
  Fritz Thiedemann, in 1959 on Retina, Godewind and Meteor

7 riders have each ridden two clear rounds on different horses in the same Derby:
  Fritz Thiedemann, in 1958 on Finale and Meteor
  Raimondo d'Inzeo, in 1962 on Merano and Posillipo
  Nelson Pessoa, in 1963 on Gran Geste and Espartaco
  Hartwig Steenken, in 1974 on Kosmos and Simona III

Ulrich Meyer zu Bexten, in 1974 on Floto and Wembly, and in 1983 on Merano and Marco
Eddie Macken, in 1976 on Boomerang and Boy
Franke Sloothaak, in 1984 on Golan and Warkant

Most clear rounds—horses

3 Meteor, in 1951, 1958, 1959
  Posillipo, in 1956, 1961, 1962
  Gran Geste, in 1963, 1965, 1968
  Dozent II, 1964, 1966, 1968
  Royale (ex Queensway Royale), 1983, 1984, 1986
  Gladstone, in 1977, 1983, 1984

Hickstead—British Jumping Derby

1961 Seamus Hayes (Ire)—Goodbye III
1962 Pat Smythe (GB)—Flanagan
1963 Nelson Pessoa (Bra)
      —Gran Geste
1964 Seamus Hayes (Ire)—Goodbye III
1965 Nelson Pessoa (Bra)
      —Gran Geste
1966 David Broome (GB)
      —Mister Softee
1967 Marion Coakes (GB)—Stroller
1968 Alison Westwood (GB)
      —The Maverick VII
1969 Anneli Drummond-Hay (GB)
      —Xanthos II
1970 Harvey Smith (GB)
      —Mattie Brown
1971 Harvey Smith (GB)
      —Mattie Brown
1972 Hendrik Snoek (FRG)—Shirokko
1973 Alison Dawes (GB)
      —Mr Banbury
      (ex The Maverick VII)
1974 Harvey Smith (GB)—Salvador
1975 Paul Darragh (Ire)—Pele
1976 Eddie Macken (Ire)—Boomerang
1977 Eddie Macken (Ire)—Boomerang
1978 Eddie Macken (Ire)—Boomerang
1979 Eddie Macken (Ire)
      —Carroll's Boomerang
1980 Michael Whitaker (GB)
      —Owen Gregory
1981 Harvey Smith (GB)—Sanyo Video
1982 Paul Schockemöhle (FRG)
      —Deister
1983 John Whitaker (GB)—Ryan's Son
1984 John Ledingham (Ire)—Gabhran
1985 Paul Schockemöhle (FRG)
      —Lorenzo
1986 Paul Schockemöhle (FRG)
      —Deister

Most wins—riders

4 Eddie Macken (1976, 1977, 1978, 1979)
  Harvey Smith (1970, 1971, 1974, 1981)

Most wins—horses

4 Boomerang (Carroll's Boomerang) (1976, 1977, 1978, 1979)

Most wins—countries

12 GB
 8 Ireland
 4 FRG
 2 Brazil

Clear rounds

1 horse has jumped 3 clear rounds:
 Stroller, in 1964, 1967, 1968
3 horses have jumped 2 clear rounds:
 Goodbye III, in 1961, 1964
 The Maverick VII (Mr Banbury), in 1968, 1973
 Boomerang, in 1976, 1978

14 horses have jumped 1 clear round:
 Dundrum, 1962
 Flanagan, 1962
 Mister Softee, 1966
 Xanthos II, 1969
 Donald Rex, 1970
 Mattie Brown, 1970
 Salvador, 1974
 Buttevant Boy, 1974
 Pele, 1975
 Snaffles, 1975
 Owen Gregory, 1980
 Sanyo Video, 1981
 Ryan's Son, 1983
 Deister, 1986

Jerez de la Frontera (Spain)

1985 Jan Tops (NL)—Little Madam
1986 Heinrich-Wilhelm Johannsmann (FRG)—Daniela
1987 Nick Skelton (GB)—Raffles Apollo

Millstreet—Irish Jumping Derby

1979 Paul Darragh (Ire)
      —Carroll's Heather Honey
1980 Eddie Macken (Ire)
      —Carroll's Onward Bound
1981 Paul Darragh (Ire)
      Carroll's Doreen
1982 Nick Skelton (GB)—St James
1983 James Kernan (Ire)
      —Bailey's Condy
1984 Harvey Smith (GB)
      —Sanyo Olympic Video
1985 Robert Smith (GB)
      —Sanyo Olympic Video
1986 Harvey Smith (GB)
      —Sanyo Shining Example

Newport, Rhode Island

1976 Bernie Traurig (USA)—Singapore
1977 Michael Matz (USA)—Jet Run
1978 Bernie Traurig (USA)
      —The Cardinal
1979 Melanie Smith (USA)—Calypso

1980 Peter Leone (USA)—Semi Pro
1981 Anthony d'Ambrosio (USA)
      —Sugar Ray
1982 Donald Cheska (USA)
      —Southside
1983 Buddy Brown (USA)
      —Charles Fox
1984 Buddy Brown (USA)
      —Eclair de l'Ile
1985 Donald Cheska (USA)
      —Eaden Vale
1986 Michael Matz (USA)—Bon Retour

Penina—Portuguese Jumping Derby

1973 Francisco Caldeira (Por)—Gitana

1974 Antonio Pimenta da Gama (Por)
      —Ribamar
1978 Antonio Pimenta da Gama (Por)
      —Ribamar
1979 Henrique Callado (Por)
      —Emeraode
1980 Luis Astolfi (Spa)—Dorado
1981 José Manuel Soares da Costa
      (Por)—Orpheu
1982 Luis Astolfi (Spa)—Spring Brook
1983 Antonio Pimenta da Gama (Por)
      —Ibis J
1984 Jorge Mathias (Por)—Saint Maur
1985 José Arango (Spa)—Misar
1986 Jorge Mathias (Por)—Lot of Fun

Most wins—riders

3 Antonio Pimenta da Gama, (1974, 1978, 1983)

Paul Schockemöhle and Deister tackling the Derby bank at Hickstead during their winning clear round in 1986. (Bob Langrish)

FEI International Competition

This world-wide competition was introduced by the FEI in 1979. Its unique formula enables those riders, who under normal circumstances cannot take part in international show jumping events, to compete over international courses without leaving their own country. Whether they are in Peru, or China, Norway or New Zealand, riders can compete against each other on equal terms with none of the problems and expense of long-distance travel. Riders in each participating country compete over standard, indentically-built courses designed by course designers designated by the FEI. Strict rules must be adhered to concerning the heights and widths of the obstacles; distances and dimensions; the length of poles and the depth of the cups which hold them.

The aim of the competition is to help young riders from the age of 16 onwards to gain experience over international-level courses and to raise overall jumping standards throughout the world. Any national federation which is affiliated to the FEI may organise a competition. To begin with, nations could nominate riders to different categories, but the current rules permit each country to enter only one category per year. There are three grades of competition: Category A, in which fences are a maximum 1.40 m in height; Category B, in which fences may not exceed 1.20 m; and Category C, which has a maximum height limit of 1.05m.

Each category comprises three competitions over different courses, and each competition is run over two rounds under Table A. In the case of equality of points after two rounds, the time of the second round is the deciding factor. Thus the complete competition consists of six rounds and the final score for each competitor is the total faults of the six rounds and the total of his times in the three second rounds. If two or more riders have equal total times, the fastest time in the second round of the last competition decides.

The three top-placed competitors of each participating country in each category receive diplomas, and at the end of the year the world-wide winner in each category is invited to the annual General Assembly of the FEI to receive a trophy.

The leading riders in the world-wide FEI International Jumping Competition traditionally collect their prizes at the annual FEI General Assembly. Pictured at the 1985 awards ceremony in Lisbon are (from right) HRH Prince Philip, President of the FEI; Philip Smith of South Africa, Category A winner; Mark Crean from New Zealand, Category B winner; Anne Selley from Bermuda, Category C winner and Georgina Hoare and Ken Jackson, respectively Public Relations Officer and Head of Press and Public Affairs of the sponsoring company, Tarmac.

1979

Category A

World-Wide Final Standings (top 10)

		Total F./Time
1	Greg Eurell (Aus)—Johnny Mac	0.00/247.22
2	Gonda Betrix (SA) —Elizabeth Ann's Honey Girl	4.00/209.50
3	Gavin Chester (Aus)—Blue King	4.00/218.38
4	Guy Creighton (Aus)—Mikneil	4.00/218.47
5	Anneli (Drummond-Hay) Wucherpfennig (SA)—White Horse Whisky	12.00/203.90
6	Mariane Gilchrist (Aus)—Goldray	12.00/238.21
7	Klaus Degener (SA)—Husquarna Utamara	15.00/238.80
8	Tony Lewis (SA)—Jongleur	16.00/224.40
9	Jan Broek (NL)—Faroek Z	16.00/251.10
10	Errol Wucherpfennig (SA)—Hunters' Moon	19.00/234.40

Participating nations: 8 (Aus, CRC, Den, NL, Nor, SA, Spa, Swe)

Final Standings by Country

(Where no result is given for a participating country, it means that no rider completed all three competitions; in some instances only one or two riders completed the three competitions.)

		Total F./Time
Australia		
1	Greg Eurell—Johnny Mac	0.00/247.22
2	Gavin Chester—Blue King	4.00/218.38
3	Guy Creighton—Mikneil	4.00/218.47
Costa Rica		
1	Jean-René Dechamps—Sam	28.00/230.90
Denmark		
1	Jan Skaermose—Phoenix	63.75/299.40
2	Liselotte Ternvig—Tin Tin	83.75/285.80
Netherlands		
1	Jan Broek—Faroek Z	16.00/251.10
2	Hermann Seiger—Chipantico	19.50/260.00
3	Willy van der Ham—Leanca Z	28.0/225.90
South Africa		
1	Gonda Betrix—Elizabeth Ann's Honey Girl	4.00/209.50
2	Anneli (Drummond-Hay) Wucherpfennig —White Horse Whisky	12.00/203.90
3	Klaus Degener—Husquarna Utamara	15.00/238.80

1980

Category A

World-Wide Final Standings (top 10)

		Total F./Time
1	Mickey Louw (SA)—Epol Appraise	0.00/219.46
2	Gonda Betrix (SA) —Elizabeth Ann's Honey Girl	4.00/226.67
3	Piet Raymakers (NL)—Eurotex Ducal	8.00/250.90
4	Lachlan McLaughlan (SA) —Vat 69 Bye and Bye	12.00/237.32
5	Peter Cavanagh (Aus)—Strong Brandy	12.00/263.46
6	Anton Ebben (NL)—Jumbo Design	16.00/269.33
7	John Ledingham (Ire)—Mullacrew	20.00/236.15
8	Jack Doyle (Ire)—Hardley	20.00/238.60
9	Greg Eurell (Aus)—Johnny Mac	20.00/255.65
10	Peter Winton (Aus)—Hengist	24.00/244.72

Participating nations: 10 (Aus, Den, Egy, Ire, Lux, NL, Nor, SA, Swe, Ven)

Final Standings by Country

		Total F./Time
Australia		
1	Peter Cavanagh—Strong Brandy	12.00/263.46
2	Greg Eurell—Johnny Mac	20.00/255.65
3	Peter Winton—Hengist	24.00/244.72
Denmark		
1	Niels Hansen—Nighttimes Playboy	37.00/289.40
2	Kim Richter—Janus	45.00/336.20
3	Liselotte Ternvig—Flux Toptani	58.75/279.00
Egypt		
1	Khalid M. Ali—Nasrallah	39.00/230.60
2	Ahmed El Sawaf—Salam	45.50/262.80
3	Adham Hammad—Kozak	88.00/307.80
Ireland		
1	John Ledingham—Mullacrew	20.00/236.15
2	Jack Doyle—Hardley	20.00/238.60
Luxemburg		
1	Angie Lefèbvre—Tramontane	40.00/280.57
2	Carlo Rollinger—Caesar	72.00/252.23
3	Alain Wilhelm—Soldan	78.75/282.70
Netherlands		
1	Piet Raymakers—Eurotex Ducal	8.00/250.90
2	Anton Ebben—Jumbo Design	16.00/269.33
3	Emiel Hendrix—Livius	28.00/257.25
South Africa		
1	Mickey Louw—Epol Appraise	0.00/219.46
2	Gonda Betrix —Elizabeth Ann's Honey Girl	4.00/226.67
3	Lachlan McLaughlan—Vat 69 Bye and Bye	12.00/237.32
Venezuela		
1	Luis Rincones—Salsifi	24.50/303.89
2	Jorge Machado—Progreso	51.50/262.30

Number of riders who completed the competition: 34

1981

Category A

World-Wide Final Standings (top 10)

		Total F./Time
1	Anneli (Drummond-Hay) Wucherpfennig (SA)—White Horse Nebraska	0.00/225.11
2	Mickey Louw (SA)—Epol Appraise	4.00/208.31
3	Philip Smith (SA)—Linden Rock	4.00/216.65
4	Lindsay Ball (Aus)—Kopje King	4.00/230.77
5	Gonda Betrix (SA) —Elizabeth Ann's Isis Bridge	8.00/210.51
6	Gail Foxcroft (SA)—Desert King	12.00/240.55
7	Greg Eurell (Aus)—Johnny Mac	12.00/244.89
8	Alain Wilhem (Lux)—Soldan	12.00/253.11
9	George Myburg (SA)—Toyota Merriment	16.00/220.54
10	Lachlan McLaughlan (SA) —Vat 69 Bye and Bye	20.00/218.04

Participating nations: 10 (Aus, CRC, Den, Lux, NL, Nor, SA, Spa, Swe, Ven)

Final Standings by Country

	Total F./Time
Australia	
1 Lindsay Ball—Kopje King	4.00/230.77
2 Greg Eurell—Johnny Mac	12.00/244.89
3 Clarrie Ridley—Mr Shrimpton	23.00/235.22
Denmark	
1 Lindy Fogh Pedersen—Meny	83.00/261.70
2 Liselotte Ternvig—Flux Toptani	92.00/262.90
Luxemburg	
1 Alain Wilhelm—Soldan	12.00/253.11
2 Théo Coppelmanns—Nosy Parker	28.50/303.95
3 Carlo Rollinger—Caesar	71.25/258.86
Netherlands	
1 Gerrit Veeneman—Ricardo	20.00/237.00
2 Rob Eras—Isocratus	25.50/239.00
3 Frans van Herten—Prescot	26.00/246.00
South Africa	
1 Anneli (Drummond-Hay) Wucherpfennig —White Horse Nebraska	0.00/225.11
2 Mickey Louw—Epol Appraise	4.00/208.31
3 Philip Smith—Linden Rock	4.00/216.65
Spain	
1 Luis Cabanas—Cronos	199.00/270.50
Sweden	
1 Peter Eriksson—Caraff	42.00/262.10
Venezuela	
1 Ruben Rojas-Perez—Paramaconi	74.00/283.40
2 Leopoldo Paoli—Solo	76.00/231.70

1981

Category B

World-Wide Final Standings (Top 10)

	Total F./Time
1 Pierre Wentzel (SA)—Red Ferry	0.00/203.11
2 Peter Levor (SA)—Ballad King	0.00/205.35
3 Oscar Pacheco (Ven)—Bambu	0.00/217.70
4 Jack Eadon (Aus)—Skidora	0.00/222.99
5 Ton Klumpers (NL)—Odin	0.00/255.24
6 Bill Johnson (SA)—Straight Leff	3.00/226.70
7 Jos Vogels (NL)—Boris	3.00/238.90
8 Kevin Connolly (SA)—Foolsfold	4.00/205.55
9 Jenny Robertson (Aus)—Koyuna	4.00/220.83
10 Sue Hoffmann (SA)—Em Ess Silvers Judy	4.00/226.89

Participating nations: 14 (Alg, Aus, CRC, Den, Egy, Kuw, Lux, NL, Nor, SA, Spa, Tpe, Ven, Zai)

Final Standings by Country

	Total F./Time
Algeria	
1 Boualam Ayouz—Rochad	28.00/251.10
2 Kouider Boukhari—Laurassi	61.00/247.70
3 Abdelhafid Henni—Faci	72.00/245.10
Australia	
1 Jack Eadon—Skidora	0.00/222.99
2 Jenny Robertson—Koyuna	4.00/220.83
3 Sally Boyle—Leesburg	4.00/232.98

	Total F./Time
Costa Rica	
1 Carole Ares—Sam	8.00/277.10
2 Fabio Pacheco—Princesa	21.00/274.60
3 Mario Camacho—Cleopatra	28.00/270.40
Denmark	
1 Jens Trabjerg—Hurricane	12.00/239.10
2 Kurt Jensen—Nicolaj	20.75/270.90
3 Olav Drehn—Willow Dale	27.00/244.50
Egypt	
1 Mohamed Hamdy—Bolbol	32.00/262.00
2 Ahmed El Sawaf—Salam	36.00/239.00
3 Youssef Olama—Mabrouk	44.00/243.00
Kuwait	
1 Nadia Al Mutawa—Feydan	4.00/272.76
Luxemburg	
1 Paul Zeutzius—Las Vegas	23.00/287.33
2 Angie Lefèbvre—Taquirou	36.50/303.89
3 René Lentz—Joyeuse	76.75/267.81
Netherlands	
1 Ton Klumpers—Odin	0.00/255.24
2 Jos Vogels—Boris	3.00/238.90
3 Roger van Dorst—Country Moretus	12.00/230.27
Norway	
1 Geir Gulliksen—Westpark	24.00/307.86
2 Kristin Engebretsen—Sogrape	44.00/280.75
3 Jan Tonnessen—Highway	58.25/323.26
South Africa	
1 Pierre Wentzel—Red Ferry	0.00/203.11
2 Peter Levor—Ballad King	0.00/205.35
3 Bill Johnson—Straight Leff	3.00/226.70
Spain	
1 Francisco Almansa—Farruco	19.00/254.70
Venezuela	
1 Oscar Pacheco—Bambu	0.00/217.70
Zaire	
1 Manuella Belotti—Camp Clair	20.00/292.00

1982

Category A

World-Wide Final Standings (top 10)

	Total F./Time
1 Guy Creighton (Aus)—Mikneil	0.00/206.66
2 Darryl Gershow (SA)—Agent Again	0.00/219.80
3 Anneli (Drummond-Hay) Wucherpfennig (SA)—White Horse Nebraska	3.00/197.70
4 Wayne Dale (SA)—Butterfly	4.00/189.20
5 James Young (SA)—ISC Yankee Dodger	4.00/207.20
6 Alfredo Sone (Chi)—Trumao	4.00/222.56
7 G. Bertrand (Fra)—Hussard	6.00/222.11
8 Björn Johannessen (Nor)—LS Logger	6.00/275.25
9 Seun Kok (SA)—Objective Personnel	8.00/200.30
10 Ilan Hirschowitz (SA)—Royal Enforcer	11.00/212.30

Participating nations: 8 (Aus, Chi, Den, Fra, NL, Nor, SA, Swe)

Final Standings by Country

	Total F./Time
Australia	
1 Guy Creighton—Mikneil	0.00/206.66
2 Sheridan Morley—Silverson	20.00/226.05
3 Andrea Macdonald—On Approval	24.00/233.17

Chile
1 Alfredo Sone—Trumao   4.00/222.56

Denmark
1 Henrik Nielsen—Geyser   16.00/252.30
2 Lindy Fogh Pedersen—Kalule   44.00/245.20

France
1 G. Bertrand—Hussard   6.00/222.11
2 N. Wahlen—Fleur de Mai   12.00/223.59
3 P. Duhard—Jeleda du Vivier   18.00/258.96

Netherlands
1 Dion van Groesen—Ne Soucie   15.00/233.93
2 Hank Melse—Funny Face   19.00/258.01
3 Martin de Vries—Monarch   24.50/248.07

Norway
1 Björn Johannessen—LS Logger   6.00/275.25

South Africa
1 Darryl Gershow—Agent Again   0.00/219.80
2 Anneli (Drummond-Hay) Wucherpfennig
   —White Horse Nebraska   3.00/197.70
3 Wayne Dale—Butterfly   4.00/189.20

Sweden
1 Maria Gretzer—Tartuffe   24.00/249.57
2 Lotta Strand—Gambler   80.75/265.00

Number of riders who completed the competition: 46

1982

Category B

World-Wide Final Standings (top 10)

		Total F./Time
1	Elizabeth Assaf (Bra)—Pirro	0.00/162.13
2	Marcos da Silva Fernandes (Bra)—Simbad	0.00/189.73
3	Ivan Galvao de Camargo (Bra)—Venus	4.25/174.16
4	Antonio Alegria Simoes (Bra)—Chat Noir	4.25/186.96
5	Teresa Guzzinati (Per)—Sundance Kid	8.00/174.14
6	Alice Linares (Ven)—Caramelo	11.00/197.10
7	Alberto Ettedgui (Ven)—Fireside	12.00/190.90
8	Becky de Sanoja (Ven)—Picaflor	12.00/191.80
9	Saleb Sakakini (Egy)—N. Elsafa	12.00/211.60
10	Carole Ares (CRC)—Sam	16.00/195.80

Participating nations: 9 (Alg, Bra, CRC, Egy, Kuw, Per, Tun, Ven, Zai)

Final Standings by Country

		Total F./Time
Algeria		
1	Amar Berrabah—Sahraoui	20.00/200.80
2	El Hadi Mouderres—El Djazair	21.75/194.50
3	Abdelkader Kanoun—Saphir	24.00/181.30
Brazil		
1	Elizabeth Assaf—Pirro	0.00/162.13
2	Marcos da Silva Fernandes—Simbad	0.00/189.73
3	Ivan Galvao de Camargo—Venus	4.25/174.16
Costa Rica		
1	Carole Ares—Sam	16.00/195.80
Egypt		
1	Saleb Sakakini—N. Elsafa	12.00/211.60
2	A. Kabary—Mr Swed	24.00/210.00
3	Mohamed Hamdy—Bolbol	31.00/220.40

Kuwait
1 Nadia Al Mutawa—Feydan   16.00/206.83
2 Sami Al Modaf—Exite   19.50/205.36
3 Fahad Al Sabah—Charlotte Rose   32.00/216.65

Peru
1 Teresa Guzzinati—Sundance Kid   8.00/174.14
2 Raul Vargas—Quemazon   31.00/217.04

Tunisia
1 Mourad Touhami—Kaabi   48.50/217.10
2 Hedi Baccouchi—Alouane   52.00/198.10
3 Habib Khiari—Dahbi   82.50/230.90

Venezuela
1 Alice Linares—Caramelo   11.00/197.10
2 Alberto Ettedgui—Fireside   12.00/190.90
3 Becky de Sanoja—Picaflor   12.00/191.80

Number of riders who completed the competition: 44

1983

Category A

World-Wide Final Standings (top 10)

		Total F./Time
1	Anneli (Drummond-Hay) Wucherpfennig (SA)—Tarmac Storm Finch	0.00/196.27
2	Rolf-Göran Bengtson (Swe)—Corragan	0.00/200.81
3	Heather Hillcoat (SA)—Tongaat Dual	0.00/209.03
4	Darryl Gershow (SA)—Bold Husar	0.00/212.76
5	Ann Hort (SA)—Kiss Poll	0.00/231.19
6	Judy Stegman (SA)—Autumn H. My Kingdom	3.00/225.17
7	Trevor Glass (SA)—Tugmaster	3.00/229.43
8	Barry Taylor (SA)—Powerforce	4.00/181.32
9	Lester Sanders (SA)—Bischoffs High Hopes	4.00/189.08
10	Piet Mooy (NL)—Rocco	4.00/192.09

Participating nations: 8 (Aus, Chi, Den, Fra, NL, Nor, SA, Swe)

Final Standings by Country

		Total F./Time
Australia		
1	John Patterson—Silverwood	8.00/233.39
2	Andrea McDonald—On Approval	8.00/234.51
3	Jeff Bickmore—Wylie	12.00/233.46
Chile		
1	Gustavo Rosselot—Malaquis	4.00/236.00
Denmark		
1	Lindy Fogh Pedersen—Grandis	20.00/236.90
2	Peter Kragh Andersen—Lepanto	48.25/263.60
3	Ib. Lunding—Orloff	65.25/265.40
France		
1	Charles Barbot—Juduka	10.50/256.64
2	Charly Bourratière—Estelle	23.75/242.17
3	Thierry Catala—Ksar du Vauptain	29.00/235.01
Netherlands		
1	Piet Mooy—Rocco	4.00/192.09
2	Hank Melse—Servus	4.00/196.03
3	Jan Tops—Little Madam	8.00/196.75
Norway		
1	Geir Aknessaeter—Another Guy	54.00/247.87

South Africa

	Total F./Time
1 Anneli (Drummond-Hay) Wucherpfennig —Tarmac Storm Finch	0.00/196.27
2 Heather Hillcoat—Tongaat Dual	0.00/209.03
3 Darryl Gershow—Bold Husar	0.00/212.76

Sweden

1 Rolf-Göran Bengtson—Corragan	0.00/200.81
2 Lotta Strand—Gambler	28.50/226.55

Number of riders who started the competition: 224

Number of riders who completed the competition: 70

1983

Category B

World-Wide Final Standings (top 10)

	Total F./Time
1 Carole Ares (CRC)—Sam	0.00/207.00
2 Nadia Al Mutawa (Kuw)—Classic	0.00/223.59
3 Cornelia Fieberg (CRC)—Tocuman	0.00/247.30
4 H. H. Kamel (Egy)—Sali Al Nabi	6.00/231.00
5 Belkacem Cheriane (Alg)—Amiral	7.00/207.00
6 Fernando Miro Quesada (Per)—Brimbao	7.00/244.12
7 Abdelkader Kanoun (Alg)—Saphir	8.00/192.00
8 Mario Camacho (CRC)—Cleopatra	10.00/249.90
9 Juan José Mostajo (Per)—Beau Geste	11.00/179.07
10 Abdullah Sabah (Kuw)—Mist	11.00/219.71

Participating nations: 8 (Alg, Bra, CRC, Egy, Kuw, Per, Tun, Zai)

Final Standings by Country

	Total F./Time
Algeria	
1 Belkacem Cheriane—Amiral	7.00/207.00
2 Abdelkader Kanoun—Saphir	8.00/192.00
3 El Hadi Mouderres—El Djazair	12.00/215.00
Costa Rica	
1 Carole Ares—Sam	0.00/207.00
2 Cornelia Fieberg—Tocuman	0.00/247.30
3 Mario Camacho—Cleopatra	10.00/249.90
Egypt	
1 H. H. Kamel—Sali Al Nabi	6.00/231.00
2 Saleb Sakakini—Feh El Baraka	12.00/207.00
3 Kh. M. Ali—Mabrouka	18.00/243.00
Kuwait	
1 Nadia Al Mutawa—Classic	0.00/223.59
2 Abdullah Sabah—Mist	11.00/219.71
3 Gemila Al Mutawa—Siccachant	13.00/229.46
Peru	
1 Fernando Miro Quesada—Brimbao	7.00/244.12
2 Juan José Mostajo—Beau Geste	11.00/179.07
3 Licia Prado—Digno	11.00/225.53
Tunisia	
1 Mourad Touhami—Kaabi	28.00/237.20
2 Badreddine Halleb—Afif	40.75/250.20
3 Mourad Manchoul—Raad	83.75/225.70
Zaire	
1 J. L. Namwisi—Worthy Gold	30.50/250.20
2 L. Bournigaud—Feather Stone	44.75/288.00

Number of riders who started the competition: 146

Number of riders who completed the competition: 52

1984

Category A

World-Wide Final Standings (top 10)

	Total F./Time
1 Lester Sanders (SA)—M+R High Hopes	0.00/190.21
2 Lindy Fogh Pedersen (Den)—Grandis	0.00/202.40
3 Guillermo Cordoba (Arg)—Casual	3.00/196.09
4 Kathy Kitterman (Arg)—Going	3.00/201.44
5 Philp Smith (SA)—Tabriz	4.00/193.48
6 Gonda Betrix (SA)—Sagorins Houselights	4.00/197.50
7 Gerrit Veeneman (NL)—Orli Drum	4.00/209.51
8 Francisco Galli (Arg)—Virtual	4.00/231.84
9 Jan Tops (NL)—Little Madam	7.00/216.01
10 George Myburg (SA)—Toyota Cloud Star	8.00/200.82

Participating nations: 7 (Arg, Den, Egy, Jap. NL, SA, Swe)

Final Standings by Country

	Total F./Time
Argentina	
1 Guillermo Cordoba—Casual	3.00/196.09
2 Kathy Kitterman—Going	3.00/201.44
3 Francisco Galli—Virtual	4.00/231.84
Denmark	
1 Lindy Fogh Pedersen—Grandis	0.00/202.40
2 Björn Ikast—Chasseur	20.00/225.10
3 Sören Kundsen—Chiquitta	23.00/224.90
Japan	
1 Shuichi Toki—Parachina	20.00/225.69
2 Takashi Tomura—La Silk	31.50/247.20
3 Masayo Ozawo—Brother Jin	43.25/217.80
Netherlands	
1 Gerrit Veeneman—Orli Drum	4.00/209.51
2 Jan Tops—Little Madam	7.00/216.01
3 Eric van der Vleuten—Expolisar	12.00/192.90
South Africa	
1 Lester Sanders—M+R High Hopes	0.00/190.21
2 Philip Smith—Tabriz	4.00/193.48
3 Gonda Betrix—Sagorins Houselights	4.00/197.50

Number of riders who started the competition: 162

Number of riders who completed the competition: 50

1984

Category B

World-Wide Final Standings (top 10)

	Total F./Time
1 Alejandro Melgarejo (Chi)—Solitario	0.00/183.70
2 Alfredo Sone (Chi)—Aconcagua	0.00/187.80
3 Roberto Salazar (CRC)—Pinta	0.00/206.65
4 Luiz Stockler (Bra)—Belito Blanco	0.00/208.46
5 Gonzalo Gamboa (Col)—Sagitario	0.00/209.00
6 Nadia Al Mutawa (Kuw)—Feydan	0.00/218.76
7 René Suarez (Col)—Resguardo	0.00/238.90
8 Chung-Kyun Suh (Kor)—Sinjin	1.00/265.48
9 Carole Ares (CRC)—Pop Pinkerton	3.00/213.30
10 Luis Matallana (Per)—Cochamal	3.00/263.83

Participating nations: 12 (Alg, Bol, Bra, Chi, Col, CRC, Kor, Kuw, Lux, Per, Tpe, Tun)

Final Standings by Country

	Total F./Time

Algeria
1 Mohamed Daoudi—Jeu de Kate	9.00/242.10
2 Abdelkader Kanoun—Saphir	12.00/222.60
3 Karim Ikhanazen—Jacow	12.00/251.50

Bolivia
1 Fernando Jordan—Arrogante	4.00/231.70
2 José Zapata—Satinador	7.50/227.30
3 Oscar Escobar—Galante	8.00/216.80

Brazil
1 Luiz Stockler—Belito Blanco	0.00/208.46
2 Lucia Goncalves—I'll Be Lucky	4.00/236.79
3 Gerson Monteiro—Chancellor	8.00/203.84

Chile
1 Alejandro Melgarejo—Solitario	0.00/183.70
2 Alfredo Sone—Aconcagua	0.00/187.80
3 Alfonso Anguita—Cherry Creek	4.00/223.10

Colombia
1 Gonzalo Gamboa—Sagitario	0.00/209.00
2 René Suarez—Resguardo	0.00/238.90
3 Hugo Gamboa—Quenqueno	7.00/202.20

Costa Rica
1 Roberto Salazar—Pinta	0.00/206.65
2 Carole Ares—Pop Pinkerton	3.00/213.30
3 Jorge Ruenes—Sagitario	8.00/224.70

Korea
1 Chung-Kyun Suh—Sinjin	1.00/265.48
2 Chang-Moo Shin—Bering Jack	4.00/242.53
3 Jae-Ung Ma—Dae Dang	15.75/232.18

Kuwait
1 Nadia Al Mutawa—Feydan	0.00/218.76
2 Gemila Al Mutawa—Middle Hill	8.25/246.10
3 Selwa Kadi—Rockford	21.00/245.83

"Show jumpers how Guinness gives you strength"

An advertisement from the 1960s, when Guinness was involved in show jumping sponsorship. (With permission of Guinness Archive)

Luxemburg
1 Paul Zeutzius—Las Vegas	18.00/243.75
2 Carlo Rollinger—Nautilius	26.00/227.86
3 Bea Neu—Blötz	36.00/227.82

Peru
1 Luis Matallana—Cochamal	3.00/263.83
2 Raul Vargas—Petrarca	8.00/209.89
3 Juan José Mostajo—Leonardo	8.00/210.86

Taipei
1 Han-Wen Huang—Parsher Boy	8.00/235.26
2 Huan-Hsiang Hsieh—Tao Hsiang	32.00/267.60
3 Shan-Mei Lee—Newborn	102.50/267.95

Tunisia
1 Khalifa Gahbiche—Prince	25.00/250.40
2 Naceur Gasmi—Lamouri	43.00/254.00
3 Mourad Manchoul—Raad	47.00/247.50

Number of riders who started the competition: 248

Number of riders who completed the competition: 117

1984

Category C

World-Wide Final Standings (top 10)

	Total F./Time
1 Myriam Armant (Zai)—Touch and Go	0.00/197.68
2 Vittorio Barba (Phi)—Olympia	0.00/218.84
3 Mariella Virata (Phil)—Avianca	0.00/226.48
4 J. H. Thorigne (Zai)—Puma	8.00/209.13
5 Michael de Leon (Phi)—Zodiac	9.00/261.01
6 Ahmad Basitt (Mal)—Miss Kiora	9.00/263.81
7 Andrea Somic (Sin)—Surprise	10.00/238.28
8 Manuel Montilla (Phi)—Silver King	10.00/277.97
9 Catherine Hull (Sin)—Checkmate	11.00/221.73
10 J. C. Bartz (Zai)—The Hobbit	12.00/204.97

Participating nations: 4 (Mal, Phi, Sin, Zai)

Final Standings by Country

	Total F./Time

Malaysia
1 Ahmad Basitt—Miss Kiora	9.00/263.81
2 Akilo Kume—Precious	17.00/300.89
3 Khairuddin—Top Hand	19.00/234.84

Philippines
1 Vittorio Barba—Olympia	0.00/218.84
2 Mariella Virata—Avianca	0.00/226.48
3 Michael de Leon—Zodiac	9.00/261.01

Singapore
1 Andrea Somic—Surprise	10.00/238.28
2 Catherine Hull—Checkmate	11.00/221.73
3 Yasmin Amir—Cloudy	12.00/213.18

Zaire
1 Myriam Armant—Touch and Go	0.00/197.68
2 J. H. Thorigne—Puma	8.00/209.13
3 J. C. Bartz—The Hobbit	12.00/204.97

Number of riders who started the competition: 45

Number of riders who completed the competition: 22　▶

William Steinkraus

Outside the world of horses, one of William Steinkraus' chief enjoyments is playing chamber music (he is an accomplished viola player). To those who have seen him ride this comes as no surprise, for he is an artist in the saddle, too: one of the most stylishly effective horsemen the sport of show jumping has ever seen.

Born in Cleveland, Ohio, on 12 October, 1925, he learnt to ride as a child and began competing in early 1939. His riding activities were not restricted to junior jumping; since at that time there were not enough junior classes to keep young show jumpers busy, it was usual for them to show open jumpers and hunters as well, and the all-round experience was obviously of great benefit to aspiring horsemen. The climax of Steinkraus' junior career came in 1941 when he won both of the United States' National Equitation Championships—one for riding on the flat, the other over fences.

Following service in the Far East during the Second World War, with the United States Army's last mounted regiment, he returned home to pursue his equestrian activities. After the 1948 Olympic Games the US Cavalry, which had formerly supplied riders to represent their country abroad, was disbanded, leaving the United States without an international team. It was to fill this gap that the United States Equestrian Team was formed and in 1951 William Steinkraus joined this fledgling enterprise. Four years later, in 1955, he was appointed its captain.

For 21 years he competed at the highest level with a succession of brilliant horses, all of whom performed with the smoothness and economy of effort that was to become a hallmark of the USET, and which earned the admiration of riders and spectators throughout the world.

Undoubtedly a factor which contributed to this admiration was the type of Thoroughbred horse which the USET favoured for so many years. Often ex-racehorses, these big, quality animals, beautifully trained and stylishly ridden, brought an elegance to show jumping which is not always in evidence. William Steinkraus nominates Democrat, Riviera Wonder, Ksar d'Esprit, Sinjon, Snowbound, Main Spring and Bold Minstrel as the best horses he has ridden. Of these, the first six were Thoroughbred, Main Spring was half bred and Bold Minstrel seven-eighths bred.

Steinkraus rode in his first Nations Cup in 1951 at Toronto, had his first win in that same Cup in 1956 and by the end of 1972 had ridden in 39 official winning teams. His winning mounts were First Boy (1), Ksar d'Esprit (6), Riviera Wonder (3), Trail Guide (2), Sinjon (11), Unusual (1), Snowbound (6), Bold Minstrel (4), Fleet Apple (2) and Main Spring (3). His Grand Prix successes included Aachen, New York, Toronto, Harrisburg, Rotterdam and Ostend, and he twice won the King George V Gold Cup at London's Royal International Horse Show, in 1956 (when he jumped the only two clear rounds of the competition, on First Boy and Night Owl, and nominated First Boy the winner) and again in 1964 with Sinjon. In the Pan American Games he won two team gold medals, with Riviera Wonder in 1959 and Sinjon in 1963, as well as a team silver in 1967, when his mount was the Royal Minstrel gelding, Bold Minstrel, owned by W. D. Haggard III.

Steinkraus made his Olympic debut at Helsinki in 1952, winning a team bronze medal and finishing 11th individually with Hollandia. In 1956, riding Night Owl, he finished equal 15th individually, an achievement he repeated in Rome in 1960 with Riviera Wonder. Rome also brought a team silver medal—in the separate Nations Cup Steinkraus rode Miss E. R. Sears' grey gelding Ksar d'Esprit.

After missing the 1964 Tokyo Games, he achieved the pinnacle of his career at Mexico in 1968: the individual gold medal. Riding the Princess de la Tour d'Auvergne's brown Thoroughbred gelding Snowbound, he became the first United States rider to win this supreme title. In the first round, over a tremendously testing course, Steinkraus and Snowbound scored one of only two clears in the entire competition, and with just one fence down in the second round they finished a decisive 4 faults ahead of their nearest rivals.

Four years later in Munich Steinkraus, making his last Olympic appearance, showed that he had lost none of his artistry. After he had ridden Snowbound into equal 22nd place in the individual event, a leg injury prevented the horse from taking part in the team event, so his rider switched to Main Spring, a Canadian-bred gelding who had been donated to the USET by W. D. Haggard III. Steinkraus and Main Spring went brilliantly, recording the best overall score and one of only three clear rounds in the whole contest. This performance helped the United States team to win the silver medal: they finished only 0.25 faults behind the victorious team from the Federal Republic of Germany.

Steinkraus retired as a riding member of the USET at the end of the Toronto Royal Winter Fair horse show in November 1972. Naturally, when he looks back on his distinguished career, the highlight that stands out is winning the gold medal in Mexico. However, in his capacity as Chairman of the USET he derived as much satisfaction, if of a rather different sort, from the performance of the United States team when they won the Olympic gold at Los Angeles in 1984 and the 1986 World Championship in Aachen.

A book editor by profession, he enjoys hunting, fishing, golf and skiing and in spite of his many commitments—which include being a national and an FEI judge—he finds time to make a young horse or two, both hunters and jumpers. He still competes at small, local shows to start off the young horses.

William Steinkraus and Main Spring at Lucerne in 1972. It was with this horse that Steinkraus won a team silver medal at that year's Olympics. (Findlay Davidson)

1985

Category A

World-Wide Final Standings (top 10)

		Total F./Time
1	Philip Smith (SA)—Cloud Nine	0.00/187.98
2	Justo Albarracin (Arg)—Virtual de Tatu	3.00/199.10
3	Johny Mendes (SA)—Aces Wild	3.00/207.47
4	Lester Sanders (SA)—High Hopes	4.00/167.90
5	Jorge Llambi (Arg)—Sorprendente	4.00/174.19
6	Errol Wucherpfennig (SA)—Courier	4.00/174.83
7	Hugo Dircie (Arg)—Monte Quemado	4.00/177.09
8	Michelle Myburg (SA)—Handmit	4.00/177.95
9	Federico Castaing (Arg)—Yaxtan	4.00/181.15
10	P. Vercruysse (Bel)—Wimpel	4.00/196.01

Participating nations: 4 (Arg, Bel, Den, SA)

Final Standings by Country

		Total F./Time
Argentina		
1	Justo Albarracin—Virtual de Tatu	3.00/199.10
2	Jorge Llambi—Sorprendente	4.00/174.19
3	Hugo Dircie—Monte Quemado	4.00/177.09
Belgium		
1	P. Vercruysse—Wimpel	4.00/196.01
2	A. Verlooy—One Eleven	16.00/174.54
3	P. Delcourt—Alwin	24.00/204.49
Denmark		
1	Niels K. Hansen—Gazelle	8.00/188.80
2	Søren Knudsen—Chiquita	11.00/201.10
3	Bjørn Ikast—Grey Lady	31.75/211.10
South Africa		
1	Philip Smith—Cloud Nine	0.00/187.98
2	Johny Mendes—Aces Wild	3.00/207.47
3	Lester Sanders—High Hopes	4.00/167.90

Number of riders who started the competition: 195

Number of riders who completed the competition: 75

1985

Category B

World-Wide Final Standings (top 10)

		Total F./Time
1	Mark Crean (NZ)—Missouri	0.00/175.10
2	Diego Vallejo (Col)—Campestre	0.00/181.30
3	Daniel Bedoya (Bol)—Amaretto	0.00/191.12
4	Richard Hampton (NZ)—Rich Hill	0.00/194.10
5	William Lopez (Col)—Buenos Aires	0.00/196.50
6	Alfredo Sone (Chi)—Huincha Negra	0.00/205.90
7	Ignacio Flores (Chi)—Motivo	0.00/219.40
8	Victor Rodriguez (Chi)—Soplito	3.00/188.60
9	Juan Manuel Rivas (Col)—Cauplican	3.00/211.30
10	Juan Carlos Garcia (Col)—Dije	4.00/170.00

Participating nations: 15 (Alg, Bol, Chi, Col, CRC, Egy, Fin, Gre, Lux, Ind, Kor, Kuw, NZ, Tpe, Tun)

Final Standings by Country

		Total F./Time
Algeria		
1	Kamel Ikhanazen—Myosotis II	15.00/216.50
2	Mohamed Daoudi—Jeux de Kate	16.00/207.70
3	Kamel Ait Ali—Faci II	20.00/208.10
Bolivia		
1	Daniel Bedoya—Amaretto	0.00/191.12
2	Jorge Antequera—Galante	4.00/200.00
3	Jorge Lopez—Huracan	12.00/211.70
Chile		
1	Alfredo Sone—Huincha Negra	0.00/205.90
2	Ignacio Flores—Motivo	0.00/219.40
3	Victor Rodriguez—Soplito	3.00/188.60
Colombia		
1	Diego Vallejo—Campestre	0.00/181.30
2	William Lopez—Buenos Aires	0.00/196.50
3	Juan Manuel Rivas—Cauplican	3.00/211.30
Costa Rica		
1	Roberto Salazar—Pinta	4.00/218.25
2	Carole Ares—Pop Pinkerton	4.00/219.55
Egypt		
1	Khaled Aly—Ashet Elasany	4.00/213.00
2	Sayed Mouawad—Farag	4.00/226.20
3	Omar Mamdouh—Basel	12.00/229.30
Finland		
1	Raimo Aaltonen—Romanze	7.00/206.23
2	Patricia Winckelmann Zilliacus —Kuwait Enterprize	8.00/211.83
3	Karl Fazer—Ultimatum	13.00/234.15
Greece		
1	I. Lalaouni—Sharka	12.00/232.81
2	Th. Papakostas—Sleave Na Mon	28.00/262.37
3	E. Mitsis—Roxani	32.00/258.50
India		
1	Capt G. M. Khan—North Shore	4.00/214.74
2	Capt J. S. Ahluwalia—Elixir	8.00/213.14
3	Dfr Mahabir Singh—Amar II	11.00/196.58
Luxemburg		
1	Ange Lefèbvre—Cherun	23.25/232.81
2	Paul Zeutzius—Las Vegas	26.75/220.00
3	Patricia Fortin—Irma F	36.75/221.48
Korea		
1	Kim Sung Whan—Box Z	8.00/206.88
2	Suh Chung Kyun—Sinjin II	8.00/236.81
3	Jeon Jai Sik—Berinjack	35.00/261.40
Kuwait		
1	Sami Al Mudaf—Ballendine	4.00/193.08
2	Nadia Al Mutawa—Feydan	4.00/193.98
3	Dervilla Campbell—Sweet Briar	6.00/153.35
New Zealand		
1	Mark Crean—Missouri	0.00/175.10
2	Richard Hampton—Rich Hill	0.00/194.10
3	Colin McIntosh—Resolution	4.00/183.10
Taipei		
1	Ming-Kuen Jou—Bon Bore	24.00/205.00
2	Bill Yeh—Staumpy	36.00/216.85
3	Huan-Shyang Shieh—Taur-Shiang	43.00/239.62
Tunisia		
1	Mourad Manchoul—Raad 2	10.00/249.79
2	Riadh Meziane—Dhahbi	25.00/298.65
3	Mohamed Abassi—Kabi	27.00/254.07

Number of riders who started the competition: 364

Number of riders who completed the competition: 158

1985

Category C

World-Wide Final Standings (top 10)

		Total F./Time
1	Anne Selley (Ber)—Night Mare	0.00/192.51
2	Marina Curtis-Evans (Ber)—Shalimar	0.00/194.49
3	Mariella Virata (Phi)—Avianca	0.00/203.79
4	Marcelino de Leon (Phi)—Zodiac	0.00/237.03
5	Lorraine Bottreau (Sin)—Tobasco	0.00/240.27
6	Anna Jayme (Phi)—Baroness	3.00/275.25
7	Joan Taplin (Ber)—Silver Seabright	4.00/195.59
8	Kathryn Madeiros (Ber)—Consider It Done	4.00/199.00
9	G. P. Heslop (Ber)—Brampton Lad	4.00/199.04
10	Catriona Maclean (Sin)—Shrimpy	4.00/212.32

Participating nations: 7 (Ber, Chn, Cyp, Mal, Phi, Sin, Zai)

Final Standings by Country

		Total F./Time
Bermuda		
1	Anne Selley—Night Mare	0.00/192.51
2	Marina Curtis-Evans—Shalimar	0.00/194.49
3	Joan Taplin—Silver Seabright	4.00/195.59
China		
1	Chao Lu—Mi Ge	4.00/241.40
2	Ge Er Deng Tu—Guo Guo	7.00/277.56
3	Meng Ke—Black Wind	8.00/260.39
Cyprus		
1	Stephanos Serafim—Just George VI	24.00/274.14
2	D. Bennett—Bambino	31.50/268.80
3	Nikos Andreou—Westport	43.00/261.60
Malaysia		
1	Ahman Basid—Miss Kiora	12.00/288.30
2	M. Toye—Diamond Boy	19.00/312.80
3	Awi Naim—Senyum	20.00/294.30
Philippines		
1	Mariella Virata—Avianca	0.00/203.79
2	Marcelino de Leon—Zodiac	0.00/237.03
3	Anna Jayme—Baroness	3.00/275.25
Singapore		
1	Lorraine Bottreau—Tobasco	0.00/240.27
2	Catriona Maclean—Shrimpy	4.00/212.32
3	Peter Abisheganaden—Magnum Red	8.00/220.05
Zaire		
1	C. Guisse—Sachem	11.25/218.36
2	N. Fichter—Oasis II	16.00/212.50

Number of riders who started the competition: 104

Number of riders who completed the competition: 48

1986

Category A

World-Wide Final Standings (top 10)

		Total F./Time
1	Barry Taylor (SA)—Powerforce	0.00/199.95
2	Kim Richter (Den)—Janus	0.00/210.40
3	Gail Foxcroft (SA)—Harry's Game	0.00/221.59
4	André Ferreira (SA)—Irish Magic	4.00/194.09
5	Erik Bigler (Den)—Scirocco	4.00/200.30
6	Robert McConnochie (SA)—Aposcope	4.00/206.39
7	Judy Stegeman (SA)—Kingdom	4.00/223.30
8	Bryce McCall (SA)—Hamadan	5.50/203.96
9	Viviane Duchini (Arg)—Number One	8.00/186.93
10	José Maria Rega (Uru)—Berretin	8.00/188.43

Participating nations: 5 (Arg, Den, NZ, SA, Uru)

Final Standings by Country

		Total F./Time
Argentina		
1	Viviane Duchini—Number One	8.00/186.93
2	Daniel Rodriguez—Graff	8.00/201.28
3	Andres Baxter—Bora Bora	8.00/209.78
Denmark		
1	Kim Richter—Janus	0.00/210.40
2	Erik Bigler—Scirocco	4.00/200.30
3	Bjorn Ikast—Blue Water Grey Lady	8.00/193.60
New Zealand		
1	Geordie Bull—Gratis	20.00/206.30
2	Donna Smith—Ernie Might	28.00/198.50
3	Angela Ilston—Mechanical	28.00/224.10
South Africa		
1	Barry Taylor—Powerforce	0.00/199.95
2	Gail Foxcroft—Harry's Game	0.00/221.59
3	André Ferreira—Irish Magic	4.00/194.09
Uruguay		
1	José Maria Rega—Berretin	8.00/188.43
2	Brigido Rivero—Gendarme	11.00/189.36
3	Daniel Freyre—Free Way	12.50/207.80

Number of riders who started the competition: 146

Number of riders who completed the competition: 63

1986

Category B

World-Wide Final Standings (top 10)

		Total F./Time
1	Pedro Rojas (Ven)—Corralero	0.00/165.55
2	Bernardo Naveillan (Chi)—Exitosa	0.00/170.80
3	Magnus Lillkvist (Fin)—Black Horse Turbo	0.00/175.52
4	Alberto Posada (Col)—Juan Valdez	0.00/176.40
5	Cindy Smith (Zim)—Lucillon	0.00/213.70
6	Alfonso Anguita (Chi)—Prestigioso	3.00/221.50
7	Raimo Aaltonen (Fin)—Royal Chocolate	4.00/176.11
8	Matijaz Cik (Yug)—Santa Maria	4.00/188.97
9	Kimmo Kinnunen (Fin)—Fallera	4.00/192.40
10	Boualem Ayouz (Alg)—Rochd	4.00/195.00

Participating nations: 16 (Alg, Chi, Col, Egy, Fin, Gre, Ind, Kor, Per, Phi, Syr, Tpe, Tun, Ven, Yug, Zim)

Final Standings by Country

		Total F./Time
Algeria		
1	Boualem Ayouz—Rochd	4.00/195.00
2	Kamel Anazene—No Problem	8.00/184.00
3	Mohamed Khakhaz—Ashbourn Royal	12.00/197.00

1986

Chile

	Total F./Time
1 Bernardo Naveillan—Exitosa	0.00/170.80
2 Alfonso Anguita—Prestigioso	3.00/221.50
3 Eduardo Muñoz—Anakena	7.00/189.90

Colombia

1 Alberto Posada—Juan Valdez	0.00/176.40
2 Hernando Carrasco—Konkivo	9.00/215.10
3 Gonzalo Gamboa—Halcon	10.75/242.20

Egypt

1 Adham Hammad—Last Chance	8.00/189.90
2 Khaled Assem—Toot	8.00/199.60
3 Karim Habashi—Dalila	8.50/223.70

Finland

1 Magnus Lillkvist—Black Horse Turbo	0.00/175.52
2 Raimo Aaltonen—Royal Chocolate	4.00/176.11
3 Kimmo Kinnunen—Fallera	4.00/192.40

Greece

1 P. Koytsogiannis—Double Success	11.00/207.60
2 M. Marinopoyloy—Golden Exchange	16.00/190.30
3 E. Drakatoy—Pop Star	16.00/199.50

India

1 Capt J. S. Ahluwalia—Gautam	39.00/211.76
2 Maj R. S. Kalha—Mountain Ash	45.50/250.08
3 Dfr Mahavir Singh—North Shore	56.25/216.91

Korea

1 Son Bum Yong—Chances Are	8.00/220.47
2 Kim Hyung Chil—Mudeungsan	24.25/233.27
3 Park So Woon—Oscar de Mai	31.50/233.17

Peru

1 Ileana de Miro Quesada—La Abeja Maya	8.00/196.23
2 Adela de Graña—Kenji	12.00/191.94
3 Ricardo Moncada—Datil	19.50/224.55

Philippines

1 Vittorio Barba—Huckleberry	4.50/183.32
2 Mariella Virata—Avianca	17.50/194.50
3 Steven Virata—Flying Tiger	40.75/223.41

Syria

1 Ghassan Kassar—Miki Mouse	4.50/236.96
2 Lufti Tassabehji—Fakhraddin	51.50/255.64

Taipei

1 Bill Yeh—Stumpy	27.75/218.24
2 Chi-Hsian Tsau—Persian Boy	34.00/226.79
3 Han-Wen Huang—Bonbore	40.50/235.03

Tunisia

1 Fethi Triki—Hamada	12.00/213.46
2 Taieb Ben Naceur—Levante	15.00/223.36
3 Taoufik Meziane—Boustene	16.00/217.44

Venezuela

1 Pedro Rojas—Corralero	0.00/165.55
2 Oscar Francius—Sandor	7.00/179.57
3 Alberto Perez—Halcon	8.00/174.43

Yugoslavia

1 Matijaz Cik—Santa Maria	4.00/188.97
2 Aco Slavic—Don	41.00/223.34
3 Marko Brojan—Anita	51.00/200.47

Zimbabwe

1 Cindy Smith—Lucillon	0.00/213.70
2 Yvonne Thompson—Gratuity	5.00/194.94
3 Adele Malan—Mixed Spice	24.00/192.66

Number of riders who started the competition: 301

Number of riders who completed the competition: 133

Category C

World-Wide Final Standings (top 10)

	Total F./Time
1 Carole Ares (CR)—Pop Pinkerton	0.00/180.01
2 Alexandra Macaya (CR)—Izalco	0.00/190.10
3 Ge Er Deng Tu (Chn)—Sai Fu	0.00/195.40
4 Magali Vanderbuerie (Zai)—Suroit	0.00/207.53
5 James Ng (Sin)—Cloudy	0.00/222.70
6 Sue Philip (Sin)—Eastern Monarch	0.00/223.70
7 Ignacio Esquivel (CR)—Piccolo	3.00/177.76
8 Pamela Mahoney (Ber)—Captain Sam	4.00/175.96
9 Kathryn Madeiros (Ber)—Consider It Done	4.00/178.77
10 Kathy Reynell (Ber)—Right Reaction	4.00/182.80

Participating nations: 8 (Ber, Chn, CRC, Cyp, Esa, Ina, Sin, Zai)

Final Standings by Country

Bermuda

	Total F./Time
1 Pamela Mahoney—Captain Sam	4.00/175.96
2 Kathryn Madeiros—Consider It Done	4.00/178.77
3 Kathy Reynell—Right Reaction	4.00/182.80

China

1 Ge Er Deng Tu—Sai Fu	0.00/195.40
2 Ji En Si—Golden Star	4.00/189.30
3 Meng Ke—Black Wind	8.00/209.00

Costa Rica

1 Carole Ares—Pop Pinkerton	0.00/180.01
2 Alexandra Macaya—Izalco	0.00/190.10
3 Ignacio Esquivel—Piccolo	3.00/177.76

Cyprus

1 Harry Roberts—Scimitar	36.00/248.94
2 Nicos Andreou—Just Josper	36.25/279.84
3 Stefano Seraphim—Khalife	48.00/280.02

El Salvador

1 Gerardo Magaña—Moro	4.00/206.35
2 Felipe Umaña—Don Quijote	7.00/210.46
3 Katia Stubig—Kapushka	8.00/192.02

Indonesia

1 Country K.—Aldanity	10.00/258.00
2 Tenrie Palanbarg—Shilla	19.00/245.00
3 Aadi Habsono—Gagalri	40.00/234.00

Singapore

1 James Ng—Cloudy	0.00/222.70
2 Sue Philip—Eastern Monarch	0.00/223.70
3 Sandra Jourdain—Black Mak	8.00/232.00

Zaire

1 Magali Vanderbuerie—Suroit	0.00/207.53
2 Elisabeth Giuliano—Python	4.00/192.24
3 Patrick Kauffmann—Happy Star	4.00/205.40

Number of riders who started the competition: 121

Number of riders who completed the competition: 69

National Championships

Australia

Year	Champion
1960	Kevin Bacon—Ocean Foam
1961	Art Uytendahl—Brahmin
1962	Art Uytendahl—Madison Square
1963	Bert Jacobs—Red King
1964	John Fahey—Bonvale
1965	Peter Rymill—Bundanoon
1966	Jeff Evans—Cygnet Rambler
1967	Art Uytendahl—Trafalgar Square
1968	Wayne Roycroft—Allomba
1969	Kevin Bacon—Rajah
1970	Kevin Bacon—Simon
1971	Guy Creighton—Johnny Reb
1972	John Fahey—Warwick
1973	Lindsay Ball—Burgundy
1974	Jeff Evans—Cygnet Rambler
1975	Mariane Gilchrist—Gold Ray
1976	Guy Creighton—Little John
1977	Les Bunning—Gay Scott
1978	John Fahey—The Fall
1979	John Fahey—Red Rocket
1980	Guy Creighton—Spring Melody
1981	Not held
1982	Peter Mullins—Silveneer
1983	Peter Mullins—Silveneer
1984	Ken Graham—Happy Jack
1985	Colleen Brook —Carlbrook Rebound
1986	Gavin Chester—Rossmore

Most wins—riders

4 John Fahey (1964, 1972, 1978, 1979)

Most wins—horses
2 Cygnet Rambler (1966, 1974)
  Silveneer (1982, 1983)

High Jump Record

On 21 July, 1978 at Cairns Show Katrina Towns and Big John cleared 7 ft 8 in (2.336 metres) to set a new Australian high jump record (the record set in 1941 at this same show by Rukin Lass and Peninsula, who both jumped 8 ft 5 in [2.565 metres], was achieved prior to the formation of the Equestrian Federation of Australia and is not officially recognised).

Puissance Record

In November 1978 Gavin Chester riding Rockefella cleared 7 ft 7¼ in (2.31 metres) at Warrnambool, Victoria.

Brazil's National Champion in 1984 and 1986, Vitor Alves Teixeira on Tipiton Marcolab. (Elizabeth Furth)

Belgium

Year	Champion
1951	Georges Poffé—Hicamboy
1952	Georges Poffé—Hicamboy
1953	Charles de Selliers de Moranville —Cambridge
1954	Georges Poffé—Hicamboy
1955	Françoise van der Haegen —Etincelle B
1956	Françoise van der Haegen —Etincelle B
1957	Prince Ruspoli—Furstin
1958	Raymond Lombard—Dandy
1959	Françoise van der Haegen —Schlincel
1960	Françoise van der Haegen —Schlincel
1961	J. P. Seynaeve—Dorn
1962	J. P. Seynaeve—Dorn
1963	Paul Daout—Christophe
1964	P. Charon—Jordy
1965	Georges Hernalsteen—Wildling
1966	François Mathy—Laurenzen
1967	Jean-Baptiste Bouckaert—Orient
1968	Jean Baptiste Bouckaert—Orient
1969	P. Vercoutère—Royal Caen
1970	François Mathy—Laurenzen
1971	Jean-Baptiste Bouckaert—Orient
1972	François Mathy—Laurenzen
1973	Patrick Ronge—White City
1974	Patrick Ronge—White City
1975	Jules Ceulemans—Grey Mist
1976	Stanny van Paesschen—Porsche
1977	Ferdi Tyteca—Passe Partout
1978	Christian Huysegoms—Katapulte
1979	Eric Wauters—Rossantico
1980	Mark Goossens—Orkaan
1981	Edgar-Henri Cuepper—Cyrano
1982	Ferdi Tyteca—Ransome
1983	Philippe Vandelannoitte—Opollo
1984	Philippe Lejeune—Faon Rouge
1985	Eric Wauters—Mrs Carlsberg
1986	Stanny van Paesschen —Intermezzo

Most wins—riders

4 Françoise van der Haegen (1955, 1956, 1959, 1960)

Most wins—horses

3 Hicamboy (1951, 1952, 1954)
  Laurenzen (1966, 1970, 1972)
  Orient (1967, 1968, 1971)

Brazil

Year	Champion
1956	Nelson Pessoa
1957	Gianni Samaja
1958	Nelson Pessoa
1959	Antonio Carlos de Carvalho
1960	Nelson Pessoa
1961	Rodolfo Lara Campos
1962	Renyldo Guimaraes Ferreira
1963	Not held
1964	Eloy Menezes
1965	Renyldo Guimaraes Ferreira

1966	Gianni Samaja
1967	Roberto Kalil
1968	Oscar Sotero da Silva
1969	Roberto Luiz Joppert
1970	Gianni Samaja
1971	Roberto Luiz Joppert
1972	Antonio Carlos de Carvalho
1973	Jorge Gerdau Johannpeter
1974	Luiz Felipe de Azevedo
1975	José Roberto Reynoso Fernandez
1976	José Roberto Reynoso Fernandez
1977	Luiz Felipe de Azevedo
1978	José Roberto Reynoso Fernandez
1979	Elizabeth Menezes
1980	Andreas Weinchenck
1981	José Roberto Reynoso Fernandez
1982	Elizabeth Menezes
1983	Paulo Stewart
1984	Vitor Alves Teixeira
1985	Luiz Felipe Azevedo
1986	Vitor Alves Teixeira

Most wins

4 José Roberto Reynoso Fernandez
(1975, 1976, 1978, 1981)

Bulgaria

Class L=height of jumps 1.30 metres
Class T=height of jumps 1.50–1.60
metres

1977	Class L	Plamen Peinov—Effort
	Class T	Dimitar Guenov—Gloria
1978	Class L	Genko Sabev—Tseh
	Class T	Vassil Marinov—Pramo
1979	Class L	Dimitar Guenov —Mollier
	Class T	Boris Pavlov —Montblanc
1980	Class L	Jenya Kulinsky —Vosmorka
	Class T	Krassimir Gavazov —Elastick
1981	Class T	Boris Pavlov —Montblanc
1982	Class T	Givko Gelev—Gaer
1983	Class T	Panayot Dimitrov —Kadet
1984	Class T	Anelia Anguelova —Molnar
1985	Class L	Nikola Dimitrov—Bimbo
	Class T	Peter Yankov—Temp
1986	Class L	Ivan Ivanov —Tamerland
	Class T	Givko Gelev—Meteor

Puissance record

The Bulgarian record in the puissance is
1.90 metres (6 ft 2¾ in), a height which
was jumped by Todor Ratshev riding
Schema during the National Show
Jumping Championships in 1977.

Canada

1982	Michel Vaillancourt
1983	Ian Millar
1984	Hugh Graham
1985	Not held
1986	Ian Millar—Warrior

Dunhill Equestrian of the Year Award

(Discontinued after 1984)

1977	John Simpson
1978	Mark Laskin
1979	Mark Laskin
1980	Mark Laskin
1981=	Mark Laskin
=	Alan Brand
1982	Hugh Graham
1983	Ian Millar
1984	Ian Millar

Puissance record

At the 1985 Royal Agricultural Winter Fair
in Toronto, Alexa Bell riding Ferner
cleared 7 ft 4½ in (2.25 metres) to set a
new ladies' indoor world record for the
puissance.

Denmark

1968	Per Siesbye—Fernando
1969	Per Siesbye—Fernando
1970	Lisbeth Krogsgaard—Flax
1971	Per Siesbye—Fernando
1972	John Jensen—Didrik
1973	Birgit Helt-Hansen—Sharok
1974	Connie N. G. Holm—Pils
1975	Finn Saksø Larsen—Temptation
1976	Finn Saksø Larsen—Temptation
1977	Erik Bigler—Flair
1978	Per Siesbye—Dunardre
1979	Henrik R. Nielsen —Titus the Monk
1980	Henrik Carlsen—Lurifax
1981	Erik Bigler—Hassan
1982	Per H. Hansen—Jack
1983	Erik Bigler—Hassan
1984	Liselotte Ternvig—Flux Toptani
1985	John Byrialsen—World Cup
1986	Lone Kromann—Qludy

Most wins—riders

4 Per Siesbye (1968, 1969, 1971, 1978)

Most wins—horses

3 Fernando (1968, 1969, 1971)

Puissance record

The greatest height jumped by a Danish
rider in a puissance is 2.20 metres
(7 ft 2½ in) which was cleared at Lucerne
in 1986 by Bjørn Ikast and Southern
Cross Blue Water.

Finland

1948	Mauno Roiha—Roa
1950	Mauno Roiha—Roa
1951	Mauno Roiha—Roa
1953	Kauko Paananen—Lassi
1954	Reino Kuistila—Jane Pet
1956	Reino Kuistila—Jane Pet
1957	Arvi Tervalampi—Marras
1958	Viktor Jansson—Asta II
1959	Eino Brisk—Leija
1960	Kauko Paananen—Lassi
1961	Jaakku Palin—Lowing
1962	Reino Pölönen—Rekas
1963	Aarne Vartiainen—Barbara
1964	Reino Pölönen—Rekas
1965	Brita Dahlström—Barbara
1966	Märta Rosenius—Duell
1967	Brita Dahlström—Sans Souci
1968	Märta Rosenius—Duell
1969	Silja Pursiainen—Rolf
1970	Kristian Maunula—Nowator
1971	Christopher Wegelius—No Girls
1972	Silja Pursiainen—Ben Hur
1973	Christopher Wegelius—No Girls
1974	Christopher Wegelius —Solar Lady
1975	Kristian Maunula—Last Chance
1976	Kristian Maunula —Highland Queen
1977	Christopher Wegelius —Trigger Hill
1978	Magnus Lillkvist —Main Attraction
1979	Tom Gordin—Monday Morning
1980	Veikko Heikkilä—Amigo
1981	Christopher Wegelius —Monday Morning
1982	Tom Gordin—Belmont
1983	Raimo Aaltonen—Mr Jason
1984	Tom Gordin—Stowaway
1985	Christine Procope—Ferdinand
1986	Kristian Maunula—Kingsize

Most wins—riders

5 Christopher Wegelius (1971, 1973,
1974, 1977, 1981)

Most wins—horses

3 Roa (1948, 1950, 1951)

France

1950	Bertrand du Breuil
1951	Guy Lefrant
1952	Daniel Lamour
1953	Georges Calmon
1954	Pierre Jonquères d'Oriola
1955	Guy Lefrant
1956	Pierre Jonquères d'Oriola
1957	Bernard de Fombelle
1958	Pierre Jonquères d'Oriola
1959	Pierre Jonquères d'Oriola
1960	Michel Boutte
1961	Bernard Geneste
1962	François Fabius
1963	Jean-Pierre Cancre
1964	Bernard de Fombelle
1965	Michel Pelissier

Gilles Bertran de Balanda, twice Champion of France, riding the powerful Selle Français stallion Galoubet Malesan. (Findlay Davidson)

1966	Michel Raoul-Duval
1967	Michel Raoul-Duval
1968	Bernard Geneste
1969	Jerôme Chabrol
1970	Marcel Rozier
1971	Marcel Rozier
1972	Xavier Delalande
1973	Marc Houssin
1974	Marcel Rozier
1975	Marc Houssin
1976	Christophe Cuyer
1977	Alain Hinard
1978	Hervé Godignon
1979	Gilles Bertran de Balanda
1980	Frédéric Cottier
1981	Laurent Elias
1982	Pierre Durand
1983	Michel Robert
1984	Gilles Bertran de Balanda
1985	Michel Robert
1986	Pierre Durand

Most wins

4 Pierre Jonquères d'Oriola (1954, 1956, 1958, 1959)

Federal Republic of Germany

Men's Championship

1959	Hans Günter Winkler—Halla
1960	Hermann Schridde—Flagrant
1961	Alwin Schockemöhle—Freiherr
1962	Hermann Schridde—Ilona
1963	Alwin Schockemöhle—Freiherr
1964	Not held
1965	Peter Schmitz—Amsella
1966	Gerd Wiltfang—Ferdl/Ferrara
1967	Alwin Schockemöhle —Donald Rex/Wimpel III
1968	Not held
1969	Hartwig Steenken —Simona III/Porta Westfalica
1970	Hartwig Steenken —Simona III/Der Lord
1971	Gerd Wiltfang—Sieno/Askan
1972	Not held
1973	Hartwig Steenken —Simona III/Kosmos
1974	Paul Schockemöhle —Agent/Talisman
1975	Alwin Schockemöhle —Rex the Robber/Warwick Rex
1976	Not held
1977	Hendrik Snoek—Gaylord
1978	Sönke Sönksen—Kwept
1979	Gerd Wiltfang—Roman
1980	Paul Schockemöhle—Deister
1981	Franke Sloothaak—Argonaut
1982	Paul Schockemöhle—Deister
1983	Paul Schockemöhle—Deister
1984	Karsten Huck—Calando
1985	Michael Rüping—Silbersee
1986	Paul Schockemöhle—Deister

Most wins—riders

5 Paul Schockemöhle (1974, 1980, 1982, 1983, 1986)

Most wins—horses

4 Deister (1980, 1982, 1983, 1986)

Ladies' Championship

1959	Helga Köhler—Amalva
1960	Helga Köhler—Pesgö
1961	Anna Clement—Flugwind
1962	Romi Röhr—Tanja
1963	Maria Günther—Sambesi
1964	Ute Richter—Scholli
1965	Karin Möller—Saskia
1966	Romi Laurenz—Freier
1967	Bertl Kreuder—Markant/Parsus
1968	Gisela Franken—Echo
1969	Madeleine Winter—Patella
1970	Sylvia Kempter —Spielerin/Daphne
1971	Lene Nissen-Lembke —Cottage Incident/Cottan
1972	Marion Snoek —Jo d'Amour/Janeau
1973	Lene Nissen-Lembke —Onassis/Abeste
1974	Hannelore Raab—Wakuba
1975	Madeleine Winter —Bwana/Dacapo
1976	Marion Henkel—Greco
1977	Lene Nissen-Lembke—Mosquito
1978	Lene Nissen-Lembke—Mosquito
1979	Iris Bayer—Cavalierist
1980	Lene Nissen-Lembke—Mowgli
1981	Iris Bayer—Trabant
1982	Iris Bayer—Pandur
1983	Petra Gleich—Lord
1984	Sabine Knepper—Rio Grande
1985	Iris Bayer—Zampano
1986	Iris Bayer—Pandur

Most wins—riders

5 Lene Nissen-Lembke (1971, 1973, 1977, 1978, 1980)
  Iris Bayer (1979, 1981, 1982, 1985, 1986)

Most wins—horses

2 Mosquito (1977, 1978)
  Pandur (1982, 1986)

High Jump Record

The Federal Republic of Germany's high jump record (over a wall) was established on 15 July 1985 in a competition at Aachen when Willibert Mehlkopf riding Hanns List's 12-year-old Holstein gelding, Wabbs, cleared 2.30 metres (7 ft 6½ in). This beat the previous record of 2.28 metres (7 ft 5¾ in), set up in Rhineland earlier that same year by Gerhard Bongardt riding Altreck.

Great Britain

1945	Nat Kindersley—Maguire
1946	R. Hall—Sparky
1947	Nat Kindersley—Maguire
1948	Seamus Hayes (Ire)—Limerick
1949	Seamus Hayes (Ire)—Sheila
1950	Seamus Hayes (Ire)—Sheila
1951	Alan Oliver —Red Admiral/Red Knight
1952	Donald Beard—Costa
1953	Harry Llewellyn—Foxhunter
1954	Alan Oliver—Red Admiral
1955	Ted Williams —Larry/Sunday Morning
1956	Ted Williams —Pegasus*/Montana
1957	Ted Edgar—Jane Summers
1958	Paddy McMahon—Tim II
1959	Alan Oliver—John Gilpin
1960	Harvey Smith—Farmer's Boy
1961	David Broome—Discutido
1962	David Broome —Wildfire III/Grand Manan
1963	Harvey Smith—O'Malley
1964	Liz Broome—Jacopo

*Nominated first

1965 Peter Robeson—Firecrest
1966 Andrew Fielder—Vibart
1967 David Broome—Mister Softee
1968 Marion Coakes—Stroller
1969 Alan Oliver—Pitz Palu
1970 Alan Oliver—Sweep III
1971 Marion Mould—Stroller
1972 Aileen Ross—Trevarrion
1973 David Broome—Sportsman
1974 Pip Nicholls—Timmie
1975 Harvey Smith—Speakeasy
1976 John Whitaker—Ryan's Son
1977 Caroline Bradley—Berna
1978 Graham Fletcher
        —Buttevant Boy
1979 David Broome—Sportsman
1980 Derek Ricketts
        —Hydrophane Coldstream
1981 Nick Skelton—St James
1982 Mark Fuller—Punchdale
1983 Jeff McVean (Aus)
        Hello Le Val
1984 Michael Whitaker
        —Overton Amanda
1985 Peter Richardson—Foxwood
1986 David Broome—Phoenix Park
1987 Robert Smith—April Sun

Most wins—riders

6 David Broome (1961, 1962, 1967, 1973, 1979, 1986)

Most wins—horses

2 Maguire (1945, 1947)
  Sheila (1949, 1950)
  Red Admiral (=1st 1951, 1954)
  Stroller (1968, 1971)
  Sportsman (1973, 1979)

Ladies' Championship

1947 Iris Kellett (Ire)—Rusty
1948 Lady Dudley—Princess
1949 A. Hinchcliffe—Victory Boy
1950 A. Dickinson—Paddy
1951 Pat Rose—Without Reserve
1952 Pat Smythe—Prince Hal
1953 Pat Smythe—Tosca
1954 Dawn Palethorpe
        —Earlsrath Rambler
1955 Pat Smythe—Flanagan
1956 Anne Morley—Nugget
1957 Pat Smythe—Prince Hal
1958 Pat Smythe—Flanagan
1959 Pat Smythe—Mr Pollard
1960 Judy Shepherd—Thou Swell
1961 Pat Smythe—Scorchin
1962 Pat Smythe—Flanagan
1963 Ann Townsend—Dunboyne III
1964 Liz Broome—Bess
1965 Cancelled owing to equine flu
        epidemic
1966 C. Warburton—Nautilus II
1967 Jean Goodwin—Hobo
1968 Jean Goodwin—Hobo
1969 Valerie (Clarke) Barker
        —Brandy Jim
1970 Shirley Edwards—Bright Morning
1971 Ann Coleman—Havana Royal
1972 Alison (Westwood) Dawes
        —The Maverick VII

1973 Ann Backhouse—Cardinal III
1974 Ann Moore—Psalm
1975 Liz (Broome) Edgar
        —Everest Mayday
1976 Marion (Coakes) Mould
        —Elizabeth Ann (ex Dunlynne)
1977 Amanda Rooney—Barbarella
1978 Sally Horner (Aus)—Bay Rum
1979 Ann Wilson—Owen Gregory
1980 Maureen Holden—Mr Vee
1981 Lesley McNaught
        —One More Time
1982 Liz (Broome) Edgar
        —Everest Forever
1983 Sue Pountain—Ned Kelly VI
1984 Emma-Jane Brown—Guilty
1985 Sue Pountain—Ned Kelly VI
1986 Gillian Greenwood—Sky Fly
1987 Deborah Dolan (USA)—Albany

Most wins—riders

8 Pat Smythe (1952, 1953, 1955, 1957, 1958, 1959, 1961, 1962)

Most wins—horses

3 Flanagan (1955, 1958, 1962)

High Jump Record

In 1978, at Olympia, 20-year-old Nick Skelton and the Everest Stud's German-bred Lastic cleared 7 ft 7⁵⁄₁₆ in (2.32 metres) at their third attempt to set a new British record. The previous record, set at Olympia in 1937 by Donald Beard riding Fred Foster's Swank, stood at 7 ft 6¼ in (2.29 metres).

Greece

1954 K. Triboukas
1955 S. Ladopoulos
1956 S. Ladopoulos
1957 S. Nisiotis
1958 S. Nisiotis
1959 E. Dabasi
1960 A. Kiriakidis
1961 T. Razelos
1962 K. Koutras
1963 N. Papamichael
1964 F. Bravos
1965 M. Agapitos
1966 I. Moireas
1967 A. Manolitsis
1968 D. Lambadarios
1969 F. Serpieris
1970 A. Kipreos
1971 A. Kipreos
1972 F. Bravos
1973 A. Kipreos
1974 N. Skenther
1975 G. Fragogiannis
1976 N. Skenther
1977 A. Kipreos
1978 N. Skenther
1979 A. Kipreos
1980 G. Fragogiannis
1981 A. Milonas
1982 A. Milonas
1983 G. Rosiadis
1984 K. Grazios

1985 G. Kastianos
1986 D. Lambadarios

Most wins

5 Aris Kipreos (1970, 1971, 1973, 1977, 1979)

2nd Category Championship (Positive Cup)

1980 K. Kiriakidis
1981 A. Diamadidis
1982 R. Snaddon
1983 E. Snaddon
1984 A. Diamadidis
1985 Th. Dallas
1986 D. Lambadarios

Ladies' Championship (Longines Cup)

1983 N. Papaliou
1984 N. Papaliou
1985 N. Papaliou
1986 D. Papalios

Men's Championship (Lancia Cup)

1983 N. Papadopoulos
1984 N. Iliadis
1985 K. Somoglou
1986 D. Lambadarios

Panhellenic Winners (Seniors)

1979 D. Lambadarios—Winotu
1980 G. Fragogiannis—Fleole
1981 Ch. Dimitriadi—Quincy Jones
1982 F. Bravos—Constellation
1983 F. Bravos—S. Namon
1984 D. Lambadarios—Go for Gold
1985 D. Lambadarios—Go for Gold
1986 D. Lambadarios—Go for Gold

Ireland

1985 Harry Marshall—Avallon
1986 Vina Lyons—Listerine Giltspur

Liechtenstein

Men's Championship

1986 Thomas Batliner—Foxstone

Women's Championship

1986 Isabelle Beck—Urano

Puissance Record

The greatest height jumped by a rider from Liechtenstein in a puissance is 2.15 metres (7 ft 5⁄8 in), which was cleared in Salzburg in 1985 by Thomas Batliner riding Nicolai.

Netherlands

1948	N. Uytendaal
1949	K. Hensen
1950	W. Scheeren
1951	Jacob, Baron van Lynden
1952	Jacob Rijks
1953	Joachim Joseph Gruppelaar
1954	Jacob Rijks
1955	Wiel Hendrickx
1956	M. M. Koster
1957	W. Scheeren
1958	L. C. M. Uytendaal
1959	W. Scheeren
1960	Irene Jansen
1961	Anton Ebben
1962	Tjeerd Velstra
1963	Jan Maathuis
1964	Tjeerd Velstra
1965	Jan Maathuis
1966	H. A. Ernst
1967	Jan Maathuis
1968	Jan Maathuis
1969	Jan Maathuis
1970	Anton Ebben
1971	F. van Herten
1972	Henk Nooren
1973	Rob Eras
1974	Henk Nooren
1975	Johan Heins
1976	H. J. M. Wouters van den Oudenweijer
1977	Henk Nooren
1978	Anton Ebben
1979	W. van der Ham
1980	Piet Raymakers
1981	Henk Nooren
1982	Henk Nooren
1983	Rob Ehrens
1984	Emiel Hendrix
1985	Emiel Hendrix
1986	T. Holtus

Most wins

5 Jan Maathuis (1963, 1965, 1967, 1968, 1969
  Henk Nooren (1972, 1974, 1977, 1981, 1982)

New Zealand

1953	D. Holden—Starlight
1954	M. Meredith—Paragon
1955	H. V. Thompson—Kilfi
1956	W. A. Meech—Weinagain
1957	P. Holden—Rum
1958	R. B. Hansen—Sportsmaster
1959	E. Upritchard—Landrover
1960	E. Upritchard—Landrover
1961	C. Mould—Treason
1962	R. W. Hyem—Coronation
1963	H. V. Thompson—Cassidy
1964	C. Matthews—Syndicate
1965	D. Robertson—Lady Vanquish
1966	Stuart Mitchell—Walnut
1967	P. Teki—Lucky Steve
1968	Stuart Mitchell—Walnut
1969	C. Clarke—Town Boy
1970	D. Hamilton—Henry Lea
1971	R. McVicar—Fan Fare

1972	B. Anderson—Cardiff Lass
1973	John Cottle—Rifleman
1974	A. D. Yorke—Big Red
1975	Chris Smith (Aus)—Sanskrit
1976	Sue Cawston—Matlock
1977	Harvey Wilson—Old Smuggler
1978	Jeff McVean (Aus)—Claret
1979	Doug Isaacson—Chicago
1980	Mary Gordon (Aus)—TNT
1981	John Cottle—Footman
1982	Ian Campbell—Calico Joe
1983	Maurice Beatson—Nationwide
1984	Maurice Beatson—Nationwide
1985	David Asimus (Aus) —Golden Grand
1986	Maurice Beatson —Jeffersen Junior

Most wins—riders

3 Maurice Beatson (1983, 1984, 1986)

Most wins—horses

2 Landrover (1959, 1960)
  Walnut (1966, 1968)
  Nationwide (1983, 1984)

Puissance

In 1984 at Hastings (outdoor show) Skud ridden by Allan Goodall jumped 2.13 metres (6 ft 11⅞ in). The fence was a treble bar.

Norway

1970	Hanne Kirkerud
1971	Rita Stephansen Smith
1972	Eddie Bull
1973	Ewy Lindrup
1974	Amund Wormstrand
1975	Eddie Bull
1976	Per Atle Danielsen
1977	Ellen Islann
1978	Per Atle Danielsen
1979	Per Atle Danielsen
1980	Ove Hansen
1981	Ove Hansen
1982	Geir Håkon Jensen
1983	Ove Hansen
1984	Ove Hansen
1985	Ove Hansen
1986	Ove Hansen

Most wins

6 Ove Hansen (1980, 1981, 1983, 1984, 1985, 1986)

Poland

1931	Wojciech Bilinski—Rabuś
1932	Zygmunt Rucinski—Roksana
1933	Roman Pohorecki—Olaf
1934	Wilhelm Lewicki—Kikimora
1935	Karol Rommel—Sahara
1936	Tadeusz Sokolowski—Zbieg II
1937	Karol Rommel—Dyngus
1938	Bronisław Skulicz—Dunkan
1939–1952	Not held
1953	Czesław Matlawski—Alchemik
1954	Władysław Byszewski—Besson
1955	Maciej Swidzinski—Argun

1956	Władysław Byszewski—Besson
1957	Marian Kowalczyk—Pregor
1958	Władysław Byszewski—Besson
1959	Marian Babirecki—Don Hubertus
1960	Stanisław Kubiak—Wareg
1961	Władysław Byszewski—Dukat
1962	Stanisław Kubiak—Wareg
1963	Antoni Pacynski—Don Hubertus
1964	Andrzej Orlos—Bao Day
1965	Jan Kowalczyk—Ronceval
1966	Jan Kowalczyk—Drobnica
1967	Jan Kowalczyk—Drobnica
1968	Not held
1969	Jan Kowalczyk—Blekot
1970	Jan Kowalczyk—Blekot
1971	Piotr Wawryniuk—Poprad
1972	Marian Kozicki—Bronz
1973	Jan Kowalczyk—Blekot
1974	Jan Kowalczyk—Blekot
1975	Jan Kowalczyk—Darlet
1976	Henryk Hucz—Bertyn
1977	Jan Kowalczyk—Darlet
1978	Jan Kowalczyk—Darlet
1979	Jan Kowalczyk—Artemor
1980	Jan Kowalczyk—Artemor
1981	Krzysztof Ferenstein—Kobryń
1982	Jan Kowalczyk—Artemor
1983	Marek Orłos—Torreador
1984	Jan Kowalczyk—Festyn
1985	Grzegorz Kubiak—Gabon
1986	Jan Kowalczyk—Harlem

Most wins—riders

15 Jan Kowalczyk (1965–67, 1969–70, 1973–75, 1977–80, 1982, 1984, 1986)

Most wins—horses

4 Blekot (1969, 1970, 1973, 1974)

High Jump Record

2.07 metres (6 ft 9½ in), jumped at Gniezno (Poland) in 1985 by Ordynek, ridden by Robert Sydow.

Puissance Record

At the Olsztyn CSIO in 1969 Via Vitae, ridden by Wiesław Dziadczyk, jumped 2.20 metres (7 ft 2½ in).

Portugal

1955	João Cruz Azevedo—Fagulha
1956	Alvaro Sabbo—Licorne
1957	Eduardo Netto de Almeida —Jacare
1958	Henrique Callado—Martingil
1959	Vasco Ramires—Apache
1960	Eduardo Netto de Almeida —Joc de l'Ile
1961	Eduardo Netto de Almeida —Joc de l'Ile
1966	Antonio Pimenta da Gama —Mistral
1967	Manuel Malta da Costa—Alentejo
1968	Vasco Ramires—Namur du Payre
1970	Alvaro Sabbo—Marau
1972	Antonio Pimenta da Gama —Espora

Jan Kowalczyk

Jan Kowalczyk has been National Show Jumping Champion of Poland on 15 occasions and he has also twice won the national eventing championship, which gives him a record that has probably never been equalled by any rider anywhere in the world.

His unprecedented run of 15 National Championships began in 1965. He retained the title until 1971 when Piotr Wawryniuk was successful. Kowalczyk then notched up a hat-trick in 1973, 1974 and 1975, lost to Henryk Hucz in 1976, but won again in 1977 to 1980, inclusive, and has since been successful in 1982, 1984 and 1986. His three-day event championship wins came in 1958 and again in 1966.

He was born on 18 December 1941 at Drogomysl, in south-west Poland, the son of a stud farm worker, and competed for the first time in 1954 at the age of 13. A soldier by profession, he has benefited from the instruction of two former cavalry officers, Jan Mossakowski (a member of the winning Polish Nations Cup team at Spa in 1935) and Wiktor Olędzki.

Up to 1987 Jan Kowalczyk had no fewer than 402 wins to his credit on his home ground, plus 49 at the CSIOs of Aachen, Bratislava, Budapest, London, Lucerne, Olsztyn, Rome, Rotterdam, Salzburg, Sopot and Trinwillershagen. Riding the good mare Drobnica he went particularly well in the 1967 European Championships, winning the first leg, finishing equal first in the second, and fifth in the fourth and final part, which left him equal fourth overall behind David Broome, Harvey Smith and Alwin Schockemöhle.

Despite such good form he was for many years singularly unlucky at Olympic level. Shortly before the 1968 Games Drobnica started to refuse and he was forced to ride the reserve horse, Braz, in the team event, in which Poland could finish only eleventh. Then in Munich in 1972 his gelding Chandzar was taken ill and died in his stable the

Jan Kowalczyk, 15 times champion of Poland. (Findlay Davidson)

night before the individual competition. He was finally rewarded with success at the Moscow Games in 1980. Riding Artemor, he put up the best performance of the Polish team to help clinch the team silver, and went on to win the individual gold, thanks to two splendid rounds with only one fence down in each.

Jan Kowalczyk is still competing, and there is no reason to suppose that he will not add to that amazing tally of victories before he hangs up his boots.

1973	Francisco Caldeira —Gran Senhor	
1974	José Marchueta—Harpy Prince	
1975	Antonio Pimenta da Gama —Ribamar	
1976	José Antonio Balula Cid —Lotus II	
1977	Antonio Pimenta da Gama —Ribamar	
1978	Luis Xavier de Brito—Balluche	
1979	Luis Lupi—My Hope	
1980	Luis Xavier de Brito—Balluche	
1981	José Manuel Soares da Costa —Helios D	

1982 Francisco Caldeira—Rubi II
1983 Jorge Mathias—Saint Maur
1984 Jorge Oliveira—Killy des Neiges
1985 Luis Xavier de Brito—Mister X
1986 João Azevedo e Silva —Laurier Rose V

Most wins—riders

4 Antonio Pimenta de Gama (1966, 1972, 1975, 1977)

Most wins—horses

2 Joc de l'Ile (1960, 1961)

Ribamar (1975, 1977)
Balluche (1978, 1980)

High Jump Record

In 1952, at Caldas da Rainha, Henrique Callado and Caramulo jumped 2.20 metres (7 ft 2½ in).

Long Jump Record

In 1906, in Lisbon, Forever, ridden by Ruy d'Andrade, cleared 7.36 metres (24 ft 1¾ in).

South Africa

1955	Bob Grayston—Guardsman
1956	G. Peerman—Hoboe
1957	E. Guthrie—Bold Fighter
1958	Bob Grayston—Captain Bligh
1959	L. Taylor—Du Roco
1960	L. Taylor—Du Roco
1961	Gonda Butters—Gunga Din
1962	William Angus—Rigoletto
1963	Yvonne Johnson—Arrow
1964	Mickey Louw—Jurigo
1965	Gonda Butters—Eldorado
1966	George Myburg—The Laird
1967	Gonda Butters—Ratification
1968	Mickey Louw—Marlon
1969	Gonda Butters—Ratification
1970	Peter Levor—Esprit
1971	Peter Levor—Esprit
1972	Ian Harrop-Allain—Honest Dez
1973	Mickey Louw—Torch Sign
1974	Gonda (Butters) Betrix—Format
1975	Mickey Louw—Ford Appraise
1976	Peter Götz—Toyota's Thales
1977	Peter Götz—Toyota's Thales
1978	Anthony Lewis—Jongleur
1979	Gonda (Butters) Betrix —Honey Girl
1980	Gonda (Butters) Betrix —Isis Bridge
1981	Heather Hillcoat—Chevrolet Dual
1982	Errol Wucherpfennig —Compass Line
1983	André Ferreira—Irish Magic
1984	Philip Smith—Cloud Nine
1985	Anneli (Drummond-Hay) Wucherpfennig—Storm Finch
1986	Peter Götz—Toyota Gossiper

Most wins

7 Gonda (Butters) Betrix (1961, 1965, 1967, 1969, 1974, 1979, 1980)

Inter-provincial Team Championship

1958	W. Province
1959	Transvaal
1960	Transvaal
1961	Transvaal
1962	W. Province
1963	Natal
1964	W. Province
1965	Transvaal
1966	Transvaal
1967	Transvaal
1968	Transvaal
1969	Transvaal
1970	Transvaal
1971	W. Province
1972	Transvaal
1973	Transvaal
1974	SWA
1975	Transvaal
1976	Transvaal
1977	Transvaal
1978	Natal
1979	OFS and NCHS
1980	Transvaal
1981	Transvaal
1982	E. Cape
1983	SADF
1984	Transvaal
1985	W. Province
1986	Transvaal

High Jump Record

in 1973 Fancy That, ridden by his owner, Mickey Louw, jumped 2.280 metres (7 ft 5¾ in) at Pietermaritzburg. This beat the previous record of 2.185 metres (7 ft 2 in), set by Peter Levor on Format in Johannesburg in 1969.

Long Jump Record

In 1975 André Ferreira, riding Mrs. I. G. van der Merwe's horse, Something, jumped 8.40 metres (27 ft 6¾ in) in Johannesburg. This is the current official world long jump record.

Spain

1960	Francisco Goyoaga—Kif Kif
1961	Francisco Goyoaga—Kif Kif
1962	Alfonso Quéipo de Llano—Eolo IV
1963	José Alvarez de Bohorques —Quizás
1964	Francisco Goyoaga—Kif Kif
1965	José Alvarez de Bohorques —Quizás
1966	Not held
1967	Luis Antonio Alvarez Cervera —Bampur
1968	Alfredo Goyeneche, Marqués Artasona—On Dit
1969	Luis Jaime Carvajal, Duque Aveyro—Vilaya
1970	Alfonso Segovia—Albaycín
1971	Alfonso Segovia—Tic Tac
1972	Luis Antonio Alvarez Cervera —Cambalache
1973	Fernando Lazcano—La Panocha
1974	Luis Antonio Alvarez Cervera —Acorne
1975	Luis Jaime Carvajal, Duque Aveyro—Kurfust
1976	Luis Antonio Alvarez Cervera —Thor
1977	Luis Antonio Alvarez Cervera —Acorne
1978	Alfonso Segovia—White Oak
1979	Alfonso Segovia—Akrobat
1980	Luis Antonio Alvarez Cervera —Romeo
1981	Eduardo Pérez—Etiope
1982	Luis Antonio Alvarez Cervera —Romeo
1983	Alejandro Zambrano—Tipitón
1984	Luis Astolfi—Coreven Steepers
1985	Juan Andrés Ruiz de Alda —Lingere
1986	Pedro Sánchez Alemán—Lobato

Most wins—riders

7 Luis Antonio Alvarez Cervera (1967, 1972, 1974, 1976, 1977, 1980, 1982)

Most wins—horses

3 Kif Kif (1960, 1961, 1964)

High Jump Record

In 1948, at Bilbao, Jaime García Cruz and Bengalí jumped 2.22 metres (7 ft 3½ in).

Long Jump Record

In 1951, in Barcelona, Fernando López del Hierro and Amado Mío cleared 8.30 metres (27 ft 2¾ in).

Sweden

1946	Stig Holm
1947	Tor Eliasson
1948	Kurt Wiksell
1949	Greger Lewenhaupt
1950	Tor Eliasson
1951	B. Janse
1952	Hans Helge Rasmussen
1953	Carl Jan Hamilton
1954	Gunnar Palm
1955	Gunnar Palm
1956	Douglas Wijkander
1957	Tor Burman
1958	Kurt Wiksell
1959	Dag Nätterqvist
1960	Dag Nätterqvist
1961	Christer Roswall
1962	Per-Erik Cedermark
1963	Dag Nätterqvist
1964	Gunnar Sandén
1965	Dag Nätterqvist
1966	Uno Lantz
1967	Georg Ekström
1968	Dag Nätterqvist
1969	Jan-Olaf Wannius
1970	Åke Hultberg
1971	Marianne von Geijer
1972	Åke Hultberg
1973	Åke Hultberg
1974	Åke Hultberg
1975	Jan-Olaf Wannius
1976	Jan-Olaf Wannius
1977	Jan-Olaf Wannius
1978	Åke Hultberg
1979	Leif Holgersson
1980	Leif Holgersson
1981	Leif Holgersson
1982	Björn Carlsson
1983	Peter Eriksson
1984	Leif Nilsson
1985	Peter Eriksson
1986	Lotta Emanuelsson—Kings Slater

Most wins

5 Dag Nätterqvist (1959, 1960, 1963, 1965, 1968)
Åke Hultberg (1970, 1972, 1973, 1974, 1978)

High Jump Record

2.08 metres (6 ft 9⅞ in), jumped by Anders Normann on Watergate.

Switzerland

1957	Werner Brenzikofer
1958	Samuel Bürki
1959	Paul Weier
1960	Viktor Morf
1961	Paul Weier
1962	Max Hauri
1963	Alexandre von Erdey
1964	Paul Weier
1965	Arthur Blickenstorfer
1966	Monica Bachmann
1967	Paul Weier
1968	Paul Weier
1969	Paul Weier
1970	Monica Bachmann
1971	Francis Racine
1972	Kurt Maeder
1973	Markus Fuchs
1974	Willi Melliger
1975	Walter Gabathuler
1976	Walter Gabathuler
1977	Walter Gabathuler
1978	Walter Gabathuler
1979	Walter Gabathuler
1980	Jürg Notz
1981	Bruno Candrian
1982	Heidi Robbiani
1983	Willi Melliger
1984	Markus Fuchs
1985	Willi Melliger
1986	Thomas Fuchs

Most wins

6 Paul Weier (1959, 1961, 1964, 1967, 1968, 1969)

Turkey

1971	Nurettin Yaran—Tunca
1972	Ateş Dağli—Ulaş
1973	Feyzi Atabek—Peter Pan
1974	Feyzi Atabek—Peter Pan
1975	Kaya Oktayören—Miranda
1976	Atila Inoğlu—Hakan
1977	Ömer Yilmaz—Yüksel
1978	Bülent Bora—Chopin
1979	Bülent Bora—Chopin
1980	Resit Özlen—Kimo
1981	Feyzi Atabek—Ares
1982	Feyzi Atabek—Rainlover
1983	Ata Zorlu—Binboğa
1984	Feyzi Atabek—Ares
1985	Ali Ersin—Cornet
1986	Ata Zorlu—Laredo

Most wins—riders

5 Feyzi Atabek (1973, 1974, 1981, 1982, 1984)

Most wins—horses

2 Peter Pan (1973, 1974)
Chopin (1978, 1979)
Aves (1981, 1984)

USA

United States Equestrian Team Show Jumping Championship

1981	Michael Matz—Honest Tom
1982	Conrad Homfeld—Balbuco
1983	Michael Matz—Chef
1984	Conrad Homfeld—Abdullah
1985	Leslier Burr Lenahan—McLain
1986	Katie Monahan—Bean Bag

American Grandprix Association Rider of the Year

(Since 1981 Mercedes Rider of the Year)

1978	Melanie Smith
1979	Conrad Homfeld
1980	Conrad Homfeld
1981	Michael Matz
1982	Katie Monahan
1983	Leslie Burr Lenahan
1984	Michael Matz
1985	Robert Gage
1986	Katie Monahan

USSR

All-Union Show Jumping Competitions (USSR Cup)

1938	E. Levin—Diktovka
1946	G. Anastasev—Galka
1947	Ya. Savchenko—Kazbek
1948	V. Lagosh—Navigator
1949	A. Truupyld—Fanza
1950	N. Shelenkov—Ersh
1951	N. Shelenkov—Ersh
1952	A. Kiselev—Rangi
1953	A. Pinding—Sadé
1954	T. Kulikovskaya—Tryum
1955	B. Lilov—Diagramma
1956	A. Belitsky—Karabin
1957	V. Zemskov—Emitent
1958	B. Lilov—Myatezh
1959	V. Utkin—Plastun
1960	V. Raspopov—Kodeks
1961	A. Belitsky—Plastun
1962	E. Shabailo—Boston
1963	Yu. Soskov—Ensemble
1964	I. Semenov—Sibiryak
1965	Yu. Skoblilov—Rok
1966	A. Purtov—Svecha
1967	G. Samosedenko—Aeron
1968	V. Nenakhov—Zaur
1969	V. Matveev—Krokhotny
1970	Yu. Zyabrev—Grim
1971	V. Lisitsyn—Penteli

1972	P. Tkachenko—Ranok
1973	Yu. Zyabrev—Grim
1974	V. Poganovsky—Grim
1975	G. Samosedenko—Luch
1976	A. Nebogov—Equador
1977	V. Poganovsky—Fazan
	All-round champion: Ya. Belinsky—Even
1978	V. Nenakhov—Izolomit
	All-round champion: V. Poganovsky—Fazan
1979	V. Chukanov—Gepatit
1980	N. Koropatnik—Polzunok
	All-round champion: N. Korolkov—Espadron
1981	V. Chukanov—Gepatit
1982	V. Poganovsky—Prospekt
1983	Z. Sharka—Fastsidas
1984	V. Poganovsky—Prospekt
1985	V. Poganovsky—Prospekt
1986	Z. Klimovas—Despotas
	Young Horse Champion: R. Udrakis—Dekoratsiya

Most wins—riders

5 Victor Poganovsky (1974, 1977, 1982, 1984, 1985)

Most wins—horses

3 The Thoroughbred, Grim (1970, 1973, 1974)
The Trakehner, Prospekt (1982, 1984, 1985)

High Jump Record

In 1953, at Moscow Racecourse, the Trakehner, Kover, ridden by Igor Lysogovsky, Merited Master of Sport, cleared 2.25 metres (7 ft 4½ in).

Long Jump Record

In 1946 Nikolai Shelenkov, an officer in the Red Army, cleared 8.20 metres (26 ft 10⅞ in) on the mare Burya (Nikolai Shelenkov died in December 1985). This is still the official long jump record of the USSR.

In 1950, in Ashkhabad, an Akhal-Teke stallion called Perepel cleared 8.72 metres (28 ft 7⁵⁄₁₆ in). This jump, however, is not officially recognized.

Zaire

1982	Marie-Claude Turlot—New-Crete
1984	Michel Deckkers—Camp Clair
1985	Elisabeth Giuliano—Python

High Jump Record

In 1971, at the Cercle Hippique de Kinshasa, Horace, ridden by André Roquet, cleared 1.96 metres (6 ft 5¹⁄₁₆ in).

Index

Page numbers in italics refer to illustrations

Adigüzel, Ülgen 165
Adzemov, Ivan 156
Aguirre, Carlos 151
Aksel, Mehmet 165
Alanyali, Toufan 154
Albanese, Sergio 178
Alberding, Kay 171
Aldazabal, L. 194
Alegria-Simoes, Antonio 150
Aliev, Mehmed 162
Allen, Roisin 198
Alvarez Cervera, Luis 166, 167
Alvaro, Hector 194, 195
Alvisi, Alessandro 15
Amaya, Jorge 150
Ambrosetti, Fabrizzio 190
Andersen, Sten 183
Anderson, Bryan 174
Anderson, John Carl 174
Andersson, Linda 202
Andreotis, Yanis 165
Angelova, Amelia 163
Angioni, Stephano 179
Anguelov, Todor 164
Antoniewicz, Michael 17, 45
Apostolopoulos, N. 161
Aramburu, Manuel 196, 197
Aranda, Dieter 197
Argüelles, J. 179
Arles-Dufour, Bertrand 183, 191
Arrambide, Hugo 140
Arredondo, Sergio 150
Arrenda, Guillermo 149
Arts, Miss 178
Ascarraga, Jaime 152
Ashmore, Joe 179
Asmaev, Viktor 37
Aspirides, Angelos 163
Asselay, Pierre 166
Asselberghs, George 178, 192
Atabek, Feyzi 155, 156, 157, 161,
  162, 163, 165
Atanasova, Emilia 162
Atanossova, Tzvetana 161
Athanassiades, Emanuela 162, 164,
  165
Athanassiu, Dan 154
Augustinov, Stephan 155, 156
Aydin, Nuray 164
Azambuja, A. J. 194

Baccaglini, Paola 181
Bachmann, Monica (see Weier,
  Monica)
Bacigalupo, Andrea 181
Backhouse, Ann (née Townsend)
  143, 146, 179
Badulescu, Ruxandra 161, 162, 163
Bagusat, Bernd 179, 180, 191
Bagusat, Michael 179
Baillie, John 181, 191, 192, 193
Bamber, John 198
Barbot, Marie-Christine 199
Barbot, Philippe 198, 199
Baricelli, Gerardo 195
Barker, C. David 140, *146*, 148
Barker, Ian 190
Barker, William 181
Barlagen, Tonko 188
Barnes, Mary 179, 191, 192
Barnes, Sheila 180, 192, 193
Barone, Barbara 151
Barrios, Pablo 195
Barros, Antonio 195
Barros, Antonio Marcos 196
Barry, Kevin 184
Bartalucci, Duccio 166
Bartels, Thomas 182

Bartzoglou, Panayotis 165
Bates, Zoë 188
Batur, Murat 161
Beard, Carole 179
Beerbaum, Ludger 171
Bell, Angela 202
Bell, Vicky 199
Beltrão, José 19
Belvisi, François 199
Bembo, Gian Piero 178, 191
Benakopoulos, Stelios 163
Benedetto, James 174
Berker, Mehmet 157
Bernaldo, Juan Nardiz 166
Bernasconi, Paolo 187
Berretta, J. 194, 195
Bertran de Balanda, Gilles 49, 69,
  166, 182, *231*
Bertran de Balanda, Isabelle 182, 183
Bertran de Balanda, Pierre 18
Best, Gregory 174
Bettoni, Vicenzo 166
Bevis, Robert 198
Binetti, Giovanna 181, 191
Bischoff, Alexandra 190
Björnstjerna, Carl 17
Blagojevic, Jovan 155, 156
Blaton, Evelyne 148, 198
Blessmann, Marcelo 195
Blessman, Luciano 195
Blickenstorfer, Kurt 170
Blum, Egan 185
Bobik, Janusz 37
Bogdanou, Amalia 162, 163
Bogo, Deborah 196
Bohlmann, Klaus 184
Bom, Trudy 199
Bora, Bülent 154, 165
Borges de Almeida, Anibal 16
Borisov, Jivko 157, 161, 163, 164
Bornudd, Lotta 202
Bort, Jennifer 174
Bost, Roger-Yves 171, 172, 173, 188
Botte, Beatrice 189
Bourdeleau, Marie-Claude 179
Bourdy, Hubert 167
Bozan, Alexandru 154, 155, 156, 157,
  160, 161, 162, 163, 165
Bozan, Razvan 165
Bozick, Jay 174
Bradley, Caroline 48, *48*, 57, 69, 142,
  145, 148
Brandt, Heinz 19, 142
Bravos, Fotis 156, 157, 162, 163, 164,
  165
Brink, Conni 185
Brookes, Norton 179
Broome, David 28, 31, 44, 48, 49, 51,
  52, 57, 69, 138, *138*, 139, 140, 141,
  146, 147, 148, *148*
Broome, John 180
Brown, Buddy 48, 69, 151, 152
Brown, John 186
Brucco, Esteban 194
Brüggemann, Detlef 170
Brugman, Hans 180
Buchholz, Rainer 180
Bucur, Ionel 163, 165
Bühler, Hans E. 16
Buldanlioğlu, Barbara 161, 162
Burchmore, Sadie Ann 198
Burdsall, Katharine 31, 49, 67, 69,
  144
Burke, Vincent 189
Burr, Leslie (see Burr-Lenehan,
  Leslie)
Burr-Lenehan, Leslie (née Burr) 31,
  38, 66, 69, 71, 152

Cacciandra, Giulio 15, 45
Caffaratti, Ettore 15, 45
Cagnat, Jean-Michel 181
Campos, Rafael 149
Canales, Ricardo 195
Cancre, Adeline 187
Cancre, Jean-Pierre 178
Cancre, Michèle (see d'Orgeix-
  Cancre, Michele)
Candrian, Bruno 138, 142
Can, Rafet 161
Capa, Tunc 155, 165
Caram, Pablo 194
Cardenas, Fernando 197
Cariou, Jean 14, *14*, 44, 45, 46
Carli, S. 180
Carlon, Barbara 183
Carlsen, Lisa 174
Carnejo, Monica 174
Caron, Patrick 49, 134, 166
Carrasco, Hernando 197
Carr, Arthur 21
Carty, John 187
Carty, Justin 185
Carvalho, Antonio 149
Cash, Alejandro 195, 196
Casio, Stacy 174
Castagna, Rudolfo 181, 191
Castaing, Federico 194
Castellini, Emanuele 181, 191
Castellini, Gualtiero 180
Ceballos, Pablo 195
Chamberlin, Harry D. 19, 45
Chaouqui, Bachir 167
Chapman, Lynn 185
Chapot, Frank 26, 32, 44, 52, 140,
  149, 150, 152
Chapot, Mary (née Mairs) 150, 152
Charles, Hanley 189
Cherkaoui, Fikri 167
Cheska, Donald 62, 69, 152
Chopping, Harold 174
Chornawaka, Norma 151
Christov, Dimo 156, 157
Chukanov, Viateslav 37
Claudiu, Gheorghe 164, 165
Clement, Anna 142, 143, 147
Coakes, Douglas 179, 180, 191, 192,
  193
Coakes, Marion (see Mould, Marion)
Cohen, Susan 143
Coleman, Ann 184
Collard Bovy, Lionel 187
Colombo, Daniela Moira 196
Connors, Gillian 202
Constantin, Albert 164, 165
Costello, Tom 198
Costello, Dermot 198
Cottier, Frédéric 49, 69, 142
Coumans, André 15
Courtney, Linda 189
Cresswell, Michael 179, 180, 191, 192
Crisan, Radu 157
Cristi, Oscar 23, 24, 44, 46, 149, 150
Crow, Camille 199, 202
Cuepper, Edgar-Henri 34, 40
Curtis, Charlie 184
Curti, Gilles 180, 181

Daaleu, A. 154
Daems-Vastapane, Veronique 186,
  187, 191, 193
Dagg, Philip 198
Dagli, Ateş 155
Dahler, Dirk 186
Dahlgren, Agneta 199
Daigneux, Fabienne 198
Dallas, Ronnie 50

Dallas, Theodorakis 161
Daly, Louise 202
Damman, Jean 182
Damm, Carlos 150
Danescu, Anghel 154
d'Anno 178
Darbier, Bernard 179
Darragh, Paul 183, 184, 191
Daudré, Yves 178
David, Ioana 160, 161, 163, 164, 165
Dawes, Alison (née Westwood) 54,
  145
Dawson, Marilyn 184
Day, Jim 30, 150
Deac, Gruia 157, 160, 164, 165
de Almeida, José Dias 180
de Aveyro, Jaime 166
de Bellegarde, Lt 14
de Blicquy, Claude du Roy 179
de Blommaert de Soye, Emmanuel
  13, 14
de Bohorques, José Alvarez 51, 57,
  159, 166
de Bruine, Jan Adrianus 19
de Bruycker, Daniella 186, 191
de Champsavin, Louis 14
de Fombelle, Bernard 139, 166
de Fresne, Annie 174
de Gaiffier d'Hestroy, Herman 15
d'Harcourt, Joaquin 149
de la Garza, Jaime 149
Delaveau, Patrice 49, 171, 173, 188,
  191
Delaveau, Stephane 189, 190, 191
DeLeyer, Harry 169, *169*
Delfini, Riccardo 197
Delforge, J. P. 179
Delia, Carlos 51, 56, 57, 149, 150
della Casa, Michele 166
Dello Joio, Norman 61, 63, 64, 69,
  70, 144, 151
Deloch, Ernst 14
de los Trujillos, José Alvarez 17
de Medici, Marquis Lorenzo 139, 166
Demeersman, Dirk 198
Demirci, Gülay 162
de Muynck, Freddy 172
Deppe, Michael 182
Dermody, Eddie 199
Deroullers, J. P. 185
Deslauriers, Mario 64, 69, 71
Destree, Hubertus 181
Desutter, Olivier 172, 189
Deuerer, Hans-Jürgen 188
de Wit, Antonio 166
d'Inzeo, Piero 25, *25*, 26, 28, 33, 44,
  46, 49, 139, 140, 147, 175, *176*, 177
d'Inzeo, Raimondo 25, *25*, 26, 27, 28,
  33, 44, 46, 50, 51, 55, 56, 57, 159,
  175, 176, 177, *177*
di San Marzano, C. Asinari 15
Dickinson, Helena 171, 198
Dimitriadu, Christina 160, 162
Dimitrov, Nikola 157, 160, 161, 162
Dinev, Juri 157
Dircie, Hugo 195
Dizioğlu, Murat 161
do Funchal, Luis Marquez 19
Docherty, Michael 182, *182*
Dokic, R. 155
Doney, Jackie 181
d'Orgeix, Chevalier Jean 21, 45, 86
d'Orgeix-Cancre, Michèle (née
  Cancre) 143, 144
d'Oriola, Pierre Jonquères 23, 24, 28,
  29, 29, 30, 44, 45, 46, 49, 50, 51,
  51, 56, 57, 139, 147, 158, *158*, 159, *159*
d'Oultremont, Herman 15

Doyle, Edward 198
Dragič, Milana 165
Drakatou, Helene 164
Drapela, Pablo 194, 195
Drummond-Hay, Anneli (see Wucherpfennig, Anneli)
Dufort d'Astafort, Michel 14
Duggan, Thomas 189
Dunlap, Moffat 150
Durand, Pierre 49, 65, 69, 167
Dürrer, Markus 170, 173

Ebben, Anton 48, 142
Echeverria, Ricardo 23, 149
Edgson, James 198
Edwards, Carl 171, 173
Egmore, Jonathan 171, 189
Ehrens, Rob 138
Elbers, Josef 188
Elder, Jim 30, 41, 150, 151, 152, 169
Emanuelsson, Anna 199
Emanuelsson, Charlotte 199
Empain, Diane 182
Endicott, Michael 174
Englebert 178
Ense, Anke 190
Eras, Rob 184
Erdoğan, Levent 157
Ernst, Jos 181
Ersin, Ali 161, 162, 165
Eryildiz, Cuneyt 163
Escobar, William 195
Eskilsson, Robert 202
Estatjio, Alicia 194
Etiman, Neylan 161
Eurich, Stacey 174

Fabich, Otto 161
Fabius, F. 179
Fabius, Laurent 181
Fargis, Joe 38, 39, 40, 44, 46, 69, 151
Farias, Alejandro 195
Farias, G. C. 194
Farje, Carlos 195
Fasciolo, Fabio 195
Ferenstein, Krzysztof 182
Fernandes, Ricardo Guida 196
Fernandez, Frederico 174
Fernandez, José 150
Fernandez, José Roberto 181
Ferreira, Renyldo 149, 150
Fielder, Andrew 181, 191
Filipucci, Marco 181
Filis, Cristian 160
Finesi, Fabrizio 166
Fischer, Roland 41
FitzAlan-Howard, Lady Sarah 179, 180, 191, 192, 193
Flass, Guido 188
Fleischer, Peter 157, 160
Fletcher, Graham 41
Fragogiannis, Georges 156, 157, 160, 162, 164
Fragoso Pires, Rafael 194
Fraissinet, Ines 185
Francome, John 184, 184
Frauenfelder, Dieter 185
Freer, Michael 179
Freitag, Renate 179
Frei, René 182
Freyer, Sigismund 14
Freyre, Daniel 194
Frühmann, Thomas 41, 69
Fuchs, Markus 134, 183, 184, 185, 191
Fuchs, Thomas 69, 138, 184, 185, 192

Gabathuler, Walter 134, 138
Gagnon, Francis 174
Gahan, Heather 187
Gallegos, Oscar 196
Gallon, Martyn 198
Garcia Cruz, Jaime 21
Garcia Fernández, Julio 17
Garcia, Juan 197
Garcia, Juan Carlos 197
Gardères, Dominique Maximien 14
Gasagrande, Jean 170
Gascoine, Emma 190, 199, 202
Gascoine, Vicky 186, 187, 188, 191
Gaskell, Amanda 198
Gavilán y Ponce de Léon, Marcelino 21

Gaw, Philip 202
Gayat, Jean-Charles 171, 172, 188, 189, 191, 192, 193
Gayford, Tom 30, 150, 151
Gaytan, Eduardo 197
Gemmel, Alison 199
Gemuseus, Alphonse 16, 16, 44, 45, 46
Gentchev, Kamen 161
Georgieva, Galina 162
Georgiev, Liuben 156
Germany, Jean 187, 191, 192
Ghedini, Francesca 181
Giannini, Filippo 170
Giraud, Philippe 183
Givaudan, Arline 144
Göbel, Michael 185
Gockel, Michael 181
Godoy, Carolina 195
Godoy, Mireya 197
Goffert, Joachim 198
Gómez Portugal, Jesus 37
Gönenli, Hayal 155, 156
Gönenli, Nail 154
Gontika, Kira 164
Goranov, Oleg 155, 156
Goris, Hilde 186
Govoni, Gianni 190
Goyeneche, A. 179
Goyeneche, J. 179
Goyoaga, Francisco, 49, 50, 51, 56, 57, 201
Goyoaga-Elizalde, Paola 144
Graham, Hugh 69, 152
Gramtchev, Dobrin 162
Grandjean, Charles 183, 184, 191, 193
Gravemeier, Kurt 185, 186
Grazios, Constantin 161, 163
Grazios, Georges 161, 162, 163
Greenough, Gail 54, 54, 56, 57, 69
Greenwood, Gillian 171, 172, 172, 189
Greenwood, Julie 190
Gremme, Robert 186
Grenon, Caroline 174
Greter, Johan Jacob 19
Griffin, Ashley 173
Grubb, Tim 38, 41, 69
Guasch, Ricardo 151
Gubaira, Teodoro 197
Gudjamanis, Panayotis 164
Guenov, Dimitar 154, 155, 156, 157, 160
Guerdat, Philippe 138
Guerra, Jaime 174, 196
Guertsou, Carina 160
Guevara, Gonzalo 195
Guidi, C. 180
Guiliani, Mario 196
Gzowski, Kazimierz 17

Haegeman, Aimé 14
Halcartegaray, Esteban 194
Hall Hall, Michael 182, 182, 184, 191
Hallberg, Ernst 17, 46
Hamel, Françoise 178
Hammad, Kabbari 166
Haneş, Octavian 165
Hansen, Karl 17
Hansson, Lisbeth 188
Harmsen, Sven 170
Hartmann, Wieslaw 37
Hasse, Kurt 19, 20, 44, 46
Hatton, Anne 187
Haughey, Eimear 185
Hauser, Dieter 185
Heed, Anna 202
Heffer, Mark 171, 188, 198
Heffer, Philip 171, 172, 173, 198
Hegner, Rolf 187
Heijbroek 178
Heins, Johan 48, 138, 142, 147, 148
Helak, Stanislaw 186
Hellfrich, Gerd 186
Hemerijck, Rik 190
Hendrix, Emiel 138, 184
Herbert, Bernd 188
Herman, Gigi 174
Hermesmeier, Dirk 170, 173
Hermon, Christian 170
Hernalsteens, George 178, 192

Hernandez, Jorge 173
Hernandez-Izquierdo, Fernando 151
Herrera, Francisco 195
Higareda, Edouardo 151
Hill, Richard 187
Hinrichsen, Gerd 178
Hirsch, Monika 171, 173
Hoepner, Wolfgang 178
Hoffmann, Karl-Ludwig 178
Homfeld, Conrad 38, 39, 44, 46, 48, 49, 54, 54, 61, 65, 66, 69, 70, 71
Honrubia, Alberto 167
Hottendorf, Maren 198
Howard, Marion 186
Huck, Karsten 180, 181
Huerkamp, Dirk 170, 171
Huet, Lan 180
Hughes, Marion 199
Humen, Nikki 174
Hunter, Janet 130, 171
Hvioru, Cornel 155

Ignatovici, Vasa 163
Iliades, Denis 163, 164
Iliadis, Theagenis 162, 163
Iliev, Mihail 157
Ilin, Corneliu 154, 155, 156, 160
Ilin, Ligia 164, 165
Ineichen, Christian 187
Inglefield, Clare 199
Inglis, Duncan 172
Innoolou, A. 154
Ionescu, Gabriela 154
Ionescu, G. 154
Ionescu, Petre 165
Irwin, Alan 198
Irwin, Beverley Anne 199
Iskarov, Ilian 164
Isnard, Françoise 194
Itajahy, Claudia 194, 195
Ivanovici, Dusko 163

Jacobs, Piet 187
Jacquin, Lisa 67, 69
Jalabi, Capt 166
Jamagne, Marie-Luce 178, 179
Jankov, Petar 156
Jansen, Irene 143, 144, 147
Jarasinski, Kurt 28
Jasinski, Stanislaw 186
Johanpeter, André 70, 194, 195
Johansson, Jessica 199, 202
Johansson, Svante 171, 173, 199
Johnsey, Debbie 30, 148, 185, 192
Jostes, Peter 188, 189
Jouy, Philippe 179
Jünemann, Ulrich 182, 183
Jurici, Rajka 161, 163

Kaczmarek, Bronislaw 180
Kahny, Georg 185
Kalender, Kirk 190
Kalmik, Metin 155, 156
Kamcil, Atif 154
Kane, Michael 180
Kaplangi, Bülent 157
Kappler, Chris 174
Karagülle, Hulki 156, 161
Katchev, Valentin 154
Katchov, Hristo 160, 161
Katsianos, Georges 165
Kavanagh, Feargal 186
Kavur, Z. 155
Kazis, Michel 164
Kazmier, Bronislaw 180
Kelly, Edward 189
Kelly, Jill 187, 192
Kempter, Sylvia 183
Kenn, Jürgen 170
Kernan, James 185, 186, 192
Kerr, Barbara (née Simpson) 55, 151
Kersic, Alenka 161, 165
Kidd, Jane 179, 191, 192, 193
Kidd, John 180, 191, 192, 193
Kilman, Gustaf 14
Kim, Seong Joong 168
Kim, Sung Hwan 168
Kinnear, Fiona 183
Kipreos, Aris 156, 157, 160
Kirchhoff, Ulrich 172
Kisseuv, Milio 154
Kliijnee, René 185

Klinkhamer, Sandra 190
Kloepper, Alfons 188
Klumpers, Ton 170
Knepper, Sabine 170
Knorren, Wolfgang 183
Koc, Salih 155
Köhler, Helga 144
Koleva, Galina 163
Konieczny, Andrzej 186
Koning, Béatrice 179
Koof, Norbert 49, 53, 53, 56, 57, 138, 185
Koopmans, Abe 187
Koppany, Sandra 196
Korolkov, Nikolai 37, 38, 44, 46
Kostantinov, Krassimir 163
Koster, Miss 178
Kowalczyk, Jan 37, 37, 38, 44, 46, 234, 234
Koyuncuoğlu, Mine 165
Kozicki, Marian 37
Krastev, Liuben 156
Kraus, Ulla 188
Krizan, Janos 182
Krogsgaard, Lisbeth 183
Krolikiewicz, Adam 16
Kronenberger, Paul 183
Kuhn, Charles 18
Kuipers, Jan 188
Kun, Wolfgang 183, 184
Kursinski, Anne 31, 69, 152
Kurttepeli, Merve 165
Kusner, Kathy 32, 54, 56, 144, 150
Kyle, John 183

Laame, Henri 15
Labye, Didier 189
Laenens, Hetty 181
Laffargue, Guy 181
Lalaouni, Iona 165
Lambadarios, Dimitri 160, 164
Lang, Stefan 171
Lanni, Matthew 199
Lapointe, Richard 174
Larraguibel, Alberto 149, 152
Larrain, Joaquin 149, 150
Larrazabal, Carlos 195
Larrondo, Guido 151
Laskin, Mark 41, 69
Latham, Rutherford 167
Laubscher, Jochen 185
Lauda, Keli 163
Laufer, Andrej 165
Lauffer, Olivier 186
Lavin, Eugenio 151
Lawlor, Colette 198
Lederman, Alexandra 199
Lefèbvre, Janou (see Tissot, Janou)
Lefrant, Guy 28, 159, 166
Legrand, Eugenie 190, 202
Leguen, François 202
Leibel, Terry 151
Leitenberger, Monika 145
Leman, Gregoire 198
Lenssens, Johan 172, 189, 192
Lequio di Assaba, Tommaso 15, 15, 16, 44, 46
Leredde, Xavier 167, 185, 186, 187
Leroyer, Eric 166, 185
Letherbarrow, Vicki 202
Leuenberg, Mario 149
Levallois, Eric 171, 188
Lewenhaupt, Carl Gustaf 14, 15, 44
Lewis, Annette 171
Lewis, Michelle 188
Liappi, Lila 156, 160
Ligges, Fritz 32, 38, 44
Lima, Rodrigo Ullmann 196
Linget, Philippe 170
Llambi, Jorge 151
Llewellyn, Harry 21, 22, 22, 23, 44, 46
Locken, Manuel 195
Logotheti, Elizabeth 160
López Quesada, Carlos 166
López, José L. 194
López, Rene 195
Lorre, A. 180
Loubaris, Karim 167
Loudon, A. A. 178
Loughran, Ann-Marie 173, 174

Loverdos, Panayotis 164
Lowry, Margi 185
Lozanova, Velisava 163
Lucardi, Jorge 149
Luciana, Sabina 186
Lundqvist, Helena 202
Lundström, Åge 16
Luther, Hauke 171, 172
Luther, Peter 38, 49, 138
Luther, Thiess 171
Lütke-Westhues, Alfons 25
Lutturgue, G. 180
Luxardo, Maria Luisa 197
Lynch, Emma 202
Lyons, Mandy 187
Lyons, Vina 189, 198
Lytle, Jill 173

Ma, Jae Woong 168
Mac, Michael 188, 198
Macken, Eddie 52, 53, 56, 57, 61, 69,
    142, 147, 153, 153
Madcur, Roberto 196
Mäder, Kurt 184
Madson, Tracy 173
Maia, Dalton Camargo 196
Maigret, Christian 181
Mairs, Mary (see Chapot, Mary)
Makin, Tony 179
Malloy, Vivi 174
Mancinelli, Graziano 29, 32, 33, 44,
    46, 52, 140, 159, 178, 191
Manfredi, Lucio 185
Marchis, Horatiu 161, 164
Marcon, Nelson 195, 196
Margaride, Luiz de Menezes 16
Marian, Simion 154
Mariles Cortés, Humberto 21, 24, 44,
    45, 46, 86, 87, 87, 149
Marinkov, Vladan 181
Marinopoulou, Marina 162, 163, 164
Marinov, Ivo 161
Marisci, Tania 161
Marissen, Sacha 189
Markslag, Yolanda 188
Martens, Marlene 186
Martins, Helder de Souza 16
Martin, Frank 15
Marusic, Tania 160
Maslin, Jabeena 180, 193
Masters, Shaina 173
Mathers, Natalie 174
Mathy, Bernard 190, 202
Mathy, François 34, 36, 44, 46
Mathy, François (jnr), 190
Matran, Liviu 157, 160
Matz, Michael 48, 49, 53, 62, 69, 71,
    151, 152
Maurer, Antonio 173, 195
Mayorga, Pedro 149
Mazilu 156
McCartan, Jim 187
McCashin, Arthur 23
McConnell, Trevor 187
McEvoy, Michele 55, 56
McGarry, Declan 187
McMahon, Brian 186, 186, 187, 192
McMahon, Paddy 141, 147
McNaught, Lesley 188, 191, 192, 193
Meimarides, Costis 16, 165
Meimarides, Nikola 160
Melliger, Willi 69, 134, 138
Mello, Pedro 195
Melo, Celso Figueira 196
Mena e Silva, Luis 19
Mendoza, Cesar 23, 149
Meulman, Simone 202
Meyer, Bernard 14
Michael, Emma 199
Middleton, Christine 179
Millar, Ian 41, 66, 69, 151, 152
Millar, Terrance 151, 152
Milner, Gillian 187, 188
Milonas, Aris 160, 162
Miloutinovic, Milan 155, 156, 164
Minassian, E. 195
Mirel, Engin 154, 155
Mitov, Tichomir 165
Mitovski, Miltcho 154
Mitterer, Joseph 181
Mladenovic, V. 156
Mocanu, Stelian 165

Möhr, Thomas 188
Moisei, Mariana 160, 161, 164
Molinuevo, Argentino (snr) 149
Möller, Rinne 182, 183, 192
Mollet, Margreth 186, 187, 192
Monahan, Katie, 31, 49, 61, 69, 71
Montana, Alejandro 197
Montenegro, Mariana 197
Monteyne, Marianne 182
Montoya, Francisco 197
Moon, Un Jin 168
Moore, Ann 33, 145, 145, 181, 182,
    182, 183, 191, 192, 193
Moore, Barbara 183
Moreau, Charles 166
Morelli, Carmen 196, 197
Moretti, Giuseppe 169
Morgan, Iain 171, 189
Morrison, Kim 173, 174
Morris, George 26, 149
Mosset, Elisabeth 186
Mosset, Erich 170
Mostajo, Juan José 196, 197
Mould, Marion (née Coakes) 29, 31,
    54, 56, 129, 129, 142, 145, 180, 181,
    191, 192
Moutsis, Georges 164
Mousinho de Albuquerque, José 16
Moyersoen, Filippo 134, 166
Mudaf, Sami A. Al 168
Mudrici, Dragan 163
Mühlbauer, Thomas 190
Mulhall, M. 194
Müller, Frank 171
Mullins, Gerry 69
Murat, Ibrahim 154, 155
Murphy, Dennis 48, 151
Murphy, Peter 199, 202
Muskantor, Diana 202
Mutawa, Gamila M. Al 168
Mutawa, Nadia M. Al 168

Naday, K. 194
Nagel, Carsten 188
Naidenov, Boiko 164
Nairz, Andreas 185
Nakano, Yoshihiro 168
Nater, Brigitte 182, 183, 192
Navarro Morenés, José 17, 21
Navellán, Francisco 195
Navet, Eric 187, 191
Neagu, Mircea 157, 160, 162, 163,
    164, 165
Nedeltav, Peter 157
Nedkov, Naiden 165
Newsham, Alexandra 202
Nicolae, George 156
Nicolas, Jean-Marc 182, 183, 193
Nicolet, Pierre 170, 173
Nicoll, Henry 21
Niemann, Hans-Michael 179
Niemann, Ralf 198
Nieto, Raul 152
Niewald, Jürgen 180
Nikolae, George 155, 157
Nikolov, Marian 161, 162, 163
Nikolov, Vaselin 163
Nishi, Baron Takeichi 19, 19
Nooren, Henk, 48, 138, 184
Norling, Daniel 15
Nossi, C. 180
Notz, Jürg 183, 184, 185, 191, 192
Novo, Lalla 144

Okçuoğlu, Levin 154, 157
Oktayuren, Kaya 160
Okuno, Ryuzo 168
Oliver, Vivienne 180
Ollieric, Jean 179
Ollieric, Philippe 179
Öncü, Kemal 157, 163
Oouzlouztu 155
Oppes, Salvatore 25, 26, 139, 148
Orlandi, Vittorio 33
Ornia, Oswaldo 194, 195
Orozco, Alejandro 195, 196
Orsini, Luca 190
Orthuber, Eva-Maria 190
Osacar, Jorge 150
Ottens, Hans-Jorn 188
Ott, Klaus 185
Ozan, Volkan 155, 156

Özkan, Hakan 161
Özlen, Reşit 157, 161, 162

Pachoud, Dany 184
Pacynski, Antoni 180
Pacynski, Tomasz 180
Pade, Klaus 178, 179, 192
Padilha, Paula 195
Palethorpe, Dawn (see Wofford,
    Dawn)
Palmizzi, Gian 170, 173
Panca, Theodor 161
Papa, Laura 165
Papadopoulos, Nicolas 163
Papakonstantinou, Helene 157
Papalios, Dorina 165
Parker, Christopher 186
Parot, Hubert 34, 141, 166
Parot, Sylvie 189, 198, 199
Parra, Francisco 189
Pasarin, Georg 160
Patron, Yves 189
Patsarikas 156
Paullier, Rafael 194
Pavlov, Boris 154, 155, 156, 157, 160,
    161, 162, 164
Peinov, Plamen 157, 160
Pekin, Sefika 165
Pelissier, Sophie 190
Penades, Enrique 194
Pérez de las Heras, Elisa 151
Pérez de las Heras, Joaquin 37, 38,
    44, 46, 151
Pérez, Alejandro 150
Peric, M. Lagos 195
Permbeck, Linda 202
Pessoa, Nelson 64, 69, 134, 140, 149,
    150, 159
Pettinari, Sandro 196, 197
Philippaerts, Ludo 188
Pignolet, Alain 172
Pincius, Vasile 154
Piper, Zoran 165
Pisier, Armelle 179
Pitrola, Gabriel 196
Planchard, J. L. 179
Plate, Ulf 171, 188
Poganovsky, Viktor 37
Pollman-Schweckhorst, Alois 171
Polyakov, Y. 187
Popa, Ion 157, 160, 161, 162
Popescu, Dania 160, 161, 162, 163
Popescu, George 155, 156
Porter, Mandy 174
Poulet, Philippe 187
Powell, Karen 174
Prasek, Janusz 186
Preda, Mircea 160
Prentice, Joanne 199
Puricelli, Emilio 134, 166
Pyrah, Malcolm 48, 49, 53, 56, 57,
    138, 142

Quinones, Hector 195
Quintella, Antonio 196

Rabelo, Francisco Leite 149
Rabouan, Isabelle 199, 202
Raducanu, Tite 164, 165
Radu, Ilioi 164
Raitchev, Rossen 164
Rambaud, Hugues 183
Ranchigataï, Vlad 155
Rancigaj, Eva 160
Ranghianu, Monica 157
Rang, Henri 20, 46
Raper, Lynne 181, 191, 193
Rapalli, Monica 178
Rashkov, Kroum 155
Ratchev, Todor 154
Rätcheev, Oskar 155, 156, 157, 160
Ravano, Giuseppe 179, 180, 191
Rayment, Margo 173
Rayton, Pamela 187
Razo, Luis 151
Rees, Beverley 199
Refait, Martine 178, 179, 192
Reid, John 182, 192
Reitter, Barbara 190
Renwick, John 202
Ricciotti, Francesco 181
Richardson, Rebecca 184
Richter, Hans 174

Ricketts, Derek 48
Riedl, George 41
Riemann, Dietrich 183, 184
Ritters, Hans-Werner 178
Riva, Giulio 170
Rivera, Alberto 152
Riviere, Alfredo Luis 197
Riviere, Carlos 197
Rizopoulos, Pavlos 165
Robbiani, Heidi 40, 138, 142, 148,
    206
Robert, Michel 49, 53, 57, 134
Robeson, Peter 13, 25, 29, 44
Roche, Michel 34
Rodriguez, Gerardo 173
Rodriguez, Manuel 149
Rodriguez, Ruben 173, 174, 196
Roger Smith, Althea 180, 193
Roger Smith, Sarah 181, 192
Roggemans, André 178
Roguet, André 171, 188
Roguet, Christophe 190, 192
Roguet, Marc 34
Rojas, Leopoldo 149
Rojas, Pedro José 197
Rolt, Pablo 196
Rombouts, Marcel 188
Ronge, Patrick 184
Rosencrantz, Fredrik 14
Rosiadis, Georges 162, 163
Rosselot, G. 194
Röthlisberger, Beat 182, 183, 192
Rovaldi, Giorgio 181
Rozier, Marcel 30, 34, 44
Rozier, Philippe 67, 167, 188
Rozier, Thierry 171
Ruchti, Carlos 149
Runge, Ralf 171
Rüping, Michael 138
Russell, John W. 23
Russev, Emil 163

Sa Mota, Roberta 196
Sabah, Barah S. Al 168
Sabev, Dzenko 154
Sagan, Cheryl 174
Sales, Alex 173
Salinas, Carlos 151
Salmen, Gerhard 178
Salvador, Javier 190
Salvati, Alberto 178
San Clemente, Fernando 195
San Felice, P. 194
Sanclaudio, Andres 197
Sarç, Alev 165
Sargent, Jane 188, 198
Saversnik, E. 156
Savu, Arina 164
Scalabre, Eric 202
Scarpa, Barbara 190
Schmal, Cees 180
Schmidt, Hans-Joachim 181
Schneider, Gerhard 157
Schockemöhle, Alwin 26, 30, 34, 35,
    36, 44, 45, 46, 140, 141, 147, 148,
    178, 203
Schockemöhle, Paul 34, 38, 44, 49,
    61, 62, 69, 138, 142, 146, 147, 148,
    153, 217
Schridde, Hermann 28, 29, 30, 44, 46,
    140, 158, 178
Schulter, Gerard 199
Schulze-Siehoff, Hendrick 183
Scolari, Bruno 170, 187
Segovia, Alfonso 166, 167
Seigner, G. 14
Sellinger, Frank 69, 151
Senderos, Fernando 151
Sergopoulo 156
Serpieris, F. 156
Serventi, Giulia 142, 143, 145, 147
Severo, Antonio 196
Seyalloğlu, Halil 156
Sforza, Alberto Riario 178
Shapiro, Neal 32, 33, 44, 46
Sherman, Pam 174
Shopov, Stefan 154
Shore, Keith 198
Shuaib, Tariq H. 168
Sigismund, Cathy 173
Silan, Emine 156, 157, 162, 164
Simonetti, Americo 70, 150

Simon, Hugo 40, 41, *41*, 42, 52, *60*, 61, 62, 63, 69, 70, 71, 142
Simpson, Barbara (see Kerr, Barbara)
Simpson, Debbie 173
Simpson, John 151
Skelton, Nick 41, 49, 54, 65, 69, 128, *130*, 138, 185, 186, 191
Skenther, Nikolas 157, 160
Skountzos, Makis 164, 165
Slattery, Sinead 199
Sloothaak, Franke 38, 40, 138, 184, 185, 187
Smismans, Michel 189, 191
Smith, Harvey 52, 138, 140, 141, *215*
Smith, Janet 180
Smith, Melanie 31, 38, 42, 61, 62, 63, 69, 70, 71, 151
Smith, Nigel 189
Smith, Peter 199
Smith, Robert 187, 192
Smith, Stephen 189
Smith, Steven 38, 187, 191, 192
Smulders, Irma 187
Smythe, Pat 12, *13*, 25, 44, *45*, 142, 143, *143*, 144, 146, 147, 148
Şnautil, Majda 165
Snoek, Hendrik 181
Snoek, Marion 183, 184, *185*, 191, 193
Sone, Alfredo 70, 195
Sönksen, Sonke 34, 141, 148
Sotiriou 156
Southern, Linda 173, 174
Soveza 156
Spasojevic, Rodmilo 155, 156
Spassov, Margarit 155, 156
Speglie, B. 156
Spens, Mallowry 182
Stackfleth, Peter 179
Ståhle, Axel 16
Steenken, Hartwig 32, 52, *52*, 57, 141, 147, 148
Stefanescu, Christina 163
Steinkraus, William 23, 26, *30*, 31, 32, 44, 149, 150, 152, 224, 225, *225*
Stewart, Duggie 22, 23
Stewart, Paulo 70, 195, 196
Stoianova, Theodora 162
Stoica, Aurelian 156
Stoica, Florin 161, 162, 163, 164
Stoika, Alexandrou 154, 155
Stojanov, Najdan 163
Storme, Alain 184, 185, 192
Storme, Thierry 181, 182
Stretta, Alberto 179
Stuber, Werner 187
Subercaseaux, Alicia 194
Sunkel, Peter 184

Sutton, Paul 172
Suvasdici, Dejan 163
Svensson, Patrick 199
Swail, Conor 202
Swail, Marcus 199
Szosland, Kazimierz 17
Sztyrle, Federico 195
Sztyrle, Guido 195

Taaken, Uriel 199
Targett, Louise 199
Tasca, Lucio 179
Tavazzani, F. 180
Tazzer Valencia, Gerardo 37, 151, 152
Tebbel, Rene 190
Teich, Cristine 187
Tenev, Milan 155
Teologlou 156
Thelning, Åke 16, 46
Thiedemann, Fritz 24, 25, 26, 44, 45, 46, 47, *47*, 49, 51, 56, 57, 139, 147, 159
Thirouin, Max 189, 190, 191
Thiry, Myriam 182
Thürnagel, Stefan 184
Tidball, Laura (see Tidball-Balisky, Laura)
Tidball-Balisky, Laura (née Tidball) 69, 173
Tihomirov, Nikolai 155, 156
Tilger, Achim 170
Tincu, Ion 164, 165
Tissot, Janou (née Lefèbvre) 24, 28, 30, 44, 54, *55*, 56, 144, 145, 179
Todea, Silvana 165
Todorov, Todor 164
Toki, Shuichi 168
Tolerton, Margaret 186
Tomura, Takashi 168
Tops, Jan 170, 187
Totzev, Jachar 157
Touil, Ahmed 167
Townsend, Ann (see Backhouse, Ann)
Traherne, Gay 182, *182*, 191, 192, 193
Travers, Eileen 198
Trissino, Gian Giorgio 14
Turkington, Colin 199
Tyteca, Ferdi 184
Tzanev, Todor 165

Udrakis, Rajmondas 172
Ugarte, Natalia 195
Ulrich, Giaginta 181
Up, Neslihan 164, 165
Uriate, F. 179
Uriza Castro, Rubén 21, 44, 46, 86

Utgel, Fercham 155
Uzan, Stephane 170, 173

Vacchelli, Caterina 188
Vaillancourt, Michel 36, 41, 151
Valdés Lacarra, Alberto 37
Valdés Ramos, Alberto 21, 149
Valente, Giullermo 196
Valerio, Alessandro 15
Valev, Evelin 163
Vallance, Stephen 187
van Belle, Mike 172, 173
van de Poële, Georges 14
Vandewalle, Stefan 189, 190, 191
van den Bosch, Danny 188, 189
van den Brook, Nicolle 199
van der Veken, Thierry 181
van der Vleuten, Eric 170, 173, 188
van Ginhoven, Jessica 195
van Langendonck, Constant 14
van Malsen, Tanja 188
van Paesschen, Eva 184
van Paesschen, Stanny 34, 185
van Schaik, Henri Louis 19
van Spaendonck, San 180
Vanderhaegen, Françoise 178, 192
Vanwijn, Ben 172, 189
Varas, Rene 151
Vard, Taylor 198
Vasilev, Dimitar 163, 164
Vassilev, Mitko 154, 155, 157
Velea, Dumitru 154, 156, 157, 161, 162, 163, 164
Velitchov, Radomir 165
Ventura, František 18, *18*, 45
Verdes, Camelia 154
Verlooy, Axel 188
Vilain, Yves 198
Vinals Contreras, Roberto 149, 152
Vingerhoets, Marc 186
Vlad, Constantin 156, 157, 160
Vlad, N. 156
von Barnekow, Marten 19
von Braun, Georg 16
von Buchwaldt, Achaz 138
Von der Weid, Henri 16
von Dreusche, Peter 180
von Hohenau, Wilhelm 14
von Kröcher, Rabod Wilhelm 14
von Opel, Heinz 180
von Platthy, Jozsef 20
von Preussen, Friedrich Karl 14
von Rosen, Clarence 19, 45
von Rosen, Hans 14, 15, 44, 45
von Zychlinski, Hasso 180, 191
Vortsman, N. 178
Voulgarakis, Demetre 162, 163
Vourtea, Marius 155

Wagner, Udo 198
Walker, Cheryl 185
Walsh, Michael 189
Walters, Marsha 174
Watson, Mennell 186, 187
Wauters, Eric 34, 134
Weber, Willie 170
Weier, Monica (née Bachmann) 144, 145
Weier, Paul 141
Westwood, Alison (see Dawes, Alison)
Wettstein, Frank 182
Whitaker, John 34, 38, 41, 42, 49, 69, 70, 71, *130*, 138, 142, 144
Whitaker, Michael 38, 49, 71, *130*, 138, 186, 187, 192
White, Jan 179, 191, 192, 193
White, Paul 183
White, Wilf *13*, 22, 23, 25, 44, 46
Wieja, Norbert 180
Wieken, Dick 48
Wiel, Heber 185
Wiley, Hugh 149, 150
Williams, Monica 196
Wilson, Marnie 199
Wilson-Kay, Fiona 184
Wiltfang, Gerd 32, 49, 53, 56, 57, 138, 142, 144, 148
Winkler, Hans Günter 25, *25*, 26, 28, 30, 32, 34, 44, 46, 50, *50*, 55, 56, 57, 72, 139, 140, 141, 153, 159, 175, 200, *200*, 201
Wittmer, Pascale 189, 192
Wofford, Dawn (née Palethorpe) 143
Woodward, Robert 181
Worziger, Ulrich 183
Wucherpfennig, Anneli (née Drummond-Hay) 54, 56, 135, *135*, 144, 145, 148

Yankov, Gueorgui 157
Yankov, Petar 155
Yaran, Nurettin 155
Yardley, Carole 198
Yoffe, Fernando 194
Yucel, Fehran 154

Zacharapolou, Helena 163
Zaveustnik, Eva 155
Zambilci, Esin 161
Zemp, Werner 187
Zeredo, Walmor (jnr) 194
Zoer, Jenny 199
Zorlu, Ata 161, 162, 163
zu Rantzau, Breido Graf 181, 182, 192
Zubiaurre, Maria 194
Zúñiga, Gastón 150

Competitions

Asian Games 168

Balkan Championships 154–165

Derbies
Falsterbo (Sweden) 215
Finn Derby (Finland) 216
Hamburg (FRG) 216
Hickstead (Great Britain) 216–217
Jerez de la Frontera (Spain) 217
Millstreet (Ireland) 217
Newport, Rhode Island (USA) 217
Penina (Portugal) 217

European Championships, 136–148

FEI International Jumping Competition 218–228

Grand Prix
Aachen 203–204
American Gold Cup 204
American Invitational (Tampa) 204
Amsterdam 204
Antwerp 204
Barcelona 204–205
Berlin 205
Bratislava 205
Bordeaux 205

Brussels 205–206
Calgary 206
Cleveland 206
Dortmund 206–207
Dublin 207
Gothenburg 207
Harrisburg 207
s'Hertogenbosch 207–208
King George V Gold Cup 208
Lisbon 208–209
London (Olympia) 209
Lourenço Marques 209
Lucerne 209–210
Madrid 210
New York 210–211
Nice 211
Olsztyn 211
Paris (Coupe) 211–212
Paris (Le Jumping) 212
Paris (Salon du Cheval) 212
Queen Elizabeth II Cup 212
Rome 212–213
Rotterdam 213
Royal International Horse Show 213
South Africa 213
Toronto 213–214
Vienna 214
Washington 214

High Jump Records 132–133

International Show Jumping Festival (Rotterdam 1980) 41–42

Junior American Championships, 194–197
Junior European Championships, 178–193

Long Jump Records 133–134

Masters Games 169
Mediterranean Games 166–167

National Championships
Australia 229
Belgium 229
Brazil 229–230
Bulgaria 230
Canada 230
Denmark 230
Finland 230
France 230–231
Federal Republic of Germany 231
Great Britain 231–232
Greece 232
Ireland 232
Liechtenstein 232

Netherlands 233
New Zealand 233
Norway 233
Poland 233
Portugal 233–234
South Africa 235
Spain 235
Sweden 235
Switzerland 236
Turkey 236
USA 236
USSR 236
Zaire 236
Nations Cups 75–128

Olympic Games, 14–47

Pan American Games, 149–152
Pony European Championships, 198–202
President's Cup 130–131
Puissance Records 134

World Championships, 48–57
World Cup, 60–71

Young Riders American Championships, 173–174
Young Riders European Championships, 170–173